TWENTIETH CENTURY BRITISH LITERATURE

TWENTIETH CENTURY

A Reference Guide

Frederick Ungar Publishing Co., New York

BRITISH LITERATURE:

and Bibliography

Compiled and edited by

RUTH Z. TEMPLE
Professor of English
The City University of New York
(Brooklyn College)

With the assistance for the author bibliographies of
MARTIN TUCKER
Associate Professor of English
Long Island University

PREFACE

This book is addressed to the student of contemporary British literature. None of the existing reference guides has been especially designed for him; yet, confronted with a subject of daunting abundance and complexity, he surely needs help—and so perhaps does his primary resource, the reference librarian.

The study of the contemporary always has its special hazards; in our day these are increased by the mass of the literary product. Reticence being out of date, authors publish late and soon on themselves, their friends, their enemies. Journals having multiplied as readers became more numerous and more diverse, their contributors are legion, and many of these, unreconciled to the ephemeral nature of their craft, assiduously collect reviews and articles in volumes. Academic critics, too, abound, on both sides of the Atlantic, and form or follow this or that critical mode. Nor is the modern battle of the books a simple skirmish between two parties. Christened the "gay science" before the century began, literary criticism has become more solemn, more scientific, and more various, until at midpoint the twentieth century was labeled the age of criticism.

Part I is designed as a reference guide to the books about British books of this period. Most of the divisions listed in the Table of Contents are self-explanatory, but a few need comment. In the first section are listed some of the primary materials of literary history: authors' journals, autobiographies and reminiscences of authors and of people who knew authors, memoirs and biographies of authors by their acquaintances or friends.* Formal literary histories, however (except for histories of a genre, which are with that genre), will be found in the section with that heading, and there, too, are studies of literature in its relation to politics, economics, social theory, philosophy, and the other arts. Obviously, categories can only roughly be imposed on the impure stuff of literary criticism; in one sense all the books in the sections Collections of Essays through Poetry are literary criticism, and the reader is therefore advised, if he fails to find something in one section, to look in another. The most tenuous distinction, probably, is that between Literary Criticism and Collections of Essays. Under the former, appear books of literary criticism

---

* Collected letters are not included but will be found in the author bibliographies.

in the narrow sense—that is, on theory and technique of criticism, including formal aesthetics—and in the wide sense, the study of literature
as art, but only when more than one genre is discussed and when a
specific theme unifies the book—for example, an approach to literature
such as the Freudian or the Marxist or the anthropological. Many modern
"books," unfortunately, masquerade as such by virtue of an introduction
written to unify what began as random articles. Some of these may have
crept into Literary Criticism, but they are more probably in Collections,
the place for books which have no unifying theme and may indeed include very diverse matter, perhaps reviews of novels, plays, and poetry,
together with lectures, and chapters of informal reminiscence. Annotations
here indicate the titles of important general essays on modern literature
as well as the particular authors discussed, when they are among those
whose bibliographies appear in this book. Annotations of books in
other sections, though listing these authors, are primarily designed
to indicate nature and value—that is, to provide some perspective—
and, indeed, so is the selection of books. There are fashions in
scholarship and criticism as in ladies' shoes, and the student of one
generation is likely to be unaware that things ever looked different
—that instead of Northrop Frye and Meyer Abrams there were Irving
Babbitt and John Livingston Lowes, that the "new criticism" meant
Spingarn's discipleship to Croce, not Cleanth Brooks's search for ironic
meaning. The twentieth century thus far has a commendable number of
landmarks and lighthouses, none of which should be neglected by the
literary traveler. The most important of these, I hope, are here. Part I
does not pretend to completeness—an aim in modern bibliography only
to be approached as limit. Moreover, it is, and not least in the annota-
tations, which are matters of judgment, an individual performance and
consequently idiosyncratic. The user is thus assured of the satisfying
opportunity to remedy omissions and to register dissent.

In Part II are listed the works themselves. Substantially a reprint
from *A Library of Literary Criticism: Modern British Literature* (N.Y.,
Ungar, 1966), but brought more nearly up to date and with certain items
added, it consists of the bibliographies of some 400 modern British
authors. The description of those bibliographies in the Introduction to
that book is appropriate here.

In general, "British" means writers of English, Irish, Welsh, or Scottish
origin, or those of Commonwealth—or ex-Commonwealth—origin who
have lived mainly in the British Isles. Auden is here, although he is now
a citizen of the United States. Exceptional cases are two "Britons" by
their own election, Americans who chose to live in England: Henry
James and Logan Pearsall Smith. "Modern" needs definition, too.
Although most of these writers both lived and won their recognition in
this century, some were known by 1900 (for example, Conrad and Henry

James) and two did not live on into the century that discerned their merits (Hopkins and Samuel Butler). On the other hand, some famous authors who did live on, outliving their creativity, are not included (e.g. Swinburne). A number of authors are here who though not "creative" writers occupy an honorable position on the literary scene: art historians, art critics, biographers, literary critics academic and otherwise. And, also for their relevance to that scene, some entertainers: Hall Caine, Marie Corelli, Angela Thirkell, Edgar Wallace, P. G. Wodehouse.

Each author's bibliography is arranged in chronological order and the genre of each book is indicated. For each author are noted a bibliography of his work, if one has been published, and if possible one or two books about him—an early life by a contemporary together with a recent critical study or, if there is one, the definitive biography.

In the preparation of the author bibliographies, Martin Tucker and I were helped by my colleague at Brooklyn College, Jack Kalmar, by Dr. Sylvia England and Dr. Joy Grant in London and by Dr. Frances Barasch, Barbara Goldberg, and Catherine Stimpson in New York. For the bibliographies in Part I, I was helped by Robert Scotto and in the preparation of the manuscript by Geneva Sayre. To all these we are deeply grateful. No book of this kind could, of course, be compiled without the resources generously made available by libraries. We have used those of Brooklyn College, to whose Chief of the Humanities Division, Mr. Alex S. Preminger, I am especially indebted, the British Museum, Columbia University, Long Island University, New York City at 42nd Street, and Smith College.

RUTH Z. TEMPLE

The City University of New York
(Brooklyn College)

ABBREVIATIONS

bibliog. bibliographical or bibliography
biog. biography
c. century
circul. circulation
coll. collected or collection
comp. compiled (by)
crit. criticism
ed. edited (by) or editor or edition
enlgd. enlarged
esp. especially
et al. and others
hist. history
ill. illustrated or illustrations
incl. including
introd. introduction
lib. library
lit. literature or literary
n.d. no date (of publication) given
orig. originally
pub. published
q.v. quem vide (see the item)
ref. reference
repr. reprint or reprinted (As used in annotation of collections, this means that the essays collected were originally printed in periodicals.)
rev. revised (by) or revision
sect. section
sel. selected (by) or selection
ser. series
suppl. supplementary
tr. translated (by)
vol. volume
WC World's Classics (series)

CONTENTS

PART TWO

PART ONE

NOTE ON FORM

In the listings that follow, original date of publication is given in square brackets; place, publisher, and date of latest edition are given and, if nearly or quite simultaneous in America and England, the data for both. If no place precedes publisher, *London* is to be understood. BC/Longmans means: published for the British Council by Longmans, Green and Company. If book is a paperback, its series name is given in parentheses after publication date (e.g. Anchor, Bison, Galaxy, Vintage).

BIBLIOGRAPHY OF BIBLIOGRAPHIES

NOTE. The British national bibliography, corresponding to the American *Library of Congress Author Catalog,* is the *Catalogue of the Printed Books in the Library of the British Museum* (Wm. Clowes and Sons, 1881–1900, 95 vols.) now called *General Catalogue of Printed Books* in an ed. 1965. This lists by author books supplied to the British Museum as the copyright library of Great Britain.

General Reference

COLLINSON, Robert L. *Bibliographies:* Subject and National. A Guide to Their Contents, Arrangement and Use. [1951] rev., enlgd. N.Y., Hafner, 1962.
>Annotated list of most important bibliogs. in most fields.

LOWRY, George. *A Searcher's Manual.* Shoe String Pr., 1965.

NORTHUP, Clark S[utherland]. *A Register of Bibliographies of the English Language and Literature.* New Haven, Conn., Yale Univ. Pr., 1925.

VAN PATTEN, Nathan. *An Index to Bibliographies and Bibliographical Contributions Relating to the Work of American and British Authors, 1923–1932.* Stanford, Calif., Stanford Univ. Pr., 1934.

WALFORD, A[rthur] John (with assistance of L. M. Payne). *Guide to Reference Material.* Library Assoc., 1959. Suppl., 1962.
>British equivalent of Winchell.

WINCHELL, Constance M. *Guide to Reference Works.* 7th ed. based on 6th by Isadore Gilbert Mudge. Chicago, Am. Lib. Assoc., 1951. 3 supplements, to 1958.
>The standard work. Indispensable.

Bibliographies of English Literature
(Contemporary or Including Contemporary)

THE CONCISE CAMBRIDGE BIBLIOGRAPHY OF ENGLISH LITERATURE, 600–1950. Ed. George Watson. Cambridge Univ. Pr., 1958.
>Partial list of the writings of some eighty 20th c. writers. Very brief list of lit. hist. and crit., anthologies and periodicals. Revision in pro-

3

gress. CBEL (*The Cambridge Bibliography of English Literature*, ed. F. W. Bateson, 4 vols., 1940 ; Supplement by George Watson, 1957) covers Eng. lit. only to 1900 though a 20th c. volume is in progress.

CUTLER, B[radley] D[wyanne]. *Modern British Authors:* Their First Editions. N.Y., Greenberg, 1930.
> 19th and 20th c. authors. Ref. list of bibliogs.

EASTWOOD, W[ilfred] and J. T. GOOD. *Signposts:* A Guide to Modern English Literature. Cambridge Univ. Pr. for the National Book League, 1960.
> Very brief introd. by genres followed by lists of books by genre (e.g. one collection per poet, 2 or 3 novels per novelist) ; section on war poetry by wars ; section on lit. crit. etc.

ENGLISH LITERATURE FROM THE SIXTEENTH CENTURY TO THE PRESENT. [1962] Rev. BC/Longmans, 1966.
> Selective bibliog. of lit. and crit. incl. best eds. and current cheap eds. Lists of collections, anthologies.

MILLETT, Fred B. *Contemporary British Literature:* A Critical Survey and 232 Author-Bibliographies. 3d rev. enlgd. ed. based on 2d rev. enlgd. ed. by John M. Manly and Edith Rickert. [1921] N.Y., Harcourt, Brace, 1940.
> Coverage up to 1935. Author bibliogs. chronol. under genre, complete and admirably accurate. Selected critical bibliog. for each incl. periodical essays. The only compilation of the kind.

NATIONAL BOOK COUNCIL. *British Book News* (title varies). 1940—
> Monthly. A selection of recent books.

SMITH, F. Seymour. *The Best Books of the War:* A List of Books Published between 1939 and 1945. Printed for Private Circul. by H. Smith, 1947.

————*What Shall I Read Next?* A Personal Selection of Twentieth Century English Books. Cambridge Univ. Pr. for the National Book League, 1953.

Special Reference Guides
for Students of English Literature

> NOTE. For evaluation of many scholarly studies, up to 1958, of individual writers as well as of genres and movements, see *Contemporary Literary Scholarship:* A Critical Review, ed. Lewis Leary (for the Committee on Literary Scholarship and the Teaching of English of the National Council of Teachers of English) (N.Y., Appleton-Century-Crofts, 1958). An excellent summary of bibliog. materials available for the student of Eng. literature is Alex Preminger's "English Literature," *Library Trends,* Vol. 15, no. 3 (Jan., 1967), pp. 522–49, repr. in *Bibliography: Current State and Future Trends,* ed. Robert B. Downs and Frances B. Jenkins (Urbana, Univ. of Illinois Press, 1967).

ALTICK, Richard D. and Andrew WRIGHT. *Selective Bibliography for the Study of English and American Literature*. N.Y., Macmillan, 1960. (paper).
> With introd. on the use of scholarly tools. Practical in selection and arrangement. A good book for the student to own.

BATESON, F. W. *A Guide to English Literature*. Garden City, N.Y., Doubleday, 1965 (Anchor).
> By period, with discussion of each as well as bibliog., the latter fully and sometimes picturesquely annotated. Easier to read than to use for reference because of the format, though there is an index. Somewhat idiosyncratic in coverage and not altogether reliable as to detail.

BOND, Donald F., comp. *A Reference Guide to English Studies* (a revision of the *Bibliographical Guide to English Studies* by Tom Peete Cross). Chicago, Univ. of Chicago Pr., 1962 (Phoenix).
> Excellent revision of a work standard since 1919. General introd. to literary research. Good indexes.

KENNEDY, Arthur G. and Donald B. SANDS. *A Concise Bibliography for Students of English*. [1940] Stanford, Calif., Stanford Univ. Pr., 1960 (4th ed.) (paper).
> By far the most inclusive. Indispensable reference work, usable and exact. Index of authors, editors, etc.

Genre Bibliographies

BELL, Inglis and Donald BAIRD. *The English Novel, 1578–1956:* A Checklist of Twentieth Century Criticism. Denver, Colo., Alan Swallow, 1958.
> Relatively meagre selection of crit.

KUNTZ, Joseph, ed. *Poetry Explication:* A Checklist of Interpretation since 1925 of British and American Poems Past and Present. [1950] rev. Denver, Colo., Alan Swallow, 1962.

LECLAIRE, L. *General Analytical Bibliography of Regional Novelists of the British Isles, 1800–1950*. Paris, Les Belles Lettres, 1954.
> Section 3 on regional novel proper since 1870, incl. bibliog. notes, titles, scenes of novels.

THURSTON, Jarvis et al. *Short Fiction Criticism:* A Checklist of Interpretation since 1925 of stories, and novelettes (Am., Brit., Continental) 1800–1958. Denver, Colo., Alan Swallow, 1960.

WALKER, Warren S. *Twentieth-Century Short Story Explication:* Interpretations 1900–1960 inclusive of Short Fiction since 1800. Hamden, Conn., Shoe String Pr., 1961. Supplements, 1961–63, 1963–64.
> Crit. in books, monographs and periodicals, mostly after 1920. Covers same ground as Thurston but is much more inclusive. The two supplement one another.

Author Bibliographies
(Collective and Series)

NOTE. The periodical *English Literature in Transition 1880–1920* (founded 1957 at Purdue Univ., Lafayette, Ind., as *English Fiction in Transition*) publishes bibliographies of works by and on (these annotated) the authors of this period.

BIBLIOGRAPHIES OF MODERN AUTHORS. First series, ed. Henry Danielson. Bookman's Journal ; N.Y., Drake, 1921.
> Most of material orig. in *Bookman's Journal*, though all rev. to date. *Incl.* Beerbohm, R. Brooke, de la Mare. Drinkwater, Dunsany, Flecker, Gissing, Mackenzie, Masefield, A. Symons, H. Walpole.

———— Second Series, ed. and comp. Charles A. and Helen W. Stonehill, John Castle, 1925.
> *Incl.* Davidson, K. Mansfield (periodical contrib. only), A. Meynell.

———— Third Series, ed. P[ercy] H. Muir. Bookman's Journal, 1931.
> *Incl.* M. Hewlett, R. Firbank.

BLOCK, Andrew. *Key Books of British Authors 1600–1932*. Dennis Archer, 1933.
> One book per author, selected criticism (very brief excerpts) of it quoted from journals, etc. Index of titles.

GAWSWORTH, John (pseud. of Terence Ian Fytton Armstrong). *Ten Contemporaries: Notes toward Their Definitive Bibliography*. First Series. Ernest Benn, 1933.
> *Incl.* Abercrombie, Rhys Davies, Gibson, S. Hudson, R. Nichols, E. Sitwell.

———— Second Series. Joiner and Steele, 1933.
> Bibliog. of and autobiog. essay by each. *Incl.* D. Richardson, O'Flaherty, S. Benson, Onions, E. M. Delafield, L. A. G. Strong, Collier, H. E. Bates.

SOHO BIBLIOGRAPHIES. Rupert Hart-Davies, 1951—
> *Incl.* No. 1, Allan Wade, *Yeats*, 1951 ; No. 2, John Carter and John Sparrow, *A. E. Housman*, 1952 ; No. 3, A. E. Gallatin and L. M. Oliver, *Max Beerbohm*, 1952 ; No. 4, G[eoffrey] L. Keynes, *Rupert Brooke*, 1959 ; No. 5, J. J. Slocum and H[erbert] A. Cahoon, *Joyce, 1882–1941*, Yale, 1953 ; No. 6, Cecil Woolf, *Norman Douglas*, 1954 ; Cecil Woolf, *Frederick Rolfe [Baron Corvo]*, 1957 ; No. 8, Leon Edel and Dan Laurence, *Henry James*, 1957 ; No. 9, B[rownlee] J. Kirkpatrick, *Virginia Woolf*, 1957 ; No. 10, Geoffrey L. Keynes, *Sassoon*, 1962 ; No. 11, R. Fifoot, *Edith, Osbert and Sacheverell Sitwell*, 1963 ; No. 12, W. Roberts, *D. H. Lawrence*, 1963 ; No. 16, Miriam J. Benkovitz,

Ronald Firbank, 1963 ; No. 19, B[rownlee] J. Kirkpatrick, *E. M. Forster*, 1965.

Annual Bibliographies

NOTE. Much information useful to scholars and writers is to be found in the annual volume of *Writers' and Artists' Year Book* (Black, 1906—), incl. lists of current periodicals and of publishers, Eng. and Am., with addresses ; also directory of literary agents, societies etc. See for current bibliog. information from periodicals *Bibliographic Index:* A Cumulative Bibliography of Bibliographies (N.Y., H. W. Wilson Co., 1945—), quarterly with annual cumulations.

BRITISH NATIONAL BIBLIOGRAPHY, ed. A. J. Wells. Council of the British National Bibliography, 1950—
Annual vol. with cumulative index at 5-year intervals ; for current year, weekly supplements with index for month in last issue of month, and quarterly cumulations. Record of British book public by year, based on records of Copyright Office, British Museum. Full information about each book incl. Dewey Decimal catalogue number, which indicates subject classification. Also subject index. Until 1950 the annual bibliogs. that must be consulted are Whitaker's (see below) and the next item.

THE ENGLISH CATALOGUE OF BOOKS. Publishers' Circular, 1801—
Continuation of earlier catalogues. Based on weekly booklets of *Publishers' Circular and Booksellers' Record,* thus dependent on co-operation of publishers. Annual volumes and cumulation at irregular intervals, e.g. 1801–1952 (1864–1952, 16 vols.) ; 1952–1955 (1956). By author and title.

THE REFERENCE CATALOGUE OF CURRENT LITERATURE. J. Whitaker and Sons, 1874—.
Published at irregular intervals, listing books in print at date of publication, e.g. Dec. 31, 1960 (1961). By title, author, subject. Corresponds to American *Publishers' Trade List Annual* (N.Y., Bowker, 1873—) with annual index since 1957: *Subject Guide to Books in Print*. This should be consulted for English books, as should American *Paperbound Books in Print* (N.Y., Bowker, 1955—), and *English Paperbound Books in Print* (J. Whitaker and Sons). Other useful sources for current books are the following: *Oxford University Press General Catalogue* (N.Y. and London, Oxford Univ. Pr., 17th ed. 1965), listing books pub. by Oxford and Clarendon Presses, arranged by Dewey Decimal System (thus by subject) with alphabetical list ; *A*

Catalogue of Books, published by the Syndics of the Cambridge Univ. Pr. (Bentley House, 1952), listing all Cambridge Press books published before Jan. 1, 1952 now in print "or likely to be repr. at some future date" (preceding issue 1938).

WHITAKER'S CUMULATIVE BOOK LIST. J. Whitaker and Sons, 1924—.

Quarterly with annual cumulations ; based on weekly *The Publisher and Bookseller.* Genre of book is indicated.

For current listing of books about books see *Scholarly Books in America*: A Quarterly Bibliography of University Press Publications. Chicago, Univ. of Chicago Pr., 1959—.

SOURCES FOR BIOGRAPHY

For current material on living authors, see *Contemporary Authors:* The International Bio-bibliographical Guide to Current Authors and Their Works (Detroit, Gale Research Co., 1962) ; (quarterly), *Biography Index:* A Quarterly Index to Biographical Material in Books and Magazines (N.Y., H. W. Wilson Co., 1946—, with annual cumulation) ; *Current Biography:* Who's News and Why (N.Y., H. W. Wilson Co., 1940— monthly Sept. through July, with annual cumulation).

BATES, E[rnest] Stuart. *Inside Out:* an Introduction to Autobiography. Oxford, Blackwell, 1936–37. 2 vols.
> *Incl.* Bridges, de la Mare, Doughty, Drinkwater, D. H. Lawrence, Gosse, G. Moore, O'Flaherty, J. C. Powys, H. Read, D. Richardson, L. Strachey, A. Symons, Yeats. Extensive bibliog. ; in vol. 2 an index of autobiographers.

BOASE, Frederic. *Modern English Biography:* Supplement. 3 vols. Truro, Eng., Netherton and Worth for the author, 1908–1912.

BROWNING, D[avid] C. *Everyman's Dictionary of Biography:* English and American. Compiled after John W. Cousin by D. C. Browning. Dent, 1958.
> Supersedes Cousin's *Biographical Dictionary of English Literature* [Everyman Lib.]. New authors from the last fifty years, some still writing. 2300 biographies, incl. Scottish, Irish, American ; lowbrow as well as highbrow, few scholars unless popularly known. Dates exact to day where available. Mostly 2 or 3 sentences of biog., though major figures may have 2 pages, with sel. bibliog.

CHURCH, Richard. *British Authors:* A Twentieth Century Gallery. BC/ Longmans, 1943.
> "Miniature word-portraits" of 57 modern British authors. About 2 small pp. and photo for each. *Incl.* some popular authors (Edgar Wallace), historians (Guedalla), critics (Lynd).

HOEHN, Matthew, ed. *Catholic Authors:* Contemporary Biographical Sketches 1930–1947. Newark, N.J., St. Mary's Abbey, 1948. Also: *Catholic Authors 1948–1952.* Ibid., 1952.
> Written by ed. or anon. contributors. Not limited to English-speaking.

KUNITZ, Stanley J[asper] and Howard HAYCRAFT. *Twentieth Century Authors:* A Biographical Dictionary of Modern Literature (incl. 1850 biogs. and 1700 portraits). N.Y., Wilson, 1942, repr. 1950. First Supplement by Stanley J. Kunitz and Vineta Colby. Ibid., 1955.

Supersedes *Living Authors* (1931) and *Authors Today and Yesterday* (1933). Standard. Wide and various in coverage, generally reliable.

STEPHEN, Leslie and Sydney LEE, eds. *Dictionary of National Biography*. Smith, Elder, 1885–1901 (66 vols.). Repr. (22 vols.) 1908–1909 ; 1921–1922 ; 1937–1938. Last two repr. Oxford Univ. Pr. Vol. XXII of repr. is First Supplement. Second: 1913 ; Third: 1921 ; Fourth: 1930 ; Fifth: 1949 ; Sixth: 1959.

Policy is to include no living persons, so supplements must be consulted for modern authors. Only the eminent included. Reliable biographies and sel. bibliog.

REFERENCE BOOKS

NOTE. For British material, see Theodore Besterman, *British Sources of Reference and Information: A Guide to Societies, Works of Reference and Libraries,* compiled under the direction of Aslib (for BC by Aslib, 1947).

GRIGSON, Geoffrey, ed. *The Concise Encyclopedia of Modern World Literature.* Hutchinson, and N.Y., Hawthorn Bks., 1963.
    Ill. with photographs of most authors incl. Highly selective. Readable but rather unsystematic. Short essay (paragraph to a page) on each author: a few biographical facts, general characterization and evaluation of *oeuvre*, synopsis and crit. of one or more works. Liberal quotation from the poets.

HARVEY, Paul. *Oxford Companion to English Literature* [1932] 3d ed. Oxford, Clarendon Pr., 1946, repr. 1955.
    Identification of authors, books, characters.

MULGAN, John, ed. *The Concise Oxford Dictionary of English Literature.* [1939] 2d ed. rev. Oxford, Clarendon Pr., 1963.
    Abridgement of above with additional material, e.g. articles on periods of literary history and on general subjects.

SCOTT, A. F. *Current Literary Terms:* A Concise Dictionary. Macmillan, 1964 ; N.Y., St. Martin's Pr., 1966.
    Alphabetical reference book ; definitions and quotations.

SHIPLEY, Joseph T[wadell], ed. *Dictionary of World Literature:* Criticism, Forms, Technique. [1943] Rev. ed. N.Y., Philosophical Library, 1953.
    Broad coverage ; very brief to extensive entries of uneven quality. Some bibliog.

WRITERS' AND ARTISTS' YEAR BOOK: A Directory. Adam and Charles Black, (58th year) 1965.
    Names and addresses of British and American journals, newspapers, publishers, agencies and societies, literary prizes, markets for writing. Also short pieces on copyright, indexing, translating, libel, preparation and submission of mss., correcting proof. A valuable reference book.

JOURNALS

Part I. A selected list of English journals that, for articles and reviews, were or are the most useful for students of modern English literature.

> NOTE. Abbreviations used in the text are included. Place of publication unless given is London. For a description of the policies of the most important of these, see Ruth Z. Temple, Introduction to *A Library of Literary Criticism:* Modern British Literature, eds. Ruth Z. Temple and Martin Tucker (N.Y., Frederick Ungar, 1966). For information about British periodicals see *Guide to Current British Periodicals,* ed. Mary Toase (London Library Assoc., 1962), and for a complete listing, see *The British Union Catalogue of Periodicals:* A Record of the Periodicals of the World from the Seventeenth Century to the Present Day in British Libraries (Butterworths, 1955–58, 4 vols.; Supplement to 1960, 1962; from March 1964 with annual cumulations incorporating the *World List of Scientific Periodicals*); for a guide to materials in British periodicals (corresponding roughly to *Reader's Guide to Periodical Literature*), see *Subject Index to Periodicals* (Library Assoc., 1915–61), annual, superseded for literary materials by *The British Humanities Index* (quarterly with annual cumulations, 1962—), *SIP* is far less inclusive and trustworthy, than *Reader's Guide* or *International Index to Periodicals* (now *The Social Science and Humanities Index*), the American guides.

The Academy and Literature, 1869–1916 (The Academy, 1969—absorbed Literature, 1902)

The Athenæum, 1828–1921 (merged then with The Nation) (*Ath*)

The Bookman, 1891–1934 (absorbed then by The London Mercury) (*BkmL*)

The Calendar of Modern Letters, 1925–1927 [repr. with introd. Malcolm Bradbury, 3 vols. Frank Cass, 1966]

The Criterion, 1929–1939 (title varies)

The Critical Quarterly, University of Hull, 1959—

Encounter, 1953— (*Enc*)

The Egoist, 1914–1919

The English Review, 1908–1937 (merged then with The National Review)

Essays in Criticism, Oxford, 1951—

Essays and Studies by Members of the English Association, Oxford, 1910— (annual)

The Fortnightly Review, 1865–1934, The Fortnightly, 1934–1954 (absorbed then by The Contemporary Review, still publishing) (*FR*)

The Guardian (title from 1959 of The Manchester Guardian, Manchester, 1821—)

Horizon, 1940–1950 (*Hor*)

John o'London's Weekly, 1919–1954 (merged then with Time and Tide) (*JOL*)

The Illustrated London News, 1842— (*ILN*)

Life and Letters, 1928–1935, Life and Letters Today, 1935–1950 (*LL*)

The Listener, 1929— (now The Listener and BBC Television Review) (*List.*)

The London Magazine, 1954—

The London Mercury, 1919–1939 (merged then with Life and Letters Today) (*LM*)

The London Quarterly Review, 1853–1931 (title then changed to The London Quarterly and Holborn Review—)

The Manchester Guardian Weekly, Manchester, 1919—

The Month, 1863— (title varies)

The Nation, 1907–1921 (merged then with The Athenæum) (*NationL*)

The Nation and Athenæum, 1921–1931 (merged then with The New Statesman)

The National and English Review, 1937—

The New Statesman, 1913–Feb. 1931 ; June 1957— (see next item) (*NS*)

The New Statesman and Nation, Feb. 1931–June 1957 (*NSN*)

The Nineteenth Century and After, 1901–1950, then The Twentieth Century, q.v.

The Observer, 1791— (*Obs*)

The Review, 1962— (on poetry)

A Review of English Literature, 1960— (one review per issue but a fair proportion of articles on contemporary literature)

The Saturday Review of Politics, Literature, Science and Art, 1885–1938 (subtitle varies) (*SR*)

Scrutiny, 1932–1953 (*Scy*)

The Spectator, 1828— (*Spec*)

Time and Tide, 1920— (incorporated John o'London's Weekly, 1954) (*TT*)

The Times Literary Supplement, 1902— (*TLS*)

The Twentieth Century, 1951— (continuation of The Nineteenth Century and After)

See also, especially for its interviews with living authors, The Paris Review, Paris, 1953—

> NOTE. A unique tool for the student is *Notes and Queries*: For Readers and Writers, Collectors and Librarians (Oxford Univ. Pr., 1849—[subtitle varies])

Part II. A list of periodicals that publish bibliographies of contemporary English literature.

> NOTE. No attempt is made to list the very numerous American periodicals, scholarly, popular, and "little," which carry articles or re-

views of contemporary English literature. *Explicator* (Columbia, So. Carolina, 1942—) is unique in being made up of poetry explications with occasional reviews and an annual checklist of the explications incl. For a list of periodicals by categories, with description, see Arthur G. Kennedy and Donald B. Sands, *A Concise Bibliography for Students of English* (Stanford, Calif., Stanford Univ. Pr., fourth ed. rev. 1963). For a guide to recent material, see *An Index to Book Reviews in the Humanities* (Williamston, Mich., Phillip Thomson, 1960—), quarterly index to reviews of fiction and nonfiction in over 600 periodicals; also *Index to Little Magazines* (Denver, Colo., Alan Swallow, 1943-60, annual). *Abstracts of English Studies* (National Council of Teachers of English: Boulder, Colo., Univ. of Colorado, 1958—) publishes abstracts of a selection of articles from periodicals; ten monthly issues and an annual volume, cumulated.

English Literature in Transition, 1880–1920 (formerly English Fiction in Transition) Purdue Univ., 1957—. Mainly devoted to publication of annotated bibliographies of works by and about authors of this period. Unique and important.

Études anglaises, Paris, 1937— (suspended March 1943–Feb. 1952). Incl. reviews and summaries of periodical literature.

Journal of Aesthetics and Art Criticism, Cleveland, Ohio, 1941—. Annual selective bibliog. of aesthetics and art criticism.

Modern Drama, Lawrence, Kansas, 1958—. Current bibliog. quarterly.

Modern Fiction Studies, Purdue Univ., 1955—. Current annotated bibliog. in each issue.

Publications of the Modern Language Association of America, N.Y., 1884—. May issue annually has list of publications in English and the other modern languages and literatures, books and periodical articles classified and cross-referenced. (1922–1956 lists work by Am. scholars only.) Bibliog. issue pub. as separate vol. (N.Y. Univ. Pr.) 1964 (for 1963)—. Bibliographies 1921–1962 repr. N.Y., Kraus Reprint Corp., 1965.

Review of English Studies: A Quarterly Journal of English Literature and the English Language, London, 1925—. Summary of periodical literature in each issue.

Tulane Drama Review. New Orleans, La., Tulane Univ., 1956—. In summer issue, annual bibliog. of Am. publications in theatre.

Twentieth Century Literature: A Scholarly and Critical Journal, Denver, Colo., 1954—. Current bibliog. in each issue.

Two indispensable annual bibliographies of current scholarly material:

Modern Humanities Research Assoc. Annual Bibliography of English Language and Literature, Cambridge, 1921 (for 1920)—.

The Year's Work in English Studies, pub. by The English Association, London, 1920 (for 1919/20)—. Classified by literary periods, annotated.

HISTORY

BELGION, Montgomery. *Our Present Philosophy of Life*. Faber and Faber, 1929.
>Our "present philosophy" as expounded by Shaw, Gide, Freud and B. Russell.

NEW CAMBRIDGE MODERN HISTORY, Vol. XII, 1898–1945. Cambridge Univ. Pr., 1960.

COLLIER, John and Iain LANG, *Just the Other Day:* An Informal History of Great Britain Since the War. Hamish Hamilton, 1932.
>Refers to many writers.

DAY LEWIS, C[ecil], ed. *The Mind in Chains:* Socialism and the Cultural Revolution. F. Muller, 1937.
>Essays by various hands. Culture, progress and the English tradition.

ENSOR, R[obert] C[harles] K[irkwood]. *England, 1870–1914. Oxford History of England,* Vol. XIV. Oxford Univ. Pr., 1936.

FURTH, Charles. *Life Since 1900*. [1956] Allen and Unwin, 1960.
>The main events and the temper of the times, in chapters on roughly 10-year periods.

GORER, Geoffrey. *Exploring English Character,* N.Y., Criterion Bks., 1955.
>Study of contemporary society based on interviews and questionnaires ; by a social anthropologist.

GRAVES, Robert and Alan HODGE. *The Long Week-End:* A Social History of Great Britain 1918–1939. Faber and Faber, 1940.

GREEN, Martin. *A Mirror for Anglo-Saxons:* A Discovery of America ; A Rediscovery of England. N.Y., Harper, 1960.
>Partly repr. Lower-class Englishman, educated at Cambridge, self-exiled and repatriated, comments on British scene.

GRETTON, R[ichard] H[enry] *A Modern History of the English People* 1880–1922. 3 vols. in one. Vol. I, 1880–1898 (1912) ; Vol. II, 1898–1910 (1914) ; Vol. III, 1910–1922 (1930). Martin Secker, n.d.
>Standard work covering all aspects incl. literature. Readable.

HALÉVY, Élie. *A History of the English People:* Epilogue 1895–1914. E. I. Watkin, tr. [French 1926] Penguin Bks., 1939–40.

HARRIS, R. W. *An Historical Introduction to the Twentieth Century.* Blandford Pr., 1966.

HEARD, Gerald. *Those Hurrying Years:* An Historical Outline 1900–1933. Chatto and Windus, 1934.
>By decades.

HEARNSHAW, F[ossey] J[ohn] C[obb], ed. *Edwardian England, A.D. 1901–1910.* Benn, 1933.
> Lectures by various authors at King's College, Univ. of London, 1932–33. On various aspects, incl. literature (by Abercrombie).

JARMAN, T. L. *A Short History of Twentieth-Century England, 1868–1962.* N.Y. [New Am. Lib. of World Lit.] Mentor Bks.; London, Blandford Pr. as *Democracy and World Conflict, 1868–1962,* 1963.
> Short, systematic. Maps, ill., brief bibliog.

LASSELL, Margaret. *Wellington Road.* Routledge and Kegan Paul, 1962.
> Case history of contemporary family life on low economic level in housing estate in suburb of a big city.

LAVER, James. *The Age of Optimism:* Manners and Morals, 1848–1914. Weidenfeld and Nicolson, 1966.
> Unsystematic. Anecdotes. Lavishly ill.

LEAVIS, F[rank] R. and Denys THOMPSON. *Culture and Environment:* The Training of Critical Awareness. Chatto and Windus, 1962.

MARRIOTT, Sir [John] A[rthur] R[ansome]. *Modern England 1885–1945:* A History of My Own Times. [1934] Methuen, 1948.

MAUROIS, André. *The Edwardian Era.* Tr. Hamish Miles. N.Y., Appleton-Century, 1933.

NOWELL-SMITH, Simon, ed. *Edwardian England, 1901–1914.* London and N.Y., Oxford Univ. Pr., 1964.
> Chapters by various hands on all aspects of the life of the period. Ill. Readable and useful.

PETRIE, Sir Charles. *The Edwardians.* N.Y., Norton, 1965.
> Ill. Informal, readable.

POTTER, Stephen. *The Muse in Chains:* A Study in Education. Cape, 1937.
> History of literary education and the effect of literature on education. *Incl.* Saintsbury.

SOMERVELL, D[avid] C[hurchill]. *Modern Britain, 1870–1950.* [1941] 8th ed. enlgd. Methuen, 1952.

SPENDER, J[ohn] A[lfred]. *Great Britain:* Empire and Commonwealth, 1886–1935. Cassell, 1936.
> "The principal sources of history for the period."

TAYLOR, A[lexander] J[ohn] P(ercivale]. *English History, 1914–1945. Oxford History of England,* Vol. XV. Oxford Univ. Pr., 1965.

TUCHMAN, Barbara W. *The Proud Tower:* A Portrait of the World Before the War, 1890–1914. N.Y., Macmillan, 1965.
> Impressionistic history with emphasis on the anecdotal and on personal detail; esp. on England and France.

WILLIAMS, Neville. *Chronology of the Modern World, 1763–1965.* Barrie and Rockliff, 1966.

WILLIAMS, Raymond. *Culture and Society: 1780–1950.* [1958] N.Y., Harper, 1966 (Torchbk.).

Unique. Independent leftist account of critical history of idea of culture in England. Specific reference to Gissing, Shaw, Hulme, D. H. Lawrence, Eliot, Orwell.

————The Long Revolution. Chatto and Windus, 1961.

Unusual kind of book, well executed. *Incl.* chapters on "The Creative Mind" ; "The Analysis of Culture" ; "The Growth of the Reading Public" ; "The Growth of the Popular Press" ; "The Growth of 'Standard English' " ; "The Social History of English Writers" ; "The Social History of Dramatic Forms" ; "Realism and the Contemporary Novel" ; "Britain in the 1960s." List of authors used, from Aristotle to Butler (*The Electoral System in Great Britain*).

WINGFIELD-STRATFORD, Esmé. *The Harvest of Victory, 1918–1926.* Routledge, 1935.

Preface: "My Victorian trilogy was an effort to assist in the comprehension, from a British standpoint, of the Prewar age. In this and subsequent volumes I am trying to do the same for our immediate past." Incl. chapter on literature: "Culture against Life."

————*The Victorian Aftermath, 1901–1914.* Routledge, 1933.

Last vol. of Victorian trilogy: I, *The Victorian Tragedy* ; II, *The Victorian Sunset,* 1932. Also pub. as *The Victorian Cycle* (N.Y., Morrow, 1935. Vol. I of Am. ed. entitled *Those Earnest Victorians.*). Very useful as well as readable books for general survey of period.

GENERAL HISTORIES OF MODERN LITERATURE

NOTE. For periodic surveys of the state of letters in England, see the pamphlets pub. for the British Council by Longmans, Green: William Allen, *The Year's Work in Literature, 1949* (1950); John Hayward, *Prose Literature since 1939* (1947); John Lehmann, ed., *The Year's Work in Literature, 1949–1950* (1951) [no more pub.]; Alan Pryce-Jones, *Prose Literature, 1945–1950* (1951). See also under Drama, Novel and Poetry. The pamphlets devoted to individual authors are being repr., several authors to one vol., as an American ed.: *British Writers and Their Work*, ed. Bonamy Dobrée and T. O. Beachcroft, American ed. J. W. Robinson, by Univ. of Nebraska as Bison Books.

ANNALS OF ENGLISH LITERATURE 1475–1950: The Principal Publications of Each Year, Together with an Alphabetical Index of Authors and Their Works. 2nd. ed., corr. Oxford Univ. Pr., 1961.
Necessarily very selective.

BATHO, Edith C[lare] and Bonamy DOBRÉE. *The Victorians and After, 1830–1914*. [1918] 2nd ed. rev. Cressett Pr., 1950. Vol. IV of *Introductions to English and American Literature*, ed. Bonamy Dobrée.
With a chapter on the economic background by Guy Chapman. Introd. only, and as such useful. Chapters on genres. Half the book consists of bibliog., also by genre: incl. history, travel, science, theology, philosophy, nonsense-parody, sport as well as the obvious headings. Sel. bibliog. of authors' works with paragraph summing up characteristics of each author. Despite series title, this vol. contains Eng. authors only.

BAUGH, Albert C[roll] et al. *A Literary History of England*. N.Y., Appleton-Century-Crofts, 1948.
"The Nineteenth Century and After, 1789–1939" by S[amuel] C[laggett] Chew. The first small-scale critical history of Eng. literature after Legouis and Cazamian; not very useful for contemporary literature. Brief, almost aphoristic treatment of modern writers (e.g. one paragraph on Forster). Extensive bibliog. footnotes.

BOYD, Ernest. *Ireland's Literary Renaissance*. [1916]. Rev. ed. N.Y., Knopf, 1922.
Factual and critical account of the literature produced in Ireland during the preceding 30 years under the impulse of the Celtic Renascence.

BRETT-JAMES, Antony. *The Triple Stream:* Four Centuries of English, French, and German Literature. Bowes and Bowes, 1953.
>   Parallel columns by year; chronological listing of selected major literary events, publication of books, dates of writers' births and deaths, *incl.* the 20th c. to 1930.

CLARKE, David Waldo. *Modern English Writers.* Essential Eng. Lib., 1947.
>   A survey by author: Hardy, Conrad, Kipling, Bennett, Galsworthy, Lawrence, Shaw, Wells, Maugham, Masefield, Priestley.

COMPTON-RICKETT, Arthur. *A Primer of English Literature.* Rev. enlgd. ed. of *A History of English Literature From the Earliest Times to 1916.* [1918] (In Series: *The Teaching of English*) Nelson, 1928.
>   Relevant section: "Present-Day Tendencies in English Literature." Short sections on genres and individual writers *incl.* Davidson, Kipling, Watson, Shaw, Wells, Bennett, Chesterton. Critical and well written. Useful for reputations at date of writing.

CONNOLLY, Cyril. *The Modern Movement:* One Hundred Key Books from England, France, and America, 1880–1950. N.Y., Atheneum, 1966. Pt. I: 1880–1920; II: 1920–1930; III: 1930–1940; IV: 1940–1950.
>   Each part has brief introd.; each book short (paragraph) description. Not much more than highly selective bibliog.

CUNLIFFE, J[ohn] W[illiam]. *English Literature During the Last Half-Century.* [1919] 2nd ed. rev. enlgd. N.Y., Macmillan, 1927.
>   By authors, *incl.* Hardy, Butler, Gissing, Shaw, Barrie, Kipling, Conrad, Wells, Galsworthy, Bennett, the Irish movement, the new poets, the new novelists. Sel. bibliog.

———— *English Literature in the Twentieth Century.* N.Y., Macmillan, 1933.
>   Introductory chapter on the age; chapters on individual authors (major only) and "Georgian Novelists" (*incl.* Conrad, Hardy, V. Woolf); "The Irish Renaissance"; "Essays, Journals and Travel"; "Masefield and the New Georgians." Bibliog. Author less at home in the new.

DAICHES, David. *The Present Age: After 1920.* Cresset Pr., 1958. (Am. ed. *The Present Age in British Literature.* Bloomington, Indiana Univ. Pr., 1958) Vol. V in Series: *Introductions to English Literature.* Replacement of Edwin Muir, *The Present Age: 1914* (Cresset Pr., 1939).
>   About half the book is extensive bibliogs. of authors and sel. critical bibliog.

EVANS, B[enjamin] Ifor. *English Literature Between the Wars.* [1948] 2nd. ed. Methuen, 1949, repr. 1951.
>   Lectures and essays on Forster, Joyce, D. H. Lawrence, Huxley, V. Woolf, Yeats, Eliot, "The Theatre"; "The Younger Generation"; "The New Biography."

FORD, Boris, ed. *The Modern Age.* Vol. VII of *The Pelican Guide to English Literature.* [1961] 2nd. ed. Penguin Bks., 1963.

Essays, uneven in quality, on random aspects of modern lit. by a variety of contributors.

FRASER, G[eorge] S[utherland]. *The Modern Writer and His World.* [1935] 3rd. ed. rev. Penguin Bks., 1964.

Critical and discerning. By genres and movements. The best introd. to the subject.

GOSSE, Edmund [William] and Richard GARNETT. *English Literature: An Illustrated Record.* [1926] New ed., 4 vols. in 2, with suppl. chapter on literature 1892–1922 by John Erskine. N.Y., Macmillan, 1935.

By general critics, not scholars, for general reader.

GWYNN, Stephen. *Irish Literature and Drama in the English Language: A Short History.* Nelson, 1936.

Incl. esp. A. E., Joyce, G. Moore, O'Casey, Robinson, Shaw, Synge, Yeats.

ISAACS, J[acob]. *An Assessment of Twentieth-Century Literature.* Secker and Warburg, 1951.

Six BBC Third Programme lectures by a perceptive critic: "The Assessment of Contemporary Literature"; "The Age of Anxiety"; "The Stream of Consciousness"; "Culture, Chaos, and Order"; "T. S. Eliot and Poetic Drama"; "The Verdict."

KENNEDY, J[ohn] M[cFarland]. *English Literature 1880–1905.* Stephen Swift, 1912; Boston, Small and Maynard, 1913.

Incl. Beerbohm, Symons, and chapters on Wells, Shaw, Gissing, Yeats, G. Moore, the Celtic Revival, Cunninghame Graham. Contemporary account, partisan but provocative and never dull.

LALOU, René. *Panorama de la littérature anglaise contemporaine.* [1926] Paris, Simon Kra, 1929.

By author: *incl.* Butler, Hardy, Kipling, Chesterton, Wells, Shaw, G. Moore, Yeats, Synge, Stephens, Joyce, Conrad, Galsworthy, Bennett.

LAW, Hugh Alexander. *Anglo-Irish Literature.* Dublin and Cork, Talbot Pr., 1926.

From Swift to after WW I. Last 50 pp. on moderns, *incl.*, briefly treated, Lady Gregory, Yeats, Synge Robinson, O'Casey, A. E., Ervine, Shaw, Katharine Tynan, Stephens, Colum, Joyce, G. Moore.

LEGOUIS, Émile and Louis CAZAMIAN. *A History of English Literature. Incl. Modern Times* (1660–1947) by Louis Cazamian, tr. W. D. MacInnes and the author [French 1924] Dent, 1947, repr. 1957. New ed. with new chapters on period 1914 to the sixties by Raymond Las Vergnas, bibliographies by Donald Davie and Pierre Legouis (*incl.* Book VIII, new chapters, 1964). Dent, 1965.

For long a standard history, with emphasis on criticism of authors.

LONGAKER, Mark and Edwin C. BOLLES. *Contemporary English Literature.* N.Y., Appleton-Century-Crofts, 1953

By authors under genres and movements; many authors, brief critical comment. Survey book; selected facts, short bibliog. of works and of history and criticism of literature.

MACDONAGH, Thomas. *Literature in Ireland:* Studies Irish and Anglo-Irish. Dublin, Talbot Pr., 1916.
> By one of the Irish Revolutionary Brotherhood.

MAIR, G[eorge] H. *Modern English Literature 1450–1959.* With Additional Chapter [on 20th c.] by A. C. Ward. [1911] Rev. ed. Oxford Univ. Pr., 1960.
> Series: Home University Lib. Student's handbook ; brief.

MORRIS, Lloyd R. *The Celtic Dawn:* A Survey of the Renascence in Ireland 1889–1916. N.Y., Macmillan, 1917.

NICOLSON, Harold. *The Development of English Biography.* Leonard and Virginia Woolf, 1927.
> Hogarth Lectures on Lit. One chapter on the present age, *incl.* Strachey, Gosse.

O'CONNOR, William Van. *The New University Wits and the End of Modernism.* Carbondale, Southern Illinois Univ. Pr., 1963.
> Important essays on English writers since World War II, *incl.* "A New Literary Generation" ; Larkin, Wain, Murdoch, Amis ; "The Other Writers" ; "The New Hero and a Shift in Literary Conventions" ; "A Postscript on Period Styles."

PARRY, Thomas. *History of Welsh Literature.* Tr. from Welsh by [H.] Idris Bell. N.Y. and London, Oxford Univ. Pr., 1955.
> Appendix by the translator on the 20th c., *incl.* Gwyn Jones.

ROUTH, H. V. *English Literature and Ideas in the Twentieth Century:* An Inquiry into Present Difficulties and Future Prospects. N.Y., Longmans, Green, 1948.
> Ca. 1900–1940s. "I believe that I have included and discussed every name which serves the spirit of twentieth-century literature." Authors separately and rather briefly considered under periods.

SAMPSON, George. *The Concise Cambridge History of English Literature.* [1941] Cambridge Univ. Pr. ; N.Y., Macmillan, 1943.
> Fairly brief section called "Late-Victorian and Post-Victorian Literature"—a diagnostic title. Author not really sympathetic to contemporary literature. Highly personal history. Substantial bibliog.

SCOTT-JAMES, R[olfe] A[rnold]. *50 Years of English Literature, 1900–1950.* With a Postscript 1951 to 1955. [1951] Longmans, Green, 1956.
> By an editor of *LM.* Many minor authors incl. Very conservative, so especially valuable on the Edwardians.

STEWART, J[ohn] I[nnes] M[ackintosh]. *Eight Modern Writers.* Vol. XII of *The Oxford History of English Literature,* eds. F. P. Wolson and Bonamy Dobrée. Oxford, Clarendon Pr., 1963.
> Hardy, James, Shaw, Conrad, Kipling, Yeats, Joyce, D. H. Lawrence. Long introd. on literature from 1880. More critical than factual, and idiosyncratic criticism, but always diverting.

SUTHERLAND, James. *On English Prose.* Toronto, Toronto Univ. Pr., 1966.

History of Eng. prose style from the 14th to the 20th c.; *incl.* D. H. Lawrence, V. Woolf.

SWINNERTON, Frank. *The Georgian Scene:* A Literary panorama. (Eng. ed., *The Georgian Literary Scene:* A Panorama, Heinemann, 1935) N.Y., Farrar and Rinehart, 1934.

Assessment of the work and importance, with comments on the personality and life, of many authors, most of them known to the author. Indispensable.

TINDALL, William York. *Forces in Modern British Literature 1885–1946.* [1947] Rev. ed. N.Y., Vintage, 1956.

Unique and indispensable.

VAN DOREN, Carl and Mark. *American and British Literature Since 1890.* [1925] Rev. ed. London and N.Y., Appleton-Century-Crofts, 1939.

By authors. Elementary level.

VINES, Sherard. *Movements in Modern English Poetry and Prose.* Oxford Univ. Pr., 1929.

"The sketching of an outline of literary events." Late Victorian period through WWI.

WARD, A[lfred] C. *Illustrated History of English Literature.* Vol. III: *Blake to Bernard Shaw.* Longmans, Green, 1955.

————*The Nineteen Twenties:* Literature and Ideas in the Post-War Decade. [1930] 2d. ed., Methuen, 1933.

Incl. selected reading list of books pub. 1920–1930.

————*Twentieth-Century English Literature, 1901–1960.* 1st ed. Methuen, 1928, as *Twentieth-Century Literature, 1901–1925*; rev. subsequently by decades. N.Y., Barnes and Noble, 1964.

By genre, with bibliographical footnotes. Good.

WILLIAMS, Sir Harold [Herbert]. *Modern English Writers: Being a Study* of Imaginative Literature 1890–1914. [1918] 3rd ed. rev. Sidgwick and Jackson, 1925.

————*Outline of Modern English Literature, 1890–1914.* Sidgwick and Jackson, 1920.

From *Modern English Writers* with some revision and additions. Very brief critical descriptions. Poetry takes up half the book.

SPECIAL STUDIES OF MODERN LITERATURE

CAMPOS, Christophe. *The View of France from Arnold to Bloomsbury.* London and N.Y., Oxford Univ. Pr., 1965.
> Ill. Relations with French literature and life of writers *incl.* James, G. Moore, Bennett, the Bloomsbury group.

CHARQUES, Robert D. *Contemporary Literature and the Social Revolution.* Secker, 1933.

CAUDWELL, Christopher (*pseud.* of Christopher St. John Sprigg). *Further Studies in a Dying Culture.* Ed. with pref. Edgell Rickword. Bodley Head, 1949.

————*Studies in a Dying Culture.* Lane, 1938.
> Studies in "bourgeois" aesthetics, history, psychology, philosophy, religion, from a Marxist point of view.

COWLEY, Malcolm and Bernard SMITH, eds. *Books That Changed Our Minds.* N.Y., Doubleday, 1939.
> Essays by well-known critics on influential books, *incl.* authors Freud, Veblen, Dewey, Boas, Beard, Parrington, Lenin, Spengler ; David Daiches on I. A. Richards ; "An Afterword on the Modern Mind."

DECLARATION. MacGibbon and Kee, 1958.
> "Revolutionary" authors state their position. *Incl.* Kenneth Tynan, Osborne, Lessing, Colin Wilson, Wain.

DOBRÉE, Bonamy. *Modern Prose Style.* [1934] 2nd ed. Oxford Univ. Pr., 1964.

ELLIS, Havelock. *The World of Dreams.* [1911] New ed. Boston and N.Y., Houghton Mifflin, 1926.

FRAZER, James M. *The Golden Bough.* [1911–1915] Abgd. ed. [1922] N.Y., Macmillan, 1951.

HOFFMAN, Frederick J. *The Mortal No:* Death and the Modern Imagination. (Reissue of *Freudianism and the Literary Mind,* Baton Rouge, Louisiana State Univ. Pr., 1945). Princeton, N.J., Princeton Univ. Pr., 1964.
> The Freudian theory and its impact on literature, *incl.* D. H. Lawrence.

HOGGERT, Richard. *The Uses of Literacy:* Changing Patterns in English Mass Culture. [1957] Boston, Beacon Pr., 1961 (paper).
> By a university lecturer in English, of working-class origin.

HOPPER, Stanley R[omaine], ed. *Spiritual Problems in Contemporary Literature:* A series of Addresses and Discussions. N.Y., Inst. for Religious and Social Studies (Harper, distrib.), 1952.

Incl. J. J. Sweeney, "Religion and the Artist's Situation" ; A. Salomon, "Sociology and the Literary Artist" ; Irwin Edman, "Philosophy and the Literary Artist" ; Horace V. Gregory, "Mutations of Belief in the Contemporary Novel."

JOHNSTONE, J[ohn] K. *The Bloomsbury Group:* A Study of E. M. Forster, Lytton Strachey, Virginia Woolf, and their Circle. Secker and Warburg ; N.Y., Noonday Pr., 1954.

Important study of influential writers.

KRUTCH, Joseph Wood. *The Modern Temper:* A Study and a Confession. [1931] N.Y., Harcourt, Brace and World, 1956.

Classic study of the thought and mood of the twenties.

LEAVIS, F[rank] R. *Two Cultures?* The Significance of C. P. Snow, with an Essay on Sir Charles Snow's Rede Lecture by Michael Yudkin. New Preface for American Readers by Leavis. Chatto and Windus ; N.Y., Pantheon Books, 1963.

LEWIS, Wyndham. *Time and Western Man.* [1927] Boston, Beacon Pr., 1957 (paper).

Author's characteristic theory applied to poetry, philosophy, science, etc. Authors discussed *incl.* Joyce.

LUCAS, F[rank] L[aurence]. *Style.* [1955] N.Y., Collier Books, 1962.

Lectures at Cambridge by a distinguished stylist, with ample ill. from French and Eng. lit., *incl.* modern.

MEYERHOFF, Hans. *Time in Literature.* Berkeley and Los Angeles, Univ. of Calif. Pr., 1960.

Time in literature in relation to the self and to nature.

MURRY, J[ohn] Middleton. *The Problem of Style.* [1922] N.Y., and London, Oxford Univ. Pr., 1956. (Galaxy).

Theoretical and with reference to English literature in general.

NOTT, Kathleen. *The Emperor's Clothes.* [1953] Heinemann, 1953 ; Bloomington, Indiana Univ. Pr., 1954.

Contradicts the "neo-scholastic" claim that humanism is dead. *Incl.* Hulme, Eliot, C. S. Lewis, Sayers, Greene.

O'CONNOR, William Van. *Modern Prose:* Form and Style. N.Y., Crowell, 1959.

ORTEGA Y GASSET, José. *The Modern Theme.* Tr. James Cleugh. [1931] N.Y., Harper Torchbooks, 1961.

Rationalism, relativity.

SAPIR, Edward. *Culture, Language and Personality:* Selected Essays, ed. David G. Mandelbaum. Cambridge Univ. Pr., and Berkeley and Los Angeles, Univ. of Calif. Pr., 1961.

By a famous professor of anthropological linguistics.

SLOCHOWER, Harry. *No Voice is Wholly Lost:* Writers and Thinkers in War and Peace. N.Y., Creative Age Pr., 1945.

Incl. Aldous Huxley, D. H. Lawrence, Belloc, Santayana, Eliot, Joyce, Shaw. Loss of traditional individual value in modern literature and turn to synthesis of Marx and Freud.

SPENDER, Stephen. *The Struggle of the Modern*. Berkeley and Los Angeles, Univ. of Calif Pr., 1963 ; paperback ed. 1965.

"This is a book of personal reflections about those qualities in litera-ture and art in the present century which I consider modern." (Introd.)

STARKIE, Enid. *From Gautier to Eliot:* The Influence of French on Eng-lish Literature 1851–1939. Hutchinson, 1960.

Introd. survey for the neophyte ; oversimplified.

SYPHER, Wylie. *Loss of the Self in Modern Literature and Art.* [1962] N.Y., Random House, 1964. (Vintage).

——————*Rococo to Cubism in Art and Literature:* Transformations in Style, in Art and Literature, from the 18th to the 20th Century. N.Y., Random House, 1960.

Ill. *Incl.* Eliot.

TEMPLE, Ruth Zabriskie. *The Critic's Alchemy:* A Study of the Introduc-tion of French Symbolism into England. [1953] New Haven, Conn. Col-lege and Univ. Pr., 1962 (paper).

Incl. Gosse, G. Moore, A. Symons, as poets and critics.

THORNDIKE, Ashley H. *Literature in a Changing Age*. N.Y., Macmillan, 1920.

Incl. "Changing Literature" ; "The Reading Public" ; "The Literary In-heritance" ; "Beauty and Art" ; "The Future."

TURNELL, Martin. *Modern Literature and Christian Faith*. Darton, Long-man and Todd, 1961.

Lauriston Lectures 1959. *Incl.* D. H. Lawrence, Forster, V. Woolf, Greene.

VAHANIAN, Gabriel. *Wait Without Idols*. N.Y., Braziller, 1964.

Exploration of human situation of post-Christian man in Western Christian literary tradition. *Incl.* Eliot, Auden.

WESTON, Jessie. *From Ritual to Romance*. [1920] Garden City, N.Y., Doubleday, 1957 (Anchor).

Anthropological studies used to explain myth in its literary appear-ances.

WILSON, Edmund. *Axel's Castle:* A Study in the Imaginative Literature of 1870–1930. [1936] N.Y., Scribner's, 1959.

Early and now classic treatment of Symbolism in English literature and its relation to the French movement. *Incl.* Yeats, Eliot, Joyce.

AUTOBIOGRAPHIES, DIARIES, MEMOIRS, REMINISCENCES

NOTE. Memoirs and reminiscences, as understood here, may be auto-biographical or biographical. Formal biographical studies by scholars not personally acquainted with the subject of the biographies are not included. Certain autobiographies disguised as fiction are included and labelled (n), as are certain *romans à clef* using actual authors as characters. Since most of these books have not been reprinted, only the date of original publication is included.

See the useful guide: William Matthews, *British Autobiographies:* An Annotated Bibliography of British Autobiographies Published or Written before 1951 (Berkeley, Univ. of Calif. Pr., 1955). As the arrangement is alphabetical, the only way to find modern autobiographies is to know the authors or read through, but the listing is commendably full. See also the same author's *British Diaries*: an Annotated Bibliography of British Diaries Written between 1442 and 1942 (Berkeley and Los Angeles, Univ. of Calif. Pr., 1950), arranged by years, under years by authors alphabetically. Place and date of pub. given and each entry is annotated for type of contents. Index of names provided.

ABINGTON, Adrian. *Beginnings,* 1935.
    Incl. novelists, e.g. Pritchett.

ACTON, Harold [Mario Mitchell]. *Grand Men,* 1954 (ill.). *Memoirs of an Aesthete,* 1948.

AGATE, James. *Ego.* Autobiography in nine parts: 1935, 1936, 1940, 1942, 1944, 1945, 1946, 1948. (*Ego 8* and *9* pub. as *Later Ego,* introd. and notes Jacques Barzun, 1951.)

ALDINGTON, Richard. *Life for Life's Sake:* A Book of Reminiscences, 1941.

————*Pinorman:* Personal Recollections of Norman Douglas, Pino Orioli and Charles Prentice, 1954.

ANSTEY, F[rederick]. *A Long Retrospect,* 1936.

ARCHER, William. *Real Conversations Recorded by William Archer,* with 12 Portraits, 1904.
    Incl. Hardy, Moore, Pinero, Phillips.

ARIC, Mrs. Eliza. *My Sentimental Self,* 1922.
    Novelist who knew G. Moore and Independent Theatre.

ARLEN, Michael. *The London Venture,* 1920.

ARMSTRONG, Martin. *Victorian Peep-Show,* 1938.

ATHERTON, Gertrude. *Adventures of a Novelist,* 1932

AUDEN, W[ystan] H[ugh]. *Louis MacNeice,* 1963.

BAILEY, John C[ann]. *Letters and Diaries 1864–1931,* ed. by his wife (Sarah Bailey), 1935.

BAIN, James S. *A Bookseller Looks Back,* 1940.

BARING, Maurice. *Comfortless Memory,* 1928.
Posthumously pub. narrative which, preface says, would supply missing fragment of B.'s biography.

———— *The Puppet Show of Memory,* 1922.

BARKER, George. *The Dead Seagull,* 1950 (a,n).

———— *The True Confession of George Barker,* 1950.

————*The True Confession of George Barker* (Book Two), 1965.

BAX, Clifford. *Evenings in Albany,* 1942.

———— *Ideas and People,* 1936.

———— *Inland Far,* 1925.

———— *Rosemary for Remembrance,* 1948.

————*Some I Knew Well,* 1951.

BEERBOHM, Max. *Leaves from the Garland,* 1926.

———— *Seven Men* [1919] *and Two Others,* enlgd. 1950 (s,r).

BEACH, Sylvia. *Shakespeare and Company,* 1966 [1959].

BEHAN, Brendan. *Borstal Boy,* 1958.

———— *Confessions of an Irish Rebel,* 1965.

BEHAN, Brian. *With Breast Expanded,* 1964.

BEHAN, Dominic. *My Brother Brendan,* 1965.

BEHRMAN, S. N. *The Suspended Drawing Room,* 1966.

BELL, Clive. *Old Friends:* Personal Recollections, 1956.

BELLOC, Hilaire. *The Cruise of the "Nona,"* 1925.

BENNETT, Arnold. *Books and Persons, 1908–1911,* 1917.

———— *Frank Swinnerton,* 1920.

————*Journal,* 1929 (Am. ed. *Journal of Things New and Old,* 1930).

————*The Journals,* ed. Newman Flower: I (1896–1910), 1932; II (1911–1921), 1932; III (1921–1928), 1933.

———— *Journals,* sel. and ed. Frank Swinnerton, 1954.

————*Paris Nights and Other Impressions of Places and People,* 1913. *Incl.* life in England 1907–1911.

———— *Things That Have Interested Me,* 1906, 1907, 1921, 1923, 1925.

————*The Truth about an Author,* 1903.

BENSON, A[rthur] C[hristopher]. *The Diary of A. C. Benson,* ed. Percy Lubbock, 1926.

————*The House of Quiet,* An Autobiography, 1904.

————*Memories and Friends,* 1924.

Incl. James, R. Brooke.

————*Rambles and Reflections,* 1926.

Incl. mostly Gissing.

BENSON, E[dward] F[rederic]. *As We Are:* A Modern Revue, 1932.
Effect of 1914 War ; chapter on aspects of times *incl.* Joyce.

———— *As We Were:* A Victorian Peep-Show, 1930.
Up to 1890's.

———— *Final Edition,* 1940.

BENTLEY, Phyllis. *O Dreams, O Destinations,* 1962.

BERESFORD, J[ohn] D[avys]. *What I Believe,* 1938.

————*Writing Aloud,* 1928.

BERNSTEIN, Herman. *Celebrities of Our Time:* Interviews (Shaw, H. Ellis), 1924.

BETJEMAN, John. *Summoned by Bells,* 1960 (a,p).

BLANCHE, Jacques-Émile. *More Portraits of a Lifetime,* 1918–1938, tr. and ed. Walter Clement, 1939.

Incl. G. Moore, James, H. Nicolson, Granville-Barker, Walkley.

————*Portraits of a Lifetime:* the Late Victorian Era, the Edwardian Pageant 1870–1914 (*Mes Modèles,* 1928), tr. and ed. Walter Clement, 1937 (Am. ed. 1938).

Incl. Hardy, James, G. Moore.

BLATHWAYT, Raymond. *Looking Down the Years,* 1935.

BLOOM, Ursula, *Rosemary for Stratford-on-Avon,* 1966.
Childhood memories of Edwardian Stratford, *incl.* Marie Corelli.

BLOOMFIELD, Paul. *Half the Battle:* Harrow, Oxford, London (the 'Thirties), 1936.

BLUNDEN, Edmund. *Guest of Thomas Hardy,* 1964.

————*Undertones of War,* 1928.

————*Winter Nights,* A Reminiscence, 1928 (p).

BLUNT, Wilfrid Scawen. *My Diaries:* Being a Personal Narrative of Events 1888–1914, 1919–1920.

BOTTRALL, Margaret. *Personal Records:* A Gallery of Self-Portraits, 1961.

BOTTOME, Phyllis. *The Challenge,* 1952.

———— *The Goal,* 1962.

———— *Search For a Soul,* 1947.

BOWEN, Elizabeth. *Bowen's Court,* 1942.

————*Seven Winters:* Memories of a Dublin Childhood [1942], and *Afterthoughts:* Pieces about Writing, 1962.

————*The Shelbourne Hotel,* 1951. (Eng. ed. *The Shelbourne:* A Centre in Dublin Life for More Than a Century)

Incl. G. Moore.

──────*A Time in Rome,* 1960.

BOYD, E[rnest] A[ugustus]. *Portraits Real and Imaginary,* Being Memories and Impressions of Friends and Contemporaries, 1924.

BREIT, Harvey. *The Writer Observed,* 1956.
> (Interviews, pub. in *New York Times* Book Section, with 18 of these authors.)

BRENAN, Gerald. *A Life of One's Own:* Childhood and Youth [1894–1919], 1962.

BRIDGES, Robert. *Henry Bradley,* 1926.

──────*Three Friends,* Memoirs of Digby Mackworth Dolben, Richard Watson Dixon, Henry Bradley, 1932.

BRIDIE, James. *One Way of Living,* 1939.

BRITTAIN, Vera. *Testament of Youth,* 1933.

BROOKE, Jocelyn. *The Birth of a Legend:* A Reminiscence of Arthur Machen and John Ireland, 1964.

──────*The Dog at Clambercrown,* 1955 (n,a).

──────*The Goose Cathedral,* 1950 (n,a).

──────*The Military Orchid,* 1948 (n,a).

──────*The Mine of Serpents,* 1949 (n,a).

BROOKFIELD, A[rthur] M[ontague]. *Annals of a Chequered Life,* 1930.

BROWN, Ivor. *The Way of My World,* 1954.

BRYHER, Winifred. *The Heart to Artemis:* A Writer's Memoirs, 1963.

BUCHAN, John. *Francis and Riversdale Grenfell,* 1920.

──────*Memory Hold-the-Door* (Am. ed. *Pilgrim's Way*), 1940.

BUTLER, Samuel. *The Notebooks of Samuel Butler,* ed. Henry Festing Jones, 1912. See also *Samuel Butler's Notebooks,* sel. and ed. Geoffrey Keynes and Brian Hill, 1951 ; *Selections from the Notebooks,* ed. A. T. Bartholomew, 1912.

──────*The Way of All Flesh,* 1903 (a,n) and *Ernest Pontifex, or The Way of All Flesh,* ed. with introd. and notes Daniel F. Howard, 1965.
> The latter is a reconstruction from ms. of novel before its recasting by Henry Festing Jones.

CAMPBELL, Roy. *Broken Record,* 1934.

──────*Light on a Dark Horse,* 1901–1935, 1951.

CARPENTER, Edward. *My Days and Dreams,* 1916.

──────*The Story of My Books,* 1916.

CARR, Mrs. J[oseph] [William] Comyns (Alice). *Reminiscences,* ed. Eve Adam, 1925.
> *Incl.* James, Shaw, Barrie, Hardy, Corelli, Gosse.

CARR, J[oseph] [William] Comyns. *Strange Memories,* 1920.

CARSWELL, Catherine Roxburgh. *Lying Awake:* An Unfinished Autobiography with Other Posthumous Papers, ed. John Carswell, 1950.

CARY, Joyce. *A House of Children,* 1941 (n,a).

CASEY, Marie. *Tides and Eddies,* 1966.

CHAPMAN, Guy. *A Passionate Prodigality:* Fragments of Autobiography, [1935] 1966.

CHESTERTON, G[ilbert] K[eith]. *The Autobiography of G. K. Chesterton,* 1936.

CHURCH, Richard. *The Golden Sovereign,* 1957.

————*Over the Bridge,* 1955.

————*A Stroll Before Dark,* 1965.

———— *The Voyage Home,* 1964.

CLARK, Barrett H. *Intimate Portraits:* Being Recollections of Maxim Gorky, John Galsworthy, Edward Sheldon, George Moore, Sidney Howard and Others, 1951.

CLARKE, Austin. *Twice Round the Black Church,* 1962.

CLODD, Edward, *Memories,* 1916.

COLLIER, John. *Just the Other Day,* 1932.

COLUM, Mary. *Life and the Dream,* 1947.

COLUM, Padraic. *My Irish Year,* 1912.

————(with Mary Colum). *Our Friend James Joyce,* 1958.

COMFORT, Alex. *The Silver River,* 1936.

COMPTON-RICKETT, Arthur. *I Look Back:* Memories of Fifty Years, 1933.

CONNOLLY, Cyril. *Enemies of Promise and Other Essays:* An Autobiography of Ideas, 1938 (rev. ed. 1949, 1960).
Pt. III. A Georgian Boyhood.

———— *The Unquiet Grave:* A Word Cycle (by Palinurus) [1945], 1966. Reminiscence and observations incl. some diary.

CONRAD, JESSIE. *Joseph Conrad and His Circle,* 1935.

————*Joseph Conrad as I Knew Him,* 1926.

CONRAD, Joseph. *The Mirror of the Sea,* 1906.

————*Some Reminiscences* (also pub. as *A Personal Record*), 1912.

COPPARD, A[lfred] E[dward]. *It's Me, O Lord!,* 1957.

COWARD, Noel. *Future Indefinite,* 1954.

———— *Present Indicative,* 1937.

CRONIN, A[rchibald] J[oseph]. *Adventures in Two Worlds* [1935], 1952.

CUMBERLAND, Gerald (pseud.) [Charles F. Kenyon]. *Set Down in Malice,* A Book of Reminiscences, 1919.

———— *Written in Friendship,* A Book of Reminiscences, 1923.

DAICHES, David. *Two Worlds,* 1956.

DANE, Clemence (pseud. of Winifred Ashton). *London Has a Garden,* 1964.

DAVIES, Rhys. *No Escape,* 1954.

DAVIES, W[illiam] H[enry]. *The Autobiography of a Super-Tramp,* 1908.

———— *Beggars,* 1909.

———— *Later Days,* 1925.

———— *A Poet's Pilgrimage,* 1918.

DIXON, Ella Hepworth. *As I Knew Them:* Sketches of People I Have Met on the Way, 1930.

D[OOLITTLE], H[ilda]. *Bid Me to Live,* 1965 (n,a).
   Roman à clef incl. Aldington, D. H. Lawrence.

DOUGLAS, Norman. *Late Harvest,* 1956.

————*Looking Back,* An Autobiographical Excursion, 1933.

DOYLE, Arthur Conan. *Memories and Adventures,* 1924.

———— *The Wanderings of a Spiritualist,* 1921.

DRAPER, Muriel [Gurdon]. *Music at Midnight,* 1929.
   Reminiscences of literary and musical people, London, before 1914.

DRINKWATER, John. *Discovery 1894–1913,* 1932.

———— *Inheritance,* 1931.

———— (with Albert Rutherston) *Claude Lovat Fraser,* 1923.

DU MAURIER, Angela. *Old Maids Remember,* 1966.

DUNCAN, Ronald [Frederic Henry]. *All Men Are Islands,* 1964 (a).
   The succeeding items are repr. of articles written as weekly feature of *The London Evening Standard* and signed "Jan." They are in effect the diary of a countryman, reporting Duncan's experiences and observations on his farm.

———— *The Blue Fox,* 1951.

———— *Home Made Home,* 1947.

———— *Jan at the Blue Fox,* 1952.

———— *Jan's Journal,* 1949.

———— *Journal of a Husbandman,* 1944.

DUNSANY, Lord (Edward John Moreton Drax Plunkett, Baron Dunsany). *Patches of Sunlight,* 1938.

———— *The Sirens Wake,* 1945.

EGLINTON, John (pseud.). *Irish Literary Portraits,* 1935.
   Some repr. from *LL* and N.Y. *Dial. Incl.* Yeats, A. E., G. Moore, Joyce.

———— *A Memoir of A. E.,* George William Russell, 1937.

EHRENBURG, Ilya. *People and Life, 1891–1921,* tr. Anne Bostock and Yvonne Kapp, 1961 (Am. ed. *Childhood and Youth,* 1962).

ELLIS, Havelock. *Impressions and Comments,* [1920] rev. ed. 1926 ; *Second Series* 1914–1920, [1921] rev. ed. 1926 ; *Third Series* 1920–1923, 1925. The three series collected as *Fountain of Life,* 1930.
   Random reflections by way of journal entries on books, society, etc.

————*My Life:* Autobiography, 1939.

ERVINE, St. John. *Some Impressions of My Elders*, 1922.

FAUSSET, Hugh I'Anson. *A Modern Prelude*, 1933.

FAY, W. G. and Catherine Carswell. *The Fays of the Abbey Theatre*, An Autobiographical Record, 1935.

FELBERMANN, Heinrich. *The Memoirs of a Cosmopolitan*, 1936.

FIELD, Michael (pseud.) (Katherine Harris Bradley and Edith Emma Cooper). *Works and Days:* From the Journal of Michael Field, ed T. and D. C. Sturge Moore, 1933.

FORBES-ROBERTSON, Sir John. *A Player Under Three Reigns*, 1925.

FORD, Ford Madox (born Ford Madox Hueffer). *Ancient Lights and Certain New Reflections* (Am. ed. *Memories and Impressions*, A Study in Atmospheres), 1911.

———— *It Was the Nightingale*, 1933.

————*Joseph Conrad*, A Personal Remembrance, 1924.

———— *No Enemy*, 1929.

————*Portraits from Life*, 1937. Eng. ed. *Mightier than the Sword:* Memories and Criticisms, 1938.
    Incl. James, Conrad, Hardy, Wells, D. H. Lawrence, Galsworthy, W. H. Hudson.

————*Reminiscences 1894–1914*, 1931. Am. ed. *Return to Yesterday*, 1932.

———— *Thus to Revisit*, 1921.
    Incl. Hudson, Conrad, James, Flint, some Imagists, "vers libre."

FRANKAU, Gilbert. *Self-Portrait: A Novel of His Life*, 1940.

FRY, Roger. *Goldsworthy Lowes Dickinson*, 1932.

GALSWORTHY, John. *Memorable Days*, 1924.

GARNETT, David. *The Familiar Faces*, 1962. (a, Vol. III).

———— *The Flowers of the Forest* (a, Vol. II), 1954.

———— *The Golden Echo* (a, Vol. I), 1953. (Also title of series.)

GERHARDI, William. *Memories of a Polyglot*, 1931.

GIBBINGS, Robert. *Lovely is the Lea*, 1945.

GIBBS, Philip. *Crowded Company*, 1949.

———— *Life's Adventures*, 1957.

———— *The Pageant of the Years*, 1946.

GIBSON, Wilfrid. *Wild Career*, 1935.

GISSING, George. *Selections, Autobiographical and Imaginative*, 1929.

GOGARTY, Oliver St. John. *As I was Going Down Sackville Street:* A Phantasy in Fact, 1937.

———— *Going Native*, 1941.

————*It Isn't This Time of Year At All:* An Unpremeditated Autobiography, 1954.

———— *Mourning Becomes Mrs. Spendlove and Other Portraits*, 1948.
Incl. Joyce, Yeats.

GOLDING, Louis. *Adventures in Living Dangerously*, 1930.

————*Louis Golding's Boxing Tales*, 1948.

———— *The World I Knew*, 1940.

GOLDING, William. *The Hot Gates*, 1965.

GOLDRING, Douglas. *The Nineteen Twenties:* A General Survey and Some Personal Memories, 1945.

————*Odd Man Out*: The Autobiography of a Propaganda Novelist, 1935.

————*Privileged Persons*, 1955.
Real and imaginary characters in "period" pieces of fiction, written over 30 yrs., designed to hold up mirror to age.

————*South Lodge:* Reminiscences of Violet Hunt, Ford Madox Ford and the *English Review* Circle, 1943.

GORE, John. *Edwardian Scrapbook*, 1951.

GRAVES, Robert. *Goodbye to All That*, 1929. (a).

———— *Occupation: Writer*, 1951.

———— *Steps*, 1958.

GREEN, Henry. *Pack My Bag:* A Self-Portrait, 1940.

GREGORY, Lady (Isabella Augusta, Lady Gregory). *Journals 1916–1930*, ed. Lennox Robinson, 1946.

————*Our Irish Theatre:* A Chapter of Autobiography, 1913.

GREIN, Jacob [T.]. *The World of the Theatre:* Impressions and Memories, 1920–1921, 1921.
Repr. from *ILN. Incl.* Galsworthy, Shaw, Beerbohm, Mackenzie, Milne.

GRIGSON, Geoffrey. *The Crest on the Silver*, 1950.

GWYNN, Stephen. *Duffer's Luck:* A Fisherman's Adventures, 1924.

———— *Experiences of a Literary Man*, 1926.

———— *Fishing Holidays*, 1904.

HAGGARD, H[enry] Rider. *The Days of My Life*, 1926.

HAMILTON, G[eorge] Rostrevor. *Rapids of Time:* Sketches from the Past, 1965.

HANLEY, James. *Broken Water:* An Autobiographical Excursion, 1937.

HARDY, Florence (Emily). *The Early Life of Thomas Hardy, 1840–1891*, 1928.

———— *The Later Years of Thomas Hardy 1892–1928*, 1930.
The two pub. as *The Life of Thomas Hardy, 1840–1928*, 1962. Author, H.'s second wife, describes these as "compiled largely from contemporary notes, letters, diaries, and biographical memoranda, as well as from oral information in conversations extending over many years." Thus they appear to constitute in effect H.'s autobiography.

HARDY, Thomas. *Thomas Hardy's Notebooks* and Some Letters from Julia Augusta Martin, ed. Evelyn Hardy, 1955.

HARPER, J. Henry. *I Remember*, 1934.

HARRAP, George G. *Some Memories: 1901–1935*, 1935.

HARRIS, Frank. *Confessional*, 1930.

————*Frank Harris, His Life and Adventures:* An Autobiography, introd. Grant Richards, 1947.

———— *My Life*, 1925——

———— *My Life and Loves* [4 vols., 1922–1927], ed. John F. Gallagher, 1963.

————*On the Trail,* My Reminiscences as a Cowboy, 1930.

HEPPENSTALL, Rayner. *Four Absentees*, 1960.
  Incl. Orwell, D. Thomas, Murry.

————*The Intellectual Part*, 1963.

HERBERT, A[lan] P[atrick]. *Independent Member*, 1950.

HIBBERT, H[enry] G[eorge]. *Fifty Years of a Londoner's Life*, 1916.

———— *A Playgoer's Memories*, 1920.

HILTON, James. *To You, Mr. Chips*, 1938.
  One chapter of autobiog. incl.

HOLLOWAY, John. *A London Childhood*, 1966.

HOPE, Anthony. *Memories and Notes*, 1927.

HOPKINS, Gerard Manley. *The Notebooks and Papers*, ed. Humphry House, 1937. Rev. enlgd. as *Journals and Papers,* completed Graham Storey, 1959.

HOUSEHOLD, Geoffrey. *Against the Wind:* An Autobiography, 1958.

HOUSMAN, A[lfred] E[dward]. *Some Poems, Some Letters, and a Personal Memoir by Laurence Housman,* 1938.

HOUSMAN, Laurence. *A.E.H.,* 1938.

———— *The Unexpected Years*, 1937.

HUDSON, W[illiam] H[enry]. *Far Away and Long Ago*, 1918.

HUGHES, Richard. *Richard Hughes, An Omnibus* (with an autobiographical introd.), 1931.

HUNEKER, James Gibbons. *Steeplejack,* 2 vols., 1920.
  Incl. Conrad, Shaw, Beerbohm.

HUNT, Violet. *The Flurried Years* (Am. ed. *I Have This to Say*), 1926.
  Incl. Ford.

HUTCHINSON, R[oy] C[oryton]. *Interim*, 1945.

HUXLEY, Aldous. *Aldous Huxley, 1894–1963*, ed. Julian Huxley, 1965.
  Incl. essay by Aldous Huxley dictated the day before his death.

———— *Point Counterpoint*, 1928 (n).
  Roman à clef, incl. D. H. Lawrence.

IRISH RENAISSANCE. A Gathering of Essays, Memoirs, and Letters from the *Massachusetts Review*, ed. Robin Skelton and Daniel R. Clarke, 1966.

ISHERWOOD, Christopher. *Lions and Shadows:* An Education in the Twenties, 1938 (n,a).

JAMES, Alice. *The Diary of Alice James,* ed. Leon Edel, 1965.

JAMES, Henry. *An Autobiography,* ed. Frederick W. Dupee, 1956. *Incl. A Small Boy and Others,* 1913 ; *Notes of a Son and Brother,* 1914 ; *The Middle Years,* 1917.

————*The Notebooks,* ed. F. O. Mathiessen and Kenneth B. Murdock, 1947.

JAMESON, Storm. *No Time Like the Present,* 1933.

JEROME, JEROME K[lapka]. *My Life and Times,* 1926.

————*On the Stage—and Off,* 1885.

JOHNSTON, Denis. *Nine Rivers from Jordan,* 1955.

JONES, Gwyn. *The First Forty Years,* 1957.

JONES, Sir Lawrence. *An Edwardian Youth,* 1956.

KAYE-SMITH, Sheila. *All the Books of My Life,* 1956.
———— *Three Ways Home,* 1937.

KERNAHAN, Coulson. *Celebrities:* Little Stories about Famous Folk, 1923.

————*In Good Company:* Some Personal Recollections of . . . , 1917.
    Incl. Phillips.

KEYNES, John M[aynard]. *Two Memoirs:* Dr. Melchior, a Defeated Enemy, and My Early Beliefs, 1949.

KIPLING, Rudyard. *Something About Myself,* 1937.

KNIGHT, Dame Laura. *The Magic of a Line,* 1965.
    80 years of this artists's life.

KOESTLER, Arthur. *Arrow in the Blue,* 1942.

———— *The Invisible Writing,* 1954.

———— *Scum of the Earth,* 1941.
    Experiences in France, Aug. 1939–June 1940.

LADD, Henry. *With Eye of the Past,* 1928.

LAVER, James. *The Age of Optimism* (1848–1914), 1966.

———— *Edwardian Promenade,* 1958.

LAWRENCE, FRIEDA. *The Memoirs and Correspondence,* ed. E. W. Tedlock, 1961.

———— *Not I but the Wind* . . . , 1934.

LAWRENCE, T[homas] E[dward]. *The Mint,* 1955.

———— *Secret Dispatches from Arabia,* 1939.

————*Seven Pillars of Wisdom:* A Triumph, 1926. Abgd. as *Revolt in the Desert,* 1926.

————*T. E. Lawrence to his Biographer, Liddell Hart,* 1939.

———— *T. E. Lawrence to his Biographer, Robert Graves,* 1939.

LEE, Laurie. *Cider with Rosie* (Am. ed. *The Edge of Day*), 1959. (n, a).

LEGALLIENNE, Richard. *From a Paris Garret,* 1936.

RICHARD LeGALLIENNE: a Centenary Memoir-Anthology, ed. Clarence Raymond Decker, 1966.

LEHMANN, John. *Ancestors and Friends,* 1962.

————*I Am My Brother,* 1960 (a, Vol. II).

———— *The Whispering Gallery,* 1955 (a, Vol. I).

————, ed., *Coming to London,* 1957.
Reminiscences written for *The London Magazine* by Plomer, L. Woolf, Pritchett, Barker, Priestley, Bowen, Grigson, Murry, Isherwood, Pryce-Jones, Sansom, J. Brooke, Macaulay, E. Sitwell.

LESLIE, Shane. *American Wonderland,* 1936.

———— *The End of a Chapter,* 1919.

———— *The Film of Memory,* 1938.

———— *Long Shadows:* A Book of Reminiscences, 1966 (later Victorian, Edwardian and Georgian periods).

LESSING, Doris. *In Pursuit of the English,* 1960.

LEWIS, C[ecil] Day. *The Buried Day,* 1960.

LEWIS, C[live] S[taples]. *Surprised by Joy,* 1955.

LEWIS, (Percy) Wyndham. *Blasting and Bombardiering,* 1937.
Recollections of Eliot, Joyce, James, Pound.

LINKLATER, Eric. *A Year of Space,* 1953.

LOWNDES, Mrs. Belloc. *The Merry Wives of Westminster,* 1946.

LUBBOCK, Percy. *Shades of Eton,* 1929.

LUCAS, E[dward] V[errall]. *Reading, Writing and Remembering,* 1932.

LUHAN, Mabel Dodge. *Intimate Memories,* 1933–1937 (4 vols.).

MACCARTHY, Desmond. *Memories,* 1953.
Incl. Bennett, Wells, Strachey, Galsworthy, Maugham, W. H. Davies, Kipling, Hardy, Joyce, Sassoon, L. P. Smith, Doyle, R. Fry, Beerbohm, James, R. Brooke, Blunt.

MACCARTHY, Lillah (Lady Keeble). *Myself and My Friends,* 1933.

MCFEE, William. *Harbours of Memory,* 1921.

MACKENZIE, Compton. *Literature in My Time,* 1933.
On his own reading and his reflections on men and movements *incl.* Hardy, Noyes, Masefield, Butler, Galsworthy, Bennett, Wells, Conrad, "The Aesthetic Movement."

————*My Life and Times, Octave I:* 1883–1891, 1963 ; *Octave II:* 1891–1900, 1963 ; *Octave III:* Vintage Oxford Years and Debut as a Writer, 1964 ; *Octave IV:* 1907–1915, 1965 ; *Octave V:* 1915–1923, 1966.

MACNEICE, Louis. *The Strings Are False,* 1965 (unfinished a).

MALLOCK, W[illiam] H[urrell]. *Memories of Life and Literature,* 1920.

MACMILLAN, Harold. *Winds of Change, 1914–1939,* 1966.

MARSH, Sir Edward [Howard]. *A Number of People:* A Book of Reminiscences, 1939.
> *Incl.* Baring, Bridges, Gosse, James, R. Brooke, H. Munro.

MARTIN, Kingsley. *Father Figures:* A First Volume of Autobiography 1897–1931, 1966.

MASEFIELD, John. *Grace before Plowing,* 1966 (fragments of autobiography of early years).

———— *John M. Synge,* 1915.

———— *New Chum,* 1944.

———— *So Long to Learn,* 1952.

———— *Some Memories of W. B. Yeats,* 1940.

. MASSINGHAM, Harold. *Remembrance,* 1941.

MASTERS, John. *Bugles and a Tiger,* 1956.

———— *The Road Past Mandalay,* 1961.

MAUGHAM, Robin. *Somerset and all the Maughams,* 1966.

MAUGHAM, W[illiam] S[omerset]. *Cakes and Ale,* or The Skeleton in the Cupboard, 1930 (n,b).
> *Roman à clef, incl.* Hardy.

———— *Of Human Bondage,* 1915 (n,a).

————*The Partial View,* 1954. Contains *The Summing Up* (1938) and *A Writer's Notebook* (1949) with a new preface.
> *The Summing Up* according to M. is not autobiog. or book of recollections but effort "to sort out my thoughts on the subjects that have chiefly interested me during the course of my life."

———— *Strictly Personal,* 1941.

———— *The Writer's Point of View,* 1951.

MEYERSTEIN, E[dward] H[arry] W[illiam]. *Of My Early Life,* ed. Rowland Watson, 1957.

MEYNELL, Viola. *Alice Meynell:* A Memoir, 1929.

———— *Francis Thompson and Wilfrid Meynell:* A Memoir, 1952.

MILNE, A[lan] A[lexander]. *It's Too Late Now,* 1939.

————*Year In, Year Out,* 1952.

MONAHAN, Michael. *Adventures in Life and Letters,* [1912] rev. 1925.

MOORE, George. *Avowals,* [1919], 1926.
> M.'s typical informal discursive monologue, ranging widely over literature and art. Reminiscence, real and imaginary, idiosyncratic views.

———— *A Communication to My Friends,* 1933.

———— *Confessions of a Young Man,* 1888.
> His Paris "education," ironic in tone. Contemporary literary movements and men.

————*Conversations in Ebury Street,* [1924] rev. 1930.
> English and French authors and friends.

———— *Hail and Farewell,* Trilogy: *Ave,* 1911 ; *Salve,* 1912 ; *Vale,* 1914.
M.'s connection with the Irish Renascence.

———— *Impressions and Opinions,* 1891.

MORGAN, Charles. *The House of Macmillan 1843–1943,* 1943.

MOTTRAM, R[alph] H[ale]. *Another Window Seat,* 1957.

————*Autobiography With a Difference,* 1938.

———— *Vanities and Verities,* 1958.

———— *The Window Seat,* 1954.

MUIR, Edwin. *The Story and the Fable,* 1940. Rev. enlgd. as *An Autobiography,* 1954.

MURRAY, Gilbert. *An Unfinished Autobiography,* ed. J. Smith, 1960.

MURRY, John Middleton. *Between Two Worlds,* 1935.

————*Katherine Mansfield and Other Literary Portraits,* 1949.

———— *Reminiscences of D. H. Lawrence,* 1933.

———— *Son of Woman,* the Story of D. H. Lawrence, 1931.

———— (with Ruth E. Mantz) *The Life of Katherine Mansfield,* 1935.

NAPIER, Priscilla. *A Late Beginner,* 1966.

NEWBOLT, Sir Henry. *The Later Life and Letters of Sir Henry Newbolt,* ed. Margaret Newbolt, 1942.

————*My World as in My Time 1862–1932,* 1932.

NICHOLS, Beverley. *A Case of Human Bondage,* 1966.
On Maugham.

———— *All I Could Never Be:* Recollections, 1949.

———— *The Sweet and Twenties,* 1958.

NICOLSON, Harold. *Diaries and Letters, 1930–39,* ed. Nigel Nicolson, 1966.

NOYES, Alfred. *Two Worlds for Memory,* 1953.

O'CASEY, Sean, *Mirror in My House,* Autobiographies, 2 vols., [1956],
1958. Contains Vol. I: *I Knock at the Door* and *Swift Glances Back at Things That Made Me* (1939), *Pictures in the Hallway* (1942), *Drums Under the Windows* (1945) ; Vol. II: *Inishfallen, Fare Thee Well* (1949), *Rose and Crown* (1952), *Sunset and Evening Star* (1954).

O'CONNOR, Frank. *An Only Child,* 1961.

O'CONNOR, Mrs. T[homas] P[lower] (Elizabeth Paschal). *I, Myself,* 1911.

O'DONOVAN, John. *Shaw and the Charlatan Genius, a Memoir,* 1966.

O'FAOLAIN, Sean. *Vive Moi!,* 1964.

OMMANNEY, Francis Downes. *The River Bank,* 1966.

ORCUTT, William Dana. *In Quest of the Perfect Book,* Reminiscences and Reflections of a Bohemian, 1926.
Incl. Shaw, James, Hewlett.

ORWELL, George. *Down and Out in Paris and London,* 1933.

O'SULLIVAN, Seumas (pseud. of James Starkey). *Essays and Recollections,* 1944.

OWEN, Wilfred. *Journey From Obscurity:* Wilfred Owen 1893–1918 (Memoirs of the Owen Family) ; I *Childhood*, 1963 ; II *Youth*, 1964 ; III *War*, 1965.

OXFORD AND ASQUITH, Earl of. *Memories and Reflections 1852–1957*, 2 vols., 1958.

PEARSON, Hesketh. *Hesketh Pearson by Himself*, 1966.

PLOMER, William. *At Home*, 1958.

———— *Double Lives*, 1943.

POTTER, Stephen. *Steps to Immaturity*, 1959.

POWYS, John Cooper. *Autobiography*, 1934.

————*The Religion of a Sceptic*, 1925.

———— *Still the Joy of It*, 1956.

PRIESTLEY, J[ohn] B[oynton]. *Delight*, 1949.

————*Midnight on the Desert:* A Chapter of Autobiography, 1937.

————*Rain upon Godshill:* A Further Chapter of Autobiography, 1939.

PRITCHETT, V[ictor] S[awdon]. (Author of preface) *Why Do I Write?* An Exchange of Views Between Elizabeth Bowen, Graham Greene and V. S. Pritchett, 1948.

PUDNEY, John. *Who Only England Know:* Log of a War-Time Journey of Unintentional Discovery of Fellow-Countrymen, 1943.

QUILLER-COUCH, Arthur. *Memoir of Arthur John Butler*, 1917.

———— *Memories and Opinions:* An Unfinished Autobiography, ed. S. C. Roberts, 1945.

RAVERAT, Gwendolyn Mary (Darwin). *Periodic Piece:* A Cambridge Child-hood, 1952.

READ, Herbert. *The Innocent Eye*, 1933 (incl. *In Retreat*, 1925) Eng. ed. *Annals of Innocence and Experience* [1940], 1947, includes later material.

————*The Contrary Experience: Autobiographies* [incl. *The Innocent Eye* and pt. 2 of *Annals* with new unpub. material], 1963.

REES, Goronwy. *A Bundle of Sensations:* Sketches in Autobiography, 1961.

REID, Forrest. *Apostate*, 1926.

————*Private Road*, 1940.

RETINGER, J. H. *Conrad and his Contemporaries:* Souvenirs, 1943.

RHYS, Ernest. *Everyman Remembers*, 1931.

———— *Wales England Wed*, 1940.

RICHARDS, Grant. *Author Hunting by an Old Literary Sportsman:* Memo-ries of Years Spent Mainly in Publishing, 1897–1925, [1934] new ed. 1960.

————*Memories of a Misspent Youth 1872–1896*, 1932.

RIDING, Laura. *Contemporaries and Snobs*, 1928.

ROBERTS, Sir Sydney. *Adventures with Authors*, 1966.

ROBINSON, Lennox. *Curtain Up*, 1942.

———— *Pictures in a Theatre:* A Conversation Piece, 1947.

———— (with Tom Robinson and Nora Dorman) *Three Homes,* 1938.

ROTHENSTEIN, Sir John, *Summer's Lease:* Autobiography 1901–1938, 1965 (Vol. I).

———— *Brave Day, Hideous Night,* 1966 (Vol. II).

ROTHENSTEIN, Sir William. *Men and Memories:* Recollections: Vol. I 1872–1900, Vol. II 1900–1922 [1931–32], 1937.

————*Since Fifty: Men and Memories, 1922-1938,* 1940.

ROWSE, A[lfred] L[eslie]. *A Cornish Childhood,* 1942.

———— *A Cornishman at Oxford:* The Education of a Cornishman, 1965.

RUSSELL, Bertrand. *The Autobiography, 1872–1914,* 1967.

————*Portraits from Memory,* [1951], 1956.
> *Incl.* "Adaptation: an Autobiographical Epitome"; "Six Autobiographical Talks"; "How to Grow Old"; "Reflections on my 80th Birthday"; "Portraits from Memory" *incl.* Shaw, Wells, Conrad, D. H. Lawrence. Also essays: "How I Write" and on Orwell.

A. E. (George William Russell). *The Living Torch,* ed. Monk Gibbon, 1937.
> "A. E.'s table talk, a note-book of his ideas and ideals."

SACKVILLE-WEST, Edward. "Sketches for an Autobiography" in *Orion,* Vol. III (1946), pp. 51–58 ; Vol. IV (1947), pp. 7–15.

SACKVILLE-WEST, Victoria. *The Edwardians,* 1930 (n).
> Background authentic.

SANTAYANA, George. *Persons and Places:* Vol. I *The Background of my Life,* 1944, Vol. II *The Middle Span,* 1945, Vol. III *My Host the World,* 1953 [English ed. *Persons and Places: The Background of my Life*].

SAROYAN, William. *Not Dying,* 1966.

SASSOON, Siegfried. *The Complete Memoirs of George Sherston,* 1937. Contains *Memoirs of a Fox-Hunting Man,* 1928 (repr. 1954) ; *Memoirs of an Infantry Officer,* 1930 ; *Sherston's Progress,* 1936.

————*The Old Century and Seven More Years,* 1938.

———— *Siegfried's Journey 1916–1920,* 1945.

———— *The Weald of Youth,* 1942.

SHAW, George Bernard. *Shaw Gives Himself Away,* 1939.

———— *Sixteen Self Sketches,* 1949.

SHUTE, Nevil. *Slide Rule,* the Autobiography of an Engineer, 1954.

SIDGWICK, Ethel. *Mrs. Henry Sidgwick,* A Memoir, 1938.

SICHEL, Walter S[ydney]. *The Sands of Time:* Recollections and Reflections, 1923.

SITWELL, Edith. *Taken Care Of:* An Autobiography, 1965.

SITWELL, Osbert. *Great Morning!* (a, Vol. III), 1947.

————*Laughter in the Next Room* (a, Vol. IV), 1948.

————*Left Hand, Right Hand!* (a, Vol. I and title of series), 1944.

————*Noble Essences* (a, Vol. V), 1950.

—————*The Scarlet Tree* (a, Vol. II), 1946.

————— *Tales My Father Taught Me*, 1962.

SITWELL, Sacheverell. *All Summer in a Day*, 1926. (Autobiographical fantasy.)

SMALLEY, George W. *Anglo-American Memories*, 1911.

SMITH, Logan Pearsall. *A Portrait of Logan Pearsall Smith,* Drawn from His Letters and Diaries and Introduced by John Russell, 1950.

————— *Robert Bridges, Recollections,* 1931.

————— *Unforgotten Years,* 1938.

SMYTH, [Dame] Ethel [Mary]. *As Time Went On,* 1936 (ill.).

————— *Impressions that Remained:* Memoirs, 1919, new ed. 1923. 2 vols.

—————*Streaks of Life,* 1921 (Autobiographical papers).

————— *What Happened Next,* 1940 (ill.).

SPARROW, [John Walter] Gerald. *Confessions of an Eccentric,* 1965.

SPENDER, Stephen. *World Within World,* The Autobiography of Stephen Spender, 1951.

SQUIRE, J[ohn] C[ollings]. *The Honeysuckle and the Bee,* 1937.

—————*Reflections and Memories,* 1935.
   Incl. Flecker, Freeman.

STARK, Freya. *Beyond Euphrates,* 1951.

————— *The Coast of Incense* 1933–39, 1953.

————— *Dust in the Lion's Paw* 1939–46, 1961.

————— *The Freya Stark Story,* 1953. Condensation of autobiography to 1939.

————— *Traveller's Prelude,* 1950.

STANSKY, Peter, and William ABRAHAMS. *Journey to the Frontier: Julian Bell and John Cornford, Their Lives in the 1930s,* 1966.

STARKIE, Enid. *A Lady's Child,* 1941.

STEEN, Marguerite. *Looking Glass:* An Autobiography, 1966.

STEIN, Gertrude. *The Autobiography of Alice B. Toklas,* 1933.
   S.'s life written as autobiography of her companion. Paris, literary figures, artists.

STEIN, Leo. *Journey into the Self,* Being the Letters, Papers and Journals of Leo Stein, ed. Edmund Fuller, 1950.

STERN, G[ladys] B[ronwyn]. *All in Good Time,* 1954.

—————*And Did He Stop and Speak to You?,* 1957.
   Incl. Beerbohm, Betjeman, Kaye-Smith, Sherriff, Maugham.

————— *Another Part of the Forest,* 1941.

————— *Benefits Forgot,* 1949.

————— *Monogram,* 1936.

————— *A Name to Conjure With,* 1953.

————— *The Way it all Worked Out,* 1956.

STRONG, L[eonard] A[lfred] G[eorge]. *Shake Hands and Come Out Fighting*, 1938.

———— *Green Memory*, 1961.

STUART, Francis. *Things to Live For*, 1934.

SUTRO, Alfred. *Celebrities and Simple Souls*, 1933.

SWINNERTON, Frank. *Background with Chorus:* A Footnote to Changes in English Literary Fashion between 1901 and 1917, 1956.
> *Incl*. James, Gissing.

———— *Figures in the Foreground:* Literary Reminiscences 1917–1940, 1963.

———— *Frank Swinnerton: Personal Sketches* together with Notes and Comments on the Novels, by Arnold Bennett, H. G. Wells and Grant Overton, 1920.

SYMONS, Arthur. *Confessions*. A Study in Pathology, 1930.

———— *From Toulouse-Lautrec to Rodin*, with Some Personal Impressions, 1929.

————*Mes Souvenirs* (on Verlaine), 1931.

———— *Notes on Joseph Conrad*, with Some Unpublished Letters, 1925.

SYNGE, J[ohn] M[illington]. *The Autobiography of J. M. Synge*, Constructed from the Manuscripts by Alan Price, 1966.

THIRKELL, Angela. *Three Houses*, 1931.

THOMAS, Dylan. *A Child's Christmas in Wales* [1954], rev. ed. 1959.

THOMAS, Edward. *The Childhood of Edward Thomas:* A Fragment of Autobiography, 1938.

———— *The Woodland Life*, 1897.

TICKNOR, Caroline. *Glimpses of Authors*, 1922.
> Reminiscences, anecdotes. *Incl*. James.

TOKLAS, Alice B. *What Is Remembered*, 1963.

TOMLINSON, H[enry] M[ajor]. *A Mingled Yarn*, 1953.

TOYNBEE, Philip. *Friends Apart:* A Memoir of Esmond Romilly and Jasper Ridley in the Thirties, 1954.

TREVELYAN, George Macaulay. *An Autobiography and Other Essays*, 1949.

———— *Scenes from Italy's War*, 1919.

TREWIN, J[ohn] C[ourtney]. *Up from the Lizard*, [1949] 1953.

TUELL, Anne K. *Mrs. Meynell and Her Literary Generation*, 1925.

TYNAN, Katharine. *Memories*, 1924.

———— *The Middle Years*, 1916.

———— *Twenty-Five Years:* Reminiscences, 1913.

———— *The Wandering Years*, 1922.

———— *The Years of the Shadow*, 1919.

UNWIN, Stanley. *Truth About Publishing*, rev. 1960.

VACHEL, Horace Annesley. *Distant Fields,* 1938.

———— *Fellow-Travellers,* 1923.

———— *In Sober Livery,* 1949.

———— *Methuselah's Diary,* 1950.

———— *More from Methuselah,* 1951.

———— *Now Came Still Evening On,* 1946.

———— *Twilight Grey,* 1948.

———— *Where Fancy Beckons,* 1938.

VAN DRUTEN, John. *Playwright at Work,* 1953.

————*The Way to the Present,* 1938.

———— *The Widening Circle,* 1957.

VULLIAMY, C[olwyn] E[dward]. *Calico Pie,* 1940.

VYVYAN, C. C. *Coloured Pebbles,* 1964.

———— *Journey up the Years,* 1966.

————*Roots and Stars,* 1962.

WAIN, John. *Sprightly Running,* 1962.

WALLACE, Edgar. *Edgar Wallace:* A Short Autobiography, 1929.

———— *My Hollywood Diary:* The Last Work of Edgar Wallace, 1932.

———— *People:* A Short Autobiography, 1926.

WALPOLE, Hugh. *The Apple Trees*: Four Reminiscences, 1932.
James, Galsworthy, Masefield, Ervine.

WARD, Mrs. Humphrey. *A Writer's Recollections,* 1918.

WARNER, Sylvia Townsend. *Teacher,* 1963.

WAUGH, Alec. *The Early Years,* 1962.

————*Myself When Young:* Confessions, 1923.

———— *Thirteen Such Years,* 1932.

WAUGH, Arthur. *One Man's Road:* Being a Picture of Life in a Passing
Generation, 1931.

WAUGH, Evelyn. *A Little Learning,* 1964.

———— *The Ordeal of Gilbert Pinfold,* 1957 (n,a)

———— *Sword of Honor,* 1966. Rev. ed. of trilogy: *Men at Arms,* 1952 ;
Officers and Gentlemen, 1955 ; *Unconditional Surrender* (Am. ed. *The End
of the Battle*), 1961 (n,a).

WELCH, Denton. *The Denton Welch Journals,* ed. Jocelyn Brooke, 1952.

———— *Maiden Voyage,* 1943.

WELLESLEY, Dorothy. *Far Have I Travelled,* 1952.

———— *Sir George Goldie,* Founder of Nigeria, 1934.

WELLS, H[erbert] G[eorge]. *Experiment in Autobiography:* Discoveries
and Conclusions of a Very Ordinary Brain (since 1866), 1934.

WHIPPLE, Dorothy. *The Other Day*: An Autobiography, 1936.
A best-selling novelist's journal kept through many years.

———— *Random Commentary,* 1965. Second part of autobiography.

WHITALL, James. *English Years,* 1936.

WHITE, T[erence] H[anbury]. *America at Last:* American Journal of T. H. White, 1965.

WILLEY, Basil. *Spots of Time,* A Retrospect of the Years 1897–1920, 1965.

WILLIAMS, Emlyn. *George,* An Early Autobiography, 1961.

WILLIAMS, Raymond. *Second Generation,* 1965.

WILLIAMSON, Henry. *Goodbye, West Country* (diary), 1937.

———— *Genius of a Friendship:* T. E. Lawrence, 1941.

———— *The Sun in the Sands,* 1945.

———— *The Wet Flanders Plain,* 1929.

WILLIAMSON, Hugh Ross. *The Walled Garden,* 1956.

WILSON, Angus. *The Wild Garden,* or, Speaking of Writing, 1963.

WINTER, Ella. (Wife of Lincoln Steffens and then Donald Ogden Stewart.) *And Not to Yield,* 1963.

WODEHOUSE, P[elham] G[renville]. *America, I Like You,* 1956.

WOLFE, Humbert. *Now a Stranger,* 1933.

———— *Portraits by Inference,* 1934.

————*The Upward Anguish,* 1938.

WOOLF, Leonard. *Beginning Again:* An Autobiography of the Years 1911–1918, 1964.

————*Growing:* An Autobiography of the Years 1904–1911, 1961.

———— *Sowing:* An Autobiography of the Years 1880–1904, 1960.

WOOLF, Virginia. *A Writer's Diary,* ed. Leonard Woolf, 1953. Excerpts esp. on composition and literary opinions.

YEATS, William Butler. *The Autobiography,* 1938. Contains: *Reveries over Childhood and Youth,* 1915 ; *The Trembling of the Veil,* 1922 ; *Dramatis Personae* 1896–1902, 1935. The first two were also published together as *Autobiographies,* 1926.

———— *Pages from a Diary,* 1944.

ZWEIG, Stefan. *The World of Yesterday:* An Autobiography [1943], tr. anon., 1965.

NOTE. Annotation of volumes in the following sections of Part I includes, besides a brief comment on the nature of the book, titles of important essays and the names of authors treated, but only the authors whose bibligraphies appear in *Twentieth Century British Literature*. If this list does not exhaust the contents of the book, it will be preceded by the abbreviation *incl*.

COLLECTIONS OF ESSAYS

THE AUTHOR AND THE PUBLIC: Problems of Communication. Introd. by C. V. Wedgwood. Hutchinson, 1957.
> P.E.N. Congress, London, July, 1956. Sections as follows with addresses by *inter alios*: "The Author and the Public"—Priestley, A. Wilson, R. Lehmann; "Criticism"—M. Kennedy, Empson, Pritchett; "History and Biography"—Wedgwood, Rowse, Forster; "Contemporary Techniques in Poetry"—Spender; "The Technique of the New Mass-Communication Media"—P. Bentley; "The Importance of Minority Literature"—Michison; "Contemporary Techniques in Fiction"—W. Cooper, L. P. Hartley; Inaugural Speech by C. Morgan.

ADCOCK, A[rthur] St. John. *The Glory that Was Grub Street:* Impressions of Contemporary Authors. Ill. E. O. Hoppé. Low, Marston; N.Y., Stokes, 1928.
> *Incl.* Shaw, Chesterton, Dane, Ervine, Gosse, Guedalla, Hichens, A. E. Housman, Huxley, Jacobs, Jerome, Jameson, E. V. Lucas, Lynd, Machen, Tomlinson, Webb, R. West.

———— *Gods of Modern Grub Street:* Impressions of Contemporary Authors. Ill. E. O. Hoppé. Low, Marston; N.Y., Stokes, 1923.
> *Incl.* Hardy, Belloc, Bennett, Beresford, Buchan, W. H. Davies, de la Mare, Doyle, Drinkwater, Galsworthy, Kaye-Smith, Kipling, Mackenzie, Masefield, Mason, Maugham, Milne, Noyes, Sinclair, Swinnerton, Walpole, Wells.

AGATE, James. *Agate's Folly:* A Pleasaunce. Chapman and Hall, 1925.
> Very short, informal, topical essays *incl*. M. Baring.

———— *Alarums and Excursions*. N.Y., Doran, 1922.
> Reviews and essays, *incl*. Shaw, Drinkwater.

———— *Here's Richness!* An Anthology of and by James Agate. Harrap, 1942.
> *Incl.* Monkhouse, Galsworthy, Pinero.

AIKEN, Conrad [Potter]. *A Reviewer's ABC:* Collected Criticism from

1916 to the Present, Introd., ed. Rufus A. Blanshard. N.Y., Meridian Bks, 1958.

> I. Views on Literature and Criticism; II. A Reviewer's ABC. *Incl.* Bennett, Bridges, Eliot, Galsworthy, Gissing, Hardy, A. E. Housman, Huxley, James, D. H. Lawrence, Wyndham Lewis, MacNeice, Masefield, G. Moore, J. C. Powys, Richardson, D. Thomas, V. Woolf.

——*Scepticisms;* Notes on Contemporary Poetry. N.Y., Knopf, 1919.

> Repr. from periodicals. *Incl.* Hueffer [Ford], D. H. Lawrence, Masefield, R. Nichols, J. C. Powys, de la Mare, Graves, Gibson, Eliot, Hodgson, Monro, "A Treasury of War Poetry."

ALDINGTON, Richard. *Literary Studies and Reviews*. Allen and Unwin, 1924.

> *Incl.* Eliot, Joyce, "The Poet and his Age."

ALLEN, Walter, comp. and ed. *Writers on Writing*. N.Y., Dutton, 1949. (paper).

> On novel and poetry. Definitions and descriptions, mostly very short. Only a few moderns, *incl.* Conrad, de la Mare, Eliot, Ford, James, D. H. Lawrence.

ALLSOP, Kenneth. *Scan*. Hodder and Stoughton, 1965.

> Samples of his periodical contributions, *incl.* reviews, prefaced by an account of his life.

ALTICK, Richard D. *The Scholar Adventurers*. [1950] N.Y., The Free Pr.; London, Collier-Macmillan, 1966. (paper).

> Expert reports of some famous scholarly discoveries *incl.* "The Search for Sambir [Conrad]." Excellent introductory book on the methods and rewards of fact-hunting.

BARZUN, Jacques. *The Energies of Art:* Studies of Authors Classic and Modern. N.Y., Harper, 1956.

> *Incl.* Hardy, James.

BAKER, Denys Val, ed. *Modern British Writing*. N.Y., Vanguard, 1947.

> Stories, poems, essays, *incl.* on Koestler, H. Williamson, R. Warner, D. H. Lawrence.

BARING, Maurice. *Punch and Judy and Other Essays*. Heinemann; Garden City, N.Y., Doubleday, Page, 1924.

> *Incl.* Yeats, Barrie.

BEERBOHM, Max. *A Christmas Garland*. [1912] N.Y., Dutton, 1922; Heinemann, 1932.

> Parodies of: James, "The Mote in the Middle Distance"; Kipling, A. C. Benson, Wells, Hardy, Harris, Bennett, Galsworthy, Conrad, Gosse, Belloc, Shaw, Hewlett, G. Moore.

BENNETT, Arnold. *Books and Persons:* Being Comments on a Past Epoch, 1908–1911. [1917] Chatto and Windus, 1920.

> Repr. from *New Age* (signed "Jacob Tonson"). *Incl.* very short essays on novel, criticism, a British Academy of Letters, and Conrad, Jacobs, Cunningham Grahame, Wells, Chesterton, Kipling, Galsworthy, A. C. Benson, James, Hudson, Masefield.

———— *Things That Have Interested Me*. First, Second and Third Series. N.Y., Doran, 1921, 1923, 1926.

Many short pieces from journals ; on the times and a few on books.

BLACKMUR, R[ichard] P. *The Double Agent:* Essays in Craft and Elucidation. N.Y., Arrow Eds., 1935.

Incl. D. H. Lawrence, Eliot, Butler, James, "A Critic's Job of Work."

————*The Expense of Greatness*. N.Y., Arrow Eds., 1940.

Incl. T. E. Lawrence, Hardy, Yeats, A. E. Housman, "A Featherbed for Critics."

———— *The Lion and the Honeycomb:* Essays in Solicitude and Critique. [1935] N.Y., Harcourt, Brace and World, 1955. (Harvest).

BOGAN, Louise. *Selected Criticism*. N.Y., Noonday Pr., 1955.

Repr. from journals ; *incl*. E. Sitwell, V. Woolf, Hopkins, Auden, MacNeice, Yeats, Spender, James, Bowen, Joyce, Compton-Burnett, Rodgers, Graves, Betjeman, D. H. Lawrence, D. Thomas.

BOWEN, Elizabeth. *Collected Impressions*. N.Y., Knopf, 1950.

Reviews, repr. from *NSN, incl*. Heppenstall, V. Woolf, Compton-Burnett, Forster, Huxley, Barrie, Conrad, D. H. Lawrence, G. Moore.

BOYD, E[rnest] A[ugustus]. *Appreciations and Depreciations:* Irish Literary Studies. Unwin, 1917 ; N.Y., Lane, 1918.

Partly repr. from various periodicals. *Incl*. A. E., Eglinton, Dunsany, Shaw.

———— *Literary Blasphemies*. London and N.Y., Harper, 1927.
Incl. James, Hardy.

BRAYBROOKE, Patrick. *Peeps at the Mighty*. Phila., Lippincott, 1927.

Short essays on special phases of, *inter alios,* Wells, Beerbohm, A. C. Benson, Chesterton, Bennett.

———— *Some Goddesses of the Pen*. C. W. Daniel, 1927.
Incl. Kaye-Smith, Macaulay, Sidgwick.

————*Some Victorian and Georgian Catholics:* Their Art and Outlook. Burns, Oates and Washbourne, 1932.

Incl. A. Meynell, Conrad, Noyes, Katharine Tynan.

BREWSTER, Dorothy. *East-West Passage:* a Study in Literary Relationships. Allen and Unwin, 1954.

Influence of Russian literature on England and America, *incl*. James, G. Moore, Ellis, Gosse, Shaw, Forster, V. Woolf, D. H. Lawrence, Murry, Pritchett.

CECIL, David. *The Fine Art of Reading* and Other Literary Studies. N.Y., Bobbs-Merrill, 1957.

Incl. "The Fine Art of Reading" ; "The Forms of English Fiction" ; Conrad, de la Mare.

————*Poets and Story-Tellers:* A Book of Critical Essays. N.Y., Macmillan, 1949.

Incl. V. Woolf, Forster.

CHAMBERS, R[aymond] W. *Man's Unconquerable Mind:* Studies of English Writers from Bede to A. E. Housman and W. P. Ker. Cape, 1939.
>*Incl.* on A. E. Housman and Ker as philologists at Univ. College, London.

CHARLESWORTH, Barbara. *Dark Passages:* The Decadent Consciousness in Victorian Literature. Madison, Univ. of Wisconsin Pr., 1965.
>*Incl.* A. Symons.

CHEVRILLON, André. *Three Studies in English Literature:* Kipling, Galsworthy, Shakespeare. Tr. anon. [French 1901, 1918] N.Y., Doubleday, Page, 1923.

CHESTERTON, G[ilbert] K[eith]. *Heretics.* [1905] N.Y., Dodd, Mead, 1923.
>*Incl.* Kipling, Shaw, Wells, "Christmas and the Aesthetes," G. Moore, Lowes Dickinson, "Celts and Celtophiles."

CHILD, H[arold] H[annynton]. *Essays and Reflections.* Cambridge Univ. Pr., 1948.
>Repr. from *TLS* and *Times* (London). *Incl.* Barrie, Yeats. de la Mare, Archer, Forster.

CHISLETT, William, Jr. *Moderns and Near-Moderns.* N.Y., Grafton Pr., 1928.
>*Incl.* James, Shaw, Synge, Lady Gregory, Yeats, Dunsany, Lang.

CHUBB, Edwin W[atts]. *Stories of Authors:* British and American. N.Y., Macmillan, 1926.
>Incidents in the lives of authors *incl.* Kipling, Conrad, Galsworthy, Barrie, Shaw.

CONNOLLY, Cyril. *The Condemned Playground:* Essays 1927–1944. [1945] Routledge, 1953.
>*Incl.* on the modern novel, reviewers, Joyce, A. E. Housman.

———— *Enemies of Promise.* [1938] Rev. ed., Garden City, N.Y., Doubleday 1960. (Anchor).
>Part I: provocative distinction of "mandarins" (Strachey, V. Woolf), "dandies" (Firbank, Eliot, Huxley), and "new realists" (*incl.* W. Lewis).

———— *Ideas and Places.* Weidenfeld and Nicolson, 1953.
>Repr. from journals, esp. many brief topical editorials from *Horizon* by its editor. Not primarily on literature, but answers to questionnaires on the cost of letters by 21 living authors ; also "The Literature of Disengagement" ; L. P. Smith.

———— *Previous Convictions:* Selected Writings of a Decade. N.Y., Harper and Row, 1963.
>*Incl.* James, Douglas, Gissing, Eliot, D. H. Lawrence, Joyce, Orwell, MacNeice, D. Thomas, Welch, E. Sitwell, modern verse.

COMPTON-RICKETT, Arthur. *Portraits and Personalities.* Selwyn and Blount, 1937.
>*Incl.* Barrie, Hardy, Bennett, Shaw, Wells, Chesterton, Priestley, V. Woolf, Strachey, the Sitwell family.

CRONIN, Anthony. *A Question of Modernity*. Secker and Warburg, 1966.
> *Incl.* esp. Joyce and Beckett ; also Yeats, Eliot, Logue, F. R. Leavis.

DAHLBERG, Edward and Herbert READ. *Truth is More Sacred:* A Critical Exchange on Modern Literature. Routledge and Kegan Paul ; N.Y., Horizon Pr., 1961.
> *Incl.* Joyce, D. H. Lawrence, James, Graves, Eliot.

DAICHES, David. *New Literary Values:* Studies in Modern Literature. Edinburgh, Oliver and Boyd, 1936.
> *Incl.* Hopkins, Owen, Joyce, Masefield, and general topics.

DE LA MARE, Walter. *Private View*. Faber and Faber, 1953.
> Repr. from *TLS, Edinb. Rev.,* etc. ; *incl.* "Creative Criticism," James, Conrad, Hardy, Flecker, Yeats, Bridges, E. Thomas, W. H. Davies, Gosse, A. Meynell ; "Georgian Poetry" ; "Metaphor" ; "Pure English."

DOBRÉE, Bonamy. *The Lamp and the Lute:* Studies in Six Authors. Oxford, Clarendon Pr., 1929.
> *Incl.* Hardy, Kipling, Forster, D. H. Lawrence, Eliot. Rev., enlgd. ed. (Frank Cass ; N.Y., Barnes and Noble, 1964) *incl.* also Durrell.

DOUGLAS, Norman. *Experiments*. N.Y., McBride, 1925.
> *Incl.* T. E. Lawrence, D. H. Lawrence ; "Fiction" ; "Poetry."

EASTMAN, Max. *The Literary Mind:* Its Place in an Age of Science. N.Y., Scribner's, 1935.
> *Incl.* "The Swan-Song of Humane Letters" ; "The Cult of Unintelligibility" ; "The Tendency Towards Pure Poetry" ; "Poets Talking to Themselves" ; "The Future of Literature: Are Poetry and Drama Dying?" ; "A Note on I. A. Richards' Psychology of Poetry."

EGLINTON, John (pseud. of W. K. Magee), W[illiam] B[utler] Yeats, A. E. [George William Russell], and W. Larminie. *Literary Ideals in Ireland*. Unwin, 1899.
> Eglinton, "What Should Be the Subjects of a National Drama?" ; Yeats, "A Note on National Drama" ; Eglinton, "National Drama and Contemporary Life" ; Yeats, "John Eglinton and the Spiritual Life" ; Eglinton, "Mr. Yeats and Popular Poetry" ; A. E., "Literary Ideals in Ireland" ; Larminie, "Legends as Material for Literature" ; Yeats, "The Autumn of the Flesh" ; A. E., "Nationality and Cosmopolitanism in Literature."

ELIOT, T[homas] S[tearns]. *Selected Essays, 1917–1932*. [1932] enlgd. Faber, 1951 ; N.Y., Harcourt, Brace, 1950.
> *Incl.* "Tradition and the Individual Talent" ; "The Function of Criticism" ; and on Murray. The 1950 ed. *incl.* also (from *Essays Ancient and Modern*, 1936) "Religion and Literature" (1935) and "Modern Education and the Classics" (1932). See also sections Criticism, Drama and Poetry.

ELLIS, Geoffrey Uther. *Twilight on Parnassus:* A Survey of Post-War Fiction and Pre-War Criticism. Michael Joseph, 1939.
> *Inc.* Strachey, Hardy, W. Lewis, Kipling, E. Waugh, Macaulay, Huxley, O. Sitwell, Bell, Firbank, Shaw, Wells, Belloc, Chesterton, D. H.

Lawrence, V. Woolf, Joyce, Garnett, Forster, Powell, Gerhardi, Bennett.

ELLIS, Havelock. *From Marlowe to Shaw:* The Studies 1876–1936 in English Literature of Havelock Ellis. Ed. John Gawsworth. Williams and Norgate, 1950.

Incl. on Carpenter, Hardy, Shaw, Wells, Conrad, G. Moore, Murry. Prefatory letter of Hardy.

————— *My Confessional:* Questions of Our Day. Boston and N.Y., Houghton Mifflin, 1934.

Incl. "The Place of Art in Life" ; "Science and Art" ; and on G. Moore.

ELLMAN, Richard, ed. *Edwardians and Late Victorians.* N.Y., Columbia Univ. Pr. 1960. (English Institute Essays).

Incl. on G. Moore, Yeats, Wells, Shaw, criticism.

ELLMAN, Richard and Charles FEIDELSON, Jr., eds. *The Modern Tradition:* Backgrounds of Modern Literature. N.Y., Oxford Univ. Pr., 1965. Quotations from 19th-20th c. authors to illustrate aspects of "modernism."

ELTON, Oliver. *Essays and Addresses.* Arnold, 1939.

Incl. "The Nature of Literary Criticism" ; Bridges, Saintsbury.

ELWIN, Malcolm. *Old Gods Falling.* N.Y., Macmillan, 1939.

Full and useful critical essays on G. Moore, Gosse, James, Lang, A. Symons, Saintsbury, Kipling, Haggard, Doyle, Quiller-Couch, Hewlett, Hope, Caine, Corelli, Bennett, Wells, Galsworthy.

ENRIGHT, D[ennis] J[oseph]. *The Apothecary's Shop:* Essays on Literature. Phila., Dufour, 1957.

Mostly repr. from periodicals: *EC, Scy,* etc. Incl. "Criticism for Criticism's Sake" ; "Literature, Criticism and Belief" ; "Prosaic Engineering in *The Waste Land*" ; "To the Lighthouse or To India?" ; Auden ; "On Not Teaching *The Cocktail Party*" ; "The Use of Poetry" ; "The Brain-Washed Muse: Some Thoughts on Tradition" ; "The Fountain of Living Waters [modern poetry]."

ERVINE, St. John G. *Some Impressions of My Elders.* N.Y., Macmillan, 1922.

Repr. from *The North American Review,* 1920–1921. Incl. A. E., Bennett, Chesterton, Galsworthy, G. Moore, Shaw, Wells, Yeats.

FAUSSET, Hugh I'Anson. *Poets and Pundits:* Essays and Addresses. Cape, 1947.

Incl. "The Cult of Symbolism" ; Hopkins, de la Mare, Blunden.

FERNANDEZ, Ramon. *Messages.* Tr. Montgomery Belgion. N.Y., Harcourt, Brace, 1927.

"Of Philosophical Criticism" ; "Autobiography and the Novel" ; on Freud and modern thought, Conrad, Eliot.

FIGGIS, Darrell, *Studies and Appreciations.* Dent, 1912.

Incl. Synge, Watson, Yeats, W. H. Davies, Trench, Bridges.

FORD, Ford Madox [Hueffer]. *The Critical Attitude*. Duckworth, 1911, repr. (The Reader's Library), 1915.

> Theory and brief survey, *incl*. Barrie, Maugham, Pinero, Barker, Galsworthy, Shaw, James, Conrad, G. Moore, Wells, Bennett, Kipling.

FONTAINE. *Aspects de la littérature anglaise (1918–1940)*. (Numéro spécial de *Fontaine,* revue mensuelle des lettres françaises et de la littérature internationale, 1944).

> *Incl*. essays, tr. into French, by notable English writers, e.g. Baring, Bowen, Bowra.

FORSTER, E[dward] M[organ]. *Abinger Harvest*. [1936] Edward Arnold, 1961.

> *Incl*. R. Fry, Reid, Eliot, V. Woolf, Firbank, Conrad, T. E. Lawrence, Blunt.

————*Two Cheers for Democracy*. [1938] Edward Arnold ; N.Y., Harcourt, Brace, 1951.

> Essays, articles, broadcasts, mostly after 1936. *Incl*. "What I Believe" ; "Anonymity: an Enquiry" ; "Art for Art's Sake" ; "The Duty of Society to the Artist" ; "Does Culture Matter?" ; "The Raison d'Être of Criticism in the Arts" ; "English Prose between 1918 and 1939" ; "An Outsider on Poetry" [new poets, 1949] ; Orwell, Carpenter, Butler, V. Woolf, Eliot, Auden and Isherwood, Reid.

FREEMAN, John. *English Portraits and Essays*. Hodder and Stoughton, 1924. Repr. from *LM*. *Incl*. de la Mare, Hewlett, Gosse, Mackenzie.

————*The Moderns:* Essays in Literary Criticism. Scott, 1916. Repr. from *LM*. *Incl*. Shaw, Wells, Hardy, James, Conrad, Bridges.

GALSWORTHY, John. *Candelabra:* Selected Essays and Addresses. N.Y., Scribner's, 1933.

> On drama, art, and "Castles in Spain" (an address) ; "Reminiscences of Conrad" ; "The Faith of a Novelist" ; "Literature and Life" ; "The Creation of Character in Literature" (Romanes Lecture, 1931).

GARNETT, Edward. *Friday Nights:* Literary Criticisms and Appreciations, First Series. N.Y., Knopf, 1922.

> *Incl*. W. H. Hudson, Conrad, Doughty, D. H. Lawrence, "The Contemporary Critic."

GOGARTY, Oliver St. John. *Intimations*. N.Y., Abelard Pr. ; Constable (as *Rolling Down the Lea*), 1950.

> Essays, some repr. from *Town and Country, incl*. G. Moore, Joyce.

————*A Weekend in the Middle of the Week,* N.Y., Doubleday, 1958.

GOSSE, Edmund. *Aspects and Impressions*. Cassell, 1922.

> *Incl*. James, Butler.

————*Books on the Table*. Heinemann, 1921.

> *Incl*. E. V. Lucas, Hewlett, Saintsbury, Barrie, Doughty, de la Mare.

———— *Leaves and Fruit*. Heinemann, 1927.

> *Incl*. Sassoon, E. Sitwell, Gissing, Butler.

————*More Books on the Table*. Scribner's, 1923.
Incl. A. E. Housman.

————*Questions at Issue*. Heinemann, 1893.
Incl. Kipling.

———— *Selected Essays*. Heinemann, 1928.
Incl. G. Moore.

———— *Silhouettes*. Heinemann, 1925.
Incl. Lang, Saintsbury, Phillpotts, G. Moore.

————*Some Diversions of a Man of Letters*. Heinemann, 1919.
Incl. Hardy, R. Brooke, Flecker, Marsh, Bottomley, W. H. Davies, Baring, R. Nichols, Graves, Sassoon, Strachey.

GOLDRING, Douglas. *Reputations:* Essays in Criticism. N.Y., Seltzen, 1920.
Incl. Flecker, "Three Georgian Novelists" (Mackenzie, Walpole, Cannan) ; D. H. Lawrence, Wells, Gissing, Bennett ; "The War and the Poets" ; "Low Tastes" ; "Looking Back" (reminiscences).

GRAY, James. *On Second Thought*. Oxford Univ. Pr., 1946.
Reviews of 50 modern authors.

GREENE, Graham. *The Lost Childhood*. N.Y., Viking, 1952.
Mostly short reviews, some from periodicals *NS, Spec, TT, LM, Hor, The Month,* etc. *Incl*. James, de la Mare, Ford, Munro, Richardson, Doyle, Rolfe, Conrad, Hope, Buchan, Butler, Ellis, Read, B. Nichols.

GREGORY, Horace. *The Shield of Achilles:* Essays and Beliefs in Poetry. N.Y., Harcourt, Brace, 1944.
Incl. G. Moore, Yeats, D. H. Lawrence, V. Woolf.

GUEDALLA, Philip. *A Gallery*. Constable ; N.Y., Putnam, 1924.
Incl. Hardy, Wells, Shaw, Bennett, Conrad, Galsworthy, Mackenzie.

————*Masters and Men*. Constable, 1923.
Partly repr. from periodicals ; *incl*. Saintsbury, Chesterton, "The Critics."

———— *Men of Letters*. Hodder and Stoughton, 1927.
Collected essays first pub. in *Supers and Supermen, Masters and Men* and *A Gallery*.

———— *Supers and Supermen:* Studies in Politics, History and Letters. Unwin, 1920.
Repr. from *NS, Ath,* etc. *Incl*. James, Barrie, Chesterton, Blunt.

HAMILTON, Cosmo. *People Worth Talking About. N.Y.,* Robert M. McBride, 1933.
Incl. Conrad, Shaw, Barrie, Kipling, Wells, Galsworthy, Chesterton, Beerbohm, Doyle, Coward, E. F. Benson, Hardy, Gosse.

HARRIS, Frank. *Contemporary Portraits*. N.Y., Kennerley, 1915.
Incl. Davidson.

————. ————. Second Series. N.Y., the author, 1919.
Incl. Shaw, G. Moore, Kipling, Dunsany.

————. ————. Third Series. N.Y., the author, 1920.

Incl. Wells, Galsworthy, Cunninghame-Graham, Chesterton, A. Symons.

————.————. Fourth Series. N.Y., Brentano's, 1923.
Incl. Barrie, Blunt, Trench, Beerbohm.

————*Latest Contemporary Portraits.* N.Y., Macaulay, 1927.
Incl. A. E., Hardy, A. E. Housman.

HIBBARD G[eorge] R[ichard], ed. *Renaissance and Modern Essays in Honour of Vivian de Sola Pinto.* Routledge and Kegan Paul, 1966.
Contributors *incl.* Mario Praz and Blunden.

HILDRICK, Wallace. *Word for Word:* A Study of Author's Alterations with Exercises. Faber and Faber, 1966.
Excerpts from mss. of writers from Pope on, *incl.* James, Hardy, Butler, D. H. Lawrence, V. Woolf.

HOUGH, Graham. *Image and Experience:* Reflections on a Literary Revolution. Lincoln, Univ. of Nebraska Pr., 1960.
Incl. Imagism, D. H. Lawrence, R. Fry, G. Moore, Conrad.

HEPPENSTALL, Rayner. *The Fourfold Tradition:* Notes on the French and English Literatures with Some Ethnological and Historical Asides. N.Y., New Directions, 1961.
Part II: 1900–1950, *incl.* D. H. Lawrence, James, Eliot, Yeats, V. Woolf. Part II: After 1950, *incl.* Snow, Wain, Amis, Beckett. Random and iconoclastic observations on what interests the author, a novelist and critic.

HIND, C[harles] Lewis. *Authors and I.* London and N.Y., Lane, 1921.
Weekly contributions to *The Christian Science Monitor* 1919–1920. *Incl.* Barrie, Beerbohm, Belloc, Bennett, Chesterton, Conrad, W. H. Davies, Drinkwater, Dunsany, Galsworthy, Gosse, Cunninghame Graham, Hardy Hewlett, the Housmans, James, Kipling, Lang, E. V. Lucas, Masefield, A. Meynell, Phillips, G. Moore, Quiller-Couch, Sassoon, Shaw, Walpole, Watson, Wells, Yeats.

———— *More Authors and I.* N.Y., Dodd, Mead, 1922.
Short essays from *The Christian Science Monitor.* 50 authors, *incl.* "F. Anstey," Archer, Bridges, Cunninghame Graham, Davidson, Ervine, Gibbs, Gissing, W. H. Hudson, Hueffer [Ford], Jacobs, Machen, de la Mare, Marriott, Noyes, A. E., Synge, Walkley.

HOLLOWAY, John. *The Charted Mirror:* Literary and Critical Essays. Routledge and Kegan Paul, 1960.
Incl. Hardy, James, W. Lewis, "Early Epic and Modern Poetry"; "'Tank in the Stalls': Notes on the School of Anger"; and four essays on modern criticism. The author's *Studies in Argument:* the Victorian Sage (Macmillan; N.Y., St. Martin's Pr., 1953) *incl.* Hardy.

HOWE, Irving. *A World More Attractive:* A View of Modern Literature and Politics. N.Y., Horizon Pr., 1963.
Repr. from periodicals over 13 years; general essays on politics and culture. *Incl.* T. E. Lawrence, Gissing.

HUNEKER, James Gibbons. *Essays,* sel. H. L. Mencken. N.Y., Scribner's, 1929.

 Incl. Shaw, Wilde.

————*The Pathos of Distance:* A Book of a Thousand and One Moments. N.Y., Scribner's, 1913.

 Incl. G. Moore, Synge, Yeats.

———— *Unicorns.* N.Y., Scribner's, 1917.

 Incl. James, Joyce, G. Moore, "Style and Rhythm in English Prose."

ISAACS, J[acob]. *An Assessment of Twentieth Century Literature.* Secker and Warburg, 1951.

 Six BBC Third Programme Broadcasts: "The Assessment of Contemporary Literature"; "The Age of Anxiety"; "The Stream of Consciousness"; "Culture, Chaos and Order"; "T. S. Eliot and Poetic Drama"; "The Verdict."

JAMESON, Storm. *The Writer's Situation and Other Essays.* Macmillan, 1950.

 Incl. "The Writer's Situation"; "The Form of the Novel"; "The Novelist Today: 1949"; Auden; "Between the Wars"; "A Crisis of the Spirit"; "The Responsibilities of a Writer."

KAZIN, Alfred. *Contemporaries.* Boston, Little, Brown, 1962.

 Incl. Greene, D. H. Lawrence, Durrell, D. Thomas, Behan, Katharine Tynan, "The Function of Criticism Today."

KENNER, Hugh. *Flaubert, Joyce and Beckett:* The Stoic Comedians. Boston, Beacon Pr., 1962.

KERMODE, Frank. *Puzzles and Epiphanies:* Essays and Reviews 1958–1961. N.Y., Chilmark Pr., 1962.

 Incl. D. Jones, Forster, Joyce, Isherwood, Powell, Betjeman, Beckett, Snow, E. Waugh, Greene, W. Golding, Durrell.

KNIGHT, Grant C. *Superlatives.* N.Y., Knopf, 1925.

 Essays on the "greatest" creations in literature *incl.* certain characters of James, G. Moore, Conrad.

KNIGHTS, L. C. *Explorations:* Essays in Criticism Mainly on the Literature of the Seventeenth Century. [1947] N.Y., N.Y. Univ. Pr., 1964. (paper).

 Incl. James, Yeats.

LAS VERGNAS, Raymond. *Chesterton, Belloc, Baring.* Tr. C. C. Martindale. N.Y., Sheed and Ward, 1938.

LEAVIS, F[rank] R[aymond]. *The Common Pursuit.* [1952] Penguin, 1963.

 Repr. from periodicals, esp. *Scy. Incl.* Eliot, Hopkins, James, D. H. Lawrence, C. Williams, W. Lewis, Forster; "The Progress of Poesy"; "Literary Criticism and Philosophy."

————*For Continuity.* Cambridge, Eng., G. Fraser, The Minority Pr., 1933.

 Incl. "The Literary Mind"; "What Is Wrong with Criticism?";

"Arnold Bennett: American Version"; "Restatements for Critics";
" 'This Poetical Renascence' "; Joyce, D. H. Lawrence.

————*The Great Tradition.* [1948] Garden City, N.Y., Doubleday
1954. (Anchor).
Incl. Conrad, James.

————, ed. *Towards Standards of Criticism:* Selections from *The Calendar
of Modern Letters, 1925–1927.* Wishart, 1933.
Three sections: on fiction, poetry, general criticism; index of books
reviewed, authors and articles.

LEGALLIENNE, Richard. *Attitudes and Avowals:* With Some Retrospective
Reviews. John Lane, 1910.
Repr. from various journals *incl. FR, Academy. Incl.* Hewlett, Philips,
A. Symons, Yeats, Watson.

LEHMANN, John. *The Open Night.* Longmans; N.Y., Harcourt, Brace,
1952.
Essays and one lecture. *Incl.* "The Search for the Myth"; Yeats, V.
Woolf, James, Conrad, Joyce, E. Thomas, R. Brooke, A. Lewis, Owen;
"The Poet in the Modern World."

————, ed. *The Craft of Letters in England:* A Symposium [at Internat.
Congress of P.E.N. in London]. Crescent Pr., 1956.
"Biography" by J. I. M. Stewart; "The Personal Story" by A. Pryce-
Jones; "Twenty-five Years of the Novel" by F. Wyndham; "Experiment
and the Future of the Novel" by P. Toynbee; "Poetry: Tradition and
Belief" by R. Fuller; "The Poet and His Medium" by G. S. Fraser;
"The Author and the Theatre" by T. C. Worsley; "The New Criticism"
by L. D. Lerner; "The Bloomsbury Tradition and English Literary
Criticism" by P. Bloomfield; "Historical Writing" by C. V. Wedg-
wood; "The Literature of Ideas" by M. Cranston; "The Progress of
Translation" by E. de Mauny.

LEVIN, Harry, ed. *Perspectives of Criticism.* Cambridge, Mass., Harvard
Univ. Pr., 1950.
By W. J. Bate and others; *incl.* The Celtic Revival, Yeats, Synge.

LEWIS, C[ecil] Day, ed. *The Mind in Chains:* Society and the Cultural
Revolution. Muller, 1927.
Incl. "A Marxist Interpretation of Literature," by E. Upward; "The
Theatre," by Barbara Nixon; "Art under Capitalism and Socialism,"
by Anthony Blunt; "Culture, Progress and English Tradition," by
Edgell Rickword.

LEWIS, [Percy] Wyndham. *Men Without Art.* [1934] N.Y., Russell and
Russell, 1964.
Incl. Eliot, James, V. Woolf, and essays on literature in general.

————*Paleface:* The Philosophy of the Melting Pot. Chatto and Windus,
1929.
Repr. in part from *Enemy Number 2. Incl.* D. H. Lawrence, Joyce,
Shaw.

LINKLATER, Eric. *The Art of Adventure*. Macmillan, 1948.
  Incl. Bridie, E. Waugh.

LONGAKER, [John] Mark. *Contemporary Biography*. Phila., Univ. of
Penna. Pr., 1934.
  Incl. "The Vogue of Contemporary Biography" ; L. Strachey, Gue-
  dalla, Belloc.

LUCAS, F[rank] L[aurence]. *Authors Dead and Living*. Chatto and Win-
dus ; N.Y., Macmillan, 1926.
  Incl. Masefield, de la Mare, Bottomley, W. H. Davies, Rosenberg,
  S. Warner.

LYND, Robert. *The Art of Letters*. Unwin, 1920, and N.Y., Scribner's, 1921.
  Repr. *Incl*. Saintsbury, Gosse, the Georgians, "The Theory of Poetry" ;
  "The Critic as Destroyer" ; "Book Reviewing."

———— *Books and Authors*. Cobden-Sanderson, 1922, and N.Y., Putnam's,
1923.
  Personal descriptions, intermingled with critical observations ; *incl*.
  Beerbohm, Bennett, Conrad, Wells, Huxley, Tomlinson, Eliot, Douglas.

———— *Books and Writers*. [1942] Rev. ed., Dent, 1945, repr. 1952.
  Foreword by Richard Church on Lynd. Posthumous collection of
  essays many from JOL over signature John o'London. Section on
  Criticism and Critics *incl*. Bennett ; "A Passion for Style" ; "The Liter-
  ary Life" ; "Books and Their Authors" ; James, Yeats, Shaw, Kipling,
  Hardy, Wells, Eliot, Joyce.

————*Old and New Masters*. Unwin ; N.Y., Scribner's, 1919.
  Repr. from: *NationL, NS,* etc. *Incl*. Chesterton, Belloc, James, Synge,
  Flecker, Conrad, Shaw, Masefield, Yeats, Lady Gregory, Cunning-
  hame-Graham, Corelli, Squire, Kipling, Hardy.

MACCARTHY, Desmond. *Criticism*. Putnam, 1932.
  The second volume of his collected journal articles during 20 years. *Incl*.
  Butler, Yeats, Eliot, Garnett, Huxley, D. H. Lawrence, Joyce.

———— *Experience*. Putnam, 1935.
  Third volume of collected articles, mostly from *NS* ; *incl*. Belloc,
  James.

————*Humanities*. MacGibbon and Kee, 1953.
  Posthumous collection made by T. R. Fyvel, preface [on MacCarthy]
  by David Cecil. *Incl*. essays on theatre ; Joyce, Maugham, Coward,
  Huxley ; Eliot (3 essays), Mansfield, V. Lee, Bennett ; "Reviewers and
  Professors."

———— *Portraits*. Putnam, 1931.
  First volume of collected articles. *Incl*. Blunt, Conrad, James, G.
  Moore, Caine.

———— *Remnants*. N.Y., Dutton, 1920.
  Repr. from journals ; *incl*. Butler, Shaw.

MACY, John A. *The Critical Game*. N.Y., Boni and Liveright, 1922.

Incl. Conrad, Hardy, Wells, Masefield, G. Moore, Joyce, D. H. Lawrence.

MAIS, S[tuart] P[etre] B[rodie]. *Books and Their Writers.* N.Y., Dodd, Mead, 1920.

Incl. Mackenzie, Douglas, Swinnerton, Dane, Richardson, Squire, Sassoon, B. Nichols, A. Meynell, "Saki".

————*From Shakespeare to O. Henry:* Studies in Literature. N.Y., Dodd, Mead, 1923.

Incl. Butler, Masefield, R. Brooke, Hardy.

———— *Some Modern Authors.* Richards, 1923.

Incl. A. E., Eglinton, Dunsany, Shaw.

MANN, Thomas. *Past Masters and Other Essays.* Tr. H. T. Lowe-Porter, Secker ; N.Y., Knopf, 1933.

Repr. from German journals. *Incl.* Conrad.

MARTIN, Harold C. *Style in Prose Fiction.* N.Y., Columbia Univ. Pr., 1959. (English Institute Essays).

Incl. Hardy, James.

MAUROIS, André. *Prophets and Poets.* Tr. Hamish Miles. London and N.Y., Harper, 1935.

Incl. Kipling, Wells, Shaw, Chesterton, Conrad, Strachey, D. H. Lawrence, Huxley, Mansfield.

MÉGROZ, R[odolphe] L[ouis]. *Five Novelist Poets of Today.* Joiner and Steele, 1933.

Incl. de la Mare, Strong, Armstrong, O. Sitwell, D. H. Lawrence.

MIGHTIER THAN THE SWORD: The P.E.N. Herman Ould Memorial Lectures. St. Martin's Pr., 1964.

Foreword C. V. Wedgwood. On novel, drama, poetry, history, etc. by Morgan, Priestley, B. Russell, E. Sitwell, Rowse, Wedgwood, etc.

MILLER, J[oseph] Hillis. *Poets of Reality:* Six Twentieth-Century Writers. Cambridge, Mass., Belknap Pr. of Harvard Univ. Pr., 1965.

Incl. "The Poetry of Reality" ; Conrad, Yeats, Eliot, D. Thomas.

MOORMAN, Charles. *Arthurian Triptych:* Mythic Materials in Charles Williams, C. S. Lewis, and T. S. Eliot. Berkeley and Los Angeles, Univ. of Calif. Pr., 1960.

MORGAN, Charles [Langbridge]. *Reflections in a Mirror.* First Series. Macmillan, 1944.

From *TLS* ; *incl.* Hardy. Second Series (Macmillan, 1946) *incl.* Blunden, R. Nichols.

————*The Writer and His World:* Lectures and Essays. Macmillan, 1960. *Incl.* "The Artist in the Community" ; "The Independence of Writers" ; "A Defence of Story-Telling" ; "Dialogue in Novels and Play" ; "On Learning to Write." Essays uncollected at his death.

MORLEY, Christopher. *Essays.* N.Y., Doubleday, Doran, 1928.

Repr. from journals ; *incl.* R. Brooke, Gissing, Doughty.

MORTIMER, Raymond. *Channel Packet.* Hogarth Pr., 1942.

Repr. from journals, *Hor., NSN* etc. *Incl.* V. Woolf, A. E. Housman, Strachey.

MUIR, Edwin. *Essays on Literature and Society.* Hogarth Pr., 1949. Enlgd. ed. [six new pieces]. Cambridge, Mass., Harvard Univ. Pr., 1966.
Mostly on classics of English literature, *Incl.* Hardy ; "The Political View of Literature" ; "The Decline of the Novel."

————*Transition:* Essays on Contemporary Literature. N.Y., Viking, 1926.
Incl. Joyce, D. H. Lawrence, V. Woolf, S. Hudson, Huxley, Strachey, Eliot, E. Sitwell, Graves, contemporary poetry, contemporary fiction.

———— *Latitudes,* Melrose, n.d.
Some repr. from *NS, Ath, The Freeman* (N.Y.). *Incl.* "A Plea for Psychology in Literary Criticism" ; "The Truth about Art" ; "North and South" [European literature] ; Conrad ; the Shaw-Wells generation ; some aphorisms.

————*We Moderns:* Enigmas and Guesses. Allen and Unwin, 1918 ; N.Y., Knopf, 1920.
Repr. from *The New Age* ; *incl.* Chesterton, Galsworthy, Hardy, G. Moore, Shaw, Wells.

MURDOCH, Walter. *Collected Essays.* Angus and Robertson, 1938.
Incl. Conrad, Joyce, Squire, B. Russell.

MURRY, J[ohn] M[iddleton]. *Aspects of Literature.* Collins, and N.Y., Knopf, 1920.
Incl. E. Thomas, Yeats, Hopkins, Butler, Hardy, Masefield.

———— *Countries of the Mind:* Essays in Literary Criticism. Collins, 1922.
Incl. de la Mare, Doughty ; "A Critical Credo."

———— ———— Second Series. Oxford Univ. Pr., 1931.
Eleven of the 14 essays from *TLS* ; *incl.* "Metaphor" ; "Pure Poetry" ; "Reason and Criticism" ; "The Metaphysic of Poetry."

———— *Discoveries:* Essays in Literary Criticism. Collins, 1924.
Incl. "The Nature of Poetry" ; "The Break-up of the Novel."

———— *Selected Criticism 1916–1957.* Chosen and introd. Richard Rees. London and N.Y., Oxford Univ. Pr., 1960.
Incl. "The Function of Criticism" ; "Poetry and Prose" ; "Metaphor" ; "Reason and Criticism" ; "Reply to I. A. Richards" ; "Marxism" ; and on D. H. Lawrence and T. S. Eliot.

———— *Things to Come.* Cape, 1928.
Incl. Archer, "Poetry and Reality" ; "Poetry and Religion" ; "On Reading Novels." Sequel to *The Unknown God.*

NICHOLS, Beverley. *Are They the Same at Home?* Being a Series of Bouquets Diffidently Distributed by Beverley Nichols. Cape, and N.Y., Doran, 1927.
Very brief personal sketches. *Incl.* Arlen, Belloc, E. F. Benson, Coward, Doyle, Guedalla, Hope, Huxley, Kennedy, Lonsdale, Macaulay,

Maugham, G. Moore, B. Nichols, O'Casey, Pinero, O. Sitwell, Wallace, Walpole, Wells, R. West, Wodehouse.

NICHOLSON, Norman. *Man and Literature*. Macmillan, 1943.
Concept of man informing modern literature. *Incl.* Shaw, Galsworthy, Bennett, Wells, D. H. Lawrence, Huxley, Joyce, J. C. Powys, Forster, Bowen, Auden, Isherwood, R. Warner, Greene, Aldington, Charles Morgan, and chapter on modern poetry.

O'CONNOR, William Van. *The New University Wits and the End of Modernism*. Carbondale, Univ. Southern Ill. Pr., 1963.
"A New Literary Generation"; Philip Larkin, Wain, Murdoch, Amis; "The Other Writers" (*incl.* Conquest, Enwright, Holloway, Davie, Jennings, Thom Gun); "The New Hero and a Shift in Literary Conventions"; "A Postscript: Period Styles".

ORAGE, A[lfred] R[ichard]. *The Art of Reading*. N.Y., Farrar and Rinehart, 1930.
Repr. *Incl.* Bennett, West, A. E., D. H. Lawrence, James, Kipling, Galsworthy, Chesterton, Wells, Shaw, Beresford, Gissing.

————. *Readers and Writers, 1917–1921*. N.Y., Knopf, 1922.
Repr. from *The New Age: incl.* James, W. Lewis, Bell, Eglinton, A. Symons, A. E., Chesterton.

ORWELL, George. *Dickens, Dali and Other Studies in Popular Culture*. (English title: *Critical Essays*) Secker and Warburg, and N.Y., Reynal and Hitchcock, 1946.
Incl. "Raffles and Miss Blandish," Wells, Kipling, Yeats, Wodehouse.

————*Inside the Whale*. Gollancz, 1940.
The best of his literary essays though not repr. by author in *Critical Essays* perhaps because of their pessimistic tone. On the writer in contemporary society at beginning of WW II. Pt. II deals with Eng. writers of 20s and 30s.

OVERTON, Grant M. *Authors of the Day:* Studies in Contemporary Literature. N.Y., Doran, 1924.
Incl. Galsworthy, Conrad, V. Sackville-West, Walpole, R. West, Bennett, Swinnerton, Maugham.

————*Cargoes for Crusoes*. N.Y., Appleton, 1924.
Incl. Gibbs, Huxley, E. V. Lucas, Arlen.

PEARSON, Hesketh. *Modern Men and Mummers*. Allen and Unwin, 1921.
Incl. Shaw, Strachey, Phillips, E. F. Benson, Granville-Barker, Wells, Gosse, Caine, Conrad, Bottomley, Chesterton.

PHELPS, Gilbert, ed. *Living Writers:* Being Critical Studies Broadcast in the B.B.C. Third Programme. Sylvan Pr., 1947.
Betjeman on E. Waugh, Johnstone on O'Casey, Turner on Isherwood, Strong on Bowen, Grigson and W. Lewis, E. Sackville-West on Compton-Burnett, Macaulay on Forster, Pritchett on Orwell, D. Thomas on de la Mare, Quennell on Huxley; also on J. C. Powys and Greene.

POCOCK, Guy N. *Pen and Ink*. Dent, 1926.
'Twelve Practical Talks on the Art of Writing English Prose" and
"Little Studies of Contemporary Writers." *Incl*. Conrad, Kipling,
Masefield, Galsworthy, Cunninghame Graham, W. H. Hudson, Wells,
Lynd, Chesterton.

POUND, Ezra. *Instigations*. N.Y., Boni and Liveright, 1920.
Incl. "The Chinese Written Character" by Ernest Fenellosa. Also "In
the Vortex" ; and on James.

—————. *Literary Essays*. Ed. T. S. Eliot. Faber and Faber, and Norfolk,
Conn., New Directions, 1954.
Represents choice made by Eliot from Pound's writing over 30 years,
mostly from 4 of Pound's 6 books of critical essays. *Incl*. "A Retrospect" ; "How to Read" ; "The Serious Artist" ; "Date Line" ; "The
Prose Tradition in Verse" ; A. E. Housman, James, Yeats, D. H. Lawrence, Joyce, Eliot, W. Lewis.

POWELL, Dilys. *Descent From Parnassus*. N.Y., Macmillan, 1934.
Incl. D. H. Lawrence, Eliot, E. Sitwell, Sassoon, "Advance Guard."

POWYS, John Cooper. *Suspended Judgments*. N.Y., Shaw, 1916.
Incl. Conrad, James.

PRIESTLEY, J[ohn] B[oynton]. *Figures in Modern Literature*. Lane, 1924.
Incl. Bennett, de la Mare, Hewlett, A. E. Housman, Jacobs. Lynd,
Saintsbury, Squire.

————— *Thoughts in the Wilderness*. Heinemann, 1957.
Incl. Snow, Shaw, C. Wilson, Leavis ; "The Staggers and Naggers"
[on *NS*] ; "The Popular Press" ; "The Writer in a Changing Society."

PRITCHETT, V[ictor] S[awdon]. *Books in General*. Chatto and Windus,
1953.
All but one repr. from *NS ;* incl. T. E. Lawrence, James, Butler, Gissing, Firbank, Jacobs, W. Lewis.

————— *In My Good Books:* Essays on Literature. Chatto and Windus,
1942.
Incl. Synge and acute essay on Hardy.

—————, ed. *Turnstile One:* A Literary Miscellany from *The New States-
man and Nation*. Turnstile Pr., 1948.
Incl. R. West on Kipling ; Forster on D. H. Lawrence ; Quennell on
Conrad.

QUENNELL, Peter. *The Singular Preference:* Portraits and Essays. Collins,
1952.
Incl. Kipling, Wells.

QUILLER-COUCH, A[rthur] T[homas]. *Adventures in Criticism*. [1896]
Cambridge Univ. Pr. 1924 ; N.Y., Putnam's, 1925.
Repr. from *The Speaker*. *Incl*. Davidson, G. Moore, Hope ; "Excur-
sionists in Poetry" ; "The Popular Conception of a Poet" ; "Poets on
their Own Art."

RANSOM, John Crowe, ed. *The Kenyon Critics:* Studies in Modern Literature From *The Kenyon Review*. Cleveland and N.Y., World, 1951.
>*Incl.* "Pure and Impure Poetry" ; "Emotions in Poems" ; James, Joyce, E. Waugh, Yeats, Ford, D. Thomas, Quiller-Couch, A. E. Housman, Huxley, Eliot.

RATHBURN, Robert C. and Martin STEINMANN, Jr., eds. *From Jane Austen to Joseph Conrad:* Essays Collected in Memory of James T. Hillhouse. Minneapolis, Univ. of Minnesota Pr., 1958.
>*Incl.* Hardy, Gissing, Butler, Conrad.

READ, Herbert. *A Coat of Many Colours*. Routledge, 1945.
>*Incl.* very short essays on T. E. Lawrence, James, Ellis, English prose. Joyce, Hopkins, Saintsbury, Yeats, de la Mare, D. H. Lawrence, R. Fry, Hulme.

————Collected Essays in Literary Criticism. [1938] Faber and Faber, 1950. Am. ed., *The Nature of Literature,* N.Y., Horizon Pr., 1956.
>*Incl.* long essays on poetry in general and on Hopkins, James.

———— *Selected Writings:* Poetry and Criticism. N.Y., Horizon Pr., 1964. With foreword by Allen Tate and select bibliog. composed with the assistance of Philip Ward and Salma M. Ghanem.
>*Incl.* "The Personality of the Poet" ; "Psycho-Analysis and Literary Criticism" ; "American Bards and British Reviewers."

———— *The Tenth Muse:* Essays in Criticism. Routledge and Kegan Paul, 1957.
>*Incl.* "The Image in Modern English Poetry" ; "The Drama and the Theatre" ; "The Faith of a Critic."

REILLY, Joseph J. *Of Books and Men*. N.Y., Messner, 1942.
>*Incl.* Conrad, A. E. Housman, Baring, Chesterton, Strachey, Galsworthy, Hardy, Barrie.

REXROTH, Kenenth. *Assays*. N.Y., New Directions, 1961 (paper).
>Repr. from journals. *Incl.* "The Poet as Translator" ; The New Poetry" ; James, Wells, Durrell, Campbell.

RIDLEY, M[aurice] R[oy]. *Second Thoughts:* More Studies in Literature, Dent, 1965.
>*Incl.* important essay on Buchan.

RUSSELL, George William (A. E.). *Imaginations and Reveries*. Dublin and London, Maunsel, 1915.
>Collected from 25 years of periodical writing ; *incl.* "Nationality or Cosmopolitanism" ; "Art and Literature" ; Yeats, Stephens.

SACKVILLE-WEST, Edward. *Inclinations*. Secker and Warburg, 1949.
>Repr. from *NS, Spec., Hor., Crit., TLS*. *Incl.* James, Conrad, Bowen, Compton-Burnett, Day Lewis.

SCHELLING, Felix E[manuel]. *Appraisements and Asperities as to Some Contemporary Writers*. Phila., Lippincott, 1922.
>*Incl.* Conrad, Masefield, Drinkwater, Lynd, James.

SCOTT, Dixon. *Men of Letters.* [1916] Repr. with extra essay, Hodder and Stoughton, 1923.

    Incl. Shaw, Kipling, Barrie, James, Wells, Bennett, Granville-Barker, Beerbohm, Chesterton, Masefield, A. Meynell, Brooke.

SCOTT, Nathan A. *Rehearsals of Discomposure:* Alienation and Reconciliation in Modern Literature. N.Y., King's Crown Pr., 1952.

    Incl. D. H. Lawrence, Eliot.

SCOTT-JAMES, R[olfe] A[rnold]. *The Day Before Yesterday,* Muller, 1947. Editorial notes from *LM,* Oct. 1934-April 1939.

————*Personality in Literature.* [1913] Secker, 1931 ; N.Y., Holt, 1932.

    Incl. Shaw, Wells, Bennett, Chesterton, Synge, "Some Modern Poets" ; "Specialization in Literature" ; "Literature and Fine Art."

SCRUTINY. The following are collections of essays from this important periodical.

Determinations: Critical Essays. Chatto and Windus, 1934.

    Incl. on Richards ; "The Scientific Best Seller." Introd. Leavis.

The Importance of Scrutiny: Selections from *Scrutiny* 1932–1948. Ed. Eric P. Bentley, N.Y., Stewart, 1948 ; repr. N.Y. Univ. Pr., 1964. (Gotham Bks).

    Incl. bibliog. of contents of *Scrutiny* Vols. I-XV (1932–1948 ; 1964 ed. has contents Vols. I-XIX, 1932–1953). Also, one section: "A Modern Miscellany" ; and on Auden, Connolly, Eliot, Forster, Hulme, Joyce, Kipling, D. H. Lawrence, Richards, V. Woolf.

Scrutinies [I]. Coll. Edgell Rickword. Wishart, 1928.

    Incl. Barrie, Bennett, Chesterton, de la Mare, Galsworthy, Kipling, Masefield, G. Moore, Shaw, Wells, contemporary poetry.

Scrutinies. Vol. II. Coll. Edgell Rickword. Wishart, 1931.

    Incl. Eliot, Huxley, Joyce, D. H. Lawrence, W. Lewis, the Sitwells, Strachey, V. Woolf ; also on poetry and novel.

SHANKS, Edward. *First Essays in Literature.* Collins, 1923.

    Repr. *Incl.* Butler, de la Mare, Freeman, Masefield, Belloc, Wells, Yeats ; "Recent History of the English Novel" ; "The Position in the Theatre."

————*Second Essays on Literature.* Collins, 1927.

    Repr. *Incl.* Kipling, Conrad, Galsworthy, D. H. Lawrence, Flecker, Haggard, "The 'New' Poetry 1911–1925."

SHAW, G[eorge] B[ernard]. *Pen Portraits and Reviews.* Constable, 1932 (Vol. XXI of *Works*).

    Incl. Archer, Belloc, Bennett, Butler, Cannan, Chesterton, H. A. Jones, Beerbohm, Wells.

SHERMAN, Stuart P. *On Contemporary Literature.* N.Y., Holt, 1917.

    Incl. Wells, Bennett, G. Moore, Synge, James.

SMITH, Logan Pearsall. *Reperusals and Recollections.* N.Y., Harcourt, Brace, 1936.

    Incl. chapters on Michael Field, "Fine Writing."

SPARROW, John [Hanbury Angus]. *Controversial Essays.* Faber and Faber, 1966.

————— *Independent Essays.* Faber and Faber, 1963.

    Incl. "Great Poetry" (Warton lecture, Brit. Acad.) and repr. reviews mostly from *TLS*: A. E. Housman, Barrie, Betjeman, "The Censor as Aedile" (review of *Regina v. Penguin Books,* q.v., on *Chatterley* trial).

SPENDER, Stephen. *The Creative Element:* A Study of Vision, Despair, and Orthodoxy Among Some Modern Writers. Hamilton, 1953.

    Incl. chapters on Eliot, E. Waugh ; also Yeats, Forster, D. H. Lawrence, Orwell, Auden.

—————*The Destructive Element:* A Study of Modern Writers and Beliefs. [1935] Phila., Saifer, 1953.

    Incl. James, Yeats, Eliot, D. H. Lawrence.

—————*The Making of a Poem.* [1955] N.Y., Norton, 1962.

    Repr. articles of 15 years ; *incl.* "Reflections on Conditioned and Unconditioned Imagination" ; "Greatness of Aim" ; "The Making of a Poem" ; "Confessions and Autobiography" ; "Two Landscapes of the Novel [Butler, Forster, James, V. Woolf, Joyce]" ; "Georgian Poetry" ; "Notes of a Writer on Writing" ; A. E. Housman.

SQUIRE, J[ohn] C[ollings]. *Books in General.* [First series] Secker ; N.Y., Knopf, 1919.

    Repr. from *NS* (April 1913–Jan. 1920 over pseud. "Solomon Eagle"). *Incl.* G. Moore, Phillips, James, Joyce, Watson, Hodgson.

—————. —————. Second Series. N.Y., Knopf, 1920.

    Incl. A. E., Wells, R. Brooke, Beerbohm.

—————. —————. Third Series. London and N.Y., Hodder and Stoughton, 1921.

    Incl. E. Thomas, Kipling, Bridges, Drinkwater, "The Decay of the Novel."

————— *Books Reviewed.* N.Y., Doran, 1922.

    Repr.; *incl.* Mansfield, G. Moore, Gosse, de la Mare, "The Laureates" ; "The Elements of Poetry."

STEWART, Douglas Alexander. *The Flesh and the Spirit:* An Outlook on Literature. Sydney, Australia, Angus and Robertson, 1948.

    Incl. Yeats, Forster, Joyce, Eliot, Auden, Graves.

STOLL, E[lmer] E[dgar]. *From Shakespeare to Joyce:* Authors and Critics ; Literature and Life. Garden City, N.Y., Doubleday, Doran, 1944.

    Incl. "Literature and Life Again" ; "Psychoanalysis in Criticism" ; Kipling, Joyce.

STONIER, G[eorge] W[alter]. *Gog, Magog, and Other Critical Essays.* Dent, 1933.

    Incl. Eliot, Joyce, D. H. Lawrence, W. Lewis, Hopkins, Auden, Spender, C. Day Lewis.

STRONG, L[eonard] A[lfred] G[eorge]. *Personal Remarks.* Peter Neville, 1953.

    Repr. *Incl.* Yeats, Synge, P. Colum, O'Sullivan, Hardy, Bowen, James, Joyce, C. Day Lewis, Church, L. H. Myers, Forster, Walpole.

SYMONS, Arthur. *Dramatis Personae*. Indianapolis, Bobbs-Merrill, 1923.
Incl. "On Criticism" ; "The Decadent Movement in Literature" ; "Impressionistic Writing" ; "Paradoxes on Poets" ; Conrad, Watson.

———— *Studies in Prose and Verse*. Dent, and N.Y., Dutton, 1904.
Incl. Bridges, Yeats, Phillips ; "Fact in Literature" ; "What is Poetry?" ; prefaces to his collections of poetry (*Silhouettes, London Nights*).

TATE, Allen. *Collected Essays*. Denver, Colo., Alan Swallow, 1959.
Repr. ; incl. Richards, Hardy, Yeats, and many theoretical essays on poetry and criticism.

————*Reason in Madness:* Critical Essays. N.Y., Putnam's, 1941.
All but one repr. from journals ; incl. "The Present Function of Criticism" ; "Literature as Knowledge" ; "Tension in Poetry" ; "Understanding Modern Poetry" ; "Procrustes and the Poets" ; Hardy.

THOMPSON, E[dward] R[aymond] (his pseud. E. T. Raymond). *Portraits of the New Century:* The First Ten Years. Benn, and Garden City, N.Y., Doubleday, Doran, 1928.
Incl. "Literary Swashbucklers and Sentimentalists" ; also Beerbohm, James, Chesterton, Belloc, Shaw, Kipling, Galsworthy, Wells, Bennett, Phillips, Barrie.

THOMPSON, Francis. *Literary Criticisms by Francis Thompson:* Newly Discovered and Collected by Terence L. Connolly. N.Y., Dutton, 1948.
Repr. from *Academy, Ath., Merry England,* etc. *Incl.* bibliog. of Thompson's uncollected book reviews and literary criticism ; also on A. Meynell, A. Symons, James, Yeats, Blunt, Davidson, "Literary Ideals in Ireland."

TIMES LITERARY SUPPLEMENT. The following collections have been published from and by this journal.

The British Imagination: A Critical Survey from the Times Literary Supplement. Introd. Arthur Crook. Cassell, 1961.

The Critical Moment: Essays on the Nature of Literature. Faber and Faber, 1964.

Freeing the Mind: Articles and Letters from the "Times Literary Supplement" during March-June, 1962. Times Publ. Co., 1962.

TLS: Essays and Reviews from the Times Literary Supplement. Oxford Univ. Pr., 1962— (1 : 1962), 1963, (2 : 1963), 1964, (3 : 1964), 1965, (4 : 1965), 1966.
Reviews of the most important books in many fields, with index of other major reviews of the year.

The Writer's Dilemma: Essays First Published in the Times Literary Supplement Under the Heading "Limits of Control." Introd. Stephen Spender. London and N.Y., Oxford Univ. Pr., 1961.
Incl. Durrell, W. Golding, Sillitoe, Spender.

TILLYARD, E[ustace] M[andeville] W. *Essays Literary and Educational*. [1948] Chatto and Windus, 1962.
Incl. Conrad ; "The Origins of English Anti-Romanticism" ; "Is a New History of Criticism Possible?"

TRILLING, Lionel. *Beyond Culture:* Essays on Literature and Learning. N.Y., Viking, 1965.
> *Incl.* Hopkins, Yeats; "The Two Environments: Reflections on the Study of English"; "The Fate of Pleasure"; "The Leavis-Snow Controversy."

————*A Gathering of Fugitives.* Boston, Beacon Pr., 1956.
> Repr., mostly reviews; *incl.* Forster, Graves, Leavis: "The Novel Alive or Dead"; "Criticism and Aesthetics [Santayana]."

————*The Liberal Imagination:* Essays on Literature and Society. [1950] Garden City, N.Y., Doubleday, 1956. (Anchor).
> *Incl.* James, Kipling; "Freud and Literature"; "The Sense of the Past"; "Manners, Morals and the Novel"; "Art and Fortune"; "The Meaning of a Literary Idea."

————*The Opposing Self:* Nine Essays in Criticism. [1955] N.Y., Viking 1959. (Compass).
> *Incl.* James, Orwell.

VAN DOREN, Mark. *The Private Reader.* N.Y., Holt, 1942.
> Repr.; *incl.* Doughty, W. H. Davies, J. C. Powys, Eliot, T. E. Lawrence, Chesterton, V. Woolf.

VAN VECHTEN, Carl. *Excavations.* N.Y., Knopf, 1926.
> *Incl.* Machen, Firbank.

WAIN, John. *Essays on Literature and Ideas.* Macmillan, 1963.
> *Incl.* Hopkins, Eliot, Connolly, Betjeman, Orwell.

———— *Preliminary Essays.* N.Y., St. Martin's Pr., 1957.
> Repr. from journals, esp. *LM, Spec.; incl.* Bennett, Empson, D. Thomas; "The Literary Critic in the University."

WALDOCK, A[rthur] J[ohn] A[lfred]. *James Joyce and Others.* Williams and Norgate, 1937.
> *Incl.* James, Joyce, Hardy.

WALSH, William. *A Human Idiom:* Literature and Humanity. Chatto and Windus, and N.Y., Barnes and Noble, 1964.
> Some repr. from *NS, List., Review of English Literature, Universities Quarterly; incl.* James, Leavis, Enright, Yeats, Eliot, D. H. Lawrence, Joyce.

WARREN, Austin. *Rage for Order:* Essays in Criticism. Chicago, Univ. Chicago Pr., 1948.
> *Incl.* Hopkins (excellent), Forster, James.

WAUGH, Arthur. *Reticence in Literature and Other Papers.* J. G. Wilson, and N.Y., Dutton, 1915.
> Repr. mostly from journals; *incl.* Gissing.

————*Tradition and Change in Contemporary Literature.* Chapman and Hall, 1919.
> *Incl.* "Tradition and Change"; "The New Poetry"; "War Poetry (1914–1918)"; "The New Realism; "The Imagists"; "The Religious Novel";

Phillips, A. Symons, Flecker, D. H. Lawrence, Squire, R. Brooke, Butler, James, Freeman, Conrad, Galsworthy, E. V. Lucas.

WEST, Anthony. *Principles and Persuasions:* The Literary Essays of Anthony West. Eyre and Spottiswood, 1958.
Highly personal, often destructive, but rewarding criticism. *Incl.* on Wells (his father), Shaw, T. E. Lawrence, Walpole, Orwell, Greene, D. Johnston, Compton-Burnett.

WEST, Paul. *The Wine of Absurdity.* Univ. Park, Pa., Pennsylvania State Univ. Pr., 1966.
Incl. Yeats, D. H. Lawrence, Eliot, Greene.

WEST, Ray B., Jr., ed. *Essays in Modern Literary Criticism.* N.Y., Rinehart, 1952.
Incl. on James, Hulme, Eliot, Joyce, and well known essays by Richards, Blackmur, Tate, Brooks etc.

WEST, Rebecca. *Ending in Earnest:* A Literary Log. Garden City, N.Y., Doubleday, Doran, 1931.
Repr. from *BkmL,* 1929, 1930, as "Letters from Europe" ; *incl.* Beerbohm, Sherriff, Galsworthy, Gosse, V. Woolf, E. Waugh, D. H. Lawrence.

————*The Strange Necessity.* Garden City, N.Y., Doubleday, 1928.
Repr. from *NYHT,* esp., and *BkmL, NS ; incl.* Joyce, Bennett, H. M. Tomlinson, Hardy.

WILSON, Colin. *The Strength to Dream:* Literature and the Imagination. Gollancz, 1962.
Incl. esp. Yeats, Greene, Beckett, Wells, D. H. Lawrence, Huxley.

WILSON, Edmund. *The Bit Beneath My Teeth:* A Literary Chronicle of 1950–1965. N.Y., Farrar, Straus and Giroux, 1965.
Repr. reviews, etc.

————*Classics and Commercials:* A Literary Chronicle of the Forties. Farrar, Straus, 1950.
Incl. H. Nicolson, E. Waugh, Joyce, Huxley, Shaw, Connolly, Saintsbury, Maugham, Beerbohm, Firbank.

———— *A Literary Chronicle:* 1920–1950. Garden City, N.Y., Doubleday, 1956. (Anchor).
Sel. from *Classics and Commercials* and *The Shores of Light. Incl.* D. H. Lawrence, Eliot, Strachey, E. Waugh, Joyce, Saintsbury.

————*The Shores of Light:* A Literary Chronicle of the Twenties and Thirties. N.Y., Farrar, Straus, and Young, 1952.
Incl. James, V. Woolf, Eliot, Strachey, Butler.

————*The Triple Thinkers.* [1943] N.Y., Oxford Univ. Pr., 1963. (Galaxy).
Incl. A. E. Housman, James, Shaw ; "Is Verse a Dying Technique" ; "Marxism and Literature" ; "The Historical Interpretation of Literature."

————*The Wound and the Bow:* Seven Studies in Literature. [1941] N.Y.,
Oxford Univ. Pr., 1959. (Galaxy).
Incl. Kipling, Joyce.

WOOLF, Leonard. *Essays on Literature, History, Politics, etc.* Leonard and
Virginia Woolf, and N.Y., Harcourt, Brace, 1927.
Incl. Butler, Conrad, G. Moore.

WOOLF, Virginia. *The Captain's Death Bed and Other Essays.* Hogarth Pr.,
1950.
Incl. Hardy, Conrad; "Mr. Bennett and Mrs. Brown"; "Modern
Letters."

————*Contemporary Writers.* Hogarth Pr., 1965.
Hitherto uncollected essays, from *TLS. Incl.* Butler, Maugham, V. Lee,
Forster, N. Douglas, Bennett, Galsworthy, Walpole, L. P. Smith, C.
Mackenzie, Hewlett, Wells, W. H. Hudson, Swinnerton, Cannan,
D. Richardson, G. Moore, A. Huxley, Beresford, D. H. Lawrence.

————*The Common Reader:* First Series. [1925] Hogarth Pr., 1948.
Incl. Conrad; "Modern Fiction"; "The Modern Essay"; "How It
Strikes a Contemporary."

————. ————. Second Series. [1932] Hogarth Pr., 1948.
Book reviews from *TLS,* etc.; *incl.* Gissing and Hardy.

————*The Death of the Moth and Other Essays.* [1942] Penguin, 1961.
Incl. James, G. Moore, Forster, Strachey.

————*Granite and Rainbow.* Hogarth Pr., 1958.
Incl. James, Mansfield, H. Nicolson; "Phases of Fiction."

YEATS, John Butler. *Essays Irish and American.* Dublin, Talbot Pr., 1918.
Partly repr. from *Harper's Weekly* and *The Seven Arts;* *incl.* Butler,
Synge.

YOUNG, G[eorge] M[alcolm]. *Daylight and Champaign.* Cape, 1937.
Mostly book reviews from *TLS, NS, Obs., LL, LM. Incl.* Spender,
Dobrée, Potter, C. S. Lewis, Yeats, Armstrong, Macaulay, Belloc,
Baring, V. Sackville-West.

CRITICISM

Histories

NOTE. What will certainly be the standard history is the forthcoming Vol. V of René Wellek's *A History of Modern Criticism,* 1750–1950 (New Haven and London, Yale Univ. Pr., 1955—): *The Twentieth Century.* (Vol. IV, *The Later Nineteenth Century,* 1965, *incl.* James, A. Symons, Saintsbury, Shaw.) Like the other volumes, this will be European and American in coverage, written from a consistent point of view (for which, see below Wellek and Warren, *Theory of Literature*), fully documented, with annotated bibliographies and index. The only comparable predecessor is George Saintsbury's *A History of Criticism and Literary Taste in Europe,* 1901–1904, 3 vols. (repr. 1929–1934), also the work of a scholar of encyclopedic range but of course not useful for the twentieth century, which has been called the age of criticism. The books listed below in this section are general histories with some consideration of twentieth century authors or historical sketches of the period.

HALL, Vernon, Jr. *A Short History of Literary Criticism.* N.Y. Univ. Pr., 1963 (Gotham).
> Very brief and rather elementary treatment of a few major aspects of modern criticism. *Incl.* Richards, Eliot.

O'CONNOR, William Van. *An Age of Criticism, 1900–1950.* Chicago, Regnery, 1952.
> Notes toward a hist. of Am. criticism. Describes modes, identifies authors and classic essays. Clear, non-polemical, but especially sympathetic to New Criticism.

SHIPLEY, J[oseph] T[wadell]. *Quest for Literature:* A Survey of Literary Criticism and the Theories of Literary Forms. N.Y., Richard K. Smith, 1931.
> From ancient times to the present. Many modern authors included.

WATSON, George. *The Literary Critics:* A Study of English Descriptive Criticism. Baltimore, Penguin, 1962.
> Outline book, good introd. to subject. One chapter on James and two on 20th c. *incl.* Eliot, Richards, Empson, Leavis. Selected bibliog.

WILLIAMS, Orlo. *Contemporary Criticism of Literature,* Leonard Parsons, 1924.

"A present view of criticism." Relaxed and sensible, by kinds. *Incl.*
Murry, Eliot, Strachey, Saintsbury, Gosse, Beresford. No apparatus.

WIMSATT, W[illiam] K. and Cleanth BROOKS. *Literary Criticism:* A
Short History. N.Y., Knopf, 1962.
> Indispensable. Called by authors an "argumentative" history of literary
> argument in the West. From the Greeks through Hulme, Eliot,
> Richards, Empson. Wide-ranging documentation.

Theory and Special Studies

ADLER, Mortimer J. *Art and Prudence:* A Study in Practical Philosophy.
N.Y. and London, Longmans, Green, 1937.
> "The problem of the moral and political criticism of the fine arts,
> occasioned by the conflict in operation of two practical virtues—
> prudence and art." Theoretical discussion by an Aristotelian, with
> emphasis on the cinema.

BABBITT, Irving. *The New Laokoon:* An Essay on the Confusion of the
Arts. [1910] Boston, Houghton, Mifflin, 1926.
> A classic essay, against Romanticism.

BEARDSLEY, Monroe C. *Aesthetics:* Problems in the Philosophy of Criticism. N.Y., Harcourt, Brace, 1958. Ill.
> Excellent introd. for student of any of the arts. Vast bibliog. in notes.

BERGSON, Henri. *Laughter.* Tr. [of *Le Rire,* 1900] Cloudesley Brereton
and Fred Rothwell. N.Y., Macmillan, 1911.
> Essay on the meaning of the comic.

BETHELL, S. L. *Essays on Literary Criticism and the English Tradition.*
Dennis Dobson, n.d.
> Repr. from *New English Weekly,* spring 1945–1946. Short but useful
> book on critic's method and duty. *Incl.* Leavis, Eliot, Richards.

BLACKMUR, R[ichard] P. Language as Gesture: Essays in Poetry. N.Y.,
Harcourt, Brace, 1952.
> *Incl.* Eliot.

BROWER, Reuben Arthur. *The Fields of Light:* An Experiment in Critical
Reading. N.Y., Oxford Univ. Pr., 1951.
> How to read poetry and prose, *incl.,* V. Woolf, Forster.

————and Richard POIRIER, eds. *In Defense of Reading:* A Reader's
Approach to Literary Criticism. N.Y., Dutton, 1962.

BROWNELL, William Crary. *Criticism.* N.Y., Scribner's, 1914.
> Short but valuable essay by an American on kinds of criticism and
> critic's function.

BUCKLEY, Vincent. *Poetry and Morality:* Studies on the Criticism of
Matthew Arnold, T. S. Eliot, and F. R. Leavis. [1959] N.Y., Humanities Pr.,
1965.

BURKE, Kenneth. *Counter-Statement*. [1931] Chicago, Univ. of Chicago Pr., 1957. (Phoenix).
> Essays to "elucidate a point of view"—that of one of the foremost living critics.

———— *The Philosophy of Literary Form:* Studies in Symbolic Action. [1941] rev. abgd. by author. N.Y., Vintage, 1957.

CARNAP, Rudolf. *Meaning and Necessity:* A Study in Semantics and Modal Logic. [1947] Chicago, Univ. of Chicago Pr., 1956 (Phoenix).
> "A new method for analyzing and describing the meanings of linguistic expressions" by an influential semanticist.

CARRIT, E[dgar] F[rederick], ed. *Philosophies of Beauty from Socrates to Robert Bridges,* Being the Sources of Aesthetic Theory. [1931] Oxford Univ. Pr., 1952.
> *Incl.* selection from G. Moore, Bell, Hulme, Bridges.

CASSIRER, Ernst. *Language and Myth*. Tr. Susanne K. Langer. N.Y., Dover Publications, 1946.
> Early (1920's) essay on genesis of the theory of knowledge of an influential philosopher.

CAUDWELL, Christopher (*pseud.* of Chistopher St. John Sprigg). *Further Studies in a Dying Culture,* ed. with preface Edgell Rickword. Bodley Head, 1949.

————*Studies in a Dying Culture*. John Lane, 1938.
> Studies, from a Marxist point of view, of "bourgeois" religion, aesthetics, history, psychology, philosophy. This book and the sequel (see above item) pub. posthumously have been influential.

CAZAMIAN, Louis. *Criticism in the Making*. N.Y., Macmillan, 1929.
> By a French academic critic, on criticism and scholarship, psychology and criticism, parallels in the development of French and English literature.

CHASE, Richard [Volney]. *Quest for Myth*. Baton Rouge, Louisiana State Univ. Pr., 1949.
> "The central premise of this book is that myth is literature and therefore a matter of aesthetic experience and the imagination. . . ." Discusses various views of myth (e.g. historical, anthropological, psychoanalytical) to refute all but author's own.

CLARK, David R. and Robin SKELTON, eds. *The Irish Renaissance:* A Gathering of Essays, Letters, and Memoirs from *The Massachusetts Review*. Oxford Univ. Pr., 1966.

COLLINGWOOD, R[obin] G[eorge]. *The Principles of Art*. [1938] Oxford Univ. Pr., 1958 (Galaxy).
> Useful introd. to aesthetics for students of literature.

COLUM, Mary. *From These Roots:* The Ideas That Have Made Modern Literature. [1937] N.Y., Columbia Univ. Pr., 1944.
> From Lessing and Herder to the present in Europe, focussing on realism.

COOMBES, H[enry]. *Literature and Criticism.* [1953] Penguin, 1963.

CRANE, Ronald S., ed. *Critics and Criticism.* Ancient and Modern. [1952] Chicago, Univ. of Chicago Pr., 1957. (Also, abgd., Phoenix).

> Essays in method by a group of the "Chicago" critics, selected to show development and application of their method. *Incl.* on Richards.

————, ed. *The Languages of Criticism and the Structure of Poetry.* Toronto, Univ. of Toronto Pr., 1953.

> The Alexander lectures, Univ. of Toronto, 1951–1952. Founding critic of the "Chicago" school, arguing for his method, with many illust. from modern literature.

CROCE, Benedetto. *Aesthetic:* as Science of Expression and General Linguistic. Tr. Douglas Ainslie. 2d ed. Macmillan, 1922.

> Theory of influential modern aesthetician.

DAICHES, David. *Critical Approaches to Literature.* [1956] Longmans, Green, 1963.

> Presentation of "some of the more important ways in which literature has been discussed," under divisions: "The Philosophical Inquiry"; "Practical Criticism"; "Literary Criticism and Related Disciplines." From Plato to the present.

————*New Literary Values:* A Study of Literature for Readers and Critics. [1936] Ithaca, N.Y., Cornell Univ. Pr., 1948.

DANZIGER, Marlies K. and W. Stacy JOHNSON. *An Introduction to Literary Criticism.* Boston, Heath, 1961.

> Textbook. Introd. section by authors and anthology of essays on aspects of criticism by standard critics, all Am. except Forster, Richards.

DUCASSE, Curt John. *The Philosophy of Art.* N.Y., L. MacVeagh, Dial Pr., 1929.

> Theory of an influential modern aesthetician and criticism, from author's point of view, of other theories.

EASTMAN, Max. *The Literary Mind:* Its Place in an Age of Science. [1931] N.Y., Scribner's, 1935.

> *Incl.* "The Swan-Song of Humane Letters"; "The Cult of Unintelligibility"; The Tendency towards Pure Poetry"; "Poets Talking to Themselves"; "The Future of Literature: Are Poetry and Drama Dying?"; "A Note on I. A. Richards' Psychology of Poetry."

ELIOT, T[homas] S[tearns]. *After Strange Gods:* A Primer of Modern Heresy. N.Y., Harcourt, Brace, 1934.

> Page-Barbour lectures, Univ. of Virginia, 1933. A further development of the problem first discussed by Eliot in "Tradition and the Individual Talent," a classic essay from *The Sacred Wood* (1920), repr. in *Selected Essays* (1932) and *Selected Essays,* 1950. Also in *The Sacred Wood:* "The Perfect Critic," "Imperfect Critics."

————*To Criticize the Critic and Other Writings.* Faber and Faber, 1965.

> Title essay, 6th convocation lecture at Univ. of Leeds, 1961, unrev. at E.'s death, is an interesting review of his own critical positions. For other Eliot essays, *see* under Collections, Drama and Poetry.

ELLIOTT, Robert C. *The Power of Satire:* Magic, Ritual, Art. Princeton, N.J., Princeton Univ. Pr., 1960.
> Theoretical and historical: early connection of magic with satire and survival today of the connection. Chapt. V: "Twentieth-Century Magic" *incl.* W. Lewis, Roy Campbell.

ELLIS, Havelock. *The Dance of Life.* [1923] N.Y., Mod. Lib., 1929.
> *Incl.* the arts of dancing, thinking, writing, religion, morals.

————*The World of Dreams.* [1911] Boston and N.Y., Houghton, Mifflin, 1926.

ELLMAN, Richard and Charles FEIDELSON, Jr., eds. *The Modern Tradition:* Backgrounds of Modern Literature. N.Y., Oxford Univ. Pr., 1965.
> European (*incl.* Eng.) writers, artists, philosophers, and scientists on topics relevant to the modern tradition, e.g. literary criticism, aesthetics, symbolism. Useful compilation.

ELTON, William. *A Glossary of the New Criticism.* Chicago, Mod. Poetry Assoc., 1948. Rev. 1949 as *A Guide to the New Criticism.*

FLETCHER, Angus. *Allegory.* The Theory of a Symbolic Mode. Ithaca, N.Y., Cornell Univ. Pr., 1964.

FOSS, Martin. *Symbol and Metaphor in Human Experience.* Princeton, N.J., Princeton Univ. Pr., 1949.
> Philosophical analysis of symbol and metaphor in their relation to myth, music, the fine arts, law, ethics, poetry, drama.

FRANK, Joseph. *The Widening Gyre:* Crisis and Mastery in Modern Literature. New Brunswick, N.J., Rutgers Univ. Pr., 1963.
> Repr. By a disciple of Worringer. *Incl.* "Modern Poetry," "The Parallel with the Plastic Arts," "The Meaning of Spatial Form," "The Dehumanization of Art."

FOWLER, Roger, ed. *Essays on Style and Language:* Linguistic Approaches to Literary Style. Routledge and Kegan Paul, 1966.
> Analysis of texts from *Beowulf* to Philip Larkin by practitioners of the new linguistics. Very novel.

FRYE, Northrop. *Anatomy of Criticism.* Four Essays. Princeton, N.J., Princeton Univ. Pr., 1957.
> Application of Blakean symbolism and Biblical typology to the working out of a highly organized system of criticism dependent on myth, symbol and numerology. A controversial classic.

GARDNER, Helen [Louise]. *The Business of Criticism.* Oxford Univ. Pr., 1959.
> Two sets of lectures: "The Profession of a Critic"; "The Limits of Criticism."

GILBERT, Katherine. *Studies in Recent Aesthetic.* Chapel Hill, Univ. of North Carolina Pr., 1927.
> Six essays on philosophy of beauty. *Incl.* on theories of Bosanquet, Bergson, Croce, Santayana.

GREENE, T[heodore] M[eyer]. *The Arts and the Art of Criticism.* Princeton, N.J., Princeton Univ. Pr., 1947.
> Excellent introd. to theory.

GREENLAW, Edwin. *The Province of Literary History.* Baltimore, Johns Hopkins Pr. and London, Oxford Univ. Pr., 1931.
> "The purpose is to study the history of civilization through literature rather than to study authors and their works as literary phenomena." Counterweight to Wellek and Warren, *Theory of Literature,* q.v.

GUÉRARD, Albert. *Art for Art's Sake.* N.Y., Lothrop Lee and Shepard, 1936.
> Perceptive explanation of a commonly misunderstood theory.

HANNA, Thomas. *The Bergsonian Heritage.* N.Y., and London, Columbia Univ. Pr., 1962.
> Papers read at two Bergson centennial celebrations (Hollins College and Paris, 1959). Useful remarks on the philosopher who had the most influence on literature of the early 20th c. in England and France. See esp. Enid Starkie's paper which refers to B.'s connection with French literature.

HAEZRAHI, Pepita. *The Contemplative Activity:* A Study in Aesthetics. N.Y., Abelard-Schuman, 1956.
> Useful introductory study.

HAZLITT, Henry. *The Anatomy of Criticism:* a Trialogue. N.Y., Simon and Schuster, 1933.
> Graceful and stimulating discussion.

HOFSTADTER, Albert and R. KUHNS, eds. *Philosophies of Art and Beauty:* Selected Readings in Aesthetics from Plato to Heidegger. N.Y., Mod. Lib., 1964.
> Standard. Bibliog. footnotes.

HOSPERS, John. *Meaning and Truth in the Arts.* Chapel Hill, Univ. of North Carolina Pr., 1946.
> Useful theoretical discussion for students of literature.

HULME T[homas] E[rnest]. *Further Speculations,* ed. Sam Hynes. Minneapolis, Univ of Minnesota Pr., 1955.
> Repr. from journals, mostly from *The New Age,* except for the previously unpub. "Diary from the Trenches." One short essay "Literary Criticism." With useful introd. on H.'s life and thought.

——————*Notes on Language and Style,* ed. Herbert Read. Seattle, Univ. of Washington Pr., 1929.
> Notes from H.'s mss. excluded from *Speculations.*

——————*Speculations:* Essays on Humanism and the Philosophy of Art, ed. Herbert Read, with a foreword [on H.] by Jacob Epstein. [1924] Routledge and Kegan Paul, 1955.
> The most important collection of this influential thinker. *Incl.* on Eliot.

HUTCHINSON, G[eorge] E[velyn]. *The Itinerant Ivory Tower:* Scientific and Literary Essays. Oxford Univ. Pr., and New Haven, Conn., Yale Univ. Pr., 1953.

    Incl. R. West, Eliot.

HUXLEY, Aldous. *Literature and Science*. Chatto and Windus, 1963.

HYMAN, Stanley Edgar. *The Armed Vision:* A Study in the Methods of Modern Criticism. [1948] N.Y., Vintage Bks., 1955 (rev., abgd.).

    Indispensable. Exposition of 12 critical modes, *incl*. theories of Eliot, Caudwell, Empson, Richards.

————, ed. *The Critical Performance:* An Anthology of Literary Criticism of Our Century. N.Y., Vintage Bks., 1956.

    Intended as supplement to above item. Essays sel. to show method of various critics, *incl*. Murray, Eliot, Read, Richards, Empson, Caudwell, Auden.

JESPERSON, Otto. *Growth and Structure of the English Language*. [1905] Garden City, N.Y., Doubleday, 1955 (Anchor).

    Classic study by a great philologist.

JONES, Phyllis M. Jones, ed. *English Critical Essays: Twentieth Century*. Oxford Univ. Pr., 1933 (WC).

    The best-known 20th c. critics on various authors or topics, e.g. H. W. Garrod, "The Profession of Poetry" ; Murry, "Pure Poetry" ; Bridges, "Poetic Diction in English" ; Abercrombie, "The Function of Poetry in the Drama" ; Charles Williams on Bridges ; Dobrée on Hardy ; Read on Hopkins ; V. Woolf, "Modern Fiction."

KRIEGER, Murray. *The New Apologists for Poetry*. Minneapolis, Univ. of Minnesota Pr., 1956.

    Perceptive discussion of modern critical modes, by critic, *incl*. Richards, Hulme, Eliot. Excellent account of New Criticism ; preferable to Richard Foster's *The New Romantics:* A Reappraisal of the New Criticism (Bloomington, Indiana Univ. Pr., 1962).

KRUTCH, Joseph Wood. *Experience and Art:* Some Aspects of the Esthetics of Literature. N.Y., Smith and Haas, 1932.

LANGER, Susanne K. *Feeling and Form:* A Theory of Art Developed from *Philosophy in a New Key*. N.Y., Scribner's, 1953.

    "In effect Vol. II of the study in symbols that began with" *Philosophy* [see below]. Critique of art based on semantic theory. Two very influential books.

————*Philosophical Sketches*. Oxford Univ. Pr., and Baltimore, Johns Hopkins Pr., 1962.

    Work in progress toward a new book, developing and modifying theory explained in earlier two.

————*Philosophy in a New Key:* A Study in the Symbolism of Reason, Rite, and Art. [1942] Penguin, 1948.

    A classic. Application of Gestalt psychology to art.

————, ed. *Reflections on Art:* A Source Book of Writings by Artists, Critics, and Philosophers. Baltimore, Johns Hopkins Pr., 1958.

    Less useful for literature than for the other arts.

LEE, Vernon (*pseud.* of Violet Paget). *The Handling of Words* and Other Studies in Literary Psychology. John Lane, 1923.
> Interesting essays by a neglected author, amateur student of aesthetics. *Incl.* Kipling, Hardy, James, "Aesthetics of the Novel."

LEMON, Lee T. *The Partial Critics*. N.Y., Oxford Univ. Pr., 1965.
> On the various contemporary critical approaches, esp. as applied to poetry.

LERNER, Lawrence. *The Truest Poetry:* An Essay on the Question What Is Literature? Hamilton, 1960.
> Discussion by perceptive critic of current theories (*incl.* Richards's) with illustration from literature incl. modern. *Incl.* "The Opinions of the Novelists."

LEVI, Albert William. *Literature, Philosophy, and the Imagination*. Bloomington, Indiana Univ. Pr., 1962.
> Various types of the literary imagination.

LEWIS C[live] S[taples]. *An Experiment in Criticism*. Cambridge Univ. Pr., 1961.
> Stimulating book. Theory of criticism based on reader's reactions.

LEWIS, Wyndham. *Men Without Art*. [1934] N.Y., Russell and Russell, 1964.
> *Incl.* Eliot, James, V. Woolf ; "The Greatest Satire is Non-Moral" ; "The Materialism of the Artist" ; "Anti-Artist" ; his own theory of literature ; Appendix: "The Taxicab Driver's Test for 'Fiction'."

LISTOWELL, W[illiam] F[rancis]. *A Critical History of Modern Aesthetics*. Allen and Unwin, 1933.

LIVINGSTON, Ray. *The Traditional Theory of Literature*. [1957]. Oxford Univ. Pr., and Univ. of Minnesota Pr., 1962.

LUCAS, F. L. *Style*. [1955] N.Y., Collier Bks., 1962.
> Lectures at Cambridge Univ. Useful remarks by a distinguished stylist.

MELCHIORI, Giorgio. *The Tightrope Walkers:* Essays on Mannerism in Modern English Literature. Routledge and Kegan Paul, 1956.
> Highly provocative discussion. *Incl.* James, Hopkins, Joyce, Eliot, D. H. Lawrence, C. Fry, Green, D. Thomas.

MEYERHOFF, Hans. *Time in Literature*. Berkeley and Los Angeles, Univ. of Calif. Pr., 1960.
> Short, simple and useful introd. to concept of time in the modern world. Not primarily concerned with literature. For the seminal discussion of time in literature, see Georges Poulet, *Etudes sur le temps humain* (Paris, Plon, 1950--), of which Vol. II, *La Distance intérieure,* tr. Elliott Coleman as *Studies in Human Time* (Baltimore, Johns Hopkins Pr., 1956). Poulet's book considers French writers from Montaigne to Proust and has an appendix, supplied for the translated edition, on Am. literature, *incl.* James, Eliot. The concept of space as applied to art is the subject of *La Poétique de l'espace* (Paris, Presses universitaires de France, 1958) by Gaston Bachelard, distinguished philo-

sopher (of science). Tr. Maria Jolas as *The Poetics of Space* (N.Y., Orion Pr., 1964).

MONTAGUE, C[harles] E[dward]. *A Writer's Notes on his Trade*. Chatto and Windus, and Garden City, N.Y., Doubleday, 1930.

MOORE, T[homas] Sturge. *Armour for Aphrodite:* an Essay on Aesthetics. Cayme Pr., 1929.

———— *Art and Life*. Methuen, 1910.

MOULTON, Richard Green. *The Modern Study of Literature:* an Introduction to Literary Theory and Interpretation. Chicago, Univ. of Chicago, Pr. 1915.
   A teacher of literature tries to organize the discipline. Good introd- for serious reader.

NOTT, Kathleen. *The Emperor's Clothes*. Heinemann, 1953.
   "The New Philistinism" the author's label for attitude she finds characteristic of the "Augustinian" novelists and others, as Eliot, Hulme, whom she attacks. Contention is that even sincere religious faith when it becomes dogmatic results in insincerity.

MULLER, Herbert J[oseph]. *Science and Criticism*. Oxford Univ. Pr., and New Haven, Conn., Yale Univ. Pr., 1943.
   Gestalt psychology shown as useful to literary critics.

OGDEN, C. K. and I. A. RICHARDS. *The Meaning of Meaning:* A Study of the Influence of Language upon Thought and of the Science of Symbolism. Routledge, 1923.
   Too important to 20th c. aesthetics to omit although most students of literature will find it daunting.

PEPPER, Stephen C. *The Basis of Criticism in the Arts*. Cambridge, Mass., Harvard Univ. Pr., 1945.

PEYRE, Henri. *Writers and their Critics:* A Study of Misunderstanding. Ithaca, N.Y., Cornell Univ. Pr., 1944.
   Messenger lectures at Cornell Univ., 1943. European in scope ; esp. 19th and 20th c. Exploration of the characteristic failure of contemporary critics to recognize genius ; with a "lesson" for the future.

PHILIPSON, Morris, ed. *Aesthetics Today*. N.Y., Meridan Bks., 1961.
   Useful collection of contemporary essays.

POLLOCK, Thomas Clark. *The Nature of Literature:* Its Relation to Science, Language, and Human Experience. Princeton, N.J., Princeton Univ. Pr., 1942.

POUND, Ezra. *The ABC of Reading*. [1934] Faber and Faber, 1961. (paper).
   Aphoristic. Author calls it a "fuller and simpler" [!] explanation of method of reading in his *How to Read* (Harmsworth, 1931).

RANSOME, John Crowe. *The World's Body*. N.Y., Scribner's, 1938.
   Essays on theory of poetry and criticism by a New Critic.

———— *The New Criticism*. Norfolk, Conn., New Directions, 1941.
   Incl. Richards, Empson, Eliot, "Wanted: an Ontological Critic."

READ, Herbert. *English Prose Style*. Bell, 1928.

——————*The Meaning of Art*. [1931 ; pub. 1932 as *The Anatomy of Art*] Faber and Faber, 1962.

——————*Reason and Romanticism*. Faber and Gwyer, 1926.
 Incl. "The Attributes of Criticism" ; "Pure Poetry" ; "The Future of Poetry" ; "Psycho-analysis and Criticism" ; "The Definition of Comedy."

—————— *The Tenth Muse:* Essays in Criticism. Routledge and Kegan Paul, 1957.
 Repr. of 40 essays pub. 1946–1956. *Incl.* "The Writer and his Region" ; "The Limits of Logic" ; "The Image in Modern English Poetry" ; "The Faith of a Critic."

RICHARDS, I[vor] A[rmstrong]. *How to Read a Page:* A Course in Efficient Reading, with an Introduction to 100 Great Words. [1942] Boston, Beacon Pr., 1959.

——————*The Philosophy of Rhetoric*. [1936] Oxford Univ. Pr., 1966. (Galaxy).
 The Mary Flexner lecture, Bryn Mawr College.

——————*Practical Criticism:* A Study of Literary Judgment. [1929] N.Y., Harcourt, Brace, n.d. (Harvest).
 Criticism is concerned with total meaning: no separation of form from content is possible. Investigation of readers' responses to poems as basis for new (psychological) technique of interpretation of poetry.

——————*Principles of Literary Criticism*. [1924] Routledge and Kegan Paul, 1949.
 Influential theory of important critic.

—————— *Speculative Instruments*. Routledge and Kegan Paul, and Chicago, Univ. of Chicago Pr., 1955.
 Coll. lectures and articles on interpretation of literature. *Incl.* on literary criticism, words, teaching, "Language and Value" ; "Poetry as an Instrument of Research."

——————, C. K. OGDEN, and James WOOD. *The Foundations of Aesthetics*. N.Y., Lear Publishers, 1925. (Ill.)
 Psychological approach to problem of aesthetic judgment in all the arts.

RIGHTER, William. *Logic and Criticism*. N.Y., Chilmark Pr. 1963.
 Stimulating and systematic treatment of method and function of criticism by theorist acquainted with literature. *Incl.* Richards, D. H. Lawrence, Leavis.

SANTAYANA, George. *The Sense of Beauty,* Being the Outline of Aesthetic Theory. [1896] N.Y., Dover Publishers, 1955.

SAPIR, Edward. *Language:* An Introduction to the Study of Speech. [1921] N.Y., Harcourt, Brace, 1949.
 The nature of language and its relation to culture and art. By a linguistic theorist.

SARTRE, Jean-Paul. *Essays in Aesthetics,* sel. and tr. Wade Baskin. N.Y., Philosophical Lib., 1963.

————*What Is Literature?* Tr. Bernard Frechtman. N.Y., Philosophical Lib., 1949.

> The writer in the modern world.

SCHORER, Mark, Josephine MILES and Gordon McKENZIE, eds. *Criticism: The Foundations of Modern Literary Judgment* [1948] rev. N.Y., Harcourt, Brace, 1958.

> *Incl.* essays by James, V. Woolf, Orwell, Auden, Spender, Hulme, Eliot, Forster, Yeats, Richards.

SCOTT, Wilbur. *Five Approaches of Literary Criticism:* An Arrangement of Contemporary Critical Essays. N.Y., Collier Bks., 1962.

> Only the arrangement is by the "author." Essays illustrating the moral, psychological, formalistic, and archetypal (myth) approaches to criticism. Essays incl. Eliot, "Religion in Literature"; Caudwell, "George Bernard Shaw"; Orwell, "Kipling"; Murray, "Hamlet and Orestes"; and (as synthesis) Blackmur's "A Critic's Job of Work."

SCOTT-JAMES, R[olfe] A[rnold]. *The Making of Literature:* Some Principles of Criticism Examined in the Light of Ancient and Modern Theory. N.Y., Holt, n.d.; London, Secker, 1928.

> Historical. Four last chapters relevant, *incl.* "Expressionism"; "The Novel"; "The Critic."

SEWARD, Barbara. *The Symbolic Rose.* N.Y., Columbia Univ. Pr., 1960.

> Illuminating study of one symbol in writers *incl.* Yeats, Eliot, Joyce.

SHUMAKER, Wayne. *Elements of Critical Theory.* [1952] Berkeley and Los Angeles, Univ. Calif. Pr., 1964.

> For students of literature: "the grammar of practice" in criticism clearly explained and illustrated.

SMITH, S. Stephenson. *The Craft of Critic.* N.Y., Crowell, 1931.

> Ostensibly specific advice for book and play reviewers; actually an informal ramble through literature.

SPENDER, Stephen. *The Struggle of the Modern.* Berkeley and Los Angeles, Univ. of Calif. Pr., 1963.

> Observations on modern literature à propos of the theme.

SPRINGARN, Joel. *The New Criticism.* N.Y., Columbia Univ. Pr., 1911.

> Columbia Univ. lecture (1910) arguing for Crocean theory of criticism. Not to be confused with the mode of criticism called New which is one of the principal inventions of this c. See also Spingarn's *Creative Criticism*: Essays on the Unity of Genius and Taste (N.Y., Holt, 1931) which *incl.* rev. of this essay together with "Dramatic Criticism"; "The Theatre"; "Prose and Verse"; "Creative Criticism."

STALLMAN, Robert Wooster, ed. *The Critic's Notebook:* Minneapolis, Univ. of Minnesota Pr., 1950.

> Brief selections from poets and critics on aspects of their art, arranged by topic.

————, ed. *Critiques and Essays in Criticism, 1920–1948,* Representing the Achievement of Modern British and American Critics. N.Y., Ronald Pr., 1949.

Very wide sampling (some 30 critics, from academic, e.g. Wellek, to poets, e.g. Spender) of the classic essays on contemporary critical theory. Excellent sel. bibliog. of modern criticism. One of the best anthologies.

STAUFFER, Donald A., ed. *The Intent of the Critic*. Princeton, N.J., Princeton Univ. Pr., 1941.

Four critics present each his own view of the critic's function: Edmund Wilson, Norman Foerster, John Crowe Ransom, W. H. Auden. See also *The Intent of the Artist,* ed. Augusto Centeno (Ibid., 1941).

SYPHER, Wylie. *Loss of the Self in Modern Literature and Art*. N.Y., Random House, 1964 (Vintage).

Contrast of 19th and 20th c. ideas of the self as ill, in art and literature by a critic who has explored the historical connections of art and literature.

TILLYARD, E[ustace] M[andeville] W[etenhall] and C[live] S[taples] LEWIS. *The Personal Heresy, a Controversy*. See under Poetry.

TINDALL, William York. *The Literary Symbol*. N.Y., Columbia Univ. Pr., 1955.

General discussion of the symbol in modern poetry and novel, European and Am.

TSCHUMI, Raymond. *A Philosophy of Literature*. Linden Pr., 1961.

ULLMANN, Stephen. *Language and Style;* Collected Papers. Oxford, Blackwell, 1964

By a semanticist whose other books should also be seen.

VALÉRY, Paul. *Aesthetics*. Tr. Ralph Manheim, introd. Herbert Read. Routledge, 1964.

VIVAS, Eliseo. *The Artistic Transaction* and Essays on Theory of Literature. Columbus, Ohio State Univ. Pr., 1963.

The author's coll. of what he regards as his best recent work on theory of criticism. Modern modes of criticism appraised.

————*Creation and Discovery*: Essays in Criticism and Aesthetics. N.Y., Noonday Pr. 1955.

On problems and theories, *incl*. James, Eliot, Richards.

WARREN, Robert Penn Warren: Collection of Critical Essays. Ed. with introd. John L. Longley, Jr. N.Y., New York Univ. Pr., 1965.

WELLEK, René. *Concepts of Criticism*. New Haven and London, Yale Univ. Pr., 1963.

Essays, mostly repr., on methods of studying literary works, ill. by ref. to European and American literature.

————and Austin WARREN. *Theory of Literature*. [1949] N.Y., Harcourt, Brace, 1956 (Harvest).

Paperback slightly rev. and minus chapter "The Study of Literature in the Graduate School." Indispensable book for every serious student of literature. A controversial classic by two scholars of critical distinction and wide literary knowledge. Only attempt in Eng.

to unite literary theory, criticism and scholarship as basis for a general theory of literature (not merely English literature). Good bibliog. and notes.

WELLS, Henry [W.]. *The Judgment of Literature.* N.Y., Norton, 1928.
Outline of aesthetics.

WEST, Alick. *Crisis and Criticism.* Lawrence and Wishart, 1937.
Short, selective book with theme. Chapters on men and modes *Incl.* Eliot, Read, Richards, Joyce.

WEST, Geoffrey (pseud. of Geoffrey Harry Wells). *Ducalion* ; or, The Future of Literary Criticism. Kegan Paul, Trench, Trubner ; N.Y., Dutton, 1930.

WHEELWRIGHT, Philip. *The Burning Fountain:* A Study in the Language of Symbolism. Bloomington, Univ. of Indiana Pr., 1954.
Incl. besides theoretical discussion of myth, language, etc., chapter on Eliot.

——— *Metaphor and Reality.* Ibid., 1962.
Based on lectures at Univ. of Bristol, etc. Many ill. from modern literature.

WHITEHEAD, Alfred North. *Symbolism:* Its Meaning and Effect. [1927] N.Y., Macmillan, 1958.
Barbour-Page lectures, Univ. of Virginia. By an influential philosopher.

——— *Process and Reality:* An Essay in Cosmology. N.Y., Humanities Pr., 1955.
Gifford lectures, Univ. of Edinburgh.

WILLIAMS, Raymond. *Reading and Criticism.* Frederick Muller, 1950.

WILSON, Angus. *The Wild Garden ;* or, Speaking of Writing. Secker and Warburg, 1963.
Mostly on his own method of writing, by a novelist.

WILSON, Colin. *The Strength to Dream:* Literature and the Imagination. Gollancz, 1962.

WINTERS, Yvor. *The Anatomy of Nonsense.* Norfolk, Conn., New Directions, 1943.
An Am. critic of distinctive position on modern literature, *incl.* Eliot.

——— *In Defense of Reason.* Routledge, 1965.
Mostly repr. from his earlier books: *Primitism and Decadence, Maule's Curse, The Anatomy of Nonsense,* but some additions. *Incl.* James, Eliot.

——— *The Function of Criticism:* Problems and Exercises. Denver, Colo., Alan Swallow, 1957 ; Routledge, 1962.
Incl. "Problems for the Modern Critic of Literature" ; "The Audible Reading of Poetry" ; Hopkins (against).

WIMSATT, W[illiam] K. *Hateful Contraries.* See under Poetry.

——— *The Verbal Icon,* and Two Preliminary Essays Written in Collaboration with Monroe C. Beardsley. Univ. of Kentucky Pr., 1954.
Written 1941–1952, some as lectures or essays, now rev. W.'s own

theory and his criticism of other contemporary modes (e.g. Chicago School).

WOOLF, Virginia. *A Writer's Diary:* Being Extracts from the Diary of Virginia Woolf, ed. Leonard Woolf. N.Y., Harcourt, Brace, 1954.

Important for author's theory of art, views on books, and report of her own method of composition. For her numerous critical essays, see under Collections.

WRITERS AT WORK: The Paris Review Interviews [First Series], ed. Malcolm Cowley. N.Y., Viking, 1958.

Authors on their own work. Excellently managed interviews. *Incl.* Forster, Cary, O'Connor, A. Wilson.

——— Second Series. Introd. Van Wyck Brooks. (Interviews and notes prepared by George Plimpton.) N.Y., Viking, 1963.

Incl. Eliot, Huxley, Durrell.

ZABEL, Morton Dauwen, ed. *Literary Opinion in America.* [1937] 3rd rev. ed., N.Y., Harper and Row, 1962. (Torchbooks) 2 vols.

Important Am. critical essays on aspects of criticism and on Am. and some Eng. writers. Essays by James, Eliot, Auden, and on Joyce, Eliot, Hopkins, D. H. Lawrence, Kipling, Yeats, V. Woolf, James. Excellent bibliog. of Am. criticism: books, essays in periodicals and collections, and a note on contemporary English criticism. Probably the best such anthology.

DRAMA

Histories

AGATE, James. *A Short View of the English Stage, 1900–1926.* Jenkins, 1926.
> By a play reviewer, for whose coll. reviews see next section.

ARCHER, William. *The Old Drama and the New.* Heinemann, and Boston, Small and Maynard, 1923.
> *Incl.* H. A. Jones, Pinero, Barrie, Shaw, Granville-Barker, Galsworthy, Masefield, Synge, Yeats, Robinson.

BOYD, E[rnest] A[ugustus]. *The Contemporary Drama of Ireland.* [1917] Boston, Little, Brown, 1928.
> *Incl.* Yeats, Synge, Colum, Lady Gregory.

BYRNE, Dawson. *The Story of Ireland's National Theatre:* the Abbey Theatre. Dublin, Talbot Pr., 1929.

CLARK, Barrett H[arper]. *A Study of the Modern Drama:* A Handbook for the Study and Appreciation of the Best Plays, European, English and American, of the Last Half Century. N.Y., Appleton, 1925.
> Outgrowth of two books: *British and American Drama of Today,* and *Continental Drama of Today.* One section on Eng., selected authors: paragraph on author, critical analysis of several plays as for student exercise ; pp. of bibliog.

———— and George FREEDLEY, eds. *A History of Modern Drama.* [1925] N.Y., Appleton-Century-Crofts, 1947.
> Standard survey of modern drama by country.

CUNLIFFE, J[ohn] W[illiam]. *Modern English Playwrights:* A Short History of the English Drama from 1825. London and N.Y., Harper, 1927.
> From "The Victorian Transition," *incl.* H. A. Jones, Pinero and Shaw, to "After War," *incl.* Milne, C. K. Munro, Coward, O'Casey ; "Taste and Style."

DICKINSON, T[homas] H[erbert]. *The Contemporary Drama of England.* Boston, Little, Brown, 1931.
> Survey, incl. all authors.

DUKES, Ashley. *The Youngest Drama:* Studies of Fifty Dramatists. Benn, 1923.
> European coverage. Very brief characterizations of: Barrie, Bennett, Galsworthy, Granville-Barker, H. A. Jones, Masefield, Maugham, Pinero, Shaw, Synge, Ervine, C. K. Munro, Milne, Drinkwater, Flecker.

ELLIS-FERMOR, Una. *The Irish Dramatic Movement*. [1939] 2nd ed., Methuen, 1954.

> Very thorough though brief ; chapters on aspects of movement and on main authors ; bibliog.

GASCOIGNE, Bamber. *Twentieth Century Drama*. Hutchinson, 1962.

> On groups by decades, with section on style, and by dramatists, *incl.* Eliot, Beckett, Osborne, Wesker, Behan, Pinter.

GASSNER, John. *Masters of the Drama*. N.Y., Dover Pub., 1945.

> History from the beginnings ; *incl.* Shaw, Irish Renascence.

———— and Ralph G. ALLEN. *Theatre and Drama in the Making*. Boston, Houghton Mifflin, 1964. 1 vol.

GWYNN, Stephen. *Irish Literature and Drama in the English Language*. Nelson, 1936.

> *Incl.* James, Stephens, Joyce.

HART, Olive Ely. *The Drama in Modern Wales:* A Brief History of Welsh Playwrights from 1900 to the Present Day. Phila., Univ. of Pennsylvania Pr., 1928.

> Very brief ; *incl.* Evans, R. Hughes, E. Williams.

KITCHIN, Lawrence. *Drama in the Sixties:* Form and Interpretation. Faber and Faber, 1966.

> By type, *incl.* avant-garde, epic realism. Mostly from *Listener* and BBC Third Programme.

LUMLEY, Frederick. *Trends in Twentieth Century Drama:* A Survey Since Ibsen and Shaw. Fair Lawn, N.J., Essential Bks., 1956.

MALONE, Andrew E. *The Irish Drama*. Constable, and N.Y., Scribner's, 1929.

> *Incl.* Yeats, Lady Gregory, G. Moore, Shaw, A. E., Synge, Ervine, Colum, Robinson, O'Casey, Dunsany.

MORGAN, A[rthur] E[ustace]. *Tendencies of Modern English Drama*. Glasgow, The Univ. Pr., and N.Y., Scribner's, 1924.

> From the early Victorians through Dunsany, Flecker, Bottomley, Abercrombie, *incl.* the Irish drama, chapters on Drinkwater, Galsworthy, Granville-Barker, Masefield. Full discussion of separate plays.

NICOLL, Allardyce. *British Drama*. [1925] Harrap, 1962, 5th ed. rev.

> Chap. VII on 20th c. Standard ; good brief survey. Brief bibliog. of critical and historical studies.

REYNOLDS, Ernest Randolph. *Modern English Drama:* A Survey of the Theatre from 1900. [1949] Rev. ed., Harrap, 1950.

> Useful brief survey "dealing with conditions in the theatre and tendencies of dramatic development" ; dramatists grouped by theme, tendency, etc. Ill.

ROBINSON, Lennox. *Ireland's Abbey Theatre:* A History, 1899–1951. Sidgwick and Jackson, 1951.

> By a playwright with personal experience of the Abbey Theatre.

TAYLOR, John Russell. *Anger and After:* A Guide to the New British Drama. Methuen, 1962.

> *Incl.* Osborne, Wesker, Pinter.

———— *The Rise and Fall of the Well-Made Play.* 1966.

> From Robertson (1867) to Rattigan.

THOULESS, Priscilla. *Modern Poetic Drama.* Oxford, Blackwell, 1934.

> Detailed examination of works of: Phillips, Flecker, Binyon, Masefield, Gibson, Drinkwater, Abercrombie, Davidson, Hardy, A. Symons, Yeats, Bottomley, T. S. Moore.

TREWIN, J[ohn] C[ourtenay]. *The Birmingham Repertory Theatre,* 1913–1963. Barrie and Rockliff, 1963.

————*Drama, 1945–1950.* BC/Longmans, 1951.

> Very brief survey, *incl.* Shaw, Priestley, Bridie, Coward, Lonsdale, O'Casey, C. Fry, Eliot, Rattigan, Ustinov.

———— *The English Theatre.* Paul Elak, 1948.

> Brief history with emphasis on modern period.

———— *The Theatre Since 1900.* Andrew Dakers, 1951.

————*The Turbulent Thirties:* A Further Decade of the Theatre. MacDonald, 1960.

> Survey by year. Ill. by Raymond Manders and Joe Mitchenson.

———— *Verse Drama Since 1800.* Cambridge Univ. Pr., 1956.

> Outline.

————ed. *The Year's Work in the Theatre,* 3 vols., 1948–9, 1949–50, 1950–51. BC/Longmans, 1949–51.

VERNON, Frank. *The Twentieth-Century Theatre.* Harrap, and N.Y., Houghton Mifflin, 1924.

> A survey.

Theory and Special Studies

ABEL, Lionel. *Metatheatre:* A New View of Dramatic Form. N.Y., Hill and Wang, 1963.

> Theory of modern drama ; *incl.* Beckett, Joyce.

AGATE, James. *Alarums and Excursions.* N.Y., Doran, 1922.

> Reviews, essays and reminiscences ; *incl.* Shaw, Monkhouse, Drinkwater, Walkley, R. Hichens, Mason, Bennett.

————*The Amazing Theatre.* Harrap, 1939.

> Reviews. *Incl.* L. Housman, Priestley, Kennedy, Shaw, Wolfe, Ervine, F. L. Lucas, Bridie, Coward, Van Druten, Dunsany, Morgan, E. Williams, Synge, Levy, Eliot, Rattigan, O'Casey, Sayers.

———— *Ego 8 ;* Continuing the Autobiography of James Agate. Harrap, 1946.

> Reviews, mostly on actors' performances ; for others in this series of "Egos" see sect. Autobiographies.

————*The Contemporary Theatre, 1925*. Chapman and Hall, 1926.
> Reviews. *Incl*. Hardy, O'Casey, Robinson, Arlen, Coward, Lonsdale, Maugham, Shaw, Granville-Barker, Pinero, Galsworthy.

———— *First Nights*. Nicholson and Watson, 1934.
> Reviews.

————*At Half-Past Eight:* Essays of the Theatre. N.Y., Bernard G. Richards, 1923.
> Reviews. *Incl*. Ervine, Barrie, Galsworthy, Shaw, Drinkwater, Pinero, Bennett, Sutro, Maugham, Murray.

————*Immoment Toys:* A Survey of Light Entertainment on the London Stage, 1920–1943. Cape, 1945.
> Musicals, etc.; *incl*. Lonsdale, Coward.

————*Those Were the Nights:* A Collection of Newspaper Cuttings of Dramatic Criticisms, 1880–1906. Hutchinson, 1947.
> Reviews and reminiscences of actors and actresses.

———— *Thursdays and Fridays*. [1941] Hutchinson, 1947.
> Reviews. *Incl*. Bennett, Phillips, Chesterton, Baring, Wallace, Bax, James, Galsworthy.

BALMFORTH, Ramsden. *The Ethical and Religious Value of the Drama*. Allen and Unwin, 1925.
> *Incl*. Shaw, Galsworthy, Hardy.

———— *The Problem-Play and Its Influence on Modern Thought and Life*. Allen and Unwin, 1928.
> Relation of drama to life organized by life topics and not of first importance for drama.

BEERBOHM, Max. *Around Theatres*. [1924, 2 vols.] Repr., 1 vol., Hart-Davis, 1953
> Sel. of M. B.'s reviews as drama critic of *Sat. Rev. (SR)* for 12 years, from 1898. Important and lively. *Incl*. Vol. I. Shaw, Archer, Walkley, G. Moore, Hardy, H. A. Jones, Pinero, Barrie, Kipling, A. Symons; Vol. II: Yeats, Synge, Shaw, Barrie, Sutro, Doyle, Conrad, Granville-Barker, Masefield, L. Housman, Baring, Jerome, James, Galsworthy.

BENTLEY, Eric. *The Dramatic Event:* An American Chronicle. N.Y., Horizon Pr., 1954.
> *Incl*. O'Casey, Yeats.

———— *In Search of Theater*. N.Y., Knopf, 1953.
> *Incl*. Shaw, Yeats.

BOAS, Frederick S[amuel]. *From Richardson to Pinero;* Some Innovators and Idealists. Murray, 1936; N.Y., Columbia Univ. Pr., 1937.
> *Incl*. very full study of Pinero.

BROWN, John Mason. *Broadway in Review*. N.Y., Norton, 1940.
> Reviews, esp. Carroll, Morgan, Milne.

CARROLL, Sydney W[entworth]. *Some Dramatic Opinions*. White, 1924.
> *Incl*. Synge, Conrad, Barrie.

CHANDLER, F[rank] W[adleigh]. *Aspects of Modern Drama.* [1914] N.Y., Macmillan, 1929.
> Based on lectures at Columbia Univ. and Univ. of Cincinnati; by themes; bibliog.; chapter on Shaw.

CORDELL, Richard. *Henry Arthur Jones and the Modern Drama.* N.Y., Long and Smith, 1932.
> Three chapters on Jones; 6 on other dramatists. Perceptive criticism.

DONOGHUE, Denis. *The Third Voice:* Modern British and American Verse Drama. Princeton, N.J., Princeton Univ. Pr., 1959.
> *Incl.* esp. Auden, Eliot (6 chapters), C. Fry, Yeats.

DUKES, Ashley. *Modern Dramatists.* Palmer, 1911 and Chicago, Sergel, 1912.
> European Coverage. *Incl.* Shaw, Granville-Barker, Galsworthy.

ELIOT, T[homas] S[tearns]. *The Aims of Poetic Drama.* Galleon, 1949.
> Presidential Address to The Poets' Theatre Guild. Coll. in *Selected Essays* (Faber and Faber, 1951).

————*Poetry and Drama.* Cambridge, Mass., Harvard Univ. Pr., 1951.
> Theodore Spencer Memorial Lecture, 1950. Coll. in *On Poetry and Poets* (Faber and Faber; N.Y., Farrar, Straus, 1957).
> Principally on his own experience in writing poetic drama. See also "Rhetoric and Poetic Drama" (1919) in *Selected Essays,* 1932 and 1950.

ELLEHAUGE, Martin. *Striking Figures among Modern English Dramatists.* Copenhagen, Levin and Munksgaard, 1931.
> Critical chapter on each; *incl.* Synge, Galsworthy, Granville-Barker, Cannan, Drinkwater, Abercrombie, Masefield, Bottomley, Barrie. Bibliog.

ELLIS-FERMOR, Una. *The Frontiers of Drama,* with an introd. Allardyce Nicoll and bibliog. Harold Brooks. [1945] Methuen, 1964.

ERVINE, St. John G[reer]. *The Theatre in My Time.* Rich and Cowan, and N.Y., Loring and Mussey, 1933.
> Author's recollections of drama (1883–1933). Brief references to Archer, Barrie, Galsworthy, Granville-Barker, L. Housman, Murray, Sherriff, H. A. Jones, Pinero, Shaw, *inter alios.*

ESSLIN, Martin. *The Theatre of the Absurd.* Garden City, N.Y., Doubleday, 1961 (Anchor); London, Eyre and Spottiswoode, 1962.
> *Incl.* Beckett, Pinter.

FERGUSSON, Francis. *The Idea of Theater.* Princeton, N.J., Princeton Univ. Pr., 1949.
> A classic; thematic study of the importance of the *theater* in drama; *incl.* Shaw, Eliot.

GRANVILLE-BARKER, Harley. *On Dramatic Method.* N.Y., Hill and Wang, 1962.

———— *The Use of the Drama.* Princeton, N.J., Princeton Univ. Pr., 1945.

GREIN, Jacob T[homas]. *The New World of the Theatre:* 1923–1924. Hopkinson, 1924.

Repr. from *ILN* ; *incl.* Shaw, G. Moore, Trench, Conrad.

———— *The World of the Theatre:* Impressions and Memoirs, 1920–1921. Heinemann, 1921.

Repr. from *ILN ; incl.* Galsworthy, Shaw, Beerbohm, Mackenzie, Hutchinson, Milne.

HAMILTON, Clayton M. *Seen on Stage.* N.Y., Holt, 1920.

Incl. Shaw, Ervine, Dunsany.

HENDERSON, Archibald. *European Dramatists.* Cincinnati, Ohio, Stewart and Kuld, 1913.

Incl. Shaw, Granville-Barker.

HOWE, P[ercival] P[resland]. *Dramatic Portraits.* Martin Secker, 1913.

Repr. *Incl.* Pinero, H. A. Jones, Barrie, Shaw, Granville-Barker, Galsworthy.

JAMESON, Storm. *Modern Drama in Europe.* Collins, 1920.

Incl. Jones, Pinero, Bennett, Masefield, Phillpotts, Shaw, Granville-Barker, Drinkwater, Abercrombie, Barrie, Synge.

KITCHIN, Laurence. *Drama in the Sixties.* Faber, 1966.

Theatre of Cruelty, of the Aburd. etc. Scholarly study.

KRUTCH, Joseph Wood. *"Modernism" in Modern Drama:* A definition and an Estimate. Ithaca, N.Y., Cornell Univ. Pr., 1953.

Messenger Lectures, Cornell Univ., 1952. *Incl.* Shaw, Synge.

LEWISOHN, Ludwig. *The Drama and the Stage.* N.Y., Harcourt, Brace, 1922.

Incl. Shaw, Barrie, Archer, Maugham.

MACCARTHY, Desmond. *Drama.* Putnam, 1940.

Reviews ; *incl.* Granville-Barker, Galsworthy, Joyce, Shaw, Maugham, Coward, E. Wallace, Barrie, R. Hughes, O'Casey.

————*Theatre.* MacGibbon and Kee, 1954 ; N.Y., Oxford Univ. Pr., 1955. Reviews and broadcasts ; *incl.* Galsworthy, Granville-Barker, Maugham, Coward, Barrie, Shaw, Synge, G. Moore, de la Mare, Freeman, Blunt, Beerbohm, L. Housman, Gosse.

MONTAGUE, C. E. *Dramatic Values.* 2nd ed., Methuen, 1911.

Repr. *Incl.* Synge, Shaw, Masefield, theory of drama.

O'CASEY, Sean. *The Flying Wasp:* A Laughing Look-Over of What Has Been Said about the Things of the Theatre by the English Dramatic Critics. Macmillan, 1937.

PEACOCK, Ronald. *The Art of the Drama.* Routledge and Kegan Paul, 1957.

On theory.

————*The Poet in the Theatre.* [1946] N.Y., Hill and Wang, 1960.

Incl. Eliot, James, Shaw, Synge, Yeats, "Tragedy, Comedy and Civilization."

PHELPS, W[illiam] L[yon]. *The Twentieth-Century Theater:* Observations on the Contemporary English and American Stage. N.Y., Macmillan, 1918.

ROBINSON, Lennox, ed. *The Irish Theatre, 1939:* Lectures Delivered During the Abbey Theatre Festival, Dublin, Aug., 1938. Macmillan, 1939.
Essays on early history of the Abbey Theatre, *incl.* Synge, Lady Gregory, Yeats, the rise of the realistic movement, O'Casey, Gallic drama, problem plays.

SHAW, Bernard. *Shaw on Theatre,* ed. E. J. West. N.Y., Hill and Wang, 1958. Samples of early to latest writing on particular plays and books as well as on his own theory and technique of play writing.

STRACHEY, Lytton. *Spectatorial Essays.* [1964] N.Y., Harcourt, Brace and World, 1965.
Incl. Granville-Barker.

STRATFORD-UPON-AVON STUDIES 4. *Contemporary Theatre.* N.Y., St. Martin's Pr., 1962.
Incl. Shaw, O'Casey, Auden and Isherwood, Priestley, Eliot, Osborne, C. Fry, Beckett, Wesker, Pinter. Useful bibliog. of criticism.

SUTTON, Graham. *Some Contemporary Dramatists:* Leonard Parsons, 1924.
Incl. Granville-Barker, Dane, Drinkwater, Ervine, Maugham, Milne, Monkhouse, C. K. Munro, Flecker.

THOMPSON, A[lan] R[eynolds]. *The Anatomy of Drama.* Berkeley, Univ. of Calif. Pr., 1942.
"A proper study of plays ... becomes also a study of civilizations." Theory of drama by elements and types of plays. On modern drama: "The Dilemma of Modern Tragedy" ; "The Modern Drama" ; "Drama and Poetry." Large, rather discursive book. See also the author's *The Dry Mock:* A Study of Irony in Drama (Berkeley, Univ. of Calif. Pr., 1948).

TREWIN, J[ohn] C[ourtenay]. *Dramatists of Today.* London and N.Y., Staples Pr., 1953.
Incl. essays on: Shaw, Maugham, Masefield, O'Casey, Lonsdale, Bax, Bridie, Eliot, Priestley, Dane Ervine, Carroll, Johnston, Sherriff, Coward, E. Williams, C. Fry, Rattigan, Ustinov, MacDougall.

————*A Play Tonight.* Elek Books, 1952.
Repr. reviews, 1949–1952.

TYNAN, Kenneth. *Curtains.* N.Y., Atheneum Pr., 1961.
Penetrating criticism in reviews for *New Yorker, NS. Incl.* Shaw, Pinero, Rattigan, Priestley, Coward, Morgan, Sherriff, Eliot, O'Casey, Beckett, Herbert, Greene, Osborne, Ustinov, Behan, Dennis, D. Thomas, "The Angry Young Movement."

WALBROOK, H[enry] M[ackinnon]. *Nights at the Play.* Ham-Smith, 1911.
Repr. reviews from *The Pall Mall Gazette* ; *incl.* James, Shaw, Pinero, Sutro, Galsworthy, Barrie, Jerome, Lady Gregory, Synge, Robinson, Masefield.

———— *A Playgoer's Wanderings.* Leonard Parsons, 1926.
Incl. James, Barrie, Archer, Shaw, Pinero.

WALKLEY, A[rthur] B[ingham]. *Drama and Life.* Methuen, 1907.
Repr. from *Times,* except 2 from *Edinburgh Review ; incl.* Pinero, Barrie, Shaw, and general essays on theatre. See also Walkley's other collections of short reviews mostly from *Times: Pastiche and Prejudice:* Essays Chiefly on the Drama, 1921 ; *More Prejudice,* 1923, *incl.* Shaw, E. V. Lucas, Granville-Barker ; *Still More Prejudice,* 1925.

———— *Dramatic Criticism.* J. Murray, 1903.
Three lectures at Royal Institution, 1903. "The Ideal Spectator" ; "The Dramatic Critic" ; "Old and New Criticism."

WILLIAMS, Raymond. *Drama From Ibsen to Eliot.* Chatto and Windus, 1952.
Selected authors, *incl.* Shaw, Synge, O'Casey, Yeats, Eliot, Auden, C. Fry.

———— *Modern Tragedy:* Essays on the Idea of Tragedy in Life and in the Drama and on Modern Tragic Writing from Ibsen to Tennessee Williams, Chatto and Windus, and Stanford, California, Stanford Univ. Pr., 1966.
Incl. D. H. Lawrence, Eliot.

WEYGANDT, Cornelius. *Irish Plays and Playwrights.* Boston and N.Y., Houghton Mifflin, 1913.
Incl. Yeats, G. Moore, A. E., Lady Gregory, Synge, Colum, Robinson, Ervine.

YEATS, W[illiam] B[utler]. *The Cutting of an Agate.* N.Y., Macmillan, 1912.
Incl. Lady Gregory, Synge, "Poetry and Tradition" ; "The Tragic Theatre." These essays are also to be found in *Essays,* Vol. IV of *Collected Ed.* (N.Y., Macmillan, 1924).

———— *Discoveries.* Dun Emer Pr., 1907.
"The Play of Modern Manners" ; "Has the Drama of Contemporary Life a Root of its Own?" ; "The Subject Matter of Drama."

———— *Drama.* Macmillan, 1919.

NOVEL

Histories

NOTE. For assessments of the novel at intervals, see the excellent short studies, ill. with photographs of the authors, pub. for the British Council by Longmans, Green: Henry Reed, *The Novel since 1939* (1946, repr. 1948) ; P. H. Newby. *The Novel 1945–1950* (1951) ; Walter Allen, *The Novel Today* (1955, rev. 1960) ; Anthony Burgess, *The Novel Today* (1963).

ALLEN, Walter. *The English Novel:* A Short Critical History. [1945] N.Y., Dutton, 1958 (Everyman paper).
> By author, with details on their novels, *incl.* "The Novel from 1881–1914" ; "1914 and After." Sober, even pedestrian.

————— *The Modern Novel in Britain and the United States.* (Eng. ed. *Tradition and Dream*) N.Y., Dutton, 1964.
> The most up-to-date history. By decades through "War and Post-War." Conventional, middle-of-the-road criticism, emphasis on trends and relationships.

ALLSOP, Kenneth. *The Angry Decade:* a Survey of the Cultural Revolt of the Nineteen-Fifties. Peter Owen, and N.Y., British Book Center, 1958.
> *Incl.* Beckett, Amis, Osborne, Dennis, Braine, C. Wilson, Murdoch, A. Wilson.

BAKER, E[rnest] A[lbert]. *The History of the English Novel* (10 vols.)
> Vol. IX. *The Day Before Yesterday.* Witherby, 1938.
> *Incl.* Hardy, Gissing, "Esthetes and Eclectics," James, "The Romances."

> Vol. X. *Yesterday.* Witherby, 1939.
> *Incl.* Conrad, Kipling, Bennett, Galsworthy, Wells, D. H. Lawrence, "Some Women Novelists" ; "The Scots Group and Some Irish."
> Substantial consideration of the authors ; less on movements and relations.

BATES, H[erbert] E[rnest]. *The Modern Short Story:* A Critical Survey. [1945] Boston, The Writer Inc., 1965.

BLAZE DE BURY, Yetta. *Les Romanciers anglais contemporains.* Paris, Perrin, 1900.
> *Incl.* Moore, Hardy, Kipling.

CAZAMIAN, Madeleine L. *Le Roman et les idées en Angleterre, 1860–1914:* Les Doctrines d'action et l'aventure, 1880–1914. Paris, Les Belles lettres, 1955.

> History-of-ideas approach to novel. Thoroughly informed and documented. Extensive critical bibliog. and selected bibliog. of authors. Long sections on Conrad, Kipling, Galsworthy, Wells ; minor figures by types of novel.

CHEVALLEY, Abel. *The Modern Novel.* Tr. Ben Ray Redman. [French 1921] N.Y. Knopf, 1925.

> Many minor figures. Incl. bibliog. of French books on English novel and novelists.

CROSS, Wilbur L. *The Development of the English Novel.* [1927] N.Y., Macmillan, 1949.

> *Incl.* James, Hardy, Kipling.

EDGAR, Pelham. *The Art of the Novel from 1700 to the Present.* N.Y., Macmillan, 1933.

> By author. Major modern figures Hardy through Lawrence. Bibliog.

FORD, Ford Madox. *The English Novel from the Earliest Days to the Death of Joseph Conrad.* Philadelphia, Lippincott, 1929.

FRIERSON, William C[oleman]. *The English Novel in Transition, 1885–1940.* Norman, Univ. of Oklahoma Pr., 1942.

> By periods and movements. Many novelists mentioned ; foreign influences discussed. Better on pre-war period ; rest slighter.

GEROULD, Gordon Hall. *The Patterns of English and American Fiction:* A History. Boston, Little, Brown, 1942.

> *Incl.* moderns, Hardy to Kaye-Smith. Minor writers, e.g. E. F. Benson, Mackenzie, Walpole.

GINDIN, James. *Postwar British Fiction:* New Accents and Attitudes. Berkeley and Los Angeles, Univ. of Calif. Pr., 1962.

> Not a history and not genuinely critical. Chapters on Sillitoe, Amis, Lessing, Wain, C. Wilson, Murdoch, Golding, Snow, Durrell, even dramatists Wesker and Osborne. Some mention of Dennis, Hinde, Larkin, Tracy. Short biog. sketches. No index. By an American for Americans.

GOULD, Gerald. *The English Novel Today.* John Castle, 1924.

> By groups, *incl.* minor writers of temporary importance ; also D. H. Lawrence and Joyce (attacked).

KARL, Frederick R. *A Reader's Guide to the Contemporary English Novel.* Thames and Hudson, 1963 ; N.Y., Noonday Pr., 1962.

> Much the best book on contemporaries. Excellent criticism ; no biog. Chapters on Beckett, Durrell, Snow, Greene, Bowen, Cary, Orwell, E. Waugh, Green, Compton-Burnett, "The Angries," Powell, A. Wilson and Dennis, W. Golding, Murdoch, Rex Warner, Newby, "Composite."

KETTLE, Arnold. *An Introduction to the English Novel.* Hutchinson, 1951–1953. 2 vols.

> Vol. II James to the present, *incl.* Green, Greene, Cary, Compton-Burnett. Marxist approach.

KNIGHT, Grant C[ochran]. *The Novel in English.* N.Y., Richard Smith, 1931.

> From the beginnings to 1914, with short summation from 1914. *Incl.* Walpole, Swinnerton, Firbank, Phillpotts, Garnett, Aldington, Sherriff as well as major figures.

LOVETT, Robert Morss and Helen Sard HUGHES. *The History of the Novel in England.* Boston and N.Y., Houghton Mifflin, 1932.

> Chapter on Edwardians and one on Georgians. General and very brief treatment.

MCCULLOUGH, Bruce Walker. *Representative English Novelists:* Defoe to Conrad. N.Y. and London, Harper, 1946.

> *Incl.* H. James, Hardy, G. Moore, Galsworthy, Conrad, Bennett ; one novel each.

MARBLE, Annie R[ussell]. *A Study of the Modern Novel, British and American, since 1900.* N.Y. and London, Appleton. 1928.

> By tendency, *incl.* minor authors.

PRIESTLEY, J[ohn] B[oynton]. *The English Novel.* [1927] T. Nelson, 1940.

> Last section (25 pp.) on present, mostly major figures.

SHEPPERSON, Archibald Bolling. *The Novel in Motley,* A History of the Burlesque Novel in English. Cambridge, Mass., Harvard Univ. Pr., 1936.

> *Incl.* Barrie, Caine, Corelli, Doyle, Haggard, Hardy, James, Jerome, Kipling.

SPEARE, Morris Edmund. *The Political Novel:* Its Development in England and America. N.Y., Oxford Univ. Pr., 1924.

> More about Am. novel than about English and more about theory than about authors.

STEVENSON, Lionel. *The English Novel:* A Panorama. Boston, Houghton Mifflin, 1960.

> Very brief mention of most moderns. Last two chapters (about 30 pp.): 1895–1915 ; Since 1915.

VORWINCKEL, Ernst. *Der englische Roman der Neuesten Zeit und Gegenwart:* Stilformen und Entwicklungslinien. Berlin, Herbig, 1926.

> By tendency, incl. many minor authors.

WAGENKNECHT, F. C. *Cavalcade of the English Novel* from Elizabeth to George VI. [1943] N.Y. Holt, 1960.

> Full, well-informed, genuinely critical. Chapters on major novelists and consideration of minor ones. Extensive treatment of de la Mare.

WALPOLE, Hugh, et. al. *Tendencies of the Modern Novel,* ed. H. R. Westwood. Allen and Unwin, 1934.

> One essay for each country. English chapter by Walpole.

WARD, A[lfred] C[harles]. *Aspects of the Modern Short Story,* English and American. Univ. of London Pr., 1924 ; N.Y., MacVeagh, 1925.

> History, by author, *incl.* James, Kipling, Wells, Conrad, Quiller-Couch, de la Mare, Doyle, Freeman, Jacobs, Mansfield. 22 portraits. Bibliog.

WEYGANDT, Cornelius. *A Century of the English Novel.* N.Y., Appleton-Century, 1925.

> About half on 20th c. Survey from Scott to Conrad *incl.* L. Housman, E. F. Benson, Machen, Hewlett, Cannan, Mackenzie, Beresford, Walpole, Delafield, Onions, T. F. Powys, Swinnerton, de la Mare, as well as major figures.

WEST, Paul. *The Modern Novel.* Hutchinson, 1963.

> European, incl. English, and American. Relationships well studied, but so wide in scope as to be somewhat superficial.

Theory and Special Studies

ALDRIDGE, John W., ed. *Critiques and Essays on Modern Fiction, 1920–1951,* Representing the Achievement of Modern American and British Critics. N.Y., Ronald Pr., 1952.

> Eng. and (esp.) Am. critics, mostly well-known, on aspects of the technique of fiction and in particular on the work of Conrad, Joyce, D. H. Lawrence, Huxley. Biog. notes on the critics ; sel. bibliog. of criticism of modern fiction comp. Robert Wooster Stallman. Large and good anthology.

ALLEN, Walter Ernest. *Reading a Novel.* Phoenix House, 1949.

ALLOTT, Miriam [ed.]. *Novelists on the Novel.* Routledge and Kegan Paul, 1959 ; N.Y., Columbia Univ. Pr., 1962.

> Brief selections from novelists incl. a few 20th c. ones: Conrad, James, Hardy, V. Woolf, D. H. Lawrence, Huxley, Ford, Compton-Burnett. Longer selections, but without precise indication of sources, are brought together in *Novelists on Novelists,* ed. Louis Kronenberger (Garden City, N.Y., Doubleday, 1962).

AMES, Van Meter. *Aesthetics of the Novel.* Chicago, Univ. of Chicago Pr., 1928.

AUERBACH, Erich. *Mimesis: The Representation of Reality in Western Literature.* Tr. from the German [1946] Willard Trask. Garden City, N.Y., Doubleday, 1957. (Anchor).

> Realism in the novel. Only V. Woolf of modern Eng. writers.

BEACH, Joseph Warren. *The Twentieth Century Novel:* Studies in Technique. N.Y., Century, 1932.

> Detailed consideration of major novels, Continental, Am. and Eng. Suggestive though some over-use of labels (e.g. "beyond impressionism").

BEEBE, Maurice. *Ivory Towers and Sacred Founts:* The Artist as Hero in Fiction from Goethe to Joyce. N.Y. Univ. Pr., 1964.

> *Incl.* Conrad, H. James, Joyce. Discursive ; wide rather than precise despite subtitle.

BENNETT, Arnold. *The Author's Craft*. Hodder and Stoughton, 1914.

BENTLEY, Phyllis. *Some Observations on the Art of Narrative*. Home and Van Thal, 1946.

> Short essay by a novelist, *incl.* on V. Woolf, Richardson.

BOOTH, Wayne C. *The Rhetoric of Fiction*. Chicago and London, Univ. of Chicago Pr., 1961.

> Contrast of conventional with modern techniques of fiction, to the advantage of the former. Extensive discussion of Joyce, Conrad, James. Excellent bibliog. of books on fiction. A controversial classic.

BRAYBROOKE, Patrick. *Novelists, We Are Seven*. Phila., Lippincott, 1926.

> *Incl.* Sinclair, Walpole, R. West.

———— *Philosophies in Modern Fiction*. C. W. Daniel, 1929.

> Very brief analysis of attitudes of a number of writers, *incl.* Barrie, Belloc, Bennett, Chesterton, Hardy, Kipling, Sinclair, Walpole, Wells, R. West.

———— *Some Catholic Novelists: Their Art and Outlook*. Burns, Oates, and Washbourne, 1931.

> Chesterton, Belloc, Gibbs, Kaye-Smith, Katharine Tynan.

————*Some Goddesses of the Pen*. C. W. Daniel, 1927.

> *Incl.* Kaye-Smith, Macaulay.

BREWSTER, Dorothy and Angus BURRELL. *Modern Fiction*. N.Y., Columbia Univ. Pr., 1934.

> Based on Columbia Univ. Courses in modern fiction. Some essays from following item, though rev. Chapters on single authors or books. *Incl.* Gissing, Conrad, Maugham, Bennett, Sinclair, D. H. Lawrence, Joyce, V. Woolf, Huxley, Mansfield, Coppard.

———— *Dead Reckonings in Fiction,* London and N.Y., Longmans, Green, 1924.

> *Incl.* Conrad, James, Mansfield, Sinclair, D. H. Lawrence.

BROWN, Edward Killoran. *Rhythm in the Novel*. Toronto Univ. Pr., 1950.

> Lectures. Stimulating technical study, *incl.* of Forster's *Passage to India*.

BULLETT, Gerald W. *Modern English Fiction:* A Personal View. H. Jenkins, 1926.

> "The Background," Wells, Bennett, Galsworthy, Conrad, Forster, "Eccentricities" ; "The Short Story" ; "Summary of Omissions."

BURGUM, Edwin Berry. *The Novel and the World's Dilemma*. [1947] Russell and Russell, 1963.

> Social consciousness approach, *incl.* Joyce, V. Woolf, Huxley.

CANBY, Henry S[eidel]. *Definitions:* Essays in Contemporary Criticism. N.Y., Harcourt, Brace, 1922.

Largely repr. *Incl*. Conrad, Hardy, James, Butler, "On Fiction" ; "The New Generation."

CARRUTHERS, John (pseud. of John Young Thompson Greig) *Scheherazade,* or The Future of the Novel. Kegan Paul, Trench, Trubner, 1927.
Brief essay on forces molding the novel of the future.

CARY, Joyce. *Art and Reality*. Ways of the Creative Process. N.Y., Harper ; Cambridge Univ. Pr., 1958.
Clarke lectures, Trinity College, Cambridge, 1956. A novelist on his own craft.

CHATTOPADHYAYA, Sisir. *The Technique of the Modern English Novel*. Calcutta, Mukhapadhyay, 1959.
Attempt "to take up the novel where critics like Percy Lubbock, E. M. Forster and Edwin Muir left it." Emphasis on new methods of characterization, annihilation of story-telling, and, esp., on language. *Incl*. James, Richardson, Joyce, V. Woolf, Conrad. (Univ. of London thesis.)

CHURCH, Margaret. *Time and Reality:* Studies in Contemporary Fiction. Chapel Hill, Univ. of North Carolina Pr., 1963.
One section on Eng. novel: Joyce, V. Woolf, Huxley. Rather obvious where sound, and not penetrating.

COLLINS, Norman. *The Facts of Fiction*. Gollancz, 1932 ; N.Y., Dutton, 1933.
Biographical *incl*. Hardy, James, G. Moore, D. H. Lawrence.

COMFORT, Alex. *The Novel and Our Time*. Phoenix House, and Denver, Colo., Alan Swallow, 1948.
Short essay on theory and technique.

COOK, Albert. *The Meaning of Fiction*. Detroit, Mich., Wayne State Univ. Pr., 1960.
From the beginning, *incl*. James, D. H. Lawrence, Conrad. Encumbered with terminology.

COOPER, Frederic T. *Some English Story Tellers:* A Book of the Younger Novelists. N.Y., Holt, 1912.
By author. *Incl*. Conrad, de Morgan, Hewlett, Phillpotts, Kipling, Galsworthy, Bennett, Hope, Sinclair, Hichens.

CROSS, Wilbur L. *Four Contemporary Novelists*. N.Y., Macmillan, 1930.
Conrad, Bennett, Galsworthy, Wells.

DAICHES, David. *The Novel and the Modern World*. [1939] Univ. of Chicago Pr., 1960.
Rather routine discussion. *Incl*. Galsworthy, Mansfield, esp. Conrad, Joyce, V. Woolf, Huxley.

DREW, Elizabeth. *The Modern Novel* ; Some Aspects of Contemporary Fiction. N.Y., Harcourt, Brace, 1926.
For the general reader. Many novelists but esp. Galsworthy, Wells, Bennett, Conrad.

———— *The Novel* ; A Modern Guide to Fifteen English Masterpieces. N.Y., Dell, 1963.

Introductory. *Incl*. Hardy, Conrad, D. H. Lawrence, James.

DUHAMEL, Georges. *Essai sur le roman*. Paris, Lesage, 1925.
On technique, by a novelist.

DUJARDIN, Édouard. *Le Monologue intérieur:* son apparition, ses origines dans l'oeuvre de James Joyce. Paris, Messein, 1931.
By the novelist who first used interior monologue.

DYSON, A. E. *The Crazy Fabric:* Essays in Irony. N.Y., St. Martin's Pr., 1965.
Incl. Orwell, E. Waugh.

EDEL, Leon. *The Modern Psychological Novel, 1900–1950*. [1955] rev. enlgd. Grossett and Dunlap, 1965. (Universal Lib.).
General discussion of many novelists.

FOLLETT, Helen T. and Wilson. *Some Modern Novelists:* Appreciations and Estimates. N.Y., Holt, 1918.
Incl. Gissing, James, Hardy, de Morgan, Phillpotts, Bennett, Wells, Galsworthy, Conrad, "The Younger Generation."

FOLLETT, Wilson. *The Modern Novel ;* A Study of the Purpose and the Meaning of Fiction. Rev. ed. N.Y., Knopf, 1923.
Principles of criticism of fiction. By types of novel, as satire, romance.

FORSTER, E. M. *Aspects of the Novel*. [1927] N.Y., Harcourt, Brace, 1954.
Clark lectures, Trinity College, Cambridge Univ. Urbane and stimulating remarks on novels from the author's characteristic point of view. A classic.

FOX, Ralph Winston. *The Novel and the People from a Communist Viewpoint*. [1937] sec. ed. Cobbett Pr., 1948.
Little on Eng. novel.

FRIEDMAN, Melvin. *Stream of Consciousness:* A Study in Literary Method. New Haven, Conn., Yale Univ. Pr. ; London, Oxford Univ. Pr., 1955.
Esp. Richardson, V. Woolf, Joyce.

GARDINER, Harold C[harles], S. J. *Norms for the Novel*. [1953] N.Y., Doubleday, 1960.
Religious approach to novel in general.

GEORGE, W[alter] L[ionel]. *A Novelist on Novels*. Collins, 1918.
Incl. D. H. Lawrence, Kaye-Smith, and other contemporaries in general essays taking a dim view of the present state of the novel.

GOODMAN, Paul. *The Structure of Literature*. Chicago, Univ. of Chicago Pr., 1954.
Esp. on various uses of plot as unifying device in novel and drama.

GORDON, Caroline. *How to Read a Novel*. [1953] N.Y., Viking, 1964.
Informal essay, with special attention to James.

GRABO, Carl. *The Art of the Short Story*. N.Y., Scribner's, 1913.

————*The Technique of the Novel.* N.Y., Scribner's, 1928.
Elements of the novel examined in many contemporaries.

GREEN, Thomas Hill. *An Estimate of the Value and Influence of Works of Fiction in Modern Times,* ed. Fred Newton Scott. Ann Arbor, Mich., George Wahr, 1911.
Theoretical essay ; novel compared with other forms.

GREENBLATT, Stephen Jay. *Three Modern Satirists:* Evelyn Waugh, Orwell and Huxley. New Haven, Conn., Yale Univ. Pr., 1965.

GREGOR, Ian and Brian NICHOLAS. *The Moral and the Story.* Faber, 1962.
Not especially provocative examination of one novel each of several novelists, French and Eng., *incl.* G. Moore, Hardy, James, Greene.

HALL, James. *The Tragic Comedians:* Seven Modern British Novelists. Indianapolis, Univ. of Indiana Pr., 1963.
Huxley, Forster, E. Waugh, Cary, Hartley, Green, Powell. Seven chosen as best each of his kind. Two, three or four novels of each discussed ; theme in each chapter. Interesting.

HARDY, Barbara. *The Appropriate Form ;* An Essay on the Novel. Athlone Pr., Univ. of London, 1964.
Stimulating and original technical criticism. *Incl.* James, Forster, Hardy, D. H. Lawrence.

HARVEY, W. J. *Character and the Novel.* Ithaca, N.Y., Cornell Univ. Pr., 1966.
Argues own theory ; for an "open" novel: "loose, baggy monsters."

HENDERSON, Philip. *The Novel Today:* Studies in Contemporary Attitudes. John Lane, 1936.
Incl. D. H. Lawrence, Joyce, V. Woolf, Forster, W. Lewis, Galsworthy, Wells, Huxley, Jameson.

HOARE, Dorothy. *Some Studies in the Modern Novel.* Chatto and Windus, 1938.
Original. James, V. Woolf, Forster, D. H. Lawrence, Hardy, Conrad, G. Moore and Joyce, Mansfield.

HOWE, Irving. *Politics and the Novel.* N.Y., Horizon Pr., 1957.
Incl. Conrad, James, Orwell.

HUMPHREY, Robert. *Stream of Consciousness in the Modern Novel.* [1954] Berkeley and Los Angeles, Univ. of California Pr., 1962.
Valuable discussion, esp. of V. Woolf, Joyce, Richardson.

JAMES, Henry. *The Art of the Novel,* with introd. Richard P. Blackmur. [1934] N.Y., Scribner's, 1950.
James's prefaces to his own novels written for the New York ed. See also *Henry James and H. G. Wells: A Record of Their Friendship, Their Debate on the Art of Fiction and Their Quarrel* [based on their correspondence], eds. Leon Edel and Gordon Ray (Urbana, Univ. of Illinois Pr., 1958).

―――――*The Art of Fiction and Other Essays,* ed. Morris Roberts. Oxford
Univ. Pr., 1948.
　　Incl. "The Art of Fiction" ; "The New Novel" ; "Criticism."

JOHNSON, R[eginald] B[rimley]. *Some Contemporary Novelists (Men),*
Leonard Parsons, 1922.
　　Incl. Cannan, Walpole, Beresford, D. H. Lawrence, Mackenzie, For-
　　ster, Buchan, Swinnerton. Mainly biog.

―――――*Some Contemporary Novelists (Women),* Leonard Parsons, 1920.
　　Incl. Sinclair, Macaulay, Kaye-Smith, Sidgwick, V. Meynell, Richard-
　　son, V. Woolf, Stella Benson, Delafield, Dane.

KARL, Frederick and Marvin MAGALANER. *A Reader's Guide to Great
Twentieth Century English Novels,* N.Y., Noonday Pr., 1959.
　　Analysis of novels by Conrad, D. H. Lawrence, Joyce, Forster, V.
　　Woolf, Huxley.

KENNEDY, Margaret. *The Outlaws on Parnassus.* [1958] N.Y., Viking
Pr., 1960.
　　Spirited defence of story-telling with diversified examples from Eng.
　　novel.

KIELY, Benedict. *Modern Irish Fiction.* A Critique. Dublin, Golden Eagle
Bks., 1950.
　　Numerous writers considered under topical headings ; *incl.* Bowen,
　　Greene, Isherwood, Joyce, G. Moore, O'Connor, O'Faoláin,
　　O'Flaherty, A. E. Reid, Stephens, Synge, Stuart, Yeats.

KUMAR, Shiv K. *Bergson and the Stream of Consciousness Novel.* N.Y.
Univ. Pr., 1963.
　　Incl. Richardson, V. Woolf, Joyce. K. argues persuasively for influ-
　　ence of Bergson rather than Jung on development of this technique.

LATHROP, Henry Burrowes. *The Art of the Novelist.* N.Y., Dodd, Mead,
1919 ; Harrap, 1920.
　　Technique for the general reader. Some modern novels referred to.

LAWRENCE, Margaret. *The School of Femininity.* N.Y., Stokes, 1936 (Eng.
ed. *We Write as Women*).
　　Incl. D. Du Maurier, G. B. Stern, R. Macaulay, Jameson, Bentley, P.
　　Bottome, Kaye-Smith, Sinclair, M. Kennedy, E. M. Delafield, "Eliza-
　　beth," V. Sackville-West, Radclyffe Hall, M. Webb, Mansfield, Dane,
　　V. Woolf.

LEAVIS, F. R. *The Great Tradition:* A Study of the English Novel. [1948]
Garden City, N.Y., Doubleday, 1954 (Anchor).
　　Incl. James, Conrad.

LEAVIS, Q[ueenie] D. *Fiction and the Reading Public.* [1932] Chatto
and Windus, 1965 ; N.Y., Russell and Russell, 1966.
　　Traces quantitative increase and qualitative decline in fiction-reading
　　public, esp. 19th c. A classic.

LEGGETT, H. W. *The Idea in Fiction.* Allen and Unwin, 1934.

Elements of the novel discussed with regard to Bennett, Galsworthy, Huxley, Maugham etc.

LESSER, Simon O. *Fiction and the Unconscious.* [1957] N.Y., Vintage, 1962.
Preface by Ernest Jones indicates approach of this study: psycho-analytical. Some essays repr. from *PR, MFS* etc.

LEVER, Katherine. *The Novel and the Reader:* a Primer for Critics. N.Y., Crofts, 1961.

LEWIS, R[ichard] W. B. *The Picaresque Saint:* Representative Figures in Contemporary Fiction. [1956] Phila., Lippincott, 1958.
Greene and Continental authors.

LIDDELL, Robert. *Some Principles of Fiction.* Cape, 1953 ; Indianapolis, Univ. of Indiana Pr., 1954.
Discursive rather than systematic, by perceptive critic. Very full reference to modern fiction.

———— *A Treatise on the Novel.* [1947] Cape, 1953.
On technique, contrasts of modern with earlier novel. Much quotation from novelists on their craft.

LODGE, David. *Language of Fiction:* Essays in Criticism and Verbal Analysis of the English Novel. Routledge and Kegan Paul, and N.Y., Columbia Univ. Pr., 1966.
Pioneering application to novel of method of verbal analysis usual in criticism of poetry. Besides theoretical sections, specific treatment of Hardy, James, Wells, Amis.

LUBBOCK, Percy. *The Craft of Fiction.* [1921] N.Y., Viking, 1957.
Discursive and wide-ranging treatment of technique with special, and admiring, reference to James. A classic.

McCARTHY, Mary. *On the Contrary.* N.Y., Farrar, Straus, and Cudahy, 1961.
Repr. "The Fact in Fiction" ; "Characters in Fiction."

MCCORMICK, John. *Catastrophe and Imagination:* An Interpretation of the Contemporary English and American Novel. N.Y. and London, Longmans, 1957.
Applies critical doctrines of Blackmur and Eliot. Inc. living authors and compares Eng. and Am. novels. By tendencies and techniques.

MANSFIELD, Katherine. *Novels and Novelists,* ed. J. Middleton Murry. Boston, Beacon Pr., 1930.
Ath. reviews, 1919–1920. Very brief, mostly multiple, *incl.* many very minor works as well as D. Richardson, V. Sackville-West, H. M. Tomlinson, May Sinclair, Walpole etc.

MENDILOW, Adam Abraham. *Time and the Novel.* Peter Nevill, 1952.
Time as related to technique of the novel not exclusively modern. For other treatments of time in literature see under Criticism: Meyerhoff, Poulet.

MILLER, James E., Jr. *Myth and Method:* Modern Theories of Fiction. Lincoln, Univ. of Nebraska Pr., 1960 (Bison Bks.).

> Misleading title for small coll. of standard, often-repr. essays on aspects of fiction, *incl.* James, "The Art of Fiction"; Conrad, "Preface" to *The Nigger of the Narcissus*; Bowen, "Notes on Writing a Novel"; Forster, "Pattern and Rhythm."

MIZENER, Arthur. *The Sense of Life in the Modern Novel.* Boston, Houghton Mifflin, 1964.

> Mostly repr. reviews and mostly on Am. lit. *Incl.* Hardy, Powell.

MONROE, N. Elizabeth. *The Novel and Society: A Critical Study of the Modern Novel.* Chapel Hill, Univ. of North Carolina Pr., 1941.

> Author finds novel in state of decay. Chapters on 6 "non-decadent" women novelists *incl.* only V. Woolf of English.

MOSKOWITZ, Sam, *Explorers of the Infinite:* Shapers of Science Fiction. N.Y., World, 1963.

> Repr. articles 1957–1963. *Incl.* Doyle, Wells.

MUELLER, William R. *The Prophetic Voice in Modern Fiction.* [1959] Garden City, N.Y., Doubleday, 1966. (Anchor).

> Relation to Bible of certain modern novels. *Incl.* Joyce, Greene.

MUIR, Edwin. *The Structure of the Novel.* [1929] N.Y., Harcourt, Brace, 1938.

> Series: Hogarth Lectures on Literature. Short, theoretical, valuable.

MULLER, Herbert. *Modern Fiction:* A Study of Values. N.Y. and London, Funk and Wagnalls, 1937.

> General chapters and chapters on authors: Hardy, G. Moore and Gissing, Bennett, Galsworthy, Maugham, Conrad, D. H. Lawrence, Joyce, "V. Woolf and Feminine Fiction"; Huxley. Gestalt psychological approach.

MYERS, Walter L. *The Later Realism:* A Study of Characterization in the British Novel. Chicago, Univ. of Chicago Pr., 1927.

> Modern authors used as illust. of realism newly defined.

O'CONNOR, Frank. *The Lonely Voice:* A Study of the Short Story. Cleveland, World, 1963.

> *Incl.* Kipling, Joyce, Mansfield, D. H. Lawrence, Coppard, "The Irish Writers." Critical discussion, forthright and personal, by an author famous for his own stories.

——*The Mirror in the Roadway:* A Study of the Modern Novel. N.Y., Knopf, 1956.

> *Incl.* James, Hardy, D. H. Lawrence, Joyce. See comment above.

O'CONNOR, William Van, ed. *Forms of Modern Fiction.* Oxford Univ. Pr., and Minneapolis, Univ. of Minnesota Pr., 1948. (Essays Coll. in Honor of Joseph Warren Beach).

> *Incl.* O'Connor, "The Novel in Our Time"; Tate, "Techniques of Fiction"; Mark Schorer, "Technique as Discovery"; Trilling, "Manners, Morals and the Novel"; and on Joyce, D. H. Lawrence, Forster, Huxley, Conrad, V. Woolf, Greene. Excellent anthology.

O'FAOLAIN, Sean. *The Short Story*. Collins, 1948 ; N.Y., Devin Adair, 1951.
    Stories, comment esp. on Continental writers but one relevant section:
    "The Technical Struggle."

————— *The Vanishing Hero:* Studies of the Hero in the Modern Novel.
N.Y., Grosset and Dunlap ; London, Eyre and Spottiswoode, 1956. (Subtitle of Eng. ed.: Novelists of the Twenties).
    Based on Christian Gauss Lectures, Princeton Univ., 1953. Stimulat-
    ing criticism, *incl.* Huxley, E. Waugh, Greene, Bowen, V. Woolf, Joyce.

ORTEGA Y GASSET, José. *The Dehumanization of Art and Notes on
the Novel,* Tr. Helen Weyl. [Spanish 1925. Am. 1948] Garden City, N.Y.,
Doubleday, 1956. (Anchor).
    Provocative remarks on modern vs. earlier art, esp. novel.

OVERTON, Grant. The Philosophy of Fiction. N.Y. Appleton, 1928.

PRITCHETT, V[ictor] S[awdon]. *The Living Novel*. Chattto and Windus,
1946 ; N.Y., Reynal and Hitchcock, 1947.
    Reviews of this excellent critic repr. from *NS. Incl.* Gosse, Wells,
    Bennett, D. H. Lawrence, Conrad. Expanded as *The Living Novel and
    Later Appreciations* (N.Y., Random House, 1964): *incl.* 27 new essays
    from *NS* among which Butler, Gissing, Kipling, Saki, Jerome, For-
    ster, Galsworthy, Durrell, W. Golding.

————— *The Working Novelist*. Chatto and Windus, 1965.
    Repr. *Incl.* Ford, Galsworthy, Beckett, Durrell, Kipling, Forster,
    W. Golding, Gissing, Jerome, Saki, T. E. Lawrence, Powell, Conrad.

RAJAN, B., ed. *The Novelist as Thinker (Focus Four)*. Dennis Dobson,
1947.
    Incl. Huxley, E. Waugh, Isherwood, L. H. Myers.

ROLPH, G. H., ed. *The Trial of Lady Chatterley:* Regina v. Penguin Books
Ltd. Penguin Bks., 1961.
    Complete testimony of famous authors at famous trial.

ROMBERG, Bertil. *Studies in the Narrative Technique of the First Person
Novel*. Stockholm, Almqviist, 1962.
    More statistical than critical.

SAVAGE, D. S. *The Withered Branch*. Eyre and Spottiswoode, 1950.
    Tendentious criticism of a Leavisite. *Incl.* attacks on Huxley, Joyce,
    V. Woolf.

SCHOLES, Robert and Robert KELLOG. *The Nature of Narrative*. N.Y.,
Oxford Univ. Pr., 1966.
    "New" view of narrative in the new novel, *incl.* Joyce, D. H. Lawrence.

SCHORER, Mark, ed. *Modern British Fiction:* Essays in Criticism. N.Y.,
Oxford Univ. Pr. ; 1961 (Galaxy 1962).
    Incl. useful essays on Hardy, Conrad, Ford, Forster, D. H. Lawrence,
    Joyce, V. Woolf.

SHAPIRO, Charles, ed. *Contemporary British Novelists*. Carbondale, Univ.
of Southern Ill. Pr., 1965.
    Crosscurrents series. Stimulating and sensible appraisals of ten: Amis,

Durrell, W. Golding, Murdoch, Lessing, Powell, Sillitoe, Snow, Spark, A. Wilson.

SIMON, Irène. *Formes du roman anglais de Dickens à Joyce.* Bibliothèque de la Faculté de philosophie et lettres de l'Université de Liège (Fascicule CXVIII), 1949.

Incl. James, Joyce, V. Woolf.

THIBAUDET, Albert. *Le Liseur de romans.* Paris, Crès, 1925.

On various kinds of novels, by a great French critic.

TILLOTSON, Kathleen. *The Tale and the Teller.* Rupert Hart-Davis, 1959.

Inaugural lecture Bedford College, Univ. of London.

Incl. James, de Morgan.

TILLYARD, E[ustace] M. W. *The Epic Strain in the English Novel.* Chatto and Windus, 1958.

Eng. academic critic finds epic characteristics in Bennett's *Old Wives' Tale,* Joyce's *Ulysses,* and Conrad's *Nostromo.*

VAN GHENT, Dorothy. *The English Novel,* Form and Function. N.Y., Rinehart, 1953.

For the general reader and student, an accompaniment to the reading of 18 novels, *incl.* Hardy, *Tess* ; James, *The Portrait of a Lady ;* Conrad, *Lord Jim ;* Joyce, *A Portrait of the Artist as a Young Man ;* Lawrence, *Sons and Lovers.* Elementary in tone but eccentric in point of view, a disconcerting combination.

VERSCHOYLE, Derek, ed. *The English Novelists:* A Survey of the Novel by Twenty Contemporary Novelists. Chatto and Windus, 1936.

Essays of generally high quality on Butler, James, Hardy and Conrad, D. H. Lawrence and Huxley, Forster and V. Woolf, Joyce.

WALPOLE, Hugh, et. al. *Tendencies of the Modern Novel.* Peter Smith, 1934.

WARD, A[lfred] C[harles]. *Aspects of the Modern Short Story.* N.Y., MacVeagh, 1925.

Examination of one story by each of following: James, Kipling, Wells, Conrad, Quiller-Couch, de la Mare, Doyle, Jacobs, Masefield.

WESCOTT, Glenway. *Images of Truth:* Fiction Writing in a Time of Troubles. [1939] N.Y., Harper, 1960. (Colophon).

Incl. Maugham.

WHARTON, Edith. *The Writing of Fiction.* N.Y., Scribner's, 1925.

WOOLF, Virginia. *Mr. Bennett and Mrs. Brown.* Hogarth Pr., 1928.

Read to The Heretics, Cambridge, May 18, 1924, repr. in *Granite and Rainbow* (Hogarth Pr., 1958).

See also "Modern Fiction" [written 1919] in the *Common Reader* (First Series) under Collections. These two essays constitute a manifesto of the experimental novel in the twenties.

ZABEL, Morton Dawen. *Craft and Character in Modern Fiction.* N.Y., Viking, 1957.

Repr. Useful essays on various authors, *incl.* Hardy, Butler, James, Conrad, Forster, Ford, Greene, Maugham.

POETRY

Encyclopedias

THE CONCISE ENCYCLOPEDIA OF ENGLISH AND AMERICAN POETS AND POETRY, ed. Stephen Spender and Donald Hall. Hutchinson 1963. (New Horizon Bks).

> From the beginning to the present. Alphabetical by poets; *incl.* short account of life and work, pictures of poets; also definition of terms, etc.

ENCYCLOPEDIA OF POETRY AND POETICS, ed. Alex Preminger with Frank J. Warnke and O. B. Hardison. Princeton, N.J., Princeton Univ. Pr., 1965.

> History of world poetry from the beginning, *incl.* movements, prosody, critical terminology; no biography or criticism of individual poets. 1000 entries, 20 to 20,000 words each. Useful.

Histories

> NOTE. For periodic assessments of the state of poetry see the excellent short studies, mostly ill. with photographs of poets, published by Longmans, Green for the British Council: Stephen Spender, *Poetry Since 1939* (1946, repr. 1948); Geoffrey Moore, *Poetry To-Day* (1958); R. N. Currey, *Poets of the 1939–1945 War* (1960); Elizabeth Jennings, *Poetry To-Day* (*1957–60*) 1961.

BLACKBURN, Thomas. *The Price of an Eye.* Longmans, 1961.

> History and criticism of 20th c. English poetry: major figures.

BUSH, Douglas. *English Poetry,* The Main Currents from Chaucer to the Present. N.Y., Oxford Univ. Pr., 1952.

> Modern period pp. 193–217. Panorama.

COFFMAN, Stanley K., Jr. *Imagism.* A Chapter in the History of Modern Poetry. Norman, Univ. of Oklahoma Pr., 1951.

COHEN, J[ohn] M[ichael]. *Poetry of this Age,* 1908–1958. Arrow Bks. and Hutchinson, 1960.

> All European poetry, grouped by tendency. English authors *incl.* Yeats, Muir, Owen, Graves, Eliot, D. Thomas, Auden, E. Sitwell, Larkin, R. S. Thomas.

COLLINS, H. P. *Modern Poetry*. Cape, 1925.

> A survey, *incl.* chapters on Owen, A. E. Housman.

DEUTSCH, Babette. *Poetry in Our Time:* A Critical Survey of Poetry in The English-Speaking World, 1900 to 1960. 2nd ed., rev. enlgd., Garden City, N.Y., Doubleday, 1963. (Anchor).

> Perceptive appraisal by a poet ; poets grouped in interesting ways. Critical analysis with some textual commentary.

———— *This Modern Poetry*. N.Y., Norton, 1935.

> By movements ; a preparation, perhaps, for the preceding item.

DURRELL, Lawrence. *A Key to Modern British Poetry*. Peter Nevill (as *Key to Modern Poetry*) ; Norman, Univ. of Oklahoma Pr., 1952.

> Lectures for British Council to graduate English teachers in Argentina, 1948. Apologia for complexities of modern poetry and introd. to certain poets and movements.

ELTON, Oliver. *The English Muse, A Sketch*. Bell, 1933.

> Historical introd. to poetry which the author, an historian of English literature, declines to call *history* ; emphasis on poetry for its own sake. Last 2 chapters on "Later Poetry Meredith to Monro."

GRIERSON, Herbert J. C. and J[ames] C. SMITH. *A Critical History of English Poetry*. [1944] Rev. ed. 1947 ; Chatto and Windus, 1962.

> Three short chapters on 20th c. poetry ; selected bibliog. of books on poetry.

HUGHES, Glenn. *Imagism and the Imagists*. [1931] Bowes and Bowes, 1960.

> Good history of the movement. See also the excellent introd. by William Pratt to *The Imaginist Poem*, ed. Pratt (N.Y., Dutton, 1963, paper).

JOHNSTON, John Hubert. *English Poetry of the First World War:* A Study in the Evolution of Lyric and Narrative Form, Princeton, N. J., Princeton Univ. Pr., 1964.

> By poets *incl.* R. Brooke, R. Nichols, Sorley, Sassoon, Blunden, Owen, Rosenberg, Read, D. Jones. Bibliog.

MÉGROZ, Rodolphe Louis. *Modern English Poetry, 1882–1932*. Nicholson and Watson, 1933.

> Survey by movements and tendencies.

MORTON, David *The Renaissance of Irish Poetry, 1880–1930*. N.Y., Washburn, 1929.

> Introd. for Am. reader. Lyric poetry shown as an outgrowth of older poetry. More loving than informing ; much quotation.

OMOND, T. S. *English Metrists:* Being a Sketch of English Prosodical Criticism from Elizabethan Times to the Present Day. Oxford, Clarendon Pr., 1921.

> Standard book, though 1900–1920 treated in "Postscript" only: *incl.* Saintsbury.

PINTO, Vivian de Sola. *Crisis in English Poetry, 1880–1940*. [1951] N.Y., Harper, 1966. (Torchbks).

Very brief, selective history for students. Originally for Hutchinson's Univ. Lib. Series.

RIDING, Laura and Robert GRAVES. *A Survey of Modernist Poetry.* Heinemann, 1927.

ROSS, Robert H. *The Georgian Revolt, 1910–1922:* Rise and Fall of a Poetic Ideal. Carbondale, Southern Illinois Univ. Pr., 1965.

    The poets, their work, and reception of the 6 vols. of *Georgian Poetry.*

SAINTSBURY, George. *Historical Manual of English Prosody.* [1910] Macmillan, 1930.

    Pioneering work, still standard, though only Bridges of moderns included.

SCARFE, Francis. *Auden and After:* The Liberation of Poetry, 1930–1941. [1942] Routledge, 1945.

    Arranged by poets, most of them young at the time, as was the author, also a poet.

Theory and Special Studies

ABRAMS, Meyer H., ed. *Literature and Belief.* N.Y., Columbia Univ. Pr., 1958. English Institute Essays.

    Essays on theory of poetry by Abrams, Bush, Cleanth Brooks, Walter Ong, Nathan A. Scott, Jr., and Louis L. Martz.

ALVAREZ, A[lfred]. *The Shaping Spirit:* Studies in Modern English and American Poets. (Am. ed., *Stewards of Excellence*) Chatto and Windus; N.Y., Scribner's, 1958.

    Incl. Eliot, Yeats, Empson, Auden, D. H. Lawrence; "Art and Isolation." By a perceptive poet, sympathetic to the new poetry.

ARCHER, William. *Poets of the Younger Generation.* Lane, 1902.

    Incl. Binyon, Quiller-Couch, Davidson, A. E. Housman, A. E., D. H. Lawrence, Kipling, A. Meynell, Newbolt, Phillips, A. Symons, Trench, Watson, Yeats. Useful for the reputation of these poets as the century began.

BARFIELD, Owen. *Poetic Diction:* A Study in Meaning. Faber and Gwyer, 1928.

BARTLETT, Phyllis. *Poems in Process.* N.Y., Oxford Univ. Pr., 1951.

    Valuable study of the making of poems, based on study of mss. *Incl.* Yeats, A. E., Auden, Bridges, Eliot, Hopkins, A. E. Housman, D. H. Lawrence, Spender, Sassoon, E. Sitwell.

BATESON, F[rederick] W[ilse]. *English Poetry:* A Critical Introduction. London and N.Y., Longmans, Green, 1950.

    Last two chapters on two poems by L. Johnson and Auden; also "Toward a Poetry-Reading Elite."

BEATTY, Jerome and William H. MATCHETT. *Poetry:* From Statement to Meaning. N.Y., Oxford Univ. Pr., 1965.

> Introd. to reading poetry, for the beginner.

BERRY, Francis. *Poetry and the Physical Voice.* Routledge and Kegan Paul, 1962.

> Interesting theory, illus. by reference to modern poets, *incl.* Hopkins, Yeats, Eliot, Auden ; bibliog.

———— *Poets' Grammar:* Person, Time, and Mood in Poetry. Routledge and Kegan Paul, 1958.

> Analysis of grammar to illuminate texts, by experimental critic. Bibliog. footnotes.

BLACKMUR, R[ichard] P. *Form and Value in Modern Poetry.* Garden City, N.Y., Doubleday, 1957. (Anchor).

> Critical essays, repr. from *Language as Gesture* (1952), by an important New Critic. *Incl.* Hardy, Yeats, Eliot, H. Read, D. H. Lawrence, "A Critic's Job of Work" ; "Lord Tennyson's Scissors: 1912-1950."

BODKIN, Maud. *Archetypal Patterns in Poetry:* Psychological Studies of Imagination. [1934] Oxford Univ. Pr., 1963 (Galaxy).

> A classic.

BOWRA, C[ecil] M[aurice]. *The Creative Experiment.* N.Y., Grove Pr., 1948.

> *Incl.* Eliot.

———— *In General and Particular.* Weidenfeld and Nicolson, 1964.

> Mostly addresses ; *incl.* "Poets and Scholars" ; "Poetry and the First World War" ; "The Prophetic Element [in poetry]."

———— *The Heritage of Symbolism.* Macmillan, 1943.

> Only Yeats, of English authors.

BRÉMOND, Henri. *Prière et Poésie.* Paris, Grasset, 1926.

> On the theory of pure poetry.

BRENNER, Rica. *Ten Modern Poets.* N.Y., Harcourt, Brace, 1930.

> *Incl.* de la Mare, A. E. Housman, Kipling, Masefield, Noyes.

———— *Poets of Our Time.* N.Y., Harcourt, Brace, 1941.

> *Incl.* Eliot, Auden, Spender, Yeats.

BRONOWSKI, J[acob]. *The Poet's Defence.* Cambridge Univ. Pr., 1939.

> Examination of poets' belief as to the worth of poetry and criticism ; *incl.* A. E. Housman, Yeats.

BROOKE-ROSE, Christine. *A Grammar of Metaphor.* Secker and Warburg, 1958.

> Unusual and valuable study. Introd. on history of the analysis of metaphor ; kinds of metaphor, ill. by analysis of particular poets, *incl.* Yeats and D. Thomas.

BROOKS, Cleanth. *Modern Poetry and the Tradition.* [1939] Chapel Hill, Univ. of North Carolina Pr., 1965.

> *Incl.* Eliot, Yeats, Auden. Important for position of this New Critic.

————— *The Well Wrought Urn:* Studies in the Structure of Poetry. [1947] N.Y., Harcourt, Brace, 1960 (Harvest).

> *Incl.* study of a Yeats poem and chapters on the author's critical theory.

BULLOUGH, Geoffrey. *The Trend of Modern Poetry.* [1934] Oliver and Boyd, 1949.

> *Incl.* Yeats, de la Mare, E. Sitwell, Read, D. H. Lawrence, Eliot.

CAUDWELL, Christopher (pseud. of Christopher St. John Sprigg). *Illusion and Reality:* A Study of the Sources of Poetry. Macmillan, 1937.

> *Incl.* "The Death of Mythology" ; "The Development of Modern Poetry" ; "The Characteristics of Poetry" ; "The World and the 'I' " ; "The Psyche and Phantasy" ; "Poetry's Dream-Work" ; "The Organisation of the Arts" ; "The Future of Poetry."

CHURCH, Richard. *Eight for Immortality.* Dent, 1941.

> *Incl.* W. H. Davies, de la Mare, Yeats, Blunden, V. Sackville-West, Eliot, Graves ; full biography and critical studies.

COLLINS, John Churton. *Studies in Poetry and Criticism.* Bell, 1905.

> *Incl.* review of collected works of Watson.

CRUM, Ralph B. *Scientific Thought in Poetry.* N.Y., Columbia Univ. Pr., 1931.

> *Incl.* Davidson.

DAICHES, David. *Literary Essays.* Oliver and Boyd, 1956.

> *Incl.* D. Thomas.

————— *Poetry and the Modern World:* A Study of Poetry in England Between 1900 and 1939. Chicago, Univ. of Chicago Pr., 1940.

> Not a history ; by a critic who is perhaps sounder on prose.

DAVIE, Donald. *Articulate Energy:* An Enquiry into the Syntax of English Poetry. Routledge, and N.Y., Harcourt, Brace, 1955.

> *Incl.* general considerations (e.g., "What is Modern Poetry?") and study of theory and/or practice of various writers, *incl.* Hulme, Susanne Langer, D. Thomas, Ernest Fenellosa, Yeats, Northrop Frye.

————— *Purity of Diction in English Verse.* Chatto and Windus, 1952.

DE LA MARE, Walter. *Poetry in Prose.* N.Y., Oxford Univ. Pr., 1937.

> Warton Lecture on English Poetry, British Academy, 1935. Delightful and valuable essay on distinctions between styles of English prose and poetry.

DOBRÉE, Bonamy. *The Broken Cistern.* Cohen and West, 1954.

> Clark Lectures, Cambridge, 1952–1953. Examines the question why modern poetry is not read.

DREW, Elizabeth. *Poetry:* A Modern Guide to its Understanding and Enjoyment. N.Y., Norton, 1959.

> *Incl.* modern poetry.

————— and Joseph L. SWEENEY. *Directions in Modern Poetry.* N.Y., Norton, 1940.

> Guide to technique, etc., rather than to separate authors.

DUNCAN, Joseph Ellis. *The Revival of Metaphysical Poetry:* The History of a Style, 1800 to the Present. Oxford Univ. Pr.; Minneapolis, Univ. of Minnesota Pr., 1959.

> *Incl.* "The Metaphysical Revival 1872–1912"; "Yeats, Donne and the Metaphysicals"; "Eliot and the Twentieth-Century Revival"; "Metaphysicals and Critics since 1912"; "The Metaphysical Florescence."

EASTMAN, Max. See under Criticism.

ELIOT, T[homas] S[tearns]. *On Poetry and Poets.* Faber, and N.Y., Farrar, Straus, 1957.

> Coll. articles and lectures. *Incl.* Yeats, Kipling, "The Music of Poetry"; "What is Minor Poetry?"; The Social Function of Poetry"; "The Three Voices of Poetry"; "The Function of Criticism" [1956].

—————— *The Use of Poetry and the Use of Criticism.* [1933] N.Y., Barnes and Noble, 1955.

> The Charles Eliot Norton lectures, Harvard Univ., 1932–1933. For other Eliot essays, see also in Collections, Criticism, and Drama.

ELLIOTT, G[eorge] R. *The Cycle of Modern Poetry.* Princeton, N.J., Princeton Univ. Pr., 1929.

> Essays on the difficulties of modern poetry; *incl.* Hardy.

EMPSON, William. *Seven Types of Ambiguity:* A Study of its Effects in English Verse. [1930] Rev. ed. Chatto and Windus, 1947; N.Y., New Directions, n.d.

> A classic of modern criticism. Extension of I. A. Richards' doctrine, applied to poetry, *incl.* Eliot, Hopkins, Yeats.

—————— *Some Versions of Pastoral:* A Study of Pastoral Form in Literature. [1935] Chatto and Windus, 1950.

> A landmark in modern criticism; not specifically on modern literature but relevant thereto.

FENELOSSA, Ernest. *The Chinese Written Character as a Medium for Poetry.* Nott, 1936.

> Important document for modern poetry esp. Imagism.

FLOWER, Desmond, ed. *The Pursuit of Poetry:* A Book of Letters About Poetry Written by English Poets, 1550–1930. Cassell, 1939.

> *Incl.* Hopkins to Bridges and Canon Dixon; William Barnes to Gosse; Bridges to Coventry Patmore; R. Brooke to Flecker; Flecker to Frederick Savary; D. H. Lawrence to Catherine Carswell; Hardy to Noyes; A. E. Housman to Seymour Adelman.

FRASER, G[eorge] S[utherland]. *Vision and Rhetoric:* Studies in Modern Poetry. Faber and Faber, 1959.

> By a perceptive critic. *Incl.* Yeats, Graves, Eliot, Auden, MacNeice, Empson, Spender, D. Thomas.

GRAVES, Robert. *The Common Asphodel:* Collected Essays on Poetry, 1922–1949. Hamilton, 1949.

> A poet on his contemporaries. *Incl.* Bridges, Eliot, D. H. Lawrence, Sassoon, E. Sitwell, S. Sitwell, Yeats.

————*Contemporary Techniques of Poetry:* A Political Anthology. Hogarth Pr., 1925.

>Analysis of poetry by diction, metre, etc.; conservative vs. Left Wing; many references to contemporary poetry.

———— *On English Poetry:* Being an Irregular Approach to the Psychology of this Art, From Evidence Mainly Subjective.

————*Poetic Unreason and Other Studies.* C. Palmer, 1925.

>"What is bad poetry?"; "Definition of Poetic Analysis"; "Poetic Genius."

GROOM, Bernard. *The Diction of Poetry From Spenser to Bridges.* Toronto, Univ. of Toronto Pr., 1955.

>" . . . result of almost life-long study of the diction of English poetry." Based on earlier essays. Historical considerations; *incl.* only Bridges of 20th c.

GROSS, Harvey. *Sound and Form in Modern Poetry:* A Study of Prosody from Thomas Hardy to Robert Lowell. Ann Arbor, Univ. of Michigan Pr., 1964.

>Less ambitious and less systematic than the subtitle indicates.

HAMILTON, G[eorge] Rostrevor. *Poetry and Contemplation*: A New Preface to Poetics. Cambridge Univ. Pr., 1937.

>Theory of poetry by a poet.

———— *The Tell-Tale Article:* A Critical Approach to Modern Poetry. Heinemann, 1949.

>Three essays, *incl.* Eliot.

HEATH–STUBBS, John. *The Darkling Plain:* Romanticism in English Poetry from Darling to Yeats. Eyre and Spottiswoode, 1950.

>Study of the theme of romanticism in a number of poets, *incl.* Hopkins, Bridges, Doughty, Blunt, Yeats.

HENDERSON, Philip. *The Poet and Society.* Secker and Warburg, 1939.

>*Incl.* Hopkins, Yeats, Eliot, Auden.

HOLLOWAY, John. *The Lion Hunt:* A Pursuit of Poetry and Reality. Routledge and Kegan Paul, 1965.

———— *Widening Horizons in English Verse.* Routledge and Kegan Paul, 1966.

>From lectures at Univ. of Chicago, 1965; problems in the development of poetry.

HOUSMAN, A[lfred] E[dward]. *The Name and Nature of Poetry.* Cambridge Univ. Pr., and N.Y., Macmillan, 1933.

>Leslie Stephen Lecture at Cambridge. Housman's romantic notion of poetry; observations on poems and description of his method of composition.

HUNGERLAND, Isabel C. *Poetic Discourse.* Berkeley and Los Angeles, Univ. of Calif. Pr., 1958.

>Analysis by a professional philosopher. Bibliog. footnotes.

HUXLEY, Aldous. *On the Margin,* Notes and Essays [1923] Collected Ed. (Works) Chatto and Windus, 1948.
>*Incl.* "The Subject Matter of Poetry" ; on Edward Thomas.

HYMAN, Stanley Edgar. *Poetry and Criticism:* Four Revolutions in Literary Taste. N.Y., Atheneum Pr., 1961.
>Based on lectures at Wayne State Univ. Section IV is "Modern Literature," *incl.* Eliot.

ISAACS, J[acob]. *The Background of Modern Poetry.* [1951] N.Y., Dutton, 1958.
>Lectures in the BBC Third Programme, 1948–1951 ; sympathetic, perceptive ; good introductory explanation of ideas and trends.

JAMES, D[avid] G. *Scepticism and Poetry:* An Essay on the Poetic Imagination. [1937] N.Y., Barnes and Noble, 1960.
>Takes issue with Richards on the poetic imagination (with special reference to Coleridge).

JARRELL, Randall. *Poetry and the Age.* N.Y., Vintage, 1955.
>Repr. reviews ; mostly on Am. poets, but *incl.* de la Mare, Comfort.

JONES, Llewelyn. *First Impressions:* Essays on Poetry, Criticism and Prosody. N.Y., Knopf, 1925.
>*Incl.* de la Mare, Yeats, Abercrombie, T. S. Moore, A. Meynell, "Criticism in General" ; "The Periphery of Poetry" ; "Free Verse and its Propaganda" ; "Four Younger Women Poets."

KERMODE, Frank. *The Romantic Image.* [1957] N.Y., Viking, 1964.
>Important book, tracing pattern in modern poetry from the '90s to the present. *Incl.* Yeats, A. Symons, Hulme.

KERNAHAN, Coulson. *Five More Famous Living Poets.* Butterworth, 1928.
>*Incl.* de la Mare, Kaye-Smith, Watson.

——— *Six Famous Living Poets:* Introductory Studies. Butterworth, 1926.
>*Incl.* Masefield, Kipling, Newbolt, Baring, Noyes, Drinkwater.

LANGBAUM, Robert Woodrow. *The Poetry of Experience:* The Dramatic Monologue in Modern Literary Tradition. Chatto and Windus, 1957.
>*Incl.* Eliot, Hopkins, Joyce, Yeats.

LEAVIS, F[rank] R[aymond]. *New Bearings in English Poetry.* [1932] Ann Arbor, Univ. of Michigan Pr., 1960.
>*Incl.* Eliot, Hopkins, "Poetry and the Modern World" ; "The Situation at the End of World War I" ; "Epilogue, Retrospect, 1950." By a leading critic, early proponent of Eliot.

LEWIS, C[ecil] Day. *A Hope for Poetry.* [1934] Repr. with postscript, 1936. Oxford, Blackwell, 1942.
>Important discussion of modern poetry by a poet.

——— *The Poetic Image.* N.Y., Oxford Univ. Pr., 1947.
>Clarke lectures, Cambridge Univ., 1964. This aspect of poetic technique examined in wide range of Eng. poetry.

LOWES, John Livingston. *Convention and Revolt in Poetry.* [1919] Boston, Houghton Mifflin, 1928.
  Lectures at Lowell Institute, Boston, 1918.

MARITAIN, Jacques. *Creative Intuition in Art and Poetry.* [1953] N.Y., Noonday Pr., 1955. (Meridian Bks).
  The A. W. Mellon Lectures in the Fine Arts, Washington, 1952. Exposition of the distinctive position of a leading critic and philosopher.

MAYNARD, Theodore. *Our Best Poets, English and American.* N.Y., Holt, 1922.
  Chapter on each poet, criticism and quotation ; incl. Chesterton, A. Meynell, C. Williams, de la Mare, Hodgson, Yeats, Belloc, Squire, W. H. Davies, Abercrombie, Binyon, Masefield.

MACNEICE, Louis. *Modern Poetry, A Personal Essay.* Oxford Univ. Pr., 1938.
  Sheds more light on the author (a poet) than on ostensible subject.

MILES, Josephine. *Eras and Modes in English Poetry.* [1957] 2d. ed., rev. enlgd. Berkeley and Los Angeles, Univ. of Calif. Pr., 1964.
  From Donne through Hopkins and Yeats.

MONRO, Harold. *Some Contemporary Poets,* Parsons, 1920.
  Useful short studies of many, mostly young, poets, by a contemporary.

MUIR, Edwin. *The Estate of Poetry.* Chatto and Windus, and Cambridge, Mass., Harvard Univ. Pr., 1962.
  The Charles Eliot Norton Lectures, 1955–1956.

NOWOTTNY, Winifred. *The Language Poets Use.* N.Y., Oxford Univ. Pr., 1962.
  Based on lectures to students of English at Univ. of London. Novel and very valuable analysis of workings of elements of poetry: language, idiom, metaphor, schematization and abstraction, ambiguity, symbolism and obscurity.

NOYES, Alfred. *Some Aspects of Modern Poetry.* Hodder and Stoughton, 1924.
  Incl. A. Meynell.

O'CONNOR, William Van. *Sense and Sensibility in Modern Poetry.* Chicago, Univ. of Chicago Pr., 1948.
  Some repr. from journals. By tendencies and techniques with wide reference to poets.

ORR, Peter, ed. *The Poet Speaks Out.* Routledge and Kegan Paul, 1966.
  Broadcast interviews with 45 contemporary poets of their own writing, from Blunden and Read to younger poets. Introd. by Kermode.

POTTLE, Frederick A. *The Idiom of Poetry.* [1941] Ithaca, N.Y., Cornell Univ. Pr., 1946.
  Messenger Lectures, Cornell Univ. Theory of poetry [as communication] and criticism approached psychologically, with ill, esp. from Wordsworth.

PRATT, William Crouch. *Revolution Without Betrayal*. Nashville, Tenn., Vanderbilt Univ. Pr., 1957.
> *Incl*. James, Eliot.

PRESCOTT, Frederick Clarke. *The Poetic Mind*. [1922] N.Y., Macmillan, 1926.
> Pioneer American application to poetry of Freud's theory of dreams. Useful introductory book on the creative process, even though its psychology is not now altogether up to date.

————*Poetry and Myth*. N.Y., Macmillan, 1927.
> Early and still valuable examination of myth in relation to literature; "proper reading and interpretation of poetry" to be reached through recognition of the nature of poetry and of mind.

PRESS, John. *The Chequer'd Shade:* Reflections on Obscurity in Poetry. [1958] Oxford Univ. Pr., 1963 (Galaxy).
> Mainly on contemporary poetry; general discussion with quotations for illus. but not for explication.

————*The Fire and the Fountain:* An Essay on Poetry. [1955] Methuen, 1965 (Univ. Paperback).

————*Rule and Energy:* Trends in British Poetry Since the Second World War. London and N.Y., Oxford Univ. Pr., 1963.
> G. Elliston Poetry Foundation lectures at Univ. of Cincinnati. The poets who have emerged since 1939 presented with enthusiasm.

READ, Herbert. *In Defence of Shelley and Other Essays*. Heinemann, 1936.
> On obscurity in poetry; parallels with Eng. painting; Hopkins.

————*Phases of English Poetry*. [1928] Rev. ed., Norfolk, Conn., Direction 19, 1951.
> Brief, selective, provocative historical sketches by a poet. *Incl*. "Pure Poetry," "Modern Poetry."

————*Selected Writings:* Poetry and Criticism. Faber and Faber, 1963.
> Foreword by Allen Tate and good selective bibliog. *Incl*. "The Personality of the Poet"; also on correlation of poetry with other arts, incl. painting.

ROBERTS, Michael. *Critique of Poetry*. Cape, 1934.
> On technique and terminology of criticism; the difficulty of some modern poets, *incl*. Graves, Eliot, A. E. Housman [bk. reviews]; on practical criticism, *incl*. "A Philosophy of Life"; on Hulme's *Speculations*.

ROSENBERG, Harold. *The Tradition of the New*. N.Y., Horizon Pr., 1959.
> One section on poetry.

ROSENTHAL, M[asha] L[ouis]. *The Modern Poets:* A Critical Introduction. N.Y., Oxford Univ. Pr., 1960.
> Extended treatment of sel. poets, British and American, with quotation and commentary on texts quoted. *Incl*. Eliot, Hopkins, Hardy, Yeats, MacDiarmid, Muir, D. H. Lawrence, Auden, MacNeice, Spender, Day Lewis, D. Thomas, Larkin, C. Tomlinson. Bibliog.

RYLANDS, George [Humphrey Wolfestan]. *Words and Poetry*. Hogarth Pr., and N.Y., Payson and Clarke, 1928.
Introd. by L. Strachey.

SANSOM, Clive, ed. *The World of Poetry:* Poets and Critics on the Art and Functions of Poetry, Extracts Selected and Arranged by Clive Sansom. Phoenix House, 1959.
Very short selections, on various topics, from poets and critics, incl. modern.

SANTAYANA, George. *Interpretations of Poetry and Religion*. [1900] N.Y., Harper, 1957. (Torchbks).
Collection of essays repr. and rev. Controlling idea: "religion and poetry are identical in essence."

SAVAGE, Derek S. *The Personal Principle:* Studies in Modern Poetry. Routledge, 1944.
By a Leavisite ; *incl.* Yeats, Eliot, D. H. Lawrence, Auden.

SITWELL, Edith. *Aspects of Modern Poetry*. Duckworth, 1934.
Important book. Uninhibited judgments and expert analysis of texts by a poet. *Incl.* Hopkins, Yeats, W. H. Davies, Eliot, S. Sitwell, Auden, Spender, Day Lewis, W. Lewis, Bottrall ; "Notes on Innovations in Prose." "Pastors and Masters" is an attack on Leavis and Grigson.

———— *A Poet's Notebook*. Macmillan, 1943.
Notes on history and criticism of poetry.

———— *Poetry and Criticism*. Leonard and Virginia Woolf, 1925.
Hogarth Essays on Literature.

SMITH, Chard Powers. *Annals of the Poets*. N.Y., Scribner's, 1935.
Biog., Eng. and Am. Bibliog.

SOUTHWORTH, James G. *Sowing the Spring:* Studies in British Poets from Hopkins to MacNeice. Oxford, Blackwell, 1940.
Incl. chapters on Hopkins, Yeats, Binyon, D. H. Lawrence, Eliot, MacDiarmid, Day Lewis, Auden, Spender, MacNeice. Perceptive.

SPARROW, John. *Sense and Poetry*. New Haven, Conn., Yale Univ. Pr., 1934.
Anti-modern essays on the place of meaning in contemporary verse.

SQUIRE, J[ohn] C[ollings]. *Essays on Poetry*. Hodder and Stoughton, and N.Y., Doran, 1923.
Repr. from various sources. *Incl.* A. Meynell, Bridges, Hardy, A. E. Housman, Yeats, Blunden.

STANFORD, Derek. *The Freedom of Poetry:* Studies in Contemporary Verse. Falcon Pr., 1947.
Incl. Gascoyne, Comfort, Durrell, N. Moore, N. Nicholson, Raine, Todd, Ridler.

STAUFFER, Donald A. *The Nature of Poetry*. N.Y., Norton, 1946.
Rather elementary discussion of various historical theories of English poetry.

STRONG, L[eonard] A[lfred] G[eorge]. *Common Sense about Poetry.* Gollancz, 1931.

STURGEON, Mary C. *Studies of Contemporary Poets.* [1916] Rev. ed., N.Y., Dodd, Mead, 1919.
> *Incl.* Abercrombie, R. Brooke, W. H. Davies, de la Mare, Gibson, Hodgson, Hueffer (Ford), Macaulay, Masefield, Monro, Stephens, Drinkwater, Michael Field, Hardy, Squire, Yeats, contemporary women poets.

TATE, Allen. *On the Limits of Poetry:* Selected Essays, 1928–1948. W. Morrow, and N.Y., Swallow Pr., 1948.
> General essays on poetry and criticism ; poets *incl.* Hardy, Yeats, Eliot.

————, ed. *The Language of Poetry.* Oxford Univ. Pr., and Princeton, N.J., Princeton Univ. Pr., 1942.
> Mesure Series in literary criticism: essays read at Princeton. *Incl.* Wheelwright, "Poetic Myth and Reality" ; Cleanth Brooks, "The Language of Paradox" ; I. A. Richards, "The Interactions of Words" ; Wallace Stevens, "The Noble Rider and the Sound of Words."

THWAITE, Anthony. *Essays on Contemporary English Poetry:* Hopkins to the Present. Tokyo, Kenkyasha, 1957.
> Arranged by poets ; last chapter, "Poetry Since 1950," incl. both major and minor poets.

TILLYARD, E[ustace] M[andeville] W. *Poetry Direct and Oblique.* [1934] Rev. ed., Chatto and Windus, 1959.
> Criticism of texts to illustrate important critical theory ; though the texts are not modern, the theory is useful for criticism of modern poetry.

———— and, C[live] S[taples] LEWIS. *The Personal Heresy:* A Controversy. N.Y. and London, Oxford Univ. Pr., 1939.
> Three of these essays repr. from *Essays and Studies* (Eng. Assoc.). A debate on the relevance of a poet's life and intention to the interpretation of a poem. Tillyard is for the personal approach ; Lewis against. Not on modern poetry in particular, but relevant to the modern age.

TREECE, Henry. *How I See Apocalypse.* Drummond, 1946.
> On the Apocalyptic movement in poetry ; *incl.* Eliot, Hopkins, D. Thomas, Read.

TSCHUMI, Raymond. *Thought in Twentieth-Century English Poetry.* Routledge and Kegan Paul, 1951.
> *Incl.* Yeats, Muir, Eliot, Read, Day Lewis, A. E., W. J. Turner, D. H. Lawrence, Spender, Huxley, Auden.

TURNELL, Martin. *Poetry and Crisis.* Sands, 1938.
> Short essay.

UNGER, Leonard. *The Man in the Name:* Essays on the Experience of Poetry. Minneapolis, Univ. of Minnesota Pr., 1956.

VALÉRY, Paul. *The Art of Poetry*. Tr. Denise Folliot. N.Y., Pantheon, 1958.
Influential theory of a great French poet ; introd. by T. S. Eliot, whose
theory is related to Valéry's.

WAIN, John, ed. *Interpretations:* Essays on 12 English Poems. Routledge
and Kegan Paul, 1955.
Poems explicated by Oxford-Cambridge critics of post-Leavis generation. *Incl.* Dennis Ward [Hopkins] "The Windhover" ; Joseph Mar-
golis, [Eliot] "The Love Song of J. Alfred Prufrock" ; Wain, [Yeats]
"Among School Children" ; G. S. Fraser, "Epilogue on the Interpretation of the Difficult Poem."

WHALLEY, George. *Poetic Process*. Routledge and Kegan Paul, 1953.
Creativity, ill. by Eliot, Hulme, Joyce, Yeats, Synge, James, Read,
Hopkins, Bowra.

WILLIAMS, Charles. *Poetry at Present*. Oxford, Clarendon Pr., 1930.
Incl. Hardy, Bridges, A. E. Housman, Kipling, Yeats, W. H. Davies,
de la Mare, Chesterton, Masefield, Hodgson, Gibson, Abercrombie,
Eliot, E. and S. Sitwell, Graves, Blunden. See also *The English Poetic
Mind* (Oxford, Clarendon Pr., 1932).

WILLIAMS-ELLIS, A[mabel]. *An Anatomy of Poetry*. Oxford, Blackwell,
and N.Y., Macmillan, 1922.
Repr. some from *Spec*. Short studies of some modern poets in Part
V. Theoretical and general criticism. Idiosyncratic and of its time.

WIMSATT, W[illiam] K. *Hateful Contraries:* Studies in Literature and
Criticism. With an Essay on English Meter Written in Collaboration with
Monroe C. Beardsley. Lexington, Univ. of Kentucky Pr., 1965.
Incl. "What to Say About a Poem" ; "Horses of Wrath" (review of
critical theory from Romantics to Frye) ; Wimsatt's theory of tension
in poetry ; on Eliot.

WOODHOUSE, A. S. P. *The Poet and His Faith:* Religion and Poetry in
England from Spenser to Eliot and Auden. Chicago, Univ. of Chicago
Pr., 1965.
Only Eliot and Auden. Lectures sponsored by Weil Institute for Studies
in Religion and the Humanities.

WYLD, H[enry] C[ecil] [Kennedy]. *Some Aspects of the Diction of English
Poetry*, Oxford, Blackwell, 1933.
Philological. Two lectures, Univ. of London, 1933.

YEATS, William Butler. *Essays, 1931 to 1936*. Dublin, Cuala Pr., 1937.
Incl. "Modern Poetry, a Broadcast" [1936].

————*Ideas of Good and Evil*. [1903] Dublin, Maunsel, 1905, repr.
Macmillan, 1914. Also in *Essays*, Vol. IV of *Collected Edition* of *The
Works*. Macmillan, 1924.
Incl. "What is Popular Poetry?" [1902] ; "The Symbolism of Poetry"
[1900] ; "The Celtic Element in Literature" [1898] ; on Bridges
[1897].

————*Letters on Poetry from W. B. Yeats to Dorothy Wellesley.* [1940] London and N.Y., Oxford Univ. Pr., 1965. (paper).

Yeats's theory of poetry indicated.

———— "Introduction" to *The Oxford Book of Modern Verse,* ed. Yeats. Oxford Univ. Pr., 1936.

Historical sketch of the poets who were his associates in the poetic movement 1890's on.

PART TWO

PART TWO

AUTHORS INCLUDED

Abercrombie, Lascelles
AE. *See* Russell, George William
Agate, James
  (James Evershed Agate)
Aldington, Richard
Allen, Walter
  (Walter Ernest Allen)
Amis, Kingsley
Anstey, F.
  (pseud. of Thomas Anstey Guthrie)
Archer, William
Arlen, Michael
  (pseud. of Dikran Kuyumjian)
Armstrong, Martin
  (Martin Donesthorpe Armstrong)
Auden, W. H.
  (Wystan Hugh Auden)
Balchin, Nigel
Baring, Maurice
Barker, George
Barrie, J. M.
  (Sir James Matthew Barrie)
Bates, H. E.
  (Herbert Ernest Bates)
Bates, Ralph
Bateson, F. W.
  (Frederick Wilse Bateson)
Bax, Clifford
Beckett, Samuel
Bedford, Sybille
Beerbohm, Max
  (Sir Max Beerbohm)
Behan, Brendan
Bell, Clive
Belloc, Hilaire
Bennett, Arnold
Benson, E. F.
  (Edward Frederic Benson)

Benson, Stella
Bentley, Phyllis
  (Phyllis Eleanor Bentley)
Beresford, J. D.
  (John Davys Beresford)
Betjeman, John
Binyon, Laurence
Blunden, Edmund
  (Edmund Charles Blunden)
Blunt, Wilfrid Scawen
Bottome, Phyllis
Bottomley, Gordon
Bottrall, Ronald
Bowen, Elizabeth
Bowra, Maurice
  (Sir Cecil Maurice Bowra)
Bradbury, Malcolm
Braine, John
Bridges, Robert
  (Robert Seymour Bridges)
Bridie, James
  (pseud. of Osborne Henry Mavor)
Brooke, Jocelyn
Brooke, Rupert
Brooke-Rose, Christine
Brophy, Brigid
Brown, Ivor
  (Ivor John Carnegie Brown)
Bryher, Winifred
Buchan, John
  (John Buchan, Baron
  Tweedsmuir)
Burgess, Anthony
Butler, Samuel
Caine, Hall
  (Sir Hall Caine)
Campbell, Roy

119

Cannan, Gilbert

Carpenter, Edward
(Edward Childs Carpenter)

Carroll, Paul Vincent

Cary, Joyce

Caudwell, Christopher
(pseud. of Christopher St. John
Sprigg)

Cecil, David
(Lord David Cecil)

Chambers, E. K.
(Sir Edmund Kerchever Chambers)

Chesterton, G. K.
(Gilbert Keith Chesterton)

Church, Richard

Clarke, Austin

Collier, John

Colum, Padraic

Comfort, Alex
(Alexander Comfort)

Compton-Burnett, Ivy

Connolly, Cyril

Conrad, Joseph
(Teodor Józef Konrad
Korzeniowski)

Cooper, William
(pseud. of H. S. Hoff)

Coppard, A. E.
(Alfred Edward Coppard)

Corelli, Marie

Corvo, Baron. *See* Rolfe, Frederick

Coward, Noel
(Noel Pierce Coward)

Cronin, A. J.
(Archibald Joseph Cronin)

Cunninghame-Graham, R. B.
(Robert Bontine Cunninghame-
Graham)

Daiches, David

Dane, Clemence
(pseud. of Winifred Ashton)

Davidson, John

Davie, Donald

Davies, Rhys

Davies, W. H.
(William Henry Davies)

Day Lewis. *See* under Lewis

Delafield, E. M.
(pseud. of Edmée Elizabeth
Monica de la Pasture, afterwards
Dashwood)

De la Mare, Walter
(Walter John de la Mare)

De Morgan, William
(William Frend De Morgan)

Dennis, Nigel
(Nigel Forbes Dennis)

De Selincourt, Ernest

Dobrée, Bonamy

Doughty, Charles
(Charles Montagu Doughty)

Douglas, Norman

Doyle, Arthur Conan
(Sir Arthur Conan Doyle)

Drinkwater, John

Duggan, Alfred
(Alfred Leo Duggan)

Du Maurier, Daphne

Duncan, Ronald
(Ronald Frederic Henry Duncan)

Dunsany, Lord
(Edward John Moreton Drax
Plunkett, Baron Dunsany)

Durrell, Lawrence

Eglinton, John
(pseud. of William Kirkpatrick
Magee)

Eliot, T. S.
(Thomas Stearns Eliot)

Ellis, Havelock

Empson, William

Enright, D. J.
(Dennis Joseph Enright)

Ervine, St. John
(St. John Greer Ervine)

Evans, Caradoc

Fausset, Hugh I'Anson

Field, Michael
(pseud. of Katherine Harris
Bradley and Edith Emma Cooper)

Fielding, Gabriel
(pseud. of Alan Gabriel Barnsley)

Firbank, Ronald
(Arthur Annesley Ronald Firbank)

Flecker, James Elroy

Flint, F. S.
(Frank Stewart Flint)

Ford, Ford Madox
(born Ford Madox Hueffer)

Forester, C. S.
(Cecil Scott Forester)

Forster, E. M.
(Edward Morgan Forster)

Fraser, G. S.
(George Sutherland Fraser)

Freeman, John

Fry, Christopher

Fry, Roger
(Roger Eliot Fry)

Fuller, Roy
(Roy Broadbent Fuller)

Galsworthy, John

Garnett, David

Gascoyne, David

Gerhardi, William
(William Alexander Gerhardi)

Gibbons, Stella

Gibbs, Philip
(Sir Philip Hamilton Gibbs)

Gibson, Wilfrid
(Wilfrid Wilson Gibson)

Gissing, George
(George Robert Gissing)

Godden, Rumer
(Mayard Rumer Haynes Dixon)

Gogarty, Oliver St. John

Golding, Louis

Golding, William
(William Gerald Golding)

Goldring, Douglas

Gosse, Edmund
(Sir Edmund William Gosse)

Gould, Gerald

Graham, W. S.
(William Sydney Graham)

Grahame, Kenneth

Granville-Barker, H.
(Harley Granville Granville-
Barker)

Graves, Robert

Green, Henry
(pseud. of Henry Vincent Yorke)

Greene, Graham

Gregory, Lady
(Isabella Augusta, Lady Gregory)

Grierson, Herbert
(Sir Herbert John Clifford
Grierson)

Grigson, Geoffrey

Guedalla, Philip

Gunn, Thom

Gwynn, Stephen

Haggard, H. Rider
(Sir Henry Rider Haggard)

Hall, Radclyffe

Hamilton, G. Rostrevor
(George Rostrevor Hamilton)

Hanley, James

Hardy, Thomas

Harris, Frank

Hartley, L. P.
(Leslie Poles Hartley)

Hassall, Christopher
(Christopher Vernon Hassall)

Heath-Stubbs, John
(John Francis Alexander
Heath-Stubbs)

Heppenstall, Rayner

Herbert, A. P.
(Sir Alan Patrick Herbert)

Hewlett, Maurice
(Maurice Henry Hewlett)

Hichens, Robert
(Robert Smythe Hichens)

Hilton, James

Hodgson, Ralph

Holloway, John

Holtby, Winifred

Hope, Anthony
(pseud. of Sir Anthony Hope
Hawkins)

Hopkins, Gerard Manley

Housman, A. E.
(Alfred Edward Housman)

Housman, Laurence

Howard, Elizabeth Jane

Hudson, Stephen
  (pseud. of Sydney Schiff)

Hudson, W. H.
  (William Henry Hudson)

Hughes, Richard
  (Richard Arthur Warren Hughes)

Hughes, Ted

Hulme, T. E.
  (Thomas Ernest Hulme)

Hutchinson, R. C.
  (Roy Coryton Hutchinson)

Huxley, Aldous

Isherwood, Christopher

Jacobs, W. W.
  (William Wymark Jacobs)

James, Henry

Jameson, Storm

Jennings, Elizabeth

Jerome, Jerome K.
  (Jerome Klapka Jerome)

Johnson, Pamela Hansford

Johnston, Denis

Jones, David
  (David Michael Jones)

Jones, Glyn

Jones, Gwyn

Jones, Henry Arthur

Joyce, James

Kaye-Smith, Sheila

Kennedy, Margaret

Ker, W. P.
  (William Paton Ker)

Kipling, Rudyard

Koestler, Arthur

Lang, Andrew

Larkin, Philip

Laski, Marghanita

Laver, James

Lawrence, D. H.
  (David Herbert Lawrence)

Lawrence, T. E.
  (Thomas Edward Lawrence)

Leavis, F. R.
  (Frank Raymond Leavis)

Lee, Laurie

Lee, Vernon
  (pseud. of Violet Paget)

Lehmann, John

Lehmann, Rosamond

Leslie, Shane
  (Sir Shane Leslie)

Lessing, Doris
  (Doris May Lessing)

Levertov, Denise

Leverson, Ada

Levy, Benn
  (Benn Wolf Levy)

Lewis, Alun

Day Lewis, C.
  (Cecil Day Lewis)

Lewis, C. S.
  (Clive Staples Lewis)

Lewis, D. B. Wyndham
  (Dominic Bevan Wyndham Lewis)

Lewis, (Percy) Wyndham

Liddell, Robert

Linklater, Eric

Logue, Christopher

Lonsdale, Frederick

Lowry, Malcolm

Lubbock, Percy

Lucas, E. V.
  (Edward Verrall Lucas)

Lucas, F. L.
  (Frank Laurence Lucas)

Lyle, Rob

Lynd, Robert

Lyon, Lilian Bowes
  (Lilian Helen Bowes-Lyon)

Macaulay, Rose

MacCaig, Norman

MacCarthy, Desmond
  (Sir Desmond MacCarthy)

MacDiarmid, Hugh
  (pseud. of Christopher Murray
  Grieve)

MacDougall, Roger

Machen, Arthur

MacInnes, Colin

Mackail, J. W.
(John William Mackail)

Mackenzie, Compton
(Sir Compton Mackenzie)

MacNeice, Louis

Madge, Charles

Manning, Olivia

Mansfield, Katherine
(pseud. of Kathleen Beauchamp,
afterwards Mrs. John Middleton
Murry)

Marriott, Charles

Marsh, Edward
(Sir Edward Howard Marsh)

Masefield, John

Mason, A. E. W.
(Alfred Edward Woodley Mason)

Masters, John

Maugham, W. S.
(William Somerset Maugham)

Menen, Aubrey

Mew, Charlotte

Meyerstein, E. H. W.
(Edward Harry William
Meyerstein)

Meynell, Alice
(Alice Christiana Meynell,
née Thompson)

Meynell, Viola

Milne, A. A.
(Alan Alexander Milne)

Mitchison, Naomi
(Naomi Mitchison, née Haldane)

Mitford, Nancy

Monkhouse, Allan
(Allan Noble Monkhouse)

Monro, Harold

Monsarrat, Nicholas

Moore, George

Moore, Nicholas

Moore, T. Sturge
(Thomas Sturge Moore)

Morgan, Charles

Mottram, R. H.
(Ralph Hale Mottram)

Muir, Edwin

Munro, H. H. *See* Saki

Munro, C. K.
(Charles Kirkpatrick Munro)

Murdoch, Iris

Murray, Gilbert

Murry, John Middleton

Myers, L. H.
(Leopold Hamilton Myers)

Newbolt, Henry
(Sir Henry John Newbolt)

Newby, P. H.
(Percy Howard Newby)

Nichols, Beverley

Nichols, Robert

Nicholson, Norman

Nicolson, Harold
(Hon. Sir Harold George
Nicolson)

Noyes, Alfred

O'Casey, Sean

O'Connor, Frank
(pseud. of Michael O'Donovan)

O'Faolain, Sean
(Seán O'Faoláin)

O'Flaherty, Liam

Onions, Oliver
(pseud. of George Oliver)

Orwell, George
(pseud. of Eric Blair)

Osborne, John

Owen, Wilfred

Phillips, Stephen

Phillpotts, Eden

Pinero, Arthur Wing
(Sir Arthur Wing Pinero)

Pinter, Harold

Pitter, Ruth

Plomer, William
(William Charles Franklyn
Plomer)

Potter, Stephen

Powell, Anthony

Powys, John Cowper

Powys, T. F.
(Theodore Francis Powys)

Priestley, J. B.
(John Boynton Priestley)
Prince, F. T.
(Frank Templeton Prince)
Pritchett, V. S.
(Victor Sawdon Pritchett)
Pudney, John
Quennell, Peter
Quiller-Couch, A. T.
(Sir Arthur Thomas Quiller-Couch,
pseud. "Q")
Raine, Kathleen
(Kathleen Jessie Raine)
Rattigan, Terence
Read, Herbert
(Sir Herbert Edward Read)
Reid, Forrest
Richards, I. A.
(Ivor Armstrong Richards)
Rickword, Edgell
Richardson, Dorothy
(Dorothy M. Richardson)
Ridler, Anne
(Anne Ridler, née Bradby)
Roberts, Michael
Robinson, Lennox
Rodgers, W. R.
(William Robert Rodgers)
Rolfe, Frederick
(Frederick William Rolfe, pseud.
Frederick, Baron Corvo)
Rosenberg, Isaac
Ross, Alan
Rowse, A. L.
(Alfred Leslie Rowse)
Royde-Smith, Naomi
(Naomi Gwladys Royde-Smith)
Russell, Bertrand
(Earl Russell)
Russell, George William
(pseud. AE)
Sackville-West, Edward
(Baron Sackville)
Sackville-West, V.
(Hon. Victoria Sackville-West)
Saintsbury, George
(George Edward Bateman
Saintsbury)

Saki
(pseud. of Hector Hugh Munro)
Sansom, William
Sassoon, Siegfried
(Siegfried Lorraine Sassoon)
Savage, D. S.
(Derek Stanley Savage)
Sayers, Dorothy
(Dorothy Leigh Sayers)
Scarfe, Francis
Shanks, Edward
Shaw, George Bernard
Sherriff, R. C.
(Robert Cedric Sherriff)
Shute, Nevil
(pseud. of Nevil Shute Norway)
Sidgwick, Ethel
Silkin, Jon
Sillitoe, Alan
Sinclair, May
Sitwell, Edith
(Dame Edith Sitwell)
Sitwell, Osbert
(Sir Osbert Sitwell, Bart.)
Sitwell, Sacheverell
Smith, Logan Pearsall
Smith, Sydney Goodsir
Smith, Stevie
(pseud. of Florence Margaret
Smith)
Snow, C. P.
(Sir Charles Percy Snow)
Sorley, Charles
(Charles Hamilton Sorley)
Spark, Muriel
Spencer, Bernard
Spender, Stephen
Squire, J. C.
(Sir John Collings Squire)
Standish, Robert
(pseud. of Digby George Gerahty)
Stanford, Derek
Stark, Freya
Stephens, James
Stern, G. B.
(Gladys Bronwyn Stern)
Strachey, Lytton
(Giles Lytton Strachey)

Strong, L. A. G.
   (Leonard Alfred George Strong)
Stuart, Francis
Sutro, Alfred
Swinnerton, Frank
   (Frank Arthur Swinnerton)
Symons, Arthur
Symons, Julian
Synge, J. M.
   (John Millington Synge)
Thirkell, Angela
   (Angela Thirkell, née Mackail)
Thomas, Dylan
Thomas, Edward
Thomas, R. S.
   (Ronald Stuart Thomas)
Thompson, Sylvia
Tiller, Terence
Todd, Ruthven
Tolkien, J. R. R.
   (John Ronald Renel Tolkien)
Tomlinson, Charles
Tomlinson, H. M.
   (Henry Major Tomlinson)
Toynbee, Philip
Treece, Henry
Trench, Herbert
Trevelyan, G. M.
   (George Macaulay Trevelyan)
Turner, James
Turner, W. J.
   (Walter James Redfern Turner)
Tynan, Katharine
   (Mrs. Katharine [Tynan] Hinkson)
Tynan, Kenneth
Ustinov, Peter
Vachell, Horace
   (Horace Annesley Vachell)
Van Druten, John
Vulliamy, C. E.
   (Colwyn Edward Vulliamy)
Wain, John
Walkley, A. B.
   (Arthur Bingham Walkley)
Wallace, Edgar
Walpole, Hugh
   (Sir Hugh Walpole)

Warner, Rex
Warner, Sylvia Townsend
Watkins, Vernon
   (Vernon Phillips Watkins)
Watson, William
   (Sir William Watson)
Waugh, Alec
Waugh, Evelyn
Webb, Mary
   (Mary Gladys Webb, née Meredith)
Wedgwood, C. V.
   (Cicely Veronica Wedgwood)
Welch, Denton
Wellesley, Dorothy
   (Dorothy Violet [Ashton] Wellesley,
   Duchess of Wellington)
Wells, H. G.
   (Herbert George Wells)
Wesker, Arnold
West, Anthony
   (Anthony Panther West)
West, Morris
   (Morris Langlo West)
West, Rebecca
   (pseud. of Cicely Isabel Fairfield)
White, T. H.
   (Terence Hanbury White)
Williams, Charles
Williams, Emlyn
Williams, Raymond
Williamson, Henry
Williamson, Hugh Ross
Wilson, Angus
Wilson, Colin
Wodehouse, P. G.
   (Pelham Grenville Wodehouse)
Wolfe, Humbert
Woodcock, George
Woodhouse, C. M.
   (Christopher Montague
   Woodhouse)
Woolf, Leonard
Woolf, Virginia
   (Virginia Woolf, née Stephen)
Yeats, William Butler
Young, Francis Brett
Young, G. M.
   (George Malcolm Young)

NOTE ON BIBLIOGRAPHIES

Our bibliographies are based principally upon the *British Museum General Catalogue of Printed Books,* supplemented by the *British National Bibliography, Whitaker's Cumulative Book List, The English Catalogue of Books, The Cumulative Book Index, The National Union* (Library of Congress) *Catalog,* and special bibliographies where available. For some authors it was possible to use *in situ* the Catalogue of the British Museum Library. As not even these standard sources are exempt from error, we cannot hope to be so.

Except in a few cases, each specified in a headnote, the editors have attempted to list all the separate publications of the authors, excluding only (1) privately printed works and those issued in very small limited editions; (2) ephemeral works such as wartime propaganda. Translations are included only when they constitute an important part of an author's work or are of important works or works rarely translated. Books edited by an author are omitted except in the few cases where an author's reputation rests largely upon his edited work. Children's books are omitted unless famous or a significant element in the author's fame.

The works of each author are listed chronologically, and the genre of each is indicated by a letter (for explanation of which see below). Date of publication given is the earliest, whether of English or American edition. Title of an American edition is noted when it differs markedly from the British title. Reprints are noted when, occurring twenty years or more after the original publication, they indicate continuing popularity or suggest (though, of course, they do not guarantee) availability.

If a published bibliography of the author exists, it is listed at the end of his works, and there, too, appears, if possible, a source of information about him: preferably a life and works study by a contemporary of his and a recent critical study, or, failing these, a composite book in which the author is treated with some thoroughness. The last will be preceded by *See.*

GENRE ABBREVIATIONS

The genre abbreviations are self-explanatory except possibly for (n) and (s). Here (n) means usually novel but broadly any sort of fiction not a short story— romance, detective story, historical novel, etc.; (s) means a single short story or more usually a collection. Numerals preceding the genre abbreviation indicate the number of plays, stories, etc., collected in that book.

a	autobiography	p	poetry
b	biography	pd	poetic drama
c	criticism	r	reminiscence
d	drama	rd	radio drama
e	essay	s	short stories
h	history	sk	sketches
m	memoir	t	travel or topography
misc.	miscellany	tr	translation
n	novel		

AUTHOR BIBLIOGRAPHIES

LASCELLES ABERCROMBIE
1881-1938

Interludes and Poems, 1908 (p); *Mary and the Bramble*, 1910 (p); *The Sale of Saint Thomas, Act I*, 1911 (pd); *Emblems of Love, Designed in Several Discourses*, 1912 (pd); *Thomas Hardy*, 1912 (c); *Speculative Dialogues*, 1913 (e); *Deborah*, 1913 (pd); *The Epic*, 1914 (c); *Poetry and Contemporary Speech*, 1914 (c); *An Essay Towards a Theory of Art*, 1922 (c); *Four Short Plays: The Adder, The Staircase, The Deserter, The End of the World*, 1922 (pd); *Phoenix*, 1923 (pd); *Communication Versus Expression in Art*, 1923 (c); *Principles of English Prosody*, 1923 (c); *The Theory of Poetry*, 1924 (c); *The Idea of Great Poetry*, 1925 (c); *Romanticism*, 1926 (c); *Twelve Idyls*, 1928 (c); *Progress in Literature*, 1929 (c); *A Plea for the Liberty of Interpreting*, 1930 (c); *The Poems of Lascelles Abercrombie*, 1930 (p); (with others) *Revaluations, Studies in Biography*, 1931 (c); *The Sale of Saint Thomas, in Six Acts*, 1931 (pd); *Poetry, Its Music and Meaning*, 1932 (c); *Principles of Literary Criticism*, 1932 (c); *Lyrics and Unfinished Poems*, 1940 (p)

See John Gawsworth, *Ten Contemporaries, Notes toward their Definitive Bibliography*, 1932

JAMES AGATE
1877-1947

Buzz, Buzz!, 1918 (e); *Responsibility*, 1919 (n); *Alarums and Excursions*, 1922 (e); *At Half-Past Eight*, 1923 (c); *Fantasies and Impromptus*, 1923 (e); *On an English Screen*, 1924 (e); *Blessed are the Rich*, 1924 (n); *White House and Red Lion*, 1924 (e); *The Contemporary Theatre, 1923 (-1925)*, 1924-27 (c); *Agate's Folly*, 1925 (r); *The Common Touch*, 1926 (e); *A Short View of the English Stage, 1900-1926*, 1926 (c); *Playgoing*, 1927 (c); *Gemel in London*, 1928 (n); *Rachel*, 1928 (b); *Their Hour upon the Stage*, 1930 (c); *My Theatre Talks*, 1933 (c); *First Nights*, 1934 (c); *Ego, 9 pts.*, 1935, 1936, 1938, 1940, 1942, 1944, 1945, 1946, 1948 (a); *Kingdom for Horses*, 1936 (e); *More First Nights*, 1937 (c); *The Amazing Theatre*, 1939 (c); *Bad Manners*, 1939 (e); *Thursdays and Fridays*, 1941 (e); *Brief Chronicles*, 1943 (e); *Red Letter Nights*, 1944 (c); *Immoment Toys* [sic], 1945 (e); *Noblesse Oblige*, 1944 (e); *The Contemporary Theatre, 1944 and 1945*, 1946 (c); *Around Cinemas*, 1946 (c); *Thus to Revisit*, 1947 (e); *Those were the Nights*, 1947 (c); *Oscar Wilde and the Theatre*, 1947 (c); *Around Cinemas, Second Series*, 1948 (c)

James Agate, ed. Herbert van Thal, with introd. by Alan Dent, 1961 [no bibliog.]

RICHARD ALDINGTON
1892-

Images, 1910-1915, 1915 (Am. ed. *Images Old and New*) (enlgd. 1919) (p); *The Love of Myrrhine and Konallis and other Prose Poems*, 1926 (p); *Reverie, a Little Book of Poems for H.D.*, 1917 (p); *Images of War*, 1919 (p); *Images of Desire*, 1919 (p); *War and Love (1915-1918)*, 1919 (p); *The Poet and His Age*, 1922 (e); *Exile*, 1923 (p); *Literary Studies and Reviews*, 1924 (c); *Voltaire*, 1925 (b); *A Fool i' the Forest, a Phantasmagoria*, 1925 (p); *French Studies and Reviews*, 1926 (c); *D. H. Lawrence; an Indiscretion*, 1927 (e); *Rémy de Gourmont*, 1928 (c); *Collected Poems*, 1928; *Hark the Herald*, 1928 (p); *The Eaten Heart*, 1929 (p); *Death of a Hero*, 1929 (n); *A War Story*, 1930 (s); *A Dream in the*

127

Luxembourg, 1930 (Am. ed. *Love and the Luxembourg*) (p); *At All Costs*, 1930 (s); *Last Straws*, 1930 (s); *Roads to Glory*, 1930 (s); *Two Stories*, 1930 (s); *Balls, and Another Book for Suppression*, 1930 (e); *Stepping Heavenward, a Record*, 1931 (s); *The Colonel's Daughter*, 1931 (n); *Soft Answers*, 1932 (s); *All Men Are Enemies*, 1933 (n); *Women Must Work*, 1934 (n); *The Poems of Richard Aldington*, 1934 (p); *Life Quest*, 1935 (e); *Artifex: Sketches and Ideas*, 1935 (e); *The Life of a Lady*, 1936 (d); *The Crystal World*, 1937 (p); *Very Heaven*, 1937 (n); *Rejected Guest*, 1939 (n); *W. Somerset Maugham: an Appreciation*, 1939 (c); *Life for Life's Sake*, 1941 (r); *The Duke* [Arthur Wellesley, 1st Duke of Wellington], 1934 (b); *The Romance of Casanova*, 1946 (n); *Complete Poems*, 1948; *Seven Against Reeves*, 1948 (h); *Four English Portraits, 1801-1851*, 1948 (b); *The Strange Life of Charles Waterton*, 1949 (b); *D. H. Lawrence, Portrait of a Genius, But . . .* , 1950 (b); *Ezra Pound and T. S. Eliot*, 1954 (c); *A. E. Housman and W. B. Yeats*, 1955 (c); *Pinorman*, 1954 (b); *Lawrence of Arabia*, 1955 (b); *Introduction to Mistral*, 1956 (c); *Frauds*, 1957 (e); *Portrait of a Rebel; the Life and Work of R. L. Stevenson*, 1957 (b)

Translations (selective list)
French Comedies of the XVIIIth Century, 1923 (d); Rostand, *Cyrano de Bergerac* and *Voyages to the Moon and the Sun*, 1923 (d); Choderlos de Laclos, *Dangerous Acquaintances*, 1924 (n); Antoine de la Sale, *The Fifteen Joys of Marriage* [ca. 1388-ca. 1462], 1926 (e); Voltaire, *Candide and Other Romances*, 1927 (n); Julien Benda, *The Great Betrayal* [*La Trahison des Clercs*] (Am. ed. *The Treason of the Intellectuals*), 1928 (e); *Fifty Romance Lyric Poems*, 1928 (p); Rémy de Gourmont, *Selections*, 1929; Euripides, *Alcestis*, 1930 (d); Boccaccio, *The Decameron*, 1930 (s); Rémy de Gourmont, *Letters to the Amazon*, 1931; Gérard de Nerval, *Aurelia*, 1932 (n)

Also other trs. from Greek, Latin, Russian, Italian

Alister Kershaw, *A Bibliography of the Works of Richard Aldington from 1915 to 1945*, 1950; *Richard Aldington: an Intimate Portrait*, ed. Alister Kershaw and F. J. Temple, 1965

WALTER ALLEN
1911-

Innocence Is Drowned, 1938 (n); *Blind Man's Ditch*, 1939 (n); *Living Space*, 1940 (n); *The Novels of Graham Greene*, 1943 (c); *Rogue Elephant*, 1946 (n); *The Black Country*, 1947 (t); *Arnold Bennett*, 1948 (c); *Festive Baked Potato Cart*, 1948 (s); *Reading a Novel*, 1949 (rev. 1956, 1963) (c); *Dead Man Over All*, 1949 (Am. ed. *Square Peg*) (n); *Joyce Cary*, 1953 (c); *The English Novel*, 1954 (h); *Six Great Novelists*, 1955 (c); *The Novel Today*, 1955 (c); *All in a Lifetime*, 1959 (Am. ed. *Three Score and Ten*) (n); *Tradition and Dream*, 1964 (Am. ed. *The Modern Novel in Britain and the United States*) (c); *George Eliot*, 1965 (b,c)

KINGSLEY AMIS
1922-

Bright November, 1947 (p); *A Frame of Mind*, 1953 (p); *Lucky Jim*, 1954 (n); *Poems*, 1954 (p); *That Uncertain Feeling*, 1955 (n); *A Case of Samples, Poems 1946-1956*, 1956 (p); *Socialism and the Intellectuals*, 1957 (e); *I Like It Here*, 1958 (n); *New Maps of Hell*, 1960 (c); *Take A Girl Like You*, 1960 (n); *My Enemy's Enemy*, 1962 (n); *One Fat Englishman*, 1963 (n); *The James Bond Dossier*, 1965 (c); (with Robert Conquest) *The Egyptologists*, 1965 (n); *The Anti-Death League*, 1966 (n)

FREDERICK ANSTEY
1856-1934

Vice-Versa, 1882 (n); *The Giant's Robe*, 1884 (n); *The Black Poodle*, 1884 (s); *The Tinted Venus*, 1885 (n); *A Fallen Idol*, 1886 (n); *Burglar Bill*, 1888 (d); *The Pariah*, 1889 (n); *Voces Populi*, 1890 (s); *Tourmalin's Time Cheques*, 1891 (n); (with Brander Matthews) *With My Friends, Tales Told in Partnership*, 1891 (s); *The Talking Horse*, 1892 (s); *Mr. Punch's Model Music-Hall Songs and Dramas*, 1892 (p,d); *The Travelling Companions*, 1892 (d); *The Man from Blankley's*, 1893 (d); *Under the Rose*, 1894 (d); *Lyre and Lancet*,

1895 (d); *The Statement of Stella Maberly*, 1896 (n); *Baboo Jabberjee, B.A.*, 1897 (n); *Puppets at Large*, 1897 (s,d); *Paleface and Redskin*, 1898 (s); *Love Among the Lions*, 1898 (n); *The Brass Bottle*, 1900 (d); *A Bayard from Bengal*, 1902 (n); *Only Toys*, 1903 (n); *Salted Almonds*, 1906 (s); *Vice Versa, A Farcical Fantastic Play*, 1910 (d); *The Brass Bottle, A Farcical Fantastic Play*, 1911 (d); *Percy*, 1915 (s,d); *In Brief Authority*, 1915 (n); *The Last Load*, 1925 (s,e); Molière, *The Would-Be Gentleman*, 1926 (tr); Molière, *The Imaginary Invalid*, 1929 (tr); *Four Molière Comedies*, 1931 (tr); *Three Molière Plays*, 1933 (tr); *A Long Retrospect*, 1936 (r)

WILLIAM ARCHER
1856-1924

English Dramatists of Today, 1882 (c); *Henry Irving, Actor and Manager*, 1883 (c); *About the Theatre*, 1886 (c); *Masks or Faces? A Study in the Psychology of Acting*, 1888 (e); *The Prose Dramas of Henrik Ibsen*, 1890 ff (tr); *William Charles Macready*, 1890 (b); *The Theatrical "World" for 1893 (-1897)*, 5 vols., 1894-98 (c); *Study and Stage: A Year-Book of Criticism*, 1899 (c); Maeterlinck, *Interior*, 1899 (d,tr); *America Today*, 1900 (e); *Poets of the Younger Generation*, 1901 (c); *Real Conversations Recorded by Archer*, 1904; *Through Afro-America: An English Reading of the Race Problem*, 1910 (e); *The Life, Trial, and Death of Francisco Ferrer*, 1911 (b); (with Walter Ripman) *Proposals for a Simplified Spelling of the English Language*, 1911 (repr. as *New Spelling*, 1940, 1948) (e); *The Great Analysis: A Plea for a Rational World Order*, 1912 (repr. 1931) (e); *Play-Making: A Manual of Craftsmanship*, 1912 (repr. 1926, 1960) (e); *God and Mr. Wells*, 1917 (c); *India and the Future*, 1917 (e); *The Peace-President* [Woodrow Wilson], 1918 (e); *The Green Goddess*, 1921 (d); *The Old Drama and the New*, 1923 (c); *William Archer as Rationalist: A Collection of his Heterodox Writings*, ed. J. M. Robertson, 1925; *Three Plays*, 1927 (d); *On Dreams*, 1935 (e); also trs. of Brandes, Hauptmann, Kielland

Charles Archer, *William Archer: Life,*

Work and Friendships, 1931; H. Schmid, *The Dramatic Criticism of William Archer*, 1964

MICHAEL ARLEN
1895-1956

The London Venture, 1920 (a); *The Romantic Lady*, 1921 (s); *Piracy*, 1922 (n); *These Charming People*, 1923 (s); *The Green Hat*, 1924 (n); *The Man with the Broken Nose*, 1927 (s); *Ghost Stories*, 1927 (s); *Young Men in Love*, 1927 (n); *The Ace of Cads*, 1927 (s); *Lily Christine*, 1928 (n); *Young Women out of Love*, 1928 (n); *The Ancient Sin*, 1930 (s); *Babes in the Wood*, 1930 (n); *Men Dislike Women*, 1931 (n); *Man's Mortality*, 1933 (n); *Short Stories*, 1933 (s); *Hell! Said the Duchess*, 1934 (n); *The Crooked Coronet*, 1937 (s)

MARTIN ARMSTRONG
1882-

Exodus, 1912 (p); *Thirty New Poems*, 1918 (p); *The Buzzards*, 1921 (p); *The Puppet Show*, 1922 (s); *The Bazaar*, 1924 (s); *The Goat and Compasses* (Am. ed. *At the Sign of the Goat and Compasses*), 1925 (n); *Desert*, 1926 (n); *Lady Hester Stanhope*, 1927 (b); *The Stepson* (Am. ed. *The Water Is Wide*), 1927 (n); *The Three-Cornered Hat of P. Alarcón*, 1927 (d,tr); *Saint Hercules*, 1927 (s); *Sir Pompey and Madame Juno*, 1927 (s); *Laughing*, 1928 (e); *Portrait of the Misses Harlowe*, 1928 (s); *Saint Christopher's Day* (Am. ed. *All in a Day*), 1928 (n); *The Bird-Catcher*, 1929 (p); *The Sleeping Fury*, 1929 (n); *The Fiery Dive*, 1929 (s); *Adrian Glynde* (Am. ed. *Blind Man's Mark*), 1930 (n); *Collected Poems*, 1931; *The Romantic Adventures of Mr. Darby and of Sarah his Wife*, 1931 (n); *Lover's Leap*, 1932 (n); *Fifty-four Conceits, A Collection of Epigrams and Epitaphs*, 1933 (p); *The Foster-Mother*, 1933 (n); *General Buntop's Miracle*, 1934 (s); *Venus Over Lannery*, 1936 (n); *Spanish Circus*, 1937 (h); *A Case of Conscience*, 1937 (s); *The Snake in the Grass*, 1938 (n); *Victorian Peep-Show*, 1938 (a); *Simplicity Jones*, 1940 (s); *The Butterfly*, 1941 (n); *George Borrow*, 1950 (b); *Selected Stories*, 1951 (s)

See R. L. Mégroz, *Five Novelist Poets of Today*, 1933; [Bristol Public Libraries] *Martin Armstrong, Poet and Novelist: a Bibliography*, 1937

W. H. AUDEN
1907-

Poems, 1930 (rev. 1932) (p); *The Orators*, 1932 (e,p); *The Dance of Death*, 1933 (p); (with Christopher Isherwood) *The Dog Beneath the Skin*, 1935 (d); (with Christopher Isherwood) *The Ascent of F 6*, 1936 (d); *Look, Stranger!* 1936 (Am. ed. *On this Island*) (p); (with Louis MacNeice) *Letter from Iceland*, 1937 (p,e); *Spain*, 1937 (p); (with Christopher Isherwood) *On the Frontier*, 1938 (d); *Selected Poems*, 1938 (p); *Ballad of Heroes* (words for Benjamin Britten's music), 1939; (with Christopher Isherwood) *Journey to a War*, 1939 (p,t); *Some Poems*, 1940 (p); *Another Time*, 1940 (p); **New Year Letter* (Am. ed. *The Double Man*), 1941 (p); *Hymn to St. Cecilia* (words for Benjamin Britten's music), 1942; *For the Time Being* (incl. *The Sea and the Mirror*), 1945 (p); *Collected Poems*, Am. ed., 1945; *The Dyer's Hand*, 1948 (rev. 1962) (coll. e); *The Age of Anxiety*, 1948 (p); *Collected Shorter Poems, 1930-44*, 1950; *The Enchafed Flood*, 1951 (c); (with Chester Kallman) *The Rake's Progress* (libretto for Igor Stravinsky's opera), 1951; *Nones*, 1951 (p); (with Chester Kallman) *Delia* (libretto for a one-act opera), 1953; *Mountains*, 1954 (p); *The Shield of Achilles*, 1955 (p); *The Old Man's Road*, 1956 (p); *Making, Knowing and Judging* (inaugural lecture as Prof. of Poetry at Oxford Univ.), 1956; (with Chester Kallman) English version of J E. Schikaneider, *The Magic Flute* (libretto), 1957; *Selected Poetry*, 1958 (p); *Daniel* (verse narrative for the 13th c. play), 1958; *W. H. Auden: A Selection by the Author*, 1958 (p); *Homage to Clio*, 1960 (p,c); *Five Poems for Music* (of Lennox Berkeley), 1960; *Elegy for Young Lovers* (libretto for opera of Hans Henze), 1961; Goethe, *Italian Journey, 1786-88*, 1962 (tr. with Elizabeth Mayer); *Louis MacNeice*, 1963 (e,r); Brecht, *The Caucasian Chalk Circle*, 1963 (tr. with others); *Selected Essays* (repr. from *The Dyer's Hand*, 1962), 1964 (e); *About the House*, 1965 (p)

*repr. 1965

Monroe K. Spears, *The Poetry of Auden*, 1964; B. C. Bloomfield, with foreword by Auden, *W. H. Auden: a Bibliography. The Early Years Through 1955*, 1965

NIGEL BALCHIN
1908-

How to Run a Bassoon Factory, 1934 (e); *No Sky*, 1934 (n); *Business for Pleasure*, 1935 (e); *Simple Life*, 1935 (n); *The Small Back Room*, 1943 (n); *Mine Own Executioner*, 1945 (n); *Lord, I Was Afraid*, 1947 (n); *The Borgia Testament*, 1948 (n); *A Sort of Traitors*, 1949 (Am. ed. *Who Is My Neighbor*, 1950) (n); *The Anatomy of Villainy*, 1950 (e); *A Way Through the Wood*, 1951 (n); *The Fall of the Sparrow*, 1955 (n); *Last Recollections of My Uncle Charles*, 1955 (n); *Seen Dimly Before Dawn*, 1962 (n); *In the Absence of Mrs. Petersen*, 1966 (n)

MAURICE BARING
1874-1945

(by M.B.) *Pastels and Other Rhymes*, 1891 (p); (by M.B.) *Northcourt Nonsense, Triolets*, 1893 (p); (by M.B.) *Triolets, Second Series*, 1893 (p); *Hildesheim, Quatre Pastiches*, 1899 (e); *The Black Prince*, 1903 (p); *Gaston de Foix*, 1903 (d); (by M.B.) *Poems*, 1905 (p); *With the Russians in Manchuria*, 1905 (e); *Sonnets and Short Poems*, 1906 (p); *Desiderio*, 1906 (pd); *A Year in Russia*, 1907 (t); *Russian Essays and Stories*, (1908) (misc.); *Prosperpina, a Masque*, 1908 (p); *Orpheus in Mayfair*, 1909 (s); *Dead Letters, 1910* (e); *The Glass Mender* (Am. ed. *The Blue Rose Fairy Book*), 1910 (s); *Landmarks in Russian Literature*, 1910 (c); *Collected Poems of Maurice Baring*, 1911; *Diminutive Dramas*, 1911 (d); *The Grey Stocking*, 1911 (d); *The Russian People*, 1911 (e); *Letters from the Near East, 1909 and 1912*, 1913; *Lost Diaries*, 1913 (e); *Palamon and Arcite, a Play for Puppets*, 1913 (d); *The Mainsprings of Russia*, 1914 (e); *An Outline of Russian Literature*, 1914 (h); *Poems, 1914-1917*, 1918 (p); *Round the World in Any Number of Days*, 1919 (t); *Poems, 1914-1919*, 1920 (p); *R.F.C., H.Q., 1914-1918*, 1920 (m); *Manfroy*, 1920 (d); *Passing By*, 1921 (n); *A Place of Peace, "Somewhere* in London," 1922 (e); *The Puppet Show of Memory*, 1922 (a); *Overlooked*, 1922 (n); *His Majesty's Embassy*, 1923 (d); *A Triangle, Passages from Three Notebooks*, 1923 (n); *Punch and Judy*, 1924 (e); *C*, 1924 (n); *Collected Poems*, 1925; *Cat's Cradle*, 1925 (n); *Half a Minute's Silence*, 1925 (s); *Daphne Adeane*, 1926 (n); *Tinker's Leave*, 1927 (n); *When They Love*, 1928 (n); *Comfortless Memory*, 1928 (n,a); *Poems, 1892-1929*, 1929 (p); *The Coat Without Seam*, 1929 (n); *Selected Poems*, 1930 (p); *Robert Peckham*, 1930 (n); *In My End Is My Beginning*, 1931 (e); *Lost Lectures, or, The Fruits of Experience*, 1932 (e); *Friday's Business*, 1932 (n); *Sarah Bernhardt*, 1933 (c); *Unreliable History*, 1934 (misc.); *The Lonely Lady of Dulwich*, 1934 (n); *Darby and Joan*, 1935 (n); *Have You Anything to Declare?* 1937 (c); *Russian Lyrics*, 1943 (tr)

Leslie Chaundy. *A Bibliography of the First Editions of Maurice Baring* (with poems by M.B. and an introductory note on M.B. by Desmond MacCarthy), 1925; Laura Lovat, *Maurice Baring: a Postscript with some Letters and Verse*, 1947 [no bibliog.]

GEORGE BARKER
1913-

Alanna Autumnal, 1933 (p); *Thirty Preliminary Poems*, 1933 (p); *Janus*, 1935 (s); *Poems*, 1935 (p); *Calamiterror*, 1937 (p); *Lament and Triumph*, 1940 (p); *Selected Poems*, 1941 (p); *Sacred and Secular Elegies*, 1943 (p); *Eros in Dogma*, 1944 (p); *Love Poems*, 1947 (p); **The Dead Seagull*, 1950 (n); *News of the World*, 1950 (p); *The True Confession of George Barker*, 1950 (p,a); *A Vision of Beasts and Gods*, 1954 (p); *Collected Poems, 1930-1955*, 1957 (p); *Two Plays*, 1958 (d); *The View from a Blind I*, 1962 (p); *The True Confession of George Barker* (repr. Bk. I with Bk. II), 1965 (a); *Dreams of a Summer Night*, 1966 (p)

*repr. 1965

J. M. BARRIE
1860-1937

Selective Bibliography

Note. Barrie's lectures are omitted, as are the numerous selected editions and

recent reprints of the plays. Some of the principal collected editions are: *The Novels, Tales and Sketches of J. M. Barrie*, 12 vols., 1896-1911; *The Plays of J. M. Barrie* (Uniform Ed.), 11 vols., 1918-1929; *The Works of J. M. Barrie* (Uniform Ed.), 1925-; *The Plays of J. M. Barrie in One Volume*, 1928.

Better Dead, 1887 (n); *Auld Licht Idylls*, 1888 (s); *When a Man's Single*, 1888 (s); *An Edinburgh Eleven, Pencil Portraits from College Life*, 1889 (sk); *A Window in Thrums*, 1889 (s); *My Lady Nicotine*, 1890 (e); *The Little Minister*, 1891 (n); (with H. B. Marriot Watson) *Richard Savage*, 1891 (d); *A Holiday in Bed*, 1892 (sk); (with A. Conan Doyle) *Jane Annie*, 1893 (d); *A Powerful Drug*, 1893 (s); *A Tillyloss Scandal*, 1893 (s); *Two of Them*, 1893 (s); *An Auld Licht Manse*, 1893 (sk); *Life in a Country Manse*, 1894 (s); *Scotland's Lament, a Poem on the Death of R. L. Stevenson*, 1895 (p); *Margaret Ogilvie*, 1896 (b); *Sentimental Tommy*, 1896 (n); *Jess*, 1898 (s); *Tommy and Grizel* (seq. to *Sentimental Tommy*), 1900 (n); *The Wedding Guest*, 1900 (d); *Quality Street*, 1901 (d); *The Little White Bird*, 1902 (child's bk.); *Peter Pan*, produced 1905 (d); *Peter Pan in Kensington Gardens* (from *The Little White Bird*), 1906 (child's bk.); *Walker, London*, 1907 (d); *George Meredith*, 1909 (also pub. as *Neither Dorking Nor the Abbey*, 1911) (c); *Peter and Wendy* (seq. to *Peter Pan*), 1911 (child's bk.); *The Admirable Crichton*, 1914 (d); *Der Tag*, 1914 (d); *Half-Hours*, 1914 (4d); *Charles Frohman*, 1915 (e); *Shakespeare's Legacy*, 1916 (d); *Who Was Sarah Findlay? by Mark Twain, with a Suggested Solution of the Mystery by J. M. Barrie*, 1917 (e); *Echoes of the War*, 1918 (4d); *What Every Woman Knows*, 1918 (d); *Alice-Sit-by-the-Fire*, 1919 (d); *A Kiss for Cinderella*, 1920 (d); *Dear Brutus*, 1922 (d); *Mary Rose*, 1924 (d); *Peter Pan, or, The Boy Who Would Not Grow Up* (dram. of *The Little White Bird*), 1928 (d); *Shall We Join the Ladies*, 1928 (d); *The Entrancing Life*, 1930 (address on installation as Chancellor of Edinburgh Univ.); *Farewell, Miss Julie Logan: a Wintry Tale*, 1931 (s)

Bradley Dwyane Cutler, *Sir James M. Barrie: a Bibliography*, 1931; Roger Lancelyn Green, *J. M. Barrie*, 1961

H. E. BATES
1905-

The Two Sisters, 1926 (n); The Last Bread, 1926 (d); Day's End, 1928 (s); Seven Tales and Alexander, 1929 (s); Catherine Foster, 1929 (n); The Hessian Prisoner, 1930 (s); Charlotte's Row, 1931 (n); The Black Boxer, 1932 (s); The Fallow Land, 1932 (n); A German Idyll, 1932 (s); The House with the Apricot, 1933 (s); Thirty Tales, 1934 (s); The Woman Who Had Imagination, 1934 (s); Cut and Come Again, 1935 (s); Flowers and Faces, 1935 (e); The Poacher, 1935 (n); Through the Woods, 1936 (e); A House of Women, 1936 (n); Down the River, 1937 (e); Something Short and Sweet, 1937 (s); Spella Ho, 1938 (n); Country Tales, 1938 (s); The Flying Goat, 1939 (s); My Uncle Silas, 1939 (s); The Beauty of the Dead, 1940 (s); Country Tales, 1940 (s); The Modern Short Story, 1941 (c); (by "Flying Officer X") The Greatest People in the World, 1942 (s); The Heart of the Country, 1942 (e); (by "Flying Officer X") How Sleep the Brave, 1943 (s); (by "Flying Officer X") The Bride Comes to Evensford, 1943 (s); O! More Than Happy Countryman, 1943 (e); Fair Stood the Wind for France, 1944 (n); The Day of Glory, 1945 (d); The Cruise of the Breadwinner, 1946 (n); The Purple Plain, 1947 (n); Thirty-One Selected Tales, 1947 (s); The Jacaranda Tree, 1948 (n); The Country Heart (rev. of O! More Than Happy Countryman and The Heart of the Country), 1949 (e); Dear Life, 1949 (s); The Scarlet Sword, 1950 (n); Edward Garnett, 1950 (m); Colonel Julian, 1951 (s); Twenty Tales, 1951 (s); Selected Short Stories, 1951 (s); The Country of White Clover, 1952 (e); The Face of England, 1952 (e); Love for Lydia, 1952 (n); The Stories of Flying Officer "X," 1952 (s); The Nature of Love, 1953 (3n); The Feast of July, 1954 (n); The Daffodil Sky, 1955 (s); The Sleepless Moon, 1956 (n); Selected Stories, 1957 (s); Death of a Huntsman (Am. ed. Summer in Salandar), 1957 (4n); Sugar for the Horse, 1957 (s); The Darling Buds of May, 1958 (n); A Breath of French Air, 1959 (n); The Watercress Girl, 1959 (s); An Aspidistra in Babylon (Am. ed. Grapes of Pain), 1960 (n); When the Green Woods Laugh (Am. ed. Hark, Hark, the Lark!), 1960 (n); The Day of the Tortoise, 1961 (n); The Nature of Love, 1961 (4n); Now Sleeps the Crimson Petal (Am. ed. The Enchantress), 1961 (n); A Crown of Wild Myrtle, 1962 (n); The Golden Oriole, 1962 (5n); Oh! To Be in England, 1963 (n); A Moment in Time, 1964 (n); The Fabulous Mrs. V., 1964 (s); The Wedding Party, 1965 (s); The Four Beauties, 1966 (4s)

See: John Gawsworth, Ten Contemporaries: Notes Toward Their Definitive Bibliography, Sec. Series, 1933

RALPH BATES
1899-

Franz Schubert, 1934 (b); Lean Men, 1935 (n); The Olive Field, 1936 (n); Rainbow Fish, 1937 (4n); Sirocco, 1939 (s); The Miraculous Horde, 1939 (s); The Fields of Paradise, 1940 (n); The Undiscoverables, 1942 (s); The Dolphin in the Wood, 1950 (n)

F. W. BATESON
1901-

English Comic Drama, 1700-1750, 1929 (c); English Poetry and the English Language, 1934 (c); Editor of Cambridge Bibliography of English Literature, 5 vols., 1940; *English Poetry: A Critical Introduction, 1950 (c); Wordsworth: A Re-interpretation, 1954 (c); A Guide to English Literature, 1965 (c)

*Sec. ed. 1966

CLIFFORD BAX
1886-1962

Poems Dramatic and Lyrical, 1911 (p); The Rose and the Cross, 1918 (d); Square Pegs, 1920 (d); A House of Words, 1920 (p); (with Harold F. Rubenstein) Shakespeare, 1921 (d); The Cloak, 1921 (d); Antique Pageantry, 1921 (pd); Old King Cole, 1921 (d); The Traveller's Tale, 1921 (p); Polite Satires, 1922 (d); Up Stream, 1922 (d); Prelude and Fugue, 1923 (d); Nature in Palermo, 1924 (d); Studio Plays, 1924 (d); Inland Far, 1925 (r); Mr. Pepys: a Ballad-Opera, 1926 (d); Many a Green Isle, 1927 (s); Bianca Capello, 1927 (b); Socrates, 1930 (d); April in August, 1931 (d); The Immortal Lady, 1931 (d); Valiant Ladies, 1931 (3d); Farewell My Muse, 1932 (p);

Leonardo da Vinci, 1932 (b); *Pretty Witty Nell*, 1932 (b); *Twelve Short Plays*, 1932 (d); *That Immortal Sea*, 1933 (e); *The Quaker's Cello*, 1933 (d); *Tragic Nesta*, 1934 (d); *Ideas and People*, 1936 (r); *The Life of the White Devil*, 1940 (b); *Evenings in Albany*, 1942 (r); *Time with a Gift of Tears*, 1943 (n); *Whither the Theatre*, 1945 (e); *All the World's a Stage*, 1946 (b); *The Golden Eagle*, 1946 (d); *The Play of St. Lawrence*, 1947 (d); *Rosemary for Remembrance*, 1948 (a); *Circe*, 1949 (d); *Some I Knew Well*, 1951 (r)

SAMUEL BECKETT
1906-

Whoroscope, 1930 (p);* *Proust*, 1931 (c); *More Pricks than Kicks*, 1934 (s); *Echo's Bones and Other Precipitates*, 1935 (p); **Murphy*, 1938 (Fr. tr. by Beckett, 1947) (n); *Molloy*, 1951 (Eng. tr. by Patrick Bowles and Beckett, 1955) (n); *Malone Meurt*, 1951 (tr. by Beckett as *Malone Dies*, 1956) (n); *L'Innomable*, 1953 (tr. by Beckett as *The Unnamable*, 1958) (n) [the foregoing three novels written in French compose a trilogy]; *En Attendant Godot*, 1952 (tr. by Beckett as *Waiting for Godot*, 1954) (d); *Watt*, 1953 (n); *Nouvelles et Textes pour Rien*, 1955 (s,e); Jean Wahl, *Illustrations for the Bible by Marc Chagall*, 1956 (tr. by Beckett and Jean Wahl); *All That Fall*, 1957 (rd); *Fin de Partie*, suivi de *Acte sans Paroles*, 1957 (tr. by Beckett as *Endgame* and *Act without Words*, 1958) (d); *From an Abandoned Work*, 1958 (e); *Embers*, 1959 (rd); *Krapp's Last Tape*, 1960 (d); (with Olive Classe) *Bram van Velde* by J. Putnam, 1960 (tr); *Happy Days*, 1961 (tr. by Beckett as *Oh! les Beaux Jours*, 1963) (d); *Poems in English*, 1961 (p); *Comment c'est*, 1961 (tr by Beckett as *How It Is*, 1961) (n); (with others) *Selected Poems of Alain Bosquet*, 1963 (tr); *Play and Two Short Pieces for Radio* [incl. *Words and Music, Cascanda*], 1965 (d); *Poems in English* (incl. *Whoroscope*, repr., and 4 lyrics in English and French), 1965 (p); *Imagination Dead Imagine*, 1966 (n)

*repr. with *Three Dialogues with Georges Duthuit* [on modern painting], 1965
**repr. 1957.

John Fletcher, *The Novels of Samuel Beckett*, 1964; Raymond Federman, *Journey to Chaos, Samuel Beckett's Early Fiction* [incl. sel. crit. bibliog.], 1966; Josephine Jacobsen and William R. Mueller, *The Testament of Samuel Beckett*, 1966

SYBILLE BEDFORD
1911-

The Sudden View: A Mexican Journey, 1953 (also pub. as *A Visit to Don Otavio*, 1960) (t); *A Legacy*, 1956 (n); *The Best We Can Do*, 1958 (Am. ed. *The Trial of Dr. John Bodkin Adams*) (e); *The Faces of Justice*, 1961 (e); *A Favourite of the Gods*, 1963 (n)

MAX BEERBOHM
1872-1956

The Works of Max Beerbohm, 1896 (e); *The Happy Hypocrite*, 1897 (s); *More*, 1899 (e); *Yet Again*, 1909 (e); *Zuleika Dobson*, 1911 (n); *A Christmas Garland*, 1912 (enlgd. 1950) (e); *A note on "Patience,"* 1919 (c); *Seven Men*, 1919 (enlgd. 1950) (s); *And Even Now*, 1920 (e); *A Defence of Cosmetics*, 1922 (e); *A Peep Into the Past*, 1923 (e); *Around Theatres*, 1924 ([Theatre reviews 1898-1910] repr. 1953) (c); *The Guerdon*, 1925 (m); *Leaves From the Garland*, 1926 (m); *A Variety of Things*, 1928 (rept. abgd. 1953) (misc.); *The Dreadful Dragon of Hay Hill*, 1928 (s); *Lytton Strachey*, 1943 (c); *Mainly on the Air*, 1946 (enlgd. 1957) (radio talks), *Selected Essays*, 1958 (e); *Max Beerbohm's Letters to Reggie Turner*, ed. Rupert Hart-Davis, 1964; *Max in Verse: Rhymes and Parodies*, ed. J. G. Riewald, 1964 (p)

A. E. Gallatin and L. M. Oliver, *A Bibliography of the Works of Max Beerbohm*, 1952; David Cecil, *Max: A Biography*, 1964

BRENDAN BEHAN
1922-1964

The Quare Fellow, 1954 (d); *The Hostage*, 1958 (productions in Gaelic and in English) (d); *Borstal Boy*, 1958 (a); *Brendan Behan's Ireland*, 1961 (e); *Island: an Irish Sketch-book*, 1962 (t); *Hold Your Hour and Have Another*,

1963 (e); *The Scarperer*, 1964 (n); (with Paul Hogarth) *Brendan Behan's New York*, 1964 (t); *Confessions of an Irish Rebel* [seq. to *Borstal Boy*], 1964 (a); *Brendan Behan's Island*: an *Irish Sketch-book* (d r a w i n g s by Paul Hogarth), 1966 (t)

Dominic Behan, *My Brother Brendan*, 1965

CLIVE BELL
1881-

Art, 1914 (e); *Pot-Boilers*, 1918 (c); *Poems*, 1921 (p); *Since Cezanne*, 1922 (c); *The Legend of Monte della Sibilla*, 1923 (p) ; *Landmarks in Nineteenth-Century Painting*, 1927 (c); *Civilization*, 1928 (e); *Proust*, 1928 (c); *An Account of French Painting*, 1931 (h); *Enjoying Pictures, Meditations in the National Gallery and Elsewhere*, 1934 (c); *Old Friends*, 1956 (r)

HILAIRE BELLOC
1870-1953

Verses and Sonnets, 1896 (p); *The Bad Child's Book of Beasts*, 1896 (p); (H.B.) *More Beasts for Worse Children*, 1897 (p); (H.B.) *A Moral Alphabet*, 1899 (p); *Danton, a Study*, 1899 (b); *Robespierre, a Study*, 1901 (b); *Emmanuel Burden*, 1904 (n); *The Path to Rome*, 1902 (t); *The Aftermath, or, Gleanings from a Busy Life*, 1903 (c); *The Romance of Tristan and Iseult*, retold by J. Bédier, 1903 (tr); *The Old Road*, 1904 (t); *Avril, Essays on the Poetry of the French Renaissance*, 1904 (c); *Esto Perpetua, Algerian Studies and Impressions*, 1906 (t); *Hills and the Sea*, 1906 (t); *An Open Letter on the Decay of Faith*, 1906 (e); *The Historic Thames*, 1907 (h); *On Nothing and Kindred Subjects*, 1908 (e); *The Eye-Witness*, 1908 (h); *Mr. Clutterbuck's Election*, 1908 (n); *Cautionary Tales for Children*, 1908 (p); *The Pyrenees*, 1909 (t); *On Everything*, 1909 (e); *This and That and the Other*, 1909 (e); *Marie Antoinette*, 1909 (b); *A Change in the Cabinet*, 1909 (n); *On Anything*, 1910 (e); *On Something*, 1910 (e); *Verses*, 1910 (p); *Pongo and the Bull*, 1910 (n); *First and Last*, 1911 (e); *The French Revolution*, 1911 (h); *More Peers*, 1911 (p); *The Girondin*, 1911 (n); *The Four Men*, 1912 (t); *The River of*

London, 1912 (t); *Warfare in England*, 1912 (h); *The Green Overcoat*, 1912 (n); *The Book of the Bayeux Tapestry*, 1914 (e); *High Lights of the French Revolution*, 1915 (h); *A General Sketch of the European War* (also under title, *The Elements of the Great War*), 2 vols., 1915, 1916 (h); *At the Sign of the Lion*, 1916 (e); *The Last Days of the French Monarchy*, 1916 (h); *The Second Year of the War*, 1916 (h); *The Free Press*, 1918 (e); *Europe and the Faith*, 1920 (h); *The House of Commons and Monarchy*, 1920 (h); *The Mercy of Allah*, 1922 (n); *The Contrast*, 1923 (e); *On*, 1923 (e); *The Road*, 1923 (e); *Sonnets and Verse*, 1923 (p); *The Campaign of 1812 and the Retreat from Moscow*, 1924 (h); *The Cruise of the "Nona,"* 1925 (r); *Mr. Petre*, 1925 (n); *Miniatures of French History*, 1925 (h); *A History of England*, 4 vols., 1925, 1927, 1928, 1931; *The Catholic Church and History*, 1926 (e); *Short Talks with the Dead and Others*, 1926 (e); *The Emerald of Catherine the Great*, 1926 (n); *The Emerged*, 1926 (n); *The Haunted House*, 1927 (n); *Many Cities* (Am. ed. *Towns of Destiny*), 1928 (t); *A Conversation with an Angel*, 1928 (e); *How the Reformation Happened*, 1928 (h); *James the Second*, 1928 (b); *The Chanty of the "Nona,"* 1928 (p); *Belinda, a Tale of Affection in Youth and Age*, 1928 (n); *But Soft—We are Observed!* (Am. ed. *Shadowed!*), 1928 (n); *Survivals and New Arrivals*, 1929 (e); *Wandering*, 1929 (e); *Joan of Arc*, 1929 (b); *Richelieu, a Study*, 1929 (b); *The Missing Masterpiece*, 1929 (n); *Wolsey*, 1930 (b); *The Man Who Made Gold*, 1930 (n); *New Cautionary Tales*, 1930 (p); *Six British Battles*, 1931 (h); *A Conversation with a Cat and Others*, 1931 (e); *Essays of a Catholic Layman in England* (Am. ed. *Essays of a Catholic*), 1931 (e); *On Translation*, 1931 (e); *Cranmer*, 1931 (b); *Napoleon*, 1932 (b); *An Heroic Poem in Praise of Wine*, 1932 (p); *Ladies and Gentlemen, for Adults Only, and Mature at That, Verses*, 1932 (p); *The Postmaster-general*, 1932 (n); *Charles the First, King of England*, 1933 (b); *William the Conqueror*, 1933 (h); *The Tactics and Strategy of the Great Duke of Marlborough*, 1933 (h); *A Shorter History of England*, 1934 (h); *Cromwell*, 1934 (b); *Milton*, 1935 (b);

Characters of the Reformation, 1936 (b); *The County of Sussex*, 1936 (h); *The Hedge and the Horse*, 1936 (n); *The Crisis of Our Civilization*, 1937 (h); *The Crusade*, 1937 (h); *An Essay on the Nature of Contemporary England*, 1937 (e); *Sonnets and Verse* (enl.), 1938 (p); *The Great Heresies*, 1938 (h); *Monarchy, a Study of Louis XIV*, 1938 (h); *Return to the Baltic*, 1938 (t); *On Sailing the Sea*, 1939 (misc.); *The Last Rally: a Study of Charles II*, 1940 (b); *The Silence of the Sea*, 1940 (e); *On the Place of Gilbert Chesterton in English Letters*, 1940 (c); *Places*, 1942 (e); *Elizabethan Commentary*, 1942 (h); *Selected Essays*, ed. J. B. Morton, 1948 (e); *An Anthology of Prose and Verse*, ed. W. N. Roughead, 1951; *Verse*, ed. W. N. Roughead, 1954

Patrick Cahill, *The English First Editions of Hilaire Belloc*, 1953; Robert Speaight, *The Life of Belloc*, 1957

ARNOLD BENNETT
1867-1931

A Man from the North, 1898 (n); *Polite Farces for the Drawing Room*, 1900 (d); *Fame and Fiction*, 1901 (c); *Anna of the Five Towns*, 1902 (n); *The Grand Babylon Hotel*, 1902 (n); *Leonora*, 1903 (n); *The Gates of Wrath, a Melodrama*, 1903 (n); (anon.) *The Truth About an Author*, 1903 (a); *A Great Man: a Frolic*, 1904 (n); *Teresa of Watling Street*, 1904 (n); *The Loot of Cities*, 1905 (n); *Tales of the Five Towns*, 1905 (s); *Sacred and Profane Love*, 1905 (rev. ed. *The Book of Carlotta*, 1911) (n); *Things That Have Interested Me*, 1906, 1907, 1921, 1923, 1925 (r); *Whom God Hath Joined*, 1906 (n); (with Eden Phillpotts) *The Sinews of War*, 1906 (n); *The City of Pleasure*, 1907 (n); *The Ghost*, 1907 (n); *The Grim Smile of the Five Towns*, 1907 (s); *The Reasonable Life, Being Hints for Men and Women*, 1907 (e); *Buried Alive*, 1908 (n); *The Old Wives' Tale*, 1908 (n); (with Eden Phillpotts) *The Statue*, 1908 (n); *The Glimpse*, 1909 (n); *Cupid and Commonsense* (dramatization of *Anna of the Five Towns*), 1909 (d); *What the Public Wants*, 1909 (d); *Literary Taste, How to Form It, with Detailed Instructions for Collecting a Com-*

plete *Library of English Literature*, 1909 (e); *Clayhanger* (trilogy: Vol. I), 1910 (n); *Helen with the High Hand*, 1910 (dramatized version, 1914) (n); *The Card* (Am. ed. *Denry the Audacious*), 1911 (n); *The Honeymoon*, 1911 (d); *Hilda Lessways* (trilogy: Vol. II), 1911 (n); (with Edward Knoblock) *Milestones*, 1912 (d); *The Matador of the Five Towns*, 1912 (s); *Those United States* (Am. ed. *Your United States*), 1912 (t); *The Great Adventure* (dramatization of *Buried Alive*), 1913 (d); *The Old Adam* (sequel to *The Card*), 1913 (n); *The Regent*, 1913 (n); *Paris Nights*, 1913 (t); *The Author's Craft*, 1913 (c); *The Price of Love*, 1914 (n); *These Twain* (trilogy: Vol. III), 1915 (n); *The Lion's Share*, 1916 (n); *Books and Persons, 1908-1911*, 1917 (c,r); *The Pretty Lady*, 1918 (n); *The Roll-Call*, 1918 (n); *The Title*, 1918 (d); *Judith*, 1919 (d); *Sacred and Profane Love* (from the novel), 1919 (d); *Frank Swinnerton*, 1920 (r); *Body and Soul*, 1921 (d); *Lilian*, 1922 (n); *Mr. Prohack*, 1922 (n); *The Love Match*, 1922 (d); *Riceyman Steps*, 1923 (n); *Don Juan de Marana*, 1923 (d); *How To Make the Best of Life*, 1923 (e); *Elsie and the Child*, 1924 (s); *The Bright Island*, 1924 (d); (with Edward Knoblock) *London Life*, 1924 (d); *Lord Raingo*, 1926 (n); *The Woman Who Stole Everything*, 1927 (s); (with Edward Knoblock) *Mr. Prohack* (from the novel), 1927 (d); *Accident*, 1928 (n); *The Strange Vanguard*, 1928 (n); *The Savour of Life*, 1928 (e); *Mediterranean Scenes*, 1928 (t); *Imperial Palace*, 1930 (n); *Journal*, 1929 (Am. ed. *Journal of Things New and Old*), 1930; *The Night Visitor*, 1931 (s); *Venus Rising from the Sea*, 1931 (n); *Dream of Destiny, an Unfinished Novel* and *Venus Rising from the Sea* (Am. ed. *Stroke of Luck* and *Dream of Destiny*), 1932 (n); *The Journals of Arnold Bennett*, ed. Newman Flower, 3 vols., 1932-33; ([Selection], ed. Frank Swinnerton, 1954); *170 Letters to Dorothy Cheston*, 1935; *Letters to his Nephew*, ed. Richard Bennett 1936; *Arnold Bennett and H. G. Wells: A Record of a Personal and a Literary Friendship*, ed. Harris Wilson, 1960 (letters); *Letters of Arnold Bennett*, Vol. I, *Letters to J. B. Pinker*, ed. James Hepburn, 1966

Georges Lafourcade, *Arnold Bennett*, 1939; James G. Hepburn, *The Art of Arnold Bennett*, 1965

E. F. BENSON
1867-1940

Dodo, 1893 (n); *The Rubicon*, 1894 (n); *Mammon and Co.*, 1899 (n); *The Relentless City*, 1903 (n); *Account Rendered*, 1911 (n); *David Blaize*, 1916 (n); *Queen Lucia*, 1920 (n); *Colin*, 1923 (n); *Paying Guests*, 1929 (n); *Life of Alcibiades*, 1929 (b); *Ferdinand Magellan*, 1930 (b); *As We Were*, 1930 (r); *Charlotte Brontë*, 1932 (b); *As We Are*, 1932 (r); *Raven's Brood*, 1934 (n); *Queen Victoria*, 1935 (b); *Queen Victoria's Daughters*, 1938 (b); *The Trouble for Lucia*, 1939 (n); *Final Edition*, 1940 (a)

STELLA BENSON
1892-1933

I Pose, 1915 (n); *This is the End*, 1917 (n); *Twenty*, 1918 (p); *Living Alone*, 1919 (n); *The Poor Man*, 1922 (n); *Kwan-Yin*, 1922 (d); *Pipers and a Dancer*, 1924 (n); *The Little World*, 1925 (t); *The Awakening, a Fantasy*, 1925 (s); *Goodbye, Stranger*, 1926 (n); *Worlds Within Worlds*, 1928 (t); *The Man Who Missed the Bus*, 1928 (s); *Tobit Transplanted* (Am. ed. *The Far-Away Bride*), 1931 (n); *Hope Against Hope*, 1931 (s); *Christmas Formula*, 1932 (s); *Pull Devil, Pull Baker*, 1933 (b); *Mundos*, 1935 (n unf.); *Poems*, 1935 (p); *Collected Short Stories*, 1936

See: John Gawsworth, *Ten Contemporaries*, Sec. Series, 1933

PHYLLIS BENTLEY
1894-

Pedagogomania, or, The Gentle Art of Teaching, 1918 (e); *The World's Bane*, 1918 (s); *Environment*, 1922 (n); *Cat-in-the-Manger*, 1923 (n); *The Partnership*, 1928 (n); *The Spinner of the Years*, 1928 (n); *Carr*, 1929 (n); *Sounding Brass*, 1930 (d); *Trio*, 1930 (n); *Inheritance*, 1932 (n); *A Modern Tragedy*, 1934 (n); *The Whole of the Story*, 1935 (s); *Freedom Farewell*, 1936 (n); *Sleep in Peace*, 1938 (n); *The Power and the Glory* (Eng. ed. *Take Courage*), 1940 (n); *The English Regional Novel*, 1941 (c). *Here is*

America, 1941 (t); *Manhold*, 1941 (n); *The Rise of Henry Morcar*, 1946 (n); *The Brontës*, 1947 (b); *Life Story*, 1948 (n); *The Brontë Sisters*, 1950 (b); *Quorum*, 1950 (n); *Panorama*, 1952 (s); *The House of Moreys*, 1953 (n); *Noble in Reason*, 1955 (n); *Love and Money*, 1957 (s); *Crescendo*, 1958 (n); *The New Apprentice*, 1959 (d); *Kith and Kin*, 1960 (s); *The Young Brontës*, 1960 (b); *O Dreams, O Destinations*, 1962 (a); *Enjoy Books: Reading and Collecting*, 1964 (e); *Public Speaking*, 1964 (e); *Tales of the West Riding*, 1965 (s); *A Man of His Times* (3d of trilogy, incl. *Inheritance* and *The Rise of Henry Morcar*), 1966 (n)

J. D. BERESFORD
1873-1947

Jacob Stahl trilogy: Vol. I, *The Early History of Jacob Stahl*, 1911 (n); *The Hampdenshire Wonder*, 1911 (n); Stahl trilogy: Vol. II, *A Candidate for Truth*, 1912 (n); *Goslings* (Am. ed. *A World of Women*), 1913 (n); *The House in Demetrius Road*, 1914 (n); *H. G. Wells*, 1915 (c); Stahl trilogy: Vol. III, *The Invisible Event*, 1915 (n); *The Mountains of the Moon*, 1915 (n); *These Lynnekers*, 1916 (n); *Housemates*, 1917 (n); (with Kenneth Richmond) *W. E. Ford*, 1917 (b); *The Wonder*, 1917 (n); *God's Counterpoint*, 1918 (n); *Nineteen Impressions*, 1918 (s); *Jervaise Comedy*, 1919 (n); *An Imperfect Mother*, 1920 (n); *Revolution*, 1921 (n); *Signs and Wonders*, 1921 (n); *The Prisoners of Hartling*, 1922 (n); *Taken from Life*, 1922 (misc.); *Love's Pilgrim*, 1923 (n); *The Imperturbable Duchess*, 1923 (s); *Unity*, 1924 (n); *The Monkey-Puzzle*, 1925 (n); *That Kind of Man* (Am. ed. *Almost Pagan*), 1926 (n); *The Tapestry*, 1927 (n); *The Decoy*, 1927 (n); *All or Nothing*, 1928 (n); *Writing Aloud*, 1928 (e); *The Instrument of Destiny, a Detective Story*, 1928 (n); *Real People*, 1929 (n); *The Meeting Place*, 1929 (s); *Love's Illusion*, 1930 (n); *Seven, Bobsworth*, 1930 (n); *The Innocent Criminal*, 1931 (n); *The Old People* (Vol. I of trilogy), 1931 (n); *The Next Generation* (Vol. II of trilogy, Am. ed. *The Middle Generation*), 1932 (n); *The Camberwell Miracle*, 1933 (n); *The Inheritor*, 1933 (n); *The Young People* (Vol. III of trilogy), 1933 (n); *Peckover*, 1934 (n); *The Case for Faith-Healing*, 1934 (e); *On a Huge Hill*, 1935 (n); *The Unfinished Road*, 1938 (n); *What I Believe*, 1938 (a); *Snell's Folly*, 1939 (n); *Strange Rival*, 1939 (n); *Quiet Corner*, 1940 (n); *"What Dreams May Come,"* 1941 (n); (with Esmé Wynne Tyson) *Men in the Same Boat*, 1943 (n); (with Esmé Wynne Tyson) *The Riddle of the Tower*, 1944 (n); (with Esmé Wynne Tyson) *The Gift*, 1947 (n)

JOHN BETJEMAN
1906-

Mount Zion, 1931 (p); *Ghastly Good Taste*, 1933 (e); *Continual Dew*, 1937 (p); *Antiquarian Prejudice*, 1939 (p); *Old Lights for New Chancels*, 1940 (p); *Vintage London*, 1942 (t); *English Cities and Small Towns*, 1943 (t); (with Geoffrey Taylor) *English, Scottish, and Welsh Landscape, 1700-1860*, 1944 (t); *John Piper*, 1944 (c); *New Bats in Old Belfries*, 1945 (p); *Slick but not Streamlined*, ed. W. H. Auden, 1947 (p); *Selected Poems*, 1948 (chosen and with preface John Sparrow) (p); *First and Last Loves*, 1952; (e) *A Few Late Chrysanthemums*, 1954 (p); *Altar and Pew*, 1959 (p); *Collected Poems, 1958*, 1962; *Summoned by Bells*, 1960 (a,p); *A Ring of Bells*, sel. and comp. Irene Slade, 1962 (p); *Cornwall*, 1964 (t); (with Basil Fulford Lowther Clarke) *English Churches*, 1964 (t); *High and Low*, 1966 (p)

Jocelyn Brooke, *Ronald Firbank and John Betjeman*, 1963

LAURENCE BINYON
1869-1943

Persephone, 1890 (p); (with Stephen Phillips *et al.*) *Primavera, Poems by Four Authors*, 1890 (p); *Lyric Poems*, 1894 (p); *Poems*, 1895 (p); *Dutch Etchers of the 17th Century*, 1895 (c); *London Visions*, 1896 (enlgd. 1908) (p); *The Praise of Life*, 1896 (p); *The Popularization of Art*, 1896 (c); *The Supper*, 1897 (p); *John Crome and John Sell Cotman*, 1897 (c); *Porphyrion*, 1898 (p); *The Second Book of London Visions*, 1898 (p); *Western Flanders*, 1899 (t); *Thomas Girtin*, 1900 (e); *Odes*, 1901 (p);

The Death of Adam, 1903 (p); *Life and Works of J. S. Cotman*, 1903 (e); *Dream Come True*, 1905 (p); *Penthesilea*, 1905 (p); *Paris and Œnone*, 1906 (p); *Attila*, 1907 (d); *Painting in the Far East*, 1908 (c); *Japanese Art*, 1909 (e); *England*, 1909 (p); *The Flight of the Dragon* [on Chinese and Japanese art], 1911 (e); *The Art of Botticelli*, 1913 (c); *Auguries*, 1913 (p); *The Winnowing Fan*, 1914 (p); *Bombastes in the Shades*, 1915 (d); *The Art of Asia*, 1915 (c); *The Anvil*, 1916 (p); *The Cause*, 1917 (p); *For the Fallen*, 1917 (p); *The New World*, 1918 (p); *English Poetry in its Relation to Painting and the Other Arts*, 1918 (e); *Poetry and Modern Life*, 1918 (e); *The Four Years: War Poems Collected and newly Augmented*, 1919 (p); *The Secret*, 1920 (p); *Sakuntala*, by Kalidasa, a new version by L.B., 1920 (tr); *The Court Painters of the Grand Moguls*, 1921 (e); *Selected Poems*, 1922 (p); *The Drawings and Engravings of William Blake*, 1922 (e); *Ayuli*, 1923 (d); *Arthur*, 1923 (d); (with J. J. O'Brien Sexton) *Japanese Colour Prints*, 1923 (e); *The Sirens, an Ode*, 1924 (p); *Asiatic Art in the British Museum*, 1925 (e); *The Followers of William Blake*, 1925 (c); *Little Poems from the Japanese*, 1925 (tr); *The Engraved Designs of William Blake*, 1926 (c); *Tradition and Reaction in Modern Poetry*, 1926 (c); *Chinese Paintings in English Collections*, 1927 (e); *Boadicea*, 1927 (d); *The Wonder Night*, 1927 (p); Dante Alighieri, *Episodes from the Divine Comedy*, 1928 (tr); *The Idols, an Ode*, 1928 (p); *Love in the Desert*, 1928 (d); *The Poems of Nizami*, 1928 (e); *Three Short Plays*, 1930 (3d); *Landscape in English Art and Poetry*, 1931 (c); *Collected Poems*, 1931; *Akbar*, 1932 (e); *Koya San, Four Poems from Japan*, 1932 (p); *English Water-Colours*, 1933 (c); *Dante's Inferno*, 1933 (tr); *The Young King*, 1934 (d); *Brief Candles*, 1938 (d); *The North Star*, 1941 (p); *The Burning of the Leaves*, 1944 (also pub. as "Ruins" in *Horizon*, 1942 (p)

EDMUND BLUNDEN
1896-

Poems, 1914 (p); *The Harbingers*, 1916 (p); *Pastorals*, 1916 (p); *The Waggoner*, 1920 (p); *The Bonaventure*, 1922 (t); *Old*

Homes, 1922 (p); *The Shepherd*, 1922 (p); *Dead Letters*, 1923 (p); *To Nature*, 1923 (p); *Christ's Hospital, A Retrospect*, 1923 (e); *English Poems*, 1925 (p); *Far East*, 1925 (p); *Masks of Time*, 1925 (p); *More Footnotes to Literary History*, 1926 (c); *On the Poems of Henry Vaughan, With his Principal Latin Poems Carefully Translated into English Verse*, 1927 (c); *Japanese Garland*, 1928 (p); *Retreat*, 1928 (p); *Leigh Hunt's "Examiner" Examined*, 1928 (c); *Undertones of War*, 1928 (r); *Winter Nights, A Reminiscence*, 1928 (p); *Nature in English Literature*, 1929 (c); *Near and Far*, 1929 (p); *Shakespeare's Significances*, 1929 (e); *The Poems of Edmund Blunden, 1914-30*, 1930; *Leigh Hunt* (Am. ed. *Leight Hunt and His Circle*), 1930 (b); *A Poet on Poets*, 1930 (e); *A Summer's Fancy*, 1930 (p); *To Themis, Poems on Famous Trials*, 1931 (p); *Votive Tablets, Studies Chiefly Appreciative of English Authors and Books*, 1931 (c); *Halfway House*, 1932 (p); *The Face of England*, 1932 (misc.); *Charles Lamb and His Contemporaries*, 1933 (c); (with Sylvia Norman) *We'll Shift Our Ground, or, Two on a Tour, Almost a Novel*, 1933 (n); *Choice or Chance*, 1934 (p); *The Mind's Eye*, 1934 (e); *Edward Gibbon and His Age*, 1935 (c); *Keats's Publisher, John Taylor*, 1936 (m); *An Elegy*, 1937 (p); *Poems, 1930-40*, 1940 (p); *Thomas Hardy*, 1941 (b); *English Villages*, 1941 (e); *Romantic Poetry and the Fine Arts*, 1942 (c); *Shells by a Stream*, 1944 (p); *Cricket Country*, 1944 (e); *Shelley*, 1946 (b); *Shakespeare to Hardy*, 1948 (repr. 1956) (h); *Addresses on General Subjects Connected with English Literature*, 1949 (c); *Sons of Light: English Writers*, 1949 (c); *After the Bombing*, 1949 (p); *Poetry and Science*, 1949 (c); *Favorite Studies in English Literature*, 1950 (c); *Influential Books*, 1950 (c); *Reprinted Papers: Partly Concerning Some English Romantic Poets*, 1950 (c); *John Keats*, 1950 (c); *Chaucer to "B.V."* [James Thomson, 1834-82], 1950 (c); *Selection of the Prose and Poetry*, ed. K. Hopkins, 1950; *A Wanderer in Japan*, 1950 (t); *The Dede of Pittie: Dramatic Scenes*, 1953 (misc.); *Charles Lamb*, 1954 (b); *Poems of Many Years*, ed. Rupert Hart-Davis, 1957 (p); *A Hong Kong House: Poems 1951-61*,

1962 (p); *William Crowe, 1745-1829*, 1963 (a); *Guest of Thomas Hardy*, 1964 (r); *Eleven Poems*, 1966 (p)

Alec M. Hardie, *Edmund Blunden*, 1958

WILFRID SCAWEN BLUNT
1840-1922

In Vinculis, 1889 (p); *A New Pilgrimage*, 1889 (p); *Esther, Love Lyrics, and Natalia's Resurrection*, 1892 (p); *The Love-Lyrics and Songs of Proteus*, 1892 (p); *Griselda*, 1893 (p); *Satan Absolved*, 1899 (p); *Poetical Works*, 1914; *My Diaries: Being a Personal Narrative of Events, 1888-1914*, 1919, 1920

PHYLLIS BOTTOME
1884-1963

Life the Interpreter, 1902 (n); *The Master Hope*, 1904 (n); *Raw Material*, 1905 (e); *The Imperfect Gift*, 1907 (n); (with H. de Lisle Brock) *Crooked Answers*, 1911 (n); *The Common Chord*, 1913 (n); *"Broken Music,"* 1914 (n); *The Captive*, 1915 (n); *Secretly Armed* (Am. ed. *The Dark Tower*), 1916 (n); *A Certain Star*, 1917 (n); *The Second Fiddle*, 1917 (n); *The Derelict*, 1917 (s); *Helen of Troy and Rose*, 1918 (n); *A Servant of Reality*, 1919 (n); *The Crystal Heart*, 1921 (n); *The Kingfisher*, 1922 (n); (with Dorothy Thompson) *The Depths of Prosperity*, 1924 (n); *The Belated Reckoning*, 1925 (n); *Old Wine*, 1926 (n); *The Rat* (from the play by Ivor Novello and Constance Collier), 1927 (n); *Wild Grapes*, 1927 (n); *The Messenger of the Gods*, 1927 (n); *Plain Case*, 1928 (n); *Strange Fruit*, 1928 (s); *Tatter'd Loving*, 1929 (n); *Windlestraws*, 1929 (n); *Devil's Due* (also pub. as *Wind in His Fists*), 1931 (n); *The Advances of Harriet*, 1933 (n); *Innocence and Experience*, 1934 (s); *Private Worlds*, 1934 (n); *Level Crossing*, 1936 (n); *The Mortal Storm*, 1937 (n); *Alfred Adler*, 1939 (repr. 1946) (b); *Murder in the Bud* (Am. ed. *Danger Signal*), 1939 (n); *The Heart of a Child*, 1940 (n); *Masks and Faces*, 1940 (s); *Formidable to Tyrants* (Am. ed. *Mansion House of Liberty*), 1941 (e); *London Pride*, 1941 (n); *Survival*, 1943 (n); *Within the Cup*, 1943 (n); *Austria's Contribution towards Our New Order*,

1944 (e); *From the Life*, 1944 (b); *Individual Countries*, 1946 (e); *Lifeline*, 1946 (n); *Search for a Soul*, 1947 (a); *Fortune's Finger*, 1950 (s); *Under the Skin*, 1950 (n); *The Challenge*, 1952 (a); *Man and Beast*, 1953 (n); *Against Whom?* (Am. ed. *Secret Stair*), 1954 (n); *Not in Our Stars*, 1955 (e); *Belated Reckoning*, 1955 (s); *Eldorado Jane* (Am. ed. *Jane*), 1956 (n); *Walls of Glass*, 1958 (n); *The Goal*, 1962 (a)

GORDON BOTTOMLEY
1874-1948

The Mickle Drede, 1896 (p); *Poems at White Nights*, 1899 (p); *The Crier by Night*, 1902 (d); *The Gate of Smaragdus*, 1904 (p); *Midsummer Eve*, 1905 (d); *Chambers of Imagery*, 1907 (p); *Laodice and Danaë*, 1909 (d); *The Riding to Lithend*, 1909 (d); *A Vision of Giorgione*, 1910 (first London ed. 1922, rev.) (p); *Chambers of Imagery*, 2nd ser., 1912 (p); *King Lear's Wife*, 1916 (d); *King Lear's Wife and Other Plays*, 1920 (new ed. with new p, 1922) (4d); *Gruach and Britain's Daughter*, 1921 (2d); *Littleholme*, 1922 (p); *Prologue*, 1922 (p); *Poems of Thirty Years*, 1925 (p); *Frescoes from Buried Temples* (a Portfolio of Drawings by James Guthrie, with poems by G.B.), 1928; *A Parting and The Return*, 1928 (p); *Gordon Bottomley* [Selected Poems], 1928 (p); *Scenes and Plays*, 1929 (d); *Festival Preludes*, 1930 (p); *Lyric Plays*, 1932 (d); *The Acts of Saint Peter*, 1933 (d); *Choric Plays and A Comedy*, 1939 (d); *Deirdre* (in Gaelic and Eng., adapted from Alexander Carmichael Barra, story and lay by G.B.), 1944 (d); *Kate Kennedy*, 1945 (d); *Poems and Plays*, ed. Claude C. Abbott, 1953; *Poet and Painter* (*being the Correspondence between G.B. and Paul Nash, 1910-1946*), 1955

RONALD BOTTRALL
1906-

Loosening, 1931 (p); *Festivals of Fires*, 1934 (p); *Turning Path*, 1939 (p); *Farewell and Welcome*, 1945 (p); *Selected Poems*, 1946 (p); *Palisades of Fear*, 1949 (p); *Adam Unparadised*, 1954 (p); *The Collected Poems*, 1961

ELIZABETH BOWEN
1899-

Encounters, 1923 (s); *Ann Lee's*, 1926 (s); *The Hotel*, 1927 (n); *Joining Charles*, 1929 (s); *The Last September*, 1929 (n); *Friends and Relations*, 1931 (n); *To the North*, 1932 (n); *The Cat Jumps*, 1934 (s); *The House in Paris*, 1935 (n); *The Death of the Heart*, 1938 (n); *Look at All Those Roses*, 1941 (s); **Bowen's Court*, 1942 (h); *Seven Winters*, 1942 (a); *The Demon Lover*, (Am. ed. *Ivy Gripped the Steps*), 1945 (s); *English Novelists*, 1946 (c); *Anthony Trollope: A New Judgment*, 1946 (rd); (with Graham Greene and V. S. Pritchett) *Why Do I Write?* 1948 (e); (with John Perry) *Castle Anna*, 1948 (d, performed but unpublished); *The Heat of the Day*, 1949 (n); *Collected Impressions*, 1950 (c); *Early Stories*, 1950 (s); *The Shelbourne: A Centre in Dublin Life for More Than a Century* (Am. ed. *The Shelbourne Hotel*), 1951 (h); *A World of Love*, 1955 (n); *Stories by Elizabeth Bowen*, 1959 (s); *A Time in Rome*, 1960 (a); *Seven Winters and Afterthoughts*, 1962 (a,e); *The Little Girls*, 1964 (n); (with Dorothy Annie Hundhammer) *Iesu A'I Deyrnas: Llyfr Darllen Ysgrythurol I'R Ysgolion*, 1964 (s); *A Day in the Dark*, 1965 (s)

*repr. 1965 [on the Bowen family]

William Webster Heath, *Elizabeth Bowen: an Introduction to her Novels*, 1961

MAURICE BOWRA
1898-

Tradition and Design in the Iliad, 1930 (c); *Ancient Greek Literature*, 1933 (c); *Greek Lyric Poetry from Alcman to Simonides*, 1936 (c); *Early Greek Elegists*, 1938 (c); *The Heritage of Symbolism*, 1943 (c); *Sophoclean Tragedy*, 1944 (c); *A Classical Education*, 1945 (e); *From Vergil to Milton*, 1945 (c); *The Background of Modern Poetry*, 1946 (e); *Edith Sitwell*, 1947 (c); *The Creative Experiment*, 1949 (c); *The Romantic Imagination*, 1950 (c); *Inspiration and Poetry*, 1951 (e); *John Dewar Denniston, 1887-1949*, 1952 (m); *Heroic Poetry*, 1952 (c); *Problems in Greek Poetry*, 1953 (c); *Homer and His*

Forerunners, 1955 (e); *The Simplicity of Racine*, 1956 (e); *The Meaning of a Heroic Age*, 1957 (e); *The Greek Experience*, 1957 (e); *The Prophetic Element*, 1959 (e); *Mediaeval Love-Song*, 1961 (e); *Poetry and the First World War*, 1961 (e); *Primitive Song*, 1962 (e); *Pindar*, 1964 (c); *In General and Particular*, 1964 (c); *Pindar*, 1965 (c); *Landmarks in Greek Literature*, 1966 (h,c); *Poetry and Politics, 1900-1960*, 1966 (Wiles lecture at the Queens University, Belfast, 1965); *Memories, 1898-1913*, 1966 (r)

MALCOLM BRADBURY
1932-

Eating People Is Wrong, 1959 (n); *Phogey! Or How to Have Class in a Classless Society*, 1960 (e); *All Dressed Up and Nowhere to Go*, 1962 (e); *Evelyn Waugh*, 1964 (c); *Stepping Westward*, 1965 (n)

JOHN BRAINE
1922-

Room at the Top, 1957 (n); *The Vodi* (Am. ed. *From the Hand of the Hunter*), 1959 (n); *Life at the Top*, 1962 (n); *The Jealous God*, 1964 (n)

ROBERT BRIDGES
1844-1930

Poems, 1873 (p); *The Growth of Love*, 1876 (p); *Poems*, 1879; *Poems*, 1880; *Prometheus the Firegiver*, 1883 (d); *Poems* (sel. from foregoing series), 1884 (p); *Eros and Psyche*, 1885 (p); *The Feast of Bacchus*, 1889 (d); *Achilles in Scyros*, 1890 (d); *The Christian Captives*, 1890 (d); *Palicio*, 1890 (d); *The Return of Ulysses*, 1890 (d); *Shorter Poems*, 1890 (p); *Eden, an Oratorio*, 1891 (p); *Shorter Poems, Bk. V*, 1893 (p); *The Humours of the Court*, 1893 (d); *Milton's Prosody*, 1893 (c); *John Keats*, 1895 (c); *Invocation to Music, an Ode* (in honour of Henry Purcell), 1895 (p); *Ode for the Bicentenary Commemoration of Henry Purcell, with Other Poems and a Preface on the Musical Setting of Poetry* (Am. ed. *Purcell Ode and Other Poems*), 1896 (p); *A Song of Darkness and Light, an Ode*, 1898 (p); *Poetical Works* (6 vols. 1898-

1905) (p); *A Practical Discourse on Some Principles of Hymn Singing*, 1901 (e); *Now in Wintry Delights*, 1903 (p); *Peace Ode*, 1903 (p); *Demeter, a Masque*, 1905 (d); *About Hymns*, 1911 (e); *Poetical Works* (excluding the eight dramas), 1912 (p); *A Tract on the Present State of English Pronunciation*, 1913 (e); *Poems Written in the Year MCMXIII*, 1914 (p); *Ibant Obscuri, an Experiment in the Classical Hexameter*, 1916 (e); *The Chivalry of the Sea, Naval Ode*, 1916 (p); *Ode on the Tercentenary Commemoration of Shakespeare*, 1916 (p); *Lord Kitchener*, 1916 (p); *Britannia Victrix*, 1918 (p); *The Necessity of Poetry*, 1918 (e); *October*, 1920 (sel. p); *New Verse Written in 1921*, 1925 (p); *The Tapestry*, 1925 (p); *Henry Bradley*, 1926 (m); *The Influence of the Audience, Considerations Preliminary to the Psychological Analysis of Shakespeare's Characters*, 1926 (e); *The Testament of Beauty*, 1929 (p); *Collected Essays, Papers, etc.*, 1927 (misc.); *Poetry*, 1929 (c); *On Receiving Trivia From the Author*, 1930 (p); *The Shorter Poems* (enlgd. ed.) 1931 (p); *Three Friends, Memoirs of Digby Mackworth Dolben, Richard Watson Dixon, Henry Bradley*, 1932 (m); *Verses Written for Mrs. Daniel*, 1932 (p)

George L. MacKay, *A Bibliography of Robert Bridges*, 1933; John Sparrow, *Robert Bridges*, 1962 [selected bibliog.]

JAMES BRIDIE
1888-1951

Some Talk of Alexander, 1926 (d); *The Switchback*, etc., 1930 (3d); *The Anatomist*, etc., 1930 (3d); *Tobias and the Angel*, 1931 (re-issue 1961) (d); *Jonah and the Whale*, 1932 (d); *A Sleeping Clergyman*, 1933 (d); *Colonel Witherspoon*, 1934 (d); *Marriage is no Joke*, 1934 (d); *Mr. Bridie's Alphabet for Little Glasgow Highbrows*, 1934 (e); *The Black Eye*, 1935 (d); (with Claud Gurney) *Mary Read*, 1935 (d); *Mrs. Waterbury's Millenium*, 1935 (d); *Moral Plays*, with Preface "The Anatomy of Failure," 1936 (3d); *The Scottish Character*, 1937 (e); *The King of Nowhere*, etc., 1938 (4d); *The Last Trump*, 1938 (d); *The Letter-Box Rattles*, 1938 (d); *One Way of Living*,

1939 (r); *The Theatre*, 1939 (e); *What Say They*, 1939 (d); *Susannah and the Elders*, etc, 1940 (4d); *Plays for Plain People*, 1944 (6d); *The British Drama*, 1945 (c); *Tedious and Brief*, 1945 (misc.); *It Depends What You Mean*, 1948 (d); (with Moray McLaren) *A Small Stir: Letters on the English*, 1949 (e); *John Knox*, etc., 1949 (3d;) *Dr. Angelus*, 1950 (d); *Daphne Laureole*, 1950 (d); *Mr. Gillie*, 1950 (d); *The Queen's Comedy*, 1950 (d); *The Blaikie Charivari, or the Seven Prophets*, 1953 (d); *Meeting at Night*, 1956 (d)

Winifred Bannister, *James Bridie and his Theatre*, 1955 [no bibliog.]; Helen L. Lugben, *James Bridie, Clown and Philosopher*, 1966

JOCELYN BROOKE
1908-

December Spring, 1946 (p); *The Military Orchid*, 1948 (n,a); *A Mine of Serpents*, 1949 (n,a); *The Scapegoat*, 1949 (n); *The Goose Cathedral*, 1950 (n,a); *The Image of a Drawn Sword*, 1950 (n); *Wild Orchids of Britain*, 1950 (e); *Ronald Firbank*, 1951 (abgd. in *Ronald Firbank and John Betjeman*, 1962) (b,c); *The Elements of Death*, 1952 (p); *Elizabeth Bowen*, 1952 (b,c); *The Passing of a Hero*, 1953 (n); *Private View: Four Portraits*, 1954 (b); *Aldous Huxley*, 1954 (b,c); *The Dog at Clambererown*, 1955 (r,letters); *The Crisis in Bulgaria, or, Ibsen to the Rescue*, 1956 (n); *Conventional Weapons*, 1961 (n); *The Name of Greene*, 1961 (n); *The Birth of a Legend: a Reminiscence of Arthur Machen and John Ireland*, 1964 (r)

RUPERT BROOKE
1887-1915

Poems, 1911 (p); *War Sonnets in New Numbers*, 1914 (p); *The Collected Poems of Rupert Brooke*, 1915; *1914*, 1915 (p); *Lithuania*, 1915 (pd); *The Old Vicarage, Grantchester*, 1916 (p); *John Webster and The Elizabethan Drama*, 1916 (c); *Letters from America* (preface by Henry James), 1916 (e); *Selected Poems*, 1917 (p); *The Collected Poems of Rupert Brooke*, 1918 (repr. 1942); *Fragments Now First Collected, Some Being Hitherto Unpublished*, ed. R. M. G. Potter,

1925 (misc.); *A Letter to the Editor of the Poetry Review*, 1929; *The Complete Poems of Rupert Brooke*, 1932; *Twenty Poems*, 1935 (p); *Poetical Works*, ed. G. Keynes, 1946 (p); *Democracy and the Arts*, 1946 (e); *The Prose of Rupert Brooke*, ed. Christopher Hassall, 1956

Geoffrey Keynes, *A Bibliography of Rupert Brooke*, 1959; Christopher V. Hassall, *Rupert Brooke*, 1963 [no bibliog.]

CHRISTINE BROOKE-ROSE
1923-

The Languages of Love, 1957 (n); *A Grammar of Metaphor*, 1958 (c); *The Sycamore Tree*, 1958 (n); *The Dear Deceit*, 1960 (n); *The Middlemen: a Satire*, 1961 (n); *Out*, 1964 (n); *Such*, 1966 (n)

BRIGID BROPHY
1929-

The Crown Princess, 1953 (s); *Hackenfeller's Ape*, 1953 (n); *The King of a Rainy Country*, 1956 (n); *Flesh* (Am. ed. 1961), 1962 (n); *Black Ship to Hell*, 1962 (e); *The Snowball* and *The Finishing Touch*, 1964 (2n); *Mozart the Dramatist*, 1964 (e); *Don't Never Forget*, 1966 (e,c)

IVOR BROWN
1891-

Years of Plenty, 1915 (n); *Security*, 1916 (n); *The Meaning of Democracy*, 1919 (e); *English Political Theory*, 1920 (e); *Lighting up Time*, 1920 (n); *H. G. Wells*, 1923 (b); *Smithfield Preserved*, 1926 (d); *Masques and Phases*, 1926 (e); *First Player*, 1927 (c); *Parties of the Play*, 1928 (c); *Essays*, 1929 (e); *Now on View*, 1929 (e); *Art and Everyman*, 1929 (c); *Brown Studies*, 1930 (e); *Puck, our Peke*, 1931 (e); *Marine Parade*, 1932 (n); *I Commit to the Flames*, 1934 (e); *Heart of England*, 1935 (t); *Master Sanguine*, 1935 (e); *The Great and the Goods*, 1937 (n); *I Made You Possible*, 1937 (d); *Life Within Reason*, 1939 (e); (with George Fearon) *Amazing Monument*, 1939 (Am. ed. *This Shakespeare Industry*) (e); *Just Another Word*, 1943 (e); *I Give You My Word*, 1945 (e); *The Old Vic King Lear*, 1946 (c); *Say the*

Word, 1947 (e); (with others) *Britain's Heritage*, 1948 (e); *No Idle Words*, 1948 (e); *Shakespeare*, 1949* (b); *Having the Last Word*, 1950 (e); *I Break my Word*, 1951 (e); *Summer in Scotland*, 1952 (t); (with others) *Approach to Drama Criticism*, 1952 (c); *Winter in London*, 1953 (t); *Shakespeare Memorial Theatre, 1951-53*, 1953 (h); *Word in Edgeways*, 1953 (e); *The Way of My World*, 1954 (a); *Balmoral*, 1955 (t); *Chosen Words*, 1955 (e); *Dark Ladies*, 1957 (c); *J. B. Priestley*, 1957 (c); *Words in our Time*, 1958 (e); *William Shakespeare*, 1958 (c); *London*, 1960 (t); *Shakespeare in his Time*, 1960 (e); *Look at Theatres*, 1962 (e); *Mind Your Language*, 1962 (e); *Words in Season*, 1962 (e); *How Shakespeare Spent the Day*, 1963 (b); *Dickens in His Time*, 1963 (b); *Shakespeare and His World*, 1964 (c)

(*rev. 1964)

WINIFRED BRYHER
1894-

Region of Lutany, 1914 (p); *West*, 1915 (e); *Amy Lowell: A Critical Appreciation*, 1918 (c); *Bion, The Lament for Adonis*, 1918 (tr); *Development*, 1920 (n); *Arrow Music*, 1922 (p); *Film Problems of Soviet Russia*, 1929 (e); *Film in Education*, 1937 (e); *The Fourteenth of October*, 1954 (n); *Roman Wall*, 1955 (n); *Beowulf*, 1956 (n); *The Player's Boy*, 1957 (n); *Gate to the Sea*, 1959 (n); *Ruan*, 1961 (n); *The Heart to Artemis: a Writer's Memoirs*, 1963 (a); *The Coin of Carthage*, 1964 (n); *Visa for Avalon*, 1965 (n)

JOHN BUCHAN
1875-1940

Sir Quixote of the Moors, 1895 (n); *Scholar Gipsies*, 1896 (e); *John Burnet of Barns*, 1898 (n); *Grey Weather*, 1899 (s); *A Lost Lady of Old Years*, 1899 (n); *The Half-Hearted*, 1900 (n); *The Watcher by the Threshold*, 1902 (s); *A Lodge in the Wilderness*, 1906 (n); *Some Eighteenth Century Byways*, 1908 (e); *Prester John*, 1910 (n); *Sir Walter Raleigh*, 1911 (b); *The Moon Endureth*, 1912 (s); *The Marquis of Montrose*, 1913 (h); *Andrew Jameson, Lord Ardwall*, 1913 (b); *Nelson's History of the War*, 1915-1919 (repr. 1940) (h); *The Achievement of France*, 1915 (e); **The Thirty-nine Steps*, 1915 (n); *Salute to Adventurers*, 1915 (n); *Ordeal by Marriage*, 1915 (p); *The Power-House*, 1916 (n); *The Battle of Jutland*, 1916 (h); **Greenmantle*, 1916 (n); *The Battle of the Somme, First Phase*, 1916 (h); *The Battle of the Somme, Second Phase*, 1917 (h); *Poems, Scots and English*, 1917 (enlgd. 1936) (p); **Mr. Standfast*, 1918 (n); *Francis and Riversdale Grenfell*, 1920 (m); *The Path of the King*, 1921 (n); *Huntingtower*, 1922 (n); *A Book of Escapes and Hurried Journeys*, 1922 (s); *The Last Secrets*, 1923 (e); *Midwinter*, 1923 (n); **The Three Hostages*, 1924 (n); *Lord Minto*, 1924 (m); *The History of the Royal Scots Fusiliers*, 1925 (h); *John Macnab*, 1925 (n); *The Man and the Book: Sir Walter Scott*, 1925 (c); *The Dancing Floor*, 1926 (n); *Homilies and Recreations*, 1926 (e); *Witch Wood*, 1927 (n); *The Runagates Club*, 1928 (e); *Montrose*, 1928 (b); *The Courts of the Morning*, 1929 (n); (with George Adam Smith) *The Kirk in Scotland, 1560-1929*, 1930 (h); *Castle Gay*, 1930 (n); *The Blanket of the Dark*, 1931 (n); *The Gap in the Curtain*, 1932 (n); *Sir Walter Scott*, 1932 (b); *Julius Caesar*, 1932 (b); *The Magic Walking Stick*, 1932 (n); *The Massacre of Glencoe*, 1933 (h); *A Prince of the Captivity*, 1933 (n); *The Free Fishers*, 1934 (n); *Gordon at Khartoum*, 1934 (h); *Oliver Cromwell*, 1934 (h); *The King's Grace*, 1935 (h); *The House of the Four Winds*, 1935 (n); *The Island of Sheep*, 1936 (n); *Augustus*, 1937 (b); *Memory Hold-the-Door* (Am. ed *Pilgrim's Way*), 1940 (r); *Comments and Characters*, 1940 (e); *Canadian Occasions*, 1940 (e); *Sick Heart River*, 1941 (Am. ed. *Mountain Meadow*) (n); *The Long Traverse* (Am. ed. *The Lake of Gold*) 1941 (n)

*These 4 novels collected as *The Four Adventures of Richard Hannay*, 1930

Archibald Hanna, *John Buchan, 1875-1940: A Bibliography*, 1953; Janet A. Smith, *John Buchan: a Biography*, 1965; Queen's Univ., Kingston, Ont., Library, *A Checklist of Works by and about John Buchan*, 1965; J. Randolph Cox, *John Buchan, Lord Tweedsmuir: An Annotated Bibliography of Writing About Him*, in *English Literature in Transition*, Vol IX (1966), nos. 5 and 6

ANTHONY BURGESS
1917-

Time for a Tiger, 1956 (n); *The Enemy in the Blanket*, 1958 (n); (pseud. John Burgess Wilson) *English Literature—A Survey for Students*, 1958 (h); *Beds in the East*, 1959 (n); *The Doctor is Sick*, 1960 (n); *The Right to an Answer*, 1960 (n); (pseud. Joseph Kell) *One Hand Clapping*, 1961 (n); *The Worm and the Ring*, 1961 (n); *Devil of a State*, 1961 (n); *A Clockwork Orange*, 1962 (n); *The Wanting Seed*, 1962 (n); *Honey for the Bears*, 1963 (n); (pseud. Joseph Kell) *Inside Mr. Enderby*, 1963 (n); *The Novel Today*, 1963 (c); *Language Made Plain*, 1964 (e); *Nothing Like the Sun*, 1964 (n); *The Eve of Saint Venus*, 1964 (n); *Malayan Trilogy* [*Time for a Tiger, The Enemy in the Blanket, Beds in the East*], 1964 (3n); *Here Comes Everybody: an Introduction to James Joyce for the Ordinary Reader* (Am. ed. *Re Joyce*), 1965 (c); *A Vision of Battlements*, 1965 (n); *Tremor of Intent*, 1966 (n)

SAMUEL BUTLER
1835-1902

Erewhon, 1872 (n); *Evolution Old and New*, 1879 (e); *Unconscious Memory*, 1880 (e); *The Authoress of the Odyssey*, 1897 (rev. 1922) (e); *Erewhon Revisited*, 1901 (n); *The Way of All Flesh*, ed. R. A. Streatfield, 1903 (n); *Essays on Life, Art and Science*, ed. R. A. Streatfield, 1904 (e); *The Notebooks of Samuel Butler*, ed. Henry Festing Jones, 1912; *The Humour of Homer, and Other Essays*, ed. R. A. Streatfield, 1913 (e); *The Shrewsbury Edition of the Works of Samuel Butler*, ed. Henry Festing Jones and A. T. Bartholomew, 20 vols., 1923-26; *Selections from the Notebooks*, ed. A. T. Bartholomew, 1912; *Erewhon and Erewhon Revisited*, 1932 (2n); *Butleriana* [unpub. notebooks], ed. A. T. Bartholomew, 1932; *Further Extracts from the Notebooks of Samuel Butler*, ed. A. T. Bartholomew, 1934; *The Essential Samuel Butler*, sel. G. D. H. Cole, 1950; *Samuel Butler's Notebooks*, sel. and ed. Geoffrey Keynes and Brian Hill, 1951; *The Family Letters of Samuel Butler, 1841-1886*, sel. Arnold Silver, 1962; *Ernest Pontifex,*

or The Way of All Flesh, ed. [from the original ms.] with introd. and notes Daniel F. Howard, 1965 (n)

Philip Henderson, *Samuel Butler*, 1953 [no bibliog.]; Stanley B. Harkness, *The Career of Samuel Butler: A Bibliography*, 1955; Willem Gerard Bekker, *An Historical and Critical Review of Samuel Butler's Literary Works*, 1964

HALL CAINE
1853-1931

Recollections of Rossetti, 1882 (r); *Cobwebs of Criticism*, 1883 (c); *The Shadow of a Crime*, 1885 (n); *A Son of Hagar*, 1887 (n); *The Deemster*, 1887 (n); *Life of Samuel Taylor Coleridge*, 1887 (b); *The Bondman*, 1890 (h); *The Little Manx Nation*, 1891 (e); *The Scapegoat*, 1891 (n); *Captain Davy's Honeymoon*, 1893 (3s); *The Little Man Island*, 1894 (t); *The Manxman*, 1894 (h); *The Christian*, 1897 (h); *The Eternal City*, 1901 (n); *The Prodigal Son*, 1904 (n); *The Bondmen Play*, 1906 (d); *Drink*, 1906 (n); *My Story*, 1908 (a); (with Louis N. Parker) *Pete*, 1908 (d); *The White Phophet*, 1909 (n); *The Woman Thou Gavest Me*, 1913 (n); *The Master of Man*, 1921 (n); *The Woman of Knockaloe* (one ed. pub. as *Barbed Wire*), 1923 (n); *Life of Christ*, ed. G. R. Hall Caine and Sir Derwent Hall Caine, 1938 (b)

ROY CAMPBELL
1901-1957

The Flaming Terrapin, 1924 (p); *The Wayzgoose, a South African Satire*, 1928 (p); *Adamastor*, 1930 (p); *Poems*, 1930 (p); *The Georgiad, a Satirical Fantasy*, 1931 (p); *Pomegranates*, 1932 (p); *Burns*, 1932 (c); *Taurine Provence, the Philosophy, Technique and Religion of the Bullfighter*, 1932 (e); *Wyndham Lewis*, 1932 (e); *Flowering Reeds*, 1933 (p); *Broken Record*, 1934 (a); *Mithraic Emblems*, 1936 (p); *Flowering Rifle*, 1939 (p); *Sons of the Mistral*, 1941 (p); *Talking Bronco*, 1946 (p); *Collected Poems*, Vol. I (Vol. II, 1957; Vol. III, Translations, 1960), 1949 (p); *Light on a Dark Horse* (1901-1935), 1951 (a); *The Poems of St. John of the Cross*, 1951 (tr); *Lorca*, 1952 (c); *Poems of Baudelarie*, 1952 (tr); *Selected Poems*, 1955 (p);

Portugal, 1957 (t). Also trs. of Calderon, Cervantes, Lope de Vega, Eça de Queiroz, Helge Krog

David Wright, *Roy Campbell,* 1961

GILBERT CANNAN
1884-1955

Peter Homunculus, 1909 (n); *Devious Ways,* 1910 (n); Romain Rolland, *John Christopher* (Am. ed. *Jean Christophe*), 1910-13 (tr); *Little Brother,* 1912 (n); *Round the Corner,* 1913 (n); *Four Plays,* 1913 (d); *Old Mole,* 1914 (n); *Satire,* 1914 (e); *Young Earnest,* 1915 (n); *Samuel Butler,* 1915 (c); *Adventurous Love,* 1915 (p); *Windmills,* 1915 (4n); *Mendel, A Story of Youth,* 1916 (n); *Three Pretty Men* (Am. ed. *Three Sons and a Mother*), 1916 (n); *The Stucco House* (seq. to *Three Pretty Men*), 1917 (n); *Everybody's Husband,* 1917 (d); *Freedom,* 1917 (e); *Mummery,* 1918 (n); *Pink Roses,* 1919 (n); *Time and Eternity,* 1919 (n); *The Anatomy of Society,* 1919 (e); *The Release of the Soul,* 1920 (e); *Pugs and Peacocks,* 1921 (n); *Annette and Bennett,* 1922 (n); *Sembal* (seq. to *Pugs and Peacocks*), 1922 (n); *Noel, An Epic in Ten Cantos* (Cantos I-IV), 1917-18 (reissued as *Noel, An Epic in Seven Cantos,* 1922) (p); *Seven Plays,* 1923 (7d); *Love is Less Than God, the Book of Soul,* 1923 (e); *Letters from a Distance,* 1923 (e); *The House of Prophecy* (seq. to *Sembal*), 1924 (n); also tr. Chekhov, Heine, Benda

EDWARD CARPENTER
1844-1929

The Religious Influence of Art, 1870 (c); *Narcissus,* 1873 (p); *Moses* (repub. with alterations as: *The Promised Land,* 1910), 1875 (d); *Towards Democracy,* (Pts. I, II, III, 1892; Pt. IV: *Who Shall Command the Heart,* 1902; Complete, 1905), 1883 (p); *Modern Science, a Criticism,* 1885 (e); *England's Ideal,* 1887 (e); *Civilization, Its Cause and Cure,* 1889 (e); *From Adam's Peak to Elephanta, Sketches in Ceylon and India* (pub. in part as *A Visit to a Gñani,* 1911), 1892 (sk); (with Edward Maitland) *Vivisection,* 1893 (e); *St. George and the Dragon,* a play for children, 1895 (d); *Love's Coming-of-Age,* 1896 (e); (with others) *Forecasts of the Com-*

ing Century, 1897 (e); *Angels' Wings, Essays on Art and Its Relation to Life,* 1898 (e); *The Art of Creation,* 1903 (e); *Vivisection,* 1904 (e); *The Art of Creation,* 1904 (e); *Prisons, Police and Punishment,* 1905 (e); *Days with Walt Whitman,* 1906 (r,c); *Sketches From Life in Town and Country and Some Verses,* 1908 (misc.); *The Intermediate Sex, a Study of Some Transitional Types of Men and Women,* 1908 (e); *The Drama of Love and Death,* 1912 (e); *Intermediate Types Among Primitive Folk,* 1914 (e); *The Healing of Nations and the Hidden Sources of Their Strife,* 1915 (e); *My Days and Dreams,* 1916 (a); *The Story of my Books,* 1916 (a); *Towards Industrial Freedom,* 1917 (e); *Pagan and Christian Creeds, Their Origin and Meaning,* 1920 (e); *The Teaching of the Upanishads,* 1920 (e); *The Story of Eros and Psyche (retold from Apuleius) with some early verses,* 1923 (p); *Some Friends of Walt Whitman, a Study in Sex-Psychology,* 1924 (e); (with George Barnefield) *The Psychology of the Poet Shelley,* 1925 (c)

Tom Swan, *Edward Carpenter, a Study,* rev. 1929; Sheffield Public Libraries, *A Bibliography of Edward Carpenter,* 1949. See E. M. Forster, *Two Cheers for Democracy,* 1951

PAUL VINCENT CARROLL
1900-

Things That Are Caesar's, 1934 (d); *Shadow and Substance,* 1938 (d); *Plays for My Children,* 1939 (d); *The White Steed* and *Coggerers,* 1939 (2d); *Old Foolishness,* 1944 (d); *Three Plays (The White Steed, Things That are Caesar's, The Strings, My Lord, Are False),* 1944 (3d); *Green Cars Go East,* 1947 (d); *The Conspirators,* 1947 (d); *The Wise Have Not Spoken,* 1947 (d); *Two Plays (The Wise Have Not Spoken, Shadow and Substance),* 1948 (2d); *The Wayward Saint,* 1955 (d); *Irish Stories and Plays,* 1958

JOYCE CARY
1888-1957

[Arthur Cary] *Verse,* 1908 (p); *Aissa Saved,* 1932 (n); *An American Visitor,* 1933 (n); *The African Witch* 1936 (n); *Castle Corner,* 1938 (n); *Power in Men,*

1939 (repr. 1964) (e); *Mister Johnson,* 1939 (n); *Charley Is My Darling,* 1940 (n); *A House of Children,* 1941 (n,a); *Herself Surprised,* 1941 (n); *The Case for African Freedom,* 1941 (rev. enlgd. 1944) (e); *To Be a Pilgrim,* 1942 (n); *Process of Real Freedom,* 1943 (e); *The Horse's Mouth,* 1944 (n); *Marching Soldier,* 1945 (p); *Britain and West Africa,* 1946 (e); *The Moonlight,* 1946 (n); *The Drunken Sailor: a Ballad-Epic,* 1947 (p); *A Fearful Joy,* 1949 (n); *Prisoner of Grace* (Pt. I of Trilogy), 1952 (n); *Except the Lord* (Pt. II of Trilogy), 1953 (n); *Not Honour More* (Pt. III of Trilogy), 1955 (n); *Art and Reality,* 1958 (Clark lectures); *First Trilogy (Herself Surprised, To Be a Pilgrim, The Horse's Mouth),* 1958; *The Captive and the Free,* 1959 (n); *Spring Song,* 1960 (s)

Andrew Wright, *Joyce Cary: a Preface to his Novels,* 1958

CHRISTOPHER CAUDWELL
1907-1937

(All the novels except *This My Hand* are detective stories signed with the author's real name, Christopher St. John Sprigg)

The Airship, 1931 (e); (with H. Davis) *Fly with Me,* 1932 (e); *Crime in Kensington* (Am. ed. *Pass the Body*), 1933 (n); *Fatality in Fleet Street,* 1933 (n); *British Airways,* 1934 (e); *Death of an Airman,* 1934 (n); *Perfect Alibi,* 1934 (n); *Corpse with the Sunburned Face,* 1935 (n); *Great Flights,* 1935 (b); *Death of a Queen* 1935 (n); *This My Hand,* 1936 (n); *Illusion and Reality,* 1937 (e); *Let's Learn to Fly,* 1937 (e); *Six Queer Things,* 1937 (n); *Studies in a Dying Culture,* 1938 (e); *Crisis in Physics,* 1939 (e); *Poems,* 1939 (p); *Further Studies in a Dying Culture,* 1949 (e)

DAVID CECIL
1902-

(with Cynthia Asquith) *Cans and Can'ts,* 1927 (e); *The Stricken Deer: the Life of Cowper,* 1929 (b); *William Cowper,* 1932 (c); *Sir Walter Scott,* 1933 (b); *Early Victorian Novelists,* 1934 (c); *Jane Austen,* 1935 (c); *The Young Melbourne,* 1939 (b); *The English Poets,* 1941 (c); *Hardy the Novelist,* 1943 (c);

Anthony and Cleopatra, 1944 (c); *The Poetry of Thomas Gray,* 1945 (c); *Two Quiet Lives: Dorothy Osborne, Thomas Gray,* 1948 (b); *Poets and Story-Tellers,* 1949 (c); *Reading as One of the Fine Arts,* 1949 (e); *Lord Melbourne,* 1954 (b); *Walter Pater,* 1955 (c); *The Fine Art of Reading,* 1957 (e); *Victorian Novelists,* 1958 (c); *Max, a Biography,* 1964 (b); *Melbourne [The Young Melbourne* and *Lord Melbourne],* 1965 (b)

E. K. CHAMBERS
1866-1954

The History and Motives of Literary Forgeries (The Chancellor's English Essay for 1891), 1891 (e); *The Medieval Stage,* 2 vols., 1903 (repr. 1925) (h); *Notes on the History of the Revels Office under the Tudors,* 1906 (e); *The Remembrancia* [1580-1633], 1907 (h); *The Court,* 1916 (h); *Sir Thomas Malory,* 1922 (e); *The Elizabethan Stage,* 4 vols., 1923 (h); *The Disintegration of Shakespeare,* 1924 (British Academy Annual Shakespeare lecture); *Shakespeare: a Survey,* 1925 (c); *Arthur of Britain,* 1927 (h); *William Shakespeare: A Study of Facts and Problems,* 2 vols., 1930 (abgd. by Charles Williams as *A Short Life of Shakespeare with the Sources,* 1933) (b); *Matthew Arnold,* 1932 (Warton lecture); *The English Folk-Play,* 1933 (h); *Sir Thomas Wyatt, and some Collected Studies,* 1933 (c); *Eynsham under the Monks,* 1936 (h); *Sir Henry Lee: An Elizabethan Portrait,* 1936 (b); *Samuel Taylor Coleridge,* 1938 (b); *The Timelessness of Poetry,* 1940 (Eng. Assoc. Presid. Address); *A Sheaf of Studies,* 1942 (c); *Shakespearean Gleanings,* 1944 (c); *English Literature at the Close of the Middle Ages,* Vol. II of *Oxford History of English Literature,* 1945 (h,e); *Sources for a Biography of Shakespeare,* 1946 (e); *Matthew Arnold, a Study,* 1947 (c)

G. K. CHESTERTON
1874-1936

Greybeards at Play, 1900 (p); *The Wild Knight,* 1900 (p); *The Defendant,* 1901 (e); *Twelve Types,* 1902 (c); (with J. E. H. Williams) *Thomas Carlyle,* (1902 (c); *Robert Browning,* 1903 (b,c); (with F. G. Kitton) *Charles Dickens,*

1903 (c); (with others) *Leo Tolstoy*, 1903 (c); (with Richard Garnett) *Tennyson*, 1903 (c); (with Lewis Melville, pseud.) *Thackeray*, 1903 (c); *G. F. Watts*, 1904 (b); *The Napoleon of Notting Hill*, 1904 (n); *Heretics*, 1905 (e); *The Club of Queer Trades*, 1905 (s); *Charles Dickens*, 1906 (b); *The Man Who Was Thursday*, 1908 (n); *All Things Considered*, 1908 (e); *Orthodoxy*, 1908 (e); *The Ball and the Cross*, 1909 (n); *Tremendous Trifles*, 1909 (e); *George Bernard Shaw*, 1909 (c); *A Defence of Nonsense*, 1909 (e); *Alarms and Discursions*, 1910 (e); *What's Wrong with the World*, 1910 (e); *Five Types* (repr. from *Twelve Types*), 1910 (c); *William Blake*, 1910 (c); *Appreciations and Criticisms of the Works of Charles Dickens* (also pub. as *Criticisms and Appreciations of the Works of Charles Dickens*, 1933), 1911 (c); *The Ballad of the White Horse*, 1911 (p); *The Innocence of Father Brown*, 1911 (s); *A Defence of Nonsense*, 1911 (e); *Manalive*, 1912 (n); *A Miscellany of Men*, 1912 (e); *The Victorian Age in Literature*, 1913 (c); *Magic*, 1913 (d); *The Flying Inn*, 1914 (n); *London*, 1914 (e); *The Wisdom of Father Brown*, 1914 (s); *The Appetite of Tyranny, Including Letters to an Old Garibaldian*, 1915 (e); *The Crimes of England*, 1915 (e); *Poems*, 1915 (p); *Wine, Water and Song*, 1915 (p); *Divorce versus Democracy*, 1916 (e); *A Shilling for my Thoughts*, 1916, (e); *Temperance and the Great Alliance*, 1916 (e); *A Short History of England*, 1917 (h); *Utopia of Usurers*, 1917 (e); *Lord Kitchener*, 1917 (b); *Irish Impressions*, 1919 (e); *The New Jerusalem*, 1920 (e); *The Supersitition of Divorce*, 1920 (e); *The Uses of Diversity*, 1920 (e); *The Man Who Knew too Much*, 1922 (s); *Eugenics and Other Evils*, 1922 (e); *What I Saw in America*, 1922 (t); *The Ballad of St. Barbara*, 1922 (p); *St. Francis of Assisi*, 1923 (b); *Fancies Versus Fads*, 1923 (e); *The End of the Roman Road*, 1924 (e); (with others) *Number Two Joy Street, a Medley of Prose and Verse for Boys and Girls*, 1924; *The Exclusive Luxury of Enoch Oates and The Unthinkable Theory of Professor Green*, 1925 (s); *The Everlasting Man*, 1925 (e); *The Superstitions of the Sceptic*, 1925 (e); *William Cobbett*, 1925 (b); *Collected Works*, Minerva ed., 9 vols., 1926; *Collected Poems*, 1926; *The Return of Don Quixote*, 1926 (n); *The Incredulity of Father Brown*, 1926 (s); *The Catholic Church and Conversion*, 1926 (e); *The Outline of Sanity*, 1926 (e); *The Queen of Seven Swords*, 1926 (p); *The Secret of Father Brown*, 1927 (s); *Culture and the Coming Peril*, 1927 (e); *Social Reform and Birth Control*, 1927 (e); *Robert Louis Stevenson*, 1927 (c); *The Judgement of Dr. Johnson*, 1927 (d); *Gloria in Profundis*, 1927 (p); *The Sword of Wood*, 1928 (s); *Do We Agree? A Debate between G. K. Chesterton and Bernard Shaw, with Hilaire Belloc in the Chair*, 1928 (e); *Generally Speaking*, 1928 (e); *The Moderate Murderer and the Honest Quack*, 1929 (s); *The Poet and the Lunatics*, 1929 (s); *The Thing*, 1929 (e); *G.K.C. as M.C.*, 1929 (c); *New and Collected Poems*, 1929; *Ubi Ecclesia*, 1929 (p); *The Father Brown Stories* (coll.), 1929 (s); *The Grave of Arthur*, 1930 (p); *The Turkey and the Turk*, 1930 (p); *The Ecstatic Thief*, 1930 (s); *Four Faultless Felons*, 1930 (s); *Come to Think of It*, 1930 (e); *The Resurrection of Rome*, 1930 (e); *All Is Grist*, 1931 (e); *Christendom in Dublin*, 1932 (e); *Sidelights on New London and Newer York*, 1932 (e); *Chaucer*, 1932 (c); *All I Survey*, 1933 (e); *St. Thomas Aquinas*, 1933 (e); *Collected Poems*, 1933; *Avowals and Denials*, 1934 (e); *The Scandal of Father Brown*, 1935 (s); *The Well and the Shallows*, 1935 (e); *As I Was Saying*, 1936 (e); *Autobiography, 1936 (e); *The Paradoxes of Mr. Pond*, 1936 (s); *A G.K.C. Omnibus*, 1936 (misc.); *The Colored Lands*, 1938 (misc.); *End of the Armistice*, 1940 (e)

*repr. 1952

Christopher Hollis, *G. K. Chesterton*, 1950

RICHARD CHURCH
1893-

The Flood of Life, 1917 (p); *Hurricane*, 1919 (p); *Philip*, 1923 (p); *The Portrait of the Abbot*, 1926 (p); *The Dream*, 1927 (p); *Mood without Measure*, 1927 (p); *Mary Shelley*, 1928 (b); *Theme with Variations*, 1928 (p); *The Glance Backward*, 1930 (p); *Oliver's Daughter*, 1930 (n); *High Summer*, 1931 (n); *News from the Mountain*, 1932 (p); *The Prodigal Father*, 1933 (n); *The Apple of Concord*, 1935 (n); *Twelve Noon*, 1936 (p); *The Porch*, 1937 (repr. 1963) (n); *Pilgrimage*, 1938 (e); *Calling for a Spade*, 1939 (e); **The Stronghold*, 1939 (n); **The Room Within*, 1940 (n); *Eight for Immortality*, 1941 (c); *Plato's Mistake*, 1941 (e); *The Solitary Man*, 1941 (p); *The Squirrel Called Rufus*, 1941 (n); *The Sampler*, 1942 (n); *Twentieth-century Psalter*, 1943 (p); *British Authors*, 1943 (c); *Green Tide*, 1944 (e); *The Lamp*, 1946 (p); *Richard Jefferies Centenary, 1848-1948*, 1948 (c); *Collected Poems*, 1948; *Kent*, 1948 (t); *Growth of the English Novel*, 1950 (c); *Five Boys in a Cave*, 1951 (n); *Selected Lyrical Poems*, 1951 (p); *A Window on a Hill*, 1951 (e); *The Nightingale*, 1952 (n); *Portrait of Canterbury*, 1953 (t); *The Prodigal*, 1953 (d); *Over the Bridge*, 1955 (a); *Royal Parks of London*, 1956 (t); *The Dangerous Years*, 1956 (n); *The Golden Sovereign*, 1957 (a); *The Inheritors*, 1957 (p); *Small Moments*, 1957 (e); *A Country Window*, 1958 (e); *The Crab-Apple Tree*, 1959 (n); *Selected Poems*, 1959 (p); *North of Rome*, 1960 (p); *Calm October*, 1961 (e); *The Growth of the English Novel*, 1961 (c); *Prince Albert*, 1963 (b); *The Little Kingdom*, 1964 (n); *The Voyage Home*, 1964 (a); *A Stroll Before Dark*, 1965 (e); *A Look at Tradition*, 1965 (Presidential address, Eng. Assoc.); (with illust. by Imre Hofbaum) *London, Flower of Cities All*, 1966 (t)

*repr. 1965

AUSTIN CLARKE
1896-

The Vengeance of Fionn, 1917 (p); *The Sword of the West*, 1921 (p); *The Fires of Baäl*, 1921 (p); *The Cattledrive in Connaught*, 1925 (p); **The Son of Learning* [Gaelic tale turned into blank verse comedy], 1927 (d); *Pilgrimage*, 1929 (p); *The Flame*, 1930 (d); **The Bright Temptation*, 1932 (n); *The Singing-Men at Cashel*, 1936 (n); *Collected Poems*, 1936; *Night and Morning*, 1938 (n); *Sister Eucharia*, 1939 (d); *Black Fast*, 1941 (d); *As the Crow Flies*, 1943 (d); *The Viscount of Blarney*, 1944 (d); *First

Visit to England, 1945 (e); *The Second Kiss*, 1946 (d); *The Plot Succeeds*, 1950 (d); *Poetry in Modern Ireland*, 1951 (c); *The Sun Dances at Easter*, 1952 (n); *The Moment Next to Nothing*, 1953 (d); *Ancient Lights*, 1955 (p); *Too Great a Vine*, 1957 (p); *The Horse-Eaters*, 1960 (p); *Later Poems*, 1961 (p); *Twice Round the Black Church*, 1962 (r); *Forget-me-Not*, 1962 (p); *Flight to Africa*, 1963 (p); *Collected Plays*, 1963; *Poems*, 1964 (p); *Mnemosyne Lay in Dust*, (drawings by Jack Coughlin), 1966 (p)

*repr. 1965

A Tribute to Austin Clarke on his Seventieth Birthday, ed. John Montague and Liam Miller, 1966

JOHN COLLIER
1901-

His Monkey Wife, 1930 (n); *Gemini*, 1931 (p); (with Iain Lang) *Just the other Day*, 1932 (r); *Green Thoughts*, 1932 (s); *Tom's a-cold*, 1933 (n); *Full Circle*, 1933 (n); *Defy the Foul Fiend*, 1934 (n); *The Devil and All*, 1935 (s); *Variation on a Theme*, 1935 (n); *Witch's Monkey*, 1940 (n); *Presenting Moonshine*, 1941 (s); *The Touch of Nutmeg*, 1943 (s); *Fancies and Goodnights*, 1951 (s); *Pictures in the Fire*, 1958 (s); *Of Demons and Darkness*, 1965 (s)

See: John Gawsworth, *Ten Contemporaries*, Sec. Series, 1933

PADRAIC COLUM
1881-

Broken Soil (rev. as *The Fiddler's House*), 1903 (d); *The Land*, 1905 (d); *The Fiddler's House*, 1907 (d); *Wild Earth, A Book of Verse*, 1907 (enlgd. 1950) (p); *Studies*, 1907 (s); *Thomas Muskerry*, 1910 (d); (with Shane Leslie and others) *Eyes of Youth*, 1910 (p); *The Desert*, 1912 (Am. ed. *Mogu, The Wanderer*, 1917) (d); *My Irish Year*, 1912 (a); (music by H. Hughes) *Songs from Connacht*, 1913 (p); *A Boy in Eirinn*, 1913 (s); *Three Plays: The Fiddler's House, The Land, Thomas Muskerry*, 1916 (3d); *The King of Ireland's Son*, 1916 (s); *The Adventures of Odysseus and The Tale of Troy*, 1918 (repr. 1962 as *The Children's Homer*) (s); *The Boy Who Knew What the Birds

Said, 1918 (s); *The Girl Who Sat By the Ashes*, 1919 (s); *The Boy Apprenticed to an Enchanter*, 1920 (s); *The Children of Odin*, 1920 (repr. 1962) (s); *The Golden Fleece and The Heroes Who Lived Before Achilles*, 1921 (repr. 1962), (s); *The Children Who Followed the Piper*, 1922 (s); *Dramatic Legends*, 1922 (p); *Six Who Were Left in a Shoe*, 1923 (s); *Castle Conquer*, 1924 (n); *The Peep-Show Man*, 1924 (s); *At the Gateways of the Day*, 1924 (*Tales and Legends of Hawaii*, Vol. I) (s); *The Islands of the Mighty, Being the Hero Stories of Celtic Britain Retold from Mabinogion*, 1924 (s); *The Forge in the Forest*, 1925 (s); *The Voyagers*, 1925 (s); *The Bright Islands*, 1925 (*Tales and Legends of Hawaii*, Vol. II, repr. 1960) (s); *The Road Round Ireland*, 1926 (t); *Creatures*, 1927 (p); *The Fountain of Youth*, 1927 (s); *Balloon*, 1929 (d); *Old Pastures*, 1930 (p); *Cross Roads in Ireland*, 1930 (e); *Orpheus, Myths of the World*, 1930 (repr. 1959 as *Myths of the World*) (s); *Three Men*, 1931 (s); *Poems*, 1932; *A Half-Day's Ride, or, Estates in Corsica*, 1932 (t); *The Big Tree of Bunlahy*, 1933 (s); *The White Sparrow*, 1933 (s); *The Legend of St. Columba*, 1935 (s); *The Story of Lowry Maen*, 1937 (p); *Flower Pieces*, 1938 (p); *Dublin Poets and Artists*, 1939 (c); *Where the Winds Never Blew and the Cocks Never Crew*, 1940 (s); *Frenzied Prince*, 1943 (s); *Collected Poems*, 1953; *Vegetable Kingdom*, 1954 (p); *Flying Swans*, 1958 (s); *Irish Elegies*, 1958 (sec. ed. enlgd 1961) (p); (with Mary Colum) *Our Friend James Joyce*, 1958 (r); *Arthur Griffith* (Am. ed. *Ourselves Alone!*), 1959 (b); *Poet's Circuits*, 1960 (p); *Moytura: a Play for Dancers*, 1963 (d)

ALEX COMFORT
1920-

The Silver River, 1936 (a); *No Such Liberty*, 1941 (n); *France*, 1941 (p); *Into Egypt*, 1942 (d); *The Almond Tree*, 1942 (n); *A Wreath for the Living*, 1942 (p); *Cities of the Plain*, 1943 (d); *The Power House*, 1944 (n); *Elegies*, 1944 (p); *The Song of Lazarus*, 1945 (p); *Peace and Disobedience*, 1946 (e); *Art and Social Responsibility*, 1946 (e); *The Signal to Engage*, 1946 (p); *Letters From an Outpost*, 1947 (s); *The*

Novel and Our Time, 1948 (c); *Barbarism and Sexual Freedom*, 1948 (e); *On This Side Nothing*, 1949 (n); *The Pattern of the Future*, 1949 (e); *The Right Thing To Do*, 1949 (e); *Authority and Delinquency in the Modern State*, 1950 (e); *Sexual Behavior in Society*, 1950 (e); *And All But He Departed*, 1951 (p); *Delinquency*, 1951 (e); *Social Responsibility in Science and Art*, 1951 (e); *A Giant's Strength*, 1952 (n); *The Biology of Senescence*, 1956 (e) (rev. as *Ageing: The Biology of Senescence*, 1964); *Darwin and the Naked Lady*, 1961 (e); *Come Out to Play*, 1961 (n); *Haste to the Wedding*, 1962 (p); *Sex in Society*, 1963 (e); *The Process of Ageing*, 1965 (e); *Nature and Human Nature*, 1966 (e)

IVY COMPTON-BURNETT
1892-

Dolores, 1911 (n); *Pastors and Masters*, 1925 (n); *Brothers and Sisters*, 1929 (n); *Men and Wives*, 1931 (n); *More Women Than Men*, 1933 (n); *A House and Its Head*, 1935 (n); *Daughters and Sons*, 1937 (n); *A Family and a Fortune*, 1939 (n); *Parents and Children*, 1941 (n); *Elders and Betters*, 1944 (n); *Manservant and Maidservant* (Am. ed. *Bullivant and the Lambs*), 1947 (n); *Two Worlds and Their Ways*, 1949 (n); *Darkness and Day*, 1951 (n); *The Present and the Past*, 1953 (n); *Mother and Son*, 1955 (n); *A Father and His Fate*, 1957 (n); *A Heritage and Its History*, 1959 (n); *The Mighty and Their Fall*, 1961 (n); *A God and His Gifts*, 1963 (n)

Robert Liddell, *The Novels of I. Compton-Burnett*, 1955; Charles Burkhart, *Ivy Compton-Burnett*, 1965

CYRIL CONNOLLY
1903-

The Rock Pool, 1935 (n); *Enemies of Promise*, 1938 (rev. 1949) (c,r); Editor of *Horizon*, 1939-45; *The Unquiet Grave*, 1944 (c); Vercors (pseud.), *Put out the Light*, 1944 (tr. of *Le Silence de la Mer*); *The Condemned Playground, Essays: 1927-1944*, 1945 (e); *Ideas and Places*, 1953 (c); *Les Pavillons: French Pavilions of the Eighteenth Century*, 1962 (e); *Previous Convictions*, 1964 (e); *The Modern Movement, 1880-1920*, 1965 (h)

JOSEPH CONRAD
1875-1924

Almayer's Folly, 1895 (n); *An Outcast of the Islands*, 1896 (n); *The Nigger of the Narcissus*, 1897 (n); *Tales of Unrest*, 1898 (s); *Lord Jim*, 1900 (n); (with Ford Madox Hueffer) *The Inheritors*, 1901 (n); *Typhoon*, 1902 (s); *Youth*, 1902 (3s); (with Ford Madox Hueffer) *Romance*, 1903 (n); *Nostromo*, 1904 (n); *The Mirror of the Sea*, 1906 (r); *The Secret Agent*, 1907 (n); *A Set of Six*, 1908 (s); *Under Western Eyes*, 1911 (n); *'Twixt Land and Sea Tales*, 1912 (s); *Some Reminiscences* (also pub. as *A Personal Record*), 1912 (r); *Chance*, 1913 (n); *Victory*, 1915 (n); *Within the Tides*, 1915 (s); *The Shadow Line*, 1917 (n); *The Arrow of Gold*, 1919 (n); *The Rescue*, 1920 (n); *Notes on Life and Letters*, 1921 (e); *The Rover*, 1923 (n); *Works* (Uniform Ed.), 22 vols., 1923-28; (with Ford Madox Ford) *The Nature of a Crime*, 1924 (n); *Suspense*, 1925 (n); *Tales of Hearsay*, 1925 (s); *Last Essays*, 1926 (e); *Letters to His Wife*, 1927; *Letters. Joseph Conrad to Richard Curle*, ed. R. C. [Richard Curle] (also pub. as *Conrad to a Friend*), 1928; *Letters from Joseph Conrad, 1895-1924*, ed. Edward Garnett, 1928; *Letters of Joseph Conrad to Marguerite Poradowska, 1890-1920*, tr. from French and ed. John A. Gee and Paul J. Sturm, 1940; *Letters to William Blackwood and David S. Meldrum*, ed. William Blackburn, 1958; *Conrad's Polish Background; Letters to and from Polish Friends*, ed. Zadzislaw Nayder, 1964

Gérard Jean-Aubry, *Joseph Conrad: Life and Letters*, 2 vols., 1927; Gérard Jean-Aubry, *The Sea Dreamer; a Definitive Biography of Joseph Conrad*, tr. Helen Sebba, 1957; Kenneth A. Lohf and Eugene P. Sheehy, *Joseph Conrad at Mid-Century: Editions and Studies, 1895-1955*, 1957; Jocelyn Baines, *Joseph Conrad, A Critical Biography*, 1960

WILLIAM COOPER
1910-

(pseud. Harry Summerfield Hoff) *Trina*, 1934 (n); (pseud. Harry Summerfield Hoff), *Rhéa*, 1935 (n); (pseud. Harry Summerfield Hoff), *Lisa*, 1937 (n); (pseud. Harry Summerfield Hoff) *Three Marriages*, 1946 (n); *Scenes From Provincial Life*, 1950 (n); *The Struggles of Albert Woods*, 1952 (n); *The Ever-Interesting Topic*, 1953 (n); *Disquiet and Peace*, 1956 (n); *Young People*, 1958 (n); *C. P. Snow*, 1959 (c); *Prince Genji*, 1960 (d); *Scenes From Married Life*, 1961 (n); *Memoirs of a New Man*, 1966 (n)

A. E. COPPARD
1878-1957

Adam and Eve and Pinch Me, 1921 (repr. 1946) (s); *Clorinda Walks in Heaven*, 1922 (s); *Hips and Haws*, 1922 (p); *The Black Dog*, 1923 (s); *Fishmonger's Fiddle*, 1925 (repr. 1941) (s); *The Field of Mustard*, 1926 (s); *Pelagea*, 1926 (p); *Yokohama Garland*, 1926 (p); *Count Stefan*, 1928 (s); *Silver Circus*, 1928 (s); *The Collected Poems*, 1928; *The Man from Kilsheelan*, 1930 (repr. with alterations from *The Black Dog*) (s); *Fares Please! An Omnibus*, 1931 (s from *The Black Dog, The Field of Mustard* and *Silver Circus*); *The Hundredth Story of A. E. Coppard* (Am. ed. *My One Hundredth Tale*), 1931 (s); *Nixey's Harlequin*, 1931 (s); *Easter Day*, 1931 (p); *Crotty Shinkwin, a Tale of the Strange Adventure That Befell a Butcher of County Clare. The Beauty Spot, a Tale Concerning the Chilterns*, 1932 (2s); *Rummy, That Noble Game Expounded in Prose, Poetry, Diagram, and Engraving, with an Account of Certain Diversions Into the Mountain Fastnesses of Cork and Kerry*, 1932 (misc.); *Dunky Fitlow*, 1933 (s); *Ring the Bells of Heaven*, 1933 (s); *Emergency Exit*, 1934 (s); *Polly Oliver*, 1935 (s); *Cherry Ripe*, 1935 (Am. ed. has three more poems) (p); *The Ninepenny Flute*, 1937 (s); *You Never Know, Do You?* 1939 (s); *Ugly Anna*, 1944 (s); *Selected Tales* (from the 12 vols. pub. between the wars), 1946 (s); *Fearful Pleasures*, 1946 (s); *Selected Tales*, 1947 (s); *Dark-Eyed Lady*, 1947 (s); *Collected Tales*, 1948; *Lucy In Her Pink Jacket*, 1954 (s); *It's Me, O Lord!* 1957 (a)

Jacob Schwartz, *The Writings of Alfred Edward Coppard, A Bibliography* (with foreword and notes by A. E. Coppard), 1931

MARIE CORELLI
1855-1924

A Romance of Two Worlds, 1886 (n); *Vendetta*, 1886 (n); *Thelma*, 1887 (n); *My Wonderful Wife*, 1889 (s); *Ardath*, 1889 (n); *Wormwood*, 1890 (n); *The Soul of Lilith*, 1892 (n); (pub. anonymously) *The Silver Domino*, 1892 (n); *Barabbas*, 1893 (n); *The Sorrows of Satan*, 1895 (n); *The Novels*, Author's Library Ed., 8 vols., 1896-98; *The Murder of Delicia*, 1896 (repr. 1918 as *Delicia*) (n); *The Mighty Atom*, 1896 (n); *Cameos*, 1896 (s); *Ziska*, 1897 (n); *Jane*, 1900 (s); *Boy*, 1900 (n); *The Master Christian*, 1900 (n); *A Christmas Greeting of Various Thoughts, Verses, and Fancies*, 1901; *"Temporal Power"*, 1902 (n); *The Plain Truth of the Stratford-on-Avon Controversy*, 1903 (e); *God's Good Man*, 1904 (n); *Free Opinions*, 1905 (e); *The Treasure of Heaven*, 1906 (n); *Woman, or—Suffragette?* 1907 (e); *Holy Orders*, 1908 (n); *The Life Everlasting*, 1911 (n); *Innocent*, 1914 (n); *With Shakespeare in His Garden*, 1916 (e); *The Young Diana*, 1918 (n); *My "Little Bit"*, 1919 (e); *The Lover of Long Ago*, 1920 (s); *The Secret Power*, 1921 (n); *Love—and the Philosopher*, 1923 (n); *Open Confession: To a Man from a Woman*, 1925 (n); *Poems*, ed. Berthe Vyver, 1925 (p)

Eileen Bigland, *Marie Corelli: the Woman and the Legend: a Biography*, 1953 [no bibliog.]

NOEL COWARD
1899-

"I'll Leave It To You," 1920 (d); *A Withered Nosegay* (Am. ed. *Terribly Intimate Portraits*), 1922 (d); *The Rat Trap*, 1924 (d); *The Vortex*, 1924 (d); *The Young Idea*, 1924 (d); *Fallen Angels* (rev. 1958), 1925 (d); *Hay Fever*, 1925 (d); (under pseudonym Hernia Whittlebot) *Chelsea Buns*, 1925 (d,p); *Easy Virtue*, 1926 (d); *The Queen Was In The Parlour*, 1926 (d); *"This Was A Man,"* 1926 (d); *Home Chat*, 1927 (d); *The Marquise*, 1927 (d); *Sirocco*, 1927 (d); *Charles B. Cochran's 1928 Revue . . . Book of Lyrics*, 1928 (p); *Bitter Sweet*, 1929 (musical version in 1933) (d);

Private Lives, 1930 (d); *Post-Mortem*, 1931 (d); *Collected Sketches and Lyrics*, 1931 (d,p); *Cavalcade*, 1932 (d); *Design for Living*, 1933 (d); *Play Parade, Vol. I*, 1933 (d); *Conversation Piece*, 1934 (d); *Point Valaine*, 1935 (d); *Tonight at 8:30*, 3 vols., 1936 (d); *Present Indicative*, 1937 (a); *Operette*, 1938 (d); *Second Play Parade*, 1939 (d); *To Step Aside*, 1939 (s); *Curtain Calls*, 1940 (d); *Blithe Spirit* (Am. musical version, *High Spirits*), 1941 (d); *Present Laughter*, 1943 (d); *This Happy Breed*, 1943 (d); *Middle East Diary*, 1944; *Peace in Our Time*, 1947 (d); *Play Parade, Vol. I-III*, 1949-50 (d); *Star Quality*, 1951 (s); *Quadrille*, 1952 (d); *Relative Values*, 1952 (d); *The Noel Coward Song Book*, 1953 (music, p); *Future Indefinite*, 1954 (a); *Play Parade, Vol. IV*, 1954 (d); *South Sea Bubble*, 1956 (d); *Nude With Violin*, 1957 (d); *Play Parade, Vol. V*, 1958 (d); *Look After Lulu* (adaptation of *Occupetoi d'Amélie* by G. Feydeau), 1959 (d); *Pomp and Circumstance*, 1960 (n); *Waiting in The Wings*, 1960 (d); *Play Parade, Vol. VI*, 1962 (d); *The Collected Short Stories*, 1962; *Pretty Polly Barlow*, 1965 (s); *The Lyrics of Noel Coward*, 1965 (p); *Suite in Three Keys* (trilogy: *A Song at Twilight, Shadows of the Evening, Come Into the Garden Maud*), 1966

Robert Graecan, *The Art of Noel Coward*, 1953; Raymond Mander and Joe Mitchenson, *Theatrical Companion to Coward*, with appreciation by Terence Rattigan, 1957

A. J. CRONIN
1896-

Hatter's Castle, 1931 (n); *Three Loves*, 1932 (n); *Grand Canary*, 1933 (n); *Adventures in Two Worlds*, 1935 (repr. 1952) (a); *The Stars Look Down*, 1935 (n); *The Citadel*, 1937 (n); *Jupiter Laughs*, 1940 (d); *The Keys of the Kingdom*, 1941 (n); *The Green Years*, 1944 (n); *Shannon's Way*, 1948 (n); *The Spanish Gardener*, 1950 (n); *Beyond This Place*, 1953 (n); *Crusader's Tomb*, 1956 (n); *A Thing of Beauty*, 1956 (n); *The Cronin Omnibus*, 1958; *The Northern Light*, 1958 (n); *The Judas Tree*, 1961 (n); *A Song of Sixpence*, 1964 (n)

R. B. CUNNINGHAME-GRAHAM
1852-1936

Economic Evolution, 1891 (e); *Notes on the District of Menteith*, 1895 (t); (with Mrs. Cunninghame-Graham) *Father Archangel of Scotland*, 1896 (s,e); *Aurora la Cujiñi, A Realistic Sketch in Seville*, 1898 (t); *Mogreb-el-Acksa, A Journey in Morocco*, 1898 (t); *The Ipané*, 1899 (t); *Thirteen Stories*, 1900 (s); *A Vanished Arcadia*, 1901 (h); *Success*, 1902 (sk); *Hernando de Soto, Together With An Account of One of His Captains, Gonçalo Silvestre*, 1903 (b); *Progress and Other Sketches*, 1905 (sk); *His People*, 1906 (sk); *Faith*, 1909 (s); *Hope*, 1910 (s); *Charity*, 1912 (s); *A Hatchment*, 1913 (n); *Scottish Stories*, 1914 (s); *El Rio de la Plata*, 1914 (t); *Bernal Diaz del Castillo*, 1915 (b); *Brought Forward*, 1916 (s); *Cartagena and The Banks of the Sinú*, 1920 (t); *A Brazilian Mystic, Being the Life and Miracles of Antonio Conselheiro*, 1920 (b); *The Conquest of New Granada*, 1922 (h); *The Dream of the Magi*, 1923 (s); *Inveni Portam, Joseph Conrad*, 1924 (b); *The Conquest of the River Plate*, 1924 (h); *Doughty Deeds, An Account of the Life of Robert Graham*, 1925 (b); *Pedro de Valdivia*, 1926 (b); *Redeemed and Other Sketches*, 1927 (sk); *Bibi*, 1929 (s); *Thirty Tales and Sketches* (sel. Edward Garnett), 1929 (s); *José Antonio Páez*, 1929 (b); *The Horses of the Conquest*, 1930 (h); *Writ in Sand*, 1932 (s); *Portrait of a Dictator, Francisco Solano Lopez*, 1933 (b); *With the Northwest Wind*, 1934 (t); *Mirages*, 1936 (s); *Rodeo, A Collection of . . . Tales and Sketches*, 1936; *Three Fugitive Pieces*, 1960 (s)

Herbert F. West, *A Modern Conquistador, Robert Bontine Cunninghame-Graham, His Life and Works* 1932; Hugh MacDiarmid, *Cunninghame-Graham: a Centenary Study*, 1952

DAVID DAICHES
1912-

The Place of Meaning in Poetry, 1935 (c); *New Literary Values*, 1936 (c); *Literature and Society*, 1938 (c); *The Novel and the Modern World*, 1939 (rev. 1960) (c); *Poetry and the Modern World*, 1940 (rev. 1960) (c); *The King James Version of the English Bible*, 1941 (c); *Virginia Woolf*, 1942 (rev. 1963) (c); *Robert Louis Stevenson*, 1947 (c); *A Study of Literature for Readers and Critics*, 1948 (c); *Robert Burns*, 1951 (c); *Willa Cather*, 1951 (c); *Walt Whitman*, 1955 (c); *Critical Approaches to Literature*, 1956 (e); *Literary Essays*, 1956 (c); *Two Worlds*, 1956 (a); *Milton*, 1957 (c); *The Present Age after 1920* (Vol. V of *Introduction to English Literature*), 1958 (h,c); *The Present Age in British Literature*, 1958 (c); *A Critical History of English Literature*, 2 vols., 1960 (c); *George Eliot: Middlemarch*, 1963 (c); *The Paradox of Scottish Culture: the Eighteenth-Century Experience*, 1964 (e); *English Literature*, 1964 (c); *Time and the Poet*, 1965 (lecture, Univ. College of Swansea, Cardiff, Wales)

CLEMENCE DANE
1888-1965

Regiment of Women, 1917 (n); *First the Blade*, 1918 (n); *Legend*, 1919 (n); *A Bill of Divorcement*, 1921 (d); *Will Shakespeare, an Invention*, 1921 (d); *Wandering Stars, Together With The Lover*, 1924 (n); *The Way Things Happen*, 1924 (s); *Naboth's Vineyard*, 1925 (d); *Granite*, 1926 (d); *The Women's Side*, 1926 (e); *The Babyons*, 1927 (n); *Mariners*, 1927 (d); *Mr. Fox*, 1927 (d); *A Traveller Returns*, 1927 (d); *The Dearly Beloved of Benjamin Cobb*, 1927 (s); (with Helen Simpson) *Enter Sir John*, 1928 (n); (music by Richard Addinsell) *Adam's Opera*, 1928 (d); *The King Waits*, 1929 (s); *Tradition and Hugh Walpole*, 1929 (c); (with Helen Simpson) *Author Unknown*, 1930 (n); (with Helen Simpson) *Printer's Devil*, 1930 (n); *Broome Stages*, 1931 (n); (with Helen Simpson) *Re-enter Sir John*, 1932 (n); *Wild Decembers*, 1932 (d); *Recapture, A Clemence Dane Omnibus*, 1932; (music by Richard Addinsell) *Come of Age, The Text of a Play in Music and Words*, 1934 (d); (music by Richard Addinsell) *L'Aiglon*, by Edmond Rostand (adaptation), 1934 (d); *Moonlight Is Silver*, 1934 (d); *Fate Cries Out*, 1935 (s); *The Moon Is Feminine*, 1938 (n); *Herod and Mariamne* (based on a play by Friedrich Hebbel), 1938 (d); *The Arrogant History of White Ben*,

1939 (n); *Trafalgar Day, 1940*, 1940 (p); *Cousin Muriel,* 1940 (d); *England's Darling,* 1940 (d); *The Golden Reign of Queen Elizabeth,* 1941 (d); *Saviours* (also published with music by Richard Addinsell), 1942 (d); *The Lion and the Unicorn,* 1943 (d); *He Brings Great News,* 1944 (n); *Call Home the Heart,* 1947 (d); (music by Richard Addinsell) *Alice's Adventures in Wonderland and Through the Looking Glass* (dramatization of Lewis Carroll novels), 1948 (d); *The Flower Girls,* 1954 (n); *Eighty in the Shade,* 1959 (d); *Collected Plays,* Vol. I, 1961 (d); *Approaches to Drama,* 1961 (lectures); *The Godson,* 1964 (s); *London Has a Garden,* 1964 (h,r)

JOHN DAVIDSON
1857-1909

The North Wall, 1885 (n); (anon.) *Diabolus Amans,* 1885 (p); *Bruce,* 1886 (d); *Smith,* 1888 (d); *Plays,* 1889 (d); *Scaramouche in Naxos,* 1890 (d); *Perfervid,* 1890 (n); *The Great Men and a Practical Novelist,* 1891 (s); *In a Music Hall,* 1891 (p); Montesquieu, *Persian Letters,* 1892 (tr); (with C. J. Wills) *Laura Ruthven's Widowhood,* 1892 (n); *Fleet Street Eclogues,* 1893 (p); *Sentences and Paragraphs,* 1893 (e); *A Random Itinerary,* 1894 (e); *Ballads and Songs,* 1894 (p); *Baptist Lake,* 1894 (n); *Earl Lavender,* 1895 (n); *St. George's Day,* 1895 (p); *A Second Series of Fleet Street Eclogues,* 1896 (p); François Coppée, *For the Crown,* 1896 (tr); *Miss Armstrong's and Other Circumstances,* 1896 (s); *The Pilgrimage of Strongsoul,* 1896 (n); *New Ballads,* 1897 (p); *Godfrida,* 1898 (d); *The Last Ballad,* 1899 (p); *Self's the Man,* 1901 (d); *The Testament of a Vivisector,* 1901 (p); *Testament of a Man Forbid,* 1901 (p); *The Testament of an Empire-Builder,* 1902 (p); *The Knight of the Maypole,* 1903 (d); *A Rosary,* 1903 (misc.); *A Queen's Romance* (adapted from Victor Hugo, *Ruy Blas),* 1904 (d); *The Testament of a Prime Minister,* 1904 (p); *The Theatrocrat,* 1905 (d); *The Ballad of a Nun,* 1905 (p); *Selected Poems,* 1905 (p); *Holiday,* 1906 (p); *The Triumph of Mammon),* (Pt. I of trilogy, *God and Mammon),* 1907 (p); *Mammon and His Message* (Pt. II of trilogy), 1908 (p);

The Testament of John Davidson, 1908 (p); *Fleet Street,* 1909 (p); *The Man Forbid,* 1910 (e); *Poems,* 1924 (p); *Poems and Ballads,* 1959 (p); *John Davidson, A Selection of His Poems,* ed. Maurice Lindsay, 1961 (p)

J. B. Townsend, *John Davidson, Poet of Armageddon,* 1961

DONALD DAVIE
1922-

Purity of Diction in English Verse, 1952 (c); *Poems,* 1954 (p); *Articulate Energy,* 1955 (c); *Brides of Reason,* 1955 (p); *A Winter Talent,* 1957 (p); *The Forests of Lithvania,* 1959 (p); *The Heyday of Sir Walter Scott,* 1961 (c); *New and Selected Poems,* 1961 (p); *The Language of Science and the Language of Literature, 1700-1740,* 1963 (c); *Events and Wisdoms, Poems 1957-63,* 1964 (p); *Ezra Pound: Poet as Sculptor,* 1965 (c); *Boris Pasternak, The Poems of Doctor Zhivago,* 1965 (tr)

RHYS DAVIES
1903-

Aaron, 1927 (n); *The Song of Songs and Other Stories,* 1927 (s); *The Withered Root,* 1927 (n); *A Bed of Feathers,* 1929 (n); *Rings on Her Fingers,* 1930 (n); *The Stars, The World, and The Women,* 1930 (s); *Tale,* 1930 (n); *Arfon,* 1931 (n); *A Pig in a Poke,* 1931 (s); *A Woman,* 1931 (n); *The Woman Among Women,* 1931 (p); *Count Your Blessings,* 1932 (n); *Daisy Matthews and Three Other Tales,* 1932 (n); *The Red Hills,* 1932 (n); *Love Provoked,* 1933 (n); *Honey and Bread,* 1935 (n); *One of Norah's Early Days,* 1935 (n); *The Things Men Do,* 1936 (n); *A Time to Laugh,* 1937 (n); *My Wales,* 1937 (t); *Jubilee Blues,* 1938 (n); *Sea Urchin, The Adventures of Jorgen Jorgensen,* 1940 (b); *Under the Rose,* 1940 (n); *Tomorrow to Fresh Woods,* 1941 (n); *A Finger in Every Pie,* 1942 (n); *The Story of Wales,* 1943 (t); *The Black Venus,* 1944 (n); *Selected Stories,* 1945 (s); *The Trip to London,* 1946 (s); *The Dark Daughters,* 1947 (n); *Boy With a Trumpet,* 1949 (n); *Marianne,* 1951 (n); *The Painted King,* 1954 (n);

No Escape, 1954 (a); *Collected Stories*, 1955; *Perishable Quality*, 1957 (n); *The Darling of Her Heart*, 1958 (n); *Girl Waiting in the Shade*, 1960 (n)

See John Gawsworth, *Ten Contemporaries*, 1932; R. L. Mégroz, *Rhys Davies*, 1932

W. H. DAVIES
1871-1940

The Soul's Destroyer, and Other Poems, 1905 (p); *New Poems*, 1907 (p); *Nature Poems, and Others*, 1908 (p); *The Autobiography of a Super-Tramp*, 1908 (a); *Beggars*, 1909 (a); *Farewell to Poesy*, 1910 (p); *Songs of Joy and Others*, 1911 (p); *A Weak Woman*, 1911 (n); *The True Traveller*, 1912 (t); *Foliage*, 1913 (p); *The Bird of Paradise*, 1914 (p); *Nature*, 1914 (e); *Child Lovers*, 1916 (p); *Collected Poems* (Am. ed. *The Collected Poems of William H. Davies*), 1916; *Forty New Poems*, 1918 (p); *Raptures*, 1918 (p); *A Poet's Pilgrimage*, 1918 (a); *The Song of Life*, 1920 (p); *The Captive Lion*, 1921 (p); *The Hour of Magic*, 1922 (p); *Collected Poems: Second Series*, 1923; *Selected Poems*, 1923 (p); *True Travellers, A Tramps' Opera in Three Acts*, 1923 (d); *Secrets*, 1924 (p); *W. H. Davies*, 1925 (p); *A Poet's Alphabet*, 1925 (p); *Later Days*, 1925 (a); *The Song of Love*, 1926 (p); *The Adventures of Johnny Walker, Tramp*, 1926 (t); *A Poet's Calendar*, 1927 (p); *Dancing Mad*, 1927 (n); *Forty-nine Poems by W. H. Davies*, 1928 (p); *Selected Poems of W. H. Davies*, 1928 (p); *The Collected Poems of W. H. Davies, 1928*, 1928; *Moss and Feather*, 1928 (p); *Ambition*, 1929 (p); *In Winter*, 1931 (p); *Poems 1930-31*, 1932 (p); *The Lovers' Song Book*, 1933 (p); *My Birds*, 1933 (e); *My Garden*, 1933 (e); *The Poems of W. H. Davies*, 1934 (p); *Love Poems*, 1935 (p); *The Birth of Song*, 1936 (p); *The Loneliest Mountain*, 1939 (p); *Poems*, 1940 (p); *Common Joys*, 1941 (p); *Collected Poems*, 1942; *The Essential W. H. Davies*, ed. Brian Waters, 1951; *The Complete Poems of W. H. Davies*, 1963

See Richard Church, *Eight for Immortality*, 1941

E. M. DELAFIELD
1890-1943

Zella Sees Herself, 1917 (n); *The Pelicans*, 1918 (n); *The War-Workers*, 1918 (n); *Consequences*, 1919 (n); *Tension*, 1920 (n); *The Heel of Achilles*, 1921 (n); *Humbug*, 1921 (n); *The Optimist*, 1922 (n); *A Reversion to Type*, 1923 (n); *Mrs. Harter*, 1924 (n); *Messalina of the Suburbs*, 1924 (n); *The Chip and the Block*, 1925 (n); *Jill*, 1926 (n); *The Way Things Are*, 1927 (n); *The Entertainment*, 1927 (s); *The Suburban Young Man*, 1928 (n); *What Is Love?* (Am. ed. *First Love*), 1928 (n); *Women Are Like That*, 1929 (s); *Diary of a Provincial Lady*, 1930 (n); *Turn Back the Leaves*, 1930 (n); *Challenge to Clarissa* (Am. ed. *House Party*), 1931 (n); *The Provincial Lady Goes Further* (Am. ed. *The Provincial Lady in London*), 1932 (n); *Thank Heaven Fasting* (Am. ed. *A Good Man's Love*), 1932 (n); *To See Ourselves*, 1932 (d); *Gay Life*, 1933 (n); *The Glass Wall*, 1933 (d); *General Impressions*, 1933 (e); *The Provincial Lady in America*, 1934 (t); *The Provincial Lady at Home and Abroad* (collection), 1935; (anon.) *The Bazalgettes*, 1935 (n); *Faster! Faster!* 1936 (n); *As Others Hear Us*, 1937 (e); *Straw Without Bricks* (Am. ed. *I Visit the Soviets*), 1937 (t); *Nothing Is Safe*, 1937 (n); *Ladies and Gentlemen in Victorian Fiction*, 1937 (c); *Love Has No Resurrection*, 1939 (s); *Three Marriages* (Am. ed. *When Women Love*), 1939 (n); *The Provincial Lady in Wartime*, 1940 (n); *No-One Will Know Now*, 1941 (n); *Late and Soon*, 1943 (n)

WALTER DE LA MARE
1873-1956

(pseud. Walter Ramal) *Songs of Childhood*, 1902 (p); *Henry Brocken*, 1904 (s); *Poems*, 1906 (p); *M. E. Coleridge, An Appreciation*, 1907 (c); *The Three Mulla-Mulgars* (also publ. as *The Three Royal Monkeys*), 1910 (s); *The Return*, 1910 (n); *The Listeners*, 1912 (p); *A Child's Day*, 1912 (p); *The Old Men*, 1913 (p); *Peacock Pie*, 1913 (repr. 1958) (p); *The Sunken Garden*, 1917 (p); *Motley*, 1918 (p); (with Pamela Bianco) *Flora, A Book of Drawings by P.B., With Illustrative Poems*, 1919 (p);

Rupert Brooke and the Intellectual Imagination, 1919 (c); *Poems, 1901-1918* (Am. ed. *Collected Poems, 1901-1918*), 2 vols., 1920; *The Veil,* 1921 (p); *Memoirs of a Midget,* 1921 (n); *Crossings, A Fairy Play,* 1921 (d); *Story and Rhyme, A Selection by the Author,* 1921 (s,p); *Down-adown-Derry,* 1922 (p); *Thus Her Tale,* 1923 (p); (with music by W. G. Whittaker) *The Song of Shadows,* 1923 (p); (with others) *Number One Joy Street,* 1923 (p,s); *Lispet, Lispett and Vaine,* 1923 (s); *The Riddle,* 1923 (s); *Some Thoughts on Reading,* 1923 (c); *A Ballad of Christmas,* 1924 (p); *Ding Dong Bell,* 1924 (p,s); (with music by Norman Peterkin) *The Gallias,* 1924 (p); (with music by Norman Peterkin) *She's Me Forgot,* 1924 (p); *The Hostage* (cover title: *Christmas*), 1925 (s); *Broomsticks,* 1925 (s); *Miss Jemima,* 1925 (s); (with music by Norman Peterkin) *Dubbuldideery, A Monkey's Journey-Song,* 1925 (p); (with music by Norman Peterkin) *Never More Sailor,* 1925 (p); (with music by Norman Peterkin) *Song of the Water Maiden,* 1925 (p); *The Connoisseur,* 1926 (s); (with music by Ernest L. Lodge) *Mistletoe,* 1926 (p); *Alone,* 1927 (p); *Stuff and Nonsense and So On,* 1927 (p); *Lucy,* 1927 (s); *Old Joe,* 1927 (s); *Told Again, Traditional Tales,* 1927 (s); (with music by Norman Peterkin) *Once and There Was a Young Sailor,* 1927 (p); *Self to Self,* 1928 (p); *At First Sight,* 1928 (n); (with others) *Number Six Joy Street,* 1928 (s,p); *Readings, Traditional Tales,* 1928 (s); *A Snowdrop,* 1929 (p); *Stories from the Bible,* 1929 (s); *The Hostage,* 1930 (p); *News,* 1930 (p); *Poems for Children,* 1930 (p); *On the Edge,* 1930 (s); *Desert Islands and Robinson Crusoe,* 1930 (c); *To Lucy,* 1931 (p); *Old Rhymes and New,* 1st and 2nd series, 1932 (p); *Lewis Carroll,* 1932 (c); *The Fleeting,* 1933 (p); *The Walter de la Mare Omnibus,* 1933 (3n); *The Lord Fish,* 1933 (s); *A Froward Child,* 1934 (s); *Poems, 1919-1934,* 1935 (p); *Early One Morning in the Spring,* 1935 (e); *The Nap,* 1936 (s); *The Wind Blows Over,* 1936 (s); *Poetry in Prose,* 1936 (e); *This Year, Next Year,* 1937 (p); *Stories, Essays, and Poems* (Everyman ed.), 1938; *Memory,* 1938 (p); *In a Library,* 1938 (p); *Animal Stories,* 1939 (s); *Behold this Dreamer*

(anthology with introd. and commentary by de la Mare), 1939; *Haunted,* 1939 (p); *Pleasures and Speculations,* 1940 (e); *Bells and Grass,* 1941 (p); *The Picnic,* 1941 (s); *Time Passes,* 1942 (p); *Collected Poems,* 1942; *The Best Stories of Walter de la Mare,* 1942 (s); *The Old Lion* (Am ed. *Mr. Bumps and His Monkey*), 1942 (s); *Love* (anthology), 1943; *The Magic Jacket,* 1943 (s); *Collected Rhymes and Verses,* 1944; *The Scarecrow,* 1945 (s); *The Burning Glass,* 1945 (p); *The Dutch Cheese,* 1946 (s); *The Traveller,* 1946 (p); *Collected Stories for Children,* 1947 (rev. ed. 1957); *J. B. S. Chardin, 1699-1779,* 1948 (b); *Inward Companion,* 1950 (p); *Winged Chariot,* 1951 (p); *Selected Stories and Verses,* 1952; *Snow White,* 1952 (s); *Cinderella,* 1952 (s); *Private View,* 1953 (c); *O Lovely England,* 1953 (p); *Selected Poems,* 1954 (p); *Winnowing Dream,* 1954 (p); *A Beginning,* 1955 (s); *A Selection,* 1956 (s,e,p); *Ghost Stories,* 1956 (s); *The Story of Joseph,* 1958 (b); *The Story of Moses,* 1959 (b); *Jack and the Beanstalk,* 1959 (s); *Tales Told Again,* 1959 (s); *A Penny a Day,* 1960 (p); *A Choice of de la Mare's Verse,* by W. H. Auden, 1963 (p). Also *Come Hither, a Collection of Rhymes and Poems for the Young of All Ages,* made by Walter de la Mare, 1923 (rev. 1928)

Forrest Reid, *Walter de la Mare: a Critical Study,* 1929 [no bibliog.]; Leonard Clark, *A Handlist of the Writings in Book Form 1902-1952 of Walter de la Mare,* Univ. of Virginia Bibliographical Soc. Studies in Bibliog., Vol. VI, 1953-54, pp. 197-217 (repr. as Nat. Bk. League pamphlet, 1956); Kenneth Hopkins, *Walter de la Mare,* 1953

WILLIAM DE MORGAN
1839-1917

On a Pincushion, 1877 (s); *Report on the Feasibility of a Manufacture of Glazed Pottery in Egypt,* 1894 (e); *Joseph Vance: An Ill-written Autobiography,* 1906 (n); *Alice-for-Short,* 1907 (n); *Somehow Good,* 1908 (n); *It Never Can Happen Again,* 1909 (n); *An Affair of Dishonour,* 1910 (n); *A Likely Story,* 1911 (n); *When Ghost Meets Ghost,* 1914 (n); *The Old Madhouse,* 1919 (n)

NIGEL DENNIS
1912-

Boys and Girls Come Out to Play (Am. ed. *Sea Change*), 1949 (n); *Cards of Identity*, 1955 (n); *Two Plays and a Preface* (*Cards of Identity* and *The Making of Moo*), 1958 (c,2d); *Dramatic Essays*, 1962 (e); *Jonathan Swift*, 1965 (c); *A House in Order*, 1966 (n)

ERNEST DE SELINCOURT
See under S

BONAMY DOBRÉE
1891-

Restoration Comedy, 1660-1720, 1924 (h); *Essays in Biography*, 1925 (b); *Histriophone, a Dialogue on Dramatic Diction*, 1925 (c,e); *Timotheus: the Future of the Theatre*, 1925 (e); *Rochester, a Conversation between Sir George Etherege and Mr. Fitzjames*, 1926 (e); *Sir John Denham: a Conversation between Bishop Henry King and Edumund Waller*, 1927 (e); *Sarah Churchill, Duchess of Marlborough*, 1927 (b); *Restoration Tragedy, 1660-1720*, 1929 (h); *The Lamp and the Lute*, 1929 (enlgd. 1964) (c); *St. Martin's Summer*, 1932 (n); *Variety of Ways, Discussions on Six Authors*, 1932 (c); *William Penn, Quaker and Pioneer*, 1932 (b); *As Their Friends Saw Them; Bibliographical Conversations*, 1933 (b); *Giacomo Casanova, Chevalier de Seingalt*, 1933 (b); *John Wesley*, 1933 (b); *Modern Prose Style*, 1934 (repr. 1964) (c); (with G. E. Manwaring) *The Floating Republic*, 1935 (h); *English Revolts*, 1937 (h); (with Edith C. Batho) *The Victorians and After, 1830-1914*, 1938 (h); *The Unacknowledged Legislator: Conversation on Literature and Politics in a Warden's Post, 1941*, 1941 (e); (with F. P. Wilson, ed. of *Oxford History of English Literature*, 1945- (h); *English Essayists*, 1946 (c); *The Amateur and the Theatre*, 1947 (e); *The Theme of Patriotism in the Poetry of the Early Eighteenth Century*, 1949 (Warton lecture); *Rudyard Kipling*, 1951 (b,c); Jolyot de Crébillon, *The Sofa*, 1951 (tr); *Alexander Pope*, 1951 (b); *The Broken Cistern* [on English poetry], 1954 (Clark lectures; *John Dryden*, 1956 (b,c); *English Literature in the Early Eighteenth*

Century, 1700-1740 (Vol. VII of *Oxford History of English Literature*), 1959 (h); *Three Eighteenth Century Figures* (repr. of *Sarah Churchill, John Wesley, Giacomo Casanova*), 1962 (b); *Byron's Dramas*, 1962 (Byron Foundation lecture); *William Congreve*, 1964 (b,c)

See *Of Books and Humankind; Essays Presented to Bonamy Dobrée*, ed. John Butt, 1965

CHARLES M. DOUGHTY
1843-1926

On the Jöstedal-brae Glaciers in Norway, 1866 (t); *Travels in Arabia Deserta*, 1888 (t); *Under Arms*, 1890 (p); *The Dawn in Britain*, 1906 (p); *Adam Cast Forth*, 1908 (p); *Wanderings in Arabia* (ed. Edward Garnett), 1908 (t); *The Cliffs*, 1909 (pd); *The Clouds*, 1912 (pd); *The Titans*, 1916 (p); *Mansoul* (or, *The Riddle of the World*), 1920 (p); *Passages from Arabia Derserta* (sel. Edward Garnett), 1931 (t)

David G. Hogarth, *The Life of Charles M. Doughty*, 1928

NORMAN DOUGLAS
1868-1952

(with wife, Elsa FitzGibbon; under joint pseud. of Normyx) *Unprofessional Tales*, 1901 (s); *The Blue Grotto and Its Literature*, 1904 (t); *The Forestal Conditions of Capri*, 1904 (e); *Fabio Giordano's Relation of Capri*, 1906 (h); *Three Monographs* [on Capri], 1906 (h); *The Life of the Venerable Suor Serafina di Dio* [of Capri], 1907 (b); *Some Antiquarian Notes* [Capri], 1907 (t); *Siren Land*, 1911 (t); *Fountains in the Sand, Rambles Among the Oases of Tunisia*, 1912 (t); *Old Calabria*, 1915 (t); *Disiecta Membra* [Capri], 1915 (e); *Index* [Capri], 1915 (t); *London Street Games*, 1916 (e); *South Wind*, 1917 (n); *They Went*, 1920 (n); *Alone*, 1921 (t); *Together*, 1923 (t); *D. H. Lawrence and Maurice Magnus, A Plea for Better Manners*, 1924 (c); *Experiments*, 1925 (e); *In the Beginning*, 1927 (n); *Birds and Beasts of the Greek Anthology*, 1927 (e); *The Angel of Manfredonia*, 1929 (n); *Nerinda*, 1929 (s); *One Day*, 1929 (t); *How About Europe? Some Footnotes on East and West* (Am.

ed. *Good-bye to Western Culture*), 1929 (e); *Capri, Materials for a Description of the Island* (collected ed.), 1930 (t); *Three of Them*, 1930 (misc.); *Paneros, Some Words on Aphrodisiacs and the Like*, 1931 (e); *Summer Islands, Ischia and Ponza*, 1931 (t); *Looking Back, An Autobiographical Excursion*, 1933 (a); *Late Harvest*, 1946 (a); *Norman Douglas: a Selection from his Works* (introd. D. M. Low), 1955

*complete, ed. Constantine FitzGibbon, 1953

H. M. Tomlinson, *Norman Douglas*, 1952; Cecil Woolf, *A Bibliography of Norman Douglas*, 1954

ARTHUR CONAN DOYLE
1859-1930

An Extra Passenger, 1887 (n); *The Mystery of Cloomber*, 1888 (n); *A Study in Scarlet*, 1888 (n); *Micah Clark*, 1889 (n); *The Captain of the Polestar*, 1890 (s); *The Sign of the Four*, 1890 (n); *The Firm of Girdlestone*, 1890 (n); *The White Company*, 1891 (n); *The Doings of Raffles Haw*, 1892 (n); (with others) *The Fate of Fenella*, 1892 (s); *The Adventures of Sherlock Holmes*, 1892 (s); *The Speckled Band*, 1892 (s); *The Refugees* 1893 (n); *Round the Red Lamp*, 1894 (s); *The Memoirs of Sherlock Holmes*, 1894 (s); *The Parasite*, 1894 (n); *The Stark Munro Letters*, 1894-5 (s); *The Glamour of the Arctic*, 1894 (t); *Exploits of Brigadier Gerard*, 1896 (s); *Rodney Stone*, 1896 (n); *Uncle Bernac*, 1897 (n); *Songs of Action*, 1898 (p); *A Duet*, 1899 (rev. 1910) (n); *The Striped Chest*, 1900 (n); *A Story of Waterloo*, 1900 (d); *The Great Boer War*, 1900 (h); *Some Military Lessons of the War*, 1900 (h); *The Anglo-American Reunion*, 1900 (e); *The Hound of the Baskervilles*, 1901 (n); *The War in South Africa*, 1902 (h); *Adventures of Gerard*, 1904 (s); *The Return of Sherlock Holmes*, 1905 (s); *Sir Nigel*, 1906 (n); *Through the Magic Door*, 1907 (c); *The Fiend of the Cooperage*, 1908 (n); (music by A. T. Silver) *A Hunting Morning*, 1909 (p); *A Pot of Caviare*, 1910 (p); *The Blighting of Sharkey*, 1911 (n); *The Contest*, 1911 (n); *The Last Galley: Impressions and Tales*, 1911 (s); *Songs of the Road*,

1911 (p); *The Lost World*, 1912 (n); *The Case of Oscar Slater*, 1912 (e); *The British Campaign in France and Flanders*, 6 vols., 1916-20 (h); *His Last Bow*, 1917 (s); *Is Sir Oliver Lodge Right? Yes!* 1917 (e); *Some Personalia About Sherlock Holmes*, 1917 (e); *Borrowed Scenes*, 1918 (s); *Danger*, 1918 (s); *A Point of View*, 1918 (s); *The New Revelation*, 1918 (e); *The Guards Came Through*, 1919 (p); *The Vital Message*, 1919 (e); *Spiritualism and Rationalism*, 1920 (e); *The Wanderings of a Spiritualist*, 1921 (a); *Conan Doyle Stories*, 6 vols., 1922 (s); *The Coming of the Fairies*, 1922 (e); *If I Could Preach Just Once*, 1922 (e); *Collected Poems*, 1922; *Our American Adventure*, 1923 (r); *The Case for Spirit Photography*, 1923 (e); *Our Second American Adventure* 1924 (r); *Memories and Adventures*, 1924 (r); *The Great Keinplatz Experiment*, 1925 (s); *The History of Spiritualism*, 1926 (h); *The Land of Mist*, 1926 (n); *The Casebook of Sherlock Holmes*, 1927 (s); *Sherlock Holmes: The Complete Short Stories*, 1928; *Sherlock Holmes: The Complete Long Stories*, 1929 (n); *The Adventures of Sherlock Holmes*, 1930 (s); *The Complete Sherlock Holmes*, 1930, 1936, 1953; *Resignation from the Society for Psychical Research*, 1930 (e); *The Conan Doyle Historical Romances*, 1931, 1932; *Our African Winter*, 1932 (a); *Sherlock Holmes and Dr. Watson*, ed. Christopher Morley, 1944; *The Adventures of Sherlock Holmes, A Definitive Text*, 1950 (s); *The Later Adventures of Sherlock Holmes*, 1952 (s); *The Final Adventures of Sherlock Holmes*, 1952 (s)

Harold Locke, *A Bibliographical Catalogue of the Writings of Sir Arthur Conan Doyle, 1879-1928*, 1929; William S. Baring-Gould, *Sherlock Holmes: A Biography*, 1962; Pierre Nordan, *Conan Doyle*, tr. from French, 1966

JOHN DRINKWATER
1882-1937

Poems, 1903 (p); *The Death of Leander*, 1906 (p); *Lyrical and Other Poems*, 1908 (p); *Poems of Men and Hours*, 1911 (p); *Cophetua*, 1911 (pd); *An English Medley*, 1911 (d); *Puss in Boots*, 1911 (d); *Poems of Love and Earth*, 1912 (p); *The Pied Piper*, 1912 (d); *William*

Morris, 1912 (c); *Cromwell*, 1913 (p); *Lines for the Opening of the Birmingham Repertory Theatre*, 1913 (p); *The Only Legend. A Masque of the Scarlet Pierrot*, 1913 (d); *Swinburne: An Estimate*, 1913 (c); *Rebellion*, 1914 (pd); *Robin Hood and the Pedlar*, 1914 (d); *Swords and Ploughshares*, 1915 (p); *The Storm*, 1915 (pd); *June Dance*, 1916 (p); *Olton Pools*, 1916 (p); *The God of Quiet*, 1916 (pd); *Rupert Brooke. An Essay*, 1916 (c); *Poems, 1908-1914*, 1917 (p); *Tides*, 1917 (p); *X=O: A Night of the Trojan War*, 1917 (pd); *Pawns: Three Poetic Plays*, 1917 (pd); *Prose Papers*, 1917 (e); *The Poet and Tradition*, 1918 (c); *Loyalties*, 1918 (p); *Abraham Lincoln*, 1918 (d); *Poems, 1908-1919*, 1919 (p); *Lincoln, The World Emancipator*, 1920 (e); *Cotswold Characters*, 1921 (p); *Persuasion, Twelve Sonnets*, 1921 (p); *Seeds of Time*, 1921 (p); *Mary Stuart*, 1921 (d); *Oliver Cromwell*, 1921 (d); *Preludes, 1921-1922*, 1922 (p); *Selected Poems*, 1922 (p); *Some Contributions to the English Anthology*, 1922 (c); *The World and The Artist*, 1922 (e); *Collected Poems*, 3 vols., 1923; *Robert E. Lee*, 1923 (d); (with Albert Rutherston) *Claud Lovat Fraser*, 1923 (m); *The Poet and Communication*, 1923 (Conway Memorial lecture); *Victorian Poetry*, 1923 (c); *From an Unknown Isle*, 1924 (p); *From the German*, 1924 (p); *Patriotism in Literature*, 1924 (c); *Robert Burns*, 1924 (lecture, Ninety Burns Club, Edinburgh); *New Poems*, 1925 (p); *Collected Plays*, 2 vols., 1925; *Robert Burns*, 1925 (d); *The Muse in Council*, 1925 (e); *The Pilgrim of Eternity: Byron— A Conflict*, 1925 (b); *Persephone*, 1926 (p); *A Book for Bookmen*, 1926 (e); *Mr. Charles, King of England*, 1926 (b); *Bird in Hand*, 1927 (d); *The Gentle Art of Theatre-Going*, 1927 (Am. ed. *The Art of Theatre-Going*) (e); *Cromwell, A Character Study*, 1927 (Am. ed. *Oliver Cromwell, A Character Study*) (b); *John Bull Calling*, 1928 (d); *"The Other Point of View"*, 1928 (Univ. College, London, lecture); *The World's Lincoln*, 1928 (e); *Charles James Fox*, 1928 (b); *Art and the State, 1930* (Roscoe lecture); *Pepys, His Life and Character*, 1930 (b); *American Vignettes, 1860-1865*, 1931 (p); *Christmas Poems*, 1931; *Poetry and Dogma*, 1931 (Arthur Skemp Memorial lecture); *The Life and Adventures of Carl Laemmle*, 1931 (b); *Inheritance*, 1931 (a); *Midsummer Eve*, 1932 (rd); *Discovery, 1897-1913*, 1932 (a); *Summer Harvest, Poems 1924-1933*, 1933 (p); *Laying the Devil*, 1933 (d); *This Troubled World*, 1933 (e); *John Hampden's England*, 1933 (h); *Shakespeare*, 1933 (b); *A Man's House*, 1934 (d); *The King's Reign*, 1935 (b); *Garibaldi*, 1936 (d); *Collected Poems*, 1937; *Robinson of England*, 1937 (n); *English Poetry. An Unfinished History*, 1938 (h)

See Henry Danielson, *Bibliographies of Modern Authors*, 1921

ALFRED DUGGAN
1903-1964

Knight With Armour, 1950 (n); *The Conscience of the King*, 1951 (n); *The Little Emperors*, 1951 (n); *Thomas Becket of Canterbury*, 1952 (b); *The Lady for Ransom*, 1953 (n); *Leopards and Lilies*, 1954 (n); *God and My Right* (Am. ed. *My Life for My Sheep*), 1955 (n); *Julius Caesar*, 1955 (b); *Winter Quarters*, 1956 (n); *Devil's Brood*, 1957 (h); *He Died Old* (Am. ed. *King of Pontus: The Life of Mithridates Eupator*), 1958 (b); *Three's Company*, 1958 (n); *Founding Fathers* (Am. ed. *Children of the Wolf*), 1959 (n); *The Cunning of the Dove*, 1960 (n); *Family Favourites*, 1960 (n); *The King of Athelney*, 1961 (n); *The Right Line of Cerdic*, 1961 (n); *Lord Geoffrey's Fancy*, 1962 (n); *Elephants and Castles*, 1963 (n); *Besieger of Cities*, 1963 (n); *The Story of the Crusades, 1097-1291*, 1963 (h); *Count Bohemond*, 1964 (n)

DAPHNE DU MAURIER
1907-

*The Loving Spirit, 1931 (n); *I'll Never Be Young Again*, 1932 (n); *The Progress of Julius*, 1933 (n); *Gerald*, 1934 (b); *Jamaica Inn*, 1936 (n); *The Du Mauriers*, 1937 (b); *Rebecca*, 1938 (n); *Rebecca*, 1940 (d); *Come Wind, Come Weather*, 1940 (d); *Happy Christmas*, 1940 (s); *Frenchman's Creek*, 1941 (n); *Hungry Hill*, 1943 (n); *Consider the Lilies*, 1943 (s); *Spring Picture*, 1944 (s); *The Years Between*, 1945 (d); *Leading Lady*, 1945 (s); *London and Paris*, 1945 (s); *The King's General*, 1946 (n); *September Tide*, 1949 (d); *The Parasites*, 1949 (n);

My Cousin Rachel, 1951 (n); *The Apple Tree,* 1952 (s); *Early Stories,* 1954 (s); *Mary Anne,* 1954 (n); *The Scapegoat,* 1957 (n); *The Breaking Point,* 1959 (s); *The Infernal World of Branwell Brontë,* 1960 (b); *The Birds,* 1963 (s); *The Glass-Blowers,* 1963 (n); *The Flight of the Falcon,* 1965 (n)

*repr. 1966

RONALD DUNCAN
1914-

The Dull Ass's Hoof, Three Plays, 1941 (pd); *Postcards to Pulcinella,* 1944 (p); *Journal of a Husbandman,* 1944 (a); *The Rape of Lucretia,* 1946 (libretto after André Ober's play for Benjamin Britten's opera); *This Way to the Tomb,* 1946 (d); *Home Made Home,* 1947 (a); *The Eagle Has Two Heads* (adapted from Jean Cocteau), 1948 (tr); Jean Cocteau, *The Typewriter,* 1948 (tr); *Jan's Journal,* 1949 (a); *The Mongrel,* 1950 (p); *Stratton,* 1950 (d); *Our Lady's Tumbler,* 1951 (pd); *The Blue Fox,* 1951 (a); *Tobacco Cultivation in England,* 1951 (e); *The Last Adam,* 1952 (s); *Jan at the Blue Fox,* 1952 (a); *Where I Live,* 1953 (t); *Don Juan,* 1954 (pd); *The Death of Satan,* 1955 (d); *The Solitudes,* 1960 (p); *Abelard and Heloise,* 1961 (d); *Saint Spiv,* 1961 (n); Martin Walser, *The Rabbit Race,* 1963 (tr); *The Catalyst,* 1964 (d); *All Men Are Islands,* 1964 (a)

LORD DUNSANY
1878-1957

The Gods of Pegana, 1905 (n); *Time and the Gods,* 1906 (n); *The Sword of Welleran,* 1908 (s); *A Dreamer's Tales,* 1910 (s); *The Book of Wonder,* 1912 (s); *Selections from the Writings of Lord Dunsany,* introd. W. B. Yeats, 1912; *Five Plays: The Gods of the Mountain, The Golden Doom, King Argimenes and the Unknown Warrior, The Glittering Gate, The Lost Silk Hat,* 1914 (d); *Fifty-one Tales,* 1915 (s); *Tales of Wonder* (Am. ed. *The Last Book of Wonder*), 1916 (s); *A Night at an Inn,* 1916 (repr. 1957) (d); *Plays of Gods and Men,* 1917 (4d); *Tales of War,* 1918 (s); *Nowadays,* 1918 (e); *Tales of Three Hemispheres,* 1919 (s); *Unhappy Far-off Things,* 1919 (e); *If,* 1921 (d); *The Chronicles of Rodriguez* (Am. ed. *Don Rodriguez, Chronicles of Shadow Valley*), 1922 (s); *The Tents of the Arabs,* 1922 (d); *The Laughter of the Gods,* 1922 (d); *The Queen's Enemies,* 1922 (d); *Plays of Near and Far,* 1922 (d); *The King of Elfland's Daughter,* 1924 (n); *The Compromise of the King of the Golden Isles,* 1924 (d); *Alexander and Three Small Plays,* 1925 (4d); *The Amusements of Khan Kharuda,* 1925 (d); *The Evil Kettle,* 1925 (d); *The Old King's Tale,* 1925 (d); *The Charwoman's Shadow,* 1926 (n); *The Blessing of Pan,* 1927 (n); *Seven Modern Comedies,* 1928 (7d); *Fifty Poems,* 1929 (p); *The Old Folk of the Centuries,* 1930 (d); *The Travel Tales of Mr. Joseph Jorkens,* 1931 (s); *The Curse of the Wise Woman,* 1933 (s); *Lord Adrian,* 1933 (d); *Jorkens Remembers Africa,* 1934 (s); *If I Were Dictator,* 1934 (e); *Up in the Hills,* 1935 (n); *Mr. Faithful,* 1935 (d); *My Talks with Dean Spanley,* 1936 (n); *Rory and Bran,* 1936 (n); *Plays for Earth and Air,* 1937 (d); *My Ireland,* 1937 (e); *Mirage Water,* 1938 (p); *Patches of Sunlight,* 1938 (a); *The Story of Mona Sheehy,* 1939 (n); *Jorkens Has a Large Whiskey,* 1940 (s); *War Poems,* 1941 (p); *A Journey,* 1943 (p); *Wandering Songs,* 1943 (p); *Guerilla,* 1944 (n); *While the Sirens Slept,* 1944 (e); *The Donnellan Lectures, 1943* [Trinity College, Dublin; one prose, p, d], 1945 (e); *The Sirens Wake,* 1945 (a); *The Year,* 1946 (p); *A Glimpse from a Watch-Tower,* 1946 (e); *The Odes of Horace,* 1947 (tr); *The Fourth Book of Jorkens,* 1948 (s); *To Awaken Pegasus,* 1949 (p); *The Man Who Ate the Phoenix,* 1949 (n); *The Strange Journeys of Colonel Polders,* 1950 (n); *The Last Revolution,* 1951 (n); *His Fellow Men,* 1952 (n); *Little Tales of Smethers,* 1952 (s); *Jorkens Borrows Another Whiskey,* 1954 (s)

See Henry Danielson, *Bibliographies of Modern Authors, 1921;* Mark Longaker, *Lord Dunsany,* 1944; Hazel Littlefield, *Lord Dunsany, King of Dreams: a Personal Portrait,* 1959

LAWRENCE DURRELL
1912-

Quaint Fragment, 1931 (p); *Ten Poems,* 1932 (p); *Bromo Bombastes,* 1933 (n);

Transition, 1934 (p); *Pied Piper of Lovers*, 1935 (n); (pseud. Charles Norden) *Panic Spring*, 1937 (n); *Poems*, 1938 (p); *The Black Book, An Agon*, 1938 (n); *A Private Country*, 1943 (p); *Prospero's Cell* [Corcyra], 1945 (t); *Cities, Plains, and People*, 1946 (p); *Cefalû*, (Am. ed. and 1958 London ed. *The Dark Labyrinth*) 1947 (n); *On Seeming to Presume*, 1948 (p); *Deus Loci*, 1950 (p); *Sappho*, 1950 (pd); *A Key to Modern Poetry*, 1952 (c); *Reflections on a Marine Venus* [Rhodes], 1953 (t); *Private Drafts*, 1955 (p); *The Tree of Idleness*, 1955 (p); *Selected Poems*, 1956 (p); *Bitter Lemons*, 1957 (t); *Esprit de Corps: Sketches from Diplomatic Life*, 1957 (sk); *Justine* (Pt. I of *Alexandria Quartet*), 1957 (n); *White Eagles Over Serbia*, 1957 (n); *Stiff Upper Lip*, 1958 (sk); *Balthazar* (Pt. II of *Alexandria Quartet*), 1958 (n); *Mountolive* (Pt. III of *Alexandria Quartet*), 1958 (n); (with Alfred Perles, a correspondence about Henry Miller) *Art and Outrage*, 1959 (c); *Clea* (Pt. IV of *Alexandria Quartet*), 1960 (n); *Collected Poems, 1960; Acte or The Prisoners of Time* (pub. only in *Show Magazine*), 1961 (d); (with Henry Miller, ed. George Wickes) *Lawrence Durrell and Henry Miller: A Private Correspondence*, 1963; *An Irish Faustus*, 1963 (pd); *Selected Poems, 1935-1963*, 1964 (p); *Acte*, 1965 (first produced in German, 1961, now rev.) (d); *Sauve Qui Peut*, 1966 (9s)

John Unterecker, *Lawrence Durrell*, 1954; Alfred Perles, *My Friend Lawrence Durrell* [memoir with bibliog.], 1961

JOHN EGLINTON
1868-1961

Two Essays on the Remnant, 1894 (e); *Pebbles from a Brook*, 1901 (e); *Bards and Saints*, 1906 (e); *Anglo-Irish Essays*, 1917 (e); *Irish Literary Portraits*, 1935 (m); *A Memoir of A.E.*, 1937 (m); *Confidential*, 1951 (p)

See Ernest A. Boyd, *Ireland's Literary Renaissance*, 1916

T. S. ELIOT
1888-1965

Ezra Pound: His Metric and Poetry, 1917 (c); *Prufrock*, 1917 (p); *Poems*, 1919 (p); *Ara Vos Prec* (Am. ed. *Poems*), 1920 (p); *The Sacred Wood*, 1920 (c); *The Waste Land*, 1922 (p); Editor of *The Criterion*, 1923-39; *Homage To John Dryden*, 1924 (c); *Poems 1909-1925*, 1925 (p); *For Lancelot Andrewes*, 1928 (c); *Ash-Wednesday*, 1930 (p); *Anabasis, a Poem by St.-J. Perse*, 1930 (tr); *Charles Whibley*, 1931 (m); *Thoughts After Lambeth*, 1931 (e); **Selected Essays 1917-1932*, 1932 (c); *Sweeney Agonistes*, 1932 (p); ***The Use of Poetry and the Use of Criticism*, 1933 (c); *After Strange Gods*, 1934 (e); *The Rock*, 1934 (pd); *Elizabethan Essays*, 1934 (c); *Murder in the Cathedral*, 1935 (pd); *Essays Ancient and Modern*, 1936 (e); *Collected Poems 1909-1935*, 1936 (p); *The Family Reunion*, 1939 (pd); *Old Possum's Book of Practical Cats*, 1939 (p); *The Idea of a Christian Society*, 1939 (e); *Points of View* (sel. John Hayward), 1941 (c); *Later Poems, 1925-1935*, 1941 (p); *East Coker*, 1940 (p); *Burnt Norton*, 1941 (p); *The Dry Salvages*, 1941 (p); *Little Gidding*, 1942 (p); *Four Quartets* [the four preceding titles collected], 1943 (p); *What is a Classic?*, 1945 (e); *Notes Towards the Definition of Culture*, 1948 (e); *The Undergraduate Poems of T. S. Eliot*, 1948 (p); *The Cocktail Party*, 1950 (pd); *Selected Essays*, 1951 (e); *The Complete Poems and Plays 1909-1950*, 1952; *Selected Prose*, ed. John Hayward, 1953 (c); *The Three Voices of Poetry*, 1954 (e); *The Confidential Clerk*, 1954 (pd); *Essays on Elizabethan Drama*, 1956 (c); *On Poetry and Poets*, 1957 (c); *The Cultivation of Christmas Trees*, 1959 (p); *The Elder Statesman*, 1959 (pd); *Selected Poems*, 1961 (p); *Collected Plays*, 1962 (5d); *To Criticize the Critic*, 1965 (e)

*enlgd. 1951
**repr. 1964

Donald Clifford Gallup, *T. S. Eliot: a Bibliography*, rev. 1952; Northrop Frye, *T. S. Eliot*, 1963

HAVELOCK ELLIS
1859-1939

Selective Bibliography

Note: Of the essays, only those most likely to interest a student of literature are included.

Women and Marriage, 1888 (e); Emile Zola, *Germinal*, 1894 (n,tr); *Men and Women*, 1894 (e); *Studies in the Psychology of Sex*, 6 vols., 1897-1910, Vol. VII, 1928 (new ed. 1936); *Affirmations*, 1898 (c); *A Study of British Genius*, 1904 (e); *The Soul of Spain*, 1908 (repr. 1937) (t); *Sex in Relation to Society*, 1910 (e); *The World of Dreams*, 1911 (e); *Impressions and Comments*, 1914 (e); *The Erotic Rights of Women*, 1918 (e); *Impressions and Comments, 2nd Series, 1914-20*, 1921 (e); *Kanga Creek*, 1922 (n); *Little Essays of Love and Virtue*, 1922 (e); *The Dance of Life*, 1923 (e); *Casanova in Rome, in Venice, in Paris*, 1924 (e); *Impressions and Comments, 3rd Series, 1920-23*, 1924 (e); *Sonnets With Folk Songs from the Spanish*, 1925 (p); *The Art of Life*, 1929 (e); *The Colour-Sense in Literature*, 1931 (e); *Concerning Jude the Obscure*, 1931 (c); *More Essays of Love and Virtue*, 1931 (e); *Revaluation of Obscenity*, 1931 (e); *Views and Reviews, A Selection of Uncollected Articles, 1884-1932*, 1932 (e); *From Rousseau to Proust*, 1936 (c); *Selected Essays*, 1936 (e); *My Confessional. Questions of Our Day*, 1936 (e); *Poems*, 1937 (p); *Morals, Manners, and Men*, 1939 (e); *My Life*, 1939 (a); *From Marlowe to Shaw, Studies 1876-1936*, 1950 (c)

A. Calder Marshall, *Havelock Ellis*, 1959; "Havelock Ellis: An Annotated Bibliography of Primary and Secondary Works," comp. and ed. Glenn S. Burne, in *English Literature in Transition*, Vol. IX (1966), no. 2, pp. 55-107

WILLIAM EMPSON
1906-

Letter IV, 1929 (p); *Seven Types of Ambiguity*, 1930 (rev. 1947) (c); *Poems*, 1935 (p); *Some Versions of Pastoral*, 1935 (c); J. B. S. Haldane, *The Outlook of Science* and *Science and Well-Being*, put into Basic English by W.E., 1935; (with G. Garrett) *Shakespeare Survey*, 1937 (c); *English Pastoral Poetry*, 1938 (c); *The Gathering Storm*, 1940 (p); *Collected Poems*, 1949 Am. ed. (1955 Eng. ed.); *The Structure of Complex Words*, 1951 (e); *Milton's God*, 1961 (rev. 1965) (c)

See G. S Fraser, *Vision and Rhetoric*, 1959

D. J. ENRIGHT
1920-

Commentary on Goethe's Faust, 1949 (c); *The Laughing Hyena*, 1953 (p); *World of Dew: Aspects of Living Japan*, 1955 (e); *Academic Year*, 1955 (n); *Literature for Man's Sake*, 1955 (c); *Bread Rather than Blossoms*, 1956 (p); *Apothecary's Shop*, 1957 (e); *Heaven Knows Where*, 1957 (n); *Insufficient Poppy*, 1960 (n); *Some Men Are Brothers*, 1960 (p); *Addictions*, 1962 (p); *The Old Adam*, 1965 (p); *Conspirators and Poets, Reviews and Essays*, 1966 (e)

ST. JOHN ERVINE
1883-

Mixed Marriage, 1911 (d); *The Magnanimous Lover*, 1912 (d); *Francis Place, The Tailor of Charing Cross*, 1912 (e); *Eight O'Clock and Other Studies*, 1913 (e); *Mrs. Martin's Man*, 1914 (n); *Four Irish Plays*, 1914 (4d); *Jane Clegg*, 1914 (d); *Alice and a Family*, 1915 (n); *John Ferguson*, 1915 (d); *Sir Edward Carson and the Ulster Movement*, 1915 (e); *Changing Winds*, 1917 (n); *The Foolish Lovers*, 1920 (n); *The Ship*, 1922 (d); *Some Impressions of My Elders*, 1922 (r); *The Lady of Belmont*, 1923 (d); *Mary, Mary, Quite Contrary*, 1923 (d); *The Organised Theatre, A Plea in Civics*, 1924 (e); *Anthony and Anna*, 1925 (rev. 1936) (d); *Parnell*, 1925 (b); *The Wayward Man*, 1927 (n); *Four One-Act Plays*, 1928 (4d); *The Mountain*, 1928 (s); *How To Write a Play*, 1928 (c); *The First Mrs. Fraser*, 1929 (d); *The First Mrs. Fraser* (novelization of play), 1931 (n); *The Future of the Press*, 1932 (e); *The Theatre in My Time*, 1933 (c); *If I Were Dictator*, 1934 (e); *God's Soldier, General William Booth*, 1934 (b); *The Alleged Art of the Cinema*, 1934 (c); *Boyd's Shop*, 1936 (d); *People of Our Class*, 1936 (d); *Journey to Jerusalem*, 1936 (t); *Robert's Wife*, 1938 (d); *Our Heritage*, 1939 (e); *Sophia*, 1941 (n); *Is Liberty Lost?*, 1941 (e); *Friends and Relations*, 1947 (d); *Private Enterprise*, 1948 (d); *The Christies*, 1949 (d); *Craigavon, Ulsterman*, 1949 (b); *Oscar Wilde: A Present Time Appraisal*, 1951 (c); *My Brother Tom*, 1952 (d); *Bernard Shaw: His Life, Work, and Friends*, 1956 (b)

CARADOC EVANS
1879-1945

My People: Stories of the Peasantry of West Wales, 1915 (s); *Capel Sion,* 1916 (s); *My Neighbours,* 1919 (s); *Taffy,* 1923 (d); *Nothing to Pay,* 1930 (n); *Wasps,* 1933 (n); *This Way to Heaven,* 1934 (n); *The Earth Gives All and Takes All,* 1946 (s); *Pilgrims in a Foreign Land,* 1942 (s); *Mother's Marvel,* 1949 (n)

HUGH I'ANSON FAUSSET
1895-

Youth and Sensibility, 1917 (p); *The Lady Alcuin,* 1918 (p); *The Healing of Heaven,* 1920 (p); *The Spirit of Love, A Sonnet Sequence,* 1921 (p); *The Condemned and the Spirit of Love,* 1922 (p); *Poems,* 1922 (p); *Keats,* 1922 (c); *Studies in Idealism,* 1923 (c); *Tennyson,* 1923 (c); *Before the Dawn,* 1924 (p); *John Donne,* 1924 (c); *Samuel Taylor Coleridge,* 1926 (c); *Tolstoy,* 1927 (c); *William Cowper,* 1928 (c); *The Proving of Psyche,* 1929 (c); *The Modern Dilemma,* 1930 (c); *The Lost Leader, A Study of Wordsworth,* 1933 (c); *A Modern Prelude,* 1933 (a); *Between the Tides: A Summer Idyll,* 1942 (n); *Walt Whitman,* 1942 (c); *The Last Days: A Country Chronicle,* 1945 (n); *Poets and Pundits,* 1947 (e); *Towards Fidelity,* 1952 (e); *The Flame and the Light,* 1958 (e); *Fruits of Silence,* 1963 (e); *The Lost Dimension,* 1966 (e)

MICHAEL FIELD (K. BRADLEY, 1846-1914, and E. COOPER, 1862-1913)

The New Minnesinger, 1875 (p); *Bellerephôn,* 1881 (p); *Callirrhoë Fair Rosamund,* 1884 (2pd); *The Father's Tragedy, William Rufus, Loyalty or Love,* 1885 (3pd); *Brutus Ultor,* 1886 (pd); *Canute the Great, The Cup of Water,* 1887 (2pd); *Long Ago,* 1889 (p); *The Tragic Mary,* 1890 (pd); *Stephania,* 1892 (pd); *Sight and Song,* 1892 (p); *A Question of Memory,* 1893 (pd); *Underneath the Bough,* 1893 (p); *Attila, My Attila!* 1896 (pd); *The World at Auction,* 1898 (pd); *Anna Ruina,* 1899 (pd); *Noontide Branches,* 1899 (pd); *The Race of Leaves,* 1901 (pd); *Julia*

Domna, 1903 (pd); *Borgia,* 1905 (pd); *Queen Mariamne,* 1908 (pd); *Wild Honey from Various Thyme,* 1908 (p); *The Tragedy of Pardon, Diane,* 1911 (2pd); *The Accuser, Tristran de Léonois, A Messiah,* 1911 (3pd); *Poems of Adoration,* 1912 (p); *Mystic Trees,* 1913 (p); *Dedicated,* 1914 (p); *Deirdre, A Question of Memory, Ras Byance,* 1918 (3pd); *In the Name of Time,* 1919 (pd); *A Selection from the Poems of Michael Field* (comp. T. Sturge Moore), 1923 (p); *The Wattlefold* [unpub. poems, coll. Emily C. Fortey], 1930; *Works and Days: From the Journal of Michael Field* (ed. T. and D. C. Sturge Moore), 1933

See Harold Williams, *Modern English Writers,* 1918

GABRIEL FIELDING
1916-

Brotherly Love, 1954 (n); *XXVIII Poems,* 1955 (p); *In the Time of Greenbloom* [seq. to *Brotherly Love*], 1956 (n); *Eight Days,* 1958 (n); *Through Streets Broad and Narrow,* 1959 (n); *The Frog Prince,* 1952 (p); *The Birthday King,* 1962 (n); *Gentlemen in their Season,* 1966 (n)

RONALD FIRBANK
1886-1926

Odette D'Antrevernes and *A Study in Temperament,* 1905 (sk); *Vainglory,* 1915 (n); *Odette: A Fairy Tale for Weary People,* 1916 (s); *Inclinations,* 1916 (n); *Caprice,* 1917 (n); *Valmouth,* 1919 (n); *The Princess Zoubaroff,* 1920 (d); *Santal,* 1921 (n); *The Flower Beneath the Foot,* 1923 (n); *Sorrow in Sunlight,* (Am. ed. *Prancing Nigger*), 1924 (n); *Concerning the Eccentricities of Cardinal Pirelli,* 1926 (n); *The Works* (biog. memoir by Osbert Sitwell), 1928; *Santal,* 1931 (s); *The Artificial Princess,* 1934 (n); *Five Novels,* 1949 (repr.); *Three Novels,* 1950 (repr.); *The Complete Ronald Firbank,* preface Anthony Powell, 1961

Jocelyn Brooke, *Ronald Firbank,* 1951 (abgd. 1963); Miriam J. Berkowitz, *Ronald Firbank: A Bibliography,* 1963

JAMES ELROY FLECKER
1884-1915

The Bridge of Fire, 1907 (p); The Last Generation, A Story of the Future, 1908 (s); Thirty-six Poems, 1910 (p); The Grecians, A Dialogue on Education, 1910 (e); Forty-two Poems (Thirty-six Poems with six added), 1911 (p); The Scholar's Italian Book, 1911 (e); The Golden Journey to Samarkand, 1913 (p); The King of Alsander, 1914 (s); The Old Ships, 1915 (p); The Collected Poems of James Elroy Flecker, ed. J. C. Squire, 1916 (repr. 1946); The Selected Poems, 1918 (p); Collected Prose, 1920; 14 Poems, 1921 (p); Hassan, 1922 (pd); Collected Poems, 1923; Don Juan, 1925 (pd); Some Letters from Abroad of James Elroy Flecker (with reminiscences by Hellé Flecker and introd. J. C. Squire), 1930

Geraldine Hodgson, The Life of James Elroy Flecker (from letters and materials provided by his mother), 1925 [no bibliog.]; T. Stanley Mercer, James Elroy Flecker; From School to Samarkand, 1952

F. S. FLINT
1885-

In the Net of the Stars, 1909 (p); Cadences, 1915 (p); Emile Verhaeren, Love Poems, 1916 (tr); Emile Verhaeren, Plays, 1916 (tr); Jean de Bosschère, The Closed Door, 1917 (tr); Some Modern French Poets, 1919 (c); The Younger French Poets, 1920 (c); Otherworld, Cadences, 1920 (p); Paying for War and Peace, 1948 (e). Also other trs.

FORD MADOX FORD
1873-1939

The Shifting of the Fire, 1892 (n); Ford Madox Brown, 1896 (b); Poems for Pictures and for Notes of Music, 1900 (p); The Cinque Ports, A Historical and Descriptive Record, 1900 (t); (with Joseph Conrad) The Inheritors, 1901 (n); Rossetti, A Critical Essay on His Art, 1902 (b,c); (with Joseph Conrad) Romance, 1903 (n); The Face of the Night, 1904 (p); The Benefactor, 1905 (n); Hans Holbein The Younger, 1905 (c); The Soul of London, A Survey of a Modern City, 1905 (e); The Fifth

Queen, 1906 (n); The Heart of the Country, A Survey of a Modern Land, 1906 (e); An English Girl, 1907 (n); Privy Seal, 1907 (n); From Inland, 1907 (p); The Spirit of the People, An Analysis of the English Mind, 1907 (e); England and the English (Am. ed. of The Soul of London, The Heart of the Country, The Spirit of the People), 1907 (e); The Pre-Raphaelite Brotherhood, 1907 (c); The Fifth Queen Crowned, 1908 (n); Mr. Apollo, 1908 (n); Editor of The English Review, 1908-9; The "Half Moon," 1909 (n); A Call, 1910 (n); The Portrait, 1910 (n); Songs from London, 1910 (p); Ladies Whose Bright Eyes, 1911 (n); Ancient Lights and Certain New Reflections (Am. ed. Memories and Impressions, A Study in Atmospheres), 1911 (r); High Germany, 1911 (p); The Critical Attitude, 1911 (c); The Panel, 1912 (Am. adaptation Ring for Nancy) (n); The Young Lovell, 1913 (n); Mr. Fleight, 1913 (n); Collected Poems, 1913; *Henry James, 1913 (c); The Good Soldier, 1915 (n); Antwerp, 1915 (p); (with Violet Hunt) Zeppelin Nights, 1915 (sk); On Heaven, 1918 (p); Thus to Revisit, Some Reminiscences, 1921 (r); Mister Bosphorous and the Muses, 1923 (d); Women and Men, 1923 (e); The Marsden Case, 1923 (n); (with Joseph Conrad) The Nature of A Crime, 1924 (n); Some Do Not (first of the Tietjens tetralogy), 1924 (n); Joseph Conrad, A Personal Remembrance, 1924 (m); Editor of The Transatlantic Review, 1924; No More Parades (seq. to Some Do Not), 1925 (n); A Man Could Stand Up (seq. to No More Parades), 1926 (n); A Mirror to France, 1926 (e); New Poems, 1927 (p); New York Essays, 1927 (e); New York is Not America, 1927 (e); Last Post (seq. to A Man Could Stand Up), 1928 (n); A Little Less Than Gods, 1928 (n); No Enemy, 1929 (a); The English Novel, 1929 (e); When the Wicked Man, 1931 (n); Return to Yesterday, 1931 (r); The Rash Act, 1933 (n); It Was the Nightingale, 1933 (r); Henry for Hugh, 1934 (n); Provence, 1935 (t); Vive le Roy, 1936 (n); Collected Poems, 1936; The Great Trade Route [France, England, U.S.], 1937 (e); Mightier Than the Sword (Am. ed. Portraits from Life), 1938 (r); The March of Literature, 1939 (h); Parade's End (Tietjens tetralogy),

1950 (n); *The Critical Writings of Ford Madox Ford*, ed. Frank MacShane, 1964 (c); *The Bodley Head Ford Madox Ford*, ed. Graham Greene, 4 vols. through 1965 (coll.); *Letters of Ford Madox Ford*, ed. Richard M. Ludwig, 1965

*repr. 1964

David Dow Harvey, *Ford Madox Ford, 1873-1939, A Bibliography of Works and Criticism*, 1962; Frank MacShane, *The Life and Work of Ford Madox Ford*, 1965

C. S. FORESTER
1899-1966

The Paid Piper, 1924 (n); *A Pawn Among Kings*, 1924 (n); *Napoleon and his Court*, 1924 (b); *Josephine: Napoleon's Empress*, 1925 (b); *Payment Deferred*, 1926 (n); *Emmanuel II*, 1927 (b); *Love Lies Dreaming*, 1927 (n); *The Wonderful Week*, 1927 (n); *Louis XIV*, 1928 (b); *The Shadow of the Hawk*, 1928 (n); *Nelson*, 1929 (b); *Brown on Resolution*, 1929 (n); *Plain Murder*, 1930 (n); *The Annie Marble in Germany*, 1930 (t); *U 97*, 1931 (d); *Two and Twenty*, 1931 (n); *Death to the French*, 1932 (n); *The Gun*, 1933 (n); (with Carl Bechhofer Roberts) *Nurse Cavell*, 1933 (d); *The Peacemaker*, 1934 (n); *The African Queen*, 1935 (n); *Marionettes at Home*, 1935 (e); *The General*, 1936 (n); *The Happy Return*, 1937 (n); *A Ship of the Line*, 1938 (n); *Flying Colours*, 1938 (n); *Captain Hornblower*, 1939 (n); *The Earthly Paradise* (Am ed. *To the Indies*), 1940 (n); *The Captain from Connecticut*, 1941 (n); *The Ship*, 1943 (n); *The Commodore*, 1945 (n); *Lord Hornblower*, 1946 (n); *The Sky and the Forest*, 1948 (n); *Mr. Midshipman Hornblower*, 1950 (n); *Randall and the River of Time*, 1951 (n); *Lieutenant Hornblower*, 1952 (n); *Hornblower and the Atropos*, 1953 (n); *The Nightmare*, 1954 (n); *The Good Shepherd*, 1955 (n); *The Naval War of 1812*, 1957 (h); *Hornblower in the West Indies*, 1958 (n); *Hunting the Bismarck*, 1959 (h); *Hornblower and the Hotspur*, 1962 (n); *The Hornblower Companion*, 1964 (collection); *The Young Hornblower* [*Mr. Midshipman Hornblower, Lieutenant Hornblower, Horn-*

blower and the Atropos], 1964 (3n); *Captain Hornblower, R.N.* [trilogy], 1965 (3n)

E. M. FORSTER
1879-

Where Angels Fear to Tread, 1905 (n); *The Longest Journey*, 1907 (n); *A Room with a View*, 1908 (n); *Howards End*, 1910 (n); *The Celestial Omnibus*, 1911 (s); *The Story of the Siren*, 1920 (n); *Egypt*, 1920 (t); *Alexandria*, 1922 (t); *Pharos and Pharillon*, 1923 (repr. 1961) (t,h); *A Passage to India*, 1924 (n); *Aspects of the Novel*, 1927 (c); *The Eternal Moment*, 1928 (s); *A Letter to Madam Blanchard*, 1931 (n); *Goldsworthy Lowes Dickinson*, 1934 (b); *Abinger Harvest*, 1936 (e); *What I Believe*, 1939 (e); *Reading as Usual*, 1939 (c); *England's Pleasant Land: A Pageant Play*, 1940 (d); *Virginia Woolf*, 1942 (c); *The Development of English Prose Between 1918 and 1939*, 1945 (c); *Collected Short Stories*, 1948 (s); *Two Cheers for Democracy*, 1951 (e); (with Eric Crozier) adaptation as opera of Melville, *Billy Budd*, 1951 (d); *Desmond MacCarthy*, 1952 (b); *The Hill of Devi*, 1953 (letters and e); *Marianne Thornton*, 1956 (b); *Collected Short Stories* [*The Celestial Omnibus* and *The Eternal Moment*], 1965

J. B. Beer, *The Achievement of E. M. Forster*, 1962; Alan Wilde, *Art and Order: a Study of E. M. Forster*, 1964; B. J. Kirkpatrick, *A Bibliography of E. M. Forster*, 1965

G. S. FRASER
1915-

Home Town Elegy, 1944 (p); Patrice de La Tour du Pin, *The Dedicated Life in Poetry and The Correspondence of Laurent de Cayeux*, 1948 (tr); *The Fatal Landscape*, 1948 (p); *The Traveller Has Regrets*, 1948 (p); *Vision of Scotland*, 1948 (t); *News from South America*, 1949 (t); G. Marcel, *The Mystery of Being*, 1950 (tr); G. Marcel, *Men Against Humanity*, 1952 (tr); J. Mesnard, *Pascal: His Life and Works*, 1952 (tr); (with E. de Mauny) S. Moreux, *Béla Bartók*, 1953 (tr); *The Modern Writer and His World*, 1953 (rev. 1964) (c); *W. B. Yeats*, 1954 (new ed. 1962) (c); *Scotland*, 1955 (t); *Dylan Thomas*, 1957 (c); *Vision and Rhetoric*, 1959 (c); *Ezra Pound*, 1960 (c)

JOHN FREEMAN
1880-1929

Twenty Poems, 1909 (p); *Fifty Poems*, 1911 (p); *Stone Trees*, 1916 (p); *The Moderns, Essays in Literary Criticism*, 1916 (c); *Memories of Childhood*, 1918 (p); *Poems, New and Old*, 1920; *Music: Lyrical and Narrative Poems*, 1921 (p); *The Red Path and The Wounded Bird*, 1921 (p); *A Portrait of George Moore in a Study of his Work*, 1922 (c); *The Grove*, 1924 (p); *English Portraits and Essays*, 1924 (e); *Prince Absalom*, 1925 (p); *John Freeman* [Twenty Poems], 1925 (p); *Solomon and Balkis*, 1926 (p); *Herman Melville*, 1926 (b); *Collected Poems*, 1928; *Last Poems*, ed. J. C. Squire, 1930 (p); *John Freeman's Letters*, ed. Gertrude Freeman and Sir John Squire, 1936; *Literature and Locality: The Literary Topography of Britain and Ireland*, 1963 (t,e)

CHRISTOPHER FRY
1907-

A Boy with a Cart: Cuthman Saint of Sussex, 1939 (pd); *A Phoenix Too Frequent*, 1946 (pd); *The Firstborn*, 1946 (pd); *The Lady's Not for Burning*, 1949 (pd); *Thor with Angels*, 1949 (pd); J. Anouilh, *Ring Around the Moon*, 1950 (tr); *Venus Observed*, 1950 (pd); *A Sleep of Prisoners*, 1951 (pd); *An Experience of Critics*, ed. K. Webb, 1952 (c); *The Dark is Light Enough*, 1954 (pd); J. Anouilh, *The Lark*, 1955 (tr); J. Giraudoux, *Tiger at the Gates*, 1955 (tr); J. Giraudoux, *Duel of Angels*, 1958 (tr); **Curtmantle*, 1961 (pd)

*rev. 1965

Derek Stanford, *Christopher Fry* (rev. 1962)

ROGER FRY
1866-1934

Giovanni Bellini, 1899 (b); *Vision and Design*, 1920 (e); *Architectural Heresies of a Painter*, 1921 (e); *A Sampler of Castile*, 1923 (e); *The Artist and Psycho-Analysis*, 1924 (e); (with others) *Chinese Art: An Introductory Review*, 1925 (e);

Art and Commerce, 1926 (e); (with E. A. Lowe) *English Handwriting*, 1926 (e); **Transformations: Critical and Speculative Essays on Art*, 1926 (e); *Cézanne: A Study of his Development*, 1927 (c); *Flemish Art: A Critical Survey*, 1927 (c); (with others) *Georgian Art (1760-1820)*, 1929 (c); *Henri Matisse*, 1930 (b); *The Arts of Painting and Sculpture*, 1932 (c); *Goldsworthy Lowes Dickinson*, 1932 (m); *Characteristics of French Art*, 1932 (c); *Art-History as an Academic Study*, 1933 (e); *Reflections on British Painting*, 1934 (c); *Poems by Stéphane Mallarmé*, 1936 (tr); *Last Lectures* [as Slade Professor at Cambridge Univ., 1933-34], 1939 (e); *Lectures on Royal Academy Exhibitions*, 1951 (coll.)

*repr. 1956

Virginia Woolf: *Roger Fry: a Biography*, 1940

ROY FULLER
1912-

Literary Craftsmanship and Appreciation, 1934 (c); *The Beggar's Brotherhood*, 1936 (e); *Full Measure*, 1936 (n); *Fun for the Footlights*, 1936 (p); *Poems*, 1940 (p); *The Middle of a War*, 1942 (p); *A Lost Season*, 1944 (p); *Savage Gold*, 1946 (n); *With My Little Eye*, 1948 (n); *Epitaphs and Occasions*, 1949 (p); *The Second Curtain*, 1953 (n); *Counterparts*, 1954 (p); *Fantasy and Fugue*, 1954 (n); *Image of a Society*, 1956 (n); *Brutus's Orchard*, 1957 (p); *The Ruined Boys*, 1959 (n); *That Distant Afternoon*, 1959 (n); *The Father's Comedy*, 1961 (n); *Collected Poems 1936-1961*, 1962; *The Perfect Fool*, 1963 (n); *Buff*, 1965 (p); *My Child, My Sister*, 1965 (n)

JOHN GALSWORTHY
1867-1933

(John Sinjohn, pseud.) *From the Four Winds*, 1897 (s); (J. Sinjohn, pseud.) *Jocelyn*, 1898 (n); (J. Sinjohn, pseud.) *Villa Rubein*, 1900 (n); (J. Sinjohn, pseud.) *A Man of Devon*, 1901 (s); *The Island Pharisees*, 1904 (n); *The Man of Property*, 1906 (n); *The Country House*, 1907 (n); *A Commentary*, 1908 (e); *A Justification of the Censorship of Plays*, 1909 (e); *Fraternity*, 1909 (n); *Plays:*

The Silver Box; Joy; Strife, 1909 (d); *Justice,* 1910 (d); *A Motley,* 1910 (s,e); *The Spirit of Punishment,* 1910 (e); *The Little Dream: An Allegory,* 1911 (d); *The Patrician,* 1911 (n); *The Eldest Son,* 1912 (d); *The Pigeon,* 1912 (d); *The Inn of Tranquillity,* 1912 (e); *Moods, Songs and Doggerels,* 1912 (p); *For the Love of Beasts,* 1912 (e); *The Slaughter of Animals for Food,* 1913 (e); *The Dark Flower,* 1913 (n); *The Fugitive,* 1913 (d); *The Mob,* 1914 (d); *The Army Veterinary Corps,* 1915 (e); *The Free-lands,* 1915 (n); *A Bit o' Love* (suppressed first impression: *The Full Moon*), 1915 (d); *The Little Man and Other Satires,* 1915 (d); *A Sheaf,* 1916 (e); *"Your Christmas Dinner is Served,"* 1916 (e); *Beyond,* 1917 (n); *Five Tales,* 1918 (s); *The Children's Jewel Fund,* 1918 (e); *The Land: A Plea,* 1918 (e); *Five Poems,* 1919 (p); *Saint's Progress,* 1919 (n); *Addresses in America, 1919,* 1919 (e); *Another Sheaf,* 1919 (e); *The Burning Spear,* 1919 (e); *Awakening,* 1920 (n); *The Foundations,* 1920 (d); *The Skin Game,* 1920 (d); *In Chancery,* 1920 (n); *Tatterdermalion,* 1920 (s); *The Bells of Peace,* 1921 (p); *To Let,* 1921 (n); *Six Short Plays,* 1921 (d); *A Family Man,* 1922 (d); *Loyalties,* 1922 (d); *Windows: A Comedy for Idealists and Others,* 1922 (d); *The Forsyte Saga (The Man of Property; In Chancery; To Let;* with two connecting interludes: *The Indian Summer of a Forsyte; Awakening*), 1922 (3n); *Captures,* 1923 (s); *International Thought,* 1923 (e); *The White Monkey,* 1924 (n); *Memorable Days,* 1924 (r); *On Expression,* 1924 (e); *Abracadabra and Other Satires,* 1924 (e); *The Forest,* 1924 (d); *Old English,* 1924 (d); *Is England Done For?,* 1925 (e); *Caravan,* 1925 (s); *The Show,* 1925 (d); *The Silver Spoon,* 1926 (n); *Escape,* 1926 (d); *Verses New and Old,* 1926 (p); *A Talk on Playing the Game with Animals and Birds,* 1926 (e); *The Way to Prepare Peace,* 1927 (e); *Castles in Spain and Other Screeds,* 1927 (e); *Two Forsyte Interludes: A Silent Wooing and Passers-by,* 1927 (n); *Mr. Galsworthy's Appeal for the Miners,* 1928 (e); *Swan Song,* 1928 (n); *Exiled,* 1929 (d); *A Modern Comedy (The White Monkey, The Silver Spoon, Swan Song),* 1929 (3n); *The Roof,* 1929 (d); *A Rambling Discourse,* 1929 (e);

On Forsyte 'Change, 1930 (n); *Two Essays on Conrad,* 1930 (c); *The Creation of Character in Literature,* 1931 (e); *Literature and Life,* 1931 (e); *Maid in Waiting,* 1931 (n); *Flowering Wilderness,* 1932 (n); *Candelabra,* 1932 (e); *Carmen by H. Meilhac and L. Halévy,* 1932 (tr); *Over the River* (Am. ed. *One More River*), 1933 (n); *Autobiographical Letters of J. Galsworthy: A Correspondence with Frank Harris,* 1933 (a); *End of the Chapter (Maid in Waiting, Flowering Wilderness, Over the River;* the third Forsyte coll., the second being *A Modern Comedy*), 1934 (3n); *Letters from John Galsworthy, 1900-1932,* ed. Edward Garnett, 1934; *The Collected Poems of John Galsworthy,* 1934

H. V. Marrot, *A Bibliography of the Works of John Galsworthy,* 1928; H. V. Marrot, *The Life and Letters of John Galsworthy,* 1935; Ralph Mottram, *John Galsworthy,* 1953

DAVID GARNETT
1892-

(Leda Burke, pseud.) *Dope Darling,* 1919 (n); *Lady Into Fox,* 1922 (n); *A Man in the Zoo,* 1924 (n); *The Sailor's Return,* 1925 (n); *Go She Must!* 1927 (n); *The Old Dovecote,* 1928 (s); *No Love,* 1929 (n); André Maurois, *A Voyage to the Island of the Articoles,* 1929 (tr); *The Appreciation of Voltaire's Zadig,* 1929 (c); *Never Be a Bookseller,* 1929 (e); *The Grasshoppers Come,* 1931 (n); *A Terrible Day,* 1932 (n); *A Rabbit in the Air: Notes Kept While Learning to Handle an Aeroplane,* 1932 (e); *Pocahontas, or, the Nonparell of Virginia,* 1933 (n); *Beany-eye,* 1935 (n); *War in the Air,* 1941 (e); *The Golden Echo,* 1953 (a); *Aspects of Love,* 1955 (n); *Flowers of the Forest,* 1955 (a); *A Shot in the Dark,* 1958 (n); *A Net for Venus,* 1959 (n); *The Familiar Faces,* 1962 (a); *Ulterior Motives,* 1966 (n)

DAVID GASCOYNE
1916-

Roman Balcony, 1932 (p); *Opening Day,* 1933 (n); *Man's Life Is This Meat,* 1935 (p); *A Short Survey of Surrealism,* 1935 (e); André Breton, *What is Surrealism,* 1936 (tr); *Poems, 1937-1942,*

1943 (p); *A Vagrant*, 1950 (p); *Thomas Carlyle*, 1952 (c); *Night Thoughts*, 1956 (p); *Collected Poems*, ed. Robin Skelton, 1965

See Elizabeth Jennings, *Every Changing Hope*, 1961.

WILLIAM GERHARDI
1895-

Futility: A Novel on Russian Themes, 1922 (n); *Anton Chehov*, 1923 (c); *The Polyglots*, 1925 (n); *A Bad End*, 1926 (n); *Pretty Creatures*, 1927 (s); *The Vanity-Bag*, 1927 (s); *Perfectly Scandalous, or The Immorality Lady*, 1927 (also pub. as *Donna Quixote*, 1929) (d); *Jazz and Jasper: The Story of Adams and Eva* (Am. ed. *Eva's Apples*), 1928 (n); *Pending Heaven*, 1930 (n); *Memoirs of a Polyglot*, 1931 (a); (with Brian Lunn) *The Memoirs of Satan*, 1932 (s); *Resurrection*, 1934 (n); (with Hugh Kingsmill) *The Casanova Fable: A Satirical Revaluation*, 1934 (c); *Of Mortal Love*, 1936 (n); (with Prince L. zu Loewenstein) *Meet Yourself as You Really Are*, 1936 (repr. 1962) (e); *My Wife's the Least of it*, 1938 (n); *The Romanovs*, 1940 (h); *My Sinful Earth*, 1947 (n); Collected Uniform Ed. (rev.) 1947-48, 10 vols.

STELLA GIBBONS
1902-

The Mountain Beast, 1930 (p); **Cold Comfort Farm*, 1932 (n); *Bassett*, 1934 (n); *The Priestess*, 1934 (p); *Enbury Heath*, 1935 (n); *Miss Linsey and Pa*, 1936 (n); *Roaring Towers*, 1937 (s); *Nightingale Wood*, 1938 (n); *The Lowland Venus*, 1938 (p); *My American*, 1939 (n); *Christmas at Cold Comfort Farm*, 1940 (s); *The Rich House*, 1941 (n); *Ticky*, 1943 (n); *The Bachelor*, 1944 (n); *Westwood, or, The Gentle Powers*, 1946 (n); *Conference at Cold Comfort Farm*, 1949 (n); *The Match-maker*, 1949 (n); *Collected Poems*, 1950 (p); *The Swiss Summer*, 1951 (n); *Fort of the Bear*, 1953 (n); *Beside the Pearly Waters*, 1954 (s); *The Shadow of the Sorcerer*, 1955 (n); *Here Be Dragons*, 1956 (n); *White Sand and Grey Sand*, 1958 (n); *A Pink Front Door*, 1959 (n); *The Charmers*, 1965 (n)

*repr 1965

PHILIP GIBBS
1877-1962

Founders of the Empire, 1899 (e); *Australasia, The Britains of the South*, 1903 (e); *India, Our Eastern Empire*, 1903 (e); *Knowledge is Power*, 1903 (repr. 1925) (e); *Facts and Ideas*, 1905 (repr. 1925) (e); *Men and Women of the French Revolution*, 1906 (b); *The Romance of Empire*, 1906 (rev. 1924) (e); *The Romance of George Villiers* [of the Stuart Court], (Am. ed. *The Reckless Duke*), 1908 (new ed. 1930) (b); *The Individualist*, 1908 (repr. 1932) (n); *The Spirit of Revolt*, 1908 (repr. 1924) (n); *The Street of Adventure*, 1909 (repr. 1951) (n); *King's Favourite, the Love Story of Robert Carr and Lady Essex*, 1909 (b); *Intellectual Mansions, S.W.*, 1910 (n); *Oliver's Kind Women*, 1911 (n); (with Bernard Grant) *Adventures of War with Cross and Crescent* (Am. ed. *The Balkan War*), 1912 (h); *Helen of Lancaster Gate*, 1912 (n); *The New Man, A Portrait Study of the Latest Type*, 1913 (e); *The Eighth Year, A Vital Problem of Married Life*, 1913 (n); *A Master of Life*, 1913 (n); *Beauty and Nick*, 1914 (n); *The Custody of the Child*, 1914 (n); *The Tragedy of Portugal*, 1914 (e); *The Pilgrim's Progress to Culture*, ed. Helen Cramp, 1915 (e); *People of Destiny*, 1920 (Am. ed. has subtitle: *Americans as I Saw Them at Home and Abroad*) (e); *Back to Life*, 1920 (n); *Wounded Souls*, 1920 (n); *Venetian Lovers*, 1921 (s); *The Middle of the Road*, 1922 (n); *Heirs Apparent*, 1923 (n); *Adventures in Journalism*, 1923 (e); *Ten Years After*, 1924 (e); *The Reckless Lady*, 1924 (n); *Little Novels of Nowadays*, 1924 (s); *Unchanging Quest*, 1925 (n); *Young Anarchy*, 1926 (n); *Out of the Ruins*, 1927 (s); *The Age of Reason*, 1928 (n); *The Day After Tomorrow, What is Going to Happen to the World?*, 1928 (e); *Darkened Rooms*, 1929 (n); *The Hidden City*, 1929 (n); *The Novels of Philip Gibbs*, 2 vols (*A Master of Life, Little Novels of Nowadays*), 1930 (n); *The Wings of Adventure*, 1930 (s); *Since Then*, 1930 (e); *The Winding Lane*, 1931 (n); *The Golden Years*, 1931 (n); *The Anxious Days*, 1932 (n); *The Cross of Peace*, 1933 (n); *Ways of Escape*, 1933 (e); *Paradise for Sale*, 1934 (n); *European Journey*, 1934 (t); *Blood Re-*

lations, 1935 (n); *England Speaks*, 1935 (e); *Cities of Refuge*, 1936 (n); *Ordeal in England. England Speaks Again*, 1937 (e); *Across the Frontiers*, 1938 (t); *Great Argument*, 1938 (n); *Broken Pledges*, 1939 (n); *This Nettle, Danger*, 1939 (n); *Sons of the Others*, 1940 (n); *The Long Alert*, 1941 (n); *The Amazing Summer*, 1941 (n); *America Speaks*, 1942 (e); *The Interpreter*, 1943 (n); *The Battle Within*, 1944 (n); *Through the Storm*, 1945 (n); *The Pageant of the Years*, 1946 (a); *The Hopeful Heart*, 1947 (n); *The Key of Life*, 1948 (n); *Behind the Curtain*, 1948 (n); *Crowded Company*, 1949 (a); *Both Your Houses*, 1949 (n); *Thine Enemy*, 1950 (n); *The Spoils of Time*, 1951 (n); *The Cloud Above the Green*, 1952 (n); *The Journalist's London*, 1952 (e); *Called Back*, 1953 (n); *Lady of the Yellow River*, 1953 (n); *The New Elizabethans*, 1953 (e); *No Price for Freedom*, 1955 (n); *The Ambassador's Wife*, 1956 (n); *Healing Touch*, 1957 (n); *Life's Adventures*, 1957 (r); *The Curtains of Yesterday*, 1958 (n); *How Now, England*, 1958 (e); *One of the Crowd*, 1959 (n); *The Riddle of a Changing World*, 1960 (e); *Wheel of Fortune*, 1960 (n); *His Lordship*, 1961 (n); *Oil Lamps and Candlelight*, 1962 (n); *The Law-Breakers*, 1963 (n); *The War Dispatches*, 1964 (h)

WILFRID GIBSON
1878-1962

Mountain Lovers, 1902 (p); *The Queen's Vigil and other Songs*, 1902 (p); *Song*, 1902 (p); *Urlyn The Harper*, 1902 (p); *The Golden Helm*, 1903 (p); *The Nets of Love*, 1905 (p); *On the Threshold*, 1907 (pd); *The Stonefolds*, 1907 (pd); *The Web of Life*, 1908 (p); *Akra The Slave*, 1910 (p); *Daily Bread*, 1910 (rev. 1923) (p); *Womenkind*, 1912 (d); *Fires*, 1912 (p); *Borderlands*, 1914 (p); *Thoroughfares*, 1914 (p); *Battle*, 1915 (p); *Friends*, 1916 (p); *Livelihood*, 1917 (p); *Poems (1904-1917)*, 1917 (p); *Whin*, 1918 (Am. ed. *Hill Tracks*) (p); *Twenty-Three Selected Poems*, 1919 (p); *Home*, 1920 (p); *Neighbours*, 1920 (p); *Krindlesyke*, 1922 (d); *Kestrel Edge*, 1924 (pd); *I Heard a Sailor*, 1925 (p); *Collected Poems*, *1905-1925*, 1926; *Sixty-Three Poems*, 1926 (p); *The Early Whistler*, 1927 (p); *Between Fairs*, 1928 (d); *The Golden*

Room, 1928 (p); *Hazards*, 1930 (p); *Wilfrid Gibson* [Selected Poems], 1931 (p); *Highland Dawn*, 1932 (p); *Islands: Poems, 1930-32*, 1932 (p); *Fuel*, 1934 (pd,p); *Wild Career*, 1935 (a); *Coming and Going*, 1938 (p); *The Alert*, 1941 (p); *Challenge*, 1942 (p); *The Searchlights*, 1943 (p); *The Outpost*, 1944 (p); *Solway Ford* (a selection by Charles Williams), 1945 (p); *Coldknuckles*, 1947 (p); *Within Four Walls*, 1950 (d)

See John Gawsworth, *Ten Contemporaries*, 1932

GEORGE GISSING
1857-1903

Workers in the Dawn, 1880 (n); *The Unclassed*, 1884 (n); *Demos: A Story of English Socialism*, 1886 (n); *Isabel Clarendon*, 1886 (n); *Thyrza*, 1887 (n); *A Life's Morning*, 1888 (n); *The Nether World*, 1889 (n); *The Emancipated*, 1890 (n); *New Grub Street*, 1891 (n); *Denzil Quarrier*, 1892 (n); *Born in Exile*, 1892 (n); *The Odd Women*, 1893 (n); *In the Years of Jubilee*, 1894 (n); *Eve's Ransom*, 1895 (n); *The Paying Guest*, 1895 (n); *Sleeping Fires*, 1895 (n); *The Whirlpool*, 1897 (n); *Human Odds and Ends*, 1898 (s); *The Town Traveller*, 1898 (n); *Charles Dickens*, 1898 (c); *The Crown of Life*, 1899 (n); *By the Ionian Sea: Notes of a Ramble in Southern Italy*, 1901 (t); *Our Friend the Charlatan*, 1901 (n); *The Private Papers of Henry Ryecroft*, 1903 (n); *Veranilda: A Romance*, 1904 (n); *Will Warburton*, 1905 (n); *The House of Cobwebs*, 1906 (s); *The Sins of the Fathers* (Am. ed.) (ed. V. Starrett), 1924 (s); *The Immortal Dickens*, 1925 (Am. ed. *Critical Studies of the Works of Charles Dickens*) (c); *A Victim of Circumstance*, 1927 (s); *Letters to Members of his Family* (coll. Algernon and Ellen Gissing), 1927; *Selections, Autobiographical and Imaginative*, 1929 (a); *Selected Tales* (Am. ed. *Brownie*), 1929 (s); *Stories and Sketches*, 1938 (s); *The Letters of George Gissing to Eduard Bertz*, ed. Arthur C. Young, 1961; *George Gissing and H. G. Wells: Their Friendship and Correspondence*, ed. R. A. Gettman, 1961

Jacob Korg, *George Gissing: A Critical Biography*, 1963

RUMER GODDEN
1907-

Chinese Puzzle, 1936 (s); *The Lady and the Unicorn*, 1938 (n); *Black Narcissus*, 1939 (n); *Gypsy, Gypsy*, 1940 (n); *Breakfast with The Nikolides*, 1942 (n); *A Fugue in Time*, 1945 (Am. ed. *Take Three Tenses*) (n); *Bengal Journey: A Story of the Part Played by Women in the Province, 1939-1945*, 1945 (h); *The River*, 1946 (n); **A Candle for Saint Jude*, 1948 (n); *In Noah's Ark*, 1949 (p); *A Breath of Air*, 1950 (n); *Kingfishers Catch Fire*, 1953 (n); *Hans Christian Anderson*, 1955 (b); *An Episode of Sparrows*, 1956 (n); *Mooltiki*, 1957 (s,p); *The Greengage Summer*, 1958 (n); *China Court: the Hours of a City House*, 1961 (n); *Rungli-Rungliot Means in Paharia: Thus Far and No Further*, 1961 (e); *St. Jerome and the Lion*, 1961 (p); *The Battle of the Villa Fiorita*, 1963 (n). Repr. Uniform Ed. (Heinemann) 1965ff.

*repr. 1964

OLIVER ST. JOHN GOGARTY
1878-1957

An Offering of Swans, 1924 (p); *Wild Apples*, 1928 (Am. ed. *Hyperthuliana*) (p); *Poems*, 1933 (p); *As I Was Going Down Sackville Street*, 1937 (r); *Others to Adorn* (Am. ed. *Selected Poems*), 1938 (p); *I Follow Saint Patrick*, 1938 (t); *Tumbling in the Hay*, 1939 (n); *Elbow Room*, 1939 (p); *Going Native*, 1941 (a); *Mad Grandeur*, 1944 (n); *Mr. Petunia*, 1946 (s); *Perennial*, 1947 (p); (Am. ed.) *Mourning Became Mrs. Spendlove and Other Portraits*, 1948 (e); *Rolling Down the Lea*, 1950 (Am. ed. *Intimations*) (p); *Collected Poems*, 1952; *Unselected Poems*, 1954 (p); *It Isn't This Time of Year At All*, 1954 (a); *Start from Somewhere Else* 1955 (e); *A Weekend in the Middle of the Week*, 1958 (Am. ed. 1963, *The Times I've Seen: Oliver St. John Gogarty*), (e); *W. B. Yeats, a Memoir*, 1963 (m)

Ulick J. O'Connor, *Oliver St. John Gogarty: a Poet and his Times*, 1964

LOUIS GOLDING
1895-1958

Note: A number of the novels repr. in *The Collected Edition*, 1952-55.

Sorrow of War, 1919 (p); *Forward from Babylon*, 1920 (rev. 1932) (n); *Shepherd Singing Ragtime*, 1921 (p); *Prophet and Fool*, 1923 (p); *Seacoast of Bohemia*, 1923 (n); *Sunward* [Italy], 1924 (t); *Day of Atonement*, 1925 (n); J. Fayard, *Oxford and Margaret*, 1925 (tr); *Sicilian Noon*, 1925 (t); *Store of Ladies*, 1927 (n); *Luigi of Catanzaro*, 1927 (s); *The Miracle Boy*, 1927 (n); *Those Ancient Lands* [Palestine], 1928 (t); *The Prince or Somebody*, 1929 (n); *Give Up Your Lovers*, 1930 (n); *Adventures in Living Dangerously*, 1930 (r); *A Letter to Adolf Hitler*, 1932 (e); *Magnolia Street*, 1932 (n); *James Joyce*, 1933 (c); *Five Silver Daughters*, 1934 (n); *Poems Drunk and Drowsy*, 1934 (p); *Black Frailty*, 1934 (e); *Terrace in Capri*, 1934 (t); *The Doomington Wanderer*, 1934 (Am. ed. *This Wanderer*) (s); *The Camberwell Beauty*, 1935 (n); *The Pursuer*, 1936 (n); *In the Steps of Moses the Lawgiver* [journey into Sinai], 1937 (t); *The Dance Goes On*, 1937 (n); *In the Steps of Moses the Conquerer*, 1938 (t); *The Song of Songs*, 1938 (d); *Hitler Through the Ages*, 1939 (e); *Mr. Emmanuel*, 1939 (n); *The World I Knew*, 1940 (a); *Who's There Within*, 1942 (n); *No News from Helen*, 1943 (n); *The Call of the Hand* (sel. and adapted from *The Doomington Wanderer*), 1944 (s); *Pale Blue Nightgown*, 1944 (s); *Swoop of the Falcon*, 1944 (s); *The Vicar of Dunkerly Briggs*, 1944 (s); *The Man in the White Tie*, 1944 (s); *Bert and Mary*, 1945 (s); *Louis Golding Goes Travelling*, 1945 (t); *The Glory of Elsie Silver*, 1946 (n); *Bare Knuckle Lover*, 1947 (n); *Three Jolly Gentlemen*, 1947 (n); *The Dark Prince*, 1948 (s); *Louis Golding's Boxing Tales*, 1948 (r); *My Sporting Days and Nights*, 1948 (e); *Honey for the Ghost*, 1949 (n); *The Dangerous Places*, 1951 (n); *The Bare-Knuckle Breed*, 1952 (e); *The Loving Brothers*, 1952 (n); *To the Quayside*, 1954 (n); *Goodbye to Ithaca*, 1955 (t); *Teach Yourself Local Government*, 1955 (e); *Mario on the Beach*, 1956 (s); *Mr. Hurricane*, 1957 (n); *The Little Old Admiral*, 1958 (n)

Jacob E. Simons, *Louis Golding*, 1958 [no bibliog.]

WILLIAM GOLDING
1911-

Poems, 1934 (p); *Lord of the Flies,* 1954 (n); *The Inheritors,* 1955 (n); *Pincher Martin* (Am. ed. *The Two Deaths of Christopher Martin*), 1956 (n); *The Brass Butterfly,* 1958 (d); *Free Fall,* 1960 (n); *The Spire,* 1964 (n); *The Hot Gates,* 1965 (e,a)

James R. Baker, *William Golding: a Critical Study,* 1965

DOUGLAS GOLDRING
1887-1960

A Country Boy, 1910 (p); *Ways of Escape,* 1911 (t); *The Permanent Uncle,* 1912 (n); *Streets,* 1912 (p); *The Loire,* 1913 (t); *Dream Cities,* 1913 (t); *It's an Ill Wind,* 1915 (n); *In the Town,* 1916 (p); *Margot's Progress,* 1916 (n); *On the Road,* 1916 (p); *Dublin,* 1917 (t); *The Fortune,* 1917 (n); *Polly,* 1917 (n); *A Stranger in Ireland,* 1918 (t); *Foreign Parts,* 1919 (t); *The Fight for Freedom,* 1919 (d); *The Black Curtain,* 1920 (n); *Nooks and Corners of Sussex and Hampshire,* 1920 (t); *Reputations,* 1920 (e); (with Hubert Nepean) *The Solvent,* 1920 (n); *James Elroy Flecker,* 1922 (c); *Nobody Knows,* 1923 (n); *Miss Linn,* 1924 (n); *Cuckoo,* 1925 (n); *Gone Abroad* 1925 (t); *Northern Lights and Southern Shades,* 1926 (t); *The Merchant of Souls,* 1926 (n); *The Façade,* 1927 (n); *The French Riviera and the Valley of the Rhone from Avignon to Marseilles,* 1928 (t); *Sardinia,* 1930 (t); *Impacts,* 1931 (e); *The Coast of Illusion,* 1932 (n); *Liberty and Licensing,* 1932 (e); *Pacifists in Peace and War,* 1932 (e); *To Portugal,* 1934 (t); *Odd Man Out,* 1935 (a); *A Tour in Northumbria,* 1938 (t); *Pot Luck in England,* 1938 (t); *Facing the Odds,* 1940 (e); *South Lodge,* 1943 (b); *The Nineteen Twenties,* 1943 (h); *Journeys in the Sun,* 1946 (t); *Marching with the Times, 1931-1946,* 1947 (h); *The Last Pre-Raphaelite* [Ford Madox Ford], 1948 (b); *Life Interests,* 1948 (t); *Home Ground,* 1949 (t); *Foreign Parts,* 1950 (t); *Regency Portrait Painter,* 1951 (b); *Three Romantic Countries,* 1951 (t); *The South of France,* 1952 (t); *Privileged Persons,* 1955 (r)

EDMUND GOSSE
1849-1928

(with J. A. Blaikie) *Madrigals, Songs and Sonnets,* 1870 (p); *On Viol and Flute,* 1873 (enlgd. 1890) (p); *King Erik,* 1876 (d); *The Unknown Lover,* 1878 (d); *New Poems,* 1897 (p); *Gray,* 1882 (b); *A Critical Essay on the Life and Works of George Tinworth,* 1883 (c); *Seventeenth-Century Studies,* 1883 (c); *Cecil Lawson: A Memoir,* 1883 (m); *From Shakespeare to Pope,* 1885 (c); *Firdausi in Exile,* 1885 (p); *The Masque of Painters,* 1885 (d); *Raleigh,* 1886 (b); *Life of William Congreve,* 1888 (b); *A History of Eighteenth-Century Literature 1660-1780,* 1889 (c); *The Life of Philip Henry Gosse, F.R.S., by his Son,* 1890 (b); *Robert Browning: Personalia,* 1890 (m); *Gossip in a Library,* 1891 (c); *Hedda Gabler by Henrik Ibsen,* 1891 (tr); *The Secret of Narcisse: A Romance,* 1892 (n); *Questions at Issue,* 1893 (c); (with William Archer) *Ibsen, The Master Builder,* 1893 (tr); *The Jacobean Poets,* 1894 (c); *In Russet and Silver,* 1894 (p); *Critical Kit-Kats,* 1896 (c); *Undine: A Tale by F. La Motte-Fouqué,* 1896 (tr); *A Short History of Modern English Literature,* 1897 (rev. as *Modern English Literature: A Short History,* 1905) (c); *Hypolympia, or, The Gods in the Island: An Ironic Fantasy,* 1901 (n); (with Richard Garnett) *English Literature: An Illustrated Record,* 1903 (c); *The Challenge of the Brontës,* 1903 (c); *L'Influence de la France sur la Poésie Anglaise,* 1904 (tr. Henri Davray) (c); *Jeremy Taylor,* 1904 (b); *British Portrait Painters and Engravers of the Eighteenth Century, Kneller to Reynolds,* 1905 (c); *Coventry Patmore,* 1905 (b); *Sir Thomas Browne,* 1905 (b); *French Profiles,* 1905 (c); (pub. anonymously) **Father and Son: A Study of Two Temperaments,* 1907 (b); *Ibsen,* 1907 (b); *Biographical Notes on the Writings of Robert Louis Stevenson,* 1908 (c); *Swinburne: Personal Recollections,* 1909 (m); *The Autumn Garden,* 1909 (p); *Two Visits to Denmark,* 1911 (r); *The Collected Poems,* 1911; (with others) *Browning's Centenary,* 1912 (e); *Portraits and Sketches,* 1912 (e); *The Life of Swinburne,* 1912 (b); *The Future of English Poetry,* 1913 (e); *Two Pioneers of Romanticism; Joseph and*

Thomas Warton, 1915 (c); *The Life of Algernon Charles Swinburne*, 1917 (b); *Three French Moralists*, 1918 (e); *France et Angleterre: l'Avenir de leurs Relations Intellectuelles*, 1918 (e); *The Novels of Benjamin Disraeli*, 1918 (c); *Some Diversions of a Man of Letters*, 1919 (e); *Malherbe and the Classical Reaction in the Seventeenth Century*, 1920 (c); *Books on the Table*, 1921 (c); *Aspects and Impressions*, 1922 (e); *More Books on the Table*, 1923 (c); *Tallemant des Réaux, or, The Art of Miniature Biography*, 1925 (c); *Silhouettes*, 1925 (c); *Leaves and Fruit*, 1927 (c); *Selected Essays*, 2 vols., 1928 (c)

*repr. ed. William Irvine, 1965

Evan Edward Charteris, *The Life and Letters of Edmund Gosse*, 1931

GERALD GOULD
1885-1936

Lyrics, 1906 (p); *An Essay on the Nature of Lyric*, 1909 (e); *Poems*, 1911 (p); *My Lady's Book*, 1913 (p); *The Way to Peace*, 1915 (e); *Monogamy: A Series of Dramatic Lyrics*, 1918 (p); *The Helping Hand: An Essay in Philosophy and Religion for the Unhappy*, 1918 (e); *The Happy Tree*, 1919 (p); *The Coming Revolution in Great Britain*, 1920 (e); *Memorial Notice of Julian Gould*, 1920 (m); *The Journey*, 1920 (p); *Lady Adela*, 1920 (e); *The Lesson of Black Friday*, 1921 (e); *The English Novel of To-day*, 1924 (c); *The Return to the Cabbage*, 1926 (e); *Beauty, The Pilgrim*, 1927 (p); *Selected Poems*, 1928 (p); *Democritus, or The Future of Laughter*, 1929 (e); *The Musical Glasses*, 1929 (e); *Collected Poems*, 1929; *All About Women. Essays and Parodies*, 1931 (e); *Isabel*, 1932 (n); *Refuge from Nightmare*, 1933 (e); (with B. Burnham) *Falling Angel*, 1936 (d)

W. S. GRAHAM
1918-

Cage Without Grievance, 1942 (p); *The Seven Journeys*, 1944 (p); *Second Poems*, 1945 (p); *The Voyages of Alfred Wallace*, 1948 (b); *The White Theshold*, 1949 (p); *The Night Fishing*, 1955 (p)

KENNETH GRAHAME
1859-1932

Pagan Papers, 1893 (e); *The Golden Age*, 1895 (also later edns.) (s); *Dream Days*, 1898 (e,s); *The Headswoman*, 1898 (n); *The Wind in the Willows*, 1908 (s); *Fun o' the Fair*, 1929 (e); *Kenneth Grahame: Life, Letters and Unpublished Work* (ed. Patrick R. Chalmers), 1933; *The Reluctant Dragon*, 1936 (s)

Peter M. Greene, *Kenneth Grahame, 1859-1932*, 1959

HARLEY GRANVILLE-BARKER
1877-1946

(with Laurence Housman) *Prunella, or, Love in a Dutch Garden*, 1906 (d); (with William Archer) *A National Theatre: Scheme and Estimates*, 1907 (e); *Three Plays (The Marrying of Ann Leete; The Voysey Inheritance; Waste)*, 1909 (d); *The Madras House*, 1911 (d); *Anatol: A Sequence of Dialogues* by Arthur Schnitzler, paraphrased for the English Stage, 1911 (d); *Souls on Fifth*, 1916 (n); *Rococo; Vote by Ballot; Farewell to the Theatre*, 1917 (Am. ed. *Three Short Plays*) (d); (with D. C. Calthrop) *The Harlequinade: An Excursion*, 1918 (d); *Sacha Guitry, Deburau: A Comedy*, 1921 (tr); *The Exemplary Theatre*, 1922 (c); *The Secret Life*, 1923 (d); *Preface to "Macbeth,"* 1923 (c); *Preface to "The Merchant of Venice,"* 1923 (c); *Preface to "The Tragedie of Cymbeline,"* 1923 (c); (with Helen Granville-Barker) *Plays by G. Martinez Sierra*, 1923 (also pub. as *The Kingdom of God and Other Plays*, 1929) (tr); *Preface to "A Midsummer Night's Dream,"* 1924 (c); *Preface to "Love's Labour's Lost,"* 1924 (c); *From Henry V to Hamlet*, 1925 (c); *Doctor Knock* by Jules Romains, 1925 (tr); *Preface to "The Tragedie of Julius Caesar,"* 1926 (c); *Preface to "The Tragedie of King Lear,"* 1927 (c); (with Helen Granville-Barker) *Four Plays by Serafin and Joaquin Alvarez Quintero*, 1927 (tr); *His Majesty*, 1928 (d); *Prefaces to Shakespeare*, 5 series, 1927-48, ed. M. St. Clair Byrne, 1958 (c); *A National Theatre*, 1930 (e); *On Dramatic Method*, 1931 (c); (with Helen Granville-Barker) *Take Two from One: A Farce by Gregorio and Maria Martinez Sierra*, 1931 (tr); (with Helen Granville-Barker) *Four*

Comedies by Serafin and Joaquin Alvarez Quintero, 1932 (tr); Associating with Shakespeare, 1932 (c); The Study of Drama, 1934 (c); (with G. B. Harrison) A Companion to Shakespeare Studies, 1934 (c); On Poetry in Drama, 1937 (c); The Use of the Drama, 1945 (c)

Charles B. Purdom, Harley Granville-Barker: Man of the Theatre, Dramatist and Scholar, 1955

ROBERT GRAVES
1895-

Goliath and David, 1916 (p); Over the Brazier, 1916 (p); Fairies and Fusiliers, 1917 (p); Treasure Box, 1919 (p); Country Sentiment, 1920 (p); The Pier Glass, 1921 (p); The Feather Bed, 1923 (p); Whipper-Ginny, 1923 (p); On English Poetry, 1924 (c); The Meaning of Dreams, 1924 (e); Mock Beggar Hall, 1924 (p,e); (John Doyle, pseud.) The Marmosite's Miscellany, 1925 (p); Welchman's Hose, 1925 (p); My Head! My Head!, 1925 (n); Contemporary Techniques of Poetry: A Political Analogy, 1925 (c); Poetic Unreason and Other Studies, 1925 (e); John Kemp's Wager: A Ballad Opera, 1925 (d); Another Future of Poetry, 1926 (e); Impenetrability, or, The Proper Habit of English, 1926 (e); Poems (1914-26), 1927 (p); The English Ballad, 1927 (c); Lars Porsena, or, The Future of Swearing and Improper Language, 1927 (e); Lawrence and the Arabs, 1927 (Am. ed. Lawrence and the Arabian Adventure) (b); (with Laura Riding) A Survey of Modernist Poetry, 1927 (c); Mrs. Fisher, or, The Future of Humour, 1927 (e); (with Laura Riding) A Pamphlet Against Anthologies, 1928 (e); *Good-bye to All That, 1929 (a); The Shout, 1929 (s); Poems, 1929, 1929 (p); But Still it Goes On, 1930 (e); Ten Poems More, 1930 (p); Poems, 1926-1930, 1931 (p); To Whom Else?, 1931 (p); No Decency Left, 1932 (n); The Real David Copperfield, 1933 (adaptation) (n); Poems, 1930-1933, 1933 (p); Claudius the God and his Wife, Messalina, 1934 (n); Claudius the God, 1934 (n); I, Claudius, 1934 (n); Antigua Penny Puce, 1936 (Am. ed. The Penny Stamp) (n); T. E. Lawrence to his Biographer, 1938 (e); Count Belisarius, 1938 (n); Sergeant Lamb of the Ninth, 1940 (n); (with Alan Hodge) The Long Week-End: A Social History of Great Britain, 1918-39, 1940 (e); No More Ghosts: Selected Poems, 1940 (p); Proceed, Sergeant Lamb, 1941 (n); (with Alan Hodge) The Reader Over Your Shoulder, 1943 (e); The Story of Marie Powell, Wife to Mister Milton, 1943 (n); Selected Poems, 1943 (p); The Golden Fleece, 1944 (n); King Jesus, 1946 (n); The White Goddess, 1948 (rev. 1952) (e); The Common Asphodel, 1949 (c); Seven Days in New Crete, 1949 (n); The Isles of Unwisdom, 1950 (n); Hercules My Shipmate, 1951 (n); Occupation: Writer, 1951 (misc.); Poems and Satires, 1951 (p); Poems, 1953 (p); (with Joshua Podro) The Nazarene Gospel Restored, 1953 (e); The Greek Myths, 2 vols., 1955 (rev. 1962 as Greek Gods and Heroes); Homer's Daughter, 1955 (n); The Crowning Privilege, 1955 (Clark lectures); Catacrock! Mostly Stories, Mostly Funny, 1956 (s); Poems, Selected by Himself, 1957 (p); They Hanged My Saintly Billy [William Palmer of Rugeley, the poisoner], 1957 (b); (with Joshua Podro) Jesus in Rome, 1957 (n); Five Pens in Hand, 1958 (misc.); Steps, 1958 (misc.); Food for Centaurs: Stories, Talks, Critical Studies, Poems, 1960; The Penny Fiddle, 1960 (p); More Poems, 1961 (p); The More Deserving Cases: 18 Old Poems for Reconsideration, 1962 (p); New Poems, 1962 (p); Oxford Addresses on Poetry, 1962 (e); The Siege and Fall of Troy, 1962 (h); (with Raphael Patai) Hebrew Myths, 1963 (h,c); Man Does, Woman Is, 1964 (p); Collected Stories, 1964; Mammon: Oration, 1964 (e); Mammon and the Black Goddess, 1965 (e); Collected Poems, 1965; Majorca Observed (drawings by Paul Hogarth), 1965 (t); Seventeen Poems Missing from Love Respelt [in Collected Poems], 1966 (p).
Also translations: Apuleius, The Golden Ass, 1951; Manuel de Jesús Galván, The Cross and the Sword, 1954; C. Suetonius Tranquillus, The Twelve Caesars, 1957; The Anger of Achilles; Homer's Iliad, 1959

*rev. enlgd. 1957

Douglas Day, Swifter than Reason, The Poetry and Criticism of Robert Graves, 1963; F. H. Higginson, A Bibliography of the Works of Robert Graves, 1966

HENRY GREEN
1905-

Blindness, 1926 (n); *Living,* 1929 (n); *Party Going,* 1939 (n); *Pack My Bag: A Self-Portrait,* 1940 (a); *Caught,* 1943 (n); *Loving,* 1945 (n); *Back,* 1946 (n); *Concluding,* 1948 (n); *Nothing,* 1950 (n); *Doting,* 1952 (n)

Edward Stokes, *The Novels of Henry Green,* 1959

GRAHAM GREENE
1904-

Babbling April, 1925 (p); *The Man Within,* 1929 (n); *The Name of Action,* 1930 (n); *Rumour at Nightfall,* 1931 (n); *Stamboul Train,* 1932 (Am. ed. *Orient Express*) (n); *It's a Battlefield,* 1934 (rev. 1948) (n); *The Basement Room,* 1935 (s); *The Bear Fell Free,* 1935 (s); *England Made Me,* 1935 (Am. ed. *The Shipwrecked*) (n); *A Gun for Sale,* 1936 (n); *Journey Without Maps* [French Guinea, Liberia], 1936 (t); **Brighton Rock,* 1938 (n); ***The Lawless Roads,* 1939 (Am. ed. *Another Mexico*) (t); *The Confidential Agent,* 1939 (n); *The Power and the Glory,* 1940 (n); *British Dramatists,* 1942 (c); *The Ministry of Fear,* 1943 (n); *Nineteen Stories,* 1947 (s); *The Heart of the Matter,* 1948 (n); *Why Do I Write?,* 1948 (e); *The Third Man,* 1950 (n); *The Third Man and The Fallen Idol* [films by Carol Reid from n of that title and s*], 1950; ****The Lost Childhood,* 1951 (c); *The End of the Affair,* 1951 (n); *The Living Room,* 1953 (d); *Twenty-One Stories,* 1954 (s); *Loser Takes All,* 1955 (n); *The Quiet American,* 1956 (n); *The Potting Shed,* 1957 (d); *Our Man in Havana,* 1958 (n); *The Complaisant Lover,* 1959 (d); *A Burnt-Out Case,* 1961 (n); *In Search of a Character,* 1961 (a,t); *Introduction to Three Novels* [*The Power and the Glory; The Heart of the Matter; The End of the Affair*] (c); *Three Plays* [*The Living Room, The Potting Shed. The Complaisant Lover*], 1962 (3d); *A Sense of Reality,* 1963 (s); *Carving a Statue,* 1964 (d); *The Comedians,* 1966 (n)

*Most titles repr. Uniform Ed., 1947-55
**repr. 1966
***repr. 1962

Kenneth Allott, *The Art of Graham Greene,* 1951; David Pryce-Jones, *Graham Greene,* 1963

LADY GREGORY
1859-1932

Righ Seumas by Douglas Hyde (no date) (tr); *Casadh an Tsugáin, or, The Twisting of the Rope* by Douglas Hyde, 1902 (tr); *Cuchulain of Muirtemne,* 1902 (tr); *Dráma Breithe Chríosta* by Douglas Hyde, 1903 (tr); *Poets and Dreamers: Studies and Translations from the Irish,* 1903 (c,tr); *Gods and Fighting Men,* 1904 (tr); *Spreading the News,* 1904 (d); *Kincora,* 1905 (d); *The White Cockade,* 1905 (d); *The White Cockade, and The Travelling Man,* 1905 (2d); *A Book of Saints and Wonders,* 1906 (s); *Spreading the News, and The The Rising of the Moon,* (with Douglas Hyde) *The Poorhouse,* 1906 (3d); (with W. B. Yeats) *The Unicorn from the Stars,* 1908 (d); *Seven Short Plays,* 1909 (d); *The Kiltartan History Book,* 1909 (h);*The Image,* 1910 (d); *The Kiltartan Molière: The Miser; The Doctor in Spite of Himself; The Rogueries of Scapin,* 1910 (tr); *The Kiltartan Wonder Book,* 1910 (s); *The Full Moon,* 1911 (d); *Irish Folk History Plays,* 1912 (d); *New Comedies,* 1913 (d); *Our Irish Theatre: A Chapter of Autobiography,* 1914 (a); *The Golden Apple,* 1916 (d); *The Kiltartan Poetry Book: Prose Translations from the Irish,* 1919 (tr); *Visions and Beliefs in the West of Ireland,* 1920 (e); *The Dragon,* 1920 (d); *Hugh Lane's Life and Achievement,* 1921 (b); *The Image and Other Plays,* 1922 (d); *Three Wonder Plays: The Dragon, Aristotle's Bellows, The Jester,* 1922 (d); *The Story Brought by Brigit,* 1924 (d); Carlo Goldoni, *Mirandolina,* 1924 (tr); *On the Racecourse,* 1926 (d); *The Case for the Return of Hugh Lane's Pictures to Dublin,* 1926 (e); *Three Last Plays,* 1928 (d); *My First Play,* 1930 (d); *Coole,* 1931 (e); *Journals, 1916-1930,* ed. Lennox Robinson, 1946

Eileen E. Coxhead, *Lady Gregory: A Literary Portrait,* 1961 (rev. enlgd. 1966)

HERBERT J. C. GRIERSON
1866-1960

The First Half of the Seventeenth Century, 1906 (h); *The Background of English Literature* (inaugural lecture, Univ. of Edinburgh), 1915; *Lord Byron, Arnold and Swinburne* (Warton lecture), 1921; *Don Quixote, Some Wartime Reflections on its Character and Influence,* 1921 (c); *Classical and Romantic (*Leslie Stephen lecture), 1923; *The Background of English Literature,* 1926 (repr. 1963) (e); *Lyrical Poetry from Blake to Hardy,* 1928 (Am. ed. *Lyrical Poetry of the Nineteenth Century)* (repr. 1963) (c); *Crosscurrents in English Literature of the XVIIth Century,* 1929 (repr. 1958) (c); *The Flute,* 1931 (p,tr), *Sir Walter Scott, 1832-1932,* 1933 (e); *Lang, Lockhart and Biography* (Andrew Lang lecture), 1934; *Two Dutch Poets* [Peter Hooft and P. C. Boutens] (Taylorian lecture), 1936; *The Problem of the Scottish Poet,* 1936 (e); *Milton and Wordsworth, Poets and Prophets,* 1937 (repr. 1950) (c); *The University and a Liberal Education,* 1938 (e); *Sir Walter Scott, Bart.: A New Life, Supplementary to, and Corrective of, Lockhart's Biography,* 1938 (b); *Thomas Carlyle* (lecture), 1940; *Essays and Addresses,* 1940 (e); *The English Bible,* 1943 (h); *Rhetoric and English Composition,* 1944 (e); (with J. C. Smith) *A Critical History of English Poetry,* 1944 (h); *Verse Translation* (Eng. Assoc. Presid. Address), 1948; *Criticism and Creation,* 1949 (e); *Swinburne,* 1953 (b,c)

GEOFFREY GRIGSON
1905-

Several Observations, 1939 (p); *Under a Cliff,* 1943 (p); *Henry Moore,* 1944 (b); *Wild Flowers in Britain,* 1944 (e); *Samuel Palmer: The Visionary Years,* 1947 (b); *The Harp of Aeolus,* 1948 (e); *An English Farmhouse,* ed. J. Piper, 1948 (e); *Places of the Mind,* 1949 (e); *The Crest on the Silver,* 1950 (a); *West Country,* 1951 (t); *Wessey,* 1951 (t); *A Master of Our Time: A Study of Wyndham Lewis,* 1951 (c); *Essays from the Air: Twenty-nine Broadcast Talks,* 1951 (e); *Gerdenage,* 1952 (e); *Freedom of the Parish,* 1954 (t); *English Drawings,* 1955 (e); *The Englishman's Flora,* 1955 (e); *Gerard Manley Hopkins,* 1955 (c); *Art Treasures of the British Museum,* 1957 (c); *The Painted Caves,* 1957 (e); *Wiltshire Book,* 1957 (t); (with S. Célébonovic) *Old Stone Age,* 1957 (e); *English Villages in Colour,* 1958 (t); *A Herbal of All Sorts,* 1959 (e); *Country Poems,* 1959 (p); *A Shell Guide to Wild Life,* 1959 (e); *English Excursions,* 1960 (t); *Samuel Palmer's Valley of Visions,* 1960 (e); *Christopher Smart,* 1961 (c); *Poets in their Pride,* 1962 (c); *The Shell Country Alphabet,* 1966 (t)

PHILIP GUEDALLA
1889-1944

Ignes Fatui: A Book of Parodies, 1911 (e); *Metri Gratia: Verse and Prose,* 1911 (misc.); *The Partition of Europe: A Textbook of European History, 1715-1815,* 1914 (h); *Supers and Supermen: Studies in Politics, History, and Letters,* 1920 (e); *The Second Empire: Bonapartism, The Prince, The President, The Emperor,* 1922 (rev. 1932) (h); *Masters and Men,* 1923 (e); *A Gallery: Studies of Contemporary Authors and Politicians,* 1924 (e); *Napoleon and Palestine,* 1925 (Arthur Davis Memorial lecture); *Independence Day: Studies of the Principal Persons Concerned in the American Revolution,* 1926 (Am. ed. *Fathers of the Revolution)* (e); *Palmerston,* 1926 (b); *Philip Guedalla: Selected Essays,* 1926 (e); *Collected Essays,* 4 vols., 1927; *Conquistador: American Fantasia,* 1927 (e); *Bonnet and Shawl: An Album* (sketches of six Victorian women), 1928 (b); *Mary Arnold* (repr. from preceding), 1929 (b); *The Missing Muse,* 1929 (e); *The Duke,* 1931 (Am. ed. *Wellington)* (b); *Argentine Tango,* 1932 (e); *The Hundred Days* [Napoleon], 1934 (h); *The Hundred Years* (chief historical events since Victoria's accession), 1936 (h); *Idylls of the Queen* (coll. Victorian studies), 1937 (e); *The Uniform Edition of The Works,* 1937-; *Ragtime and Tango* (uncoll. pieces and coll. studies from *Conquistador, American Fantasia, Argentine Tango),* 1938 (e); *The Hundredth Year* [1936], 1939 (h); *Mr. Churchill,* 1941 (b); (with J. A. Camacho) *The Other Americas,* 1941 (broadcast talks); *The Liberators* (14 statesmen), 1942 (b); *The Two Marshals*

(Bazaine, Pétain), 1943 (b); *Middle East, 1940-42: A Study in Air Power,* 1944 (h)

THOM GUNN
1929-

Fighting Terms, 1954 (rev. 1962) (p); *Poems,* 1954 (p); *The Sense of Movement,* 1957 (p); *My Sad Captains,* 1961 (p)

STEPHEN GWYNN
1864-1950

Memorials of an Eighteenth Century Painter [James Northcote], 1898 (m); *Highways and Byways in Donegal and Antrim,* 1899 (repr. 1903) (t); *Tennyson,* 1899 (c); *The Repentance of a Private Secretary,* 1899 (n); *The Decay of Sensibility,* 1900 (e); *The Old Knowledge,* 1901 (n); *The Queen's Chronicler,* 1901 (p); *Today and Tomorrow in Ireland,* 1903 (e); *A Lay of Ossian and Patrick and Other Irish Verses,* 1903 (p); *John Maxwell's Marriage,* 1903 (n); *The Masters of English Literature,* 1904 (h); *Fishing Holidays,* 1904 (r); *Thomas Moore,* 1905 (b); *Robert Emmet* (n); *The Glade in the Forest,* 1907 (s); *A Holiday in Connemara,* 1909 (t); *The Famous Cities of Ireland,* 1915 (t); *The Life of the Right Honorable Sir Charles W. Dilke* (begun by Stephen Gwynn, completed and ed. Gertrude M. Tuckwell, 2 vols.), 1917 (b); *Mrs. Humphry Ward,* 1917 (b); *For Second Reading: Attempts to Please,* 1918 (e); *Irish Books and People,* 1919 (e); *John Redmond's Last Years,* 1919 (b); *Garden Wisdom,* 1921 (e); *The Irish Situation,* 1921 (e); *The History of Ireland,* 1923 (h); *Collected Poems,* 1923; *Ireland,* 1924 (e); *Duffer's Luck: a Fisherman's Adventures,* 1924 (r); (Am. ed.) *The Student's History of Ireland,* 1925 (h); *Experiences of a Literary Man,* 1926 (r); *The Fair Hills of Ireland,* 1926 (t); *In Praise of France,* 1927 (t); *Ireland,* 1928 (t); *Travel in Ireland,* 1928 (t); *Captain Scott* [Robert Falcon Scott, Arctic explorer], 1929 (b); *Saints and Scholars,* 1929 (b); *The Life of Sir Walter Scott,* 1930 (b); *Burgundy,* 1930 (t); *The Life of Horace Walpole,* 1932 (b); *The Life of Mary Kingsley,* 1932 (b); *The Life and Friendships of Dean Swift,* 1933 (b); *The Charm of Ireland,* 1934 (t); *Claude Monet and His Garden,* 1934 (b,e); *Mungo Park and the Quest of the Niger,* 1934 (b); *Oliver Goldsmith,* 1935 (b); *The Happy Fisherman,* 1936 (e); *Irish Literature and Drama in the English Language,* 1936 (h); *River to River: a Fisherman's Pilgrimage,* 1937 (t); *Dublin Old and New,* 1938 (t); *Henry Grattan and His Times,* 1939 (b,h); *Robert Louis Stevenson,* 1939 (b); *Salute to Valour,* 1941 (p); *Aftermath,* 1946 (p); *Memories of Enjoyment,* 1946 (e)

H. RIDER HAGGARD
1856-1925

Cetywayo and His White Neighbors, 1882 (e); *Dawn,* 1884 (n); *The Witch's Head,* 1884 (n); *King Solomon's Mines,* 1885 (n); *She,* 1887 (n); *Jess,* 1887 (n); *Allan Quatermain,* 1887 (n); *A Tale of Three Lions,* 1887 (n); *Mr. Meeson's Will,* 1888 (n); *Maiwa's Revenge,* 1888 (n); *My Fellow Laborer and the Wreck of the "Copeland,"* 1888 (n); *Colonel Quaritch,* 1888 (n); *Cleopatra,* 1889 (n); *Allan's Wife,* 1889 (s); *Beatrice,* 1890 (n); (with Andrew Lang) *The World's Desire,* 1890 (n); *Eric Brighteyes,* 1891 (n); *Nada the Lily,* 1892 (n); *Montezuma's Daughter,* 1893 (n); *The People of the Mist,* 1894 (n); *Church and State,* 1895 (e); *Joan Haste,* 1895 (n); *Heart of the World,* 1896 (n); *The Wizard,* 1896 (n); *Doctor Therne,* 1898 (n); *The Last Boer War,* 1899 (Am. ed. *A History of the Transvaal*) (h); *Swallow,* 1899 (n); *The Spring of a Lion,* 1899 (n); *A Farmer's Year,* 1899 (e); *Black Heart and White Heart,* 1900 (s); *The New South Africa,* 1900 (e); *Lysbeth,* 1901 (n); *A Winter Pilgrimage,* 1901 (t); *Rural England,* 1902 (e); *Pearl Maiden,* 1903 (n); *Stella Fregelius,* 1904 (n); *The Brethren,* 1904 (n); *A Gardener's Year,* 1905 (e); *The Poor and the Land, Being a Report on Salvation Army Colonies,* 1905 (e); *Ayesha: The Return of She,* 1905 (n); *The Way of the Spirit,* 1906 (n); *Benita,* 1906 (Am. ed. *The Spirit of Bambatse*) (n); *Fair Margaret,* 1907 (Am. ed. *Margaret*) (n); *The Ghost Kings,* 1908 (Am. ed. *The Lady of the Heavens*) (n); *The Yellow God,* 1909 (n); *The Lady of Blossholme,* 1909 (n); *Morning Star,* 1910 (n); *Queen Sheba's Ring,* 1910 (n); *Regeneration,* 1910 (e); *Rural Denmark and its Lessons,* 1911 (e); *Red Eve*, 1911 (n); *The Mahatma and the Hare*, 1911 (n); *Marie*, 1912 (n); *Child of Storm*, 1913 (n); *The Wanderer's Necklace*, 1914 (n); *A Call to Arms*, 1914 (e); *The Holy Flower*, 1915 (Am. ed. *Allan and the Holy Flower*) (n); *The Ivory Child*, 1916 (n); *Finished*, 1917 (n); *Love Eternal*, 1918 (n); *Moon of Israel*, 1918 (n); *When the World Shook*, 1919 (n); *The Ancient Allan*, 1920 (n); *The Missionary and the Witch-Doctor*, 1920 (n); *Smith and the Pharaohs*, 1920 (s); *She and Allan*, 1922 (n); *The Virgin of the Sun*, 1922 (n); *Wisdom's Daughter*, 1923 (n); *Heu-Heu*, 1924 (n); *Queen of the Dawn*, 1925 (n); *Treasure of the Lake*, 1926 (n); *The Days of My Life*, 1926 (a); *Allan and the Ice Gods*, 1927 (n); *Mary of Marion Isle*, 1929 (n); *Rudyard Kipling to Rider Haggard: The Record of a Friendship*, ed. Morton Cohen, 1965 (letters)

J. E. Scott, *A Bibliography of the Works of Sir H. Rider Haggard*, 1947; Morton Norton Cohen, *Rider Haggard: His Life and Work*, 1960

RADCLYFFE HALL
188?-1943

Twixt Earth and Stars, 1906 (p); *A Sheaf of Verses*, 1908 (p); *Poems of the Past and Present*, 1910 (p); *Songs of Three Counties*, 1913 (p); *The Forgotten Island*, 1915 (p); *The Forge*, 1924 (n); *The Unlit Lamp*, 1924 (n); *A Saturday Life*, 1925 (n); *Adam's Breed*, 1926 (n); *The Well of Loneliness*, 1928 (n); *The Master of the House*, 1932 (n); *Miss Ogilvy Finds Herself*, 1934 (s); *The Sixth Beatitude*, 1936 (n)

G. ROSTREVOR HAMILTON
1888-

The Search for Loveliness, 1910 (p); *The Making*, 1926 (p); *Epigrams*, 1928 (p); *Light in 6 Moods*, 1930 (p); *John Lord, Satirist: a Satire*, 1934 (p); *Unknown Lovers*, 1935 (p); *Poetry and Contemplation*, 1937 (c); *Memoir, 1887-1937*, 1938 (p); *The World to Come*, 1939 (e); *The Sober War*, 1940 (p); *The Trumpeter of St. George*, 1941 (p); *Apollyon*, 1941 (p); *Death in April*, 1944 (p); *Hero or Fool? A Study of*

Milton's Satan, 1944 (c); *Selected Poems and Epigrams*, 1945 (p); *Crazy Gaunt and Other Dramatic Sketches*, 1946 (d); *The Inner Room*, 1947 (p); *The Tell-tale Article*, 1949 (c); *The Carved Stone*, 1952 (p); *The Russian Sister*, 1955 (p); *Guides and Marshals*, 1956 (c); *Collected Poems and Epigrams*, 1958; *Walter Savage Landor*, 1960 (c); *Landscape of the Mind: Late Poems*, 1964 (p); *Rapids of Time: Sketches from the Past*, 1965 (r)

JAMES HANLEY
1901-

Drift, 1930 n; *Boy*, 1931 (n); *The Last Voyage*, 1931 (n); *Men in Darkness*, 1931 (s); *Aria and Finale*, 1932 (s); *Ebb and Flood*, 1932 (n); *Stoker Haslett*, 1932 (n); *Captain Bottell*, 1933 (n); *Quartermaster Clausen*, 1934 (n); *The Furys*, 1935 (n); *Stoker Bush*, 1935 (n); *At Bay*, 1935 (s); *The Secret Journey* (seq. to *The Furys*), 1936 (n); *Broken Water: An Autobiographical Excursion*, 1937 (a); *Grey Children*, 1937 (e); *Half-an-Eye*, 1937 (s); *Hollow Sea*, 1938 (n); *People Are Curious*, 1938 (s); *Between the Tides*, 1939 (1949 ed. *Towards Horizons*) (e); *Our Time is Gone* (seq. to *The Secret Journey*), 1940 (n); *The Ocean*, 1941 (repr. 1954) (n); *No Directions*, 1943 (n); *Sailor's Song*, 1943 (n); *Crilley*, 1945 (s); *What Farrar Saw*, 1946 (n); *Selected Stories*, 1947 (n); *Emily* 1948 (n); *A Walk in the Wilderness*, 1950 (n); *Winter Song* (seq. to *Our Time is Gone*), 1950 (n); *The Closed Harbour*, 1952 (n); *Collected Stories*, 1953; *Don Quixote Drowned*, 1953 (s); *The Welsh Sonata: Variations with a Theme*, 1954 (n); *Levine*, 1956 (n); *An End and a Beginning* (seq. to *Winter Song*), 1958 (n); *Say Nothing*, 1962 (n)

THOMAS HARDY
1840-1928

Desperate Remedies, 1871 (n); *Under the Greenwood Tree*, 1872 (n); *A Pair of Blue Eyes*, 1873 (repr. 1886) (n); *Far from the Madding Crowd*, 1874 (n); *The Return of the Native*, 1878 (n); *A Laodicean*, 1881 (n); *Two on a Tower*, 1882 (n); *The Mayor of Casterbridge*, 1886 (n); *The Trumpet Major*, 1888 (n); *Tess of the d'Urbervilles*, 1891

(n); *A Group of Noble Dames,* 1891
(s); *Life's Little Ironies,* 1894 (s);
Jude the Obscure, 1896 (n); *The
Well-Beloved,* 1897 (n); *Wessex Poems,*
1898 (p); *Poems of the Past and Present,*
1902 (p); *The Dynasts,* 3 pts., 1903,
1906, 1908 (pd); *Time's Laughingstocks,*
1909 (p); *A Changed Man,* 1913 (s);
Satires of Circumstance, 1914 (p);
Moments of Vision, 1917 (p);
Collected Poems, 1919; *The Works*
(Mellstock ed.), 37 vols., 1919-1920;
Late Lyrics and Earlier, 1922 (p);
Human Shows, 1925 (p); *Life and Art:
Essays, Notes and Letters,* coll. Ernest
Brennecke, 1925; *Winter Words,* 1928
(p); *The Short Stories,* 1928 (s); *Col-
lected Poems,* 1930; *Selected Poems,* ed.
G. M. Young, 1940 (p); *Letters,* ed. Carl
J. Weber, 1954; *Thomas Hardy's Note-
books and Some Letters from Julia
Augusta Martin,* ed. Evelyn Hardy,
1955; *Love Poems,* ed. Carl J. Weber,
1963 (p)

Richard Little Purdy, *Thomas Hardy,
a Bibliographical Study,* 1954; Carl J.
Weber, *Hardy of Wessex,* 1965 [rev. of
1940 ed.]

FRANK HARRIS
1856-1931

Elder Conklin, 1894 (s); *Montes the
Matador,* 1900 (s); *Mr. and Mrs.
Daventry,* 1900 (d); *The Road to
Ridgeby's,* 1901 (s); **The Bomb,* 1908
(s); *The Man Shakespeare and his
Tragic Life Story,* 1909 (b); *Shakes-
peare and his Love,* 1910 (d); *The
Women of Shakespeare,* 1911 (c);
Great Days, 1913 (n); *Unpath'd Waters,*
1913 (n); *The Yellow Ticket,* 1914 (s);
Contemporary Portraits, 1915 (c); *The
Veils of Isis,* 1915 (s); *Oscar Wilde:
His Life and Confessions,* 1916, 1918,
enlgd. ed. 1932 (Am.) (b); *Love in
Youth,* 1916 (n); *Stories of Jesus the
Christ,* 1919 (s); *Contemporary Por-
traits,* second series, 1919 (c); *Contem-
portary Portraits,* third series, 1920 (c);
A Mad Love, 1920 (n); ***My Life and
Loves,* 1923-27 (a); *Contemporary Por-
traits,* fourth series, 1919, (c); *Un-
dream'd of Shores,* 1924 (s); *Joan La
Romée,* 1926 (d); *Latest Contemporary
Portraits,* 1921 (c); *On the Trail, My
Reminiscences as a Cowboy,* 1930 (r);

Confessional, 1930 (a); *Frank Harris
on Bernard Shaw: An Unauthorised
Biography,* 1931 (b); *Oscar Wilde* (with
preface by Bernard Shaw), 1938 (b)

*repr. with introd. John Dos Passos,
1963
**ed. John F. Gallagher, 1964

Vincent Brome, *Frank Harris,* 1959

L. P. HARTLEY
1895-

Night Fears, 1924 (s); *Simonetta Per-
kins,* 1925 (n); *The Killing Bottle,* 1932
(s); *The Shrimp and the Anemone* (Am.
ed. *The West Window*), 1944 (n); *The
Sixth Heaven,* 1946 (n); *Eustace and
Hilda,* 1947 (n); *The Boat,* 1949 (n);
The Travelling Grave, 1951 (s); *My
Fellow Devils,* 1951 (n); *The Go-
Between,* 1953 (n); *The White Wand,*
1954 (s); *A Perfect Woman,* 1955 (n);
The Hireling, 1957 (n); *Eustace and
Hilda* (a trilogy composed of *The
Shrimp and the Anemone, The Sixth
Heaven,* and *Eustace and Hilda*) 1958
(3n); *Facial Justice,* 1960 (n); *Two for
the River,* 1961 (s); *The Brickfield,* 1964
(n); *The Betrayal,* 1966 (n) (sequel to
The Brickfield)

Peter Bien, *L. P. Hartley,* 1963 and
Adam International Review, XXIX
(1961), nos. 294-96

CHRISTOPHER HASSALL
1912-1963

Poems of Two Years, 1935 (p); *Devil's
Dyke,* 1936 (p); *Christ's Comet,* 1937 (d);
Penthesperon, 1938 (p); *Crisis,* 1939 (p);
Ivor Novello, *Glamourous Night,* 1939
(lyrics by C.H.); *S.O.S.—Ludlow,* 1940
(p); *The Timeless Quest: Stephen Haggard,* 1946 (b); *Notes on the Verse
Drama,* 1948 (c); *The Slow Night, Poems,
1940-1948,* 1949 (p); *Words by Request,*
1952 (misc.); *Out of the Whirlwind,* 1953
(d); *The Player King,* 1953 (d); W. Wal-
ton, *Troilus and Cressida* [opera libretto],
1954; Ivor Novello, *King's Rhapsody*
(lyrics by C.H.), 1955; *The Red Leaf,*
1957 (p); *Edward Marsh, Patron of the
Arts,* 1959 (Am. ed. *Biography of Edward Marsh*) (b); *Bell Harry,* 1963 (p);
Rupert Brooke, 1964 (b); *Ambrosia and
Small Beer: The Record of a Corres-*

pondence between Edward Marsh and Christopher Hassall, ed. Christopher Hassall, 1964

JOHN HEATH-STUBBS
1918-

Wounded Thammuz, 1942 (p); *Beauty and the Beast*, 1943 (p); *The Divided Ways*, 1946 (p); *The Charity of the Stars*, 1949 (p); *The Darkling Plain*, 1950 (c); *The Swarming of the Bees*, 1950 (p); *A Charm against the Toothache*, 1954 (p); *Charles Williams*, 1955 (c); *The Triumph of the Muse*, 1958 (p); *Helen in Egypt*, 1959 (d); *The Blue-Fly in his Head*, 1962 (p)

RAYNER HEPPENSTALL
1911-

Patins, 1932 (p); *Middleton Murry: A Study in Excellent Normality*, 1934 (c); *First Poems*, 1935 (p); *Apology for Dancing*, 1936 (e); *Sebastian*, 1937 (p); *The Blaze of Noon*, 1939 (n); *Blind Men's Flowers Are Green*, 1940 (p); *Saturnine*, 1943 (n); *Poems, 1933-45*, 1946 (p); *The Double Image*, 1947 (c); (with Michael Innes) *Three Tales of Hamlet*, 1950 (s); *Léon Bloy*, 1953 (c); *The Lesser Infortune*, 1953 (n); *My Bit of Dylan Thomas*, 1957 (c); *The Greater Infortune*, 1960 (n); *Four Absentees* [Gill, Orwell, Dylan Thomas, Middleton Murry], 1960 (r); *The Four-fold Tradition: Notes on the French and English Literatures*, 1961 (c); *The Woodshed*, 1962 (n); *The Connecting Door*, 1962 (n); *The Intellectual Part*, 1963 (a)

A. P. HERBERT
1890-

Poor Poems and Rotton Rhymes, 1910 (p); *Play Hours with Pegasus*, 1912 (p); *Half-Hours at Helles*, 1916 (p); *The Bomber Gipsy*, 1918 (p); *The Secret Battle*, 1919 (n); *The House by the River*, 1920 (n); *The Wherefore and the Why*, 1921 (p); *Light Articles Only*, 1921 (Am. ed. *Little Rays of Moonshine*) (n); *"Tinker, Tailor . . . ,"* 1922 (p); *The Man About Town*, 1923 (e); *Four One-Act Plays*, 1923 (Am. ed. *Double Demon and Other One-Act Plays*) (4d); *The Old Flame*, 1925 (n); *Laughing Ann*, 1925 (p); *She-Shanties*.

1926 (p); *Double Demon: An Absurdity in One Act*, 1926 (d); (with Nigel Playfair) *Riverside Nights: An Entertainment*, 1926 (d); *Plain Jane*, 1927 (p); *Fat King Melon and Princess Caraway*, 1927 (d); *The Red Pen*, 1927 (d); *Two Gentlemen of Soho*, 1927 (d); *Misleading Cases in the Common Law*, 1927; *The Trials of Topsy*, 1928 (n); *Honeybubble and Company*, 1928 (n); *Topsy, M.P.*, 1929 (n); (with A. Davies-Adams) *La Vie Parisienne: A Comic Opera . . .*, 1929 (d); *The Water Gipsies*, 1930 (n); *Ballads for Broadbrows*, 1930 (p); *Wisdom for the Wise*, 1930 (p); *More Misleading Cases*, 1930; *A Book of Ballads, Being the Collected Light Verse of A. P. Herbert*, 1931 (Am. ed. *Ballads for Broadbrows and Others*) (p); *Derby Day: A Comic Opera*, 1931 (d); *Tantivy Towers: A Light Opera*, 1931 (d); *Helen: A Comic Opera*, adaptation of *La Belle Hélène* by Henri Meilhac and Ludovic Halévy, 1932 (d); *No Boats on the River*, 1932 (e); *A. P. Herbert*, 1933 (anthol. of humor); *Still More Misleading Cases*, 1933; *Holy Deadlock*, 1934 (n); *Mr. Pewter*, 1934 (e); *The Old Flame*, 1935 (n); *Uncommon Law* (rev. enlgd. 1935, 1952; ed. of coll. *Misleading Cases*) 1935 (e); *What a Word!*, 1935 (e); *Mild and Bitter*, 1936 (n); *The Secret Battle*, 1936 (n); *Sip! Swallow!*, 1937 (e); *The Ayes Have It: The Story of the Marriage Bill*, 1937 (e); *General Cargo*, 1939 (e); *Siren Song*, 1940 (e); *Let Us Be Gay*, 1941, (p); *Let Us Be Glum*, 1941 (p); *Well, Anyhow . . . , or, Little Talks*, 1942 (e); *Bring Back the Bells*, 1943 (p); *A.T.1*, 1944 (p); *A Better Sky, or, Name This Star*, 1944 (p); *"Less Nonsense!"*, 1944 (p); *Light the Lights*, 1945 (p); *Big Ben*, 1946 (d); *Point of Parliament*, 1946 (e); *Leave My Old Morale Alone*, (e); *Mr. Gay's London*, 1948 (e); *Bless the Bride*, 1948 (d); *The Topsy Omnibus (The Trials of Topsy, Topsy M.P., Topsy Turvey)*, 1949 (n); *The English Laugh*, 1950 (e); *Independent Member* (announced with title *University Member*), 1950 (a); *Number Nine, or, The Mind Sweepers*, 1951 (n); (with Reginald Arkell) *Come to the Ball* (adaptation of *Die Fledermaus*), 1951 (d); *Codd's Last Case*, 1952 (e); *Full Enjoyment and Other Verses*, 1952 (p); *Pool's Pilot, or, Why Not You?*,

1953 (e); *Why Waterloo?*, 1953 (n); *The Right to Marry*, (e); *No Fine on Fun*, 1957 (e); *Made for Man*, 1958 (n); *Look Back and Laugh*, 1960 (e); *Anything But Action?*, 1960 (e); (with others) *Radical Reaction*, ed. Ralph Harris, 1961 (e); *The Secret Battle*, 1963 (e)

Gilbert H. Fabes, *The First Editions of A. E. Coppard, A. P. Herbert, and Charles Morgan*, 1933

MAURICE HEWLETT
1861-1923

The Wreath, 1894-1914 (misc.); *A Masque of Dead Florentines*, 1895 (p); *Earthwork Out of Tuscany*, 1895 (e,tr); *Songs and Meditations*, 1896 (p); *The Forest Lovers*, 1898 (n); *Pan and the Young Shepherd*, 1898 (d); *The Judgement of Borso*, 1899 (s); *Little Novels of Italy*, 1899 (s); *Madonna of the Peach-Tree*, 1899 (s); *The Paduan Pastoral*, 1899 (s); *The Life and Death of Richard Yea-and-Nay*, 1900 (n); *Saint Gervase of Plessy*, 1900 (e); *New Canterbury Tales*, 1901 (repr. 1921) (s); *The Queen's Quair*, or, *The Six Years' Tragedy*, 1904 (n); *The Road in Tuscany*, 1904 (t); *The Fool Errant*, 1905 (n); *Fond Adventures, Tales of the Youth of the World*, 1905 (s); *The Stooping Lady*, 1907 (n); *Halfway House* (trilogy, Vol. I); 1908 (n); *The Spanish Jade*, 1908 (n); *Open Country* (trilogy, Vol. II), 1909 (n); *Artemision, Idylls and Songs*, 1909 (p); *The Ruinous Face*, 1909 (n); *Rest Harrow*, (trilogy, Vol. III), 1910 (n); *Brazenhead the Great*, 1911 (n); *The Song of Renny*, 1911 (n); *The Birth of Roland*, 1911 (s); *The Agonists, A Trilogy of God and Man (Minos, King of Crete; Ariadne in Naxos; The Death of Hippolytus)*, 1911 (d); *Mrs. Lancelot*, 1912 (n); *Bendish, A Study in Prodigality*, 1913 (n); *Helen Redeemed and Other Poems*, 1913 (p); *Lore of Proserpine*, 1913, (n); *A Ballad of "The Gloster" and "The Goeber"*, 1914 (p); *Singsongs of the War*, 1914 (p); *The Little Illiad*, 1915 (n); *A Lover's Tale*, 1915 (n); *Frey and His Wife*, 1916 (n); *Love and Lucy*, 1916 (n); *Gai Saber, Tales and Songs*, 1916 (p); *The Song of the Plow, Being the English Chronicle*, 1916 (p); *Thorgils of Treadholt*, 1917 (n); *The Loving History of Peridore*

and Paravail, 1917 (p); *Gudrid the Fair*, 1918 (n); *The Village Wife's Lament*, 1918 (p); *The Outlaw*, 1919 (n); *The Light Heart*, 1920 (n); *Mainwaring*, 1920 (n); *Flowers in the Grass*, 1920 (p); *In a Green Shade, A Country Commentary*, 1920 (e); *Wiltshire Essays*, 1921 (e); *Extemporary Essays*, 1922 (e); *Last Essays of Maurice Hewlett*, 1924 (e); *The Letters of Maurice Hewlett, to which is Added a Diary in Greece*, ed. Lawrence Binyon, 1926; *Maurice Hewlett [Selected Poems]*, 1926 (p)

Percy H. Muir, *A Bibliography of the First Editions of Books by Maurice Henry Hewlett*, 1927; *See* John Freeman, *English Portraits and Essays*, 1924

ROBERT HICHENS
1864-1950

The Coastguard's Secret, 1886 (n); *The Green Carnation*, 1894 (n); *An Imaginative Man*, 1895 (n); *The Folly of Eustace*, 1896 (s); *Flames*, 1897 (n); *Byeways*, 1897 (s); *The Londoners*, 1898 (n); (with Wilson Barrett) *The Daughters of Babylon*, 1899 (n); *The Slave*, 1899 (n); *Tongues of Conscience*, 1900 (n); *The Prophet of Berkeley Square*, 1901 (s); *Felix*, 1902 (n); *The Woman With the Fan*, 1904 (n); *The Garden of Allah*, 1904 (n); *The Black Spaniel*, 1905 (s); *The Call of the Blood*, 1906 (n); *Egypt and Its Monuments*, 1908 (repr. as *The Spell of Egypt*, 1910) (t); *A Spirit in Prison*, 1908 (n); *Barbary Sheep*, 1909 (n); *Bella Donna*, 1909 (n); *The Knock on the Door*, 1909 (n); *The Holy Land*, 1910 (t); *The Dweller on the Threshold*, 1911 (n); *The Fruitful Vine*, 1911 (n); *The Near East*, 1913 (t); *The Way of Ambition*, 1913 (n); *In the Wilderness*, 1917 (n); *Mrs. Marsden*, 1919 (n); *Snake-Bite*, 1919 (s); *The Spirit of the Time*, 1921 (n); *December Love*, 1922 (n)

JAMES HILTON
1900-1954

Catherine Herself, 1920 (n); *Storm Passage*, 1922 (n); *The Passionate Year*, 1923 (n); *The Dawn of Reckoning*, 1925 (n); *The Meadows of the Moon*, 1926 (n); *Terry*, 1927 (n); *The Silver Flame*, 1928 (n); *And Now Goodbye*, 1931 (n); (Glen Trevor, *pseud.*) *Murder at School*, 1931 (Am. ed. James Hilton, *Was It Murder?*) (n); *Contango*, 1932 (n); *Knight Without Armour*, 1933 (n); *Lost Horizon*, 1933 (n); *Goodbye, Mr. Chips*, 1934 (n); *We Are Not Alone*, 1937 (n); (with B. Burnham), dramatization of *Goodbye, Mr. Chips*, 1938; *To You, Mr. Chips*, [one chapt. of autobiog. included], 1938 (s,a); *Random Harvest*, 1941 (n); *The Story of Dr. Wassell*, 1944 (b); *So Well Remembered*, 1947 (n); *Nothing So Strange*, 1948 (n); *Morning Journey*, 1951 (n); *Time and Time Again*, 1953 (n); *The Duke of Edinburgh*, 1954 (b)

RALPH HODGSON
1871-1962

The Last Blackbird, 1907 (p); *The Bull*, 1913 (p); *Eve*, 1913 (p); *The Mystery*, 1913 (repr. 1956) (p); *The Song of Honour*, 1913 (p); *Poems*, 1917 (p); *Hymn to Moloch*, 1921 (p); *Silver Wedding*, 1941 (p); *The Muse and The Mastiff, Part I*, 1942 (p); *Skylark*, 1959 (p); *Collected Poems*, ed. Colin Fenton, 1961. In addition, Hodgson published seven undated broadsides: *The Beggar, The Bird Catcher, February, The Gypsy Girl, The Late Last Rook, Playmates,* and *A Song.*

JOHN HOLLOWAY
1920-

Language and Intelligence, 1951 (e); *Victorian Sage: Studies in Argument*, 1953 (c); *Poems*, 1954 (p); *The Minute and Longer Poems*, 1956 (p); *Charted Mirror: Literary and Critical Essays*, 1960 (c); *The Fugue, and Shorter Pieces*, 1960 (p); *The Story of the Night, Studies in Shakespeare's Major Tragedies*, 1961 (c); *The Landfallers*, 1962 (p); *The Colours of Clarity*, 1964 (c); *The Lion Hunt: A Pursuit of Poetry and Reality*, 1964 (e); *Wood and Windfall*, 1965 (p); *A London Childhood*, 1966 (a)

WINIFRED HOLTBY
1898-1935

Anderby Wold, 1923 (n); *The Crowded Street*, 1924 (n); *Eutychus*, 1928 (e); *The Land of Green Ginger*, 1928 (n); *A New Voter's Guide to Party Programmes: Political Dialogues*, 1929 (e); *Poor Caroline*, 1931 (n); *Virginia Woolf*,

1932 (c); *The Astonishing Island*, 1933 (n); *Mandoa, Mandoa!*, 1933 (n); *Women and a Changing Civilisation*, 1934 (e); *Truth is Not Sober*, 1934 (s); *The Frozen Earth*, 1935 (p); *South Riding*, 1936 (n); *Letters to a Friend*, ed. Alice Holtby and Jean McWilliam, 1937

Geoffrey H. Taylor, *Winifred Holtby: A Bibliography Together with Some Letters*, 1955

ANTHONY HOPE
1863-1933

A Man of Mark, 1890 (n); *Father Strafford*, 1891 (n); *Mr. Witt's Widow*, 1892 (n); *Sport Royal*, 1893 (s); *Half a Hero*, 1893 (n); *A Change of Air*, 1893 (n); *The God in the Car*, 1894 (n); *Dolly Dialogues*, 1894 (s); **The Prisoner of Zenda*, 1894 (n); *The Indiscretion of the Duchess*, 1894 (n); *The Chronicles of Count Antonio*, 1895 (n); *The Heart of Princess Osra*, 1896 (n); *Comedies of Courtship*, 1896 (s); *Phroso*, 1897 (n); **Rupert of Hentzau*, 1898 (n); *The King's Mirror*, 1899 (n); *Quisanté*, 1900 (n); *Tristram of Blent*, 1901 (n); *The Intrusions of Peggy*, 1902 (n); *Double Harness*, 1903 (n); *Servant of the Public*, 1905 (n); *Sophy of Kravonia*, 1906 (n); *The Duke's Allotment*, 1906 (n); *Tales of Two People*, 1907 (s); *The Great Miss Driver*, 1908 (n); *Simon Dale*, 1908 (n); *Second String*, 1910 (n); *Mrs. Maxon Protests*, 1911 (n); *Young Man's Year*, 1915 (n); *Captain Dieppe*, 1918 (n); *Beaumaroy Home from the Wars*, 1919 (n); *Lucinda*, 1920 (n); *Pilkerton's Peerage*, 1921 (d); *The Adventure of Lady Ursula*, 1921 (d); *Little Tiger*, 1925 (n); *Memories and Notes*, 1927 (r); *The Philosopher in the Apple Orchard*, 1936 (d)

*repr. 1966

GERARD MANLEY HOPKINS
1844-1899

The Poems of Gerard Manley Hopkins, ed. Robert Bridges, 1918 (enlgd. 1930, enlgd. ed. W. H. Gardner, 1948); *The Letters of Gerard Manley Hopkins to Robert Bridges*, ed. Claude C. Abbott, 1935 (Vol. II, *The Correspondence of Gerard Manley Hopkins and Richard Watson Dixon*, rev. 1955); *Further*

Letters, ed. Claude C. Abbott, 1938 (rev. enlgd. 1956); *The Notebooks and Papers,* ed. Humphry House, 1937 (rev., including next item, as *Journals and Papers,* completed Graham Storey, 1959); *The Sermons and Devotional Writings,* ed. Christopher Devlin, 1959 W. H. Gardner, *Gerard Manley Hopkins,* 2 vols., 1948

A. E. HOUSMAN
1859-1936

A Shropshire Lad, 1896 (p); *Last Poems,* 1922 (p); *The Name and Nature of Poetry,* 1933 (c); *More Poems,* ed. Laurence Housman, 1936 (p); Laurence Housman, *My Brother A. E. Housman: Personal Recollections Together with 30 Unpublished Poems,* 1938; *Collected Poems,* 1939, 1953, 1956; *Manuscript Poems,* ed. Tom B. Haber, 1955; *Thirty Housman Letters to Witter Bynner,* 1957; *Complete Poems,* 1960; *Selected Prose,* ed. John *Carter,* 1961 (e) John Carter and John Sparrow, *Housman: an Annotated Check List,* rev. 1952; George L. Watson, *A. E. Housman, a Divided Life,* 1957

LAURENCE HOUSMAN
1865-1959

All-Fellows, Seven Legends of Lower Redemption with Insets in Verse, 1896 (repr. 1923) (s); *Green Arras,* 1896 (p); *Gods and Their Makers,* 1897 (repr. 1920) (s); *Spikenard,* 1898 (p); *The Little Land, with Songs from its Four Rivers,* 1899 (p); *Rue,* 1899 (p); [Anon.] *An Englishwoman's Love-Letters,* 1900 (n); [Anon.] *A Modern Antaeus,* 1901 (n); [Anon.] *The Missing Answers to "An Englishwoman's Love-Letters",* 1901; *Of Aucassin and Nicolette* (with *Amabel* and *Amoris*), 1902 (repr. 1925) (tr); *Bethlehem, a Nativity Play,* and *The Pageant of Our Lady,* 1902 (*Bethlehem,* repr. 1955) (d,p); *Sabrina Warham,* 1904 (n); *The Blue Moon,* 1904 (s); *The Cloak of Friendship,* 1905 (s); (with Harley Granville Barker) *Prunella,* 1906 (repr. 1930) (d); *Mendicant Rhymes,* 1906 (p); *The Vicar of Wakefield* (opera based on Oliver Goldsmith's novel), 1906 (lyrics); *A Chinese Lantern,* 1908 (d); *Selected Poems,* 1908 (p); *Alice in Ganderland,*

1911 (d); Aristophanes, *Lysistrata,* 1911 (tr); *Pains and Penalties, the Defence of Queen Caroline,* 1911 (d); *John of Jingalo,* 1912 (n); *The Royal Runaway and Jingalo in Revolution* (seq. to *John of Jingalo*), 1914 (n); *As Good as Gold,* 1916 (d); *Bird in Hand,* 1916 (d); *A Likely Story,* 1916 (d); *The Lord of the Harvest,* 1916 (d); *Nazareth,* 1916 (d); *The Return of Alcestis,* 1916 (d); *The Snow Man,* 1916 (d); *The Sheepfold,* 1918 (n); *The Heart of Peace,* 1918 (p); *Ploughshare and Pruninghook,* 1919 (lectures); *The Wheel,* 1919 (pd); *Gods and Their Makers,* 1920 (s); *Angels and Ministers,* 1921 (3d); *The Death of Orpheus,* 1921 (pd); *Possession, a Peep-Show in Paradise,* 1921 (d); *Selected Poems,* 1921 (p); *A Doorway in Fairyland* (sel. child's stories), also pub. as *Moonshine and Clover,* 1922; *Dethronements, Imaginary Portraits of Political Characters,* 1922 (3d); *False Premises,* 1922 (5d); *Little Plays of St. Francis,* 1922 (18d); *Followers of St. Francis,* 1923 (4d); *Echo de Paris, a Study from Life* [Oscar Wilde etc.], 1923 (d); *All-Fellows and the Cloak of Friendship,* 1923 (s); *Trimblerigg,* 1924 (n); *Odd Pairs,* 1925 (s); *The Death of Socrates,* 1925 (d); *Ironical Tales,* 1926 (s); *The Comments of Juniper,* 1926 (6d); *Uncle Tom Pudd,* 1927 (n); *The "Little Plays" Handbook,* 1927 (c); *The Life of H.R.H. the Duke of Flamborough, by Benjamin Bunny,* 1928 (n); *The Love Concealed,* 1928 (p); *Ways and Means,* 1928 (5d); *Cornered Poets,* 1929 (7d); *Turn Again Tales,* 1930 (s); *The New Hangman,* 1930 (d); *Palace Plays,* 1930 (repr. 1951) (d); *Little Plays of St. Francis, Second Series,* 1931 (18d); *The Queen's Progress, Palace Plays, Second Series,* 1932 (9d); *Ye Fearful Saints!,* 1932 (9d); *Nunc Dimittis, An Epilogue to "Little Plays of St. Francis",* 1933 (d); *Victoria and Albert, Palace Plays, Third Series,* 1933 (13d); *Four Plays of St. Clare,* 1934 (4d); *Victoria Regina, a Dramatic Biography* [Plays from *Angels and Ministers,* *Palace Plays,* *The Queen's Progress,* and *Victoria and Albert*], 1934 (d); *Little Plays of St. Francis, Complete Series in Three Volumes,* 1935 (45d); *The Golden Sovereign* (coll. plays), 1937 (d); *The Unexpected Years,* 1937 (a); *Palace Scenes: More Plays of Queen Victoria,*

1937 (d); *Collected Poems*, 1937; *What Next*, 1937 (s); *A.E.H.*, 1938 (Am. ed. *My Brother, A. E. Housman*) (b); *Gracious Majesty*, 1941 (12d); *The Preparation of Peace*, 1941 (e); *Palestine Plays*, 1942 (4d); *Samuel, the King-Maker*, 1944 (d); *Back Words and Fore Words*, 1945 (misc.); *Strange Ends and Discoveries*, 1948 (s); *Happy and Glorious, Forty-Seven Plays Selected from Victoria Regina, The Golden Sovereign, and Gracious Majesty*, 1949 (47d); *The Family Honour*, 1950 (d); *Old Testament Plays*, 1950 (5d); *The Kind and the Foolish*, 1952 (s)

See Edmund Blunden, *Votive Tablets*, 1931

ELIZABETH JANE HOWARD
1923-

The Beautiful Visit, 1950 (n); (with Robert Aickman) *We Are For the Dark*, 1951 (s); *The Long View*, 1956 (n); (with Arthur Helps) *Bettina* [Bettina (Brentano) von Arnim], 1957 (b); *The Sea Change*, 1959 (n); *After Julius*, 1965 (n)

STEPHEN HUDSON
1868-1944

War-Time Silhouettes, 1916 (s); *Richard Kurt*, 1919 (n); *Elinor Colhouse*, 1921 (n); *Prince Hempseed*, 1923 (n); *Tony*, 1924 (n); *Richard, Myrtle and I*, 1926 (n); **A True Story*, 1930 (n); *Celeste*, 1930 (s); Proust, *Time Regained*, Vol. 12 of *Remembrance of Things Past*, 1931 (tr); *The Other Side*, 1937 (n)

*repr. 1965

Richard, Myrtle and I, ed. Violet Schiff, with a biographical note and critical essay by Theophilus E. M. Boll, 1962; *See also* John Gawsworth, *Ten Contemporaries*, 1932

W. H. HUDSON
1841-1922

The Purple Land That England Lost, 1885 (n); *A Crystal Age*, 1887 (n); *Osprey, or, Egrets and Aigrettes*, 1891 (e); *The Naturalist in La Plata*, 1892 (e); (pseud. Henry Harford) *Fan*, 1892 (n); *Birds in a Village*, 1893 (e); *Bird-Catching*, 1893 (e); *Feathered Women*, 1893 (e); *Idle Days in Patagonia*, 1893 (tr); *Lost British Birds*, 1894 (e); *Letter to Clergymen, Ministers and Others*, 1895 (e); *British Birds*, 1895 (e); *Pipits*, 1897 (e); *The Trade in Birds' Feathers*, 1898 (e); *Birds in London*, 1898 (e); *Nature in Downland*, 1900 (e); *Birds and Man*, 1901 (e); *El Ombú*, 1902 (repr. 1909 as *South American Sketches*; Am. ed. *Tales of the Pampas*) (s); *Hampshire Days*, 1903 (t); *A Linnet for Sixpence!*, 1904 (e); *Green Mansions. A Romance of the Tropical Forest*, 1904 (n); *A Little Boy Lost*, 1905 (n); *The Land's End*, 1908 (t); *Afoot in England*, 1909 (t); *A Shepherd's Life: Impressions of the South Wiltshire Downs*, 1910 (t); *A Thrush That Never Lived*, 1911 (e); *Adventures Among Birds*, 1913 (e); *On Liberating Caged Birds*, 1914 (e); *Roff and a Linnet, Chain and Cage*, 1918 (e); *Far Away and Long Ago*, 1918 (a); *Birds in Town and Village* (rev. ed. *Birds in A Village*), 1919 (e); *The Book of a Naturalist*, 1919 (e); *Birds of La Plata*, 1920 (e); *Dead Man's Plack and An Old Thorn*, 1920 (s); *A Tired Traveller*, 1921 (repr. from *Adventures Among the Birds*) (e); *A Traveller in Little Things*, 1921 (t); *Seagulls in London*, 1922 (e); *A Hind in Richmond Park*, 1922 (e); *Ralph Herne*, 1923 (n); *Rare, Vanishing and Lost British Birds* (compiled from notes by Hudson by Linda Gardiner), 1923 (enlgd. ed. of *Lost British Birds*) (e); *153 Letters from W. H. Hudson*, ed. Edward Garnett, 1923 (Am. ed. *Letters from W. H. Hudson 1901-1922*; also pub. as *Letters from W. H. Hudson to Edward Garnett*, 1925); *Men, Books, and Birds*, 1925 (e); *Mary's Little Lamb*, 1929 (e); *W. H. Hudson's Letters to R. B. Cunninghame Graham*, 1941; *Letters on the Ornithology of Buenos Ayres*, 1951

George F. Wilson, *A Bibliography of the Writings of W. H. Hudson*, 1922; Morley Roberts, *W. H. Hudson, a Portrait*, 1924

RICHARD HUGHES
1901-

Gipsy-Night, 1922 (p); *The Sisters' Tragedy*, 1922 (d); **The Sisters' Tragedy and Three Other Plays*, 1924 (Am. ed. *A Rabbit and A Leg, Collected Plays*) (d); *Confessio Juvenis, Collected Poems,* 1926; *A Moment of Time,* 1926 (s); **The Innocent Voyage,* 1929 (Am. ed. *A High Wind in Jamaica*) (n); *The Spider's Palace,* 1931 (s); *Richard Hughes, An Omnibus* (with an auto-biographical introduction), 1931; *In Hazard,* 1938 (n); *The Fox in the Attic,* 1961 (Vol. I of *The Human Predicament*) (n)

*repr. 1966 at *Plays (Danger, The Sisters' Tragedy, The Man Born To Be Hanged, A Comedy of Good and Evil.* **repr. 1965

TED HUGHES
1930-

The Hawk in the Rain, 1957 (p); *Lupercal,* 1960 (p); *Meet My Folks!,* 1961 (s); (with Thom Gunn) *Selected Poems,* 1962; *The Earth-Owl,* 1963 (s)

T. E. HULME
1883-1917

The Complete Poetical Works of Hulme, appended to Ezra Pound, *Ripostes,* 1912 (repr. in *Speculations,* 1924); Henri Bergson, *An Introduction to Metaphysics,* 1913 (tr); Georges Sorel, *Réflexions sur la Violence,* 1916 (tr); *Speculations,* ed. Herbert Read, 1924 (repr. 1960) (e); *Notes on Language and Style,* ed. Herbert Read, 1929 (e); *Further Speculations,* ed. Sam Hynes, 1955 (e)

Alun Richard Jones, *The Life and Opinions of T. E. Hulme,* 1960

R. C. HUTCHINSON
1907-

Thou Hast a Devil, 1930 (n); *The Answering Glory,* 1932 (n); *The Unforgotten Prisoner* 1933 (n); *One Light Burning,* 1935 (n); *Shining Scabbard,* 1936 (n); *Testament,* 1938 (n); *The Fire and the Wood,* 1940 (n); *Interim,* 1945 (r); *Elephant and Castle,* 1949 (n); *Recollection of a Journey,* 1949 (Am. ed. *Journey with Strangers*) (n); *The Stepmother,* 1955 (n); *March the Ninth,* 1957 (n); *Image of My Father,* 1961 (Am. ed. *The Inheritor*) (n); *A Child Possessed,* 1964 (n)

ALDOUS HUXLEY
1894-1963

The Burning Wheel, 1916, (p); *The Defeat of Youth,* 1918 (p); *Leda,* 1920 (p); *Limbo,* 1920 (s); (with T. S. Eliot, F. S. Flint) *Chapbook,* 1920 (c); *Crome Yellow,* 1921 (n); *Mortal Coils,* 1922 (s); *Antic Hay,* 1923 (n); *On the Margin: Notes and Essays,* 1923 (e); *Little Mexican,* 1924 (Am. ed. *Young Archimedes*) (s); *Those Barren Leaves,* 1925 (n); *Selected Poems,* 1925 (p); *Along the Road: Notes and Essays of a Tourist,* 1925 (t); *Two or Three Graces,* 1926 (s); *Essays, New and Old,* 1926 (e); *Jesting Pilate,* 1926 (e); *Proper Studies,* 1927 (e); *Point Counter Point,* 1928 (n); *Arabia Infelix,* 1929 (p); *Holy Face,* 1929 (e); *Do What You Will,* 1929 (e); *Brief Candles,* 1930 (one Am. ed. *After the Fireworks*) (s); *Vulgarity in Literature: Digressions from a Theme,* 1930 (e); *The Cicadas,* 1931 (p); *Music at Night,* 1931 (e); *The World of Light,* 1931 (d); *Brave New World,* 1932 (n); *T. H. Huxley as a Man of Letters,* 1932 (e); *Texts and Pretexts: An Anthology with Commentaries,* 1932 (e); *Rotunda: A Selection from the Works of Aldous Huxley,* 1932; *Retrospect: An Omnibus of Aldous Huxley's Books,* 1933; *Beyond the Mexique Bay,* 1934 (s); *Eyeless in Gaza,* 1936 (n); *The Olive Tree,* 1936 (e); *What Are You Going to do About It? The Case for Constructive Peace,* 1936 (e); *Stories, Essays and Poems,* 1937; *Ends and Means,* 1937 (e); *The Gioconda Smile,* 1938 (s); *After Many a Summer,* 1939 (Am. ed. *After Many a Summer Dies the Swan*), (n); *Grey Eminence: A Study in Religion and Politics,* 1941 (e); *The Art of Seeing,* 1942 (e); *Time Must Have a Stop,* 1944 (n); *The Perennial Philosophy,* 1945 (e); *Verses and A Comedy,* 1946 (p,d); *Science, Liberty, and Peace,* 1946 (e); *The World of Aldous Huxley: An Omnibus of his Fiction and Non-Fiction over Three Decades,* ed. Charles Rolo, 1947; *The Gioconda Smile,* 1948 (d); *Ape and Essence,* 1948 (e); *Themes and Variations,* 1950 (e); *The Devils of Loudon,* 1952 (e); (with Stuart Gilbert) *Joyce, The Artificer; Two Studies of Joyce's Method,* 1952 (c); *The Doors of Perception,* 1954 (e); *The Genius and the Goddess,* 1955 (n); *Adonis and the*

Alphabet, 1956 (Am. ed. *Tomorrow and Tomorrow and Tomorrow*) (e); *Heaven and Hell*, 1956 (e); *Collected Short Stories*, 1957; *Brave New World Revisited*, 1958 (n); *Collected Essays*, 1959; *On Art and Artists*, 1960 (e); *Stories, Essays and Poems*, 1960; *Island*, 1962 (n); *Literature and Science*, 1963 (e)

Note. The Collected Edition, pub. Chatto and Windus, has 28 titles, 1966

Claire John Eschelbach and Joyce Lee Shober, *Aldous Huxley: A Bibliography 1916-1959*, 1961; *Aldous Huxley, 1894-1963*, ed. Julian Huxley [includes essay by A.H. dictated the day before his death]. 1965 (r)

CHRISTOPHER ISHERWOOD
1904-

All the Conspirators, 1928 (n); *Intimate Journals of Baudelaire*, 1930 (tr); *The Memorial*, 1932 (n); *Mr. Norris Changes Trains* (Am. ed. *The Last of Mr. Norris*), 1935 (n); (with W. H. Auden) *The Dog Beneath the Skin*, 1935 (d); (with W. H. Auden) *The Ascent of F6*, 1936 (d); (with Desmond I. Vesey) *A Penny for the Poor*, by Berthold Brecht, 1937 (Am. ed. *The Threepenny Novel*, 1958) (tr); *Sally Bowles*, 1937 (n); *Lions and Shadows*, 1938 (a); (with W. H. Auden) *On the Frontier*, 1938 (d); (with W. H. Auden) *Journey to a War*, 1939 (t); *Goodbye to Berlin*, 1939 (n); (with Swami Prabhavananda) *Bhagavad-Gita, Song of God*, 1944 (tr); *Prater Violet*, 1945 (n); *The Memorial*, 1946 (n); (with Swami Prabhavananda) Shankara's *The Crest-Jewel of Discrimination*, 1946 (tr); *The Candor and the Cows* [S. America], 1949 (t); *Vedanta for Modern Man*, 1951 (e); *The World in the Evening*, 1952 (n); *Down There on a Visit*, 1962 (n); *A Single Man*, 1964 (n); *Ramakrishna and His Disciples*, 1965 (b); *Exhumations*, 1965 (s,e,p)

See Frederick R. Karl, *A Reader's Guide to the Contemporary English Novel*, 1962

W. W. JACOBS
1863-1943

Many Cargoes, 1896 (repr. 1936) (s); *The Skipper's Wooing and The Brown Man's Servant*, 1897 (s); *Sea Urchins*, 1898 (s); *A Master of Craft*, 1900 (n); *Light Freights*, 1901 (s); *At Sunwich Port*, 1902 (s); *The Lady of the Barge*, 1902 (repr. 1943) (s); *Odd Craft*, 1903 (repr. 1936) (s); *Dialstone Lane*, 1904 (n); *Captains All*, 1905 (s); *Short Cruises*, 1907 (s); (with Herbert C. Sargent) *The Boatswain's Mate*, 1907 (d); *Salthaven*, 1908 (n); (with H. C. Sargent) *The Changeling*, 1908 (d); (with Charles Rock) *The Ghost of Jerry Bundler*, 1908 (d); (with Charles Rock) *The Grey Parrot*, 1908 (d); *Sailors' Knots*, 1909 (s); (with Horace Mills) *Admiral Peters*, 1909 (d); (with Louis N. Parker) *Beauty and the Barge*, 1910 (d); (with Louis N. Parker) *The Monkey's Paw*, 1910 (d); *Ship's Company*, 1911 (s); (with H. C. Sargent) *In the Library*, 1913 (d); (with P. E. Hubbard) *A Love Passage*, 1913 (d); *Night Watches*, 1914 (s); *The Castaways*, 1916 (n); *Deep Waters*, 1919 (n); *Keeping Up Appearances*, 1919 (d); (with Herbert C. Sargent) *The Castaway*, 1924 (d); *Establishing Relations*, 1925 (d); *Sea Whispers*, 1926 (n); *The Warming Pan*, 1929 (d); *A Distant Relative*, 1930 (d); *Master Mariners*, 1930 (d); *Matrimonial Openings*, 1931 (d); *Snug Harbour, Collected Stories*, 1931 (s); *Dixon's Return*, 1932 (d); *The Nightwatchman and Other Longshoremen: 57 Stories*, 1932 (s); *Cruises and Cargoes: Omnibus*, 1934 (s)

See J. B. Priestley, *Figures in Modern Literature*, 1924

HENRY JAMES
1843-1916

Note: The numerous recent reprints not noted. Bodley Head repr of New York ed. now in progress.

A Passionate Pilgrim, 1875 (s); *Transatlantic Sketches*, 1875 (t); *Roderick Hudson*, 1876 (n); *The American*, 1877 (n); *French Poets and Novelists*, 1878 (c); *The Europeans*, 1878 (n); *Daisy Miller*, 1879 (n); *Hawthorne*, 1879 (c); *Washington Square*, 1880 (n); *The Portrait of a Lady*, 1881 (n); *Portraits of Places*, 1883 (t); *The Bostonians*, 1886 (n); *The Princess Casamassima*, 1886 (n); *Partial Portraits*, 1888 (c); *The Reverberator*, 1888 (n); *The Tragic*

Muse, 1890 (n); *The Other House,* 1896 (n); *The Spoils of Poynton,* 1897 (n); *What Maisie Knew,* 1897 (n); *In the Cage,* 1898 (n); *The Turn of the Screw,* 1898 (n); *The Awkward Age,* 1899 (n); *The Sacred Fount,* 1901 (n); *The Wings of the Dove,* 1902 (n); *The Ambassadors,* 1903 (n); *William Wetmore Story and his Friends,* 1903 (n); *The Golden Bowl,* 1904 (n); *The American Scene,* 1907 (t); *The Novels and Tales,* "New York Edition," 26 vols., 1907-1917; *Views and Reviews,* 1908 (c); *The Outcry,* 1911 (n); *A Small Boy and Others,* 1913 (a); *Notes of a Son and Brother,* 1914 (a); *Notes on Novelists,* 1914 (c); *The Ivory Tower,* 1917 (n); *The Sense of the Past,* 1917 (n); *The Middle Years,* 1917 (a); *The Letters,* ed. Percy Lubbock, 2 vols., 1920; *The Art of the Novel* [prefaces to novels], ed. R. P. Blackmur, 1934 (c); *The Notebooks,* ed. F. O. Mathiessen and Kenneth B. Murdock, 1947; *The Scenic Art,* ed. Allan Wade, 1948 (c); *The Art of Fiction and Other Essays,* ed. Morris Roberts, 1948 (c); *The Complete Plays,* ed. Leon Edel, 1949; *The Painter's Eye: Notes and Essays on the Pictorial Arts,* sel. and ed. John L. Sweeney, 1956 (c); *Henry James: An Autobiography (A Small Boy, Notes of a Son and Brother, The Middle Years),* ed. Frederick W. Dupee, 1956; *Henry James and H. G. Wells* [letters], ed. Leon Edel and Gordon M. Ray, 1958; *The Complete Tales,* ed. Leon Edel, 1962-1964 (12 vols.)

Leon Edel and Dan H. Laurence, *A Bibliography of Henry James,* 1957 (rev. 1961); Leon Edel, *Henry James* (3 vols. of 4), 1953-63; George Monteiro, *Henry James and John Hay: The Record of a Friendship* [incl. letters], 1965

STORM JAMESON
1897-

The Pot Boils, 1919 (n); *The Happy Highways,* 1920 (n); *Modern Drama in Europe,* 1920 (c); *The Clash,* 1922 (n); *Lady Susan and Life, An Indiscretion,* 1923 (n); *The Pitiful Wife,* 1923 (n); *Three Kingdoms,* 1926 (n); *The Lovely Ship* (Part I of trilogy), 1927 (n); *Farewell to Youth,* 1928 (n); *Full Circle,* 1928 (d); *The Georgian Novel and Mr. Robinson,* 1929 (c); *The Voyage Home* (Part II of trilogy), 1930 (n); *The Decline of Merry England,* 1930 (e); *A Richer Dust* (Part III of trilogy), 1931 (n); *The Single Heart,* 1932 (n); *That Was Yesterday,* 1932 (n); *The Triumph of Time,* Trilogy, 1932 (3n); *A Day Off,* 1933 (n); *Women Against Men,* 1933 (3n); *No Time Like the Present,* 1933 (a); *Company Parade,* 1934 (n); *Love in Winter,* 1935 (n); *The Soul of Man in the Age of Leisure,* 1935 (e); *In the Second Year,* 1936 (n); *None Turn Back,* 1936 (n); *Delicate Monster,* 1937 (n); *The Moon Is Making,* 1937 (n); *The Novel in Contemporary Life,* 1938 (c); *Civil Journey,* 1939 (e); *Farewell, Night; Welcome, Day* (Am. ed. *Captain's Wife*), 1939 (n); *Here Comes A Candle,* 1939 (n); **Cousin Honore,* 1940 (n); *Europe To Let,* 1940 (n); *The Fort,* 1941 (n); *The End of this War,* 1941 (e); *Then We Shall Hear Singing,* 1942 (n); **Cloudless May,* 1943 (n); *The Journal of Mary Hervey Russell,* 1945 (n); *The Other Side,* 1946 (n); *Before the Crossing,* 1947 (n); *The Black Laurel,* 1948 (n); *The Moment of Truth,* 1949 (n); *The Writer's Situation,* 1950 (e); (with others) *Hidden Streams: Essays on Writing,* 1951 (e); *The Green Man,* 1952 (n); *The Hidden River,* 1955 (n); *Intruder,* 1956 (n); *A Cup of Tea for Mr. Thorgill,* 1957 (n); *A Ulysses Too Many* (Am. ed. *One Ulysses Too Many*), 1958 (n); *A Day Off,* 1959 (s); *Last Score, or, The Private Life of Sir Richard Ormston,* 1961 (n); *Morley Roberts: The Last Eminent Victorian,* 1961 (b); *The Road From the Monument,* 1962 (n); *A Month Soon Goes,* 1962 (n); *The Aristide Case,* 1964 (n); *The Early Life of Stephen Hind,* 1966 (n)

*repr. 1965

ELIZABETH JENNINGS
1926-

A Way of Looking, 1955 (p); *A Sense of the World,* 1958 (p); *Let's Have Some Poetry,* 1960 (e); *Every Changing Hope,* 1961 (c); *Poetry Today,* 1961 (c); *Song for a Birth or a Death,* 1961 (p); *The Sonnets of Michel Angelo Buonarroti,* 1961 (tr); *Recoveries,* 1964 (p); *Christianity and Poetry,* 1965 (e); *The Mind Has Mountains,* 1966 (p)

JEROME K. JEROME
1859-1927

On the Stage—and Off, 1885 (r); The Idle Thoughts of an Idle Fellow, 1886 (repr. 1928, 1938) (e); Barbara, 1886 (d); Sunset (founded on second Tennyson poem of "The Sisters"), 1888 (d); Stage-Land, 1889 (reissued as Twelfth Thousand) (e); *Three Men in a Boat, 1889 (repr. 1929 etc.) (n); Diary of a Pilgrimage, 1891 (e); Told After Supper, 1891 (s); John Ingerfield, 1894 (s); (with Eden Phillpotts) The Prude's Progress, 1895 (d); Sketches in Lavender, Blue and Green, 1897 (s); The Second Thoughts of an Idle Fellow, 1898 (e); *Three Men on the Bummel, 1900 (repr. 1929) (n); The Observations of Henry, 1901 (s); "Miss Hobbs", 1902 (d); Paul Kelver, 1902 (n); Tea-Table Talk, 1903 (c); American Wives and Others, 1904 (e,s); Tommy and Co., 1904 (s); Idle Ideas, 1905 (e); The Passing of the Third Floor Back, 1907 (s); The Angel and the Author—and Others, 1908 (e,s); Fanny and the Servant Problem, 1909 (d); They and I, 1909 (n); The Passing of the Third Floor Back, 1910 (d); The Master of Mrs. Chilvers, 1911 (d); Robina in Search of a Husband, 1914 (d); Malvina of Brittany, 1916 (n); All Roads Lead to Calvary, 1919 (n); Woodbarrow Farm, 1921 (d); Anthony John: a Biography, 1923 (n); The Celebrity, 1926 (d); My Life and Times, 1926 (a); The Soul of Nicholas Snyders, 1927 (d)

*repr. 1966

Alfred Moss, Jerome K. Jerome: His Life and Work, 1929 [no bibliog.]

PAMELA HANSFORD JOHNSON
1912-

Symphony for Full Orchestra, 1934 (p); This Bed Thy Centre, 1935 (n); Blessed Above Women, 1936 (n); Here Today, 1937 (n); World's End, 1937 (n); The Monument, 1938 (n); Girdle of Venus, 1939 (n); Too Dear for my Possessing, 1940 (n); (with Neil Stewart) (pseud. Nap Lombard) Tidy Death, 1940 (n); The Family Pattern, 1942 (n); Winter Quarters, 1943 (n); (with Neil Stewart) (pseud. Nap Lombard) Murder's a Swine (Am. ed. Grinning Pig), 1943 (n); The Trojan Brothers, 1944 (n); An

Avenue of Stone, 1947 (n); Thomas Wolfe (Am. ed. Hungry Gulliver), 1947 (c); A Summer to Decide, 1948 (n); The Philistines, 1949 (n); Ivy Compton-Burnett, 1951 (c); Catherine Carter, 1952 (n); Corinth House, 1954 (d); An Impossible Marriage, 1954 (n); The Last Resort (Am. ed. The Sea and the Wedding), 1956 (n); Six Proust Reconstructions (Am. ed. Proust Recaptured), 1958; The Humbler Creation, 1959 (n); The Unspeakable Skipton, 1959 (n); An Error of Judgement, 1962 (n); (with Kitty Black) Jean Anouilh, The Rehearsal, 1926 (tr); Night and Silence! Who is Here?, 1963 (n); Cork Street, Next to the Hatter's, 1965 (n)

DENIS JOHNSTON
1901-

The Moon in the Yellow River, and The Old Lady Says No!, 1932 (2d); Storm Song and A Bride for the Unicorn, 1935 (2d); (with Ernst Toller) Blind Man's Buff, 1938 (d); The Golden Cuckoo, 1954 (d); Nine Rivers from Jordan, 1955 (r); In Search of Swift, 1959 (c); Collected Plays, 1960 (Am. ed. The Old Lady Says No! and Other Plays) (d)

DAVID JONES
1895-

In Parenthesis, 1937 (n); The Anathemata: Fragments of an Attempted Writing, 1952 (p); Epoch and Artist: Selected Writings, ed. Harman Grisewood, 1959

GLYN JONES
1905-

The Blue Bed, 1937 (s); Poems, 1939 (p); The Water Music, 1944 (s); The Dream of Jake Hopkins, 1954 (p); (with Dr. T. J. Morgan, reconstruction) The Saga of Llywarch the Old, 1955; The Valley, the City, the Village, 1956 (n); The Learning Lark, 1960 (n); The Island of Apple, 1965 (n)

GWYN JONES
1907-

Richard Savage, 1935 (b); Times Like These, 1936 (n); The Nine-Days Wonder, 1937 (n); Garland of Bays,

1938 (n); *The Buttercup Field*, 1946 (s); *The Green Island*, 1946 (n); *The Still Waters*, 1948 (s); *The Walk Home: A Prospect of Wales*, 1948 (t); *The Flowers Beneath the Scythe*, 1952 (n); *Shepherd's Hey*, 1953 (s); *Welsh Legends and Folk Tales* (Retold), 1955 (s); *Scandinavian Legends and Folk Tales* (Retold), 1956 (s); *The First Forty Years*, 1957 (a); *Egil's Saga*, 1960 (tr); *The Norse Atlantic Saga*, 1964 (h)

HENRY ARTHUR JONES
1851-1929

Note: The numerous plays before 1900 omitted except the very famous one, *The Liars.*

The Renascence of the English Drama, 1895 (misc.); *The Liars*, 1897 (d); *The Lackey's Carnival*, 1900 (d); *Mrs. Dane's Defence*, 1900 (d); *Chance, The Idol*, 1902 (d); *The Princess's Nose*, 1902 (d); *Whitewashing Julia*, 1903 (d); *A Clerical Error*, 1904 (d); *Joseph Entangled*, 1904 (d); *The Heroic Stubbs*, 1906 (d); *The Hypocrites*, 1906 (d); *The Corner Stones of Modern Drama*, 1906 (c); *On Reading Modern Plays*, 1906 (c); *The Dancing Girl*, 1907 (d); *The Galilean's Victory*, 1907 (d); *The Middleman*, 1907 (d); *Literature and The Modern Drama*, 1907 (c); *Dolly Reforming Herself*, 1908 (d); *The Knife*, 1909 (d); *The Censorship Muddle and A Way Out Of It*, 1909 (e); *Fall In, Rookies!*, 1910 (d); *We Can't Be As Bad As All That!*, 1910 (d); *The Divine Gift*, 1913 (d); *Mary Goes First*, 1913 (d); *The Foundations of a National Drama*, 1913 (misc.); *The Lie*, 1915 (d); *The Theatre of Ideas, A Burlesque Allegory and Three One-Act Plays*, 1915 (e,d); *The Pacifists, A Parable in a Farce in Three Acts*, 1917 (d); *Representative Plays*, ed. Clayton Hamilton, 4 vols., 1925

Doris Arthur Jones, *The Life and Letters of Henry Arthur Jones*, 1930; Richard A. Cordell, *Henry Arthur Jones and the Modern Drama*, 1932

JAMES JOYCE
1882-1941

Chamber Music, 1907 (ed. William York Tindall, 1954) (p); *Gas from a Burner*, 1912 (p); *Dubliners*, 1914 (s); *A Portrait of the Artist as a Young Man*, 1916 (n); *Exiles*, 1918 (d); *Ulysses*, 1922 (n); *Pomes Penyeach*, 1927 (p); *Anna Livia Plurabelle* [fragment from *Work in Progress*], 1928; *Tales Told of Shem and Shaun* [three fragments from *Work in Progress*], 1929; *Haveth Childers Everywhere* [fragment from *Work in Progress*], 1928; *Tales Told of Shem and Shaun* [fragments from *Work in Progress*], 1932; *The Mime of Mick, Nick and the Maggies* [fragment from *Work in Progress*], 1934; *Collected Poems*, 1936; *Storiello as She is Syung* [fragment form *Work in Progress*], 1937; *Finnegans Wake*, 1939 (corrected edition, N.Y., 1945) (n); *Introducing Joyce, a Selection of Prose*, ed. T. S. Eliot, 1942; *Stephen Hero* (ed. from ms. by Theodore Spencer), 1944 (rev. enlgd. ed. J. J. Slocum and Herbert Cahoon, 1955) (n); *Letters of James Joyce*, Vol. I, ed. Stuart Gilbert, 1957; *The Critical Writings of James Joyce*, ed. Ellsworth Mason and Richard Ellman, 1959 (c); *Scribbledehobble: The Ur-Workbook for Finnegans Wake*, ed. Thomas E. Connolly, 1961; *A First Draft Version of Finnegans Wake*, ed. David Hayman, 1963 (n); *Letters*, Vols. II and III, ed. Richard Ellman, 1966; *Shorter Finnegans Wake*, ed. Anthony Burgess, 1966

Work in Progress became *Finnegans Wake*

John J. Slocum and Herbert Cahoon, *A Bibliography of Joyce*, 1953; Richard Ellmann, *James Joyce*, 1959

SHEILA KAYE-SMITH
1887-1956

The Tramping Methodist, 1908 (n); *Starbrace*, 1909 (n); *Spell Land*, 1910 (n); *Isle of Thorns*, 1913 (n); *Three Against the World*, 1914 (Am. ed. *The Three Furlongers*) (n); *Willow's Forge*, 1914 (p); *Sussex Gorse*, 1916 (n); *John Galsworthy*, 1916 (c); *The Challenge to Sirius*, 1917 (n); *Little England*, 1918 (Am. ed. *The Four Roads*) (n); *Tamarisk Town*, 1919 (n); *Green Apple Harvest*, 1920 (n); *Joanna Godden*, 1921 (n); *The End of the House of Alard*, 1923 (n); *Saints in Sussex*, 1923 (p); *The George and the Crown*, 1925 (n); *Anglo-Catholicism*, 1925 (e); *The*

Mirror of the Months, 1925 (e); *Joanna Godden Married* 1926 (s); *Iron and Smoke*, 1928 (n); *A Wedding Morn*, 1928 (n); *The Village Doctor*, 1929 (n); *Sin*, 1929 (e); (with John Hampden) *Mrs. Adis*, and *The Mock-Beggar*, 1929 (d); *Shepherds in Sackcloth*, 1930 (n); *The History of Susan Spray, The Female Preacher*, 1931 (Am. ed. *Susan Spray*) (n); *Songs Late and Early*, 1931 (p); *The Children's Summer*, 1932 (Am. ed. *Summer Holiday*) (n); *The Ploughman's Progress*, 1933 (Am. ed. *Gipsy Waggon*) (n); *Gallybird*, 1934 (n); *Superstition Corner*, 1934 (n); *Selina Is Older*, 1935 (Am. ed. *Selina*) (n); *Rose Deeprose*, 1936 (n); *Three Ways Home*, 1937 (a); *Faithful Stranger*, 1938 (s); *The Valiant Woman*, 1938 (n); *Ember Lane*, 1940 (n); *The Hidden Son*, 1941 (Am. ed. *Secret Son*) (n); *Tambourine, Trumpet, and Drum*, 1943 (n); (with G. B. Stern) *Talking of Jane Austen*, 1943 (Am. ed. *Speaking of Jane Austen*) (c); *Kitchen Fugue*, 1945 (e); *The Lardners and The Laurelwoods*, 1947 (n); (with G. B. Stern) *More Talk of Jane Austen*, 1950 (Am. ed. *More About Jane Austen*) (c); *The Treasures of the Snow*, 1950 (Am. ed. *The Happy Tree*) (n); *Mrs. Gailey*, 1951 (n); *Quartet in Heaven*, 1952 (b); *The Weald of Kent and Sussex*, 1953 (t); *The View from the Parsonage*, 1954 (n); *All the Books of My Life*, 1956 (a)

Robert T. Hopkins, *Sheila Kaye-Smith and the Weald Country*, 1925

MARGARET KENNEDY
1896-1967

A Century of Revolution, 1789-1920, 1922 (h); *The Ladies of Lyndon*, 1923 (n); *The Constant Nymph*, 1924 (n); (with Basil Dean) *The Constant Nymph*, 1926 (d); *A Long Week-End*, 1927 (n); *Red Sky at Morning*, 1927 (n); *Dewdrops*, 1928 (s); *The Game and The Candle*, 1928 (s); (with Basil Dean) *Come With Me*, 1928 (d); *The Fool of the Family* (seq. to *The Constant Nymph*), 1930 (n); *Return I Dare Not*, 1931 (n); *A Long Time Ago*, 1932 (n); *Escape Me Never!*, 1934 (d); *Together and Apart*, 1936 (n); *The Midas Touch*, 1938 (n); (with Gregory Ratoff) *Autumn*, 1940 (d); *Where Stands a Winged Sentry*, 1941 (a); *The Mechanized Muse*, 1942 (c); *Who Will*

Remember?, 1946 (d); *The Feast*, 1950 (n); *Jane Austen*, 1950 (c); *Lucy Carmichael*, 1951 (n); *Troy Chimneys*, 1951 (n); *The Oracles*, 1955 (Am. ed. *Act of God*) (n); *The Heroes of Clone*, 1957 (s); *Wild Swan*, 1957 (s); *The Outlaws on Parnassus*, 1958 (c); *A Night in Cold Harbour*, 1960 (n); *The Forgotten Smile*, 1961 (n); *The Twins and the Move*, 1962 (n); *Not in the Calendar*, 1964 (n)

W. P. KER
1855-1923

The Philosophy of Art, 1883 (e); *Epic and Romance*, 1897 (c); *Oration on Founders and Benefactors of University College*, 1899 (e); *Boccaccio*, 1900 (c); *The Dark Ages*, 1904 (h); *Essays on Medieval Literature*, 1905 (c); *Sturla the Historian*, 1906 (e); *Romance*, 1907 (c); *The Eighteenth Century*, 1907 (c); *Tennyson*, 1909 (e); *On the Philosophy of History*, 1909 (e); *Browning*, 1910 (c); *On the History of the Ballads, 1100-1500*, 1910 (h); *Thomas Warton*, 1911 (c); *The Literary Influence of the Middle Ages*, 1913 (c); *Jacob Grimm*, 1915 (e); *Two Essays*, 1918 (c); *The Humanist Ideal*, 1920 (e); *Joseph Ritson*, 1922 (e); *Hazlitt*, 1922 (c); *The Art of Poetry: Seven Lectures*, 1923 (c); *English Literature: Medieval*, 1924 (c); *Collected Essays*, ed. Charles Whibley, 1925; *Form and Style in Poetry*, ed. R. W. Chambers, 1928 (c); *On Modern Literature; Lectures and Addresses*, ed. Terence Spencer and James Sutherland, 1955; *Form and Style in Poetry* [sel. of crit.], 1966

J. H. P. Pafford, *W. P. Ker, 1855-1923: a Bibliography*, 1950

RUDYARD KIPLING
1865-1936
Selective Bibliography

Note: Only the best known of R.K.'s very numerous works are included. His lectures are omitted.

Departmental Ditties 1886 (p); *Plain Tales from the Hills*, 1888 (s); *Soldiers Three*, 1888 (s); *The Phantom 'Rickshaw*, 1888 (s); *The Light that Failed*, 1890 (n); *Barrack-Room Ballads*, 1892 (p); *The Jungle Book*, 1894 (s); *The*

Second Jungle Book, 1895 (s); *The Seven Seas*, 1896 (p); *Recessional*, 1897 (p); *The Slaves of the Lamp*, 1897 (n); *Captains Courageous*, 1897 (n); *Ballad of East and West*, 1899 (p); *The White Man's Burden*, 1899 (p); *Stalky & Company*, 1899 (s); *Kim*, 1901 (n); *Just So Stories for Little Children*, 1902 (s); *Puck of Pook's Hill*, 1906 (s); *Collected Verse*, 1907; *Rewards and Fairies*, 1910 (s); *The Female of the Species*, 1912 (p); *For All We Have and Are*, 1914 (p); *Rudyard Kipling's Verse, Inclusive Edition, 1885-1918*, 1919; *A Choice of the Songs from the Verse of Rudyard Kipling*, 1925; *Sea and Sussex from Rudyard Kipling's Verse*, 1926; *The Art of Fiction*, 1926 (c); *Rudyard Kipling's Verse, 1885-1926*, 1927; *A Book of Words, Selections from Speeches and Addresses Delivered Between 1906 and 1927*, 1928; *The One Volume Kipling, Authorized*, 1928 (misc.); *Poems, 1886-1929*, 1930; *The Complete Stalky & Company*, 1930 (s); *Rudyard Kipling's Verse, 1885-1932*, 1933; *All the Mowgli Stories*, 1933 (s); *Something of Myself*, 1937 (a); *Collected Works*, Bombay ed., 31 vols., 1913-38; *Rudyard Kipling's Verse*, definitive ed., 1940; *A Choice of Kipling's Verse*, ed. T. S. Eliot, 1941; *Rudyard Kipling to Rider Haggard: The Record of a Friendship*, ed. Morton Cohen, 1965 [letters]

Flora V. Livingston, *Bibliography of the Works of Kipling*, 1927, and Supplement, 1938; Charles Carrington, *Kipling: His Life and Work*, 1955; J. M. S. Tompkins, *The Art of Kipling*, rev. 1965

ARTHUR KOESTLER
1905-

Spanish Testament, [Eng. adaptation], 1937 (n); *The Gladiators*, tr. Edith Simon, 1939 (n); *Darkness at Noon*, tr. Daphne Hardy, 1941 (n); *Scum of the Earth* [author's experiences in France, Aug. 1939-June 1940], 1941 (r); *Dialogue with Death*, tr. Trevor and Phyllis Blewitt [extracted from *Spanish Testament*], 1942; *Arrival and Departure*, 1943 (n); *The Yogi and the Commisar*, 1945 (e); *Twilight Bar*, 1945 (d); *Thieves in the Night*, 1946 (n); *Insight and Outlook*, 1949 (e); *The Age of Longing*, 1951 (n); *Arrow in the Blue*, 1942 (a); *Promise and Fulfillment,*

Palestine, 1917-1949, 1952 (h); *The Invisible Writing* [sec. vol. of *Arrow in the Blue*], 1954 (a); *The Trail of the Dinosaur*, 1955 (e); *Reflections on Hanging*, 1956 (e); *The Sleepwalkers*, 1959 (e); *The Lotus and the Robot*, 1960 (e); *The Act of Creation*, 1964 (e)

ANDREW LANG
1844-1912

Ballads and Lyrics of Old France, 1872 (p, some tr); (with S. H. Butcher) *The Odyssey of Homer*, 1879 (many repr.) (prose tr); *Theocritus, Bion and Moschus*, 1880 (repr. 1922) (tr); *Ballades in Blue China*, 1880 (p); *Helen of Troy*, 1882 (p); (with Walter Leaf and Ernest Myers) *The Iliad of Homer*, 1883 (many repr.) (prose tr); *Custom and Myth*, 1884 (repr. to 1904) (e); *Ballades and Verses Vain*, sel. Austin Dobson, 1884 (p); *Rhymes à la Mode*, 1885 (p); *Books and Bookmen*, 1886 (repr. to 1912) (c); *In the Wrong Paradise* 1886 (s); *Letters to Dead Authors*, 1886 (rev. enlgd. as *New and Old Letters to Old Authors*, 1907); *The Mark of Cain*, 1886 (n); *Myth, Ritual and Religion*, 1887 (e); *Aucassin and Nicolete*, 1887 (tr); *Grass of Parnassus*, 1888 (p); *Lost Leaders*, 1889 (e); *Letters on Literature*, 1889 (c); *Life, Letters and Diaries of Sir Stafford Northcot*, 2 vols., 1890 (b); *Old Friends, Essays and Epistolary Parody*, 1890 (e); (with H. Rider Haggard) *The World's Desire*, 1890 (n); *Essays in Little*, 1891 (e); *Picadilly*, 1892 (t); *Homer and the Epic*, 1893 (c); *Ballades and Verses*, 1894 (p); *Ban and Arrière Ban*, 1894 (p); *Cock Lane and Common Sense*, 1896 (e); *The Book of Dreams and Ghosts*, 1897 (s,e); *Modern Mythology*, 1897 (e); *The Life and Letters of John Gibson Lockhart*, 1897 (b); *The Making of Religion*, 1898 (e); *Alfred Tennyson*, 1899 (c,b); *The Homeric Hymns*, 1899 (tr); *A History of Scotland from the Roman Occupation*, 4 vols., 1900-1907 (h); *Prince Charles Edward*, 1900 (b); *Magic and Religion*, 1901 (e); *The Disentanglers*, 1902 (s); *The Valet's Tragedy*, 1903 (s,e); *Historical Mysteries*, 1904; *The Clyde Mystery: A Study in Forgeries and Folklore*, 1905 (e); *New Collected Rhymes*, 1905 (p); *Adventures Among Books*, 1905 (c); *John Knox and the Reformation*, 1905 (h); *Sir Walter Scott*, 1906 (b); *Homer and His Age*, 1906, (e); *Ballades and Rhymes* (from *Ballades in Blue China* and *Rhymes à la Mode*), 1907 (p); *Tales of Troy and Greece*, 1907 (s); *The Maid of France*, 1908 (b); *Sir Walter Scott and the Border Minstrelsy*, 1910 (e); *The World of Homer*, 1910 (e); *A Short History of Scotland*, 1911 (h); *Shakespeare, Bacon and the Great Unknown*, 1912 (e); *A History of English Literature from Beowulf to Swinburne*, 1912 (h); *Oxford*, 1916 (t); *The Poetical Works*, ed. Mrs. Lang, 4 vols., 1923; *Andrew Lang*, 1926 (p); *The Lang Fairy Books*, 1929ff; *Fifty Favourite Fairy Tales Chosen from the Colour Fairy Books by Kathleen Lines*, 1963; also collections of fairy tales entitled *Blue, Red, Brown, Green, Crimson, Pink, Yellow, Grey, Lilac, Violet, Olive* and *Orange*

Roger Lancelyn Green, *Andrew Lang*, 1962

PHILIP LARKIN
1922-

*The North Ship, 1945 (p); *Jill*, 1946 (repr. 1964) (n); *A Girl in Winter*, 1947 (n); *XX Poems*, 1951 (p); *Poems*, 1954 (p); *The Less Deceived*, 1955 (p); *The Whitsun Weddings*, 1964 (p)

*repr. 1966

MARGHANITA LASKI
1915-

Love on the Super Tax, 1944 (n); *To Bed with Grand Music*, 1946 (n); *Tory Heaven*, 1948 (Am. ed. *Toasted English*) (n); *Little Boy Lost*, 1949 (n); *Mrs. Ewing, Mrs. Molesworth, and Mrs. Hodgson Burnett*, 1950 (b); *The Village*, 1952 (n); *The Victorian Chaise-Longue*, 1952 (n); *Apologies*, 1955 (e); *The Offshore Island*, 1959 (d); *Ecstasy: a Study of Some Secular and Religious Experiences*, 1961 (e)

JAMES LAVER
1899-

Selective Bibliography

Note: Of Laver's writings on art only a sample is included.

Cervantes, 1921 (p); *His Last Sebastian*, 1922 (p); *Portraits in Oil and Vinegar*, 1925 (c); *The Young Man Dances*, 1925 (p); (with George Sheringham and others) *Design in the Theatre*, 1927 (e); *A Stitch in Time, or Pride Prevents a Fall*, 1927 (p); *The Theatre and Jean Cocteau*, 1928 (c); *Love's Progress, or The Education of Araminta*, 1929 (p); *English Costume of the Nineteenth Century*, 1929 (e); *A History of British and American Etching*, 1929 (h); *Whistler*, 1930 (b); *English Costume of the Eighteenth Century*, 1931 (h); *Nymph Errant*, 1932 (n); *Wesley*, 1932 (b); *Ladies' Mistakes: Cupid's Changeling, A Stitch in Time, Love's Progress*, 1933 (p); *Winter Wedding*, 1934 (p); *Background for Venus*, 1934 (n); *The Laburnum Tree*, 1935 (s); *Panic Among Puritans*, 1936 (n); *Nostradamus, or The Future Foretold*, 1942 (e); *Homage to Venus*, 1948 (art criticism illustrated); *The First Decadent, Being the Strange Life of J. K. Huysmans*, 1954 (b); *Oscar Wilde*, 1954 (b,c); *Edwardian Promenade*, 1958 (e); *Costume*, 1963 (e); *Women's Dress in the Jazz Age*, 1964 (e); *The Age of Optimism: Manners and Morals 1848-1914*, 1966 (h)

D. H. LAWRENCE
1885-1930

The White Peacock, 1911 (n); *The Trespasser*, 1912 (n); *Love Poems*, 1913 (p); *Sons and Lovers*, 1913 (n); *The Widowing of Mrs. Holroyd*, 1914 (d); *The Prussian Officer*, 1914 (s); *The Rainbow*, 1915 (n); *Twilight in Italy*, 1916 (t); *Amores*, 1916 (p); *Look! We Have Come Through*, 1917 (p); *New Poems*, 1918 (p); *Bay*, 1919 (p); (with S. S. Koteliansky) *Leo Shestov, All Things Are Possible*, 1920 (tr); *Touch and Go*, 1920 (d); *Women in Love*, 1920 (n); *The Lost Girl*, 1920 (n); (pseud. Lawrence H. Davison) *Movements in European History*, 1921 (h); *Psychoanalysis and the Unconscious*, 1921 (e); *Tortoises*, 1921 (p); *Sea and Sardinia*, 1921 (t); *Aaron's Rod*, 1922 (n); *Fantasia of the Unconscious*, 1922 (e); *England, My England*, 1922 (s); *The Ladybird*, 1923 (Am. ed. *The Captain's Doll: Three Novelettes*) (3s); *Studies in Classic American Literature*, 1923 (c); *Kangaroo*, 1923 (n); *Birds, Beasts and Flowers*, 1923 (p); *Giovanni*

Verga, *Mastro-Don Gesualdo,* 1923 (tr); (with M. L. Skinner) *The Boy in the Bush,* 1924 (n); Giovanni Verga, *Little Novels of Sicily,* 1925 (tr); *St. Mawr,* 1925 [together with "The Princess"] (1n,1s); †*Reflections on the Death of a Porcupine,* 1925 (e); *The Plumed Serpent,* 1926 (n); *David,* 1926 (d); *Sun,* 1926 (s); *Glad Ghosts,* 1926 (s); *Mornings in Mexico,* 1927 (t); *Selected Poems,* 1928 (p); G. Verga, *Cavalleria Rusticana,* 1928 (tr); *Rawdon's Roof,* 1928 (s); *The Woman Who Rode Away,* 1928 (n); *Lady Chatterley's Lover,* 1928 (first authorized expurgated ed. 1932; first authorized unexpurgated ed. 1961) (n); *Collected Poems,* 1928; *Sex Locked Out,* 1928 (e); A. F. Grazzini, *The Story of Doctor Manente,* 1929 (tr); **The Paintings of D. H. Lawrence,* 1929 [D.H.L.'s paintings reproduced]; *Pansies,* 1929 (p); *My Skirmish with Jolly Roger,* 1929 (e); *Pornography and Obscenity,* 1929 (e); *The Life of J.Middleton Murry,*1930(b); *Nettles,* 1930 (p) *Assorted Articles,* 1930 (e); *The Virgin and the Gypsy,* 1930 (n); *Love among the Haystacks,* 1930 (s); *Apocalypse,* 1930 (s); ***The Man Who Died,* 1931 (repr. 1950) (n); *Etruscan Places,* 1932 (t); *The Letters,* ed. Aldous Huxley, 1932; *Last Poems,* ed. Richard Aldington and Giuseppe Orioli, 1932 (p); *The Lovely Lady,* 1933 (s); *The Plays,* 1934 (3d); *The Ship of Death* [from *Last Poems*], 1933 (p); *The Tales,* 1934 (s); *Selected Poems,* 1934 (p); *A Collier's Friday Night,* 1934 (d); *A Modern Lover,* 1934 (6s and unfinished novel); *The Spirit of Place,* ed. Richard Aldington, 1935 (prose anthology); *Foreword to Women in Love,* 1936 (e); *Pornography and So On,* 1936 (e); *Phoenix, Posthumous Papers,* ed. Edward D. McDonald, 1936 (misc.); *Poems,* 2 vols., coll. ed., 1939; *Stories, Essays and Poems,* coll. ed., 1940; *Fire,* 1940 (p); *Full Score,* 1943 (s); *The First Lady Chatterley,* 1944 (n); *Selected Poems,* 1947 (p); *Letters to Bertrand Russell,* ed. Harry T. Moore, 1948; *A Prelude* [his first, previously unrecorded work], 1949 (s); *Selected Essays,* 1950 (e); *Selected Letters,* sel. Richard Aldington, 1950; *Selected Poems,* sel. W. E. Williams, 1950 (p); *Selected Poems,* ed. James Reeves, 1951 (p); *Complete Short Stories,* 3 vols., 1955; *Selected Literary Criticism,* ed.

Anthony Beal, 1955 (c); *The Short Novels,* 2 vols. (n); *Complete Poems,* 3 vols., 1957; *Selected Poetry and Prose,* ed. T. R. Barnes, 1957; *Selected Letters,* ed. Diana Trilling, 1958; *The Collected Letters,* ed. Harry T. Moore, 2 vols., 1962; *The Symbolic Meaning: The Uncollected Versions of Studies in Classic American Literature,* ed. Armin Arnold, 1962 (c); *The Complete Poems,* ed. Vivian de Sola Pinto and Warren Roberts, 2 vols. 1964; *Complete Plays,* 1965

**Paintings of D. H. Lawrence,* ed. Mervyn Levy, 1964 [collected edition of reproduction of paintings by D.H.L.]
**first printed as *The Escaped Cock,* 1929, limited ed.
†repr. 1965

Harry T. Moore, *The Life and Works of D. H. Lawrence,* 1951; Graham Hough, *The Dark Sun; a Study of D. H. Lawrence,* 1956; *D. H. Lawrence; a Composite Biography,* comp. and ed. Edward Nehls, 3 vols., 1957-1958; Francis Warren Roberts, *A Bibliography of D. H. Lawrence,* 1963

T. E. LAWRENCE
1888-1935

(with C. L. Woolley) *Carchemish, Reports on the Excavations at Djerabis,* 1914; (with C. L. Woolley) *The Wilderness of Zin (Archaeological Reports),* 1915; *Seven Pillars of Wisdom: A Triumph,* 1926 (e,r); *Revolt in the Desert,* 1926 (r,t) [Abridgment of *Seven Pillars*]; *The Odyssey of Homer,* 1932 (tr) (repr. ed. Maurice Bowra, 1955); *Letters from T. E. Shaw to Bruce Rogers,* 1933; *More Letters from T. E. Shaw to Bruce Rogers,* 1936; *Crusader Castles,* 1936 (e); *The Diary of T. E. Lawrence, 1911* [Syria], 1937; *Letters,* ed. David Garnett, 1938; *T. E. Lawrence to his Biographer, Liddell Hart,* 1938 [letters]; *T. E. Lawrence to His Biographer, Robert Graves,* 1938 [letters]; *Oriental Assembly,* ed. A. W. Lawrence, 1939 (misc.); *Secret Dispatches from Arabia,* 1939 (a); *Men in Print,* ed. A. W. Lawrence, 1939 (c); *T. E. Lawrence's Letters to H. S. Ede, 1927-1935,* 1942; *The Essential T. E. Lawrence,* ed. David Garnett, 1951 (repr. 1956) (misc.); *Selected Letters,* ed.

David Garnett, 1952; *The Home Letters of T. E. Lawrence and His Brothers,* ed. M. R. Lawrence, 1954; *The Mint,* 1955 (r)

Robert Graves, *Lawrence and the Arabs,* 1927; B. H. Liddell Hart, *Lawrence in Arabia and After,* 1934; *Lawrence by His Friends,* ed. A. W. Lawrence, 1937 (abgd, 1954); Elizabeth W. Duval, *T. E. Lawrence: a Bibliography,* 1938; Richard Aldington, *Lawrence of Arabia,* 1955

F. R. LEAVIS
1895-

D. H. Lawrence, 1930 (c); *Mass Civilization and Minority Culture,* 1930 (e); *How To Teach Reading: A Primer for Ezra Pound,* 1932 (c); Ed. *Scrutiny,* 1932-1953; *New Bearings in English Poetry,* 1932 (c); (with Denys Thompson) *Culture and Environment,* 1933 (e); *For Continuity,* 1933 (c); *Revaluation: Tradition and Development in English Poetry,* 1936 (c); *Education and the University,* 1943 (e); *The Great Tradition,* 1948 (c); *The Common Pursuit,* 1952 (c); *D. H. Lawrence: Novelist,* 1955 (c); *Two Cultures: The Significance of C. P. Snow,* 1962 (Richmond lecture, Downing College, Cambridge Univ.); (with Denys Thompson) *Culture and Environment,* 1965; *Two Cultures? The Significance of C. P. Snow and Sir Charles Snow's Rede Lecture* (with essay on Snow's Rede lecture by Michael Yudkin), 1965

D. F. MacKenzie and M.-P. Allum, *F. R. Leavis, a Bibliographical Checklist, 1924-1964,* 1966

LAURIE LEE
1914-

Viktor Fischl, *The Dead Village,* 1943 (tr); *The Sun My Monument,* 1944 (repr. 1961) (p); *The Bloom of Candles,* 1947 (p); *The Voyage of Magellan,* 1948 (rd); *Peasants' Priest,* 1952 (d); *My Many-Coated Man,* 1955 (p); *A Rose for Winter,* 1955 (t); *Cider with Rosie* (Am. ed. *The Edge of Day*), 1959 (n,a); *Selected Poems,* 1960 (p); *The Firstborn,* 1964 (e)

VERNON LEE
1856-1935

Tuscan Fairy Tales, 1880 (s); *Studies of the Eighteenth Century in Italy,* 1880 (e); *Belcaro, Being Essays on Sundry Aesthetical Questions,* 1881 (e); *The Prince of the Hundred Soups,* 1882 (also pub. as *Story of a Puppet Show,* 1889) (s); *Ottilie,* 1883 (s); *The Countess of Albany,* 1883 (b); *Miss Brown,* 1884 (n); *Euphorion, Being Studies of the Antique and the Medieval in the Renaissance,* 1884 (e); *A Phantom Lover,* 1886 (s); *Baldwin: Being Dialogues on Views and Aspirations,* 1886 (e); *Juvenilia: . . . Essays on Sundry Aesthetical Questions,* 1887 (e); *Hauntings, Fantastic Stories,* 1890 (s); *Vanitas, Polite Stories,* 1892 (rev. enlgd. 1911) (s); *Althea, a Second Book of Dialogues on Aspirations and Duties,* 1894 (e); *Au Pays de Vénus,* 1894 (s); *Renaissance Fancies and Studies,* 1895 (e); *Limbo,* 1897 (e); *Genius Loci, Notes on Places,* 1899 (t); *Penelope Brandling, a Tale of the Welsh Coast,* 1903 (n); *Hortus Vitae,* 1904 (repr. 1928) (e); *Ariadne in Mantua,* 1903 (d); *The Enchanted Wood, and Other Essays on the Genius of Places,* 1905 (e); *Pope Jacynth,* 1904 (repr. Am. ed. as *Virgin of the Seven Daggers,* 1963) (n); *The Enchanted Wood, and Other Essays on the Genius of Places,* 1905 (e); *The Spirit of Rome: Leaves from a Diary,* 1905 (t); *Sister Benvenuta and the Christ Child,* 1906 (s); *The Sentimental Traveller,* 1907 (t); *Gospels of Anarchy,* 1908 (e); *Laurus Nobilis, Chapters on Art and Life,* 1909 (e); *The Beautiful,* 1910 (e); (with C. Anstruther-Thomson) *Beauty and Ugliness,* 1912 (e); *Vital Lies,* 1912 (e); *Louis Norbert,* 1914 (n); *The Tower of Mirrors,* 1914 (t); *The Ballet of the Nations, a Present-Day Morality,* 1915 (s); *Peace with Honour,* 1915 (e); *Satan the Waster: a Philosophic War Trilogy,* 1920 (d); *The Handling of Words and Other Studies in Literary Psychology,* 1923 (e); *Proteus, or The Future of Intelligence,* 1925 (e); *The Golden Keys and Other Essays on the Genius Loci,* 1925 (t); *The Poet's Eye,* 1926 (e); *For Maurice, Five Unlikely Stories,* 1927 (s); *A Vernon Lee Anthology,* sel. Irene Cooper Willis, 1929; *Music and Its*

Lovers, 1932 (e); *The Snake Lady,* 1954 (s); *Supernatural Tales,* 1955 (s)

Peter Gunn, *Vernon Lee,* 1964

JOHN LEHMANN
1907-

A Garden Revisited, 1931 (p); *The Noise of History,* 1934 (p); *Prometheus and the Bolsheviks,* 1937 (e); *Evil Was Abroad,* 1938 (n); *Down River, a Danubian Study,* 1939 (t); *New Writing in Europe,* 1940 (c); *Forty Poems,* 1942 (p); *The Sphere of Glass,* 1944 (p); *The Age of the Dragon: Poems 1931-1951,* 1951; *The Open Night,* 1952 (e); *Edith Sitwell,* 1952 (c); Ed. *London Magazine,* 1954-1961; *The Whispering Gallery,* 1955 (a); *I Am My Brother,* 1960 (a); *Ancestors and Friends,* 1962 (b); *Collected Poems, 1930-1963,* 1963

ROSAMOND LEHMANN
1903-

Dusty Answer, 1927 (n); *A Note in Music,* 1930 (n); *A Letter to a Sister,* 1931 (e); *Invitation to the Waltz,* 1932 (n); *The Weather in the Streets,* 1936 (n); *No More Music,* 1939 (d); *The Ballad and the Source,* 1944 (n); *The Gypsy's Baby,* 1946 (s); *The Echoing Grove,* 1953 (n); Jean Cocteau, *Les Enfants Terribles,* as *Children of the Game,* 1955 (tr)

SHANE LESLIE
1885-

The Landlords of Ireland at the Crossroads, 1908 (e); *Songs of Oriel,* 1908 (p); *Lough Derg in Ulster, The Story of St. Patrick's Purgatory,* 1909 (repr. 1917) (h); *A Study of the Oxford Movement,* 1909 (e); (with Padriac Colum and others) *Eyes of Youth,* 1910 (p); *The Isle of Columbcille,* 1910 (t); *Verses in Peace and War,* 1916 (p); *The End of a Chapter,* 1916 (rev. 1929) (n); *The Celt and the World,* 1917 (e); *The Irish Issue in its American Aspect,* 1918 (e); *Henry Edward Manning, His Life and Labours,* 1921 (b); *The Oppidan,* 1922 (n); *Mark Sykes, His Life and Letters,* 1923 (b); *Doomsland,* 1923 (n); *Masquerades: Studies in the Morbid,* 1924 (n); (with Francis Birrell) *Plato's*

Symposium, 1925 (tr); *The Cantab,* 1926 (n); *George the Fourth,* 1926 (b); *The Skull of Swift, An Extempore Exhumation,* 1928 (b); *The Delightful, Diverting and Devotional Play of Mrs. Fitzherbert,* 1928 (d); *The Poems of Shane Leslie,* 1928 (p); *The Greek Anthology,* sel., 1929 (tr); *A Ghost in the Isle of Wight,* 1929 (e); *The Anglo-Catholic,* 1929 (seq. to *The Cantab* (n); *Memoir of John Edward Courtenay Bodley,* 1930 (m); *The Hyde Park Pageant, a Broadside,* 1930 (p); *Jutland, A Fragment of an Epic,* 1930 (p); *Studies in Sublime Failure* [Cardinal Newman, Charles Stuart Parnell, Coventry Patmore, Lord Curzon, Moreton Frewen], 1932 (b); *Poems and Ballads,* 1933 (p); *The Oxford Movement, 1833 to 1933,* 1933 (h); *The Passing Chapter,* 1934 (e); *Fifteen Odd Stories,* 1935 (s); *The Script of Jonathan Swift,* 1935 (e); *American Wonderland,* 1936 (r); *Men Were Different* [Randolph Churchill, Augustus Hare, Arthur Dunn, George Wyndham, Wilfrid Blunt], 1937 (b); *Sir Evelyn Ruggles-Brise,* 1938 (m); *The Film of Memory,* 1938 (a); *Mrs. Fitzherbert,* 1939 (b); *Poems from the North,* 1945 (p); *The Irish Tangle for English Readers, 1946* (Am. ed. *The Irish Question*); *The Rubaiyat of the Mystics,* 1950 (p); *Salutation to Five,* 1951 (b); *Cardinal Gosquet,* 1953 (b); *Lord Mulroy's Ghost,* 1954 (d); *Ghost Book,* 1955 (e)

DORIS LESSING
1919-

The Grass Is Singing, 1950 (n); *This Was the Old Chief's Country,* 1951 (s); *Martha Quest* (Vol. I of *Children of Violence*), 1952 (n); *Five,* 1953 (5n); *A Proper Marriage* (Vol. II of *Children of Violence*), 1954 (n); *Retreat to Innocence,* 1956 (n); *The Habit of Loving,* 1957 (s); *Going Home,* 1957 (a); *A Ripple from the Storm* (Vol. III of *Children of Violence*), 1959 (n); *Each His Own Wilderness,* 1959 (d); *Fourteen Poems,* 1959 (p); *The Habit of Loving,* 1960 (s); *In Pursuit of the English,* 1960 (a); *The Golden Notebook,* 1962 (n); *Play With a Tiger,* 1962 (d); *A Man and Two Women,* 1963 (s); *African Stories,* 1964 (s); (Am. ed.) *Children of Violence,* 1964 (this contains Vol. I, *Martha Quest,* and Vol. II, *A Proper Marriage*); *Land-locked* (Vol. IV of *Children of Violence*), 1965 (n)

ADA LEVERSON
1862-1933

The Twelfth Hour, 1907 (n); *Love's Shadow*, 1908 (n); *The Limit*, 1911 (n); *Tenterhooks*, 1912 (n); *Bird of Paradise*, 1914 (n); *Love at Second Sight*, 1916 (n); all the above reissued, 1950-51; Oscar Wilde, *Letters to the Sphinx, with Reminiscences of the Author by Ada Leverson*, 1930; *The Little Ottleys: Love's Shadow, Tenterhooks, Love at Second Sight*, with a foreword by Colin MacInness, 1962

Violet Wyndham, *The Sphinx and Her Circle*, 1963

DENISE LEVERTOV
1923-

Overland to the Islands, 1958 (p); *With Eyes at the Back of Our Heads*, 1960 (p); *The Jacob's Ladder*, 1961 (p); *Here and Now*, 1962 (p); *O Taste and See*, 1964 (p); *The Jacob's Ladder*, 1965 (p)

BENN WOLF LEVY
1900-

This Woman Business, 1925 (d); *Mud and Treacle, or, The Course of True Love*, 1928 (d); *A Man with Red Hair* [from Hugh Walpole's novel], 1928 (d); *Mrs. Moonlight*, 1929 (d); *Art and Mrs Bottle, or, The Return of the Puritan*, 1929 (d); *The Devil*, 1930 (Am. ed. *The Devil Passes*) (d); (with J. Van Druten) *Hollywood Holiday*, 1931 (d); *Springtime for Henry*, 1932 (d); *The Poet's Heart: A Life of Don Juan*, 1937 (d); *The Jealous God*, 1939 (d); *Clutterbuck*, 1947 (d); *Return to Tyassi*, 1951 (d); *Cupid and Psyche*, 1952 (d); *The Great Healer*, 1954 (d); *The Island of Cipango* 1954 (d); *The Rape of the Belt*, 1957 (d); *The Truth about Truth*, 1957 (d)

ALUN LEWIS
1915-1944

Raider's Dawn, 1942 (p); *The Last Inspection*, 1943 (s); *Ha! Ha! Among the Trumpets*, 1945 (p); *Letters from India*, 1946; *In the Green Tree: Letters and*

Six Short Stories, 1949; Ian Hamilton, *Alun Lewis: Selected Poetry and Prose*, 1966

C. DAY LEWIS
1904-

Beechen Vigil, 1925 (p); *Country Comets*, 1928 (p); *Transitional Poem*, 1929 (p); *From Feathers to Iron*, 1931 (p); *The Magnetic Mountain*, 1933 (p); *A Hope for Poetry*, 1934 (c); *A Time to Dance*, 1935 (p); *Revolution in Writing*, 1935 (e); *Collected Poems 1929-1933*, 1935; *We're Not Going to Do Nothing*, 1936 (e); *The Friendly Tree*, 1936 (n); (with L. Susan Stebbing) *Imagination and Thinking*, 1936 (two addresses); *Starting Point*, 1937 (n); *Overtures to Death*, 1938 (p); *Child of Misfortune*, 1939 (n); *Poems in Wartime*, 1940 (p); *Selected Poems*, 1940 (p); *The Georgics of Virgil*, 1941 (tr); *Word Over All* (incl. *Poems in Wartime*), 1943 (p); *Selected Poems*, 1943 (p); Paul Valéry, *Le Cimetière Marin*, 1946 (tr); *The Colloquial Element in English Poetry*, 1947 (e); *Enjoying Poetry, A Reader's Guide*, 1947 (e); *The Poetic Image*, 1947 (Clark lectures, Univ. of Cambridge); *Collected Poems, 1929-1936*, 1948; *The Otterbury Incident*, 1948 (n); *Poems 1943-1947*, 1948 (p); *The Poet's Task*, 1951 (Oxford Univ., inaugural lecture); *Selected Poems*, 1951 (p); *The Grand Manner*, 1952 (Byron Foundation lecture); *The Aeneid of Virgil*, 1952 (tr); *The Lyrical Poetry of Thomas Hardy*, 1953 (Warton lecture); *An Italian Visit, 1953* (p); *Collected Poems*, 1954; *Notable Images of Virtue* [Emily Bronte, George Meredith, W. B. Yeats], 1954 (lectures, Queens Univ., Kingston, Ont.); *Christmas Eve*, 1954 (p); *Pegasus*, 1957 (p); *The Poet's Way of Knowledge*, 1957 (c); *The Buried Day*, 1960 (a); *The Gate*, 1962 (p); Virgil, *The Eclogues*, 1963 (tr); *Requiem for the Living*, 1964 (p); *The Lyric Impulse*, 1965 (Charles Eliot Norton lectures, Harvard Uuiv.) *The Room and Other Poems*, 1966 (p)

Also, under pseud. Nicholas Blake, these detective stories: *A Question of Proof*, 1935; *Thou Shell of Death*, 1936; *There's Trouble Brewing*, 1937;

The Beast Must Die, 1938; *The Smiler with the Knife*, 1939; *Malice in Wonderland*, 1940; *The Case of the Abominable Snowman*, 1941; *Minute for Murder*, 1947; *Head of a Traveller*, 1949; *Dreadful Hollow*, 1953; *The Whisper in the Gloom*, 1954; *A Tangled Web*, 1956; *End of a Chapter*, 1957; *Penknife in My Heart*, 1958; *The Widow's Cruise*, 1959; *The Sad Variety*, 1964

Clifford Dyment, *C. Day Lewis*, 1955

C. S. LEWIS
1898-1963

[Clive Hamilton, pseud.] *Spirits in Bondage: a Cycle of Lyrics*, 1919 (p); [Clive Hamilton, pseud.] *Dymer*, 1926 (repr. 1950) (p); *The Pilgrim's Regress*, 1933 (e); *The Allegory of Love*, 1936 (c); *Out of The Silent Planet* (Part I of trilogy), 1938 (n); *Rehabilitations*, 1939 (c); *(with E. M. W. Tillyard) *The Personal Heresy*, 1939 (e); *The Problem of Pain*, 1940 (e); *Broadcast Talks*, 1942 (Am. ed. *The Case for Christianity*) (e); *A Preface to Paradise Lost*, 1942 (c); *The Screwtape Letters*, 1942 (e); *Christian Behaviour*, 1943 (e); *Perelandra* (Part II of trilogy), 1943 (n); *The Abolition of Man*, 1943 (e); *Beyond Personality: The Christian Idea of God*, 1944 (e); *That Hideous Strength* (Part III of trilogy), 1945 (n); **The Great Divorce, a Dream*, 1945 (e); *Miracles, a Preliminary Study*, 1947 (e); *Vivisection*, 1948 (e); *Transposition and Other Addresses*, 1949 (Am. ed. *The Weight of Glory*) (e); *The Literary Impact of the Authorized Version*, 1950 (lecture, Univ. of London); *Mere Christianity*, 1952 (rev. ed. of *Broadcast Talks*, *Christian Behaviour*, *Beyond Personality*) (e); *The Silver Chair*, 1953 (child's bk.); *English Literature in the Sixteenth Century, Excluding Drama* (Vol. III of *Oxford History of English Literature*), 1954 (h); *The Magician's Nephew*, 1955 (child's bk.); *Surprised by Joy*, 1955 (a); *Till We Have Faces, a Myth Retold*, 1956 (n); *The Last Battle*, 1956 (child's bk.); *Reflections on the Psalms*, 1958 (e); *The Four Loves*, 1960 (e); *Miracles*, 1960 (e); *Studies in Words*, 1960 (e); *An Experiment in Criticism*, 1961 (c);

Screwtape Proposes a Toast, 1961 (bound with *The Screwtape Letters*) (e); *A Grief Observed*, 1961 (a); *They Asked for a Paper*, 1962 (c); *The Discarded Image, an Introduction to Medieval and Renaissance Literature*, 1964 (c); *Poems*, ed. Walter Hooper, 1964 (p); *Letters to Malcolm, Chiefly on Prayer*, 1964; *Letters of C. S. Lewis*, ed. with a Memoir, W. H. Lewis, 1966 [begin where (a) *Surprised by Joy* stops and continue to his death]; *Studies in Medieval and Renaissance Literature* [6 unpub. and 8 repr.] 1966 (c); *Of Other Worlds*, ed. *Walter Hooper*, 1966 (e,s)

The Chronicles of Narnia, 1950-56, 7 books for children of which the three listed above are among the best known

*repr. 1964
**repr. 1962

Roger Lancelyn Green. *C. S. Lewis*, 1963; *Light on C. S. Lewis*, ed. Jocelyn Gibb, 1965; *Patterns in Love and Courtesy, Essays in Memory of C. S. Lewis*, ed. John Lawlor, 1966

D. B. WYNDHAM LEWIS
1894-

A London Farrago, 1922 (e); *At the Green Goose*, 1923 (n); *At the Sign of the Blue Moon*, 1924 (n); *At the Blue Moon Again*, 1925 (n); *On Straw and Other Conceits*, 1927 (e); *François Villon*, 1928 (b); *King Spider: Some Aspects of Louis XI of France and his Companions*, 1929 (b); *Mr. Thake, His Life and Letters*, 1929 (b); *Emperor of the West, a Study of Charles V*, 1932 (b); *Take it to Bed*, 1944 (anecdotes); *Ronsard*, 1944 (b); *The Hooded Hawk; or, The Case of Mr. Boswell*, 1946 (c); *Four Favourites*, 1948 (b); *The Soul of Marshal Gilles de Raiz*, 1952 (b); *James Boswell: a Short Life*, 1952 (b); (with Ronald Searle) *The Terror of St. Trinian's*, 1952 (s); *Doctor Rabelais*, 1957 (b); *A Florentine Portrait* [Saint Philip Benizi (1233-1285)], 1959 (b); *Molière, the Comic Mask*, 1959 (b); *The Shadow of Cervantes*, 1962 (b)

[PERCY] WYNDHAM LEWIS
1886-1957

Ed. *Blast: Review of the Great English Vortex*, 1914, and *Blast: No. 2*, 1915;

The Ideal Giant: The Code of a Herdsman; Cantleman's Springmate, 1947 (c,s); Tarr, 1918 (rev. 1928, repr. 1951) (n); The Caliph's Design: Architects! Where is Your Vortex?, 1919 (e); (with Louis F. Fergusson) Harold Gilman: an Appreciation, 1919 (c); The Tyro, Nos. 1, 2, 1924 (e); The Art of Being Ruled, 1926 (e); The Enemy, Nos. 1, 2, 1927 (c); The Lion and the Fox: The Rôle of the Hero in Shakespeare, 1927 (repr. 1955) (c); Time and Western Man, 1927 (e); The Wild Body, 1927 (s); The Childermass, Vol. 1, 1928 (n); The Enemy, No. 3, 1929 (e); Paleface: The Philosophy of the Melting Pot, 1929 (e); The Apes of God, 1930 (n); Satire and Fiction, 1930 (c); The Diabolical Principle and the Dithyrambic Spectator, 1931 (c); Hitler, 1931 (b); The Wild Body, 1932 (e); The Enemy of the Stars, 1932 (e); Filibusters in Barbary, 1932 (e); Snooty Baronet, 1932 (n); The Old Gang and the New, 1933 (e); One-Way Song, 1933 (also pub. as Engine Fight-Talk) (repr. 1960) (p); Men Without Art, 1934 (c); Left Wings Over Europe, 1936 (e); Count Your Dead: They Are Alive!, 1937 (e); Blasting and Bombardiering, 1937 (e); The Revenge for Love, 1937 (repr. 1951) (n); The Mysterious Mr. Bull, 1938 (e); The Jews, Are They Human?, 1939 (e); The Hitler Cult, 1939 (e); America, I Presume, 1940 (e); The Vulgar Streak, 1941 (n); Anglosaxony, 1942 (e); America and Cosmic Man, 1948 (e); Rude Assignment, 1950 (a); Rotting Hill, 1951 (s); The Writer and The Absolute, 1952 (e); The Demon of Progress in the Arts, 1954 (e); Self Condemned, 1954 (n); The Human Age: Childermass (rev.), Monstre Gai and Malign Fiesta, 1955 (3n); The Red Priest, 1956 (n); (Italian ed.) Ezra Pound, 1958 (c); The Letters of Wyndham Lewis, ed. W. K. Rose, 1964

T. I. A. F. Armstrong, Apes, Japes, and Hitlerism: a Study and Bibliography of Wyndham Lewis, 1932; Geoffrey Wagner, Wyndham Lewis, 1957

ROBERT LIDDELL
1908-

The Almond Tree, 1938 (n); Kind Relations, 1939 (n); The Gantillons, 1940 (n); Watering Place, 1945 (n); A

Treatise on the Novel, 1947 (c); The Last Enchantments, 1948 (n); Unreal City, 1952 (n); Some Principles of Fiction, 1953 (c); Aegean Greece, 1954 (t); The Novels of I. Compton-Burnett, 1955 (c); Byzantium and Istanbul, 1956 (t); The Morea, 1958 (t); The Rivers of Babylon, 1959 (n); Demetrios Sicilianos, Old and New Athens, 1960 (tr); The Novels of Jane Austen, 1963 (c)

ERIC LINKLATER
1899-

Poobie, 1925 (p); Poet's Pub, 1929 (n); White-Maa's Saga, 1929 (repr. 1963); A Dragon Laughed, 1930 (p); Ben Jonson and King James, 1931 (b); Juan in America, 1931 (repr. 1956) (n); The Men of Ness, 1932 (n); Mary, Queen of Scots, 1933 (repr. 1952) (b); The Crusader's Key, 1933 (n); Magnus Merriman, 1934 (repr. 1959) (n); The Devil's in the News, 1934 (d); Robert the Bruce, 1934 (b); The Revolution, 1934 (s); The Lion and the Unicorn or What England has Meant to Scotland, 1935 (e); God Likes Them Plain, 1935 (s); Ripeness is All, 1935 (n); Juan in China, 1936 (repr. 1959) (n); The Sailor's Holiday, 1936 (n); The Impregnable Women, 1938 (repr. 1959) (n); Judas, 1939 (repr. 1956) (n); The Northern Garrisons, 1941 (h); The Cornerstones, 1941 (n); The Man on my Back, 1941 (a); The Highland Division, 1942 (h); The Raft and Socrates Asks Why, 1942 (e); The Great Ship and Rabelais Replies, 1944 (e); Crisis in Heaven, 1944 (d); Private Angelo, 1946 (n); Sealskin Trousers, 1947 (s); Art of Adventure, 1947 (e); A Spell for Old Bones, 1949 (s); Mr. Byculla, 1950 (s); Two Comedies: Love in Albania and To Meet the Macgregors, 1950 (2d); Laxdale Hall, 1951 (n); The Campaign in Italy, 1951 (h); The Mortimer Touch, 1952 (d); The House of Gair, 1953 (s); A Year of Space, 1953 (a); The Sultan and the Lady, 1954 (n); The Faithful Ally, 1954 (n); The Ultimate Viking, 1955 (e); The Dark of Summer, 1956 (n); A Sociable Plover, 1957 (s); Breakspear in Gascony, 1958 (d); Position at Noon (Am. ed. My Father and I), 1958 (n); The Merry Muse, 1959 (n); Edinburgh, 1960 (t); Roll of Honour, 1961 (n); Hus-

band of Delilah, 1962 (n); *A Man Over Forty,* 1963 (n); *A Terrible Freedom,* 1966 (n); *The Conquest of England,* 1966 (h)

CHRISTOPHER LOGUE
1926-

Wand and Quadrant, 1953 (p); *Devil, Maggot and Son,* 1956 (p); *The Man Who Told His Love* [Pablo Neruda, *20 Poemas de Amor*], 1958 (tr); *A Song for Kathleen,* 1958 (p); *Songs,* 1959 (p); *Songs from "The Lily-White Boys",* 1960 (p); Homer, *Patrocleia* [Iliad], 1962 (tr); *The Arrival of the Poet in the City,* 1964 (p)

FREDERICK LONSDALE
1881-1954

Aren't We All, 1924 (d); *The Last of Mrs. Cheyney,* 1925 (d); *Spring Cleaning,* 1925 (d); *The Fake,* 1927 (d); *The High Road,* 1927 (d); *On Approval,* 1927 (d); *Canaries Sometimes Sing,* 1929 (d); *The Street Singer,* 1929 (d); *The Devil To Pay,* 1930 (film story); *Once is Enough,* 1938 (Am. ed. *Let Them Eat Cake*) (d); *Foreigners,* 1939 (d); *But for the Grace of God,* 1946 (d); *Another Love Story,* 1948 (d); *The Way Things Go,* 1950 (d)

Frances Donaldson, *Freddy Lonsdale.* 1957

MALCOLM LOWRY
1909-1957

Ultramarine, 1933 (rev. 1963) (n), **Under the Volcano,* 1947 (n); *Hear Us O Lord from Heaven Thy Dwelling Place,* 1961 (s); *Selected Poems,* ed. Earle Birney and Margerie Lowry, 1962 (p); *Selected Letters,* ed. Harvey Breit and Margerie Bonner Lowry, 1965

*repr. 1965

PERCY LUBBOCK
1879-

Samuel Pepys, 1904 (repr. 1923) (b); *Elizabeth Barrett Browning in Her Letters,* 1906 (b); *George Calderon: A Sketch from Memory,* 1921 (m); *The Craft of Fiction,* 1921 (c); *Earlham,* 1922 (r); *Roman Pictures,* 1923 (e); *The Region Cloud,* 1925 (n); *Mary Chol-*
mondeley, 1928 (m); *Shades of Eton,* 1929 (r); *Portrait of Edith Wharton,* 1947 (b)

E. V. LUCAS
1868-1938

Bernard Barton and His Friends, 1895 (b); *All the World Over,* 1898 (p); *The Book of Shops,* 1899 (p); *Domesticities,* 1900 (e); *Four and Twenty Toilers,* 1900 (p); *The Visit to London,* 1902 (p); *England Day by Day,* 1903 (e); *Highways and Byways in Sussex,* 1904 (repr. 1934) (t); *The Life of Charles Lamb,* 2 vols., 1905 (5th ed. rev. 1910, repr. 1921) (b); *A Wanderer in Holland,* 1905 (20th ed. rev. 1931) (t); *A Wanderer in London,* 1906 (28th ed. rev. 1931) (t); *Fireside and Sunshine,* 1906 (e); *Listener's Lure,* 1906 (n); *A Swan and Her Friends* [Anna Seward], 1907 (b,h); *Character and Comedy,* 1907 (e); *Over Bemerton's,* 1908 (n); *One Day and Another,* 1909 (e); *A Wanderer in Paris,* 1909 (24th ed. rev. Audrey Lucas, 1952) (t); *Mr. Ingleside,* 1910 (n); *Old Lamps for New,* 1911 (e); (E.V.L. and G.M. [G. Morrow]), *What a Life!,* 1911 (a); *London Lavender,* 1912 (n); *A Little of Everything,* 1912 (sel.); *A Wanderer in Florence,* 1912 (14th ed. rev. 1928) (t); *Harvest Home,* 1913 (sel.); *The British School: an Anecdotal Guide to the British Painters and Paintings in the National Gallery,* 1913 (c); *Loiterer's Harvest,* 1913 (e); *Landmarks,* 1914 (n); *A Wanderer in Venice,* 1914 (5th ed. rev. 1923, repr. 1930) (t); *London Revisited,* 1916 (6th ed. rev. 1926) (t); *Cloud and Silver,* 1916 (e); *The Vermilion Box,* 1916 (n); *Variety Lane,* 1916 (e); *A Boswell of Baghdad, with Diversions,* 1917 (e); *Twixt Eagle and Dove,* 1918 (e); *The Phantom Journal,* 1919 (e); *Mixed Vintages, a Blend of Essays Old and New,* 1919 (e); *Adventures and Enthusiasms,* 1920 (e); *Specially Selected: a Choice of Essays,* 1920 (e); *David Williams, Founder of the Royal Literary Fund,* 1920 (b); *Verena in the Midst,* 1920 (n); *Roving East and West,* 1921 (t); *Rose and Rose,* 1921 (n); *Urbanities: Essays New and Old,* 1921 (e); *Edwin Austin Abbey,* 1921 (b); *Vermeer of Delft,* 1922 (b); *Genevra's Money,* 1922 (n); *Giving and Receiving,* 1922 (e); *You Know What People Are,*

1922 (sk); *Advisory Ben*, 1923 (s); *Luck of the Year*, 1923 (m,s); *A Wanderer among Pictures: a Companion to the Galleries of Europe*, 1924 (c); *Encounters and Diversions*, 1924 (e); *The Same Star*, 1924 (d); *John Constable, the Painter*, 1924 (c); *Michael Angelo*, 1924 (c); *Chardin and Vigée Le Brun*, 1924 (c); *Rembrandt*, 1924 (c); *Little Books on Great Masters* [of painting], 1924-26 (b,c); *Zigzags in France and and Various Essays*, 1925 (Am. ed. *Wanderings and Diversions*) (t); *Introducing London*, 1925 (t); *Events and Embroideries*, 1926 (e); *Selected Essays*, ed. E. A. Wodehouse, 1926 (e); *Three Hundreds and Sixty-Five Days and One More:* being selections for every mornin of the year from the writings of E. V. Lucas, 1926 (sel.); *Franz Hals*, 1926 (c); *Giorgione*, 1926 (c); *Velasquez*, 1926 (c); *Van Dyck*, 1926 (c); *Leonardo da Vinci*, 1926 (c); *A Wanderer in Rome*, 1926 (5th ed. rev. 1951) (t); *London* (*A Wanderer in London, London Revisited*), 1926 (t); The Minerva Edition of *The Works*, 1926-; *A Fronded Isle*, 1927 (e); *The More I see of Men . . . Stray Essays on Dogs*, 1927 (sel.); *Vermeer the Magical*, 1928 (b,c); *A Rover I Would Be: Essays and Fantasies*, 1928 (e); *Introducing Paris*, 1928 (t); *The Colvins and their Friends*, 1928 (b,h); *Out of a Clear Sky: Essays and Fantasies about Birds*, 1928 (sel.); *Turning Things Over*, 1929 (e); *Windfall's Eve*, 1929 (n); *If Dogs Could Write*, 1929 (misc.); *Traveller's Luck: Essays and Fantasies*, 1930 (e); *"And Such Small Deer,"* 1930 (sel.); *Down the Sky*, 1930 (n); *No-Nose at the Show*, 1931 (p); *French Leaves*, 1931 (e); *The Barber's Clock*, 1931 (s); *Visibility Good*, 1931 (e); *At the Sign of the Dove*, 1932 (e); *Lemon Verbena*, 1932 (e); *Reading, Writing and Remembering*, 1932 (r); *English Leaves*, 1933 (e); *Saunterer's Rewards*, 1933 (t); *Animals All* (*"And Such Small Deer"* and *Out of a Clear Sky*), 1934 (e); *E. V. Lucas*, 1934 (anthology of his humorous work); *At the Shrine of Saint Charles: Stray Papers on Lamb for the Centenary of his Death*, 1934 (e); *The Old Contemporaries*, 1935 (r); *Pleasure Trove*, 1935 (e); *Only the Other Day*, 1936 (e); *All of a Piece: New Essays*, 1937 (e); *As the Bee Sucks*, chosen Ernest H. Shepard, 1937 (e);

Adventures and Misgivings, 1938 (e); *Cricket All his Life: Cricket Writings in Prose and Verse*, chosen Rupert Hart-Davis, 1950; *Selected Essays*, chosen H. N. Wethered, 1954; Also a number of humorous books, many as E.V.L. with C.L.G. [Charles Larcom Graves], e.g. *Wisdom While You Wait*, 1903

John C. Farrar et al, *E. V. Lucas: Appreciations*, 1925; Audrey Lucas, *E. V. Lucas: a Portrait*, 1939 [list of bks.]

F. L. LUCAS
1894-1967

Seneca and Elizabethan Tragedy, 1922 (c); *Euripides and his Influence*, 1924 (c); *Authors Dead and Living*, 1926 (c); *The River Flows*, 1926 (n); *Tragedy in Relation to Aristotle's Poetics*, 1927 (repr. 1957) (c); *Time and Memory*, 1929 (p); *Eight Victorian Poets*, 1930 (2nd ed. *Ten Victorian Poets*, 1940) (c); *Marionettes*, 1930 (p); *Cécile*, 1930 (n); *The Wild Tulip*, 1932 (n); *Ariadne*, 1932 (p); *The Criticism of Poetry*, 1933 (c); *The Bear Dances*, 1933 (d); *Studies, French and English*, 1934 (repr. 1950) (c); (with P. D. Lucas) *From Olympus to the Styx*, 1934 (t); *Four Plays*, 1935 (d); *Poems, 1935*, 1935 (p); *The Decline and Fall of the Romantic Ideal*, 1936 (c); *The Woman Clothed with the Sun*, 1937 (s); *Doctor Dido*, 1938 (n); *A Greek Garland*, 1938 (tr); *Journal Under the Terror, 1938*, 1939 (h); *Vigil of Venus*, 1939 (tr); *Messene Redeemed*, 1940 (d); *Critical Thoughts in Critical Days*, 1942 (e); *Aphrodite*, 1948 (tr); *Greek Poetry for Everyman*, 1951 (tr); *Literature and Psychology*, 1951 (e); *From Many Times and Lands*, 1953 (p); *Greek Drama for Everyman*, 1954 (tr); *Style*, 1955 (c); *The Search for Good Sense* [Johnson, Chesterfield, Boswell, Goldsmith], 1958 (b); *The Art of Living* [Hume, Horace Walpole, Benjamin Franklin, Burke], 1958 (b); *The Greatest Problem and Other Essays*, 1960 (e); *The Drama of Ibsen and Strindberg*, 1962 (c)

ROB LYLE
1920-

Guitar, 1951 (p); (with Francisco Xavier Lizarza India) *The Destiny of Spain*, 1952 (e); *Halcyon: Poems 1943-53*, 1953 (p); *Mistral*, 1953 (e); *Heroic Elegies*, 1957 (p); *Poems from Limbo*, 1960 (p)

ROBERT LYND
1879-1949

Irish and English, Portraits and Impressions, 1908 (e); *Home Life in Ireland*, 1909 (e); *Rambles in Ireland*, 1912 (t); *The Book of This and That*, 1915 (e); *Ireland a Nation*, 1919 (h); *Old and New Masters*, 1919 (c); *The Art of Letters*, 1920 (c); *The Passion of Labor*, 1920 (e); *The Pleasures of Ignorance*, 1921 (e); *Books and Authors*, 1922 (c); *The Sporting Life*, 1922 (e); *Solomon in all his Glory*, 1922 (e); *The Blue Lion*, 1923 (e); *Selected Essays*, 1923; *The Peal of Bells*, 1924 (e); *The Money Box*, 1925 (e); *The Little Angel*, 1926 (e); *The Orange Tree*, 1926 (e); *Dr. Johnson and Company*, 1927 (b); *The Goldfish*, 1927 (e); *The Green Man*, 1928 (e); *Old Friends in Fiction*, 1929 (c); *It's a Fine World*, 1930 (e); *Rain, Rain, Go to Spain*, 1931 (e); *The Cockleshell*, 1933 (e); *"Y.Y." An Anthology of Essays* sel. Eileen Squire 1933 (e); *Both Sides of the Road*, 1934 (e); *I Tremble to Think*, 1936 (e); *In Defence of Pink*, 1937 (e); *Searchlights and Nightingales*, 1939 (e); *Life's Little Oddities*, 1941 (e); *Things One Hears*, 1945 (e); *Modern Poetry*, 1950 (c); *Essays on Life and Literature*, 1951 (e); *Books and Writers*, 1952 (c)

See J. B. Priestley, *Figures in Modern Literature*, 1924

LILIAN BOWES-LYON
1895-1949

The Buried Stream, 1929 (n); *The White Hare*, 1934 (p); *Bright Feather Fading*, 1936 (p); *Tomorrow is a Revealing*, 1941 (p); *Evening in Stepney*, 1943 (p); *A Rough Walk Home*, 1946 (p); *Collected Poems*, 1948

ROSE MACAULAY
1881-1958

Abbots Verney, 1906 (n); *The Furnace*, 1907 (n); *The Secret River*, 1909 (n); *The Valley Captives*, 1911 (n); *Views and Vagabonds*, 1912 (n); *The Lee Shore*, 1912 (n); *The Two Blind Countries*, 1914 (p); *The Making of a Bigot*, 1914 (n); *Non-Combatants and Others*, 1916 (s); *What Not: A Prophetic Comedy*, 1919 (n); *Three Days*, 1919 (p); *Potterism*, 1920 (n); *Dangerous Ages*, 1921 (n); *Mystery at Geneva*, 1922 (n); **Told by an Idiot*, 1923 (n); *Orphan Island*, 1924 (n); *A Casual Commentary*, 1925 (e); *Catchwords and Claptrap*, 1926 (e); *Crewe Train*, 1926 (n); *Twenty-Two Poems*, 1927 (p); *Keeping Up Appearances*, 1928 (Am. ed. *Daisy and Daphne*) (n); *Staying with Relations*, 1930 (n); **Some Religious Elements in English Literature*, 1931 (e); *They Were Defeated*, 1932 (Am. ed. *The Shadow Flies*) (n); *Going Abroad*, 1934 (n); *Milton*, 1934 (b); *Personal Pleasures*, 1935 (e); *I Would Be Private*, 1937 (n); *The Writings of E. M. Forster*, 1938 (c); *And No Man's Wit*, 1940 (n); *Life Among the English*, 1942 (e); *They Went to Portugal*, 1946 (e); *Fabled Shore: From the Pyrenees to Portugal*, 1949 (t); *The World My Wilderness*, 1950 (n); ***Pleasure of Ruins*, 1953 (t); *The Disguises of Love*, 1953 (n); *The Towers of Trebizond*, 1956 (n); *The End of Pity*, 1958 (s); *Letters to a Friend*, ed. Constance B. Smith, 1961; *Last Letters to a Friend*, ed. Constance B. Smith, 1962; *Letters to a Sister*, ed. Constance B. Smith, 1964

*repr. 1965
**repr. abgd. (with photos by Roloff Beny), 1965

NORMAN MACCAIG
1910-

Far Cry, 1943 (p); *The Inward Eye*, 1946 (p); *Riding Lights*, 1955 (p); *The Sinai Sort*, 1957 (p); *A Common Grace*, 1960, (p); *A Round of Applause*, 1963 (p); *Measures*, 1965 (p)

DESMOND MACCARTHY
1878-1952

The Court Theatre: 1904-1907, 1907 (h); *Lady John Russell: A Memoir with Selections from Her Diaries*, 1910 (m); (with S. Waterlow) [Jules Romains] *The Death of a Nobody*, 1914 (tr); *Remnants*, 1918 (e); Ed. *Life and Letters*, 1928-50; *Portraits*, 1931 (repr. 1954) (b); *Criticism*, 1932 (c); *William Somerset*

Maugham, 1934 (c); *Experience,* 1935 (e); *Leslie Stephen,* 1937 (lecture); *Drama,* 1940 (c); *Shaw,* 1951 (c); *Humanities,* 1953 (e); *Memories,* 1953 (e); (with B. Guinness, etc.) E. T. W. Hoffman, *The Story of a Nutcracker,* 1953 (free tr); *Theatre,* 1954 (c)

E. M. Forster, *Desmond MacCarthy,* 1952 [no bibliog.]

HUGH MACDIARMID
1892-

Sangschaw, 1925 (p in Scots); *Penny Wheep,* 1926 (p); *A Drunk Man Looks at the Thistle,* 1926 (p); *Contemporary Scottish Studies,* 1926 (c); *The Lucky Bag,* 1927 (p); *Albyn, or, Scotland and the Future,* 1927 (e); *Scotland in 1980,* 1930 (e); *The Handmaid of the Lord,* 1930 (t); *To Circumjack Cencrastus, or, The Curly Snake,* 1930 (p); *Annals of the Five Senses,* 1930 (p,e); *First Hymn to Lenin,* 1931 (p); *Warning Democracy,* 1931 (e); *Tarras,* 1932 (p); *Second Hymn to Lenin,* 1932 (p); *Scots Unbound,* 1932 (p); *Five Bits of Miller,* 1934 (p); *Scottish Scene, or, The Intelligent Man's Guide to Albyn,* 1934 (e); *Stony Limits,* 1934 (repr. with *Scots Unbound,* 1956) (p); *At the Sign of the Thistle,* 1934 (e); *Selected Poems,* 1934 (p); *Scottish Eccentrics,* 1936 (b); *Direadh,* 1938 (p); *The Islands of Scotland,* 1939 (t); *Cornish Heroic Song for Valda,* 1943 (p); *Lucky Poet,* 1943 (a); *Selected Poems,* ed. R. Crombie Saunders, 1944 (p); *Speaking for Scotland: Selected Poems* (Am. ed.), 1946; *A Kist of Whistles,* 1947 (p); *Cunninghame Graham: a Centenary Study,* 1952 (c); *Selected Poems of Hugh MacDiarmid,* ed. Oliver Brown, 1954 (p); *Francis George Scott,* 1955 (e); *In Memoriam James Joyce,* 1955 (e); *Three Hymns to Lenin,* 1957 (p); *The Battle Continues,* 1957 (p); *Burns Today and Tomorrow,* 1959 (c); *The Kind of Poetry I Want,* 1961 (p); *Collected Poems,* 1962; *The Ugly Birds Without Wings,* 1962 (e); *The Man of (Almost) Independent Mind* [David Hume], 1962 (c); *Poems to Paintings by William Johnstone, 1933,* 1963 (p); *Poetry Like the Hawthorn,* 1963 (p); *The Terrible Crystal: A Vision of Scotland,* 1964 (p); *The Ministry of Water,* 1965 (p); *The Fire of the Spirit,* 1965 (p); *The Company I've Kept,* 1966 (a)

Kenneth Buthlay, *Hugh MacDiarmid,* 1964

ROGER MACDOUGALL
1910-

The Man in the White Suit, 1949 (d); *The Gentle Gunman,* 1950 (d); *To Dorothy, A Son,* 1952 (d); *Macadam and Eve,* 1952 (d); *Escapade,* 1953 (d); *The Facts of Life,* 1955 (d); *Double Image,* 1957 (d)

ARTHUR MACHEN
1863-1947

[Leolinus Siluriensis, pseud.] *The Anatomy of Tobacco,* 1884 (repr. 1926) (e); *The Heptameron, or, Tales and Novels of Marguerite, Queen of Navarre,* 1886 (tr); *The Grande Trouvaille,* 1887 (s); *The Chronicle of Clemendy . . . the Amorous Inventions and Facetious Tales of Master Gervase Perrot,* 1888 (n); *Thesaurus Incantatus,* 1888 (n); [Rabelais] *Fantastic Tales,* 1890 (tr); *The Great God Pan and The Inmost Light,* 1894 (repr. 1913) (s); *The Memoirs of Jacques Casanova,* 1894 (repr. 1960) (tr); *The Three Imposters,* 1895 (n); *Hieroglyphics,* 1902 (e); *Dr. Stiggins, His Views and Principles,* 1906 (e); *The House of Souls,* 1906 (n); *The Hill of Dreams,* 1907 (repr. 1954) (n); *The Angels of Mons,* 1915 (s); *The Great Return,* 1915 (s); *The Terror,* 1917 (n); *Far Off Things,* 1922 (a); *The Secret Glory,* 1922 (n); *Strange Roads,* 1923 (e); *The Caerleon Edition of the Works,* 9 vols., 1923; *Things Near and Far,* 1923 (a); *Dog and Duck, A London Calendar,* 1924 (e); *The Glorious Mystery,* ed. Vincent Starrett [periodical contributions], 1924 (e); *The London Adventure,* 1924 (t); *Ornaments in Jade,* 1924 (e); *The Canning Wonder* [the Case of Elizabeth Canning], 1925 (e); *Dreads and Drolls,* 1926 (e); *Notes and Queries,* 1926 (e); *Tom o' Bedlam and his Song,* 1930 (e); *The Green Round,* 1933 (n); *The Children of the Pool.* 1936 (s); *The Cosy Room,* 1936 (s); *Holy Terrors,* 1946 (s); *Tales of Horror and the Supernatural,* 1948 (s); *The Gray's Inn Coffee House,* 1949 (e); *Bridles and Spurs,* 1951 (e)

Henry Danielson, *Arthur Machen, a Bibliography* (with notes, biographical and critical, by Arthur Machen and introd. by Henry Savage), 1923; Adrian Goldstone and Wesley Sweetser, *A Bibliography of Arthur Machen* (with list of books and articles about Machen), 1965; Aidan Reynolds and William Charlton, *Arthur Machen: A Short Account of His Life and Work*, introd. D. B. Wyndham Lewis, 1963

COLIN MACINNES
1914-

To the Victors the Spoils, 1950 (r); *June In Her Spring*, 1952 (n); *City of Spades*, 1957 (n); *Absolute Beginners*, 1959 (n); *Mr. Love and Justice*, 1960 (n); *England, Half English*, 1961 (e); (with Kenneth Clarke and B. Robertson) *Sidney Nolan*, 1961 (c); *All Day Saturday*, 1966 (n)

J. W. MACKAIL
1859-1945

(with others) *Mensae Secundae, Verses Written in Balliol College*, 1879 (p); *Thermopylae*, 1881 (Newdigate prize verse); (with H. C. Beaching and J. B. B. Nichols) *Love in Idleness*, 1883 (p); *The Aeneid of Virgil*, 1885 (tr); *The Eclogues and Georgics of Virgil*, 1889 (tr.); *Select Epigrams from the Greek Anthology*, 1890 (tr); (with H .C. Beaching) *Love's Looking Glass*, 1891 (p); *Latin Literature*, 1895 (h); *Homer, Odysseus in Phaeacia* [Bk. VI of *Odyssey*], 1896 (tr); *The Life of William Morris*, 1899 (repr. to 1950) (b); *Homer, The Odyssey*, 1903 (repr. 1932) (tr); *Virgil in English Verse*, 1903 (e); *The Progress of Poesy*, 1906 (inaugural lecture [Sheldonian Theatre]); *The Springs of Helicon, a Study in the Progress of English Poetry from Chaucer to Milton*, 1909 (h); *Milton*, 1909 (c); *Swinburne*, 1909 (Oxford Univ. lecture); *Lectures on Poetry*, 1911 (c); *Lectures on Greek Poetry*, 1911 (repr. 1926) (c); *Pervigilium Veneris*, 1912 (tr); *The Study of Poetry*, 1915 (e); *Russia's Gift to the World*, 1915 (e); *Shakespeare after Three Hundred Years*, 1916 (first annual Shakespeare lecture [Brit. Academy]); *W. J. Courthope, 1842-1917*, 1919 (e); *Pope*, 1919 (Leslie Stephen lecture); *The Case for Latin in Secondary Schools*, 1922 (e); *Virgil and his Meaning to the World of Today* (Vol. 15 of *Our Debt to Greece and Rome*), 1923 (e); *The Classics*, 1923 (Presid. Address, Classical Assoc.); *The Alliance of Latin and English Studies*, 1923 (e); *Bentley's Milton*, 1924 (Thomas Warton lecture); *The Pilgrim's Progress*, 1924 (e); *What Is the Good of Greek?*, 1924 (lecture); *Classical Studies*, 1925 (e); *James Leigh Strachan-Davidson, Master of Balliol*, 1925 (m); *Studies of English Poets*, 1926 (c); *The Lesson of Imperial Rome*, 1929 (lecture, Queen's Univ., Belfast); *The Approach to Shakespeare*, 1930 (Lord Northcliffe lectures); *Largeness in Literature*, 1930 (e); *Virgil*, 1931 (Annual lecture, Brit. Academy); *Presidential Addresses*, Brit. Academy, 1933, 1934, 1936; *Studies in Humanism*, 1938 (e)

Cyril Bailey, *John William Mackail*, 1947

COMPTON MACKENZIE
1883-

The Gentleman in Grey, 1906 (d); *Poems*, 1907 (p); *The Passionate Elopement*, 1911 (n); *Carnival*, 1912 (n); *Kensington Rhymes*, 1912 (p); *Sinister Street*, Vol. I, 1913 (n); *Sinister Street*, Vol. II, 1914 (Am. ed. Vol. I, *Youth's Encounter*, 1913; Vol. II, *Sinister Street*, 1914) (n); *Guy and Pauline* (Am. ed. *Plashers Mead*), 1915 (n); *The Early Life and Adventures of Sylvia Scarlett* (continues *Sinister Street*), 1918 (n); *Sylvia and Michael* (continues *Sinister Street*), 1919 (n); *Poor Relations*, 1919 (n); *The Vanity Girl*, 1920 (n); *Columbine*, 1920 (d); *Rich Relatives*, 1921 (n); *The Altar Steps*, 1922 (n); *The Seven Ages of Woman*, 1923 (s); (with Archibald Marshall) *Gramophone Nights*, 1923 (s); *The Parson's Progress* (seq. to *The Altar Steps*), 1923 (n); *The Heavenly Ladder* (seq. to *The Parson's Progress*), 1924 (n); *Santa Claus in Summer*, 1924 (n); *The Old Men of the Sea*, 1924 (n); *Coral* (seq. to *Carnival*), 1925 (n); *Fairy Gold*, 1926 (n); *Rogues and Vagabonds*, 1927 n); *The Life and Adventures of Sylvia Scarlett* (complete ed.), 1927 (n); *Vestal Fire*, 1927 (n); *Extremes Meet*, 1928 (n); *Extraordinary Women*, 1928 (n); *The Three Couriers*, 1929 (n); *Gallipoli Memories*, 1929 (r); *April Fools*, 1930 (n); *Told*, 1930 (n); *First Athenian Memories*, 1931 (a); *Buttercups and Daisies* (Am. ed. *For*

Sale), 1931 (n); *Our Street*, 1931 (n); *The Lost Cause*, 1931 (d); *Unconsidered Trifles*, 1932 (e); *Greek Memories*, 1932 (withdrawn from publication, reissued 1940 (r); *Prince Charlie*, 1932 (b); *Water on the Brain*, 1933 (n); *Literature in My Time*, 1933 (c); *Reaped and Bound*, 1933 (e); *The Darkening Green*, 1934 (n); *Marathon and Salamis*, 1934 (e); *Prince Charlie and His Ladies*, 1934 (b); *Catholicism and Scotland*, 1936 (e); *Figure of Eight*, 1936 (n); *Pericles*, 1937 (b); *Four Winds of Love*, 1937-1945 [*The East Wind*, 1937; *The South Wind*, 1937; *The West Wind*, 1940; *West to North*, 1940; *The North Wind*, Vol. I, 1944; *The North Wind*, Vol. II, 1945] (n); *The Windsor Tapestry*, 1938 (b); *A Musical Chair*, 1939 (e); *Aegean Memories*, 1940 (r); *The Red Tapeworm*, 1941 (n); *The Monarch of the Glen*, 1941 (n); *Calvary*, 1942 (e); *Wind of Freedom*, 1943 (e); *Keep the Home Guard Turning*, 1943 (n); *Mr. Roosevelt*, 1943 (b); *Brockhouse*, 1944 (e); *Dr. Benes*, 1945 (b); *The Vital Flame*, 1945 (e); *Whisky Galore*, 1947 (n); *All Over the Place*, 1949 (e); *Hunting the Fairies*, 1949 (n); *Coalport*, 1951 (e); *Eastern Epic*, Vol. I, 1951 (e); *I Took a Journey*, 1951 (e); *The Rival Monster*, 1952 (n); *The Queen's House*, 1953 (e); *Echoes*, 1953 (e); *Realms of Silver*, 1953 (e); *Ben Nevis Goes East*, 1954 (n); *Eastern Epic*, Vol. II, 1954 (e); *My Record of Music*, 1955 (a); *Thin Ice*, 1956 (n); *Rockets Galore*, 1957 (n); *Sublime Tobacco*, 1957 (e); *Tatting*, 1957 (n); *The Lunatic Republic*, 1959 (n); *Tight Little Island*, 1959 (n); *Greece in My Life*, 1960 (a); *Cat's Company*, 1960 (e); *Catmint*, 1961 (e); *Mezzotint*, 1961 (n); *On Moral Courage*, 1962 (e); *My Life and Times, Octave 1: 1883-1891*, 1963 (a); *My Life and Times, Octave 2: 1891-1900*, 1963 (a); *My Life and Times, 1900-1907, Octave 3: Vintage Oxford Years and Debut as a Writer*, 1964 (a); *The Stolen Soprano*, 1965 (n); *Little Cat Lost*, 1965 (s)

Leo Robertson, *Compton Mackenzie*, 1954

LOUIS MACNEICE
1907-1963

Blind Fireworks, 1929 (p); [Louis Malone, pseud.] *Roundabout Way*, 1932 (n); *Poems*, 1935 (p); *The Agamemnon of Aeschylus*, 1936 (tr); (with W. H. Auden) *Letters from Iceland*, 1937 (t); *Out of the Picture*, 1937 (d); *The Earth Compels*, 1938 (p); *I Crossed the Minch* [Outer Hebrides], 1938 (t); *Modern Poetry*, 1938 (c); *Zoo*, 1938 (e); *Autumn Journal*, 1939 (p); *The Last Ditch*, 1940 (p); *Selected Poems*, 1940 (p); *Poems, 1925-1940*, 1940 (p); *Plant and Phantom*, 1941 (p); *The Poetry of W. B. Yeats*, 1941 (c); *Meet the U.S. Army*, 1943 (e); *Christopher Columbus*, 1944 (rd); *Springboard: Poems 1941-1944*, 1944 (p); **The Dark Tower*, 1947 (rd); *Holes in the Sky: Poems 1944-1947*, 1948 (p); *Collected Poems, 1925-1948*, 1949; *Goethe's Faust* (abridged), 1951 (tr); *Ten Burnt Offerings*, 1952 (p); *Autumn Sequel*, 1954 (p); *The Other Wing*, 1954 (p); *Visitations*, 1957 (p); *Eighty-Five Poems*, 1959 (p); *Solstices*, 1961 (p); *The Burning Perch*, 1963 (p); *The Mad Islands, and The Administrator*, 1964 (2rd); *Selected Poems*, ed. W. H. Auden ,1964 (p); *The Strings Are False*, 1965 (unfinished a); *Varieties of Parable*, 1965 (Clarke lectures, Cambridge Univ.)

*repr. 1964

John Press, *Louis MacNeice*, 1965

CHARLES MADGE
1912-

The Disappearing Castle, 1937 (p); *The Father Found*, 1941 (p); *Society in the Mind*, 1964 (e)

OLIVIA MANNING
? -

The Wind Changes, 1937 (n); *The Remarkable Expedition*, 1947 (Am. ed. *The Reluctant Rescue: the Story of Stanley's Rescue of Emir Pasha from Equatorial Africa*) (b); *Growing Up*, 1948 (s); *Artist Among the Missing*, 1949 (n); *The Dreaming Shore* [West Coast of Ireland], 1950 (t); *School for Love*, 1951 (n); *A Different Face*, 1953 (n); *The Doves of Venus*, 1955 (n); *My Husband Cartwright*, 1956 (n); *The Great Fortune*, 1960 (n); *The Spoilt City* [seq. to preceding], 1962 (n); *Friends and Heroes* (Vol. III of Balkan trilogy, the last three titles), 1965 (n)

KATHERINE MANSFIELD
1885-1923

In a German Pension, 1911 (s); *Prelude,* 1918 (s); *Je Ne Parle Pas Français,* 1918 (s); *Bliss,* 1920 (s); *The Garden Party,* 1922 (s); *The Dove's Nest,* 1923 (s); *Poems,* 1923 (p); *Something Childish,* 1924 (Am. ed. *The Little Girl* (s); *Journal of Katherine Mansfield,* ed. J. Middleton Murry, 1927 (enlgd. 1954); *The Letters of Katherine Mansfield,* ed. J. Middleton Murry, 1928; *The Aloe,* 1930 (s); *Novels and Novelists,* [reviews for *Athenaeum,* 1919-20], ed. J. Middleton Murry, 1930 (c); *Stories: a Selection,* ed. J. Middleton Murry, 1930; *The Scrapbook of Katherine Mansfield,* ed. J. Middleton Murry, 1938; *Collected Stories,* 1945; *Letters to J. Middleton Murry, 1913-22,* ed. J. Middleton Murry, 1951

Ruth Elvish Mantz, *The Critical Bibliography of Katherine Mansfield,* 1931; Ruth Elvish Mantz and J. Middleton Murry, *The Life of Katherine Mansfield,* 1933; Anthony Alpers, *Katherine Mansfield,* 1954

CHARLES MARRIOTT
1869-1957

The Column, 1901 (n); *Love With Honour,* 1902 (n); *The House on the Sands,* 1903 (n); *Genevra,* 1904 (n); *Mrs. Alemere's Elopement,* 1905 (n); *The Lapse of Vivien Eady,* 1906 (n); *Women and the West,* 1906 (s); *The Remnant,* 1907 (n); *The Wondrous Wife,* 1907 (n); *The Happy Medium,* 1908 (s); *The Kiss of Helen,* 1908 (n); *A Spanish Holiday,* 1908 (t); *The Intruding Angel,* 1909 (n); *When a Woman Woos,* 1909 (n); *"Now!",* 1910 (n); *The Romance of the Rhine,* 1911 (e); *The Dewpond,* 1912 (n); *The Catfish,* 1913 (n); *Subsoil,* 1913 (n); *What a Man Wants,* 1913 (n); *The Unpetitioned Heavens,* 1914 (n); *Davenport,* 1915 (n); *Modern Art,* 1918 (c); *Modern Movements in Painting,* 1920 (c); *The Grave Impertinence,* 1921 (n); *An Order to View,* 1922 (n); *Masterpieces of Modern Art,* 1922 (c); *Pencil Drawing,* 1922 (e); *Modern English Architecture,* 1924 (c); *Eric Gill as Carver,* 1929 (c); *A Key to Modern Painting,* 1938 (c); *British Handicrafts,* 1943 (e)

EDWARD MARSH
1872-1953

Rupert Brooke, 1918 (m); *Forty-Two Fables of La Fontaine,* 1924 (tr); *More Fables of La Fontaine,* 1925 (tr); *The Fables of La Fontaine,* 1931 (tr); *A Number of People,* 1939 (r); *The Odes of Horace,* 1941 (tr); *Minima,* 1947 (p,tr); Fromentin, *Dominique,* 1948 (tr); M. L. Bibescu, *The Sphinx of Bagatelle* (tr); M. L. Bibescu, *Proust's Oriane,* 1952 (tr); *Ambrosia and Small Beer: The Record of a Correspondence between Edward Marsh and Christopher Hassall,* ed. Christopher Hassall, 1964

Christopher Hassall, *Edward Marsh,* 1959

JOHN MASEFIELD
1878-1967

Salt-Water Ballads, 1902 (p); *Ballads,* 1903 (rev. enlgd. 1910) (p); *A Mainsail Haul,* 1905 (rev. enlgd. 1913, 1954) (e); *Sea Life in Nelson's Time,* 1905 (p); *On the Spanish Main,* 1906 (e); *A Tarpaulin Muster,* 1907 (s); *Captain Margaret,* 1908 (n); *Multitude and Solitude,* 1909 (n); *The Tragedy of Nan,* 1909 (repr. 1926) (d); *The Tragedy of Pompey the Great,* 1910 (d); *Ballads and Poems,* 1910 (p); *Martin Hyde: the Duke's Messenger,* 1910 (repr. 1931) (n); *A Book of Discoveries,* 1910 (e); *Lost Endeavour,* 1910 (repr. 1923) (e); *The Everlasting Mercy,* 1911 (p); *William Shakespeare,* 1911 (rev. 1954) (c); *The Street of Today,* 1911 (n); *Jim Davis,* 1911 (repr. 1947) (n); *The Story of a Roadhouse,* 1912 (p); *The Widow in the Bye Street,* 1912 (Am. ed. *The Everlasting Mercy and The Widow in the Bye Street*) (p); *Dauber,* 1913 (p); *The Daffodil Fields,* 1913 (p); *Philip the King,* 1914 (p); *The Faithful: a Tragedy in Three Acts,* 1915 (d); *The Locked Chest; The Sweeps of Ninety-Eight,* 1916 (2d); *John M. Synge,* 1915 (r); *Sonnets and Poems,* 1916 (p); *Good Friday,* 1916 (repr. 1955) (pd); *Lollingdon Downs,* 1917 (p); *Poems,* 1917; *A Poem and Two Plays,* 1918; *Collected Poems and Plays,* 1919; *Reynard the Fox, or The Ghost Heath Run,* 1919 (p); *Enslaved,* 1920 (p); *Right Royal,* 1920 (p); *King Cole,* 1921 (p); Jean Racine, *Berenice,* 1922 (Am. ed. *Esther and Berenice*)

(2d,tr); *Melloney Hotspur*, 1922 (d); *Selected Poems*, 1922 (p); *Leather Pocket Edition of Masefield's Work*, 8 vols., 1922; *The Dream*, 1922 (p); *A King's Daughter: a Tragedy in Verse*, 1923 (pd); *The Taking of Helen*, 1923 (s); *Collected Poems*, 1923 (rev. enlgd. 1932, 1938, 1946); *Recent Prose*, 1924 (rev. 1932); *Sard Harker*, 1924 (n); *Shakespeare and Spiritual Life*, 1924 (Romanes Lecture); *The Trial of Jesus*, 1925 (d); *Collected Works*, 4 vols., 1925; *Odtaa*, 1926 (n); *Tristan and Isolt*, 1927 (pd); *The Midnight Folk*, 1927 (n); *The Coming of Christ*, 1928 (d); *Midsummer Night*, 1928 (p); *Poems*, 1929 (p); *The Hawbucks*, 1929 (n); *Easter*, 1929 (pd); *The Wanderer of Liverpool*, 1930 (misc.); *Chaucer*, 1931 (Leslie Stephen lecture); *Minnie Maylow's Story*, 1931 (s); *A Tale of Troy*, 1932 (p); *The Conway from Her Foundation to the Present Day*, 1933 (h); *End and Beginning*, 1933 (p); *The Bird of Dawning*, 1933 (n); *The Taking of the Gry*, 1934 (n); *The Box of Delights*, 1935 (n); *Victorious Troy, or The Hurrying Angel*, 1935 (n); *The Collected Works*, 5 vols., 1935-1937; *Eggs and Baker*, 1936 (n); *A Letter from Pontus*, 1936 (p); *The Square Peg, or The Gun Fella*, 1937 (n); *The Country Scene*, 1937 (p); *Dead Ned*, 1938 (n); (with Edward Seago, ill.) *Tribute to Ballet*, 1938 (p); *Live and Kicking Ned* [seq. to *Dead Ned*], 1939 (n); *Basilissa: A Tale of The Empress Theodora*, 1940 (n); *Some Memories of W. B. Yeats*, 1940 (r); *Gautama, the Enlightened*, 1941 (p); *In the Mill*, 1941 (a); *Conquer: A Tale of the Nika Rebellion in Byzantium*, 1941 (n); *A Generation Risen*, 1942 (p); *Land Workers*, 1942 (p); *Wanderings Between One and Six Years*, 1943 (p); *New Chum*, 1944 (a); *A Macbeth Production*, 1945 (e); *Thanks Before Going*, 1946 (e); *A Book of Both Sorts*, 1947 (p,e); *Badon Parchments*, 1947 (n); *A Play of St. George*, 1948 (d); *On the Hill*, 1949 (p); *In Praise of Nurses*, 1950 (p); *St. Katherine of Ledbury and Other Ledbury Papers*, 1951 (e); *So Long to Learn*, 1952 (a); *Poems: Complete Edition*, 1953; *The Bluebells*, 1961 (p); *Old Raiger*, 1964 (p); *Grace Before Ploughing*, 1966 (a of early years)

Charles H. Simmons, *A Bibliography*

of John Masefield, 1930; Geoffrey Handley-Taylor, *John Masefield, O.M.: the Queen's Poet Laureate*, 1960

A. E. W. MASON
1865-1948

Blanche de Malétroit (founded on story by R. L. Stevenson), 1894 (d); *A Romance of Wastdale*, 1895 (n); *The Courtship of Morrice Buckler*, 1896 (repr. 1938) (n); *The Philanderers*, 1897 (repr. 1938) (n); *Lawrence Clavering*, 1897 (n); *Miranda of the Balcony*, 1899 (repr. 1938) (n); *The Watchers*, 1899 (repr. 1940) (n); *Parson Kelly*, 1900 (n); *Engsign Knightley*, 1901 (s); *Clementina*, 1901 (n); *The Four Feathers*, 1902 (repr. 1960) (n); *The Truants*, 1904 (n); *Running Water*, 1907 (n); *The Broken Road*, 1907 (n); *Colonel Smith*, 1909 (d); *At the Villa Rose*, 1910 (repr. 1949) (n) (dramatized by Mason, 1928); *Green Stockings*, 1910 (d); *The Witness for the Defence*, 1911 (n; also dramatized); *The Turnstile*, 1912 (n); *The Four Corners of the World*, 1917 (s); *The Royal Exchange*, 1920 (e); *The Summons*, 1920 (n); *The Winding Stair*, 1923 (repr. 1949) (n); *The House of the Arrow*, 1924 (n); *No Other Tiger* 1927 (repr. 1948) (n); *The Prisoner in the Opal*, 1928 (n); *The Dean's Elbow*, 1930 (n); *The A. E. W. Mason Omnibus*, 1931 (3s); *The Three Gentlemen*, 1932 (n); *The Sapphire*, 1933 (n); *A Present for Margate*, 1934 (d); *Dilemmas*, 1934 (s); *They Wouldn't Be Chessmen*, 1935 (n); *Sir George Alexander and the St. James's Theatre*, 1935 (b); *Fire Over England*, 1936 (n); *The Drum*, 1937 (s); *Königsmark*, 1938 (n); *The Life of Francis Drake*, 1941 (b); *Musk and Amber*, 1942 (n); *The House in Lordship Lane*, 1946 (n)

Roger Lancelyn Green, *A. E. W. Mason*, 1952

JOHN MASTERS
1914-

Nightrunners of Bengal, 1951 (n); *The Deceivers*, 1952 (n); *The Lotus and the Wind*, 1953 (n); *Bhowani Junction*, 1954 (n); *Coromandel!*, 1955 (n); *Bugles and a Tiger*, 1956 (a); *Far, Far the Mountain Peak*, 1956 (n); *Fandango Rock*, 1959 (n); *The Venus of Konpara*, 1960 (n); *The Road Past Mandalay*, 1961 (a); *To the Coral Strand*, 1962 (n); *Trial at Monomoy*, 1964 (n)

W. S. MAUGHAM
1874-1965

Liza of Lambeth, 1897 (n); *The Making of a Saint*, 1898 (n); *Orientations*, 1899 (n); *The Hero*, 1901 (n); *Mrs. Craddock*, 1902 (rev. 1955) (n); *A Man of Honour*, 1903 (d); *The Merry-go-round*, 1904 (n); *The Land of the Blessed Virgin* (pub. as *Andalusia*, 1920), 1905 (t); *The Bishop's Apron: A Study in the Origins of a Great Family*, 1906 (n); *The Explorer*, 1907 (n); *The Magician*, 1908 (repr. 1956 with *Fragment of an Autobiography*) (n); *Lady Frederick*, 1912 (d); *Jack Straw*, 1912 (d); dramatization of *The Explorer*, 1912; *Mrs. Dot*, 1912 (d); *Penelope*, 1912 (p); *The Tenth Man*, 1913 (d); *Landed Gentry*, 1913 (d); *Smith*, 1913 (d); *The Land of Promise*, 1913 (d); *Of Human Bondage*, 1915 (many reprs.) (n); *The Moon and Sixpence*, 1919 (repr. 1941) (n); *The Unknown*, 1920 (d); *The Circle*, 1921 (d); *The Trembling of a Leaf* (contains "Rain" pub. as *Sadie Thompson*, 1928) 1921 (s); *Caesar's Wife*, 1922 (d); *East of Suez*, 1922 (d); *On a Chinese Screen*, 1922 (t); *Our Betters*, 1923 (d); *Home and Beauty*, 1923 (d); *The Unattainable*, 1923 (d); *Loaves and Fishes*, 1924 (d); *The Painted Veil*, 1925 (n); *The Casuarina Tree*, 1926 (6s); *The Constant Wife*, 1927 (d); *The Letter*, 1927 (d); *Ashenden, or The British Agent*, 1928 (s); *The Sacred Flame*, 1928 (d); *The Gentleman in the Parlour* [Rangoon to Haiphong], 1930 (t); *Cakes and Ale, or The Skeleton in the Cupboard*, 1930 (n); *The Breadwinner*, 1930 (d); *Dramatic Works*, Vol. I-VI, 1931-1934; *Six Stories Written in the First Person Singular*, 1931 (s); *The Book Bag*, 1932 (c); *The Narrow Corner*, 1932 (n); *For Services Rendered*, 1932 (d); *Ah King*, 1933 (s); *Sheppey*, 1933 (d); *Altogether* (coll. short stories), 1934 (Am. ed. *East and West*)(s); *Non-Dramatic Works*,1934-51; *Don Fernando, or Variations on Some Spanish Themes*,1935 (rev.1950)(n); *The Collected Works*, 1936-1938; *Cosmopolitans*, 1936 (s); *My South Sea Island*, 1936 (t); *The Favourite Short Stories*,

1937 (s); *Theatre*, 1937 (n); *The Summing Up*, 1938 (a); *The Round Dozen*, 1939 (s); *Christmas Holiday*, 1939 (n); *Princess September and The Nightingale*, 1939 (s); *Books and You*, 1940 (c); *The Mixture As Before*, 1940 (s); *Up at the Villa*, 1941 (n); *Strictly Personal*, 1941 (r); *The Hour Before the Dawn*, 1942 (n); *The Unconquered*, 1944 (s); *The Razor's Edge*, 1944 (n); *Then and Now*, 1946 (n); *Creatures of Circumstance*, 1947 (s); *Catalina*, 1948 (n); *Quartet*, 1948 (4s); *Great Novelists and Their Novels*, 1948 [Eng. ed. 1954, *Ten Novels and Their Authors*] (rev. enlgd. 1955 as *The Art of Fiction*)(c); *A Writer's Notebook*, 1949 (a); *Trio*, 1950 (3s); *The Complete Short Stories*, 1951; *The Writer's Point of View*, 1951 (e,r); *Encore*, 1952 (s); *The Collected Plays*, 1952; *The Vagrant Mood*, 1952 (e); *The Noble Spaniard*, 1953 [written and produced in London, 1909] (d); *The Selected Novels*, 1953; *Ten Novels and Their Authors*, 1954 (rev. 1955) (Am. ed. *Great Novelists and Their Novels*, 1948) (c); *The Partial View* [contains *The Summing Up* and *A Writer's Notebook* with new preface], 1954; *The Travel Books of William Somerset Maugham*, 1955 (t); *Points of View*, 1958 (e); *Purely for My Pleasure*, 1962 [exhibition of his painting collection]; *Selected Prefaces and Introductions of Somerset Maugham*, ed. George Shively, 1964; *The Wit and Wisdom of Somerset Maugham*, ed. Cecil Hewetson, 1966 (misc.); *A Maugham Twelve*, sel. with introd. Angus Wilson, 1966 (s)

Raymond Toole Stott, *The Writings of William Somerset Maugham: A Bibliography*. 1956; Richard A. Cordell, *Somerset Maugham: a Biographical and Critical Study*, 1937 (rev. 1961)

Note. The Uniform Ed. (33 titles) is published by Heinemann.

AUBREY MENEN
1912-

The Prevalence of Witches, 1947 (n); *The Stumbling Stone*, 1949 (n); *The Backward Bride*, 1950 (n); *The Duke of Gallodoro*, 1952 (n); *Dead Men in the Silver Market*, 1953 (a,e); *Rama Retold*, 1954 (n); *The Abode of Love*, 1957 (n); *The Fig Tree*, 1959 (n); *Rome*

Revealed, 1960 (t); *SheLa: a Satire*, 1962 (n); *Speaking the Language Like a Native* [on Italy], 1963 (t); *A Conspiracy of Women*, 1965 (n)

CHARLOTTE MEW
1870-1928

The Farmer's Bride, 1916, new ed. with 11 new poems, 1921 (Am. ed. *Saturday Market*, 1921) (p); *The Rambling Sailor*, 1929 (p); *Collected Poems*, ed. with biog. memoir A. Monro, 1953

E. H. W. MEYERSTEIN
1889-1952

The Door, 1911 (p); *Three Odes*, 1914 (p); *Ode to Truth*, 1915 (p); *Symphonies*, 1915 (p); *The Witches' Sabbath*, 1917 (p); (with Wilfrid Blair) *Black and White Magic*, 1917 (p); *Symphonies: Second Series*, 1919 (p); *Heddon*, 1921 (d); *Mysteria Mundi*, 1921 (p); *Wade's Boat*, 1921 (p); *The Trireme*, 1921 (n); *In Merlin's Wood*, 1922 (p); *Voyage of Ass*, 1922 (p); *The Monument*, 1923 (d); *Odes on Several Contemplative and Metaphysical Subjects*, 1923 (p); *Ratscastle: a Kentish Interlude*, 1924 (pd); *The Pleasure Lover*, 1925 (n); *Grobo*, 1925 (n); *The Boy: a Modern Poem*, 1928 (p); *Terence in Love*, 1928 (n); *The First Christmas*, 1930 (p); *A Life of Thomas Chatterton*, 1930 (b); *New Symphonies*, 1933 (p); *The Pageant*, 1934 (s); *Goemagog and Corineus*, 1934 (p); *A Letter to a Naturalist*, 1935 (p); *Selected Poems*, 1935 (p); *Terence Duke* ˙ (*The Pleasure Lover*, *In Love*, *The Windfall*), 1935 (3n); *The Elegies of Propertius*, 1935 (tr); *New Odes*, 1936 (p); *Séraphine*, 1936 (n); *A Boy of Clare*, 1937 (p); *Briancourt*, 1937 (p); *Joshua Slade*, 1938 (n); *Sonnets. In Exitu Israel. Peace: an Ode*, 1939 (p); *Four People*, 1939 (n); *Eclogues*, 1940 (p); *The Visionary*, 1941 (p); *In Time of War*, 1943 (p); *Azure*, 1944 (p); *Kathleen: a Sonnet Sequence*, 1945 (p); *Division*, 1946 (p); *A Bristol Friendship: Thomas Chatterton and John Baker*, 1947 (Wedmore Memorial lecture); *Redcliff Hill*, 1948 (d); *Three Sonnets*, 1948 (p); *Quartets for Four Voices*, 1949 (p); *The Delphic Charioteer*, 1951 (p); *Robin Wastraw*, 1951 (n); *Tom Tallion*, 1952 (n); *The Unseen Beloved*, 1953 (p); *Phoebe*

Thirsk, 1953 (n); *Verse Letters to Five Friends*, 1954 (p); *Of My Early Life*, ed. Rowland Watson, 1957 (a); *Bollond*, 1958 (s); *Some Letters of E. H. W. Meyerstein*, ed. Rowland Watson, 1959; *Some Poems*, ed. M. Wollman, 1960 (p) [Bristol Public Libraries] *Edward H. W. Meyerstein, Poet and Novelist. A Bibliography*, 1938

ALICE MEYNELL
1847-1922

(A. C. Thompson) *Preludes*, 1875 (p); *The Poor Sisters of Nazareth*, 1889 (e); *The Rhythm of Life*, 1893 (e); (with W. Farrar) *William Holman Hunt, His Life and Works*, 1893 (b); *Poems*, 1893 (p); *The Colour of Life*, 1896 (e); *The Children*, 1896 (e); *Other Poems*, 1896 (p); *London Impressions* (with etchings and photogravure pictures by William Hyde), 1898 (e); *The Spirit of Place*, 1899 (e); *John Ruskin*, 1900 (e); *Venture: The Madonna*, 1901 (e); *Later Poems*, 1902 (repr. as *The Shepherdess*, 1914) (p); *Children of the Old Masters* (Italian School), 1903 (e); René Bazin, *The Nun*, 1908 (tr); *Ceres' Runaway*, 1909 (e); *Mary, the Mother of Jesus*, 1912 (e); *Poems*, 1913 (p); *Childhood*, 1913 (e); *Essays*, 1914 (e); *Ten Poems*, 1915 (p); *Poems on the War*, 1916 (p); *A Father of Women*, 1917 (p); *Hearts of Controversy*, 1917 (e); *The Second Person Singular*, 1921 (e); *The Last Poems*, 1923 (p); *Selected Poems and Prose*, ed. Albert A. Cock, 1928; *Wayfaring*, 1929 (e); *Selected Poems*, 1930 (p); *The Poems of Alice Meynell*, Complete Ed., ed. Frederick Page, 1940 (p); *The Poems of Alice Meynell*, Centenary Ed., ed. Sir Francis Meynell, 1947 (p); *Alice Meynell, 1847-1922: Catalogue of the Centenary Exhibit of Books, Mss., Letters and Portraits*, 1947; *Prose and Poetry*, Centenary Vol., ed. F.P. etc. [Frederick Page etc.], with biog. and crit. introd. V. Sackville-West, 1947; *The Wares of Autolycus*, chosen and with introd. P. M. Fraser, 1965 (sel. e); *Selected Poems* (from *Collected Poems*, 1921; *Last Poems*, 1923; *Preludes*, 1875), 1965 (p)

Anne K. Tuell, *Mrs. Meynell and Her Literary Generation*, 1925; Viola Meynell, *Alice Meynell, a Memoir*, 1929;

Terence L. Connolly, *Alice Meynell: Centenary Tribute*, 1948 (list of bks.). *See* Charles A. and H. W. Stonehill. *Bibliographies of Modern Authors*, Sec. Series, 1925

VIOLA MEYNELL
1886-1956

Martha Vine, 1910 (n); *Cross-in-Hand Farm*, 1911 (n); *Lot Barrow*, 1913 (n); *Modern Lovers*, 1914 (n); *Columbine*, 1915 (n); *Narcissus*, 1916 (n); *Julian Grenfell*, 1918 (e); *Second Marriage*, 1918 (repr. 1935) (n); *Verses*, 1919 (p); *Antonia*, 1921 (n); *Young Mrs. Cruse*, 1924 (s); *A Girl Adoring*, 1927 (n); *Alice Meynell: A Memoir*, 1929 (m); *The Frozen Ocean*, 1930 (p); *Follow Thy Fair Sun*, 1935 (n); *Kissing the Rod*, 1937 (s); *First Love*, 1947 (s); *Ophelia*, 1951 (n); *Louise*, 1954 (s); *Francis Thompson and Wilfrid Meynell: A Memoir*, 1952 (m); *Collected Stories*, 1957

See Reginald B. Johnson, *Some Contemporary Novelists* (Women), 1920

A. A. MILNE
1882-1956

Lovers in London, 1905 (e); *The Day's Play*, 1910 (e); *The Holiday Round*, 1912 (e); *Once a Week*, 1914 (e); *Happy Days, 1915 (e); Once on a Time*, 1917 (n); *Make-Believe*, 1918 (d); *Not That It Matters*, 1919 (e); *First Plays*, 1919 (5d); *If I May*, 1920 (e); *Mr. Pim*, 1921 (n); *Mr. Pim Passes By*, 1921 (d); *Second Plays*, 1921 (5d); *The Sunny Side*, 1921 (e); *The Stepmother*, 1921 (d); *Red House Mystery*, 1922 (n); *The Artist*, 1923 (d); *Three Plays*, 1923 (3d); *The Man in the Bowler Hat*, 1923 (d); *The Truth About Blayds*, 1923 (d); *The Dover Road*, 1923 (d); *Success* 1923 (d); *Vespers*, 1924 (p); *When We Were Very Young*, 1924 (child's bk.); *For the Luncheon Interval*, 1925 (p); *Ariadne*, 1925 (d); *A Gallery of Children*, 1925 (child's bk.); *To Have the Honour*, 1925 (d); *Four Plays*, 1926 (4d); *Winnie-the-Pooh*, 1926 (child's bk.); *The Boy Comes Home*, 1926 (d); *Portrait of a Gentleman in Slippers*, 1926 (child's bk.); *Now We Are Six*, 1927 (child's bk.); *The House at Pooh*

Corner, 1928 (child's bk.); *The Ascent of Man*, 1928 (e); *The Ivory Door*, 1928 (d); *The Fourth Wall* (Am. ed. *The Perfect Alibi*), 1929 (d); (from Kenneth Grahame's *The Wind in the Willows*) *Toad of Toad Hall*, 1929 (child's bk.); *The Secret*, 1929 (s); *By Way of Introduction*, 1929 (e); *The Christopher Robin Story Book*, 1929 (child's bk.); *Michael and Mary*, 1930 (d); *Two People*, 1931 (n); *The Christopher Robin Verses*, 1932 (child's bk.); *Four Day's Wonder*, 1933 (n); *Other People's Lives*, 1935 (d); *Miss Elizabeth Bennett*, 1936 (d); *It's Too Late Now*, 1939 (a); *Sarah Simple*, 1939 (d); *Behind the Lines*, 1940 (p); *The Ugly Duckling*, 1941 (d); *Chloe Marr*, 1946 (n); *Birthday Party*, 1948 (s); *The Norman Church*, 1948 (p); *A Table Near the Band*, 1950 (s); *Before the Flood*, 1951 (d); *Year In, Year Out*, 1952 (a)

See Frank Swinnerton, *The Georgian Scene*, 1934.

NAOMI MITCHISON
1897-

The Conquered, 1923 (n); *When the Bough Breaks*, 1924 (s); *Cloud Cuckoo Land*, 1925 (n); *The Laburnum Branch*, 1926 (p); *Black Sparta*, 1928 (s); *Anna Comnena*, 1928 (b); *Barbarian Stories*, 1929 (s); *The Hostages*, 1930 (s); *The Corn King and the Spring Queen*, 1931 (n); (with L. E. Gielgud) *The Price of Freedom*, 1931 (d); *The Powers of Light*, 1932 (s); *The Delicate Fire*, 1933 (s,p); *Naomi Mitchison's Vienna Diary*, 1934 (t); *Beyond this Limit*, 1935 (s); *We Have Been Warned*, 1935 (n); *The Fourth Pig*, 1936 (s,p); *An End and a Beginning*, 1937 (d); (with R. H. Crossman) *Socrates*, 1937 (b); *The Moral Basis of Politics*, 1938 (e); *The Blood of the Martyrs*, 1939 (n); *The Kingdom of Heaven*, 1939 (e); (with L. E. Gielgud) *As It Was in the Beginning*, 1939 (d); *The Bull Calves*, 1947 (n); *The Big House*, 1950 (n); (with Denis Macintosh) *Spindrift*, 1951 (d); *Lobsters on the Agenda*, 1952 (n); *Travel Light*, 1952 (n); *Graeme and the Dragon*, 1954 (s); *The Swan's Road*, 1954 (h); *To the Chapel Perilous*, 1955 (n); *The Land the Ravens Found*, 1955 (s); *Little Boxes*, 1956 (s); *Behold Your King*,

1957 (n); *The Far Harbour,* 1957 (s); *Five Men and a Swan,* 1957 (s,p); *Judy and Lakshmi,* 1959 (s); *The Rib of the Green Umbrella,* 1960 (s); *The Young Alexander the Great,* 1960 (b); *Memoirs of a Spacewoman,* 1962 (n); *When We Become Men,* 1965 (n); *Return to the Fairy Hill,* 1966 (t)

See Gerald Gould, *The English Novel of Today,* 1924

NANCY MITFORD
1904-

Highland Fling, 1931 (n); *Christmas Pudding,* 1932 (n); *Wigs on the Green,* 1933 (n); *Pigeon Pie,* 1940 (n); *The Pursuit of Love,* 1945 (n); *Love in a Cold Climate,* 1949 (n); A. Roussin, *La Petite Hutte,* 1951 (tr); Madame de Lafayette, *The Princess de Clèves,* 1950 (tr); *Madame de Pompadour,* 1954 (b); *Omnibus,* 1956 (s); *Noblesse Oblige,* 1956 (e); *The Blessing,* 1957 (s); *Voltaire in Love,* 1957 (b); *Don't Tell Alfred,* 1960 (n); *The Water Beetle,* 1962 (e); *The Sun King: Louis XIV at Versailles,* 1966 (h)

See Frederick R. Karl, *A Reader's Guide to the Contemporary English Novel,* 1962

ALLAN MONKHOUSE
1858-1936

Books and Plays, 1894 (e); *A Deliverance,* 1898 (n); *Love in a Life,* 1903 (n); *The Words and the Play,* 1910 (e); *Dying Fires,* 1912 (n); *Mary Broome,* 1912 (d); *The Education of Mr. Surrege,* 1913 (d); *Four Tragedies,*1913 (d); *War Plays,*1916 (d); *Men and Ghosts,* 1918 (n); *True Love,*1919 (n); *My Daughter Helen,* 1922 (n); *The Conquering Hero,*1923 (d); *First Blood,* 1924 (d); *The Grand Cham's Diamond,* 1924 (d); *Marmaduke,* 1924 (d); *Sons and Fathers,* 1925 (d); *Suburb,* 1925 (n); *O Death, Where is thy Sting?,* 1926 (d); *Selected Essays,* 1926 (e); *Alfred the Great,* 1927 (n); *The King of Barvender,* 1927 (d); *The Rag,* 1928 (d); *Nothing Like Leather,* 1930 (d); *Paul Felice,* 1930 (d); *Farewell Manchester,* 1931 (n); *Cecilia,* 1932 (d)

See John W. Cunliffe, *Modern English Playwrights,* 1927

HAROLD MONRO
1879-1932

Poems, 1906 (p); *Judas,* 1907 (p); *The Evolution of the Soul* [of Christ], 1907 (e); *Before Dawn: Poems and Impressions,* 1911 (p); *The Chronicle of a Pilgrimage: Paris to Rome on Foot,* 1912 (t); *Children of Love,* 1914 (p); *Trees,* 1916 (p); *Strange Meetings,* 1917 (p); *Some Contemporary Poets,* 1920 (c); *Real Property,* 1922 (p); *One Day Awake: a Morality,* 1922 (d); *Seventeen Poems,* 1927 (p); *The Earth for Sale,* 1928 (p); *The Winter Solstice,* 1928 (p); *Elm Angel,* 1930 (p); *Collected Poems,* ed. Alida Monro, 1933; *Recent Poetry, 1923-1933,* ed. Alida Monro, 1933 (p); *The Silent Pool,* chosen by A. Monro, 1942 (p)

Joy Grant, *Harold Monro and the Poetry Bookshop,* 1967

NICHOLAS MONSARRAT
1910-

Think of Tomorrow, 1934 (n); *At First Sight,* 1935 (n); *The Whipping Boy,* 1937 (n); *This Is the Schoolroom,* 1939 (n); *H.M. Corvette,* 1942 (s); *East Coast Corvette,* 1943 (s); *Corvette Command,* 1944 (s); *Three Corvettes,* 1945 (3s); *H.M. Frigate,* 1946 (r); *Depends What You Mean By Love,* 1947 (3s); *My Brother Denys,* 1948 (r); *The Cruel Sea,* 1951 (n); *"H.M.S. Marlborough Will Enter Harbour,"* 1952 (s); *The Story of Esther Costello,* 1953 (n); *The Tribe That Lost Its Head,* 1956 (n); *The Ship That Died of Shame,* 1959 (s); *The Nylon Pirates,* 1960 (n); *The White Rajah,* 1961 (n); *Smith and Jones,* 1963 (n); *A Fair Day's Work,* 1964 (n); *Something to Hide,* 1965 (n); *Life Is A Four-Letter Word* (Vol. I, *Breaking In*), 1966 (a)

GEORGE MOORE
1852-1933

Worldliness, 1874 (d); *Flowers of Passion,* 1878 (p); (with B. Lopez) *Martin Luther,* 1879 (d); *Pagan Poems,* 1881; *A Modern Lover,* 1883 (rev. as *Lewis Seymour and Some Women,* 1917) (n); *A Mummer's Wife,* 1885 (n); *Literature at Nurse, or, Circulating Morals,* 1885 (e); *A Drama in Muslin,*

1886 (rev. as *Muslin*, 1915) (n); *A Mere Accident*, 1887 (n); *Parnell and His Island*, 1887 (e); *Spring Days*, 1888 (n); *Confessions of a Young Man*, 1888 (r); *Mike Fletcher*, 1889 (n); *Vain Fortune*, 1890 (n); *Impressions and Opinions*, 1891 (c); *Modern Painting*, 1893 (c); *The Strike at Arlingford*, 1893 (d); *Esther Waters*, 1894 (n); *The Royal Academy*, 1895, 1895 (c); *Celibates*, 1895 (s); *Evelyn Innes*, 1898 (n); *The Bending of the Bough*, 1900 (d); *Sister Theresa*, 1901 (sec. ed. rewritten, 1909) (n); *The Untilled Field*, 1903 (s); *The Lake*, 1905 (n); *Memoirs of My Dead Life*, 1906 (r); *Reminiscences of the Impressionist Painters*, 1906 (r); *The Apostle*, 1911 (rev. 1923) (d); *Hail and Farewell*, *Trilogy: Ave*, 1911, *Salve*, 1912 (a); *Esther Waters*, 1913 (d); *Elizabeth Cooper*, 1913 (d); *Vale*, 1914 [last vol. of trilogy] (a); *The Brook Kerith*, 1916 (n); *A Story-Teller's Holiday*, 1918 (e); *Avowals*, 1919 (r,c); *The Coming of Gabrielle*, 1920 (d); *Héloïse and Abélard*, 1921 (n); *In Single Strictness*, 1922 (rev. as *Celibate Lives*, 1927) (s); *Conversations in Ebury Street*, 1924 (r); Longus, *The Pastoral Loves of Daphnis and Chloe*, 1924 (tr); *Moore versus Harris, an Intimate Correspondence*, 1925; *Ulick and Soracha*, 1926 (n); *Peronnik the Fool*, 1926 (s); *The Making of an Immortal*, 1927 (d); *Letters from George Moore to Edward Dujardin, 1886-1922*, tr. by John Eglinton, 1929; *Aphrodite in Aulis*, 1930 (rev. 1931) (n); *A Flood*, 1930 (s); *The Passing of the Essenes*, 1930 (d); *George Moore in Quest of Locale*, 1931 (e); *The Talking Pine*, 1932 (c); *A Communication to my Friends*, 1933 (m); (with W. B. Yeats) *Diarmuid and Grania*, 1951 (d); *Letters to Lady Cunard 1895-1933*, ed. Rupert Hart-Davis, 1957

Joseph Hone, *The Life of George Moore*, 1936; A. Norman Jeffares, *George Moore*, 1965; Jean C. Noël, *George Moore, l'homme et l'oeuvre*, Paris, 1966

NICHOLAS MOORE
1918-

A Book for Priscilla, 1941 (p); *A Wish in Season*, 1941 (p); *The Island and the Cattle*, 1941 (p); *The Carbaret, The Dancer, The Gentlemen*, 1942 (p); *Three Poems*, 1944 (p); *The Glass Tower*, 1944 (p); *Buzzing Around With a Bee*, 1948 (p); *Recollections of the Gala: Selected Poems, 1943-48*, 1950 (p); *Henry Miller*, 1953 (c); *The Bearded Iris*, 1956 (p)

T. STURGE MOORE
1870-1944

Maurice de Guérin, *The Centaur, The Bacchante*, 1899 (tr); *The Vinedresser*, 1899 (p); *Altdorfer*, 1900 (e); *Aphrodite Against Artemis*, 1901 (d); *The Centaur's Booty*, 1903 (p); *Danaë*, 1903 (p); *The Rout of the Amazons*, 1903 (p); *Absalom*, 1903 (d); *The Gazelles*, 1904 (p); *Pan's Prophecy*, 1904 (p); *Poems, Collected in One Volume*, 1904 (p); *Theseus, Medea, and Lyrics*, 1904 (p); *To Leda*, 1904 (p); *The Little School, a Posy of Rhymes*, 1905 (p); *Albert Dürer*, 1905 (b); *Corregio*, 1906 (b); *Art and Life*, 1910 (e); *Mariamne*, 1911 (p); *A Sicilian Idyll and Judith, a Conflict*, 1911 (p); *The Sea is Kind*, 1914 (p); *Hark to These Three Talk About Style*, 1915 (e); *Some Soldier Poets*, 1919 (c); *The Powers of the Air*, 1920 (d); *Danaë, Aforetime, Blind Thamyris*, 1920 (p); *Tragic Mothers*, 1920 (d); *Judas*, 1923 (p); *Roderigo of Bivar*, 1925 (d); *Armour for Aphrodite*, 1929 (c); *Mystery and Tragedy*, 1930 (2pd); *Nine Poems*, 1930; *The Poems of T. S. Moore, 1931-33*, 1933 (p); *Selected Poems of T. Sturge Moore*, 1934 (p); *The Unknown Known*, 1939 (p); *William Butler Yeats and T. Sturge Moore: Their Correspondence, 1901-1937*, 1953

Frederick L. Gywnn, *Sturge Moore and the Life of Art*, 1952

CHARLES MORGAN
1894-1958

The Gunroom, 1919 (n); *My Name Is Legion*, 1925 (n); *Portrait In a Mirror*, 1929 (also pub. as *First Love*), (n); *The Fountain*, 1932 (n); *Epitaph on George Moore*, 1935 (c); *Sparkenbroke*, 1936 (n); *The Simple Things in Life*, 1937 (e); *The Flashing Stream*, 1938 (rev. 1945 (d); *The Voyage*, 1940 (n); *The Empty Room*, 1941 (n); *Ode to France*, 1942 (p); *The House of Macmillan, 1843-1943*, 1943 (h); *Reflections in a Mirror*, 1944 (e); *The Artist in the Community*, 1945 (e); *Reflections in a*

Mirror, second series, 1946 (e); *The Judge's Story*, 1947 (n); *The Liberty of Thought and the Separation of Powers* [Zaharoff lecture], 1948 (e); *The River Line*, 1949 (n); *A Breeze of Morning*, 1951 (n); *Liberties of the Mind*, 1951 (e); *The River Line*, 1949 (d); *The Burning Glass*, 1954 (d); *Dialogue in Novels and Plays*, 1954 (c); *On Learning to Write*, 1954 (Presid. address, Eng. Assoc.); *Challenge to Venus*, 1957 (n); *The Writer and his World*, 1960 (e)

Gilbert H. Fabes, *The First Editions of A. E. Coppard, A. P. Herbert and Charles Morgan*, 1933

R. H. MOTTRAM
1883-

(J. Marjoram, pseud.) *Repose*, 1907 (p); *New Poems*, 1909 (p); *The Spanish Farm*, 1924 (n); *Sixty-four, Ninety-four!*, 1925 (n); *The Crime at Vanderlynden's*, 1926 (n); *Our Mr. Dormer*, 1927 (n); *The Spanish Farm Trilogy, 1914-1919*, 1927 (n); *The English Miss*, 1928 (n); *The Apple Disdained*, 1928 (s); *Boroughmonger*, 1929 (n); *The New Providence*, 1930 (e); (with others) *Three Personal Records of the War* (Am. ed. *Three Men's War*), 1930 (r); *Poems Old and New*, 1930 (p); H. Daniel-Rops, *The Misted Mirror*, 1930 (tr); *Europa's Beast* (Am. ed. *A Rich Man's Daughter*), 1930 (n); *The Headless Hound*, 1931 (s); *The Lost Christmas Present*, 1931 (s); *Caste Island*, 1931 (n); *John Crome of Norwich*, 1931 (b); *Dazzle*, 1932 (n); *Through the Menin Gate*, 1932 (r); *Home for the Holidays*, 1932 (n); *The Lame Dog* (Am. ed. *At the Sign of the Lame Dog*), 1933 (n); *A Good Old-Fashioned Christmas*, 1933 (n); *East Anglia*, 1933 (t); *The Banquet*, 1934 (s); *Strawberry Time*, 1934 (s); *Bumphrey's*, 1934 (n); *Early Morning*, 1935 (n); *Portrait of an Unknown Victorian*, 1936 (b); *Noah*, 1937 (e); *Time to be Going*, 1937 (n); *Autobiography With a Difference*, 1938 (a); *There Was a Jolly Miller*, 1938 (n); *Miss Lavington*, 1939 (n); *Trader's Dream*, 1939 (e); *You Can't Have it Back*, 1939 (n); *The Ghost and the Maiden*, 1940 (n); *The World Turns Slowly Round*, 1942 (n); *The Corbells at War*, 1943 (n); *Buxton the Liberator*, 1946 (n); *Visit to the Princess*, 1946 (n); *The Gentleman of Leisure*, 1948 (n); *Come to the Bower*, 1949 (n); *One Hundred and Twenty-eight Witnesses*, 1951 (n); *The Part that is Missing*, 1952 (n); *The Broads*, 1952 (t); *If Stones Could Speak*, 1953 (t); *John Galsworthy*, 1953 (c); *The Window Seat*, 1954 (a); *Over the Wall*, 1955 (n); *For Some We Loved*, 1956 (b); *Scenes that are Brightest*, 1956 (n); *Another Window Seat*, 1957 (a); *Vanities and Verities*, 1958 (r); *No One Will Ever Know*, 1958 (n); *Young Man's Fancies*, 1959, (n); *Musetta*, 1960 (n); *Time's Increase*, 1961 (n); *To Hell, with Crabb Robinson*, 1962 (n); *Happy Birds*, 1963 (n)

Gilbert H. Fabes, *The First Editions of Ralph Hale Mottram*, 1934

EDWIN MUIR
1887-1959

[E. Moore, pseud.] *Enigmas and Guesses*, 1918 (c); *Latitudes*, 1924 (c); *First Poems*, 1925 (p); *Chorus of the Newly Dead*, 1926 (p); *Transition, Essays on Contemporary Literature*, 1926 (c); *The Marionette*, 1928 (n); *The Structure of the Novel*, 1928 (e); *John Knox*, 1929 (b); *The Three Brothers*, 1931 (n); *Poor Tom*, 1932 (n); *Variations on a Time Theme*, 1934 (p); *Scottish Journey*, 1935 (t); *Scott and Scotland: The Predicament of the Scottish Writer*, 1936 (e); *Journeys and Places*, 1937 (p); *The Present Age from 1914*, 1939 (c); *The Story and the Fable*, 1940 (rev. and enlgd. as *An Autobiography*, 1954) (a); *The Narrow Place*, 1943 (p); *The Voyage*, 1946 (p); *The Scots and their Country*, 1946 (e); *Essays on Literature and Society*, 1949 (e); *The Labyrinth*, 1949 (p); *Prometheus*, 1954 (p); *One Foot in Eden*, 1956 (p); *Collected Poems, 1921-1951*, ed. J. C. Hall, 1952; *Collected Poems, 1921-1958*, 1960; *Selected Poems*, ed. T. S. Eliot, 1965 (p); (with Willa Muir) tr. Franz Kafka as follows: *The Castle*, 1930; *The Great Wall of China*, 1933; *The Trial*, 1937; *America*, 1949; *In the Penal Settlement*, 1949; also, with Willa Muir, tr. Gerhart Hauptmann, C. Heuser, L. Feuchtwanger, Sholem Asch, etc.

*rev. 1965

Elgin W. Mellown, *Bibliography of the Writings of Edwin Muir* (with sel. list of critical studies), 1964, rev. enlgd. 1966; P. H. Butter, *Edwin Muir*, 1962

C. K. MUNRO
1889-

At Mrs. Beam's, 1923 (d); *The Rumour*, 1923 (d); *Storm, or The Battle of Tinderley Down*, 1924 (d); *Progress*, 1924 (d); *The Mountain, or The Story of Captain Yevan*, 1926 (d); *Bluestone Quarry*, 1931 (d); *Three Plays*, 1932 (3d); *The True Woman, a Handbook for Husbands and Others*, 1932 (e); *Watching a Play*, 1933 (e); *The Fountains in Trafalgar Square*, 1952 (e)

See Graham Sutton, *Some Contemporary Dramatists*, 1924

IRIS MURDOCH
1919-

Sartre, 1953 (c); *Under the Net*, 1954 (n); *The Flight from the Enchanter*, 1956 (n); *The Sandcastle*, 1957 (n); *The Bell*, 1958 (n); *A Severed Head*, 1961 (n); *An Unofficial Rose*, 1962 (n); *The Unicorn*, 1963 (n); (with J. B. Priestley) dramatization of *A Severed Head*, 1964 (d); *The Italian Girl*, 1964 (n); *The Red and the Green*, 1965 (n); *The Time of the Angels*, 1966 (n)

A. S. Byatt, *Degrees of Freedom: The Novels of Iris Murdoch*, 1965

GILBERT MURRAY
1866-1957

Greek Comic Verse, 1886 (tr); *The Place of Greek in Education*, 1889 (inaugural lecture, Univ. of Glasgow); *A History of Ancient Greek Literature*, 1897 (Am. ed. *Literature of Ancient Greece*, 1956) (h); *Andromache*, 1900 (d); *Carlyon Sahib*, 1900 (d); *The Hippolytus and The Bacchae of Euripides, with The Frogs of Aristophanes*, 1902 (tr); *The Electra of Euripides*, 1905 (tr); *The Trojan Women of Euripides*, 1905 (tr); *The Medea of Euripides*, 1906 (tr); *The Rise of the Greek Epic*, 1907 (repr. 1924) (h); *The Early Greek Epic*, 1908 (h); *The Interpretation of Greek Literature*, 1909 (c); *The Iphigenia in Taurus of Euripides*, 1910 (tr); Soph-

ocles, *Oedipus, King of Thebes*, 1911 (tr); *The Story of Nefrekepta*, 1911 (p); *Four Stages of Greek Religion*, 1912 (second ed. *Five Stages of Greek Religion*, 1925) (h); *The Rhesus of Euripides*, 1913 (tr); *Euripides and His Age*, 1913 (h); *Hamlet and Orestes, a Study in Traditional Types*, 1914 (c); *The Alcestis of Euripides*, 1915 (tr); *Religio Grammatici*, 1918 (Pres. Address, Classical Assoc.); *Aristophanes and the War Party*, 1919 (Am. ed. *Our Great War and the Great War of "The Ancient Greeks"*) (e); *Satanism and the World Order*, 1920 (e); *The Agamemnon of Aeschylus*, 1920 (tr); *The Choëphoroe of Aeschylus*, 1920 (tr); *Essays and Addresses*, 1921 (Am. ed. *Tradition and Progress*) (e); *The Eumenides of Aeschylus*, 1925 (tr); *The Classical Tradition in Poetry*, 1927 (e); *The Oresteia* [of Aeschylus], 1928 (tr); *The Suppliant Women* [of Aeschylus], 1930 (tr); *Prometheus Bound* [of Aeschylus], 1931 (tr); *Aristophanes, a Study*, 1933 (c); *Then and Now*, 1935 (e); *Liberality and Civilization*, 1938 (e); *Stoic, Christian and Humanist*, 1940 (e); *Aeschylus, the Creator of Tragedy*, 1940 (c); *David Samuel Margoliouth*, 1942 (b); *A Conversation with Bryce*, 1944 (c); *Myths and Ethics*, 1944 (e); *Greek Studies*, 1946 (c); *The World of Learning*, 1947 (e); *Andrew Lang: The Poet*, 1948 (c); *Hellenism and the Modern World*, 1953 (e); *Collected Plays of Euripides*, 1955 (tr); *The Meaning of Freedom*, 1957 (e); *An Unfinished Autobiography*, ed. J. Smith, 1960 (a); *Humanist Essays* [sel. from *Essays and Addresses*, 1921 and *Stoic, Christian, and Humanist*, 1940], 1965 (e)

*repr. 1946

See: Essays in Honour of Gilbert Murray, eds. J.A.K.T. [J. A. K. Thomson] and A.J.T. [A. J. Toynbee], 1936; *Greek Poetry, Essays to be Presented to Professor Gilbert Murray on his Seventieth Birthday*, 1936

JOHN MIDDLETON MURRY
1889-1957

Fyodor Dostoevsky, 1916 (c); (with S. S. Koteliansky) *Pages from the Journal of an Author, Fyodor Dostoevsky*, 1916 (tr); *Still Life*, 1916 (n); *The Evolution*

of an Intellectual, 1916 (a); The Critic
in Judgment, or Belshazzar of Barons
Court, 1919 (c); Aspects of Literature,
1920 (c); Cinnamon and Angelica, 1920
(d); Poems, 1916-1920, 1921 (p); Countries of the Mind, 1922 (c); The
Problem of Style, 1922 (c); The Things
We Are, 1922 (n); Pencillings, 1923 (e);
(with S. S. Koteliansky) Dostoevsky,
Letters and Reminiscences, 1923 (tr);
The Voyage, 1924 (n); Discoveries, 1924
(c); To the Unknown God, 1924 (e);
Wrap Me Up in My Aubusson Carpet,
1924 (e); Keats and Shakespeare, 1925
(c); The Life of Jesus, 1926 (Am. ed.
Jesus, Man of Genius) (b); Things to
Come (seq. to The Unknown God), 1928
(e); God, 1929 (e); D. H. Lawrence,
1930 (c); Studies in Keats, 1930 (c); Son
of Woman, The Story of D. H. Lawrence, 1931 (b); Countries of the Mind,
Sec. Series, 1931 (c); The Fallacy of
Economics, 1932 (e); The Necessity of
Communism, 1932 (e); (with Ruth E.
Mantz) The Life of Katherine Mansfield, 1935 (b); Reminiscences of D. H.
Lawrence, 1933 (r,c); William Blake,
1933 (b); Between Two Worlds, 1935
(a); Shakespeare, 1936 (c); The Necessity of Pacifism, 1937 (e); The Pledge
of Peace, 1938 (e); Heaven and Earth,
1938 (e); The Defence of Democracy,
1939 (e); The Price of Leadership, 1939
(e); Studies in Keats, New and Old,
1939 (c); The Betrayal of Christ by the
Churches, 1940 (e); Adam and Eve, 1944
(e); The Challenge of Schweitzer, 1948
(e); Looking Before and After, 1948 (e);
The Free Society, 1948 (e); Katherine
Mansfield and Other Literary Portraits,
1949 (r,c); The Mystery of Keats, 1949
(c); John Clare and Other Studies, 1950
(c); The Conquest of Death [Benjamin
Constant's Adolphe, with commentary],
1951 (tr); Community Farm, 1952 (a);
Jonathan Swift, 1954 (b,c); Swift, 1955
(c); Keats, 1955 (c); Unprofessional
Essays, 1956 (c); Love, Freedom and
Society [on D. H. Lawrence, Schweitzer,
etc.], 1957 (e); Select Criticism, 1916-
1957, chosen Richard Rees, 1960 (c)

Philip Mairet, John Middleton Murry,
1956

L. H. MYERS
1881-1944

Arvat, A Dramatic Poem, 1908 (pd);
The Orissers, 1922 (n); The Clio,
1925 (n); The Near and the Far, 1929
(n); Prince Jali (seq. to preceding), 1931
(n); The Root and the Flower [the two
preceding novels and Rajah Amar], 1935
(n); Strange Glory, 1936 (n); The Pool
of Vishnu, 1940 (n); The Near and the
Far [preceding title with The Root and
the Flower], 1943 (n)

G. H. Bantock, L. H. Myers: A Critical
Study, 1956

HENRY NEWBOLT
1862-1938

Taken from the Enemy, 1892 (n); Mor-
dred, 1895 (pd); Admirals All, 1897 (p);
The Island Race, 1898 (p); The Sailing
of the Long-Ships, 1902 (p); The Year
of Trafalgar, 1905 (h); The Old
Country, 1906 (n); Clifton Chapel, 1908
(p); Songs of Memory and Hope, 1909
(p); The New June, 1909 (n); Collected
Poems, 1897-1907, 1910; The Twymans,
1911 (n); Poems: New and Old, 1912 (p);
Drake's Drum, 1914 (p); Aladore, 1914
(n); The King's Highway, 1915 (p); A
New Study of English Poetry, 1917 (c);
St. George's Day, 1918 (p); The Book
of the Long Trail, 1919 (e); Poetry and
Time, 1919 (c); A Naval History of the
War, 1914-18, 1920 (h); The Book of
Good Hunting, 1920 (e); Studies Green
and Gray, 1926 (e); A Child is Born,
1931 (p); My World As In My Time,
1862-1932, 1932 (a); Selected Poems,
1940 (p); The Later Life and Letters of
Sir Henry Newbolt, ed. Margaret Newbolt, 1942 (b)

See Coulson Kernahan, Six Famous
Living Poets, 1922

P. H. NEWBY
1918-

A Journey to the Interior, 1945 (n);
Agents and Witnesses, 1947 (n);
Mariner Dances, 1948 (n); The Snow
Pasture, 1949 (n); The Loot Runners,
1949 (s); Maria Edgeworth, 1950 (c);
The Young May Moon, 1950 (n); The
Novel, 1945-50, 1951 (c); A Season in
England, 1951 (n); A Step to Silence,
1952 (n); The Retreat, 1953 (n); The
Picnic at Sakkara, 1955 (n); Revolution
and Roses, 1957 (n); Ten Miles from
Anywhere, 1958 (s); The Guest and His

Going, 1959 (n); *The Barbary Light,* 1962 (n); *One of the Founders,* 1965 (n)

See Frederick R. Karl, *A Reader's Guide to the Contemporary English Novel,* 1962

BEVERLEY NICHOLS
1899-

Prelude, 1920 (n); *Patchwork,* 1921 (n); *Self,* 1922 (n); *Twenty-Five,* 1926 (a); *Crazy Pavements,* 1927 (n); *Are They the Same at Home?,* 1927 (e); *The Star-Spangled Manner,* 1928 (a); *Women and Children Last,* 1931 (e); *For Adults Only,* 1932 (e); *Down the Garden Path,* 1932 (e); *Evensong,* 1932 (n); (with Edward Knoblock) *Evensong,* 1933 (d); *A Thatched Roof,* 1933 (e); *Cry Havoc!,* 1933 (e); *Failures,* 1933 (d); *A Village in a Valley,* 1934 (e); *Mesmer,* 1935 (d); *The Fool Hath Said,* 1936 (e); *No Place Like Home,* 1936 (e); *News of England,* 1938 (e); *Green Grows the City,* 1939 (e); *Revue,* 1939 (n); *Men do Not Weep,* 1941 (e); *Poems,* ed. J. W. Mackail, 1943; *Verdict on India,* 1944 (e); *All I Could Never Be,* 1949 (m); *Shadow of the Vine,* 1949 (d); *Uncle Samson,* 1950 (e); *Merry Hall,* 1951 (e); *A Pilgrim's Progress,* 1952 (e); *Laughter on the Stairs,* 1953 (e); *No Man's Street,* 1954 (n); *The Moonflower,* 1955 (Am. ed. *The Moonflower Murder*) (n); *Death to Slow Music,* 1956 (n); *The Rich Die Hard,* 1957 (n); *The Sweet and Twenties,* 1958 (h); *Murder by Request,* 1960 (n); *Forty Favourite Flowers,* 1965 (e); *A Case of Human Bondage,* [on W. S. Maugham], 1966 (r); *Powers That Be,* 1966 (e)

ROBERT NICHOLS
1893-1944

Invocation, War Poems and Others, 1915 (p); *Ardours and Endurances,* 1917 (p); *The Budded Branch,* 1918 (p); *Aurelia,* 1920 (p); *The Smile of the Sphinx,* 1920 (s); *A Year's Grain,* 1921 (p); *Guilty Souls,* 1921 (d); *Fantastica,* 1923 (s); (with Norah Nichols) *Winter Berries,* 1924 (p); (with A. Mujamori) *Masterpieces of Chikamatsu,* 1926 (tr); (with Jim Tully) *Twenty Below,* 1927 (d); *Under the Yew, or, The Gambler Transformed,* 1928 (n); *Epic Wind,* 1928 (p); (with Maurice Browne) *Wings Over*

Europe, 1929 (d); I. S. Turgenev, *Hamlet and Don Quixote,* 1930 (tr); *Fisbo, or, The Looking-Glass Loaned,* 1934 (p)

See John Gawsworth, *Ten Contemporaries,* 1932 and Sherard Vines, *Movements in Modern English Poetry and Prose,* 1927

NORMAN NICHOLSON
1914-

Men and Literature, 1943 (e); *The Fire of the Lord,* 1944 (n); *Five Rivers,* 1944 (p); *The Old Men of the Mountains,* 1946 (pd); *The Green Shore,* 1947 (n); *Rock Face,* 1948 (p); *Cumberland and Westmorland,* 1949 (t); *H. G. Wells,* 1950 (rev. enlgd. 1957) (b); *William Cowper,* 1951 (b); *The Pot Geranium,* 1954 (p); *The Lakers,* 1955 (e); *A Match for the Devil,* 1955 (pd); *Provincial Pleasures,* 1959 (e); *Birth by Drowning,* 1960 (pd); *Selected Poems,* 1966 (p)

See Derek Stanford, *The Freedom of Poetry,* 1947

HAROLD NICOLSON
1886-

Sweet Waters, 1921 (n); *Paul Verlaine,* 1921 (b); *Tennyson,* 1923 (repr. 1962) (b); *Byron, The Last Journey,* 1924 (b); *Swinburne,* 1926 (b); *The Development of English Biography,* 1927 (e); *Some People,* 1927 (repr. 1951) (b); *Sir Arthur Nicolson, Bart.* (Am. ed. *Portrait of a Diplomatist*), 1930 (b); *Swinburne and Baudelaire,* 1930 (c); *People and Things,* 1931 (e); *The New Spirit in Literature,* 1931 (c); *Public Faces,* 1932 (n); *Peacemaking, 1919,* 1933 (e); *Curzon, The Last Phase, 1919-1925,* 1934 (b); *Dwight Morrow,* 1935 (b); *Politics in the Train,* 1936 (e); *Helen's Tower,* 1937 (b); *The Meaning of Prestige,* 1937 (e); *The Painted Bed,* 1937 (n); *Small Talk,* 1938 (e); *Diplomacy,* 1939 (repr. 1950) (e); *Marginal Comment,* 1939 (e); *The Poetry of Byron,* 1943 (c); *Sweden and the New Europe,* 1943 (e); *The Desire to Please,* 1943 (b); *Friday Mornings, 1941-1944,* 1944 (e); *The Congress of Vienna,* 1946 (repr. 1961) (h); *The English Sense of Humour,* 1946 (e); *Tennyson's Two Brothers,* 1947 (b); *Voyage to Wonderland,* 1947 (e); *Benjamin Constant,* 1949 (b); *Com-*

Hand of Kornelius Voyt, 1939 (n); *The Italian Chest*, 1939 (s); *Cockcrow, or Anybody's England*, 1940 (n); *The Story of Ragged Robyn*, 1945 (n); *Poor Man's Tapestry*, 1946 (n); *Arras of Youth*, 1949 (n); *A Penny for the Harp*, 1952 (n); *Bells Rung Backwards* (5 stories from *Collected Ghost Stories*), 1953 (s); *A Shilling to Spend*, 1965 (unfinished n)

See John Gawsworth, *Ten Contemporaries*, Sec. Series, 1933

GEORGE ORWELL
1903-1950

Down and Out in Paris and London, 1933 (many repr.) (a); *Burmese Days*, 1934 (n); *A Clergyman's Daughter*, 1935 (n); *Keep the Aspidistra Flying*, 1936 (repr. 1954) (n); *The Road to Wigan Pier*, 1937 (e); **Homage to Catalonia*, 1938 (e); *Coming Up for Air*, 1939 (n); *Inside the Whale*, 1940 (c); *The Lion and the Unicorn: Socialism and the English Genius*, 1941 (e); *Animal Farm. A Fairy Story*, 1945 (many repr.) (n); *Critical Essays* (Am. ed. *Dickens, Dali and Others*), 1946 (c); *The English People*, 1947 (e); *Nineteen Eighty-Four*, 1949 (many repr.) (n); *Shooting an Elephant*, 1950 (e); *England, Your England* (Am. ed. *Such, Such Were the Joys*), 1953 (e); *The Orwell Reader: Fiction, Essays, and Reportage*, introd. Richard Rovere, 1956; *Selected Essays*, 1957 (e); *Collected Essays*, 1961

**ed. Lionel Trilling, 1952

John Atkins, *George Orwell: A Literary and Biographical Study* [1954], 1965; Edward Morley Thomas, *George Orwell*, 1965

JOHN OSBORNE
1929-

Look Back In Anger, 1957 (d); *The Entertainer*, 1957 (d); (with Anthony Creighton) *Epitaph for George Dillon*, 1958 (d); *The World of Paul Slickey*, 1959 (musical comedy); *Luther*, 1961 (d); *A Subject of Scandal and Concern*, 1961 (e); *Plays for England: The Blood of the Bambergs and Under Plain Cover*, 1963 (2d); Filmscript for Fielding's *Tom Jones*, 1964; *Inadmissible Evidence*, 1965

(d); *A Patriot for Me*, 1966 (d); *A Bond Honoured* (tr. from Lope de Vega), 1966 (d)

See John Russell Taylor, *Anger and After* (Am. ed. *The Angry Theatre*), 1962

WILFRED OWEN
1893-1918

Poems, 1920 (p); *The Poems of Wilfred Owen*, with notices of his life and work by Edmund Blunden, 1931; *The Collected Poems*, ed. C. Day Lewis, 1963; *Poems of Wilfred Owen*, with memoir and notes Edmund Blunden, 1966 (p)

Note: Only four poems were published during his lifetime, and these were in periodicals; seven were included in *Wheels: Fourth Cycle*, 1919, ed. Edith Sitwell.

Dennis S. R. Welland, *Wilfred Owen, A Critical Study*, 1960; Harold Owen, *Journey from Obscurity: Wilfred Owen 1893-1918* (Memoirs of the Owen family, I, *Childhood*, 1963; II, *Youth*, 1964; III, *War*, 1965); William White, *Wilfred Owen (1893-1918): A Bibliography*, 1966 (No. 1 of Serif Series in Bibliography)

STEPHEN PHILLIPS
1868-1915

Orestes, 1884 (p); (with others) *Primavera. Poems by Four Authors*, 1890 (p); *Eremus*, 1894 (p); *Christ in Hades*, 1896 (repr. 1917) (p); *Poems*, 1898 (p); *Paolo and Francesca*, 1900 (repr. 1952) (pd); *Marpessa*, 1900 (p); *Herod*, 1901 (pd); *Ulysses*, 1902 (pd); *The Sin of David*, 1904 (pd); *Nero*, 1906 (pd); *Faust*, freely adapted from Goethe by S. P. and J. C. Carr, 1908; *New Poems*, 1908 (p); *Pietro of Siena*, 1910 (pd); *The New Inferno*, 1910 (p); *The King*, 1912 (pd); *Lyrics and Dramas*, 1913; *Armageddon*, 1915 (d); *Panama*, 1915 (p); *Harold*, 1927 (d)

See William Lyon Phelps, *The Twentieth Century Theater*, 1918

EDEN PHILLPOTTS
1862-1960

Selective Bibliography

The entries for Phillpotts occupy eight

double-column pages in the British Museum Catalogue of printed books. His first novel was published in 1891, and when he hit his stride, from 1938 to 1958, he published from two to five novels a year. Some of the novels may be classified as industrial novels (e.g. *The Spinners,* 1918); some, among the best known, as Dartmoor novels. Besides these, he published plays, fairy stories, mystery stories (e.g., *Bred in the Bones,* 1932 [Book of Avis. I]), "human boy" stories (e.g., *The Human Boy,* 1899, *The Human Boy Again,* 1908, *The Complete Human Boy,* 1930), poems, short stories, and essays. Included in the following list are samples of Phillpotts' enormous production, with emphasis on the regional (Dartmoor) writings.

My Adventure in the Flying Scotsman, 1888 (s); *The End of a Life,* 1891 (n); *In Sugar-Cane Land,* 1893 (e); *Down Dartmoor Way,* 1895 (s); *My Laughing Philosopher,* 1896 (e); *Children of the Mist,* 1898 (n); *Sons of the Morning,* 1900 (n); *The River,* 1902 (n); *My Devon Year,* 1903 (e); *The Secret Woman,* 1905 (n; dramatized 1912, rev. ed. of play 1935); (with Arnold Bennett) *Sinews of War,* 1906 (Am. ed. *Doubloons*) (n); *My Garden,* 1906 (e); *The Portreeve,* 1906 (n); *The Virgin in Judgement,* 1907 (n); *The Whirlwind,* 1907 (n); (with Arnold Bennett) *The Statue,* 1908 (n); *The Mother,* 1908 (Am. ed. *The Mother of the Man*) (n; dramatized 1913); *The Three Brothers,* 1909 (n); *The Thief of Virtue,* 1910 (n); *Dance of the Months,* 1911 (e); *The Beacon,* 1911 (n); *Demeter's Daughter,* 1911 (n); *The Forest on the Hill,* 1912 (n); *Widecombe Fair,* 1913 (repr. 1947) (n); *My Shrubs,* 1915 (e); *Brunel's Tower,* 1915 (n); *The Farmer's Wife,* 1916 (d); *A Shadow Passes,* 1918 (e,p); *Miser's Money,* 1920 (n); *Orphan Dinah,* 1920 (n); *A West Country Pilgrimage,* 1920 (t); *The Bronze Venus,* 1921 (n); *Cherrystones,* 1923 (p); *Children of Men,* 1923 (n); *Thoughts in Prose and Verse,* 1924; *A Harvesting,* 1924 (p); *Brother Man,* 1926 (p); (with Adelaide Eden Phillpotts) *Yellow Sands,* 1926 (d); *Selected Poems,* 1926 (p); *The Jury,* 1927 (n); *The Widecombe Edition of the Dartmoor Novels,* 20 vols., 1927-28; *Brother Beast,*

1928 (p); *Brother Man,* 1928 (s); *Fun of the Fair,* 1928 (s); *A West Country Sketch Book,* 1928 (sk); *Eden Phillpotts: Selected Tales,* 1929 (s); *Essays in Little,* 1931 (e); *West Country Plays* (*Buy a Broom, A Cup of Happiness,* (with Adelaide Eden Phillpotts) *The Good Old Days*), 1933 (3d); *Dartmoor Omnibus* (*Orphan Dinah, The Three Brothers, Children of Men, The Whirlwind*), 1933 (n); *A Year with Bisshe-Bantam,* 1934 (e); *A Dartmoor Village,* 1937 (p); *Fall of the House of Heron,* 1948 (n); *The Enchanted Wood,* 1948 (p); *There Was An Old Man,* 1958 (n)

Percival Hinton, *Eden Phillpotts: A Bibliography of First Editions,* 1931; Waveney Girvan, ed., *Eden Phillpotts, An Assessment and a Tribute,* 1953 [no bibliog.]

ARTHUR WING PINERO
1855-1934

Mayfair, 1885 (an adaptation of Sardou's *Maison neuve*) (d); *The Profligate,* 1887 (d); *The Cabinet Minister,* 1889 (d); *Hester's Mystery,* 1890 (d); *Lady Bountiful,* 1891 (d); *The Times,* 1891 (d); *The Hobby-Horse,* 1892 (d); *The Magistrate,* 1892 (d); *Dandy Dick,* 1893 (d); *Sweet Lavender,* 1893 (d); *The Schoolmistress,* 1894 (d); *The Second Mrs. Tanqueray,* 1894 (d); *The Weaker Sex,* 1894 (d); *The Amazons,* 1895 (d); *The Benefit of the Doubt,* 1895 (d); *The Notorious Mrs. Ebbsmith,* 1895 (d); *The Princess and the Butterfly,* 1896 (d); (with others) *The Beauty Stone,* 1898 (d); *Trelawny of the "Wells",* 1898 (d); *The Gay Lord Quex,* 1899 (d); *The Money Spinner,* 1900 (d); *Iris,* 1901 (d); *Letty,* 1903 (d); *Robert Louis Stevenson, the Dramatist, a Lecture,* 1903 (repub. 1914); *A Wife Without a Smile,* 1904 (d); *His House in Order,* 1905 (d); *In Chancery,* 1905 (d); *The Rocket,* 1905 (d); *The Squire,* 1905 (d); *The Thunderbolt,* 1907-8 (d); *Mid-Channel,* 1908-9 (d); *Preserving Mr. Panmure,* 1910 (d); *The "Mind the Paint" Girl,* 1912 (d); *The Widow of Wasdale Head,* 1912 (d); *Playgoers,* 1913 (d); *The Big Drum,* 1915 (d); *Mr. Livermore's Dream,* 1916 (d); *The Freaks,* 1917 (d); *The Social Plays of Arthur Wing Pinero,* ed. Clayton Hamil-

ton, 1917-1919; *Quick Work*, 1918 (d);
The Enchanted Cottage, 1921 (d); *A
Seat in the Park*, 1922 (d); *Dr. Harmer's
Holidays*, 1924 (d); *A Private Room*,
1926 (d); *Child Man*, 1928 (d)

Henry H. Fyfe, *Sir Arthur Pinero's Plays
and Players*, 1930

HAROLD PINTER
1930-

The Dumbwaiter, 1960 (d); *The Room*,
1960 (d); **The Birthday Party*, 1960 (d);
The Caretaker, 1960 (d); *A Slight Ache*,
1961 (d); *Three Plays*, 1962; *The Collection* and *The Lover*, 1963 (2d); *A
Night Out*, 1963 (d); *The Homecoming*,
1965 (d)
*rev. 1965

RUTH PITTER
1897-

First Poems, 1920 (p); *First and Second
Poems*, 1927 (p); *Persephone in Hades*,
1931 (p); *A Mad Lady's Garland*, 1934
(p); *A Trophy of Arms*, 1936 (p); *The
Spirit Watches*, 1939 (p); *The Rude
Potato*, 1941 (p); *The Bridge*, 1945 (p);
On Cats, 1947 (p); *Urania* [Poems from
earlier vols.], 1950 (p); *The Ermine*,
1953 (p); *Still by Choice*, 1966 (p)

WILLIAM PLOMER
1903-

*Turbott Wolfe, 1925 (n); *Notes for
Poems*, 1927 (p); *I Speak of Africa*, 1927
(7s, 3n, 2 plays for puppets); *The Family
Tree*, 1929 (p); *Paper Houses*, 1929 (n);
Sado, 1931 (Am. ed. *They Never Come
Back*) (n); *The Case is Altered*, 1932 (n);
The Fivefold Screen, 1932 (p); *The
Child of Queen Victoria*, 1933 (s); *Cecil
Rhodes*, 1933 (b); *The Invaders*, 1934
(n); *Ali, the Lion* [Ali of Tebeleni,
pasha of Jannina, 1741-1822], 1936 (b);
Visiting the Caves, 1936 (p); *Selected
Poems*, 1940 (p); *Double Lives*, 1943
(a); *The Dorking Thigh*, 1945 (p);
[William D'Arfey, pseud.] *Curious Re-
lations*, 1945 (s); *Four Countries*, 1949
(s); *Museum Pieces*, 1952 (n); *Gloriana*,
1953 (opera libretto); *A Shot in the
Park*, 1955 (p); *Borderline Ballads*, 1955
(p); *At Home*, 1958 (r); *Collected Poems*,
1960; *Taste and Remember*, 1966 (p)
*repr. 1965

STEPHEN POTTER
1900-

The Young Man, 1929 (n); *D. H. Lawrence: a First Study*, 1930 (s); *Coleridge and S.T.C.*, 1935 (c); *The Muse
in Chains: a Study in Education*, 1937
(e); *The Theory and Practice of Gamesmanship*, 1947 (e); *Some Notes on Lifemanship*, 1950 (e); *One-upmanship*, 1952
(e); *Potter on America*, 1956 (e); *The
Magic Number: The Story of "57"*, 1959
(h); *Steps to Immaturity*, 1959 (r); *Super-
manship*, 1959 (e); *Three-Upmanship*
[*Gamesmanship, Lifemanship, One-
Upmanship*], 1962 (e); *Anti-Woo* (*Gam-
bits for Young Lovers, The First Lifemanship Guide*), 1965 (e)

ANTHONY POWELL
1905-

Afternoon Men, 1931 (n); *Venusberg*,
1932 (n); *From a View to a Death*, 1933
(n); *Agents and Patients*, 1936 (n);
What's Become of Waring, 1939 (n) ;
John Aubrey and His Friends, 1948 (b);
A Dance to the Music of Time, consist-
ing of the following novels: *A Question
of Upbringing*, 1951; *A Buyer's
Market*, 1952; *The Acceptance World*,
1955; *At Lady Molly's*, 1957; *Casanova's
Chinese Restaurant*, 1960; *The Kindly
Ones*, 1962; *The Valley of Bones*, 1964;
The Soldier's Art, 1966

Bernard Bergonzi, *Anthony Powell* (in
Paul Bloomfield, *L. P. Hartley and
Anthony Powell*), 1962

JOHN COWPER POWYS
1872-1963

Odes, 1896 (p); *Poems*, 1899; *Twelve
Lectures on Carlyle, Ruskin, Tennyson*,
1900; *Six Lectures on Selected Plays of
Shakespeare*, 1901; *Visions and Revi-
sions, a Book of Literary Devotions*,
1915 (rev. 1955) (c); *Wood and Stone*,
1915 (n); *Rodmoor*, 1916 (n); *Con-
fessions of Two Brothers, John Cowper
Powys, Llewelyn Powys*, 1916 (r); *One
Hundred Best Books*, with commentary,
1916 (c); *Suspended Judgments*, 1916
(e); *Wolf's-bane; Rhymes*, 1916 (p);
Mandragon, 1917 (p); *The Complex
Vision*, 1920 (a,e); *Samphire*, 1922 (p);
Psychoanalysis and Morality, 1923 (c);
The Religion of a Sceptic, 1925 (a);
Ducdame, 1925 (n); *The Mean-*

ing of Culture, 1929 (e); Wolf Solent, 1929 (n); The Owl, the Duck, and—Miss Rowe! Miss Rowe!, 1930 (s); (with Bertrand Russell) Debate! Is Modern Marriage a Failure?, 1930; In Defence of Sensuality, 1930 (e); Dorothy M. Richardson, 1931 (c); *A Glastonbury Romance, 1932 (repr. 1955) (n); A Philosophy of Solitude, 1933 (e); Weymouth Sands, 1934 (Am. ed.; Eng. ed. Jobber Skald, 1935; rev. 1963) (n); Autobiography, 1934 (a); The Art of Happiness, 1935 (e) [text of Am. ed. differs]; *Maiden Castle, 1936 (n); Morwyn, or The Vengeance of God, 1937 (n); The Enjoyment of Literature (also pub. as The Pleasures of Literature), 1938 (e); Owen Glendower, 1940 (n); Mortal Strife, 1941 (e); The Art of Growing Old, 1944 (e); Pair Dadeni, or, "The Cauldron of Rebirth," 1946 (e); Obstinate Cymric: Essays 1935-1947, 1947 (e); Dostoievsky, 1947 (c); Rabelais: His Life, The Story Told by Him, Selections Therefrom Newly Translated, and an Interpretation of His Genius and His Religion, 1948; Porius: A Romance of the Dark Ages, 1951 (n); The Inmates, 1952 (n); In Spite Of: A Philosophy for Everyman, 1953 (e); Atlantis, 1954 (n); The Brazen Head, 1956 (n); Lucifer, 1956 (p); Still the Joy of It, 1956 (r); Up and Out, 1957 (s); The Letters of J. C. Powys to Louis Wilkinson, 1935-56, ed. L. Wilkinson, 1958; Homer and the Aether (paraphrase of The Iliad), 1959; All or Nothing, 1960 (n); A Selection from his Poems, ed. Kenneth Hopkins, 1964 (p)

*repr. 1966

Note. Macdonald has 10 titles in print.

L. E. Siberell, A Bibliography of the First Editions of John Cowper Powys, 1934; George Wilson Knight, Saturnian Quest: A Study of the Prose Works of John Cowper Powys, 1965; H. P. Collins, John Cowper Powys: Old Earth Man, 1966 [no bibliog.]

T. F. POWYS
1875-1953

An Interpretation of Genesis, 1908 (repr. 1929) (e); The Soliloquy of a Hermit, 1916 (Eng. ed. as Soliloquies of a Hermit, 1918) (e); Black Byrony, 1923 (n); The Left Leg, 1923 (s); Mark Only,

1924 (n); Mr. Tasker's Gods, 1925 (n); Mockery Gap, 1925 (n); Innocent Birds, 1926 (n); Feed My Swine, 1926 (s); A Strong Girl and The Bride, 1926 (2s); A Stubborn Tree, 1926 (s); What Lack I Yet?, 1926 (s); The Rival Pastors, 1926 (s); Mr. Weston's Good Wine, 1927 (n); The Dewpond, 1928 (s); The House with the Echo, 1928 (s); Fables, 1929 (repr. as No Painted Plumage, 1934) (s); Christ in the Cupboard, 1930 (s); The Key of the Field, 1930 (s); Uncle Dottery, 1930 (s); Uriah on the Hill, 1930 (s); The White Paternoster, 1930 (s); Kindness in a Corner, 1930 (n); Unclay, 1931 (n); The Only Penitent, 1931 (s); When Thou Wast Naked, 1931 (s); The Tithe Barn and The Dove and the Eagle, 1932 (2s); The Two Thieves, 1932 (3s); Captain Patch, 1935 (s); Coat Green, or The Better Gift, 1937 (s); Bottle's Path, 1946 (s); God's Eyes A-Twinkle, sel. C. Prentice, 1947 (s); Rosie Plum, ill. John Ward, 1966 (s)

Henry Coombes, T. F. Powys, 1960; Reginald C. Churchill, The Powys Brothers, 1962

J. B. PRIESTLEY
1894-

[N.B. Most of Priestley's works have been kept in print so reprints are not noted here.]

The Chapman of Rhymes, 1918 (p); Brief Diversions, Being Tales, Travesties and Epigrams, 1922; Papers from Lilliput, 1922 (e,p); I For One, 1923 (e); Figures in Modern Literature, 1924 (c); The English Comic Characters, 1925 (c); George Meredith, 1926 (b); Talking, 1926 (e); The English Novel, 1927 (c); Open House, 1927 (e); Adam in Moonshine, 1927 (n); Benighted, 1927 (Am. ed. The Old Dark House) (n); Thomas Love Peacock, 1927 (b); Apes and Angels, 1928 (e); Too Many People, 1928 (e); (with Hugh Walpole) Farthing Hall, 1929 (n); The Good Companions, 1929 (n); English Humour, 1929 (e); The Balconinny, 1929 (e); The Town Major of Miraucourt, 1930 (e); Angel Pavement, 1930 (n); The Works of J. B. Priestley, 1931; Dangerous Corner, 1932 (d); Faraway, 1932 (n); Self-Selected Essays, 1932 (e); I'll Tell You Everything, A Frolic, 1933 (n); *Albert Goes Through*, 1933 (n); *Wonder Hero*, 1933 (n); *The Roundabout*, 1933 (d); (with Gerald Bullett) *English Journey, Autumn, 1933*, 1934 (t); *Eden End*, 1934 (d); *Laburnum Grove*, 1934 (d); *Four-in-Hand*, 1934 (misc.); *Cornelius*, 1935 (d); *Duet in Floodlight*, 1935 (d); (with Knoblauch) *The Good Companions*, 1935 (d from novel); *Three Plays and a Preface*, 1935 (3d); (with George Billam) *Spring Tide*, 1936 (d); *Bees on the Boat Deck*, 1936 (d); *They Walk in the City*, 1936 (n); *Time and the Conways*, 1937 (d); *I Have Been Here Before*, 1937 (d); *Two Time Plays* (the two preceding plays), 1937 (2d); *Midnight on the Desert: A Chapter of Autobiography*, 1937 (a); *People at Sea*, 1937 (d); *The Doomsday Men*, 1938 (n); *When We Are Married*, 1938 (d); *Mystery at Greenfingers*, 1938 (d); *Rain upon Godshill: A Further Chapter of Autobiography*, 1939 (a); *Johnson Over Jordan . . . And All About It*, 1939 (d,e); *Let the People Sing*, 1939 (n); *Postscripts*, 1940 (e); *Out of the People*, 1941 (p); *Three Plays*, 1943 (3d); *Daylight on Saturday*, 1943 (n); *They Came to a City*, 1944 (d); *Four Plays*, 1944 (4d); *Three Men in New Suits*, 1945 (n); *Three Comedies*, 1945 (3d); *How Are They at Home*, 1945 (d); *The Secret Dream: an Essay on Britain, America, and Russia*, 1946 (e); *Bright Day*, 1946 (d); *Russian Journey*, 1946 (t); *An Inspector Calls*, 1947 (d); *Jenny Villers*, 1947 (n); *The Long Mirror*, 1947 (d); *The Plays of J. B. Priestley*, 3 vols., 1948; *The Linden Tree*, 1948 (d); *The Golden Fleece*, 1948 (d); *The High Toby: A Play for the Toy Theatre*, 1948 (d); *Ever Since Paradise*, 1949 (d); *Home is Tomorrow*, 1949 (d); *Delight*, 1949 (a,e); *Bright Shadow*, 1950 (d); *Going Up*, 1950 (s); *Summer Day's Dream*, 1950 (d); *The Priestley Companion: A Selection*, 1951 (misc.); *Festival at Farbridge*, 1951 (n); *Private Rooms*, 1953 (d); *Mother's Day*, 1953 (d); *The Other Place*, 1953 (e); *Try It Again*, 1953 (d); *A Glass of Bitter*, 1954 (d); *Low Notes on a High Level*, 1954 (n); *The Magicians*, 1954 (n); *Treasure on Pelican*, 1954 (d); (with Jacquetta Hawkes) *Journey Down a Rainbow* [New Mexico and Texas], 1955 (t); *The Scandalous Affair of Mr. Kettle and Mrs. Moon*, 1956 (d); *All About Our-*selves*, ed. Eric Gillet, 1956 (e); *The Writer in a Changing Society*, 1956 (e); *The Art of the Dramatist*, 1957 (e); *Thoughts in the Wilderness*, 1957 (e); *Topside, or, The Future of England*, 1958 (e); *The Glass Cage*, 1958 (d); *The Story of Theatre*, 1959 (h); *William Hazlitt*, 1960 (b,c); *Literature and Western Man*, 1960 (e); *Saturn Over the Water*, 1961 (n); *Charles Dickens*, 1961 (b); *The Thirty-First of June, a Tale of True Love, Enterprise, and Progress in the Arthurian and Ad-Atomic Ages*, 1961 (s); *The Shapes of Sleep*, 1962 (n); *Margin Released*, 1962 (r); *Sir Michael and Sir George*, 1964 (n); *Man and Time*, 1964 (e); (with Iris Murdoch) *A Severed Head*, 1964 (dramatization of Murdoch's novel); *Lost Empires*, 1965 (n); *The Moment and Other Pieces*, 1966 (repr. e and lectures)

David Hughes, *J. B. Priestley, an Informal Study of His Work*, 1958; Gareth Lloyd Evans, *J. B. Priestley, the Dramatist*, 1964

F. T. PRINCE
1912-

Poems, 1938 (p); *The Italian Element in Milton's Verse*, 1954 (e); *Soldiers Bathing*, 1954 (p); *The Doors of Stone*, 1963 (p)

V. S. PRITCHETT
1900-

Marching Spain, 1928 (repr. 1933) (r); *Clare Drummer*, 1929 (n); *The Spanish Virgin*, 1930 (s); *Shirley Sanz*, 1932 (n); *Nothing Like Leather*, 1935 (n); *Dead Man Leading*, 1937 (n); *You Make Your Own Life*, 1938 (s); *In My Good Books*, 1942 (c); *It May Never Happen*, 1945 (s); *The Living Novel*, 1946 (rev. enlgd. 1964) (c); (with Elizabeth Bowen and Graham Greene) *Why Do I Write?*, 1948 (e); *Mr. Beluncle*, 1951 (n); *Books In General*, 1953 (c); *The Spanish Temper*, 1954 (t); *The Sailor; Sense of Humour*, 1956 (s); *Collected Stories*, 1956; *When My Girl Comes Home*, 1961 (s); *London Perceived*, 1962 (t); *The Key to My Heart*, 1963 (n); *Foreign Faces* (Am. ed. *The Offensive Traveller*), 1964 (t); *New York Proclaimed* (photographs by Evelyn Hofer), 1965 (t); *The Working Novelist*, 1965 (c)

JOHN PUDNEY
1909-

Spring Encounter, 1933 (p); Open the Sky, 1935 (p); And Lastly the Fireworks, 1935 (s); Jacobson's Ladder, 1938 (n); Uncle Arthur, 1939 (s); Dispersal Point and Other Air Poems, 1942 (p); The Green Grass Grew All Around, 1942 (s); South of Forty, 1943 (p); Beyond this Disregard, 1943 (p); Who Only England Know: Log of a War-Time Journey of Unintentional Discovery of Fellow-Countrymen, 1943 (a); Ten Summers: Poems 1933-1943, 1944 (p); Almanack of Hope: Sonnets, 1944 (p); Flight Above Cloud, 1944 (p); World Still There [Impressions of various parts of the world in wartime], 1945 (sk); Selected Poems, 1946 (p); It Breathed Down My Neck, 1946 (s); Low Life, 1947 (p); Estuary, 1947 (n); Commemorations, 1948 (p); The Europeans, Fourteen Tales of a Continent, 1948 (s); Shuffley Wanderers, 1948 (n); The Accomplice, 1950 (n); Hero of a Summer's Day, 1951 (n); Music on the South Bank: An Appreciation of the Royal Festival Hall, 1951 (e); His Majesty King George VI, A Study, 1952 (e); The Net, 1952 (n); A Ring for Luck, 1953 (n); Sixpenny Songs, 1953 (p); The Thomas Cook Story, 1953 (h); The Smallest Room [a history of lavatories], 1953 (h); Six Great Aviators (incl. Lindbergh, Saint-Exupéry), 1955 (b); Collected Poems (incl. bibliog.), 1957; Trespass in the Sun, 1957 (n); The Seven Skies: a Study of the BOAC and its Forerunners since 1919, 1959 (h); The Trampoline, 1959 (p); A Pride of Unicorns: Richard and David Atcherley of the RAF, 1960 (b); Thin Air, 1961 (n); The Camel Fighter, 1964 (e)

PETER QUENNELL
1905-

Masques & Poems, 1922 (p); Poems, 1926 (p); Inscription on a Fountain Head, 1929 (p); Baudelaire and the Symbolists, 1929 (repr. 1954) (c); Memoirs of the Comte de Gramont, 1930 (tr); The Phoenix-Kind, 1931 (n); A Superficial Journey Through Tokyo and Peking, 1932 (t); A Letter to Mrs. Virginia Woolf, 1932 (e); Sympathy, 1933 (s); Byron, 1934 (b); Byron: The Years of Fame, 1935 (repr. 1950) (b); Victorian Panorama, 1937 (h); Caroline of England, 1939 (b); (with George Paston, pseud.) "To Lord Byron." Feminine Profiles, Based upon Unpublished Letters, 1807-1824, 1939 (b); Byron in Italy, 1941 (b); Four Portraits [Boswell, Gibbon, Sterne, John Wilkes], 1945 (b); John Ruskin, 1949, (b); The Singular Preference, 1952 (e); Spring in Sicily, 1952 (t); Hogarth's Progress, 1955 (b); The Sign of the Fish, 1960 (e); Shakespeare, The Poet and his Background, 1964 (c)

ARTHUR QUILLER-COUCH
1863-1944

Athens, 1881 (p); Dead Man's Rock, 1887 (n); The Astonishing History of Troy Town, 1888 (Troy Town, 1928); The Splendid Spur, 1889 (n); The Blue Pavilions, 1891 (n); Noughts and Crosses, 1891 (s); The Warwickshire Avon, 1892 (t); "I Saw Three Ships", 1892 (s); Green Bays: Verses and Parodies, 1893 (enlgd. 1930) (p); The Delectable Duchy, 1893 (s); Fairy Tales Far and Near, Re-told by Q, 1895; Wandering Heath, 1895 (s); Adventures in Criticism, 1896 (c); Ia, 1896 (n); Poems and Ballads, 1896 (p); St. Ives, Being the Adventures of a French Prisoner in England by Robert Louis Stevenson (completed by A. T. Quiller-Couch), 1897 (n); The Ship of Stars, 1899 (n); Historical Tales from Shakespeare, 1899 (s); Old Fires and Profitable Ghosts, 1900 (s); The Laird's Luck, 1901 (s); The Westcotes, 1902 (n); The White Wolf, 1902 (s); Two Sides of the Face, 1903 (s); The Adventures of Harry Revel, 1903 (pub. as Harry Revel, 1931) (n); Hetty Wesley, 1903 (n); Fort Amity, 1904 (n); The Mayor of Troy, 1905 (n); Shining Ferry, 1905 (n); Shakespeare's Christmas, 1905 (s); Sir John Constantine, 1906 (n); From a Cornish Window, 1906 (e); Major Vigoureux, 1907 (n); Poison Island, 1907 (n); Merry-garden, 1907 (s); True Tilda, 1909 (n); Lady Good-for-nothing, a Man's Portrait of a Woman, 1910 (n); Corporal Sam, 1910 (s); The Sleeping Beauty and other Fairy Tales from the Old French Retold, 1910; The Roll Call of Honour, a New Book of Golden Deeds, 1911 (b); Brother Copas, 1911 (n); The Vigil of Venus, 1912 (p); Hocken and Hunken, a Tale of Troy, 1912 (n); In Powder & Crinoline, Old Fairy Tales Retold, 1913 (pub. as The Twelve Dancing Princesses, 1923); News From the Duchy, 1913 (s); Poetry, 1914 (c); Nicky-Nan, Reservist, 1915 (n); On the Art of Writing, 1916 (e); Mortallone and Aunt Trinidad, Tales of the Spanish Main, 1917 (s); Notes on Shakespeare's Workmanship, from Lectures, 1917; Memoir of Arthur John Butler, 1917 (m); Shakespeare's Workmanship, 1918 (c); Studies in Literature, 1918 (c); Foe-Farrell, 1918 (n); On the Art of Reading, 1920 (c); Selected Stories, 1921; Studies in Literature, Second Series, 1922 (c); Charles Dickens and Other Victorians, 1925 (c); Honorable Men (Livingston, Lincoln, Gordon, from The Roll Call of Honour), 1925 (b); The Age of Chaucer, 1926 (h); A Lecture on Lectures, 1927; Polperro Privateers, or, The Capture of the Burgomeister Van der Werf, 1927 (s); Victors of Peace: Florence Nightingale, Pasteur, Father Damien (previously pub. in The Roll Call of Honour), 1927 (b); The Duchy Edition of Tales and Romances by Q, 3 vols., 1928-29; Studies in Literature, Third Series, 1929 (c); Poems, 1929 (p); Paternity in Shakespeare, 1932 (Shakespeare lecture for Brit. Academy); The Poet as Citizen, 1934 (e); A Further Approach to Shakespeare, 1934 (c); Mystery Stories: Twenty Stories, 1937 (s); Cambridge Lectures, 1943 (selection); Shorter Stories, 1944 (selection); Memories and Opinions: an Unfinished Autobiography, ed. S. C. Roberts, 1945; Q. Anthology, 1948; (with Daphne du Maurier) Castle d'Or, 1962 (n)

Fred Brittain, Arthur Quiller-Couch: a Biographical Study of Q, 1948

KATHLEEN RAINE
1908-

Stone and Flower, Poems 1935-43, 1943 (p); Denis de Rougement, Talk of the Devil [La Part du Diable], 1945 (tr); Living in Time, 1946 (p); Balzac, Cousine Bette, 1948 (tr); The Pythoness, 1949 (p); William Blake, 1951 (c); Balzac, Lost Illusions, 1951 (tr); The Year One, 1951 (p); Selected Poems, 1952 (p); Coleridge, 1953 (c); The Col-

lected Potems, 1956; Blake and England, 1960 (Founder's Memorial Lecture, Girton College, Cambridge Univ.); The Hollow Hill, 1965 (p)

See G. S. Fraser, The Modern Writer and His World, rev. 1964

TERENCE RATTIGAN
1911-

French Without Tears, 1937 (d); After the Dance, 1939 (d); Flare Path, 1942 (d); While the Sun Shines, 1944 (d): Love in Idleness, 1945 (Am. ed. O Mistress Mine) (d); The Winslow Boy, 1946 (d); The Browning Version, 1949 (d); Harlequinade, 1949 (d); Playbill (the two preceding titles), 1949 (2d); Adventure Story, 1950 (d); Who Is Sylvia?, 1951 (d); The Deep Blue Sea, 1952 (d); Collected Plays, 2 vols., 1953; The Sleeping Prince, 1954 (d); Separate Tables (Table by the Window, Table Number Seven), 1954 (2d); Variation on a Theme, 1959 (d); Olivia, 1960 (d); Ross: A Dramatic Portrait, 1960 (d); Man and Boy, 1963 (d); Collected Plays, Vol. III, 1964

HERBERT READ
1893-

Songs of Chaos, 1915 (p); Naked Warriors, 1919 (p); Eclogues, 1919 (p); Mutations of the Phoenix, 1923 (p); In Retreat, 1925 (sk); English Stained Glass, 1926 (e); Reason and Romanticism, 1926 (c); Collected Poems, 1913-25, 1926; English Prose Style, 1928 (c); Phases of English Poetry, 1928 (c); The Sense of Glory, 1929 (c); Julien Benda and the New Humanism, 1930 (e); Ambush, 1930 (sk); Wordsworth, 1930 (c); The Meaning of Art (Am. ed. The Anatomy of Art), 1931 (c); The End of a War, 1931 (p); Form in Modern Poetry, 1932 (c); Art Now, 1933 (rev. enlgd. 1961) (e); The Innocent Eye, 1933 (a); Art and Industry, 1934 (c); Poems, 1914-34, 1935 (p); The Green Child, 1935 (n); In Defence of Shelley, 1936 (c); Art and Society, 1937 (e); *Collected Essays in Literary Criticism, 1938 (c); Poetry and Anarchism, 1938 (c); Annals of Innocence and Experience, 1940 (rev. 1946) (a); Thirty-Five Poems, 1940 (p); Education Through Art, 1943 (c); The

Politics of the Unpolitical, 1943 (e); *The Education of Free Men*, 1944 (e); *A World Within a War*, 1944 (p); *A Coat of Many Colours*, 1945 (e); *Collected Poem*, 1946; *The Grass Roots of Art*, 1947 (e); *Coleridge as Critic*, 1949 (c); *Education for Peace*, 1950 (e); *Contemporary British Art*, 1951 (c); *Byron*, 1951 (b,c); *The Philosophy of Modern Art*, 1952 (e); *Collected Poems*, 1953; *The True Voice of Feeling*, 1953 (c); *Anarchy and Order*, 1954 (e); *Icon and Idea*, 1955 (e); *Moon's Farm*, 1955 (p); *The Art of Sculpture*, 1956 (e); *The Tenth Muse*, 1957 (c); *A Concise History of Modern Painting*, 1959 (h); *Kandinsky*, 1959 (b); *The Parliament of Women*, 1960 (d); *Aristotle's Mother*, 1960 (d); *The Form of Things Unknown*, 1960 (e); (with Edward Dahlberg) *Truth is More Sacred*, 1961 (c); *A Letter to a Young Painter*, 1962 (e); *The Contrary Experience*, 1963 (a); *Selected Writings*, 1963 (p,c); *The Origins of Form in Art*, 1965 (e); *Henry Moore: A Study of His Life and Work*, 1965 (b,c); *Poetry and Experience*, 1966 (e); *Collected Poems, 1919-1946* (those already coll. and those uncoll. which Read wants to preserve), 1966

*repr. 1950, Am. ed. *The Nature of Literature*, 1956

Herbert Read: an Introduction to his Work by Various Hands, ed. Henry Treece, 1944; Francis Berry, *Herbert Read*, rev. 1961

FORREST REID
1876-1947

The Kingdom of Twilight, 1904 (n); *The Garden God*, 1905 (n); *The Bracknels*, 1911 (rev. as *Denis Bracknel*, 1947) (n); *Following Darkness*, 1912 (rev. as *Peter Waring*, 1937) (n); *The Gentle Lover*, 1913 (n); *W. B. Yeats*, 1915 (c); *At the Door of the Gate*, 1915 (n); *The Spring Song*, 1916 (n); *A Garden by the Sea*, 1918 (s); *Pirates of the Spring*, 1919 (n); *Pender Among the Residents*, 1922 (n); *Apostate*, 1926 (r); *Demophon*, 1927 (n); *Illustrators of the Sixties*, 1928 (c); *Walter de la Mare*, 1928 (c); *Uncle Stephen*, 1931 (n); *Brian Westby*, 1934 (n); *The Retreat*, 1936 (n); *Private Road*, 1940 (r); *Retrospective Adventures*,

1941 (e,s); *Notes and Impressions*, 1942 (e); *Poems from the Greek Anthology*, 1943 (tr); *Young Tom*, 1944 (n); *The Milk of Paradise*, 1946 (c)

Russell Burlingham, *Forrest Reid, a Portrait and a Study*, 1953

I. A. RICHARDS
1893-

(with C. K. Ogden and James Wood) *The Foundations of Aesthetics*, 1922 (e); (with C. K. Ogden) *The Meaning of Meaning, a Study of the Influence of Language upon Thought*, 1923 (e); *Principles of Literary Criticism*, 1924 (e); *Science and Poetry*, 1926 (enlgd 1935) (e); *Practical Criticism*, 1929 (c); *Mencius on the Mind*, 1932 (e); *Basic Rules of Reason*, 1933 (e); *Coleridge on Imagination*, 1934 (e); *The Philosophy of Rhetoric*, 1936 (e); *Interpretation in Teaching*, 1938 (c); *How to Read a Page*, 1943 (c); *Basic English and its Uses*, 1943 (e); *The Pocket Book of Basic English*, 1945; *The Wrath of Achilles; The Iliad of Homer*, 1951 (abgd.) (tr); *Speculative Instruments*, 1955 (e); *Goodbye Earth*, 1958 (p); *The Screens*, 1960 (p); *Tomorrow Morning, Faustus!*, 1962 (d)

W. H. N. Hotopf, *Language, Thought, and Comprehension, a Case Study of the Writings of I. A. Richards*, 1965; *See* Stanley Edgar Hyman, *The Armed Vision*, 1948

DOROTHY RICHARDSON
1872-1957

The Quakers, Past and Present, 1914 (e); *Pilgrimage*, consisting of the following novels: *Pointed Roofs*, 1915; *Backwater*, 1916; *Honeycomb*, 1917; *Tunnel*, 1919; *Interim*, 1919; *Deadlock*, 1921; *Revolving Lights*, 1923; *Trap*, 1925; *Oberland*, 1927; *Dawn's Left Hand*, 1931; *Clear Horizon*, 1935; *Dimple Hill*, 1938; *John Austen and the Inseparables*, 1930 (c)

J. C. Powys, *Dorothy Richardson*, 1931; Caesar Robert Blake, *Dorothy Richardson*, 1960; Gloria Glikin, "A Checklist of Writings by Dorothy Richardson," *English Literature in Transition*, Vol. VIII, No. 1 (1965)

EDGELL RICKWORD
1898-

Behind the Eyes, 1921 (p); *Rimbaud, the Boy and the Poet*, 1924 (b); *Invocations to Angels and The Happy New Year*, 1928 (p); *Love One Another*, 1929 (n); *Twittingpan and Some Others*, 1931 (p); Marcel Coulon, *Poet Under Saturn*, 1932 (tr); *Collected Poems*, 1947

ANNE RIDLER
1912-

Poems, 1939 (p); *The Nine Bright Shiners*, 1943 (p); *Cain*, 1943 (pd); *The Shadow Factory*, 1946 (pd); *Henry Bly*, 1950 (pd); *The Golden Bird*, 1951 (p); *The Trial of Thomas Cranmer*, 1956 (pd); *A Matter of Life and Death*, 1959 (p); *Who is My Neighbour? and How Bitter the Bread*, 1963 (2pd)

MICHAEL ROBERTS
1902-1949

These Our Matins, 1930 (p); *Newton and the Origin of Colours*, 1934 (e); *Critique of Poetry*, 1934 (c); *Poems*, 1936 (p); *The Modern Mind*, 1937 (e); *T. E. Hulme*, 1938 (b); *Orion Marches*, 1939 (p); *The Recovery of the West*, 1941 (e); *The Estate of Man*, ed. J. B. A. Smith, 1951 (e); *Collected Poems*, 1958

T. W. Eason and R. Hamilton, *A Portrait of Michael Roberts*, 1949

LENNOX ROBINSON
1886-1958

The Cross-Roads, 1910 (d); *Two Plays: Harvest, The Clancy Name*, 1911 (2d); *Patriots*, 1912 (d); *The Dreamers*, 1915 (d); *A Young Man from the South*, 1917 (repr. 1945) (n); *Dark Days* [life in Ireland], 1918 (sk); *The Lost Leader*, 1918 (repr. 1954) (d); *The Whiteheaded Boy*, 1920 (repr. 1925) (d); *Eight Short Stories*, 1920 (s); *Crabbed Youth and Age*, 1924 (d); *The Round Table*, 1924 (d); *The White Blackbird, Portrait*, 1926 (2d); *The Big House*, 1928 (d); *Plays*, 1928 (d); *Give a Dog—*, 1928 (d); *Ever the Twain*, 1930 (d); *The Far-Off Hills*, 1931 (d); *Bryan Cooper*, 1931 (b); *Is Life Worth Living?*, 1933 (rev. 1938) (d); *More Plays* (*All's Over, Then?* and *Church Street* [latter repr. 1955]), 1935 (2d); (with Tom Robinson and Nora Dorman) *Three Homes*, 1938 (r); *Killycreggs in Twilight and Other Plays*, 1939 (3d); *Curtain Up*, 1942 (a); *Towards an Appreciation of the Theatre*, 1945 (c); *Pictures in a Theatre: a Conversation Piece*, 1947 (r); *The Lucky Finger*, 1948 (d); *Palette and Plough* [Desmond O'Brien], 1948 (b); *Ireland's Abbey Theatre, 1899-1951*, 1951 (h); *Drama at Irish*, 1953 (d); *Never the Time and the Place* and *Crabbed Youth and Age*, 1953 (2d); *I Sometimes Think*, 1956 (e)

Michael J. O'Neill, *Lennox Robinson*, 1964

W. R. RODGERS
1909-

Awake, 1941 (p); *The Ulstermen and their Country*, 1947 (e); *Portrait of James Joyce*, 1950 (radio script); *Europa and the Bull*, 1952 (p); *Ireland in Colour*, 1957 (e)

FREDERICK ROLFE ("BARON CORVO")
1860-1913

Stories Toto Told Me, 1898 (s); *In His Own Image*, 1901 (repr. 1924) (s); *Chronicles of the House of Borgia*, 1901 (Am. ed. *A History of the Borgias*, 1931) (h); *The Rubaiyat of Umar Khaiyam*, 1903 (tr); *Hadrian the Seventh*, 1904 (repr. 1950) (n); *Don Tarquinio*, 1905 (repr. 1957) (n); *Don Renato*, 1909 (repr. 1963) (n); *The Desire and Pursuit of the Whole*, ed. A. J. A. Symons, 1934 (repr. 1953) (n); (with C. H. C. Pirie-Gordon) *Hubert's Arthur*, ed. A. J. A. Symons, 1935 (n); *The Songs of Meleager*, 1937 (tr); *Three Tales of Venice*, 1950 (s); *Amico di Sandro, A Fragment of a Novel*, 1951 (n); *Letters to Grant Richards*, 1952; *The Cardinal Prefect of Propaganda*, 1957 (s); *Nicholas Crabbe, or The One and the Many*, 1958 (n); *Letters to C. H. C. Pirie-Gordon*, ed. Cecil Woolf, 1959; *Don Renato, an Ideal Content: a Historical Romance*, ed. Cecil Woolf, 1963 (n); *Without Prejudice: One Hundred Letters from Frederick William Rolfe (Baron Corvo) to John Lane*, ed. Cecil Woolf, 1964

A. J. A. Symons, *The Quest for Corvo*,

1934, (with additions by Julian Symons) 1952; Cecil Woolf, *A Bibliography of Frederick Rolfe, Baron Corvo,* 1957; Cecil Woolf and Brocard Sewell, *The Clerk Without a Benefice: A Study of Frederick Rolfe, Baron Corvo's Conversion and Vocation,* 1965

ISAAC ROSENBERG
1890-1918

Night and Day, 1912 (p); *Youth,* 1915 (p); *Moses,* 1916 (pd); *Poems,* ed. Gordon Bottomley, 1922; *Collected Works,* ed. Gordon Bottomley, and Denys Harding, 1937; *Collected Poems,* ed. Gordon Bottomley and Denys Harding, 1949

See Lawrence Binyon, Introd. in Rosenberg, *Poems,* 1922

ALAN ROSS
1922-

The Derelict Day, 1947 (p); *Time was Away,* 1948 (t); *The Forties,* 1950 (e); *The Gulf of Pleasure,* 1951 (t); *Poetry, 1945-50,* 1951 (c); *The Bandit on the Billiard Table,* 1954 (rev. enlgd. as *South to Sardinia,* 1960) (t); *Something of the Sea,* 1954 (p); *To Whom it May Concern, Poems 1952-1957,* 1958 (p); *African Negatives,* 1962 (p)

A. L. ROWSE
1903-

Politics and the Younger Generation, 1931 (e); (with G. B. Harrison) *Queen Elizabeth and Her Subjects,* 1935 (e); *Sir Richard Grenville of the Revenge,* 1935 (repr. 1963) (b); *Poems of a Decade, 1931-41,* 1941 (p); *Tudor Cornwall: Portrait of a Society,* 1941 (repr. 1963) (e); *A Cornish Childhood,* 1942 (a); *The Spirit of English History,* 1943 (e); *The English Spirit,* 1944 (e); *Poems Chiefly Cornish,* 1944 (p); *West Country Stories,* 1945 (s); *Poems of Deliverance,* 1946 (p); *The Use of History,* 1946 (e); *The End of an Epoch,* 1947 (e); *The West in English History,* (e); *The England of Elizabeth. The Structure of Society,* 1950 (h); **The English Past,* 1951 (e); *An Elizabethan Garland,* 1953 (e); *L. Romier: L'Ancienne France,* 1953 (tr); *The Expansion of Elizabethan England,* 1955 (h); *The*

Early Churchills, 1956 (b); *The Elizabethans and America,* 1958 (h); *The Later Churchills,* 1958 (b); *Poems, Partly American,* 1959 (p); *All Souls and Appeasement,* 1961 (e); *Raleigh and the Throckmortons,* 1962 (b); *William Shakespeare,* 1963 (b); *Christopher Marlowe: a Biography* (Am. ed. *Christopher Marlowe: His Life and Work),* 1964 (b); *A Cornishman at Oxford: The Education of a Cornishman,* 1965 (a); *Shakespeare's Southampton,* 1965 (b); *The Elizabethans and America,* 1965 (Trevelyan Lectures, Cambridge Univ.); *Bosworth Field: From Medieval to Tudor England,* (Eng. title *Bosworth Field and the Wars of the Roses),* 1966 (h)

*Times, Persons, Places (rev. ed. of *The English Past),* 1965

NAOMI ROYDE-SMITH
? -1964

A Private Anthology, 1924 (p); *The Tortoiseshell Cat,* 1925 (n); *The Housemaid,* 1926 (d); *A Balcony,* 1927 (d); *John Fanning's Legacy,* 1927 (n); *Skin Deep, or Portrait of Lucinda,* 1927 (n); *The Lover,* 1928 (s); *Children in the Wood* (Am. ed. *In the Wood),* 1928 (n); *Summer Holiday, or Gibraltar* (Am. ed. *Give Me My Sin Again),* 1929 (n); *Mafro, Darling,* 1929 (d); *The Island,* 1930 (n); *Pictures and People,* 1930 (r); *The Delicate Situation,* 1931 (n); *The Mother,* 1931 (n); *Mrs. Siddons,* 1931 (d); *The Double Heart, a Study of Julie de Lepinasse,* 1931 (b); *Madame Julia's Tale,* 1932 (s); *The Bridge,* 1932 (n); *The Incredible Tale,* 1932 (n); *Pilgrim from Paddington,* 1933 (p); *The Private Life of Mrs. Siddons* (Am. ed. *Portrait of Mrs. Siddons),* 1933 (b); *David,* 1933 (n); *The Queen's Wigs,* 1934 (p); *Private Room,* 1934 (d); *Jake,* 1935 (n); *All Star Cast,* 1936 (n); *For Us in the Dark,* 1937 (n); *Miss Bendix,* 1938 (n); *The Altar-Piece,* 1939 (n); *Urchin Moor,* 1939 (n); *The Younger Venus,* 1939 (n); *Jane Fairfax,* 1940 (n); *Outside Information,* 1941 (e); *The Unfaithful Wife,* 1941 (n); *Mildensee,* 1943 (n); *Fireweed,* 1944 (n); *The State of Mind of Mrs. Sherwood,* 1946 (b); *Love in Mildensee,* 1948 (s); *The Iniquity of Us All,* 1949 (n); *The Idol and the Shrine* [the Life of M. de Guérin], 1949 (b); *Rosy Trodd,* 1950 (n);

The New Rich, 1951 (n); *She Always Caught the Post,* 1953 (n); *All Night Sitting,* 1954 (d); *Melilot,* 1955 (n); *Love at First Sight,* 1956 (n); *The Whistling Chambermaid,* 1957 (n); *How White is my Sepulchre,* 1958 (s); *A Blue Rose,* 1959 (s); *Love and a Birdcage,* 1960 (n)

BERTRAND RUSSELL
1872-

Selective Bibliography: the works most apt to interest a student of literature.

A Critical Exposition of the Philosophy of Leibniz, with an appendix of leading passages, 1900 (repr. 1937); *The Principles of Mathematics,* 1903; *Philosophical Essays,* 1910 (e); (with Alfred North Whitehead) *Principia Mathematica,* 1910-1913; *The Problems of Philosophy,* 1912; *Our Knowledge of the External World as a Field for Scientific Method in Philosophy,* 1914; *The Philosophy of Bergson,* 1914; *Mysticism and Logic,* 1918 (repr. 1953) (e); *Roads to Freedom: Socialism, Anarchism and Syndicalism,* 1918 (Am. ed. *Proposed Roads to Freedom*) (e); *The Analysis of Mind,* 1921; (with Dora Russell) *The Prospects of Industrial Civilization,* 1923 (e); *Icarus, or, The Future of Science,* 1924 (e); *The ABC of Relativity,* 1925; *What I Believe,* 1925 (e); *On Education Especially in Early Childhood,* 1926 (Am. ed. *Education and the Good Life*) (e); *The Analysis of Matter,* 1927; *An Outline of Philosophy,* 1927 (Am. ed. *Philosophy*); *Selected Papers of Bertrand Russell,* sel. by author, 1927; *Why I Am Not a Christian,* 1927 (e); *Sceptical Essays,* 1928 (e); *Marriage and Morals,* 1929 (e); *The Conquest of Happiness,* 1930 (e); (with John Cowper Powys) *Debate! Is Modern Marriage a Failure?,* 1930; (with others) *Divorce as I See It,* 1930 (Am. ed. *Divorce*) (e); *The Scientific Outlook,* 1931 (e); *Education and the Social Order,* 1932 (Am. ed. *Education and the Modern World*) (e); *Freedom and Organization, 1814-1914,* 1934 (Am. ed. *Freedom versus Organization, 1814-1914*) (h); (with others) *The Meaning of Marx, a Symposium,* 1934; *Religion and Science,* 1935 (e); *In Praise of Idleness,* 1935 (e); *Power, A New Social Analysis,* 1938 (e); *An Inquiry into Meaning and Truth,* 1940 (e); *A History of Western Philosophy and its Connection with Political and Social Circumstances from the Earliest Times to the Present Day,* 1945 (h); *The Faith of a Rationalist,* 1947 (e); *Philosophy and Politics,* 1947 (e); *Human Knowledge: Its Scope and Limits,* 1948 (e); *Authority and the Individual,* 1949 (the Reith lectures); *Unpopular Essays,* 1950 (e); *New Hopes for a Changing World,* 1951 (e); *The Impact of Science on Society,* 1952 (e); *What Is Freedom?,* 1953 (e); *What Is Democracy,* 1953 (e); *Satan in the Suburbs,* 1953 (s); *History as an Art,* 1954 (Herman Ould Memorial lecture); *Human Society in Ethics and Politics,* 1954 (e); *Nightmares of Eminent Persons,* 1954 (s); *Portraits from Memory,* 1956 (r); *Logic and Knowledge: Essays, 1901-1950,* ed. Robert Charles Marsh, 1956 (e); *Fact and Fiction,* 1961 (e); *The Good Citizen's Alphabet,* 1963 (e); *The Autobiography,* 1967 (a)

H. W. Leggett, *Bertrand Russell,* 1950 [lists principal works]; Alan Dorward, *Bertrand Russell. A Short Guide to His Philosophy,* 1951 [select bibliog.]

GEORGE WILLIAM RUSSELL (AE)
1867-1935

[The numerous political essays and pamphlets omitted.]

Homeward: Songs by the Way, 1894 (p); *The Future of Ireland and the Awakening of the Fires,* 1897 (e); *The Earth Breath,* 1897 (p); *Ideals in Ireland: Priest or Hero?,* 1897 (e); *Literary Ideals in Ireland—Nationality and Cosmopolitanism in Literature,* 1899 (e); *An Artist of Gaelic Ireland,* 1902 (e); *The Nuts of Knowledge,* 1903 (p); *The Divine Vision,* 1903 (p); *Controversy in Ireland,* 1904 (e); *The Mask of Apollo,* 1904 (s); *By Still Waters,* 1906 (p); *Some Irish Essays,* 1906 (e); *Deidre,* 1907 (d); *The Hero in Man,* 1909 (e); *The Renewal of Youth,* 1911 (e); *Collected Poems,* 1913 (sec. ed. 1926); *Gods of War,* 1915 (p); *Imaginations and Reveries,* 1915 (e); *The Candle of Vision,* 1918 (e); *Michael,* 1919 (p); *Open Letter to the Irish People,* 1922 (e); *The Interpreters,* 1922 (e); *Voices of the Stones,* 1925 (p); *Midsummer Eve,* 1928 (p); *Dark Weeping,* 1929 (p);

Enchantment, 1930 (p); *Vale*, 1931 (p); *Song and its Fountains*, 1932 (e); *The Avatars, a Futurist Fantasy*, 1933 (s); *The House of the Titans*, 1934 (p); *Selected Poems*, 1935 (p); *Some Passages from the Letters of AE to W. B. Yeats*, 1936; *AE's Letters to Minanlabain*, 1937; *The Living Torch*, ed. Monk Gibbon, 1937 (e); *Letters from AE*, ed. Alan Denson, 1961

See Ernest A. Boyd, *Portraits Real and Imaginary*, 1924; Alan Denson, *Printed Writings by George William Russell (AE): A Bibliography*, 1961

EDWARD SACKVILLE-WEST
1901-1965

Piano Quintet, 1925 (n); *The Ruin, a Gothic Novel*, 1926 (n); *The Apology of Arthur Rimbaud: a Dialogue*, 1927 (c); *Mandrake over the Water-Carrier: a Recital*, 1928 (n); *Simpson, a Life*, 1931 (rev. 1951) (n); (with V. Sackville-West) Rainer M. Rilke, *Duineser Elegien*, 1931 (tr); *The Sun in Capricorn a Recital*, 1934 (n); *A Flame in Sunlight: The Life and Work of Thomas De Quincey*, 1936 (b); *The Rescue*, 1945 (rd); *Inclinations*, 1949 (e); "Sketches for an Autobiography," *Orion*, Vol. III (1946), pp. 51-58; Vol. IV (1947), pp. 7-15

See Vincent Sheean, *Personal History*, 1935

VICTORIA SACKVILLE-WEST
1892-1962

Poems of West and East, 1917 (p); *Heritage*, 1919 (n); *Orchard and Vineyard*, 1921 (p); *The Dragon in Shallow Waters*, 1921 (n); *The Heir*, 1922 (s); *Knole and the Sackvilles*, 1922 (h); *Challenge*, 1923 (n); *Grey Wethers*, 1923 (n); *Seducers in Ecuador*, 1924 (s); *Passenger to Teheran*, 1926 (t); *The Land*, 1926 (p); *Aphra Behn, the Incomparable Astrea*, 1927 (b); *Twelve Days: An Account of a Journey Across the Bakhtiari Mountains in South-Western Persia*, 1928 (t); *Andrew Marvell*, 1929 (b); *King's Daughter*, 1929 (p); **The Edwardians*, 1930 (n); (with Edward Sackville-West) Rainer M. Rilke, *Duineser Elegien*, 1931 (tr); *All Passion Spent*, 1931 (n); *Sissinghurst*,

1931 (p); *V. Sackville-West* [Selected Poems], 1931 (p); *Invitation to Cast Out Care*, 1931 (p); *The Death of Noble Godovary, and Gottfried Künstler*, 1932 (s); *Thirty Clocks Strike the Hour*, 1932 (s); *Family History*, 1932 (n); *Collected Poems*, 1933-; *The Dark Island*, 1934 (n); *Saint Joan of Arc*, 1936 (rev. 1948) (b); *Pepita*, 1937 (b); *Some Flowers*, 1937 (e); *Solitude*, 1938 (p); *Country Notes*, 1939 (e); *Country Notes in Wartime*, 1940 (e); *English Country Houses*, 1941 (e); *Selected Poems*, 1941; *Grand Canyon*, 1942 (n); *The Eagle and the Dove: A Study in Contrasts, St. Teresa of Avila and St. Thérèse of Lisieux*, 1943 (b); *The Garden*, 1946 (p); *In Your Garden*, 1951 (e); *In Your Garden Again*, 1953 (e); *The Easter Party*, 1953 (n); *Daughter of France* [la Grande Mademoiselle, 1627-93], 1959 (b); *No Signposts in the Sea*, 1961 (n)

*repr. 1966

Jean Muriel Wines, *A Bibliography of the Writings of V. Sackville-West*, 1958

GEORGE SAINTSBURY
1845-1933

A Short History of French Literature, 1866 (repr. to 1917) (h); *Primer of French Literature*, 1880 (h); *Dryden*, 1878 (b,c); *Marlborough*, 1886 (b); *A History of Elizabethan Literature*, 1887 (h); *Essays on French Novelists*, 1891 (c); *Corrected Impressions: Essays on Victorian Writers*, 1895 (c); *Essays in English Literature, 1780-1860*, 1895 (c); *A History of 19th-Century Literature, 1780-1895*, 1896 (h); *The Flourishing of Romance and the Rise of Allegory*, 1897 (c,e); **A Short History of English Literature*, 1898 (h); *A History of Criticism and Literary Taste in Europe*, 3 vols., 1900-04 (repr. 1929-34) (h); *The Earlier Renaissance*, 1901 (e); *Loci Critici, Selections and Notes*, 1903 (c); *A History of English Prosody*, 3 vols., 1906 (h); *Historical Manual of English Prosody*, 1910 (h); *A History of English Criticism*, 1911 (rev. enlgd. 1949) (h); *A History of English Prose Rhythm*, 1912 (h); *The English Novel*, 1913 (rev. 1919) (h); *The Peace of the Augustans: A Survey of 18th-Century Literature*, 1916 (repr. 1946) (h); *A History of the French Novel to the Close of the*

19th Century, 1917 (h); *Notes on a Cellar-Book*, 1920 (e); *A Letter Book*, 1922 (e); *A Scrap Book*, 1922; *A Second Scrap Book*, 1923; *A Last Scrap Book*, 1924; *A Consideration of Thackeray*, 1931 (c); *Prefaces and Essays*, sel. and ed. Oliver Elton, 1933; *A Last Vintage: Essays and Papers*, ed. John W. Oliver et al [with bibiography], 1950 (e)

*repr. 1966

George Saintsbury, *The Memorial Volume: Essays, Papers and Portraits*, by Oliver Elton, Sir Herbert Grierson, etc.; biographical memoir by A. Blyth Webster, Ed. A. M. Clark and A. Muir, 1945 (Am. ed. *A Saintsbury Miscellany*)

SAKI (H. H. MUNRO)
1870-1916

The Rise of the Russian Empire, 1900 (h); *The Westminster Alice*, 1902, (s); *Reginald*, 1904 (s); *Reginald in Russia*, 1910 (s); *The Chronicles of Clovis*, 1911 (repr. 1948) (s); *The Unbearable Bassington*, 1912 (repr. 1947) (n); *When William Came*, 1914 (repr. 1941) (n); *Beasts and Super-Beasts*, 1914 (repr. 1950) (s); *The Toys of Peace*, 1919 (e); *The Square Egg and Other Sketches, with Three Plays*, 1924; *The Short Stories of Saki*, 1930 (enlgd 1948) (s); *The Novels and Plays of Saki*, 1933

See Rothay Reynolds, memoir in Saki, *The Toys of Peace*, 1919; Ethel M. Munro, biography in Saki, *The Square Egg*, 1924, and in *The Short Stories*, 1930; Christopher D. Morley, *Internal Revenue*, 1933

WILLIAM SANSOM
1912-

Jim Braidy, 1943 (e); *Fireman Flower*, 1944 (s); *Three*, 1946 (s); *Westminster at War*, 1947 (e); *The Equilibriad*, 1948 (e); *South: Aspects and Images from Corsica, Italy and Southern France*, 1948 (t); *Something Terrible, Something Lovely*, 1948 (s); *The Body*, 1949 (n); *The Passionate North*, 1950 (e); *The Face of Innocence*, 1951 (n); *A Touch of the Sun*, 1952 (n); *It Was Really Charlie's Castle*, 1953 (n); *Pleasures Strange and Simple*, 1953 (e); *A Bed of Roses*, 1954 (s); *Lord Love Us*, 1954 (s); *A Contest of Ladies*, 1956 (s); *The*

Loving Eye, 1956 (n); *Among the Dahlias*, 1957 (s); *The Cautious Heart*, 1958 (n); *The Icicle and the Sun*, 1958 (t); *Blue Skies, Brown Studies*, 1961 (t); *Collected Short Stories*, 1960 (s); *The Last Hours of Sandra Lee*, 1961 (n); *The Stories of William Sansom*, 1963 (s); *Away To It All* (Europe), 1964 (t); *The Ulcerated Milkman*, 1966 (n); *Goodbye*, 1966 (n)

SIEGFRIED SASSOON
1886-1967

[anon] *Poems*, 1906 (p); [anon] *Orpheus in Dilyoeryum*, 1908 (p); [anon] *Sonnets* 1909 (p); [anon] *Twelve Sonnets*, 1911 (p); [anon] *An Ode for Music*, 1912 (p); [anon] *Hyacinth*, 1912 (p); [anon] *Melodies*, 1912 (p); [Saul Kain, pseud.] *The Daffodil Murderer*, 1913 (Chantrey Prize poem, parody of Masefield, *The Everlasting Mercy*); *Apollo in Diloeryum*, 1913 (p); [anon] *Discoveries*, 1915 (p); [anon] *Morning-Glory*, 1916; *The Redeemer*, 1916 (p); *The Old Huntsman*, 1917 (p); *Counter-attack*, 1918 (p); *Four Poems*, 1918 (p); *Picture Show*, 1919 (p); *The War Poems of Siegfried Sassoon*, 1919; [anon] *Recreations*, 1923 (p); *Selected Poems*, 1925 (p); *Lingual Exercises for Advanced Vocabularians*, 1925 (p); *Satirical Poems*, 1926 (new ed. enlgd. 1933) (p); [*Thirty-Two Poems*], 1926 (p); *The Heart's Journey*, 1927 (p); *Nativity*, 1927 (p); *To My Mother*, 1918 (p); [anon] *Memoirs of a Fox-Hunting Man*, 1928 (repr. 1954) (a,n); *In Sicily*, 1930 (p); *Memoirs of an Infantry Officer*, 1930 (a,n); [Pinchbeck Lyre, pseud.] *Poems*, 1931 (p); *To the Red Rose*, 1931 (p); *Prehistoric Burials*, 1932 (p); *The Road to Ruin*, 1933 (p); *Vigils*, 1934 (p); *Sherston's Progress*, 1936 (a,n); *The Complete Memoirs of George Sherston*, (*Memoirs of a Fox-Hunting Man*, *Memoirs of an Infantry Officer*, with the preceding title), 1937 (a,n); *The Old Century and Seven More Years*, 1938 (r); *On Poetry*, 1939 (Memorial lecture, Univ. of Bristol); *Poems Newly Selected, 1916-35*, 1940; *Rhymed Ruminations*, 1940 (p); *The Flower Show Match*, 1941 (e); *The Weald of Youth*, 1942 (r); *Siegfried Sassoon* [*Selected Poems: Augustan Poets*], 1943 (p); *Siegfried's Journey, 1916-20*,

1945 (r); *Collected Poems*, 1947; *George Meredith*, 1948 (b,c); *Common Chords*, 1950 (p); *An Adjustment*, 1955 (p); *Sequences*, 1956 (p); *The Path to Peace, Selected Poems*, 1960 (p); *Collected Poems, 1908-56*, 1961

Geoffrey Keynes, *A Bibliography of Siegfried Sassoon*, 1962; Michael Thorpe, *Siegfried Sassoon*, 1966

D. S. SAVAGE
1917-

The Autumn World, 1939 (p); *Don Quixote*, 1939 (p); *A Time to Mourn; Poems, 1934-43*, 1943 (p); *The Personal Principle*, 1944 (c); *Hamlet and the Pirates*, 1950 (c); *The Withered Branch*, 1950 (c)

DOROTHY SAYERS
1893-1957

Opus I, 1916 (p); *Catholic Tales and Christian Songs*, 1918 (s,p); *Whose Body*, 1923 (n); *Clouds of Witness*, 1926 (n); *Unnatural Death*, 1927 (n); *The Unpleasantness at the Bellona Club*, 1928 (n); *Lord Peter Views the Body*, 1928 (s); Thomas, the Troubadour, *Tristan in Brittany*, 1929 (tr); [with Robert Eustace, pseud.] *The Documents in the Case*, 1930 (n); *Strong Poison*, 1930 (n); *The Five Red Herrings*, 1931 (n); *Have His Carcase*, 1932 (n); *Hangman's Holiday*, 1933 (s); *The Dorothy L. Sayers Omnibus*, 1933 (3n); *Murder Must Advertise*, 1933 (n); *The Nine Tailors*, 1934 (n); *Gaudy Night*, 1935 (n); *Busman's Honeymoon*, 1937 (n and, with M. Saint Clare Byrne, d); *The Zeal of Thy House*, 1937 (d); *The Greatest Drama Ever Staged* [on Easter], 1938 (e); *In the Teeth of the Evidence*, 1939 (s); *He That Should Come*, 1939 (d); *The Devil to Pay*, 1939 (d); (with others) *Double Death*, 1939 (s); *Strong Meat*, 1939 (e); *Love All*, 1940 (d); *Golden Cockerel*, 1941 (rd); *The Mind of the Maker*, 1941 (e); *The Man Born to Be King*, 1941 (repr. 1951) (rd); *The Just Vengeance*, 1946 (d); *Unpopular Opinions*, 1946 (e); *Four Sacred Plays* (*The Zeal of Thy House, The Devil to Pay, He That Should Come, The Just Vengeance*), 1948 (4d); *The Comedy of Dante Alighieri the Florentine*, 1949 (tr); *The Emperor Constantine*, 1951 (d);

Introductory Papers on Dante, 1954 (c); *The New Sayers Omnibus*, 1956; *Further Papers on Dante*, 1957 (c); *The Song of Roland*, 1957 (tr); *The Poetry of Search and the Poetry of Statement and Other Posthumous Essays on Literature, Religion, and Language*, 1963 (e)

FRANCIS SCARFE
1911-

Inscapes, 1940 (p); *Forty Poems and Ballads*, 1941 (p); *Auden and After*, 1942 (c); *W. H. Auden*, 1949 (b,c); *Underworlds*, 1950 (p); *Promises*, 1950 (n); *Single Blessedness*, 1951 (n); Paul Valéry, *Reflections on the World Today*, 1951 (tr); *Unfinished Woman*, 1954 (n); *The Art of Paul Valéry*, 1954 (c); *André Chenier: His Life and Work*, 1965 (b,c)

ERNEST DE SELINCOURT
1870-1943

English Poets and the National Ideal, 1915 (e); *The Study of Poetry*, 1918 (e); *Keats*, 1921 (c); *Poetry*, 1929 (e); Editor of William Wordsworth, *The Prelude*, 1932; *Dorothy Wordsworth: A Biography*, 1933 (b); *Oxford Lectures on Poetry*, 1934 (e); Editor of *Letters of William and Dorothy Wordsworth*, 6 vols., 1935-9; *The Early Wordsworth*, 1936 (b); Editor (with Helen Darbishire) of William Wordsworth, *Poetical Works*, 5 vols., 1940-9; Editor of Dorothy Wordsworth, *Journals*, 2 vols., 1941; *Wordsworthian and Other Studies*, 1947 (c)

Helen Darbishire, "Ernest de Selincourt", from *Proceedings of the British Academy*, Vol. 29, 1944

EDWARD SHANKS
1892-1953

Songs, 1915 (p); *Poems*, 1916 (p); (with C. C. Mandell) *Hilaire Belloc, the Man and His Work*, 1916 (b,c); *The Queen of China*, 1919 (p); *The Old Indispensables*, 1919 (n); *The People of the Ruins*, 1920 (n); *The Island of Youth*, 1921 (p); *Fête Galante, a Dance-Drama . . . after Maurice Baring's Story of that Name* (dramatiz. by Ethel Smyth), 1923 (pd); *The Richest Man*, 1923 (n); *First Essays on Literature*, 1923 (c); *Bernard Shaw*, 1924 (b,c); *The Shadowgraph*, 1925 (p); *Twenty Poems*, 1926 (p); *The Beggar's Ride*, 1926 (d); *Collected Poems, 1909-25*, 1926; *Second Essays on Literature*, 1927 (c); *Bo and His Circle*, 1931 (e); *Queer Street*, 1932 (n); *Poems, 1912-32*, 1933 (p); *The Enchanted Village*, 1933 (n); *Tom Tiddler's Ground*, 1934 (n); *Old King Cole*, 1936 (Am. ed. *The Dark Green Circle*) (n); *Edgar Allan Poe*, 1937 (b,c); *My England*, 1938 (t); *Rudyard Kipling*, 1940 (c); *Elizabeth Goes Home*, 1942 (e); *The Night Watch for England*, 1942 (p); *Poems, 1939-52*, 1954

See Harold Monro, *Some Contemporary Poets (1920)*, 1920

GEORGE BERNARD SHAW
1856-1950

Selective Bibliography

The many reprints of separate plays are not indicated. Only a sampling is given of Shaw's almost innumerable essays and tracts on the subjects that interested him, such as Fabianism, socialism, censorship, the English language and its spelling, war, the Irish question. Also, this list includes only some of the selected and collected works.
Cashel Byron's Profession, 1886 (n) (rev. 1901, contains *The Admirable Bashville, or, Constancy Unrewarded*, d based on the novel, *Cashel Byron's Profession*); *An Unsocial Socialist*, 1887 (n); *The Quintessence of Ibsenism*, 1891 (enlgd. 1913) (c); *Widowers' Houses*, 1893 (d); *Plays Pleasant and Unpleasant* (Pleasant: *Arms and the Man, Candida, The Man of Destiny, You Never Can Tell*; Unpleasant: *Widowers' Houses, The Philanderer, Mrs. Warren's Profession*), 1898; *The Perfect Wagnerite*, 1898 (c); *Love Among the Artists*, 1900 (n); *Three Plays for Puritans* (*The Devil's Disciple, Caesar and Cleopatra, Captain Brassbound's Conversion*), 1901 (3d); *Man and Superman*, 1903 (d); *The Irrational Knot*, 1905 (n); *Dramatic Opinions and Essays*, 1906 (c); *John Bull's Other Island, Major Barbara; also How He Lied to Her Husband*, 1907 (3d); *The Sanity of Art*, 1908 (c); *Press Cuttings*, 1909 (d); *The Shewing-up of Blanco Posnet*, 1909 (d); *Misalliance*, 1910 (d); *Brieux: A Preface*,

1910 (c); *The Doctor's Dilemma, Getting Married, and The Shewing-up of Blanco Posnet*, 1911 (3d); *Androcles and the Lion*, 1914 (d); *Misalliance, The Dark Lady of the Sonnets, Fanny's First Play. With a Treatise on Parents and Children*, 1914 (3d,e); *Androcles and the Lion, Overruled, Pygmalion*, 1916 (3d); *Heartbreak House*, 1917 (d); *Heartbreak House, Great Catherine, and Playlets of the War* (*O'Flaherty, V.C., The Inca of Perusalem, Augustus Does His Bit, Annajanska*), 1919 (6d); *Back to Methuselah*, 1921 (d); *Saint Joan*, 1924 (d); *Translations and Tomfooleries* (*Jitta's Atonement*, tr. from the German of Seigfried Trebitsch; *The Admirable Bashville, Press Cuttings, The Glimpse of Reality, Passion, Poison and Petrification, The Fascinating Foundling, The Music-Cure*), 1926 (7d); *The Intelligent Woman's Guide to Socialism and Capitalism*, 1928 (rev. enlgd. 1937 as *The Intelligent Woman's Guide to Socialism, Capitalism, Sovietism and Fascism*) (e); *Bernard Shaw and Karl Marx. A Symposium, 1884-1889*, ed. R. W. Ellis, 1930 (e); *The Apple Cart*, 1930 (d); *Ellen Terry and Bernard Shaw: A Correspondence*, ed. Christopher St. John, 1931; *Complete Works* (standard edition), 1931-50; *Immaturity*, 1931 (written 1879) (n); *What I Really Wrote About the War*, 1931 (e); *Pen Portraits and Reviews*, 1932 (c); *Essays in Fabian Socialism* (includes *The Fabian Society, What It Has Done and How It Has Done It*, 1892; *The Impossibilities of Anarchism*, 1893; *The Common Sense of Municipal Trading*, 1904), 1932 (e); *Doctors' Delusions, Crude Criminology and Sham Education*, 1932 (e); *Our Theatres in the Nineties*, 1932 (c); *Music in London, 1890-94*, 1932 (c); *Major Critical Essays* (*The Quintessence of Ibsenism, The Perfect Wagnerite, The Sanity of Art*), 1932 (c); *The Adventures of the Black Girl in Her Search for God*, 1932 (n); *Prefaces*, 1934 (enlgd. 1938) (e); *Too True to be Good, Village Wooing, On the Rocks*, 1934 (3d); *Short Stories, Scraps and Shavings*, 1934 (s); *The Simpleton of the Unexpected Isles, The Six of Calais, The Millionairess*, 1936 (3d); *London Music in 1888-89*, 1937 (c); *In Good King Charles's Golden Days*, 1939 (d); *Geneva: A Fancied Page of History*, 1939 (d);

Shaw Gives Himself Away, 1939 (a); Everybody's Political What's What, 1944 (e); Geneva, Cymbeline Refinished and Good King Charles, 1946 (3d); The Crime of Imprisonment, 1946 (e); Sixteen Self Sketches, 1949 (a); Shaw on Vivisection, ed. G. H. Bowker, 1949; Buoyant Billions, Farfetched Fables, Skakes Versus Shav. 1950 (3d); The Complete Plays, 1950; Bernard Shaw and Mrs. Patrick Campbell: Their Correspondence, ed. Alan Dent, 1952; Selected Prose, ed. Diarmuid Russell, 1953; Advice to a Young Critic, 1955 (letters); My Dear Dorothea, 1956 (written 1877) (e); The Illusions of Socialism. With, Socialism: Principles and Outlook, 1956 (e); Bernard Shaw's Letters to Granville Barker, ed. C. B. Purdom, 1956; An Unfinished Novel, ed, Stanley Weintraub, 1958 (n); Shaw on Theatre (includes The Dying Tongue of Great Elizabeth, The Art of Rehearsal), ed. E. J. West, 1958 (e); How to Become a Musical Critic, ed. Dan H. Laurence, 1960 (c); Shaw on Shakespeare, ed. Edwin Wilson, 1961 (c); To a Young Actress; Letters to Molly Tompkins, ed. Peter Tompkins, 1961 (letters); Complete Plays with Prefaces, 1962; Platform and Pulpit, ed. Dan H. Laurence, 1962 (e); The Matter With Ireland, ed. Dan H. Laurence and David H. Greene, 1962 (e); Religious Speeches, ed. Warren Sylvester Smith, 1963; The Rationalization of Russia, ed. Harry M. Geduld, 1964 (e); The Complete Plays (1 vol.), 1965; Selected One-Act Plays (2 vols.), 1965; Collected Letters, 1874-1897 (Vol. I of 4), ed. Dan Laurence, 1965; The Complete Prefaces, 1965; Selected Non-Dramatic Writings, ed. Dan H. Laurence, 1965; Shaw's Ready-Reckoner, ed. N. H. Leigh Taylor, 1966 (misc.)

C. Lewis and Violet M. Broad, Dictionary of the Plays and Novels of Shaw, 1929; William Irvine, The Universe of G.B.S., 1949; Alfred C. Ward, Bernard Shaw, a Biography, 1951 [selected bibliog.]; B. C. Rosset, Shaw of Dublin, 1964; J. P. Smith, The Unrepentant Pilgrim, 1966

ROBERT C. SHERRIFF
1896-

Journey's End, 1929 (d); Badger's Green, 1930 (d); (with Vernon Bartlett) Journey's End, 1931 (n); The Fortnight in September, 1931 (n); (with Jeanne de Casalis) St. Helena, 1934 (d); Two Heart's Doubled, 1935 (d); The Hopkins Manuscript, 1939 (rev. as The Cataclysm, 1958) (n); (with others, from novel by James Hilton) Goodbye Mr. Chips, 1940 (screenplay); Chedworth, 1944 (n); Another Year, 1948 (n); (from stories by W. Somerset Maugham) Quartet, 1948 (screenplay); Miss Mabel, 1949 (d); Home at Seven, 1950 (d); (with W. S. Maugham, and Noel Langley, from stories by Maugham) Trio, 1950 (screenplay); (with Frederick L. Green) Odd Man Out, 1950 (screenplay); The White Carnation, 1954 (d); King John's Treasure, 1954 (n); The Long Sunset, 1956 (d); A Shred of Evidence, 1961 (d); The Wells of St. Mary's, 1961 (n)

See Raymond Williams, Drama from Ibsen to Eliot, 1952, rev. 1964

NEVIL SHUTE
1899-1960

Pied Piper, 1924 (n); Marazan, 1926 (repr. 1952) (n); So Disdained, 1928 (repr. 1951) (n); Lonely Road, 1932 (repr. 1962) (n); Ruined City, 1938 (repr. 1951) (n); Kindling, 1938 (n); What Happened to the Corbetts, 1939 (repr. 1952) (n); Ordeal, 1940 (n); Landfall, 1940 (repr. 1962) (n); An Old Captivity, 1940 (n); Pastoral, 1944 (repr. 1964) (n); Most Secret, 1945 (n); Vinland the Good, 1946 (film play); The Chequer Board, 1947 (n); No Highway, 1948 (n); A Town like Alice, 1950 (Am. ed. Legacy) (n); Round the Bend, 1951 (n); The Far Country, 1952 (n); So Disdained, 1952 (n); In the Wet, 1953 (n); Slide Rule, The Autobiography of an Engineer, 1954 (a); Requiem for a Wren, 1955 (also pub. as The Breaking Wave) (n); Beyond the Black Stump, 1956 (n); On the Beach, 1957 (n); The Rainbow and the Rose, 1958 (n); Trustee from the Toolroom, 1960 (n); Stephen Morris, 1961 (n); Three of a Kind, 1962 (n)

ETHEL SIDGWICK
1877-

Promise, 1910 (n); Le Gentleman, an Idyll of the Quarter, 1911 (n); Herself, 1912 (n); Succession, a Comedy of the

Generations (seq. to *Promise*), 1913 (n);
A Lady of Leisure, 1914 (n); *Duke
Jones* (seq. to *A Lady of Leisure*), 1914
(n); *The Accolade*, 1915 (n); *Hatchways*,
1916 (n); *Jamesie*, 1918 (n); *Madam*,
1921 (n); *Restoration, the Fairy Tale of
a Farm*, 1923 (n); *Laura, a Cautionary
Story*, 1924 (n); *The Bells of Shoreditch*,
1928 (Am. ed. *When I Grow Rich*) (n);
*Dorothy's Wedding, a Tale of Two Vil-
lages*, 1931 (Am. ed. *A Tale of Two
Villages*) (n); *Mrs. Henry Sidgwick, a
Memoir*, 1938 (m). Also plays for
children.

See Gerald Gould, *The English Novel of
Today*, 1924

JON SILKIN
1930-

The Portrait, 1951 (p); *The Peaceable
Kingdom*, 1954 (p); *The Two Freedoms*,
1958 (p); *The Re-ordering of the Stones*,
1961 (p); *Flower Poems*, 1964 (p);
Nature with Man, 1965 (p); *Poems New
and Selected*, 1966 (p)

ALAN SILLITOE
1928-

Without Beer or Bread, 1957 (p); *Saturday Night and Sunday Morning*, 1958
(n); *The Loneliness of the Long-Dis-
tance Runner*, 1959 (s); *The General*,
1960 (n); *The Rats*, 1960 (p); *The Key
to the Door*, 1961 (n); *The Ragman's
Daughter*, 1963 (s); *Road to Volgograd*,
1964 (t); *A Falling Out of Love*, 1965
(p); *The Death of William Posters*, 1965
(n)

See James Gindin. *Postwar British
Fiction*, 1962

MAY SINCLAIR
1865-1946

Nakiketas, n.d. (p); *Essays in Verse*, 1892
(p); *Audrey Craven*, 1897 (n); *Mr. and
Mrs. Nevill Tyson*, 1898 (Am. ed. *The
Tysons*, 1906) (n); *Two Sides of a
Question*, 1901 (n); *The Divine Fire*,
1904 (n); *Superseded*, 1906 (n); *The
Helpmate*, 1907 (n); *The Judgment of
Eve*, 1907 (Am. ed. *The Return of the
Prodigal*) (s); *Kitty Tailleur*, 1908 (Am.
ed. *The Immortal Moment*) (n); *The
Creators*, 1910 (n); *The Flaw in the*

Crystal, 1912 (n); *Feminism*, 1912
(e); *The Three Brontës*, 1912 (b);
The Combined Maze, 1913 (n); *The
Three Sisters*, 1914 (n); *Tasker Jevons,
the Real Story*, 1916 (Am. ed. *The
Belfry*) (n); *The Tree of Heaven*, 1917
(n); *A Defence of Idealism, Some
Questions and Conclusions*, 1917 (e);
Mary Olivier, a Life, 1919 (n); *The
Romantic*, 1920 (n); *Mr. Waddington
of Wyck*, 1921 (n); *Anne Severn and the
Fieldings*, 1922 (n); *Life and Death of
Harriett Frean*, 1922 (n); *The New
Idealism*, 1922 (e); *Uncanny Stories*,
1923 (s); *A Cure of Souls*, 1924 (n);
Arnold Waterlow, a Life, 1924 (n); *The
Dark Night*, 1924 (p); *The Rector of
Wyck*, 1925 (n); *Far End*, 1926 (n);
The Allinghams, 1927 (n); *History of
Anthony Waring*, 1927 (n); *Fame*, 1929
(s); *Tales Told by Simpson*, 1930 (s);
The Intercessor, 1931 (s)

See Frank Swinnerton, *The Georgian
Scene*, 1934

EDITH SITWELL
1887-1964

The Mother, 1915 (p); (with Osbert
Sitwell) *Twentieth Century Harlequinade*, 1916 (p); *Clowns' Houses*, 1918
(p); *The Wooden Pegasus*, 1920 (p);
Façade, 1922 (enlgd. 1949) (p); *Bucolic
Comedies*, 1923 (p); *The Sleeping
Beauty*, 1924 (p); (with Osbert and
Sacheverell Sitwell) *Poor Young People*,
1925 (p); *Troy Park*, 1925 (p); *Poetry
and Criticism*, 1925 (e); *Edith Sitwell
[Poems]*, 1926 (p); *Elegy on Dead
Fashion*, 1926 (p); *Rustic Elegies*, 1927
(p); *Five Poems*, 1928 (p); *Popular Song*,
1928 (p); *Gold Coast Customs*, 1929
(p); *Alexander Pope*, 1930 (b,c); *Collected
Poems*, 1930; *Jane Barston, 1719-1746*,
1931 (p); *Bath*, 1932 (h); *The English
Eccentrics*, 1933 (b); *Five Variations,
on a Theme*, 1933 (p); *Aspects of
Modern Poetry*, 1934 (c); *Victoria of
England*, 1934 (b); *Selected Poems*,
1936; *I Live Under a Black Sun*, 1937
(n); (with Osbert and Sacheverell Sitwell) *Trio*, 1938 (e); *Poems New and
Old*, 1940 (p); *Street Songs*, 1942 (p);
English Women, 1942 (e); *A Poet's
Notebook*, 1943 (c); *Green Song*, 1944
(p); *The Song of the Cold*, 1945 (p);
Fanfare for Elizabeth, 1946 (b); *The*

Shadow of Cain, 1947 (p); *A Notebook on William Shakespeare*, 1948 (c); *The Canticle of the Rose: Selected Poems 1920-1947*, 1949 (p); *Poor Men's Music*, 1950 (p); *Façade and Other Poems 1920-1935*, 1950 (p); *Selected Poems*, 1952 (p); *A Book of Flowers*, 1952 (e); *Gardeners and Astronomers*, 1953 (p); *The Collected Poems*, 1957; *The Pocket Poets: Edith Sitwell*, 1960 (p); *The Outcasts*, 1962 (p); *The Queens and the Hive* [Elizabeth I], 1962 (b); *Taken Care Of: An Autobiography*, 1965 (a); *Selected Poems*, 1965 (p)

Geoffrey Singleton, *Edith Sitwell: The Hymn to Life*, 1960; Richard Fifoot, *A Bibliography of Edith, Osbert, and Sacheverell Sitwell*, 1963

OSBERT SITWELL
1892-

(with Edith Sitwell) *Twentieth Century Harlequinade*, 1916 (p); *The Winstonburg Line, Three Satires*, 1919 (p); *Argonaut and Juggernaut*, 1919 (p); *At the House of Mrs. Kinfoot*, 1921 (p); *Who Killed Cock-Robin*, 1921 (c); *Out of the Flame*, 1923 (p); *Triple Fugue*, 1924 (s); *Discursions on Travel, Art and Life*, 1925 (e); (with Edith and Sacheverell Sitwell) *Poor Young People*, 1925 (p); *Before the Bombardment*, 1926 (n); *Winter the Huntsman*, 1927 (p); *England Reclaimed*, 1927 (repr. 1949) (p); (with Sacheverell Sitwell) *All At Sea*, 1927 (d); *The People's Album of London Statues*, 1928 (e); *The Man Who Lost Himself*, 1929 (n); *Miss Mew*, 1929 (p); *Dumb Animal*, 1930 (s); *The Collected Satires and Poems of Osbert Sitwell*, 1931; *Three-Quarter Length Portrait of Michael Arlen*, 1931 (p); *Three-Quarter Length Portrait of the Viscountess Wimbourne*, 1931 (p); *Dickens*, 1932 (c); *Winters of Content*, 1932 (enlgd. 1950) (t); *Miracle on Sinai*, 1933 (n); *Brighton*, 1935 (h); *Penny Foolish*, 1935 (e); *Mrs. Kimber*, 1937 (p); *Those were the Days*, 1938 (n); (with Edith and Sacheverell Sitwell) *Trio*, 1938 (e); *Escape With Me!*, 1939 (e); *Open The Door*, 1941 (s); *A Place of One's Own*, 1941 (n); *Gentle Caesar*, 1943 (d); *Selected Poems Old and New*, 1943; *Left Hand, Right Hand!* (Vol. I of autobiog.), 1944 (a); *Sing High!*

Sing Low! 1944 (e); *A Letter to My Son*, 1944 (e); *The True Story of Dick Whittington*, 1946 (n); *The Scarlet Tree* (Vol. II of autobiog.), 1946 (a); *Alive—Alive Oh!*, 1947 (s); *Great Morning!* (Vol. III of autobiog.), 1947 (a); *The Novels of George Meredith*, 1947 (c); *Laughter in the Next Room* (Vol. IV of *Left Hand, Right Hand!*, autobiog.), 1948 (a); *Four Songs of the Italian Earth*, 1948 (p); *Demos the Emperor*, 1949 (pd); *Death of a God*, 1949 (s); *England Reclaimed and Other Poems*, 1949 (p); *Noble Essences*, 1950 (a); *Wrack at Tidesend* (Vol. II of *England Reclaimed*), 1952 (p); *Collected Stories*, 1953; *The Four Continents*, 1954 (e); *On the Continent* (Vol. III of *England Reclaimed*), 1958 (p); *Fee Fi Fo Fum!*, 1959 (n); *A Place of One's Own*, 1961 (s); *Tales My Father Taught Me*, 1962 (r); *Pound Wise*, 1963 (e); *Poems About People, or England Reclaimed* [sel. of poems from *England Reclaimed, Wrack at Tidesend, On the Continent*], 1965 (p)

See Rodolphe Louis Mégroz, *Five Novelist Poets of Today*, 1933, Richard Fifoot, *A Bibliography of Edith, Osbert, and Sacheverell Sitwell*, 1963

SACHEVERELL SITWELL
1897-

The People's Palace, 1918 (p); *Dr. Donne and Gargantua, First Canto*, 1921 (p); *The Hundred and One Harlequins*, 1922 (p); *Dr. Donne and Gargantua, Canto The Second*, 1923 (p); *The Parrot*, 1923 (p); *Southern Baroque Art*, 1924 (c); *The Thirteenth Caesar*, 1924 (p); (with Edith and Osbert Sitwell) *Poor Young People*, 1925 (p); *Exalt the Eglantine*, 1926 (p); *All Summer In A Day*, 1926 (a); *Dr. Donne and Gargantua, Canto The Third*, 1926 (p); *The Cyder Feast*, 1927 (p); *German Baroque Art*, 1927 (c); *A Book of Towers . . . of Southern Europe*, 1928 (t); *Sacheverell Sitwell* [Selected Poems], 1928 (p); *The Gothick North, A Study of Medieval Life, Art and Thought*, 1929-30 (h); *Two Poems. Ten Songs*, 1929 (p); *Dr. Donne and Gargantua, The First Six Cantos*, 1930 (p); *Beckford and Beckfordism*, 1930 (e); *Far From My Home*, 1931 (e); *Spanish Baroque Art*, 1931 (c); *Mozart*, 1932 (b);

Canons of Giant Art, 1933 (p); Liszt, 1934 (b); Touching The Orient, 1934 (sk); A Background For Domenico Scarlatti 1685-1757, 1935 (e); Dance of the Quick and the Dead, 1936 (e); Collected Poems, 1936; Conversation Pieces, 1936 (e); Narrative Pictures, 1937 (e); La Vie Parisienne, A Tribute to Jacques Offenbach, 1937 (e); Roumanian Journey, 1938 (t); (with F. Bamford) Edinburgh, 1938 (h); German Baroque Sculpture, 1938 (c); (with Edith and Osbert Sitwell) Trio, 1938 (e); Mauretania, 1940 (e); Poltergeists, 1940 (e); Sacred and Profane Love, 1940 (e); Valse des Fleurs, 1941 (sk); Primitive Scenes and Festivals, 1942 (e); The Homing of the Winds, 1942 (e); Splendours and Miseries, 1943 (e); British Architects and Craftsmen, 1945 (e); The Hunters and the Hunted, 1947 (e); The Netherlands, (e); Selected Poems, 1948; Morning, Noon and Night in London, 1948 (e); Theatrical Figures in Porcelain, 1949 (e); Spain, 1950 (t); Cupid and Jacaranda, 1952 (e); Truffle Hunt with Sacheverell Sitwell, 1953 (e); Selected Works, 1953; Portugal and Madeira, 1954 (t); Selected Works, 1955; Denmark, 1956 (t); Arabesque and Honeycomb, 1957 (e); Malta, 1958 (t); Journey to the Ends of Time, 1959 (a); Bridge of the Brocade Sash 1959 (t); Golden Wall and Mirador, 1961 (t); The Red Chapels of Banteai Srei, 1962 (e); Monks, Nuns, and Monasteries, 1965 (h,t,r)

See Charles Williams, Poetry at Present, 1930; Richard Fifoot, A Bibliography of Edith, Osbert, and Sacheverell Sitwell, 1963

LOGAN PEARSALL SMITH
1865-1946

The Youth of Parnassus, 1895 (repr. 1909) (s); Trivia, Printed from the Papers of Anthony Woodhouse, Esq., 1902 (many repr.) (e); The Life and Letters of Sir Henry Wotton, 1907 (b); Songs and Sonnets, 1909 (p); The English Language, 1912 (repr. 1952) (h); A Few Practical Suggestions [on the Work of the Society for Pure English], 1920 (e); More Trivia, 1922 (e); English Idioms, 1923 (e); Four Words: Romantic, Originality, Creative, Genius, 1924 (e); Words and Idioms: Studies in the English Langu-

age, 1925 (e); The Prospects of Literature, 1927 (e); Needed Words, 1928 (e); Afterthoughts, 1931 (aphorisms); Robert Bridges. Recollections, 1931 (r); On Reading Shakespeare, 1933 (c); All Trivia (Trivia, More Trivia, Afterthoughts, Last Words), 1933 (e); Reperusals and Re-collections, 1936 (e); Unforgotten Years, 1938 (r); Milton and His Modern Critics, 1940 (c); A Portrait of Logan Pearsall Smith, Drawn from His Letters and Diaries and Introduced by John Russell, 1950

Robert G. Hardy, Recollections of Logan Pearsall Smith, 1949

STEVIE SMITH
1902-

[The books of poetry, except the last listed, are illustrated by the author.]

A Good Time Was Had By All, 1937 (p); Novel on Yellow Paper, 1937 (repr. 1951) (n); Over the Frontier, 1938 (n); Tender Only to One, 1937 (p); Mother, What is Man?, 1942 (p); The Holiday, 1949 (n); Harold's Leap, 1950 (p); Not Waving But Drowning, 1957 (p); Some Are More Human than Others; Sketchbook, 1958 (illustrations); Cats in Colour, 1959 (illustrations); Selected Poems, 1962 (p)

SYDNEY GOODSIR SMITH
1915-

Skail Wind, 1941 (p); The Wanderer, 1943 (p); The Deevil's Waltz, 1946 (p); Carotid Cornucopius, the First Four Fitts, 1947 (p); Selected Poems, 1947 (p); Under the Eildon Tree, 1948 (p); A Short Introduction to Scottish Literature, 1951 (h); So Late Into the Night: Fifty Lyrics 1944-48, 1952 (p); Cokkils, 1953 (p); A Collection of Poems, 1954; Omens, 1955 (p); Orpheus and Eurydice, 1955 (p); The Merrie Life and Dowie Death of Colickie Meg, the Carlin Wife of Ben Nevis, 1956 (p); Figs and Thistles, 1959 (p); The Wallace, 1960 (pd)

CHARLES PERCY SNOW
1905-

Death Under Sail, 1932 (rev. 1959) (n); New Lives for Old, 1933 (n); The Search, 1934 (rev. 1958) (n); Strangers *and Brothers,* sequence of novels: *Strangers and Brothers,* 1940, *The Light and the Dark,* 1947, *Time of Hope,* 1949, *The Masters,* 1951, *The New Men,* 1954, *Homecomings,* 1956, *The Conscience of the Rich,* 1958, *Corridors of Power,* 1964; *The Affair,* 1960 (n); (with Pamela Hansford Johnson, the following plays, 1951): *Family Party, Her Best Foot Forward, The Pigeon With the Silver Foot, Spare the Rod, The Supper Dance, To Murder Mrs. Mortimer; The Two Cultures and the Scientific Revolution,* 1959 [Cambridge, Rede Lecture]; *Science and Government,* 1961 [Harvard, Godkin Lecture]; *Recent Thoughts on the Two Cultures,* 1961 [Birbeck College, lecture]; *Magnanimity,* 1962 [Univ. of St. Andrews, rectorial address]; *A Postscript to "Science and Government",* 1963 (e); *The Two Cultures, A Second Look* [expansion of *The Two Cultures* and *The Scientific Revolution*], 1964 (e)

Robert Graecen, *The World of C. P. Snow,* with bibliog. by Bernard Stone, 1962; Jerome Thale, *C. P. Snow,* 1964

CHARLES HAMILTON SORLEY
1895-1915

Letters from Germany and from the Army, ed. W. R. Sorley, 1916; *Marlborough,* 1916 (sec. ed. enlgd. 1919, repr. to 1932) (p); *The Letters of Charles Sorley,* with a chapter of biography [by Mrs. Janet Sorley], 1919; *Charles Hamilton Sorley* [Selected Poems], 1931 (p)

MURIEL SPARK
1918-

Child of Light: A Reassessment of Mary Wollstonecraft Shelley, 1951 (b); *The Fanfarlo,* 1952 (p); (with Derek Stanford) *Emily Brontë,* 1953 (b); *John Masefield,* 1953 (c); *The Comforters,* 1957 (n); *The Go-away Bird,* 1958 (s); *Robinson,* 1958 (n); *Memento Mori,* 1959 (n); *The Bachelors,* 1960 (n); *The Ballad of Peckham Rye,* 1960 (n); *The Prime of Miss Jean Brodie,* 1961 (n); *Voices at Play,* 1961 (d,s,e); *John Masefield,* 1962 (b); *Doctors of Philosophy,* 1963 (4d,6s); *The Girls of Slender Means,* 1963 (n); *The Mandelbaum Gate,* 1965 (n)

Derek Stanford, *Muriel Spark: A Biographical and Critical Study,* with bibliog. by Bernard Stone, 1963

BERNARD SPENCER
1909-1963

Aegean Islands, 1946 (p); (with others) George Sepheres, *The King of Asine,* 1948 (tr); *The Twist in the Plotting,* 1961 (p); *With Luck Lasting,* 1963 (p); *Collected Poems,* 1965

STEPHEN SPENDER
1909-

Nine Entertainments, 1928 (p); *Twenty Poems,* 1930 (p); *Poems,* 1933 (sec. ed. 1934 (p); *Vienna,* 1934 (p); *The Destructive Element,* 1935 (c); *The Burning Cactus,* 1936 (s); *Forward from Liberalism,* 1937 (e); *Trial of a Judge,* 1938 (d); *The Still Centre,* 1939 (p); (with J. B. Leishman) Rainer Maria Rilke, *Duino Elegies,* 1939 (tr); (with Goronwy Rees) *Danton's Death by Georg Büchner,* 1939 (tr); *Poems for Spain,* 1939 (p); *The New Realism,* 1939 (e); *Selected Poems,* 1940 (p); *The Backward Son,* 1940 (n); *Ruins and Visions,* 1942 (p); *Life and the Poet,* 1942 (e); (with J. L. Gili) *Selected Poems of Federico Garcia Lorca,* 1943 (tr); *Poetry Since 1939,* 1946 (c); *European Witness* [Impressions of Germany in 1945], 1946 (e); *Poems of Dedication,* 1947 (p); *Returning to Vienna,* 1947 (p); *Botticelli,* 1948 (b); *The Edge of Being,* 1949 (p); (with F. Cornford) Paul Eluard, *Le Dur Désir de Durer,* 1950 (tr); *World Within World,* 1951 (a); Rainer Maria Rilke, *The Life of the Virgin Mary,* 1951 (tr); *Learning Laughter* [A Study of Children in Israel], 1952 (e); *Shelley,* 1952 (c); Ed., *Encounter,* 1953-; *The Creative Element,* 1953 (e); *Sirmione Peninsula,* 1953 (p); *Collected Poems, 1928-1953,* 1955; *The Making of a Poem,* 1955 (e); *Engaged in Writing, and The Fool and the Princess,* 1958 (s); *Inscriptions,* 1958 (p); *Schiller, Mary Stuart,* 1958 (tr); *The Struggle of the Modern,* 1963 (c); *Selected Poems,* 1965 (p). Also trs. of Toller and Wedekind

See G. S. Fraser, *The Modern Writer and His World,* rev. 1964

J. C. SQUIRE
1884-1958

Socialism and Art, 1907 (e); Poems and Baudelaire Flowers, 1909 (p); Imaginary Speeches, and Other Parodies, 1912 (p,e); William the Silent, 1912 (b); The Three Hills, 1913 (p); Steps to Parnassus, and Other Parodies and Diversions, 1913 (p,e); The Survival of the Fittest, 1916, (p); Twelve Poems, 1916 (p); The Lily of Malud, 1917 (p); The Gold Tree, 1918 (e); Tricks of the Trade, 1917 (p,e); Poems: First Series, 1918 (p); (Solomon Eagle, pseud.) Books in General, First Series, 1918 (c); The Birds, 1919 (p); Ed., London Mercury, 1919-1934; The Moon, 1920 (p); (Solomon Eagle, pseud.) Books in General, Second Series, 1920 (c); Life and Letters, 1920 (e); (Solomon Eagle, pseud.) Books in General, Third Series, 1921 (c); Collected Parodies, 1921 (p,e); Poems, Second Series, 1922 (p); Books Reviewed, 1922 (c); (Solomon Eagle, pseud.) Essays at Large, 1922 (e); American Poems, 1923 (p); Essays on Poetry, 1923 (c); A New Song of the Bishop of London and the City Churches, 1924 (p); The Grub Street Nights Entertainments, 1924 (s); Poems in One Volume, 1926 (p); Life at the Mermaid, 1927 (e); (with John L. Balderston) Berkeley Square, 1928 (d); (with Joan R. Young) Robin Hood, 1928 (d); (adapted from Jane Austen, with Eileen H. A. Squire) Pride and Prejudice, 1929 (d); Sunday Mornings, 1930 (e); A Face in the Candlelight, 1932 (p); Outside Eden, 1933 (s); Reflections and Memories, 1935 (r); Shakespeare as a Dramatist, 1935 (c); Weepings and Wailings, 1935 (p); Flowers of Speech, 1935 (e); The Honeysuckle and the Bee, 1937 (a); Water Music, 1939 (e); Poems of Two Wars, 1940 (p); Selected Poems, 1948 (p); Collected Poems, 1959

Iolo A. Williams, John Collings Squire and James Stephens, 1922; Patrick J. F. Howarth, Squire: "Most Generous of Men", 1963

ROBERT STANDISH
1898-

The Three Bamboos, 1942 (n); Bonin, 1943 (n); The Small General, 1945 (n); Mr. On Loong, 1946 (n); The Gulf of Time, 1947 (n); Elephant Walk, 1948 (n); Gentleman of China, 1949 (n); Follow the Seventh Man, 1950 (n); Storm Centre, 1951 (n); A Worthy Man, 1951 (n); A Long Way from Pimlico, 1954 (n); Private Enterprise, 1954 (s); Honourable Ancestor, 1956 (n); Blind Tiger, 1957 (n); The Prince of Storytellers [Life of E. Phillips Oppenheim], 1957 (b); African Guinea Pig, 1958 (n); The Radio-active General, 1959 (s); The First of Trees, The Story of the Olive, 1960 (h); The Big One Got Away, 1960 (n); The Talking Dog, 1961 (s); The Cruise of "The Three Brothers", 1962 (n); Singapore Kate, 1964 (n)

DEREK STANFORD
1918-

The Freedom of Poetry, Studies in Contemporary Verse, 1947 (e); Music for Statues, 1948 (p); Christopher Fry, 1951 (c); Christopher Fry Album, 1952 (e); (with Muriel Spark) Emily Brontë, 1953 (b,c); Dylan Thomas, 1954 (rev. 1964) (c); (with Ada Harrison) Anne Brontë, 1959 (b,c); Movements in English Poetry, 1900-1958, 1959 (h); John Betjeman, 1961 (c); Muriel Spark, 1963 (b,c)

FREYA STARK
1893-

Bagdad Sketches, 1932 (sk); The Valleys of the Assassins and Other Persian Travels, 1934 (t); The Southern Gates of Arabia, 1936 (t); Seen in the Hadhramaut, 1938 (t); A Winter in Arabia, 1940 (t); Letters from Syria, 1942 (t); East is West, 1939-1943, 1945 (Am. ed. The Arab Island) (h); Perseus in the Wind, 1948 (e); Traveller's Prelude, 1950 (a); Beyond Euphrates, 1951 (a); The Coast of Incense, 1933-1939, 1953 (a); The Freya Stark Story (condensation of autobiog. to 1939), 1953 (a); Ionia, A Quest, 1954 (t); The Lycian Shore, 1956 (t); Alexander's Path, 1958 (t); Riding to the Tigris, 1959 (t); Dust in the Lion's Paw, 1939-1946, 1961 (a); The Journey's Echo: Selections, 1963 (t); Rome on the Euphrates, The Story of a Frontier, 1966 (h,t)

JAMES STEPHENS
1882-1950

Insurrections, 1909 (p); The Lonely God, 1909 (p); The Adventures of Seumas Beg: The Visit from Abroad, In The Orchard, Treasure Trove, 1910 (p); The Spy, 1910 (p); The Hill of Vision, 1912 (repr. 1922) (p); The Charwoman's Daughter, 1912 (Am. ed. Mary, Mary) (n); The Crock of Gold, 1912 (repr. 1954) (n); Five New Poems, 1913 (p); Here Are Ladies, 1913 (s); The Demi-Gods, 1914 (n); The Adventures of Seumas Beg, The Rocky Road to Dublin, 1915 (p); Songs from the Clay, 1915 (p); The Insurrection in Dublin, 1916 (e); Green Branches, 1916 (p); Reincarnations, 1918 (p); [James Esse, pseud.] Hunger, 1918 (n); Irish Fairy Tales, 1920 (s); Arthur Griffith, Journalist and Statesman, 1922 (b); Deirdre, 1923 (repr. 1962) (n); Little Things, 1924 (p); In the Land of Youth, 1924 (n); A Poetry Recital, 1925 (p); Collected Poems, 1926 (rev. enlgd. 1954); On Prose and Verse, 1928 (e); Etched in Moonlight, 1928 (s); Dublin Letters, 1928 (e); Julia Elizabeth, 1929 (d); The Outcast, 1929 (p); Theme and Variations, 1930 (p); Strict Joy, 1931 (p); Kings and the Moon, 1938 (p); A James Stephens Reader, sel. Lloyd Frankenberg, 1962; James, Seumas and Jacques: Unpublished Writings of James Stephens, ed. Lloyd Frankenberg, 1964 (misc.)

Hilary Pyle, James Stephens: His Work and an Account of His Life, 1965

G. B. STERN
1890-

Pantomime, 1914 (n); "See-Saw", 1914 (repr. 1931) (n); Twos and Threes, 1916 (n); Grand Chain, 1917 (n); A Marrying Man, 1918 (n); Children of No Man's Land, 1919 (Am. ed. Debatable Ground) (n); Larry Munro, 1920 (Am. ed. The China Shop, 1921) (n); The Room, 1922 (n); The Back Seat, 1923 (repr. 1949) (n); Smoke Rings, 1923 (s); Tents of Israel, 1924 (Am. ed. The Matriarch) (n); Thunderstorm, 1925 (n); A Deputy Was King (continues Tents of Israel), 1926 (n); (with Geoffrey Holdsworth) The Happy Meddler, 1926 (n); The Dark Gentleman, 1927 (n); Bouquet (travels in the wine-producing regions of France), 1927 (t); Jack a'Manory, 1927 (Am. ed. The Slower Judas), 1927 (s); Debonair, 1928 (n); Petruchio, 1929 (Am. ed. Modesta) (n); Mosaic (continues Tents of Israel), 1930 (n); The Shortest Night, 1931 (d); The Man Who Pays the Piper, 1931 (d); The Matriarch, 1931 (d); Little Red Horses, 1932 (Am. ed. The Rueful Mating) (n); Long-Lost Father, 1932 (n); The Rakonitz Chronicles (Tents of Israel, A Deputy Was King, Mosaic), 1932 (n); The Augs, 1933 (Am. ed. Summer's Play) (n); Pelican Walking, 1934 (s); Shining and Free: A Day in the Life of the Matriarch, 1935 (n); Monogram, 1936 (r); Oleander River, 1937 (n); The Ugly Dachshund, 1938 (s); The Woman in the Hall, 1939 (repr. 1961) (n); Long Story Short, 1939 (s); A Lion in the Garden, 1940 (n); Another Part of the Forest, 1941 (r); Dogs in an Omnibus, 1942 (n); The Young Matriach, 1942 (n); (with Sheila Kaye-Smith) Talking of Jane Austen, 1943 (c); Trumpet Voluntary, 1944 (n); The Reasonable Shores, 1946 (n); No Son of Mine, 1948 (n); Benefits Forgot, 1949 (r); A Duck to Water, 1949 (n); Ten Days of Christmas, 1950 (n); (with Rupert Croft-Cooke) Gala Night at "The Willows", 1950 (d); (with Sheila Kaye-Smith) More Talk of Jane Austen, 1950 (c); The Donkey Shoe, 1952 (n); Robert Louis Stevenson, 1952 (b,c); A Name to Conjure With, 1953 (a); Raffle for a Bedspread, 1953 (d); Johnny Forsken, 1954 (n); He Wrote "Treasure Island", 1954 (b); All in Good Time, 1954 (a); The Way It All Worked Out (seq. to preceding), 1956 (a); For All We Know, 1956 (n); And Did He Stop and Speak to You?, 1957 (r); Seventy Times Seven, 1957 (n); The Patience of a Saint, 1958 (n); Unless I Marry, 1959 (n); One is Only Human, 1960 (e); Bernadette, 1960 (b); Dolphin Cottage, 1962 (n); Promise Not to Tell, 1964 (n)

See Katherine Mansfield, Novels and Novelists, 1930

LYTTON STRACHEY
1880-1932

Some New Plays in Verse, 1908 (pd); Light Verse, 1909 (p); Landmarks in French Literature, 1912 (c); Eminent

Victorians, 1918 (b); *Queen Victoria*, 1921 (b); *Books and Characters, French and English*, 1922 (c); *Pope*, 1925 (Leslie Stephen lecture); *Elizabeth and Essex*, 1928 (b); *Portraits in Miniature*, 1931 (e); *Characters and Commentaries*, 1933 (e); *The Collected Works*, 1948, 6 vols.; *Virginia Woolf and Lytton Strachey: Letters*, ed. Leonard Woolf and James Strachey, 1956; *Spectatorial Essays* [repr. from *Spectator*, 1904-13], 1964 (c)

Charles R. Sanders, *Strachey, His Mind and Art*, 1957 [no bibliog.]; M. Holroyd, *Lytton Strachey*, Vol. I: *The Unknown Years*, 1966

L. A. G. STRONG
1896-1958

Dallington Rhymes, 1919 (p); *Dublin Days*, 1921 (p); *Twice Four*, 1921 (p); *Says the Muse to Me, Says She*, 1922 (p); *Eight Poems*, 1923 (p); *The Lowery Road*, 1923 (p); *Doyle's Rock*, 1925 (s); *Difficult Love*, 1927 (p); *At Glenan Cross*, 1928 (p); *The English Captain*, 1929 (s); *Dewer Rides*, 1929 (repr. 1949) (n); *The Jealous Ghost*, 1930 (n); *Christmas*, 1930 (p); *Northern Light*, 1930 (p); *Common Sense About Poetry*, 1931 (c); *Selected Poems*, 1931 (p); *The Big Man*, 1931 (s); *The Garden*, 1931 (repr. 1947) (n); *The Brothers*, 1932 (repr. 1946) (n); *Don Juan and the Wheelbarrow*, 1932 (s); *March Evening*, 1932 (p); *A Defence of Ignorance*, 1932 (e); *A Letter to W. B. Yeats*, 1932 (e); (with Monica Redlich) *Life in English Literature*, 1932 (e); *Sea Wall*, 1933 (n); *Corporal Tune*, 1934 (n); *The Seven Arms*, 1935 (n); *Tuesday Afternoon*, 1935 (s); *The Hansom Cab and the Pigeons*, 1935 (e); *The Last Enemy*, 1936 (n); *Call to the Swan*, 1936 (p); *Common Sense About Drama*, 1937 (c); *The Fifth of November*, 1937 (repr. 1956) (n); *The Swift Shadow*, 1937 (n); *Laughter in the West*, 1937 (n); *The Minstrel Boy, A Portrait of Tom Moore*, 1937 (b); *Odd Man In*, 1938 (s); *Shake Hands and Come Out Fighting*, 1938 (r); *The Open Sky*, 1939 (n); *Trial and Error*, 1939 (d); *The Absentee*, 1939 (d); *Sun on the Water*, 1940 (s); *English for Pleasure*, 1941 (radio talks to schools); *The Bay*, 1941 (n); *John Millington Synge*, 1941 (b); *House in Disorder*, 1941 (n); *John McCormack*, 1941 (b); *Slocombe Dies*, 1942 (n); *Authorship*, 1944 (e); *The Unpractised Heart*, 1942 (n); *The Director*, 1944 (n); *All Fall Down*, 1944 (n); *A Tongue in Your Head* [on speaking English], 1945 (e); *Sink or Swim*, 1945 (n); *Othello's Occupation*, 1945 (n); *Travellers*, 1945 (s); *Light Through the Cloud* (The Story of The Retreat, York, 1796-1946), 1946 (h); *The Doll*, 1946 (s); *Trevannion*, 1948 (n); *The Sacred River* [James Joyce], 1949 (c); *Maud Cherrill*, 1949 (b); *Which I Never*, 1950 (n); *Three Novels: The Garden, Corporal Tune, The Seven Arms*, 1950 (3n); *Darling Tom*, 1952 (s); *John Masefield*, 1952 (b); *The Writer's Trade*, 1953 (e); *The Hill of Howth*, 1953 (n); *Personal Remarks*, 1953 (e); *It's Not Very Nice*, 1954 (d); *The Story of Sugar*, 1954 (h); *Dr. Quicksilver 1660-1742*, [Thomas Dover, M.D.], 1955 (b); *Deliverana*, 1955 (h); *Flying Angel*, 1956 (e); *The Rolling Road*, 1956 (e); *The Body's Imperfection, Collected Poems*, 1957; *Treason in the Egg*, 1958 (n); *Light Above the Lake*, 1958 (n); *Instructions to Young Writers*, 1958 (e); *Green Memory*, 1961 (a)

See John Gawsworth, *Ten Contemporaries*, 1933; see Rodolphe Louis Mégroz, *Five Novelist Poets of Today*, 1933

FRANCIS STUART
1902-

We Have Kept the Faith, 1923 (p); *Women and God*, 1931 (n); *The Coloured Dome*, 1932 (n); *Pigeon Irish*, 1932 (n); *Glory*, 1933 (n); *Try the Sky*, 1933 (n); *Things to Live For*, 1934 (a); *In Search of Love*, 1935 (s); *The Angel of Pity*, 1935 (n); *The White Hare*, 1936 (n); *Racing for Pleasure and Profit in Ireland . . .*, 1937 (e); *The Bridge*, 1937 (n); *Julie*, 1938 (n); *The Great Squire*, 1939 (n); *The Pillar of Cloud*, 1948 (n); *Redemption*, 1949 (n); *The Flowering Cross*, 1950 (n); *Good Friday's Daughter*, 1952 (n); *The Chariot*, 1953 (n); *The Pilgrimage*, 1955 (n); *Victors and Vanquished*, 1958 (n); *Angels of Providence*, 1959 (n)

ALFRED SUTRO
1863-1933

Maurice Maeterlinck, *Aglavaine and*

Selysette, 1897 (tr); Maeterlinck, *The Treasure of the Humble*, 1897 (tr); Maeterlinck, *Wisdom and Destiny*, 1898 (tr); Maeterlinck, *Alladine and Palomides, Interior* [tr. William Archer], *and The Death of Tintagiles*, 1899 (tr); *The Cave of Illusion*, 1900 (d); Maeterlinck, *The Life of the Bee*, 1901 (repr. 1929) (tr); Maeterlinck, *The Buried Temple*, 1902 (tr); *Women in Love*, 1902 (8d); *The Foolish Virgins*, 1904 (d); Maeterlinck, *Monna Vanna*, 1904 (tr); *A Marriage Has Been Arranged: a Duologue*, 1904 (d); *Ella's Apology: a Duologue*, 1905 (d); *Mollentrave on Women*, 1905 (repr. 1921) (d); *A Game of Chess: a Duologue*, 1905 (d); *The Gutter of Time: a Duologue*, 1905 (d); *A Maker of Men: a Duologue*, 1905 (d); *Mr. Steinman's Corner*, 1905 (d); *The Salt of Life*, 1905 (d); *The Walls of Jericho*, 1906 (d); *The Open Door: a Duologue*, 1906 (d); *The Fascinating Mr. Vanderveldt*, 1906 (d); *John Glayde's Honour*, 1906 (d); *The Barrier*, 1907 (d); *The Man on the Kerb: a Duologue*, 1908 (d); *The Builder of Bridges*, 1909 (repr. 1921) (d); *The Man in the Stalls*, 1911 (d); *The Firescreen*, 1912 (d); *The Bracelet*, 1912 (d); *Five Little Plays*, 1912 (5d); *The Perplexed Husband*, 1913 (d); *The Two Virtues*, 1914 (d); *Freedom*, 1914 (d); *The Marriage . . . Will Not Take Place*, 1917 (d); *The Choice*, 1919 (d); *Uncle Anyhow*, 1919 (d); *The Perfect Lover*, 1921 (d); *The Laughing Lady*, 1922 (d); *The Great Well*, 1922 (d); *Far Above Rubies*, 1924 (d); *A Man with a Heart*, 1925 (d); Maeterlinck, *Ancient Egypt*, 1925 (tr); *The Desperate Lovers*, 1926 (d); Maeterlinck, *The Life of the White Ant*, 1927 (tr); *Living Together*, 1929 (d); *The Blackmailing Lady*, 1929 (d); Maeterlinck, *The Magic of the Stars*, 1930 (tr); *About Women*, 1931 (e); *Which: Lord Byron or Lord Byron, a Bet*, 1932 (e); *Celebrities and Simple Souls*, 1933 (r)

FRANK SWINNERTON
1884-

The Merry Heart, 1909 (n); *The Young Idea*, 1910 (repr. 1922) (n); *The Casement*, 1911 (n); *The Happy Family*, 1912 (n); *George Gissing*, 1912 (repr. 1924) (c); *R. L. Stevenson*, 1914 (repr. 1948) (c); *On the Staircase*, 1914 (repr. 1948) (n); *The Chaste Wife*, 1916 (n); *Nocturne*, 1917 (repr. 1948) (n); *Shops and Houses*, 1918 (n); *Women*, 1919 (e); *September*, 1919 (n); *Coquette*, 1921 (n); *The Three Lovers*, 1922 (n); *Young Felix*, 1923 (n); *The Elder Sister*, 1925 (n); *Summer Storm*, 1926 (n); *Tokefield Papers*, 1927 (new enlgd. ed. 1949) (e); *A Brood of Ducklings*, 1928 (n); *A London Bookman*, 1928 (e); *Sketch of a Sinner*, 1929 (n); *Authors and the Book Trade*, 1932 (e); *The Georgian House*, 1933 (n); *Elizabeth*, 1934 (n); *The Georgian Scene*, 1934 (English ed. *The Georgian Literary Scene*, 1935) (rev. 1950) (c); *Swinnerton, An Autobiography*, 1936 (a); *Harvest Comedy*, 1937 (n); *The Reviewing and Criticism of Books*, 1939 (Dent Memorial lecture); *The Two Wives*, 1940 (n); *The Fortunate Lady*, 1941 (n); *Thankless Child*, 1942 (n); *A Woman in Sunshine*, 1944 (n); *English Maiden*, 1946 (n); *A Faithful Company*, 1948 (n); *The Doctor's Wife Comes to Stay*, 1949 (n); *Arnold Bennett*, 1950 (c); *A Flower for Catherine*, 1950 (n); *The Bookman's London*, 1951 (t); *Londoner's Post*, 1952 (e); *Master Jim Probity*, 1952 (n); *An Affair of Love*, 1953 (n); *A Month in Gordon Square*, 1953 (n); *The Summer Intrigue*, 1955 (n); *The Adventures of a Manuscript*, 1956 (e); *Authors I Never Met*, 1956 (e); *Background with Chorus: a Footnote to Changes in English Literary Fashion between 1901 and 1917*, 1956 (e); *The Woman from Sicily*, 1957 (n); *A Tigress in Prothero*, 1959 (Am. ed. *A Tigress in the Village*) (n); *The Grace Divorce*, 1960 (n); *Death of a Highbrow*, 1961 (n); *Figures in the Foreground: Literary Reminiscences 1917-1940*, 1963 (r); *Quadrille*, 1965 (n); *A Galaxy of Fathers*, 1965 (e); *Sanctuary*, 1966 (n)

Arnold Bennett, H. G. Wells and Grant Overton, *Frank Swinnerton: Personal Sketches together with Notes and Comments on the Novels*, 1920 [no bibliog.]

ARTHUR SYMONS
1865-1945

An Introduction to the Study of Browning, 1886 (rev. 1906) (c); *Days and Nights*, 1889 (p); *Silhouettes*, 1892 (sec.

ed. enlgd. 1898) (p); Zola, *L'Assomoir*, 1894 (n,tr); *London Nights*, 1895 (rev. 1897) (p); *Collected Poems*, 1895; *Studies in Two Literatures* [English and French], 1897 (c); *Amoris Victima*, 1897 (p); Verhaeren, *Les Aubes*, 1898 (tr); *Aubrey Beardsley*, 1898 (rev. 1905) (c); *The Symbolist Movement in Literature*, 1899 (rev. 1908, 1919; repr. 1958) (c); *Images of Good and Evil*, 1899 (p); G. d'Annunzio, *The Dead City*, 1900 (n,tr); *Poems*, 2 vols., 1901; *Plays, Acting and Music*, 1903 (rev. 1909) (c); *Cities*, 1903 (e); *Lyrics*, 1903 (p); *Studies in Prose and Verse*, 1904 (c); Baudelaire, *Poems in Prose*, 1905 (tr); *Spiritual Adventures*, 1905 (s); *The Fool of the World*, 1906 (p); *Studies in Seven Arts*, 1906 (rev. 1925) (c); *Great Acting in English*, 1907 (e); *William Blake*, 1907 (c); *Lyrics*, 1907 (p); *Cities of Italy*, 1907 (t); *A Book of Parodies*, 1908 (p,e); *The Romantic Movement in English Poetry*, 1909 (c); *London*, 1909 (t); *Knave of Hearts, 1894-1908*, 1913 (p); *Gabriel d'Annunzio*, 1914 (c); *Poems*, 1914 [1889-99] (p); *Figures of Several Centuries*, 1916 (c); *Tragedies*, 1916 (pd); *Barbara Roscorla's Child*, 1917 (d); *Tristan and Iseult*, 1917 (pd); *Cities and Sea-Coasts and Islands*, 1918 (t); *Colour Studies in Paris*, 1918 (e); *The Toy Cart*, 1919 (d); *Studies in the Elizabethan Drama*, 1920 (c); *Charles Baudelaire*, 1920 (c); *Lesbia*, 1920 (p); *Cesare Borgia, Iseult of Brittany, The Toy Cart*, 1920 (3d); *Love's Cruelty*, 1923 (p); *Dramatis Personae*, 1923 (c); *The Café Royal*, 1923 (e); *Collected Works*, 9 vols., 1924; Baudelaire, *Les Fleurs du Mal, Petits Poèmes en Prose, Les Paradis Artificiels*, 1925 (tr); *Notes on Joseph Conrad, with Some Unpublished Letters*, 1925 (r); *Studies on Modern Painters*, 1925 (c); *From Catullus*, 1925 (tr); Villiers de l'Isle-Adam, *Claire Lenoir*, 1925 (tr); *Eleonora Duse*, 1926 (b); *Parisian Nights*, 1926 (e); *A Study of Thomas Hardy*, 1927 (c); *The Letters of Charles Baudelaire to His Mother*, 1927 (tr); *From Toulouse-Lautrec to Rodin with Some Personal Impressions*, 1929 (r,c); *Studies in Strange Souls* [D. G. Rosetti, A. C. Swinburne], 1929 (c); *A Study of Oscar Wilde*, 1930 (c); *Confessions, A Study in Pathology*, 1930 (r,c); *Mes Souvenirs* [on Verlaine], 1931 (r); *Wanderings*, 1931 (t); *Jezebel Mort*, 1931 (p); *A Study of Walter Pater*, 1932 (c)

Roger Lhombreaud, *Arthur Symons*, 1963 [partial bibliog.]

JULIAN SYMONS
1912-

Confusions About X, 1939 (p); *The Second Man*, 1943 (p); *The Immaterial Murder Case*, 1945 (n); *A Man Called Jones*, 1947 (n); *Bland Beginning*, 1949 (n); *A. J. A. Symons, His Life and Speculations*, 1950 (b); *The 31st of February*, 1950 (n); *Charles Dickens*, 1951 (b,c); *Thomas Carlyle*, 1952 (b,c); *The Broken Penny*, 1953 (n); *The Narrowing Circle*, 1954 (n); *Horatio Bottomley*, 1955 (b); *The Paper Chase*, 1956 (n); *The Colour of Murder*, 1957 (n); *The General Strike*, 1957 (e); *The Gigantic Shadow*, 1958 (n); *The Thirties*, 1960 (e); *Buller's Campaign* [Boer War], 1963 (h); *The End of Solomon Grundy*, 1964 (n); *Francis Quarles Investigates*, 1965 (s); *The Belting Inheritance*, 1965 (n)

JOHN MILLINGTON SYNGE
1871-1909

In the Shadow of the Glen, 1904 (d); *In the Shadow of the Glen and Riders to the Sea*, 1905 (2d); *The Well of the Saints*, 1905 (d); *The Playboy of the Western World*, 1907 (many repr.) (d); *The Aran Islands*, 1907 (e); *The Tinker's Wedding*, 1908 (d); *Poems and Translations*, ed. W. B. Yeats, 1909 (p); *Deirdre of the Sorrows*, 1910 (d); *The Works*, 4 vols., 1910; *In Wicklow, West Kerry and Connemara*, 1911 (t); *Plays by John M. Synge* (incl. extracts from notebooks and unpub. letter), 1932; *The Complete Works*, 1935; *Plays, Poems and Prose*, 1941; *Translations* (from Petrarch, Villon, etc.), ed. Robin Skelton, 1961 (tr); *Collected Works*, Vol. I, *Poems*, ed. Robin Skelton, 1962; *Poems and Plays*, ed. T. R. Henn, 1963; *The Autobiography of J. M. Synge, Constructed from the Manuscripts* by Alan Price, 1965; *Collected Works*, Vol. II: *The Aran Islands, In Wicklow, West Kerry*, and *Connemara* (with articles, reviews, and unpub. autobiog. material), ed. Alan Price, 1966

David H. Greene and Edward M. Stephens, *J. M. Synge, 1871-1909*, 1959 [book list]

ANGELA THIRKELL
1890-1961

Three Houses, 1931 (r); *Ankle Deep*, 1933 (n); *High Rising*, 1933 (n); *Wild Strawberries*, 1934 (n); *The Demon in the House*, 1934 (n); *O These Men, These Men*, 1935 (n); *The Grateful Sparrow*,* 1935 (tr); *August Folly*, 1936 (n); *The Fortunes of Harriette: The Surprising Career of Harriette Wilson*, 1936 (Am. ed. *Tribue for Harriette*) (b); *Coronation Summer*, 1937 (n); *Summer Half*, 1937 (n); *Pomfret Towers*, 1938 (n); *The Brandons*, 1939 (n); *Before Lunch*, 1939 (n); *Cheerfulness Breaks In*, 1940 (n); *Northbridge Rectory*, 1941 (n); *Marling Hall*, 1942 (n); *Growing Up*, 1943 (n); *The Headmistress*, 1944 (n); *Miss Bunting*, 1945 (n); *Peace Breaks Out*, 1946 (n); *Private Enterprise*, 1947 (n); *Love Among the Ruins*, 1948 (n); *The Old Bank House*, 1949 (n); *County Chronicle*, 1950 (n); *The Duke's Daughter*, 1951 (n); *Happy Returns*, 1952 (n); *Jutland Cottage*, 1953 (n); *What Did It Mean?*, 1954 (n); *Enter Sir Robert*, 1955 (n); *Never Too Late*, 1956 (n); *A Double Affair*, 1957 (n); *Close Quarters*, 1958 (n); *Love at All Ages*, 1959 (n); *Three Score and Ten*, 1961 (n)

*from the German

DYLAN THOMAS
1914-1953

18 Poems, 1934 (p); *Twenty-Five Poems*, 1936 (p); *The Map of Love*, 1939 (p,s); *The World I Breathe*, 1939 (p,s); *Portrait of the Artist as a Young Dog*, 1940 (s); *New Poems*, 1943 (p); *Deaths and Entrances*, 1946 (p); *Selected Writings*, ed. J. L. Sweeney, 1946; *Twenty-Six Poems*, 1950 (p); *In Country Sleep*, 1952 (p); *Collected Poems, 1934-1952*, 1952; *The Doctor and the Devils* (from story by Donald Taylor), 1953 (film script); *Quite Early One Morning*, 1954 (broadcasts); *Under Milk Wood*, 1954 (pd); *A Child's Christmas in Wales*, 1954 (rev. 1959) (r); *Adventures in the Skin Trade*, 1955 (s); *A Prospect of the Sea*, ed. Daniel Jones, 1955 (misc.); *Letters to*

Vernon Watkins, ed. Vernon Watkins, 1957; *The Beach of Falesá* (based on a story by R. L. Stevenson), 1963 (s); *Miscellany: Poems, Stories, Broadcasts*, 1963; *Me and My Bike*, 1965 (unfinished film script); *Selected Letters of Dylan Thomas*, ed. Constantine Fitzgibbon, 1966

*repr. 1966

J. Alexander Rolfe, *Dylan Thomas: a Bibliography*, 1956; John Ackerman, *Dylan Thomas: His Life and Work*, 1964; Constantine Fitzgibbon, *The Life of Dylan Thomas*, 1965

EDWARD THOMAS
1878-1917

The Woodland Life, 1897 (t,a); *Horae Solitariae*, 1902 (e); *Oxford*, 1903 (rev. 1922, repr. 1932) (t); *Rose Acre Papers*, 1904 (repr. 1910, incl. essays from *Horae Solitariae*) (e); *Beautiful Wales*, 1904 (new ed. 1924) (t); *The Heart of England*, 1906 (repr. 1932) (t); *Richard Jeffries*, 1909 (repr. 1938) (b,c); *The South Country*, 1909 (repr. 1938) (t); *Rest and Unrest*, 1910 (e); *Feminine Influence on the Poets*, 1910 (e); *Windsor Castle*, 1910 (repr. 1939) (t); *The Isle of Wight*, 1911 (t); *Light and Twilight*, 1911 (e); *Maurice Maeterlinck*, 1911 (e); *Celtic Stories*, 1911 (repr. 1922) (s); *Keats*, 1912 (b); *Algernon Charles Swinburne*, 1912 (b); *George Borrow*, 1912 (b); *Lafcadio Hearn*, 1912 (b); *Norse Tales*, 1912 (s); *The Icknield Way*, 1913 (t); *The Country*, 1913 (e); *The Happy-Go-Lucky Morgans*, 1913 (n); *Walter Pater*, 1913 (c); *In Pursuit of Spring*, 1914 (e); *Four-and-Twenty Blackbirds*, 1915 (s); *The Life of the Duke of Marlborough*, 1915 (b); *A Literary Pilgrim in England*, 1917 (t); *Poems*, 1917 (p); *Last Poems*, 1918 (p); *Collected Poems*, 1920 (new ed. 1928; Faber ed. 1936, 1949); *Cloud Castle*, 1922 (e); *Edward Thomas* [Selected Essays], 1926 (e); *Chosen Essays*, sel. Ernest Rhys, 1926 (e); *Selected Poems*, 1926 (p); *Selected Poems*, introd. Edward Garnett, 1927 (p); *The Childhood of Edward Thomas: A Fragment of Autobiography*, 1938 (a); John C. Moore, *The Life and Letters of Edward Thomas*, 1939; *The Trumpet*, 1940 (p); *The Prose of Edward Thomas*, sel. Roland Grant,

1948; *Selected Poems*, 1964 (p); *The Green Roads: Poems for Young Readers*, ed. R. S. Thomas, 1964 (p)

Robert P. Eckert, *Edward Thomas: A Biography and a Bibliography*, 1937; John Moore, *The Life and Letters of Edward Thomas*, 1939; Vernon Scannell, *Edward Thomas*, 1965

R. S. THOMAS
1913-

The Stones of the Field, 1946, (p); *An Acre of Land*, 1952 (p); *The Minister*, 1953 (p); *Song at the Year's Turning: Poems 1942-1954*, 1955 (p); *Poetry for Supper*, 1958 (p); *Tares*, 1961 (p); *The Bread of Truth*, 1963 (p); *Words and the Poet*, 1964 (e); *Pietà*, 1966 (p)

R. G. Thomas, *R. S. Thomas*, 1964

SYLVIA THOMPSON
1902-

The Rough Crossing, 1921 (n); *A Lady in Green Gloves*, 1924 (n); *The Hounds of Spring*, 1926 (n); *The Battle of the Horizons*, 1928 (n); *Chariot Wheels*, 1929 (n); *Winter Comedy*, 1931 (Am. ed. *Portrait by Caroline*) (n); *Summer's Night*, 1932 (n); *Helena*, 1933 (Am. ed. *Unfinished Symphony*) (n); *Breakfast in Bed*, 1934 (n); (with Victor Cunard) *Golden Arrow*, 1935 (d); *A Silver Rattle*, 1935 (n); *Third Act in Venice*, 1936 (n); *Recapture the Moon*, 1937 (n); *The Adventures of Christopher Columin*, 1939 (n); *The Gulls Fly Inland*, 1941 (n); *Empty Heart*, 1945 (n); *The People Opposite*, 1948 (n); *The Candle's Glory*, 1953 (n)

TERENCE TILLER
1916-

Poems, 1941; *The Inward Animal*, 1943 (p); *Unarm, Eros*, 1947 (p); *Reading a Medal*, 1957 (p); John Gower, *Confessio Amantis*, 1963 (tr)

RUTHVEN TODD
1914-

Over the Mountain, 1939 (n); *The Laughing Mulatto* [Alexandre Dumas], 1940 (b); *Ten Poems*, 1940 (p); *Until Now*, 1942 (p); *The Lost Traveller*, 1943 (n); *The Acreage of the Heart*, 1944 (p);

The Planet in My Hand, 1946 (p); *Tracks in the Snow*, 1946 (e); *Two Poems*, 1951 (p); *Loser's Choice*, 1953 (n); *A Mantelpiece of Shells*, 1954 (p); *Garland for the Winter Solstice*, 1961 (p)

J. R. TOLKIEN
1892-

A Middle-English Vocabulary, 1922 (textbook); *Beowulf, The Monsters and the Critics*, 1936 (Gollancz Memorial lecture); *The Hobbit*, 1937 (repr. 1951) (child's bk.); *Fairy Stories: a Critical Study*, 1946 (c); *Farmer Giles of Ham*, 1949 (repr. 1951) (child's bk.); *The Lord of the Rings* (trilogy: *The Fellowship of the Ring, The Two Towers, The Return of the King*), 1954-55 (3n); *The Adventures of Tom Bombadil*, 1962 (p); *Tree and Leaf*, 1964 (e)

CHARLES TOMLINSON
1927-

Relations and Contraries, 1951 (p); *The Necklace, 1955 (p); *Solo for a Glass Harmonica*, 1957 (p); *Seeing Is Believing*, 1958 (p); *A Peopled Landscape*, 1963 (p); *Poems*, 1964 (p); *American Scenes and other Poems*, 1966 (p)

*repr. 1966

H. M. TOMLINSON
1873-1958

The Sea and the Jungle, 1912 (repr. to 1956) (t); *Old Junk*, 1918 (rev. 1933); *London River*, 1921 (rev. enlgd. 1951) (sk); *Waiting for Daylight*, 1922 (sk); *Tidemarks* [The Moluccas and the forest of Malaya in 1923], 1924 (t); *Under the Red Ensign*, 1926 (Am. ed. *The Foreshore of England*) (e); *Gifts of Fortune*, 1926 (t); *Gallions Reach*, 1927 (repr. 1952) (n); *Illusion, 1915*, 1928 (e); *Côte d'Or*, 1929 (e); *Thomas Hardy*, 1929 (c); *All Our Yesterdays*, 1930 (n); *Norman Douglas*, 1931 (rev. enlgd. 1952) (c); *Out of Soundings*, 1931 (e); *The Snows of Helicon*, 1933 (n); *South to Cadiz*, 1934 (t); (with H. Charles Tomlinson) *Below London Bridge*, 1934 (t); *Mars His Idiot*, 1935 (e); *All Hands!* (Am. ed. *Pipe All Hands*), 1937 (n); *The Day Before*, 1939 (n); *The Wind is Rising*, 1941 (war diary); *The Turn of the Tide*, 1945 (t,e); *Morning Light*,

1946 (n); *The Face of the Earth*, 1950 (t); *Malay Waters*, 1951 (h); *The Haunted Forest*, 1951 (child's bk.); *A Mingled Yarn*, 1953 (a); *H. M. Tomlinson: A Selection from his Writings*, sel. Kenneth Hopkins, 1953 (misc.); *The Trumpet Shall Sound*, 1957 (s)

Isadore L. Baker, *H. M. Tomlinson: Gallions Reach*, 1953 [no bibliog.]

PHILIP TOYNBEE
1916-

The Savage Days, 1937 (n); *School in Private*, 1941 (n); *The Barricades*, 1943 (n); *Tea with Mrs. Goodman*, 1947 (Am. ed. *Prothalamium*) (n); *The Garden to the Sea*, 1953 (n); *Friends Apart, a Memoir of Esmond Romilly and Jasper Ridley in the Thirties*, 1954 (m); *The Fearful Choice*, 1958 (e); *Pantaloon, or The Valediction*, 1961 (novel in verse form); *Underdogs: Eighteen Victims of Society*, 1961 (e); (with Arnold Toynbee) *Comparing Notes*, 1963 (e); *Two Brothers: The Fifth Day of the Valediction of Pantaloon*, 1964 (novel in verse form; sequel to *Pantaloon*); *A Learned City: The Sixth Day of the Valediction of Pantaloon*, 1966 (sequel to preceding)

HENRY TREECE
1912-1966

Thirty-eight Poems, 1940; *Towards a Personal Armageddon*, 1941 (p); *Invitation and Warning*, 1942 (p); (with Nicholas Moore and F. Hendry) *Sailing Tomorrow's Seas*, 1944 (p); *The Black Seasons*, 1945 (p); *Collected Poems*, 1946; *I Cannot Go Hunting Tomorrow*, 1946 (s); *How I See Apocalypse*, 1946 (e); *The Haunted Garden*, 1947 (p); *Dylan Thomas*, 1949 (rev. 1956) (e); *The Exiles*, 1952 (p); *The Dark Island*, 1952 (n); *The Rebels*, 1953 (n); *Legions of the Eagle*, 1954 (child's bk.); *The Eagles Have Flown*, 1954 (child's bk.); *Desperate Journey*, 1954 (n); *Ask for King Billy*, 1955 (n); *Carnival King*, 1955 (d); *Hounds of the King*, 1955 (s); *The Golden Strangers*, 1956 (n); *The Great Captains*, 1956 (n); *Red Queen, White Queen*, 1958 (n); *Don't Expect Any Mercy*, 1958 (n); *The Master of Badger's Hall*, 1959 (n); *The Bombard*, 1959 (s); *A Fighting Man*, 1960 (n);

The Golden One, 1961 (s); *Jason*, 1961 (n); *The Crusades*, 1962 (h); *Electra*, 1963 (Am. ed. *Amber Princess*) (n); *Fighting Men: How Men Have Fought Through the Ages*, 1963 (h); *Killer in Dark Glasses*, 1965 (n); *The Green Man*, 1966 (n)

See *Times Literary Supplement*, Nov. 24, 1966, pp. 1072-73

HERBERT TRENCH
1865-1923

Deirdre Wed, 1901 (p); D. S. Merezhokovsky, *The Death of the Gods*, 1901 (tr); *Souvenir of the Blue Bird* [contains esssay on life and work of Maeterlinck, with account of some scenes of the play], 1910 (b,c); *Lyrics and Narrative Poems*, 1911 (p); *Ode from Italy in Time of War: Night on Mottarone*, 1915 (p); *Poems with Fables in Prose*, 1918 (p,s); *Napoleon*, 1919 (d); *The Collected Works*, 3 vols., 1924

See Darrell Figgis, *Studies and Appreciations*, 1912; Abel Chevalley, *Herbert Trench: Notice sur sa Vie et ses Oeuvres*, 1925

GEORGE MACAULAY TREVELYAN
1876-1962

England in the Age of Wycliffe, 1899 (h); *England Under the Stuarts*, 1904 (repr. 1960) (h); *The Poetry and Philosophy of George Meredith*, 1906 (c); *Garibaldi's Defence of the Roman Republic, 1848-49*, 1907 (repr. 1933 etc.) (h); *Garibaldi and the Thousand, Naples and Sicily 1859-60*, 1909 (repr. 1928) (h); *Garibaldi and the Making of Italy*, 1911 (sev. repr.) (h); *The Life of John Bright*, 1913 (b); *Clio: A Muse, and Other Essays Literary and Pedestrian*, 1913 (also pub. as *The Recreations of a Historian*, 1919) (e); *Scenes from Italy's War*, 1919 (r); *British History in the Nineteenth Century, 1782-1901* (new ed. to 1919, 1962), 1922 (h); *History of England*, 1926 (repr. 1937, 1945) (h); *Walking*, 1928 (e); *England Under Queen Ann*, 3 vols., 1930-34 (h); *Sir George Otto Trevelyan, a Memoir by His Son*, 1932 (m); *Garibaldi* [includes *Garibaldi's Defence of the Roman Republic, Garibaldi and the Thousand*, and *Garibaldi and the Making of Italy*], 1933 (h); *Grey of Fallodon*,

1937 (b); *The English Revolution, 1688-1689*, 1938 (h); *A Shortened History of England*, 1942 (h); *English Social History: A Survey of Six Centuries*, 1942 (h); *History and the Reader*, 1945 (e); *Trinity College, an Historical Sketch*, 1946 (h); *An Autobiography and Other Essays*, 1949 (a,e); *English Literature and Its Readers*, 1951 (Pres. address, Eng. Assoc.); *A Layman's Love of Letters*, 1954 (Clark lectures)

John H. Plumb, *G. M. Trevelyan*, 1951

JAMES TURNER
1909-

Jono: a Collection of Prose and Verse, 1932 (misc.); *Mass of Death*, 1937 (n); *Pastoral*, 1942 (p); *The Alien Wood*, 1945 (p); *The Hollow Vale*, 1947 (p); *My Life with Borley Rectory*, 1950 (n); *Murder at Landred Hall*, 1954 (n); *Rivers of East Anglia*, 1954 (h,t); *A Death by the Sea*, 1955 (n); *The Dolphin's Skin: Six Studies in Eccentricity*, 1956 (b); *Strange Little Snakes*, 1956 (n); *The Frontiers of Death*, 1957 (n); *The Crystal Wave*, 1957 (n); *The Shrouds of Glory: Six Studies in Martyrdom*, 1958 (b); *The Dark Index*, 1959 (n); *The Deeper Malady*, 1959 (n); *The Interior Diagram*, 1960 (p); *The Glass Interval*, 1961 (n); *Condell*, 1961 (n); *The Crimson Moth*, 1962 (n); *The Nettle Shade*, 1963 (n); *The Long Avenues*, 1964 (n)

W. J. TURNER
1889-1946

The Hunter, 1916 (p); *The Dark Fire*, 1918 (p); *The Dark Wind*, 1920 (p); *In Time Like Glass*, 1921 (p); *Paris and Helen*, 1921 (p); *Music and Life*, 1921 (e); *The Man Who Ate the Popomack*, 1922 (d); *Smaragda's Lover*, 1924 (p); *Variations on the Theme of Music*, 1924 (e); *Marigold*, 1926 (p); *Orpheus, or The Music of the Future*, 1926 (e); *Select Poems*, 1926 (p); *The Aesthetes*, 1927 (e); *Beethoven*, 1927 (b); *Musical Meanderings*, 1928 (e); *A Trip to New York and a Poem*, 1929; *Miss America*, 1930 (p); *Pursuit of Psyche*, 1931 (p); *Music: A Short History*, 1932 (sec. ed. enlgd. 1949) (h); *Facing the Music: Reflections of a Music Critic*, 1933 (e); *Wagner*, 1935 (b); *Jack and Jill*, 1934 (p); *Berlioz*, 1934 (b); *Blow for Balloons*, 1935 (n); *Henry Airbubble* (seq. to preceding), 1936 (n); *Mozart*, 1936 (b); *Music: an Introduction to its Nature and Appreciation*, 1936 (e); *Songs and Incantations*, 1936 (p); *Selected Poems, 1916-1936*, 1939 (p); *The Duchess of Popacatapetl*, 1939 (n); *English Music*, 1941 (e); *Fables, Parables and Plots*, 1943 (misc.); *English Ballet*, 1944 (e); *Fossils of a Future Time?*, 1946 (p); *Exmoor Village: a General Account by W. J. Turner, based on Factual Information from Mass-Observation*, 1947 (e)

KATHARINE TYNAN
1861-1931

Selective Bibliography

From 1895 to her death K.T. published two, three, or four novels a year and in a few years as many as six. Six were published posthumously. None of the novels is included here, but her other works, excluding children's books, are listed.

Louise de la Vallière, 1885 (p); *Shamrocks*, 1887 (p); *Ballads and Lyrics*, 1891 (p); *Cuckoo Songs*, 1894 (p); *A Cluster of Nuts*, 1894 (sk); *An Isle in the Water*, 1895 (s); *The Land of Mist and Mountain*, 1895 (s); *Miracle Plays: Our Lord's Coming and Childhood*, 1895 (d); *A Lover's Breastknot*, 1896 (p); *The Wind in the Trees*, 1898 (p); *The Land I Love Best*, 1899 (e); *Poems*, 1901 (p); *The Handsome Quaker*, 1902 (s); *Innocencies*, 1905 (p); *The Yellow Domino*, 1906 (s); *Book of Memory, Birthday Book of the Blessed Dead*, 1906 (sk); *A Little Book for John O'Mahony's Friends*, 1906 (e); *A Little Book of XXIV Carols*, 1907 (p); *The Rhymed Life of Saint Patrick*, 1907 (p); *Twenty-One Poems*, sel. W. B. Yeats, 1907 (p); *Experiences*, 1908 (p); *The Lost Angel*, 1908 (s); *Men and Maids, or, The Lover's Way*, 1908 (s); (with Frances Maitland) *The Book of Flowers*, 1909 (e); *Cousins and Others*, 1909 (s); *Ireland*, 1909 (e); *Lauds*, 1909 (p); *New Poems*, 1911 (p); *Irish Poems*, 1913 (p); *Twenty-Five Years, Reminiscences*, 1913 (r); *The Flower of Peace, a Collection of the Devotional Poetry of Katharine Tynan*, 1914 (p); *Flower of Youth*, 1915 (p); *The Holy War*, 1916 (p); *Lord Edward* [Fitzgerald]: *a Study in Romance*, 1916 (b); *The Middle Years*, 1916 (r); *Herb o' Grace, Poems in War-Time*, 1918 (p); *The Years of the Shadow*, 1919 (r); *Evensong*, 1922 (p); *The Wandering Years*, 1922 (r); *Memories*, 1924 (r); *A Dog Book*, 1926 (s); *Twilight Songs*, 1927 (p); *Collected Poems*, 1930; *Twenty-Four Poems*, 1931 (p)

See Patrick Braybrooke, *Some Catholic Novelists*, 1931

KENNETH TYNAN
1927-

He That Plays the King, 1950 (c); *Alec Guinness*, 1953 (e); (with Cecil Beaton) *Persona Grata* [short biographies of actors], 1953 (b); *Bull Fever*, 1955 (e); (with Harold Lang) *The Quest for Corbett*, 1960 (rd); *Curtains*, 1961 (c)

PETER USTINOV
1921-

House of Regrets, 1943 (d); *Beyond*, 1944 (d); *The Banbury Nose*, 1945 (d); *Top Secret*, 1945 (d); *Paris Not so Gay*, 1947 (d); *Plays about People*, 1950 (3d); *The Love of Four Colonels*, 1951 (d); *The Moment of Truth*, 1953 (d); (with Eric Ambler) *The Way Ahead*, 1956 (d); *Romanoff and Juliet*, 1957 (d); *Add a Dash of Pity*, 1959 (s); *Ustinov's Diplomats*, 1960 (e); *We Were Only Human*, 1961 (e); *The Loser*, 1961 (s); *Photo Finish*, 1962 (d); *Five Plays*, 1965 (d); *The Frontiers of the Sea*, 1966 (s)

Geoffrey Williams, *Peter Ustinov*, 1957 [no bibliog.]

HORACE ANNESLEY VACHELL
1861-1955

The Model of Christian Gay, 1895 (e); *The Romance of Judge Ketchum*, 1896 (n); *The Quicksands of Pactolus*, 1896 (n); *A Drama in Sunshine*, 1898 (n); *The Procession of Life*, 1899 (n); *John Charity*, 1900 (n); *Life and Sport on the Pacific Slope*, 1900 (t); *The Shadowy Third*, 1902 (n); *The Pinch of Prosperity*, 1903 (n); *Brothers*, 1904 (repr. 1928) (n); *The Hill*, 1905 (repr. 1925) (n); *The Face of Clay*, 1906 (n); *Her Son*, 1907 (n); *The Waters of Jordan*, 1908 (n); *The Paladin*, 1909 (repr. 1925) (n); *An Impending Sword*, 1909 (repr. 1932) (n); *The Other Side*, 1910 (repr. 1927) (n); *John Verney*, 1911 (n); *Jelf's*, 1912 (d); *Blinds Down*, 1912 (n); *Bunch Grass*, 1912 (n); *Loot from the Temple of Fortune*, 1913 (n); *Quinneys'*, 1914 (repr. 1942) (n); *Spragge's Canyon*, 1914 (n); *Quinneys'*, 1915 (d); *Searchlights*, 1915 (d); *The Triumph of Tim*, 1916 (n); *The Case of Lady Camber*, 1916 (d); *Fishpingle*, 1917 (n); *Some Happenings*, 1918 (n); *The Soul of Susan Yellam*, 1918 (n); *Whitewash*, 1920 (n); *The Fourth Dimension*, 1920 (n); *Blinkers*, 1921 (n); *Change of Partners*, 1922 (n); *Fellow-Travellers*, 1923 (r); *The Yard*, 1923 (n); *Quinneys' Adventures*, 1924 (n); *Leaves from Arcady*, 1924 (s); *Watling's for Worth*, 1925 (n); *A Woman in Exile*, 1926 (n); (with A. H. Marshall) *Mr. Allen*, 1926 (n); *Dew of the Sea*, 1927 (s); *Miss Torrobin's Experiment*, 1927 (n); *The Actor*, 1928 (n); *The Homely Ant*, 1928 (e); *Virgin*, 1929 (n); *The Enchanted Garden*, 1929 (s); *The Best of England*, 1930 (e); *Out of Great Tribulation*, 1930 (n); (with H. Simpson) *Plus Fours*, 1930 (d); *At the Sign of the Grid*, 1931 (n); *Fishpingle*, 1931 (d); *Into the Land of Nod*, 1931 (n); *The Fifth Commandment*, 1932 (n); *Experiences of a Bond Street Jeweller*, 1932 (n); *This was England*, 1933 (e); *Vicars' Walk*, 1933 (n); *The Old Guard Surrenders*, 1934 (n); *The Disappearance of Martha Penny*, 1934 (n); *Moonhills*, 1935 (n); *When Sorrows Come*, 1935 (n); *Arising Out of That*, 1935 (n); *Joe Guinney's Jodie*, 1936 (n); *My Vagabondage*, 1936 (e); *The Golden House*, 1937 (n); *Distant Fields*, 1938 (a); *Lord Samarkand*, 1938 (n); *Where Fancy Beckons*, 1938 (r); *Quinneys for Quality*, 1938 (n); *Phoebe's Guest House*, 1939 (n); *Great Chameleon*, 1940 (n); *Little Tyrannies*, 1940 (e); *Black Squire*, 1941 (n); *Gift from God*, 1942 (n); *Hilary Trent*, 1944 (n); *Averil*, 1945 (n); *Eve's Apples*, 1946; (n); *Farewell Yesterday*, 1946 (n); *Now Came Still Evening On*, 1946 (r); *Rebels*, 1947 (n); *Quiet Corner*, 1948 (n); *Twilight Grey*, 1948 (r); *Children of Sin*, 1948 (n); *In Sober Livery*, 1949 (r); *Methuselah's Diary*, 1950 (a); *More from Methuselah*, 1951 (a); *The Lamp of Golconda*, 1952 (n); *Quests*, 1954 (e)

JOHN VAN DRUTEN
1901-1957

Young Woodley, 1925 (d); *The Return of the Soldier* (adapted from Rebecca West's novel), 1928 (d); *Diversion*, 1928 (d); *After All*, 1929 (d); *Young Woodley*, 1928 (n); *A Woman On her Way*, 1930 (n); *London Wall*, 1931 (d); *There's Always Juliet*, 1931 (d); (with Benn Wolf Levy) *Hollywood Holiday*, 1931 (d); *Behold, We Live*, 1932 (d); *Somebody Knows*, 1932 (d); *The Distaff Side*, 1933 (d); *Flowers of the Forest*, 1934 (d); *Parnell*, 1936 (d); *And Then You Wish*, 1936 (n); *Most of the Game*, 1936 (d); *Gertie Maude*, 1937 (d); *The Way to the Present*, 1938 (a); *Intermezzo*, 1939 (d); *Raffles*, 1939 (d); *Leave Her to Heaven* (adapted from Ben Ames Williams' novel), 1940 (d); *Ballerina*, 1940 (d); *Old Acquaintance*, 1941 (d); *Solitaire* (adapted from Edwin Corle's novel), 1942 (d); (with Lloyd Morris) *The Damask Cheek*, 1943 (d); *McLeod's Folly*, 1943 (d); *The Voice af the Turtle*, 1944 (d); *I Remember Mama* (adapted from Kathryn Forbes's sketches, *Mama's Bank Account*), 1944 (d); *The Mermaids Singing*, 1946 (d); *The Druid Circle*, 1948 (d); *Make Way for Lucia*, 1949 (d); *Bell, Book and Candle*, 1951 (d); *I Am a Camera* (based on stories of Christopher Isherwood), 1951 (d); *I've Got Sixpence*, 1953 (d); *Playwright at Work*, 1953 (a); *The Vicarious Years*, 1955 (n); *The Widening Circle*, 1957 (a)

C. E. VULLIAMY
1886-

Charles Kingsley and Christian Socialism, 1914 (e); *Our Prehistoric Forerunners*, 1925 (h); *Unknown Cornwall*, 1925 (t); *Immortal Man: a Study of Funeral Customs and of Beliefs in Regard to the Nature and Fate of the Soul*, 1926 (e); *The Archaeology of Middlesex and London*, 1930 (h); *Voltaire*, 1930 (b); *John Wesley*, 1931 (b); *Rousseau*, 1931 (b); *James Boswell*, 1932 (b); *William Penn*, 1933 (b); *Judas Maccabeus*, 1934 (e); *Aspasia. The Life and Letters of Mary Granville, Mrs. Delany, 1700-1788*, 1935 (b); *Mrs. Thrale of Streatham*, 1936 (b); *Royal George* [George III], 1937 (b); *Out-landers: A Study of Imperial Expansion in South Africa, 1877-1902*, 1938 (h); *Crimea: The Campaign of 1854-1856*, 1939 (h); *Calico Pie*, 1940 (a); *A Short History of the Montagu Puffins*, 1941 (b); *The Polderoy Papers*, 1943 (b); *Doctor Philigo, His Journal and Opinions*, 1944 (b); *Edwin and Eleanor*, 1945 (n); *English Letter Writers*, 1945 (e); *Ursa Major: A Study of Dr. Johnson and His Friends*, 1946 (b); *Man and the Atom*, 1947 (e); *Clerical Error*, 1947 (e); *Byron*, 1948 (c); *Prodwit's Guide to Writing*, 1949 (e); *The Anatomy of Satire*, 1950 (e); *Henry Plumdew*, 1950 (n); *Rocking Horse Journey: Some Views of the British Character*, 1952 (e); *Don among the Dead Men*, 1952 (n); *The Onslow Family, 1528-1874*, 1953 (h); *The Proud Walkers*, 1955 (n); *Body in the Boudoir*, 1956 (n); *Cakes for Your Birthday*, 1959 (n); *Little Arthur's Guide to Humbug*, 1960 (e); *Justice for Judy*, 1960 (n); *Tea at the Abbey*, 1961 (n); *Floral Tribute*, 1963 (n)

JOHN WAIN
1925-

Hurry On Down, 1953 (Am. ed. *Born in Captivity*) (n); *Living in the Present*, 1955 (n); *A Word Carved on a Sill*, 1956 (p); *Preliminary Essays*, 1957 (c); *The Contenders*, 1958 (n); *A Travelling Woman*, 1959 (n); *Nuncle*, 1960 (s); *Weep Before God*, 1961 (p); *Strike the Father Dead*, 1962 (n); **Sprightly Running*, 1962 (a); *Essays on Literature and Ideas*, 1963 (e); *The Living World of Shakespeare*, 1964 (c); *The Young Visitors*, 1965 (n); *Wildtrack*, 1965 (p); *Death of the Hind Legs*, 1966 (s)

*rev. 1965

See James Gindin, *Postwar British Fiction*, 1962

A. B. WALKLEY
1855-1926

Playhouse Impressions, 1892 (c); *Frames of Mind*, 1899 (e); *Dramatic Criticism*, 1903 (3 lectures at Royal Institution); *Drama and Life*, 1907 (c); *Pastiche and Prejudice*, 1921 (c); *More Prejudice*, 1923 (c); *Still More Prejudice*, 1925 (c)

EDGAR WALLACE
1875-1932

Selective Bibliography

The Mission That Failed, 1898 (p); *Writ in Barracks*, 1900 (p); *Unofficial Despatches*, 1901 (e); *The Four Just Men*, 1905 (n); *"Smithy"*, 1906 (sk); *Smithy Abroad: Barrack-Room Sketches*, 1909; *Sanders of the River*, 1911 (s); *The People of the River*, 1912 (s); *Bosambo of the River*, 1914 (s); *Smithy's Friend Nobby*, 1914 (sk); *"Smithy", Not to Mention Nobby Clark and Spud Murphy*, 1914 (sk); *Tam o' the Scouts*, 1918 (s); *People: a Short Autobiography*, 1926 (a); *Edgar Wallace: a Short Autobiography*, 1929 (a); (with Delos W. Lovelace and Marian C. Cooper) *King Kong*, 1932 (n); *My Hollywood Diary: The Last Work of Edgar Wallace*, 1932 (a)

Also, from 1919 on, very numerous mystery or detective stories (e.g., 20 in 1926, 14 in 1927, 12 in 1928, 23 in 1929)

Margaret Lane, *Edgar Wallace*, 1938 (rev. 1964) [no bibliog.]

HUGH WALPOLE
1884-1941

The Wooden Horse, 1909 (n); *Maradick at Forty*, 1910 (n); *Mr. Perrin and Mr. Traill*, 1911 (Am. ed. *The Gods and Mr. Perrin*) (n); *The Prelude to Adventure*, 1912 (n); *Fortitude*, 1913 (n); *The Duchess of Wrexe (The Rising City: I)*, 1914 (n); *The Golden Scarecrow*, 1915 (n); *The Dark Forest*, 1916 (n); *Joseph Conrad*, 1916 (c); *The Green Mirror (The Rising City: II)*, 1917 (n); *The Secret City* (seq. to *The Dark Forest*), 1919 (n); *Jeremy*, 1919 (n); *The Captives*, 1920 (n); *The Art of James Branch Cabell*, 1920 (c); *A Hugh Walpole Anthology*, sel. by the author, with a note by Joseph Conrad, 1921; *The Young Enchanted*, 1921 (n); *The Thirteen Travellers*, 1921 (s); *The Cathedral*, 1922 (n); *Jeremy and Hamlet*, 1923 (n); *The Old Ladies*, 1924 (n); *Portrait of a Man with Red Hair*, 1925 (n); *The English Novel*, 1925 [The Rede lecture, 1925] (c); *Harmer John*, 1926 (n); *Reading*, 1926 (e); *A Stranger*, 1926 (n); *Jeremy at Crale*, 1927 (n); *Winters-moon*, 1928 (n); *The Silver Thorn*, 1928 (s); *Anthony Trollope*, 1928 (c); *My Religious Experience*, 1928 (e); (with J. B. Priestley) *Farthing Hall*, 1929 (n); *Hans Frost*, 1929 (n); *Rogue Herries (Herries Chronicles: I)*, 1930 (n); *Above the Dark Circus* (Am. ed. *Above the Dark Tumult*), 1930 (n); *Judith Paris Herries Chronicles: II)*, 1931 (n); *A Letter to a Modern Novelist*, 1932 (e); *The Apple Trees*, 1932 (r); *The Fortress (Herries Chronicles: III)*, 1931 (n); *Vanessa (Herries Chronicles: IV)*, 1933 (n); *All Souls' Night*, 1933 (s); *Captain Nicholas*, 1934 (n); *The Inquisitor*, 1935 (n); *Mr. Huffman*, 1935 (s); *A Prayer for My Son*, 1936 (n); *John Cornelius*, 1937 (n); *The Cathedral*, 1937 (d); *Head in Green Bronze*, 1938 (e); *The Joyful Delaneys*, 1938 (n); *The Haxtons*, 1939 (d); *The Sea Tower*, 1939 (n); *The Herries Chronicle (Rogue Herries, Judith Paris, The Fortress, Vanessa)*, 1939 (4n); *The Cumberland Edition of The Works*, 30 vols., 1939-40; *The Bright Pavilions*, 1940 (n); *The Freedom of Books*, 1940 (e); *Roman Fountain*, 1940 (t); *The Blind Man's House*, 1941 (n); *The Killer and the Slain*, 1942 (n); *Katherine Christian*, 1943 (n); *Women are Motherly*, 1943 (s)

Rupert Hart-Davis, *Hugh Walpole*, 1952 (repr. 1963) [bk list]

REX WARNER
1905-

Poems, 1937 (rev. as *Poems and Contradictions*, 1945) (p); *The Wild Goose Chase*, 1937 (n); *The Aerodrome*, 1941 (n); *Why Was I Killed? A Dramatic Dialogue* (Am. ed. *Return of the Traveller*), 1943 (e); *The Medea of Euripides*, 1944 (tr); *English Public Schools*, 1954 (e); *The Cult of Power*, 1946 (e); *The Prometheus Bound of Aeschylus*, 1947 (tr); *Men of Stones*, 1949 (n); *The Hippolytus of Euripides*, 1949 (tr); Xenophon, *The Persian Expedition*, 1949 (tr); *John Milton*, 1949 (b,c); *Views of Attica*, 1950 (t); *E. M. Forster*, 1950 (rev. 1960) (c); *Men and Gods* [Stories from Ovid], 1950 (tr); *Greeks and Trojans*, 1951 (e); *The Helen of Euripides*, 1961 (tr); (with pictures by Martin Hürlimann) *Eternal Greece*, 1953 (repr. 1961) (e); *Escapade,*

1953 (n); Thucydides, *The History of the Peloponnesian War*, 1954 (tr); *The Vengeance of the Gods*, 1954 (s); (with others) *New Poems*, 1954 (p); [Plutarch] *The Fall of the Roman Republic: Six Lives*, 1958 (tr); *The Young Caesar*, 1958 (n); *The Greek Philosophers*, 1958 (c); *Imperial Caesar* (seq. to *The Young Caesar*), 1958 (n); *War Commentaries of Caesar*, 1960 (tr); George Sepheres, *Poems*, 1960 (tr); *Pericles the Athenian*, 1963 (n)

SYLVIA TOWNSEND WARNER
1893-

The Espalier, 1925 (p); *Lolly Willowes*, 1926 (n); *Mr. Fortune's Maggot*, 1927 (n); *Time Importuned*, 1928 (p); *The True Heart*, 1929 (n); *Some World Far From Ours and "Stay Corydon"*, 1929 (s); *Elinor Barley*, 1930 (s); *A Moral Ending*, 1931 (s); *Opus 7*, 1931 (p); *The Salutation*, 1932 (s); *Rainbow*, 1932 (p); (with Valentine Ackland) *Whether a Dove or Seagull*, 1933 (p); *More Joy in Heaven*, 1935 (s); *Summer Will Show*, 1936 (n); *After the Death of Don Juan*, 1938 (n); *The Cat's Cradle-Book*, 1940 (s); *A Garland of Straw*, 1943 (s); *The Museum of Cheats*, 1947 (s); *The Corner That Held Them*, 1948 (n); *Somerset*, 1949 (t); *Jane Austen, 1775-1817*, 1951 (b); *The Flint Anchor*, 1954 (s); *Winter in the Air*, 1955 (s); Marcel Proust [*Contre Sainte-Beuve*] *By Way of Sainte-Beuve*, 1958 (Am. ed. *Marcel Proust on Art and Literature*) (tr); *A Spirit Rises*, 1962 (n); *A Stranger With a Bag*, 1966 (s)

See F. L. Lucas, *Authors Dead and Living*, 1926

VERNON WATKINS
1907-

Ballad of the Mari Lwyd, 1941 (p); *The Lamp and the Veil*, 1945 (p); *The Lady with the Unicorn*, 1948 (p); *Selected Poems*, 1948 (p); Heinrich Heine, *The North Sea*, 1951 (tr); *The Death Bell*, 1954 (p); *Cypress and Acacia*, 1959 (p); *Affinities*, 1962 (p)

WILLIAM WATSON
1858-1935

The Prince's Quest, 1880 (p); *Epigrams of Art, Life and Nature*, 1884 (p); *Wordsworth's Grave*, 1889 (p); *Lachrymae Musarum*, 1892 (p); *Poems*, 1892 (p); *The Eloping Angels*, 1893 (p); *Five Sonnets*, 1893 (p); *Excursions in Criticism*, 1893 (c); *Odes*, 1894 (p); *The Father of the Forest*, 1895 (p); *Hymn to the Sea*, 1895 (p); *The Purple East*, 1896 (p); *A Sonnet to Thomas Bailey Aldrich*, 1896; *The Lost Eden*, 1897 (p); *The Year of Shame*, 1897 (p); *The Hope of the World*, 1898 (p); *The Collected Poems*, 1899; *The Tomb of Burns*, 1900 (p); *Ode on the Day of the Coronation of King Edward VII*, 1902; *Selected Poems*, 1903; *For England*, 1903 (p); *Eight Poems*, 1904; *Some Poems*, 1904; *The Poems of William Watson*, ed. J. A. Spender, 1905 (p); *New Poems*, 1909 (p); *Sable and Purple*, 1910 (p); *The Heralds of the Dawn*, 1912 (d); *The Muse in Exile*, 1913 (p); *Retrogression*, 1916 (p); *Pencraft*, 1916 (e); *The Man Who Saw*, 1917 (p); *The Superhuman Antagonists*, 1919 (p); *Ireland Arisen*, 1921 (p); *Ireland Unfreed*, 1921 (p); *A Hundred Poems* [sel. from his various vols.], 1922 (p); *Poems Brief and New*, 1925 (p); *Selected Poems*, sel. by the author, 1928; *The Poems of Sir Williams Watson, 1878-1935*, 1936; *I Was an English Poet*, selection, comp. by Lady Maureen Pring Watson, 1941 (p)

Cecil Woolf, *Sir William Watson*, 1956

ALEC WAUGH
1898-

The Loom of Youth, 1917 (repr. 1929, 1941) (n); *Resentment*, 1918 (p); *The Prisoners of Mainz*, 1919 (sk); *Pleasure*, 1921 (s); *Public School Life*, 1922 (e); *The Lonely Unicorn* (Am. ed. *Roland Whately*), 1922 (n); *Myself When Young*, 1923 (r); *Card Castle*, 1924 (n); *Kept*, 1925 (n); *Love in These Days*, 1926 (n); *On Doing What One Likes*, 1926 (e); *Nor Many Waters* (Am. ed. *Portrait of a Celibate*), 1928 (n); *The Last Chukka*, 1928 (s); *Three Score and Ten*, 1920 (n); *". . . 'Sir,' She Said"*, 1930 (n); *The Coloured Countries* (Am. ed. *Hot Countries*), 1930 (t); *So Lovers Dream*, 1931 (Am. ed. *That American Woman*) (n); *"Most Women" . . .* , 1931 (t); *Leap Before You Look*, 1932 (rev. enlgd. 1934) (n); *No Quarter* (Am. ed. *Tropic Seed*), 1932 (n); *Thirteen Such Years*, 1932 (r); *Wheels Within Wheels* (Am. ed. *The*

Golden Ripple), 1933 (n); *Playing with Fire*, 1933 (n); *The Balliols*, 1934 (n); *Pages in Woman's Life*, 1934 (s); (with Adrian Alington, *et al.*) *Beginnings*, 1935 (e); *Jill Somerset*, 1936 (n); *Eight Short Stories*, 1937 (s); *Going Their Own Ways*, 1938 (n); *No Truce with Time*, 1941 (n); *His Second War*, 1944 (e); *Galaxy*, ed. E. Myers, 1944 (e); *Unclouded Summer*, 1948 (n); *The Sunlit Caribbean*, 1948 (Am. ed. *The Sugar Islands: A Caribbean Travelogue*) (t); *The Lipton Story*, 1950 (b); *Where the Clocks Chime Twice*, 1951 (t); *Guy Renton*, 1953 (n); *Island in the Sun*, 1955 (n); *Merchants of Wine* [The House of Gilbey], 1957 (h); *The Sugar Islands: a Collection of Pieces Written about the West Indies between 1928 and 1953*, 1958 (Am. ed. *Love and the Caribbean: Tales, Characters and Scenes of the West Indies*) (t); *In Praise of Wine*, 1959 (e); *Fuel for the Flame*, 1960 (n); *My Place in the Bazaar*, 1961 (s); *The Early Years*, 1962 (a); *A Family of Islands: a History of the West Indies from 1492 to 1898*, 1964 (h); *The Mule on the Minaret*, 1965 (n)

EVELYN WAUGH
1903-1966

Decline and Fall, 1928 (n); *Rossetti, His Life and Works*, 1928 (b,c); *Vile Bodies*, 1930 (n); *Labels*, 1930 (Am. ed. *A Bachelor Abroad: a Mediterranean Journal*) (t); *Remote People*, 1931 (Am. ed. *They Were Still Dancing*) (t); *Black Mischief*, 1932 (n); *A Handful of Dust*, 1934 (n); *Ninety-Two Days: The Account of a Tropical Journey Through British Guiana and Part of Brazil*, 1934 (t); *Edmund Campion*, 1935 (b); *Waugh in Abyssinia*, 1936 (t); *Mr. Loveday's Little Outing*, 1936 (s); *Scoop*, 1938 (n); *Robbery Under Law*, 1939 (Am. ed. *Mexico: an Object Lesson*) (t); *Work Suspended: Two Chapters of an Unfinished Novel*, 1942; *Put Out More Flags*, 1942 (n); *Brideshead Revisited*, 1945 (n); *When the Going Was Good* [author's selection from *Labels, Remote People, Ninety-Two Days* and *Waugh in Abyssinia*], 1946 (t); *Scott-King's Modern Europe*, 1947 (n); *The Loved One*, 1948 (n); *Wine in Peace and War*, 1949 (e); *Helena*, 1950 (n); *Men at Arms* (Vol. I of trilogy), 1952 (n);

Love Among the Ruins, 1953 (n); *Tactical Exercise*, 1954 (s); *Officers and Gentlemen* (Vol. II of trilogy), 1955 (n); *The Ordeal of Gilbert Pinfold*, 1957 (n); *The Life of the Right Reverend Ronald Knox*, 1959 (b); *A Tourist in Africa*, 1960 (t); *Unconditional Surrender* (Vol. III of trilogy), 1961 (Am. ed. *The End of the Battle*) (n); *A Little Learning*, 1964 (a); *Sword of Honour* [final version of *Men at Arms, Officers and Gentlemen, Unconditional Surrender*], 1965 (3n)

Frederick J. Stopp, *Evelyn Waugh*, 1958; Malcolm Bradbury, *Evelyn Waugh*, 1964

MARY WEBB
1881-1927

The Golden Arrow, 1916 (n); *Gone to Earth*, 1917 (n); *The Spring of Joy*, 1917 (enlgd. 1937) (e); *The House in Dormer Forest*, 1920 (n); *Seven for a Secret*, 1922 (n); *Precious Bane*, 1924 (n); *Poems and The Spring of Joy*, 1928 (p,e); *Collected Works*, 7 vols., 1928; *Armour Wherein He Trusted*, 1929 (n,s); *In Dark Weather*, 1933 (p); *The Chinese Lion*, 1937 (s); *A Mary Webb Anthology*, ed. H. B. L. Webb, 1939; *Fifty-One Poems*, 1946 (p); *The Essential Mary Webb*, ed. Martin Armstrong, 1949

Thomas Moult, *Mary Webb*, 1932 [no bibliog.]; Dorothy Patricia Harcourt, *Goodbye to Morning: a Biographical Study of Mary Webb*, 1964

C. V. WEDGWOOD
1910-

Stafford, 1593-1641, 1935 (b); *Oliver Cromwell*, 1939 (repr. 1962) (b); *The Thirty Years War*, 1938 (h); *William the Silent*, 1944 (repr. 1960) (b); *Battlefields in Britain*, 1944 (h); *Velvet Studies*, 1946 (e); (with others) *King Charles I*, 1949 (h); *Richelieu and the French Monarchy*, 1949 (h); *Reading History*, 1950 (e); *Seventeenth-Century English Literature*, 1950 (h); *The Last of the Radicals: Josiah Wedgwood, M.P.*, 1951 (b); *Montrose*, 1952 (b); *Edward Gibbon*, 1955 (b); *The Great Rebellion: The King's Peace, 1637-1641*, 1955 (h); *Literature and the Historian*, 1956 (e); *The Common Man in the Great Civil War*, 1957 (e); *The Sense of the Past*,

1957 (e); *The King's War, 1641-1647,* 1958 (h); *Poetry and Politics under the Stuarts,* 1960 (c); *Truth and Opinion,* 1960 (e); *The Trial of Charles I,* 1964 (Am. ed. *A Coffin for King Charles*) (h); *History and Hope,* 1964 (e)

DENTON WELCH
1917-1948

Maiden Voyage, 1943 (a); *In Youth is Pleasure,* 1944 (n); *Brave and Cruel,* 1948 (s); **A Voice Through a Cloud,* 1950 (n); *A Last Sheaf, Stories, Poems, Pictures,* ed. Eric Oliver, 1951; *The Denton Welch Journals,* ed. Jocelyn Brooke, 1952; *Denton Welch: Extracts from his Published Works,* ed. Jocelyn Brooke, 1963

*repr. 1966

DOROTHY WELLESLEY
1889-1956

[M.A.] *Early Poems,* 1913 (p); *Poems,* 1920 (p); *Pride,* 1923 (p); *Lost Lane,* 1925 (p); *Genesis: An Impression,* 1926 (p); *Matrix,* 1928 (p); *Deserted House,* 1930 (p); *Jupiter and the Nun,* 1932 (p); *Sir George Goldie, Founder of Nigeria,* 1934 (m); *Poems of Ten Years, 1924-1934,* 1934 (p); *Selections from the Poems of Dorothy Wellesley,* Introd. by W. B. Yeats, 1936 (p); *Lost Planet,* 1942 (p); *The Poets,* 1943 (p); *Desert Wells,* 1946 (p); *Selected Poems,* 1949 (p); *Far Have I Travelled,* 1952 (r); *Rhymes for Middle Years,* 1954 (p); *Early Light: The Collected Poems,* 1955

H. G. WELLS
1866-1946
Selective Bibliography

Included are all short-story collections and all novels, which are of various kinds: autobiographical, propagandist, sociological utopian, and some resembling science fiction. The many reprints of the more popular novels are not indicated. Of the very numerous pamphlets, tracts, and essays, only a sampling is included, to show the breadth of Wells's interests. Two principal collected editions of Wells's work are: *The Atlantic Edition,* 28 vols., 1924-27; *The Essex Edition,* 24 vols., 1926-27

(with R. A. Gregory) *Honours Physiography,* 1893 (e); *Textbook of Biology,* 1893; *The Time Machine,* 1895 (n); *The Wonderful Visit,* 1895 (n); *Select Conversations with an Uncle,* 1895 (sk); *The Stolen Bacillus,* 1895 (s); *The Wheels of Chance,* 1896 (n); *The Island of Doctor Moreau,* 1896 (n); *The Red Room,* 1896 (s); *The Invisible Man,* 1897 (n); *Thirty Strange Stories,* 1897 (s); *Certain Personal Matters,* 1897 (e); *The Plattner Story,* 1897 (s); *The War of the Worlds,* 1898 (n); *When the Sleeper Wakes,* 1899 (rev. as *The Sleeper Awakes,* 1910) (n); *A Cure for Love,* 1899 (s); *Tales of Space and Time,* 1899 (s); *The Vacant Country,* 1899 (s); *Love and Mr. Lewisham,* 1900 (n); *The First Men in the Moon,* 1901 (n); *The Sea Lady,* 1902 (n); *Twelve Stories,* 1903 (s); *Mankind in the Making,* 1903 (e); *The Food of the Gods,* 1904 (n); *Kipps,* 1905 (n); *A Modern Utopia,* 1905 (n); *In the Days of the Comet,* 1906 (n); *The Future in America,* 1906 (e); *Socialism and the Family,* 1906 (e); *Faults of the Fabian,* 1906 (e); *Reconstruction of the Fabian Society,* 1906 (e); *Will Socialism Destroy the Home?,* 1907 (e); *The War in the Air,* 1908 (n); *First and Last Things,* 1908 (rev. 1917) (e); *New Worlds for Old,* 1908 (e); *Ann Veronica,* 1909 (n); *Tono-Bungay,* 1909 (n); *The History of Mr. Polly,* 1910 (n); *The New Machiavelli,* 1911 (n); *The Country of the Blind,* 1911 (s); *The Door in the Wall,* 1911 (s); *Marriage,* 1912 (n); (with others) *The Great State,* 1912 (Am. ed. *Socialism and the Great State*) (e); *The Passionate Friends,* 1913 (n); *The Wife of Isaac Harman,* 1914 (n); *The World Set Free,* 1914 (n); *An Englishman Looks at the World,* 1914 (Am. ed. *Social Forces in England and America*) (e); *Bealby,* 1915 (n); *The Research Magnificent,* 1915 (n); *Boon,* 1915 (sk); *Mr. Britling Sees It Through,* 1916 (n); *What Is Coming,* 1916 (e); *The Soul of a Bishop,* 1917 (n); *God, the Invisible King,* 1917 (e); *Joan and Peter,* 1918 (n); *In the Fourth Year: Anticipation of World Peace,* 1918 (e); *The Undying Fire,* 1919 (n); *Russia in the Shadows,* 1920 (e); *The Outline of History,* 1920 (h); *The Salvaging of Civilisation,* 1921 (e); *The Secret Places of the Heart,* 1922 (n); *Washington and the Hope of Peace,*

1922 (Am. ed. *Washington and the Riddle of Peace*) (e); *A Short History of the World*, 1922 (h); *Men Like Gods*, 1923 (n); *The Dream*, 1924 (n); *A Year of Prophesying*, 1924 (e); *The Story of a Great Schoolmaster, Sanderson of Oundle*, 1924 (b); *The World of William Clissold*, 1926 (n); *Meanwhile*, 1927 (n); *The Short Stories of H. G. Wells*, 1927 (s); *Democracy Under Revision*, 1927 (e); *Blettsworthy on Rampole Island*, 1928 (n); *The Open Conspiracy*, 1928 (rev. 1930 as *What Are We to Do With our Lives?*) (e); *The Way the World is Going*, 1928 (e); *The King Who Was a King, the Book of a Film*, 1929; *The Treasure in the Forest*, 1929 (n); (with Julian Huxley and others) *The Science of Life Series*, 6 vols. 1929-1935; *The Autocracy of Mr. Parham*, 1930 (n); *The Valley of Spiders*, 1930 (s); *The Way to World Peace*, 1930 (e); *The Work, Wealth and Happiness of Mankind*, 1931 (e); *After Democracy*, 1932 (e); *The Bulpington of Blup*, 1933 (n); *The Scientific Romances of H. G. Wells*, 1933 (Am. ed. *Seven Famous Novels*) (7n); *The Shape of Things to Come*, 1933 (e); *Experiment in Autobiography*, 1934 (a); *Stalin-Wells Talk, the Verbatim Record and a Discussion by Shaw, Wells, Keynes, Ernst Toller and Others*, 1934 (e); *The New America*, 1935 (t); *Things to Come*, 1935 (d); *Human Happiness*, 1936 (e); *The Man Who Could Work Miracles*, 1936 (film play based on s); *The Croquet Player*, 1936 (s); *The Brothers*, 1936 (s); *The Idea of a World Encyclopaedia*, 1936 (lecture at Royal Institution); *The Anatomy of Frustration*, 1936 (e); *The Camford Visitation*, 1937 (e); *Star Begotten*, 1937 (n); *Brynhild*, 1937 (n); (with others) *Biology of the Human Race, How Animals Behave, Man's Mind and Behaviour*, 1937 (h,e); *The Brothers*, 1938 (n); *World Brain*, 1938 (e); *Apropos of Dolores*, 1938 (n); *The Fate of Homo Sapiens*, 1939 (Am. ed. *The Fate of Man*) (e); *The Holy Terror*, 1939 (n); *Travels of a Republican Radical*, 1939 (e); *The Rights of Man*, 1940 (e); *Babes in the Darkling Wood*, 1940 (s); *All Aboard for Ararat*, 1940 (e); *The New World Order*, 1940 (e); *Short Stories*, 1940; *Guide to the New World*, 1941 (e); *You Can't Be Too Careful*, 1941 (s); *The New Rights of Man*, 1942 (e); *The Conquest of Time*, 1942 (e);

Phoenix, A Summary of the Inescapable Conditions of World Reorganisation, 1942 (e); *Science and the World-Mind*, 1942 (e); *Crux Ansata, An Indictment of the Roman Catholic Church*, 1943 (e); *A Thesis on the Quality of Illusion . . .*, 1944 (e); *The Happy Turning*, 1945 (e); *Mind at the End of Its Tether*, 1945 (e); *The Short Stories*, 1948; *Henry James and H. G. Wells; a Record of their Friendship, their Debate on the Art of Fiction, and their Quarrel*, ed. Leon Edel and Gordon N. Ray, 1958; *Arnold Bennett and H. G. Wells; a Record of a Personal and a Literary Friendship*, ed. Harris Wilson, 1960 (letters); *George Gissing and H. G. Wells: their Friendship and Correspondence*, ed. Royal A. Gettmann, 1961; *The Valley of Spiders: a New Collection of Short Stories*, 1964; *Journalism and Prophecy, 1893-1946*, ed. Warren Wagar, 1966 (anthology; many pieces not before repr.); *The Complete Short Stories*, 1966 (repr. of centenary ed. 1927)

Geoffrey Harry Wells [Geoffrey West], *The Works of H. G. Wells, 1887-1925; a Bibliography, Dictionary and Subject-Index*, 1926; Vincent Brome, *H. G. Wells, a Biography*, 1951 [selected bk. list]; Inguald Raknem, *H. G. Wells and His Critics*, 1964; J. L. Kagarlitiski, *The Life and Thought of H. G. Wells*, 1966

ARNOLD WESKER
1932-

Chicken Soup With Barley (Part I of trilogy), 1959 (d); *Roots* (Part II of trilogy), 1959 (d); *I'm Talking About Jerusalem* (Part III of trilogy), 1960 (d); *The Wesker Trilogy*, 1960 (3d); *The Kitchen*, 1961 (d); *Chips With Everything*, 1962 (d); *Their Very Own and Golden City*, 1966 (d); *The Four Seasons*, 1966 (d)

See John Russell Taylor, *Anger and After*, 1962

ANTHONY WEST
1914-

On a Dark Night, 1949 (Am. ed. *The Vintage*) (n); *D. H. Lawrence*, 1950 (c); *Another Kind*, 1951 (n); *Heritage*, 1955 (n); *Principles and Persuasions*, 1958 (c); *The Trend Is Up*, 1960 (n)

MORRIS WEST
1916-

Gallows on the Sand, 1956 (n); The Big Story, 1957 (n); Kundu, 1957 (n); Children of the Sun [the depressed classes in Naples], 1957 (Am. ed. Children of the Shadows) (e); The Second Victory, 1958 (n); The Devil's Advocate, 1959 (n); Daughter of Silence, 1961 (n, also d, 1961); The Shoes of the Fisherman, 1963 (n)

REBECCA WEST
1892-

Henry James, 1916 (c); The Return of the Soldier, 1918 (repr. 1940) (n); The Judge, 1922 (repr. 1947) (n); [pseud. Lynx] (with David Low) Lions and Lambs, 1928 (e); The Strange Necessity, 1928 (c); Harriet Hume, 1929 (n); War Nurse, 1930 (n); D. H. Lawrence, 1930 (c); Arnold Bennett Himself, 1931 (e); Ending in Earnest, 1931 (c); A Letter to a Grandfather, 1933 (e); St. Augustine, 1933 (b); (with David Low) The Modern "Rake's Progress" [paintings Low, words R. West], 1934 (s); The Harsh Voice, 1935 (repr. 1948) (4n); *The Thinking Reed, 1936 (n); Black Lamb and Grey Falcon, The Record of a Journey Through Yugoslavia in 1937, 1942 (t); **The Meaning of Treason [trials of William Joyce and others], 1949 (e); A Train of Powder [criminal cases incl. Nuremburg trials], 1955 (e); The Court and the Castle, 1957 (e); The Fountain Overflows, 1957 (n); The Event and its Images, 1962 (e); The Vassall Affair, 1963 (e)

*repr. 1966
**rev. 1965 (Am. ed. The New Meaning of Treason)

George Evelyn Hutchinson, A Preliminary List of the Writings of Rebecca West, 1912-1951, 1957

T. H. WHITE
1906-1964

Loved Helen, 1929 (p); The Green Bay Tree, 1929 (p); (with Ronald M. Scott) Dead Mr. Nixon, 1931 (n); Darkness at Pemberley, 1932 (n); Farewell Victoria, 1933 (n); Earth Stopped, 1934 (n); Gone to Ground, 1935 (n); Song Through Space, 1935 (p); England Have My Bones [a diary of country life], 1936 (e); Burke's Steerage, 1938 (e); The Sword in the Stone, 1938 (repr. 1950) (n); The Witch in the Wood, 1939 (n); The Ill-Made Knight, 1941 (n); Mistress Masham's Repose, 1946 (n); The Elephant and the Kangaroo, 1947 (n); The Age of Scandal, 1950 (h); The Goshawk [falconry], 1951 (e); The Scandalmonger [on life and scandal in 18th and early 19th century England], 1952 (e); The Book of Beasts [Latin bestiary], 1954 (tr); The Master, 1957 (n); The Godstone and the Blackymor [Ireland], 1959 (t); The Once and Future King, 1959 (n); America At Last: American Journal of T. H. White, 1965 (a)

CHARLES WILLIAMS
1886-1945

The Silver Stair, 1912 (p); Poems of Conformity, 1917 (p); Divorce, 1920 (p); Poems of Home and Overseas, 1921 (p); Windows of Night, 1925 (p); The Masque of the Manuscript, 1927 (d); A Myth of Shakespeare, 1929 (d); The Masque of Perusal, 1929 (d); Poetry at Present, 1930 (c); Heroes and Kings, 1930 (p); War in Heaven, 1930 (repr. 1947) (n); Three Plays, 1931 (d,p); The Place of the Lion, 1931 (new ed. 1952) (n); Many Dimensions, 1931 (repr. 1952) (n); The Greater Trumps, 1932 (new ed. 1954) (n); The English Poetic Mind, 1932 (c); Shadows of Ecstasy, 1933 (n); Bacon, 1933 (b); Reason and Beauty in the Poetic Mind, 1933 (c); James I, 1934 (b); Rochester, 1935 (b); Queen Elizabeth, 1936 (b); Thomas Cranmer of Canterbury, 1936 (d); The Rite of the Passion, 1936 (e); Henry VII, 1937 (b); Seed of Adam, 1937 (d); Stories of Great Names, 1937 (b); Descent into Hell, 1937 (n); He Came Down from Heaven, 1938 (repr. 1950) (e); Taliessin through Logres, 1938 (p); Judgement at Chelmsford, 1939 (d); The Passion of Christ, 1939 (e); The Descent of the Dove: A Short History of the Holy Spirit in the Church, 1939 (new ed. 1950) (e); Religion and Love in Dante, 1941 (e); The New Christian Year, 1941 (e); Witchcraft, 1941 (e); The Forgiveness of Sins, 1942 (e); The Figure of Beatrice: a Study in Dante, 1943 (c); The House of the Octopus, 1945 (d); *Solway Ford*, 1945 (p); *All Hallows' Eve*, 1945 (n); *Flecker of Dean Close*, 1946 (b); *Seed of Adam*, 1948 (4d); (with C. S. Lewis) *Arthurian Torso* [includes a posthumous fragment of Williams' *The Figure of Arthur*], 1948 (p); *The Image of the City*, 1958 (c); *Collected Plays*, 1963

John Heath-Stubbs, *Charles Williams*, 1955 (including bibliog. by Linden Huddlestone); Mary Shideler, *The Theology of Romantic Love: a Study in the Writings of Charles Williams*, 1962

EMLYN WILLIAMS
1905-

A Murder Has Been Arranged, 1930 (d); *The Late Christopher Bean* (adapt. of René Fauchois, *Prenez garde à la peinture*), 1933 (d); *One Goes Alone*, 1935 (12d); *Night Must Fall*, 1935 (d); *He Was Born Gay*, 1937 (d); *The Corn Is Green*, 1937 (d); *The Light of Heart*, 1940 (Am. ed. *Yesterday's Magic*) (d); *The Morning Star*, 1942 (d); Ivan Turgenev, *A Month in the Country* (adapt.), 1943 (d); *The Druid's Rest*, 1944 (d); *The Wind of Heaven*, 1945 (d); *Guest in the House*, 1945 (d); *Spring, 1600*, 1946 (d); *Thinking Aloud*, 1946 (d); *Trespass*, 1947 (d); *Pepper and Sand: a Duologue*, 1948 (d); *The Corn Is Green*, 1950 (3d); *Accolade*, 1951 (d); *Readings from Dickens*, 1953; *Someone Waiting*, 1954 (d); *Beth*, 1959 (d); *George, an Early Autobiography*, 1961 (a); *The Collected Plays*, Vol. I, 1961

Richard Findlater [pseud.], *Emlyn Williams*, 1956 [no bibliog.]

RAYMOND WILLIAMS
1921-

Reading and Criticism, 1950 (c); **Drama from Ibsen to Eliot*, 1952 (c); (with Michael Orrom) *Preface to Film*, 1954 (e); *Drama in Performance*, 1954 (c); *Culture and Society, 1780-1950*, 1958 (h); *Advertising*, 1960 (e); *Border Country*, 1960 (n); *The Long Revolution*, 1961 (h); *Britain in the Sixties: Communications*, 1962 (e); *The Existing Alternatives in Communications*, 1962 (e); *Second Generation*, 1965 (a); *Modern Tragedy*, 1966 (e)

*rev. 1964

HENRY WILLIAMSON
1897-

The Beautiful Years (The Flax of Dream: I), 1921 (repr. 1949) (n); *Dandelion Days (The Flax of Dream II)*, 1922 (repr. 1950) (n); *The Lone Swallows*, 1922 (e); *The Peregrine's Saga* (Am. ed. *Sun Brothers*), 1923 (s); *The Dream of Fair Women (The Flax of Dream: III)*, 1924 (rev. ed. 1931) (n); *The Incoming of Summer*, 1924 (e); *A Midsummer Night*, 1924 (e); *The Old Stag*, 1926 (repr. 1946) (s); *Tarka the Otter*, 1927 (repr. 1949) (s); *The Pathway (The Flax of Dream: IV)*, 1928; *The Flax of Dream*, rev., 4 vols., 1929-31 (n); *The Linhay on the Downs*, 1929 (enlgd. 1934) (2s); *The Wet Flanders Plain*, 1929 (r); *The Patriot's Progress*, 1930 (n); *The Village Book*, 1930 (e); *The Wild Red Deer of Exmoor*, 1931 (e); *The Labouring Life*, 1932 (e); [Anon] *The Golden Falcon, or The Haggard of Love*, 1933 (repr. 1947, with author's name) (n); *On Foot in Devon*, 1933 (t); *Devon Holiday*, 1935 (r); *Salar, the Salmon*, 1935 (s); *Goodbye, West Country*, 1937 (diary); *The Children of Shallowford* [on author's children], 1939 (rev. enlgd. 1959) (a); *As the Sun Shines*, 1941 (sel.); *Genius of Friendship: T. E. Lawrence*, 1941 (m); *The Story of a Norfolk Farm*, 1941 (e); (with Lilias R. Haggard) *Norfolk Life*, 1943 (e); *The Sun in the Sands*, 1945 (a); *Tales of a Devon Village*, 1945 (s); *Life in a Devon Village*, 1945 (e); *The Phasian Bird*, 1948 (n); *The Star-Born*, 1948 (n); *The Dark Lantern*, 1951 (n); *Donkey Boy*, 1952 (n); *Tales of Moorland and Estuary*, 1953 (s); *Young Philip Maddison*, 1953 (n); *How Dear Is Life?*, 1954 (n); *A Fox Under My Cloak*, 1955 (n); *The Golden Virgin*, 1957 (n); *A Clear Water Stream*, 1958 (e); *Love and the Loveless*, 1958 (n); *A Test to Destruction*, 1960 (n); *The Henry Williamson Animal Saga*, 1960 (s); *In the Woods*, 1961 (misc.); *The Innocent Moon*, 1961 (n); *It was the Nightingale*, 1962 (n); *The Power of the Dead*, 1963 (n); *The Phoenix Generation* (12th novel in *A Chronicle of Ancient Sunlight*), 1965 (n); *A Solitary War* (13th in series), 1966 (n)

I. W. Girvan, *A Bibliography and a Critical Survey of the Works of Henry Williamson*, 1931

HUGH ROSS WILLIAMSON
1901-

The Poetry of T. S. Eliot, 1932 (c); *John Hampden*, 1933 (b); *The Rose and the Glove*, 1934 (d); *After the Event*, 1935 (d); *King James I*, 1935 (b); *Cinderella'ṣ Grandchild*, 1936 (d); *Gods and Mortals in Love*, 1935 (e); *The Seven Deadly Virtues, In a Glass Darkly, Various Heavens*, 1936 (3d); *Mr. Gladstone*, 1937 (d); *Stories from History: Ten Plays for Schools*, 1938 (10d); *Who Is for Liberty?*, 1939 (e); *George Villiers*, 1940 (b); *A.D. 33, a Tract for the Times*, 1941 (e); *Captain Thomas Schofield*, 1942 (n); *China Among the Nations*, 1943 (e); *Paul, a Bond Slave*, 1945 (rd); *Charles and Cromwell*, 1946 (b); *Queen Elizabeth*, 1947 (d); *The Story without an End* [dramatized meditations on the life, death, and resurrection of Jesus], 1947 (d); *The Arrow and the Sword* [on the deaths of William Rufus and Thomas Becket], 1947 (e); *Were You There: The Cardinal's Learning*, 1948 (d); *The Silver Bowl*, 1948 (repr. 1962) (n); *The Seven Christian Virtues*, 1949 (e); *Four Stuart Portraits* [Sir Balthazar Gerbier, Lancelot Andrewes, Sir John Eliot, Col. Thomas Rainsborough], 1949 (b); *Conversation with a Ghost*, 1950 (d); *Diamond Cut Diamond*, 1951 (d); *The Gunpowder Plot*, 1951 (h); *Sir Walter Raleigh*, 1951 (b); *Jeremy Taylor*, 1952 (b); *His Eminence of England*, 1953 (d); *Canterbury Cathedral*, 1953 (e); *The Ancient Capital: an Historian in Search of Winchester*, 1953 (t); *King Claudius*, 1954 (d); *Fool's Paradise*, 1954 (d); *James, By the Grace of God* [James II], 1955 (n); *Historical Whodunits*, 1955 (h); *The Great Prayer: Concerning the Canon of the Mass*, 1955 (e); *The Walled Garden*, 1956 (a); *The Day They Killed the King* [Charles I], 1957 (e); *Enigmas of History*, 1957 (h); *The Beginning of the English Reformation*, 1957 (h); *The Mime of Bernadette*, 1958 (d); *The Sisters*, 1958 (n); *The Challenge of Bernadette*, 1958 (e); *Sixty Saints of Christendom*, 1960 (b); *A Wicked Pack of Cards*, 1961 (n); *The Day Shakespeare Died*, 1962 (b); *The Flowering Hawthorn* [St. Joseph of Arimathea and Glastonbury], 1962 (e)

ANGUS WILSON
1913-

The Wrong Set, 1949 (repr. 1960) (s); *Such Darling Dodos*, 1950 (s); *Hemlock and After*, 1952 (n); *Emile Zola*, 1952 (c); (with Philippe Jullian) *For Whom the Cloche Tolls, A Scrapbook of the Twenties*, 1953; *Anglo-Saxon Attitudes*, 1956 (n); *The Mulberry Bush*, 1956 (d); *A Bit Off the Map*, 1957 (e); *The Middle Age of Mrs. Eliot*, 1958 (n); *The Old Men at the Zoo*, 1961 (s); *The Wild Garden, or, Speaking of Writing*, 1963 (r,c); *Late Call*, 1964 (n)

Jay L. Halio, *Angus Wilson*, 1964

COLIN WILSON
1931-

The Outsider, 1956 (e); *Religion and the Rebel*, 1957 (e); *The Age of Defeat*, 1959 (e); *Ritual in the Dark*, 1960 (n); *Adrift in Soho*, 1961 (n); (with Patricia Pitman) *Encyclopaedia of Murder*, 1961; *The Strength to Dream: Literature and the Imagination*, 1962 (c); *Man Without a Shadow*, 1963 (n); *Origins of the Sexual Impulse*, 1963 (e); *The World of Violence*, 1963 (n); *Necessary Doubt*, 1964 (n); *Rasputin and the Fall of the Romanovs*, 1964 (h); *Brandy of the Damned*, 1964 (c); *Introduction to a New Existentialism*, 1966 (e)

Sidney Ronald Campion, *The World of Colin Wilson: a Biographical Study*, 1962 [no bibliog.]

P. G. WODEHOUSE
1881-
Selective Bibliography

A number of plays, mostly in collaboration; the "Mulliner" series of collected short stories; about two humorous novels a year since 1910, a few of which, including in their titles the names of some of his best known characters, are: *Enter Psmith*, 1909; *Psmith in the City*, 1910; *Leave It to Psmith*, 1923; *The Inimitable Jeeves*, 1924; *Very Good, Jeeves*, 1930; *Brinkley Manor, a Novel about Jeeves* (Am. ed. *Right Ho, Jeeves*), 1934; *Bertie Wooster Sees It Through*, 1955; *Jeeves in the Offing*, 1960; *Frozen Assets*, 1964 (n); *Galahad at Blandings*, 1965 (n)

*Performing Flea: a Self-Portrait in

Letters, with text of 5 Berlin broadcasts, 1953 (a); *America I Like You,* 1956 (e); *Over Seventy,* 1957 (a); *Plum Pie,* 1966 (misc.)

*repr. 1961

Richard Usborne, *Wodehouse at Work,* 1961; Robert Butler Digby French, *P. G. Wodehouse,* 1966

HUMBERT WOLFE
1885-1940

London Sonnets, 1920 (p); *Shylock Reasons with Mr. Chesterton,* 1920 (p); *Circular Saws,* 1923 (s); *Labour Supply and Regulation,* 1923 (e); *Kensington Gardens,* 1924 (p); *Lampoons,* 1925 (p); *The Unknown Goddess,* 1925 (p); *Humoresque,* 1926 (p); *News of the Devil,* 1926 (p); *Cursory Rhymes,* 1927 (p); *Requiem,* 1927 (p); *The Silver Cat,* 1928 (p); *This Blind Rose,* 1928 (p); *Troy,* 1928 (p); *The Craft of Verse,* 1928 (e); *Dialogues and Monologues,* 1928 (c); *Notes on English Verse Satire,* 1929 (e); *Early Poems,* 1930 (p); *The Uncelestial City,* 1930 (p); *A Winter Miscellany,* ed. with original poems by Wolfe, 1930; *Tennyson,* 1930 (c); *Snow,* 1931 (p); *Poems,* 1931 (p); *George Moore,* 1931 (c); *Requiem,* 1931 (e); *Signpost to Poetry,* 1931 (c); *A, B, C, of the Theatre,* 1932 (p); *Now a Stranger,* 1933 (a); *Reverie of Policeman,* 1933 (pd); *Romantic and Unromantic Poetry,* 1933 (c); *Portraits by Inference,* 1934 (r); *Ronsard and French Romantic Poetry,* 1935 (The Zaharoff lecture); *The Fourth of August,* 1935 (p); *Stings and Wings,* 1935 (p); *X at Oberammergau,* 1935 (p); *P.L.M.: Peoples, Landfalls, Mountains* [France], 1936 (t); *Edmond Rostand, Cyrano de Bergerac,* 1937 (d,tr); *Don J. Ewan,* 1937 (p); *The Upward Anguish,* 1938 (a); *Out of Great Tribulation,* 1939 (p); *Kensington Gardens in Wartime,* 1940 (p)

Also translations of Greek Anthology, Heine, Ronsard, etc.

See F. L. Lucas, *Authors Dead and Living,* 1926

GEORGE WOODCOCK
1912-

The White Island, 1940 (p); *New Life to the Land,* 1942 (e); *The Centre Cannot Hold,* 1943 (p); *Railways and Society,* 1943 (e); *Anarchy or Chaos,* 1944 (e); *Homes or Hovels,* 1944 (e); *William Godwin,* 1946 (b); *The Basis of Communal Living,* 1947 (e); *Imagine the South,* 1947 (p); *A Hundred Years of Revolution, 1848 and After,* 1948 (h); *The Incomparable Aphra* [Aphra Behn], 1948 (b); *The Writer and Politics,* 1948 (e); *The Paradox of Oscar Wilde,* 1949 (b); (with I. Avakumovic) *The Anarchist Prince* [Peter Kropotkin] 1950 (b); *British Poetry Today,* 1950 (c); *Ravens and Prophets: an Account of Journeys in British Columbia, Alberta and South Alaska,* 1952 (t); *Pierre-Joseph Proudhon,* 1956 (b); *To the City of the Dead* [Mexico], 1957 (t); *Incas and Other Men,* 1959 (t); *Anarchism,* 1962 (h); *Faces of India,* 1964 (t); *Miniature Steam Locomotives,* 1964 (e)

C. M. WOODHOUSE
1917-

Apple of Discord: A Survey of Recent Greek Politics, 1948 (e); *One Omen,* 1950 (n); *Dostoievsky,* 1951 (c); *The Greek War of Independence,* 1952 (h); *Britain and the Middle East,* 1959 (e); *British Foreign Policy Since the Second World War,* 1961 (h); (with John Gilbert Lockhart) *Rhodes,* 1963 (b)

LEONARD WOOLF
1880-

The Village in the Jungle, 1913 (repr. 1926) (n); *The Wise Virgins,* 1914 (n); *International Government,* 1916 (e); (with Virginia Woolf) *Two Stories,* 1917 (s); *The Future of Constantinople,* 1917 (e); *Co-operation and the Future of Industry,* 1918 (e); *Empire and Commerce in Africa, a Study in Economic Imperialism,* 1919? (e); *International Economic Policy,* 1919? (e); *The Control of Industry by the People Through the Co-operative Movement,* 1920 (e); *Economic Imperialism,* 1920 (e); *Mandates and Empire,* 1920 (e); *Stories of the East,* 1921 (s); *Socialism and Co-operation,* 1921 (e); *The Savagery of Man,* 1925 (e); *Fear and Politics,*

1925 (e); *Essays on Literature, History, Politics, etc.*, 1927; *Hunting the High-brow*, 1927 (e); *Imperialism and Civilization*, 1928 (e); *The Way of Peace*, 1928 (e); *After the Deluge: a Study of Communal Psychology*, 1931 (e); *Quack, Quack*, 1935 (e); *The League and Abyssinia*, 1936 (e); *Barbarians at the Gate*, 1939 (Am. ed. *Barbarians Within and Without*) (e); *The Hotel*, 1939 (d); *After the Deluge, Vol. II: 1830 and 1832*, 1939 (e); *The Future of International Government*, 1940 (e); *Utopia and Reality*, 1940 (e); *The War for Peace*, 1940 (e); *Foreign Policy*, 1947 (e); *Principia Politica*, Vol. III of *After the Deluge*, 1953 (e); *Sowing: an Autobiography of the Years 1880-1904*, 1960 (a); *Growing: an Autobiography of the Years 1904-1911*, 1961 (a); *Beginning Again: an Autobiography of the Years 1911-1918*, 1964 (a)

VIRGINIA WOOLF
1882-1941

The Voyage Out, 1915 (n); (with Leonard Woolf) *Two Stories*, 1917 (s); *The Mark on the Wall*, 1917 (sk); *Night and Day*, 1919 (n); *Kew Gardens*, 1919 (s); *An Unwritten Novel*, 1920 (sk); *Monday or Tuesday*, 1921 (sk); *Jacob's Room*, 1922 (n); *Mr. Bennett and Mrs. Brown*, 1924 (c); *Mrs. Dalloway*, 1925 (n); *The Common Reader*, 1925 (c); *To the Lighthouse*, 1927 (n); *Orlando*, 1928 (n); *A Room of One's Own*, 1929 (e); *Beau Brummell*, 1930 (e); *On Being Ill*, 1930 (e); *Street Haunting*, 1930 (e); *The Waves*, 1931 (n); *The Common Reader, 2nd Series* (Am. ed. *The Second Common Reader*), 1932 (c); *A Letter to a Young Poet*, 1932 (e); *Flush*, 1933 (b); *Walter Sickert: a Conversation*, 1934 (e); *The Roger Fry Memorial Exhibition Address*, 1935 (e); *The Years*, 1937 (n); *Three Guineas*, 1938 (e); *Reviewing*, 1939 (e); *Roger Fry*, 1940 (b); *Between the Acts*, 1941 (n); *The Death of the Moth*, 1942 (e); *A Haunted House*, 1943 (s); *The Moment*, 1947 (e); *The Captain's Death Bed*, ed. Leonard Woolf, 1950 (e); *A Writer's Diary*, ed. Leonard Woolf, 1953 (a); *Virginia Woolf and Lytton Strachey: Letters*, ed. Leonard Woolf and James Strachey, 1958; *Granite and Rainbow*, 1958 (e); *Contemporary Writers*, 1965

(c); *Nurse Lugton's Golden Thimble*, 1966 (child's bk.); *Collected Essays*, ed. Leonard Woolf, 4 vols., 1966

Brownlee Jean Kirkpatrick, *A Bibliography of Virginia Woolf*, 1957; Joan Bennett, *Virginia Woolf*, enlgd. 1964; Jean Guiguet, *Virginia Woolf and Her Works*, tr. from French by Jean Stewart, 1966

WILLIAM BUTLER YEATS
1865-1939

Mosada, 1886 (p); *The Wanderings of Oisin*, 1889 (p); *The Countess Cathleen*, 1892 (pd); *The Celtic Twilight*, 1893 (misc.); *The Land of Heart's Desire*, 1894 (pd); *Poems*, 1895; *The Secret Rose*, 1897 (s); *The Tables of the Law, The Adoration of the Magi*, 1897 (s); *The Wind Among the Reeds*, 1899 (p); *The Shadowy Waters*, 1900 (p); *Cathleen ni Houlihan*, 1902 (pd); *Where There is Nothing*, 1902 (pd); *In the Seven Woods*, 1903 (p); *The Hour-Glass*, 1903 (pd); *Ideas of Good and Evil*, 1903 (e); *The King's Threshold and On Baile's Strand*, 1904 (2pd); *Stories of Red Hanrahan*, 1904 (s); *Poems, 1899-1905*, 1906; *The Poetical Works*, 2 vols., 1906-7; *Deirdre*, 1907 (pd); *Discoveries*, 1907 (e); *The Golden Helmet*, 1908 (pd); (with Lady Gregory) *The Unicorn from the Stars*, 1908 (pd); (with Lionel Johnson) *Poetry and Ireland*, 1908 (e); *The Green Helmet*, 1910 (p); *Synge and the Ireland of His Time*, 1911 (e); *The Cutting of an Agate*, 1912 (e); *Responsibilities*, 1914 (p,d); *Reveries over Childhood and Youth*, 1915 (a); *The Wild Swans at Coole*, 1917 (pd); *Per Amica Silentia Lunae*, 1918 (e); *Two Plays for Dancers*, 1919 (pd); *Michael Robartes and the Dancer*, 1920 (p); *Four Plays for Dancers*, 1921 (pd); *Later Poems*, 1922; *The Player Queen*, 1922 (pd); *Plays and Controversies*, 1923 (misc.); *The Cat and the Moon and Certain Poems*, 1924 (p); *The Bounty of Sweden*, 1925 (e); *A Vision*, 1925 (rev. 1937) (e); *Autobiographies: Reveries over Childhood and Youth and The Trembling of the Veil*, 1926 (a); *October Blast*, 1927 (p); *The Tower*, 1928 (p); *The Death of Synge*, 1928 (m); *The Winding Stair*, 1929 (p); *A Packet for Ezra Pound*, 1929 (e); *St. Patrick's Breast-plate*, 1929 (e); *Stories*

of Michael Robartes and his Friends
(with The Resurrection), 1931 (misc.);
Words for Music Perhaps, 1932 (p);
The Winding Stair, 1933 (p); The King
of the Great Clocktower, 1934 (e,p);
Wheels and Butterflies, 1934 (e,d);
Letters to the New Island, 1934 (e);
A Full Moon in March, 1935 (misc.);
Dramatis Personae, 1935 (r); Modern
Poetry, 1936 (e); Essays, 1931-1936,
1937; The Herne's Egg, 1938 (pd); New
Poems, 1938; The Autobiography
(Reveries, The Trembling of the Veil,
Dramatis Personae), 1938; Last Poems
and Two Plays, 1939; On the Boiler,
1939 (misc.); Letters on Poetry to
Dorothy Wellesley, 1940 (repr. 1964);
Last Poems and Plays, 1940; If I Were
Four-and-Twenty, 1940 (e); Pages from
a Diary, 1944 (r); Tribute to Thomas
Davis, 1947 (e); The Collected Poems,
1950; (with George Moore) Diarmuid
and Grania, 1951 (d); The Collected
Plays, 1952; W. B. Yeats and T. S.
Moore: Their Correspondence, ed.
Ursula Bridge, 1953; Letters to Katharine
Tynan, ed. Roger McHugh, 1953;
Letters, ed. Allan Wade, 1954; Variorum
Edition: Complete Poems, ed. P. Alt
and R. K. Alspach, 1957, and Plays, ed.
R. K. Alspach, 1965; Selected Criticism,
ed. A. Norman Jeffares, 1964

Richard Ellman, The Identity of Yeats,
1954; Allan Wade, A Bibliography of
the Writings of W. B. Yeats, 1958

FRANCIS BRETT YOUNG
1884-1954

(with E. Brett Young) Undergrowth,
1913 (n); Deep Sea, 1914 (n); Robert
Bridges, 1914 (c); The Dark Tower, 1915
(n); The Iron Age, 1916 (n); Five
Degrees South, 1917 (p); Marching on
Tanga, 1917 (sk); The Crescent Moon,
1918 (n); The Young Physician, 1919
(n); (with W. Edward Stirling) Captain
Swing, 1919 (d); Poems, 1916-1918,
1919; The Tragic Bride, 1920 (n); The
Black Diamond, 1921 (n); The Red

Knight, 1921 (n); Pilgrim's Rest, 1922 (n);
Woodsmoke, 1924 (n); Cold Harbour,
1924 (n); Sea Horses, 1925 (n); Portrait
of Clare, 1927 (Am. ed. Love is
Enough) (n); The Key of Life, 1928
(n); My Brother Jonathan, 1928 (n);
(with William Armstrong) The Furnace,
1928 (d); Black Roses, 1929 (n); Jim
Redlake, 1930 (Am. ed. The Redlakes)
(n); Mr. and Mrs. Pennington, 1931
(n); The House Under Water, 1932 (n);
Blood Oranges, 1932 (s); The Cage
Bird, 1933 (s); This Little World, 1934
(n); White Ladies, 1935 (n); Far Forest,
1936 (n); They Seek a Country, 1937
(n); Portrait of a Village, 1937 (n); Doctor Bradley Remembers, 1938 (n); The
Christmas Box, 1938 (s); The City of
Gold, 1939 (n); Mr. Lucton's Freedom,
1940 (Am. ed. The Happy Highway)
(n); The Ship's Surgeon's Yarn, 1940
(s); Cotswold Honey, 1940 (s); A Man
About the House, 1942 (n); The Island,
1944 (p); In South Africa, 1952 (t);
Wistanslow, 1956 (n)

Jessica Brett Young, Francis Brett
Young: A Biography, 1962 [no bibliog.]

G. M. YOUNG
1882-1959

Gibbon, 1932 (b); The Origin of the
West-Saxon Kingdom, 1934 (h); Early
Victorian England, 1830-1865, 1934 (h);
Charles I and Cromwell, 1935 (h);
Victorian England: Portrait of an Age,
1936 (h); Daylight and Champaign, 1937
(e); The Technique of Criticism, 1938
(e); The Age of Tennyson, 1939 (h);
The Government of Britain, 1941 (e);
Basic [English], 1943 (e); Why Not
Prosperity, 1943 (e); Mr. Gladstone,
1944 (b); Ourselves, 1944 (e); Rights
and Duties in the Modern State, 1946
(e); Shakespeare and the Termers, 1947
(Shakesp. lecture of Brit. Academy);
Today and Yesterday, 1948 (e); Last
Essays, 1950 (e); Stanley Baldwin, 1952
(b); (with others) The Good Society,
1953 (e); Victorian Essays, 1962 (c)

INDEX OF AUTHORS

*This index to Part One lists authors included in Collective
Studies, Histories, and Autobiographies . . . Only those authors
represented in Part Two (bibliographies) are included here.*